Interdisciplinary Advancements in Gaming, Simulations, and Virtual Environments:

Emerging Trends

Richard E. Ferdig
Research Center for Educational Technology – Kent State University, USA

Sara de Freitas
Coventry University, UK

Information Science
REFERENCE

Managing Director:	Lindsay Johnston
Senior Editorial Director:	Heather Probst
Book Production Manager:	Sean Woznicki
Development Manager:	Joel Gamon
Development Editor:	Michael Killian
Acquisitions Editor:	Erika Gallagher
Typesetters:	Adrienne Freeland, Deanna Jo Zombro
Cover Design:	Nick Newcomer, Lisandro Gonzalez

Published in the United States of America by
Information Science Reference (an imprint of IGI Global)
701 E. Chocolate Avenue
Hershey PA 17033
Tel: 717-533-8845
Fax: 717-533-8661
E-mail: cust@igi-global.com
Web site: http://www.igi-global.com

Library of Congress Cataloging-in-Publication Data

Interdisciplinary advancements in gaming, simulations and virtual environments
/ Richard E. Ferdig and Sara de Freitas, editors.
    p. cm.
  Includes bibliographical references and index.
  Summary: "This book investigates the role of games and computer-mediated
simulations in a variety of environments, including education, government, and
business, exploring psychological, social, and cultural implications of games
and simulations"--Provided by publisher.
  ISBN 978-1-4666-0029-4 (hardcover) -- ISBN 978-1-4666-0030-0 (ebook) -- ISBN
978-1-4666-0031-7 (print & perpetual access) 1. Computer-assisted
instruction. 2. Shared virtual environments. I. Ferdig, Richard E. (Richard
Eugene) II. Freitas, Sara de.

LB1028.5.I555 2012
371.33'4--dc23
                                          2011044136

British Cataloguing in Publication Data
A Cataloguing in Publication record for this book is available from the British Library.

*For our families, friends, and those who continue to advance research, policy,
and practice with electronic games and simulations*

List of Reviewers

Young Kyun Baek, *Korea National University of Education, Korea*
Michael Barbour, *Wayne State University, USA*
Dennis Beck, *University of Florida, USA*
Tugba Bulu, *Middle East Technical University, Turkey*
Vasa Buraphadeja, *University of Florida, USA*
Alison Carr-Chellman, *Penn State University, USA*
Christopher Clark, *Moves Institute Naval Post Graduate School, USA*
Yolanda Debose Columbus, *Texas A&M University, USA*
Christine Crawford, *Mayville State University, USA*
Lisa Dawley, *Boise State University, USA*
Muhammet Demirbilek, *Suleyman Demirel University, Turkey*
Michael A. Evans, *Virginia Tech, USA*
Patrick Felicia, *University College Cork, Ireland*
Thato Foko, *Meraka Institute - CSIR, South Africa*
Aroutis N. Foster, *Drexel University, USA*
Lisa Galarneau, *University of Waikato, New Zealand*
James Gall, *University of Northern Colorado, USA*
Hanan Gazit, *Virtual Reality Lab, Sehnkar College of Engineering and Design, Israel*
Ingrid Graves, *Indiana State University, USA*
Stephen Lawrence Guynup, *University of Baltimore, USA*
Richard Hartshorne, *University of Central Florida, USA*
Carrie Heeter, *Michigan State University, USA*
Hui-Yin Hsu, *New York Institute of Technology, USA*
Robert Jones, *New York University, USA*
Morris S.Y. Jong, *The Chinese University of Hong Kong, Hong Kong*
Fengfeng Ke, *Florida State University, USA*
Julian Kücklich, *University of the Arts, UK*
David J. Leonard, *Washington State University, USA*
Brian Magerko, *Georgia Institute of Technology, USA*
Pollyana Notargiacomo Mustaro, *Mackenzie Presbyterian University, Brazil*
Betul Ozkan, *University of Arizona South, USA*
Wei Peng, *Michigan State University, USA*
Andy Pulman, *Bournemouth University, UK*
Carol Luckhardt Redfield, *St. Mary's University, USA*
Symeon Retalis, *University of Piraeus, Greece*
Albert Ritzhaupt, *University of North Carolina at Wilmington, USA*
Paolo Ruffino, *University of Bologna, Italy*
Lori Shyba, *University of Calgary, Canada*
Kurt Squire, *University of Wisconsin, USA*
Vinod Srinivasan, *Texas A&M University, USA*
Laurie Taylor, *University of Florida, USA*

Table of Contents

Detailed Table of Contents

Chapter 1

  Idit Harel Caperton, World Wide Workshop Foundation, USA

This paper discusses varied ideas on games, learning, and digital literacy for 21st-century education as theorized and practiced by the author and James Paul Gee, and their colleagues. With attention to games as means for learning, the author links Gee's theories to the learning sciences tradition (particularly those of the MIT Constructionists) and extending game media literacy to encompass "writing" (producing) as well as "reading" (playing) games. If game-playing is like reading and game-making is like writing, then we must introduce learners to both from a young age. The imagining and writing of web-games fosters the development of many essential skill-sets needed for creativity and innovation, providing an appealing new way for a global computing education, STEM education, for closing achievement gaps. Gee and the author reveal a shared aim to encourage researchers and theorists, as well as policymakers, to investigate gaming with regard to epistemology and cognition.

Chapter 2

  Sasha A. Barab, Indiana University, USA
  Melissa Gresalfi, Indiana University, USA
  Tyler Dodge, Indiana University, USA
  Adam Ingram-Goble, Indiana University, USA

Education is about revealing possibility and exciting passions, empowering learners with the disciplinary expertise to meaningfully act on problematic contexts in which applying disciplinary knowledge is important. Toward this end, we have been using gaming methodologies and technologies to design curricular dramas that position students as active change agents who use knowledge to inquire into particular circumstances and, through their actions, transform the problematic situation into a known. Unlike more traditional textbooks designed to transmit facts or micro-stories, our focus is on building interactive experiences in which understanding core concepts, such as erosion or the idea of metaphor, and seeing oneself as a person who uses these to address personally meaningful and socially significant problems is valued. It is the explicit goal of this manuscript to communicate this power of educational videogames, as well as the design steps that we have been using to make this happen.

Brian C. Nelson, Arizona State University, USA
Diane Jass Ketelhut, Temple University, USA
Catherine Schifter, Temple University, USA

SAVE Science is a research project focused on creating an innovative model for assessment of learning in STEM. In SAVE Science, we are implementing game-like modules for evaluating science content and inquiry in grades 7-8, using an assessment rubric of student interactions in a virtual environment designed to capture evolving patterns of scientific understanding among students. We are also investigating two "conditions for success" for virtual environment-based assessment: managing the effects of cognitive load students experience in complex virtual environments, and helping teachers integrate technology into their pedagogy. In this paper, we provide an overview of our design approaches aimed at helping students manage the high levels of cognitive load they report experiencing in virtual environments. By reducing the perceived complexity of virtual environment-based assessments, we hypothesize that learners will be better able to attend to the processes associated with the assessments, leading to more accurate evidentiary data.

Yasmin B. Kafai, University of Pennsylvania, USA
Deborah Fields, University of California, Los Angeles, USA
Kristin A. Searle, University of Pennsylvania, USA

Millions of youth have joined virtual worlds to hang out with each other. However, capturing their interactions is no easy feat given the complexity of virtual worlds, their 24/7 availability, and distributed access from different places. In this paper, we illustrate what different methods can reveal about the dating and flirting practices of tweens in Whyville.net, a virtual world with over 1.5 million registered players in 2005 between the ages 8-16 years old. We compare findings from analyses of tweens' newspaper writings, chat records, and logfile data. Our analysis demonstrates the mixed attitudes toward flirting on Whyville and the pervasiveness of flirting as a whole, as well as the breadth and selectivity of tweens' adoption of flirting practices. We discuss how our multi-modal investigation reveals individual variation and development across practices and suggests that player expertise might contribute to the striking contrast between formal writing about dating and the frequency of it on the site. Finally, we discuss the limitations of our methodological approaches and suggest that our findings are limited to a particular space and time in the existence of Whyville and the tweens who populate it.

David Birchfield, Arizona State University, USA
Mina Johnson-Glenberg, Arizona State University, USA

Emerging research from the learning sciences and human-computer interaction supports the premise that learning is effective when it is embodied, collaborative, and multimodal. In response, we have developed a mixed-reality environment called the Situated Multimedia Arts Learning Laboratory (*SMALLab*). *SMALLab* enables multiple students to interact with one another and digitally mediated elements via 3D movements and gestures in real physical space. It uses 3D object tracking, real time graphics, and surround-sound to enhance learning. We present two studies from the earth science domain that address questions regarding the feasibility and efficacy of *SMALLab* in a classroom context. We present data demonstrating that students learn more during a recent *SMALLab* intervention compared to regular classroom instruction. We contend that well-designed, mixed-reality environments have much to offer STEM learners, and that the learning gains transcend those that can be expected from more traditional classroom procedures.

J. Alison Bryant, Consultant, USA
Anna Akerman, Adelphi University, USA
Jordana Drell, Nickelodeon/MTV Networks, USA

In this paper, the authors specifically focus on the opportunities and challenges presented by the Nintendo Wii to preschoolers in context to three key objectives in order to facilitate game development: First, to understand the range of physical and cognitive abilities of preschoolers in motion-based game play; Second, to understand how preschoolers interact with the Wii; Third, to understand the expectations of the parents of preschoolers with regard to these new gaming platforms and the purchase and play contexts within which game play occurs. In addition to reporting challenges and advantages of the motion-based play for preschoolers, the authors also discuss how the findings of this research were then implemented by the game producers to develop the first preschool-targeted game on the market in the United States.

Fulvio Frapolli, University of Fribourg, Switzerland
Amos Brocco, University of Fribourg, Switzerland
Apostolos Malatras, University of Fribourg, Switzerland
Béat Hirsbrunner, University of Fribourg, Switzerland

Existing research on computer enhanced board games is mainly focused on user interaction issues and look-and-feel, however, this overlooks the flexibility of traditional board games when it comes to game rule handling. In this respect, the authors argue that successful game designs need to exploit the advantages of the digital world as well as retaining such flexibility. To achieve this goal, both the rules of the game and the graphical representation should be simple to define at the design stage, and easy to change before or even during a game session. For that reason, the authors propose a framework allowing the implementation of all aspects of a board game in a fully flexible and decoupled way. This paper will describe the FLEXIBLERULES approach, which combines both a model driven and an aspect oriented design of computer enhanced board games. The benefits of this approach are discussed and illustrated in the case of three different board games.

Chapter 8

Studies on game-based learning usually investigate at least one of three subjects: the effects of gaming on learning performance, the effects of gaming on cognitive skills and attitudes, and learners' game-design experiences. Whether gaming relates positively to learning outcomes is still under investigation. This study examines the components contributing to the development of a literate game player and how players could cognitively grasp the design of a game scenario based on real history (namely, the game *Romance of the Three Kingdoms*). This study surveyed 497 participants in Taiwan on their knowledge of Chinese history (the Three Kingdoms period). The participants constituted two groups: participants who had years of gaming experience and participants who did not. The study examined test performance by using an independent sample t-test and one-way ANOVA and Pearson-correlation methods. The results revealed that the game players were more knowledgeable about the history of the Three Kingdoms period, had greater motivation to learn history, and were more motivated to learn history by playing the game than was the case with the non-game players.

Chapter 9

Videogames are the starting point for the general understanding of virtual space. (Grove & Williams, 1998). Academics use videogames to describe virtual space (Murray, 1997; Nitsche, 2009). Others argue that there is no understanding of virtual space, only a loose collection of articles connected by the issue of realism in rendering or behavior (Manovich, 2001). These statements point to a lack of understanding of virtual space on its own terms and set the stage for this document. This is a design document, written by a designer of virtual spaces. Its purpose is to provocatively explore user experience and task completion as forces that influence the design of virtual space. This is not a conventional research paper. The complex relationships of narrative, realism, motivation, usability, and human computer interaction (HCI) are unpacked in the videogame World of Warcraft *through a detailed examination of travel. It is proposed that the exploration of travel in a videogame can provide a toolkit of ideas for the application of narrative, realism, motivation, and usability in virtual space. Travel can inform designers on issues of user experience and task completion in virtual spaces*

This article presents an empirical study of the role of video game audio on performance. Twenty participants played *The Legend of Zelda: Twilight Princess* on the Wii console for a 45-minute session on five consecutive days. Employing a repeated measures design, the authors exposed players to one orientation session and four sound conditions, i.e., silence, remote control sounds, remote control and screen sounds, and unrelated music played on a boom-box, in a counterbalanced order. Performance was weakest when playing without sound, increasingly stronger with audio emitted by remote control only, and by remote-and-screen respectively. Surprisingly, the highest scores were earned when playing with music that was *unrelated* to players' actions or events unfolding on screen. These findings point to the challenges of processing multisensory cues during the initial stages of an elaborate role-playing game, and suggest that the most effective players swiftly develop strategies incorporating task-relevant information conveyed by both sound and images.

As educational games become more pervasive, the evolution of game design software is inevitable. This study looked at student perceptions of teacher created Serious Educational Games as part of a project striving to create a game development software where teachers and students create games as part of educational activities. The objective was to use evidence from student perceptions to inform further development of the software. A mixed method design ascertained data from 181 male and 178 females from 33 teacher created games. Results indicate that the software is relatively effective by the supporting documentation and training lacked in several areas. This information led to the creation of a commercial game development software set for release in 2010.

Problem-based learning is an instructional strategy that emphasises the accumulation and development of knowledge via an active and experiential based approach to solving problems. This pedagogical framework can be instantiated using gaming technology to provide learners with the ability to control their learning experience within a dynamic, responsive, and visually rich three-dimensional virtual environment. In this regard, a conceptual framework referred to as the Simulation, User, and Problem-based Learning (SUPL) approach has been developed in order to inform the design of 3D simulation environments based on gaming technology within a problem-based learning pedagogy. The SUPL approach identifies a series of design factors relative to the user, the problem-solving task, and the 3D simulation environment that guide the learning process and facilitate the transfer of knowledge. This paper will present a simulation environment design according to this conceptual framework for a problem-solving task within the context of an underground mine emergency evacuation. The problem-solving task will be designed to satisfy learning objectives that relate to the development of knowledge and skills for emergency evacuation of the Dominion Mining's Challenger mining operation located in South Australia.

Chapter 13

Don Heider, Loyola University Chicago, USA

Adrienne L. Massanari, Loyola University Chicago, USA

3-D virtual realms offer places for people to go interact, play games, and even do business. As these realms themselves become more sophisticated, the number of participants grows and the level and type of social interactions change. Meanwhile, scholars race to try to keep up. There is a growing, but still developing literature about interaction in virtual world. This paper explores communication and social intimacy in one such world, Second Life. In this paper, results of a four year ethnography in Second Life reveal findings that refute earlier research on computer-mediated communications, and support others while offering new findings to contribute to the growing body of knowledge.

Chapter 14

Andrew J. Wodehouse, University of Strathclyde, UK

William J. Ion, University of Strathclyde, UK

In this paper, computer gaming approaches are introduced as a viable means to structure the interaction of a product development team during concept generation. During concept generation, teams gather large amounts of information before generating new ideas and concepts. Digital technologies mean that relevant information can be sourced faster than ever, but this does not necessarily migrate into the activity of concept creation. It is suggested that cues from computer games can help integrate information as well as individuals more effectively, resulting in better conceptual output. A range of game types are evaluated with a view to their possible utilization in support of concept design. Two scenarios for the implementation of gaming methods are proposed, and one refined scenario identified as having potential for further development.

Chapter 15

Rania Hodhod, University of York, UK

Daniel Kudenko, University of York, UK

Paul Cairns, University of York, UK

Promoting ethical, responsible, and caring young people is a perennial aim of education. Efforts have been made to find ways of teaching other than traditional ones like games and role play. Narrative-based computer games are engaging learning platforms that allow collaboration of humans and computers in the creation of innovative experiences. In this paper, the authors examine the design of an adaptive, interactive narrative model that uses a student model to provide an individualized story-path and an individualized learning process. In this regard, the authors comprise strong learning objectives underpinned by effective story telling. The adaptive narrative model has been deployed in the educational game environment, AEINS, along with the use of the Socratic Method and pedagogical agents to support teaching in the ethics domain. Evaluation results indicate the usefulness of the design and provide evidence on the development of moral reasoning and the transfer of moral virtues to its users.

Jorge Arroyo-Palacios, University of Sheffield, UK
Daniela M. Romano, University of Sheffield, UK

Affective bio-feedback can be an important instrument to enhance the game experience. Several studies have provided evidence of the usefulness of physiological signals for affective gaming; however, due to the limited knowledge about the distinctive autonomic signatures for every emotion, the pattern matching models employed are limited in the number of emotions they are able to classify. This paper presents a bio-affective gaming interface (BAGI) that can be used to customize a game experience according to the player's emotional response. Its architecture offers important characteristics for gaming that are important because they make possible the reusability of previous findings and the inclusion of new models to the system. In order to prove the effectiveness of BAGI, two different types of neural networks have been trained to recognize emotions. They were incorporated into the system to customize, in real-time, the computer wallpaper according to the emotion experienced by the user. Best results were obtained with a probabilistic neural network with accuracy results of 84.46% on the training data and 78.38% on the validation for new independent data sets.

Bram van de Laar, University of Twente, The Netherlands
Boris Reuderink, University of Twente, The Netherlands
Danny Plass-Oude Bos, University of Twente, The Netherlands
Dirk Heylen, University of Twente, The Netherlands

Most research on Brain-Computer Interfaces (BCI) focuses on developing ways of expression for disabled people who are not able to communicate through other means. Recently it has been shown that BCI can also be used in games to give users a richer experience and new ways to interact with a computer or game console. This paper describes research conducted to find out what the differences are between using actual and imagined movement as modalities in a BCI game. Results show that there are significant differences in user experience and that actual movement is a more robust way of communicating through a BCI.

Stijn Hoppenbrouwers, Radboud University Nijmegen, The Netherlands
Bart Schotten, Radboud University Nijmegen, The Netherlands
Peter Lucas, Radboud University Nijmegen, The Netherlands

Many model-based methods in AI require formal representation of knowledge as input. For the acquisition of highly structured, domain-specific knowledge, machine learning techniques still fall short, and knowledge elicitation and modelling is then the standard. However, obtaining formal models from informants who have few or no formal skills is a non-trivial aspect of knowledge acquisition, which can be viewed as an instance of the well-known "knowledge acquisition bottleneck". Based on the authors' work in conceptual modelling and method engineering, this paper casts methods for knowledge modelling in the framework of games. The resulting games-for-modelling approach is illustrated by a first prototype of such a game. The authors' long-term goal is to lower the threshold for formal knowledge acquisition and modelling.

Maliang Zheng, University of York, UK
Daniel Kudenko, University of York, UK

The enjoyment of many games can be enhanced by in-game commentaries. In this paper, the authors focus on the automatic generation of commentaries for football games, using Championship Manager as a case study. The basis of this approach is a real-time mapping of game states to commentary concepts, such as "dangerous situation for team A". While in some cases it is feasible to provide such a mapping by hand-coding, in some cases it is not straight-forward because the meaning of the concepts cannot be easily formalized. In these cases, the authors propose to use inductive learning techniques that learn such a mapping from annotated game traces.

Preface

INTRODUCTION

The *International Journal of Games and Computer-Mediated Simulations* (IJGCMS) was launched in 2009 (http://www.igi-global.com/ijgcms). The journal is devoted to the theoretical and empirical understanding of electronic games and computer-mediated simulations. The journal is interdisciplinary in nature; it publishes research from fields and disciplines that share the goal of improving the foundational knowledge base of games and simulations. The journal publishes critical theoretical manuscripts as well as qualitative and quantitative research studies, meta-analyses, and methodologically-sound case studies. The journal also includes book reviews to keep readers on the forefront of this continuously evolving field. Occasional special issues from the journal provide deeper investigation into areas of interest within either gaming or simulations.

This is the second book in a series that sets out to capture the important findings and best practices of the journal articles that were published in IJGMCS over an entire year of publication. This is not meant to be a handbook of everything that has been written about games and simulations. On the contrary, this tome was created to highlight the work that has emerged through a year-long snapshot of articles published in a leading, peer-reviewed journal. This chapter begins with a brief background about the journal (text that is found in our journal mission), and then provides an overview and summary of the 19 chapters in this book. The chapter concludes with some recommendations and goals for future research, policy, and practice.

IJGCMS

One main goal of this peer-reviewed, international journal is to promote a deep conceptual and empirical understanding of the roles of electronic games and computer-mediated simulations across multiple disciplines. A second goal is to help build a significant bridge between research and practice on electronic gaming and simulations, supporting the work of researchers, practitioners, and policymakers.

There are at five guiding principles supporting this mission as well as the editorial policy of IJGCMS. The first important principle is quality and rigor. IJGCMS follows a double-blind review process to ensure anonymity and a fair review. Research articles that are published may contain either quantitative or qualitative data collection & analyses. However, articles using either method must present data to support and justify claims made within the article. Articles that simply summarize data without presenting it or the analytical techniques used, are not considered. Theoretical manuscripts are also published. However, these theoretical reviews must create new knowledge by synthesizing and critiquing past research. Simple summaries of existing literature without thoughtful and considerate analyses are not considered.

A second important principle is the notion of IJGCMS as an interdisciplinary journal. There are numerous fields and disciplines that undertake research related to games and simulations. Psychology, Education, History, Journalism, Literature, Computer Science, Engineering, Fine Arts, and Medicine are just a few of the areas where one could find gaming and simulation research. Unfortunately in academia, the notion of standing on the shoulders of giants has often meant taken a historical perspective on one's line of research. Gaining a historical backing is an important part of moving the field forward; however, failing to consider parallel work in other fields is failure to address and accept the complex natures of games and simulations. IJGCMS publishes articles from any discipline as long as the content of the work is related to games and simulations. Including multiple fields helps researchers recognize their similarities as well as introducing them to colleagues from distinctly different backgrounds.

In addition to having an interdisciplinary focus, a third principal of this journal is its international focus. There are over 18 countries represented on the Editorial Board of IJGCMS. There is no justifiable reason why our research should have disciplinary OR geographical boundaries. Drawing on work from international authors provides two interesting opportunities. First, readers are able to see one topic from multiple perspectives. For instance, how are researchers from various countries working on science simulations? Second, readers are able to see variations across countries. For instance, what are the current research topics and sets of expertise in various countries around the world?

Innovation is a fourth principle guiding the work of IJGCMS. Gaming and simulation researchers often create new concepts and technologies in their work. IJGCMS is a journal where authors who create new tools and techniques go to publish their findings; it is also a resource for readers who want to keep up with the latest and most cutting edge technologies. Special, focused issues with guest editors will also promote in-depth analyses at conceptual or technological innovations (proposals for special issues are welcomed at any time).

Finally, IJGCMS is focused on implications. Developing a strong research foundation for games and simulations is important, but only to the extent that the research impacts others. One of the main items reviewers are asked to consider when reviewing for IJGCMS is: "What are the implications of this work on other research, policy, and practice?" Each article author is asked to include direct implications for others working in similar areas, regardless of whether they be researchers, practitioners, or policy-makers.

Recommended topics for the journal include (but are not limited to) the following:

- Cognitive, social, and emotional impact of games and simulations
- Critical reviews and meta-analyses of existing game and simulation literature
- Current and future trends, technologies, and strategies related to game, simulation development, and implementation
- Electronic games and simulations in government, business, and the workforce
- Electronic games and simulations in teaching and learning
- Frameworks to understand the societal and cultural impacts of games and simulations
- Impact of game and simulation development use on race and gender game and simulation design
- Innovative and current research methods and methodologies to study electronic games and simulations
- Psychological aspects of gaming
- Teaching of games and simulations at multiple age and grade levels

During its second year in press, IJGCMS had two 'regular' or general issues and two special issue. Some work in gaming and simulations gets published in journals like IJGCMS. However, a tremendous amount of cutting-edge research in this area is first presented at conferences. In an attempt to capture these findings, IJGCMS often partners with conferences and organizations to create special issues focused on the leading research from the conference. The first special issue for 2010 was from the *American Educational Research Association* annual conference (http://www.aera.net/), and more specifically papers that were originally accepted to the *Applied Research in Virtual Environments for Learning Special Interest Group* (ARVEL SIG; http://www.arvelsig.com/). According to the SIG website, the goal of the group is to bring together educators, scholars, and practitioners who are interested in research in and on virtual environments.

The second special issue was from the annual AISB Symposium in AI and Games held in 2009 and 2010. AISB is the *Society for the Study of Artificial Intelligence and Simulation of Behavior* (http://www.aisb.org.uk/). AI and Games are one of the specific symposia topics under the broader umbrella of AISB. As previously highlighted, IJGMCS prides itself on being an international journal. The first special issue was from a major conference that happens in the United States; the second special issue was led by our international peers in the United Kingdom.

IJGCMS' editorial board consists of four separate groups (http://www.igi-global.com/ijgcms).

1. The international advisory board consists of a panel of leading experts from around the world. The advisory board provides insight and helpful recommendations to the editor; they are also available for suggestions and recommendations of future journal goals and special issues.
2. IJGCMS has a panel of associate editors. Each submission goes to one associate editor. Having a smaller number of associate editors has provided a way to maintain consistency in reviews.
3. Submissions also then go to two editorial review board members. As such, each submission receives three double-blind, peer reviews. The associate editor and the editorial review board members are matched as closely as possible based on the topic of the submission and the expertise of the reviewer. However, the reviews are double-blind. In other words, the authors do not know the identity of the reviewers assigned to their paper, nor do the reviewers know the author.
4. Finally, IJGCMS publishes a book review with almost every issue. The fourth group is a panel of co-book review editors who help select books, solicit reviewers, and edit reviews.

Journal special issues are also peer-reviewed. This can be done in a number of different ways. Often, for conference special issues, submissions are reviewed once at the submission stage, where they are accepted or rejected for presentation. Accepted papers are then offered the chance to submit for journal submission, where they are again reviewed either by the conference review panel or IJGCMS' own review board.

The four issues for 2010 produced a total of 19 peer-reviewed papers. In preparing this book, authors were given the opportunity to update their paper with new data, new findings, or related articles since the original publication of their paper. The purpose and goal of this book is to highlight the work of those authors, presenting findings that will impact the field of gaming and simulations in multiple ways.

CHAPTER HIGHLIGHTS

The work that has been published on games and simulations in IJGCMS is continuing to advance research, policy, and practice. In conclusion, one could ask, what can we learn about the current state of the field from these 19 publications? Listed below are some of the key findings from each of these studies (by chapter number).

It should be noted that the purpose of this summary is to highlight some of the main ideas identified in each chapter. It is not intended to take away from the rich insights or deep conversations included in each chapter. For instance, one of the goals of IJGCMS is to publish articles that directly impact policy, research, and practice. Each chapter in this book contains a rich description of the 'so what?' for those working in various fields. A thorough reading of each chapter will provide such detailed information.

Chapter 1 - *Toward a Theory of Game-Media Literacy: Playing and Building as Reading and Writing* (Idit Harel Caperton)

- *Game literacy is a multidimensional combination of varied practices (e.g., reading, writing, and calculating; textual, visual, and spatial cognition; interactive design, programming, and engineering; multitasking and system understanding; meaning making, storytelling, role playing, perspective taking, and exercising judgment; etc.). (2)*
- *Researchers offer solid evidence that children learn important content, perspectives, and vital 21st-century skills from playing digital games. (3)*
- *In other words, while 'systems content' may be more or less present and conveyed through game play, working on game creation arguably conveys understanding of game components and game systems through a more intimate and interdependent epistemological context... game-playing is like "reading" and game-making is like "writing" in that they must be introduced to learners hand-in-hand from a young age. (9)*
- *In a world in which the ability to imagine, represent and create, not just consume, digital media will define citizenship, measure productivity, and enable success, students can afford no less. (13)*

Chapter 2 - *Narratizing Disciplines and Disciplinizing Narratives: Games as 21st Century Curriculum* (Sasha A. Barab, Melissa Gresalfi, Tyler Dodge, & Adam Ingram-Goble)

- *We are primarily interested in the learner having the experience of being in a scenario wherein applying one's understanding of a disciplinary concept has impact on the (virtual) situation—a situation in which the learner has a significant role and which is semantically revealing, thereby helping learners appreciate the meaningfulness of the concept (its use value) for transforming problematic situation. (20)*
- *Just as the storyline narratizes the to-be-learned content, the relationship among conditions, actions, and outcomes—the anatomy of player choices—ensures that our designed game play involves disciplinizingthe narrative; that is, to make useful game play decisions the player must leverage disciplinary understandings to make meaningful play choices. (20)*
- *Curriculum designers might benefit from an examination of how gaming methodologies and technologies situatively embody the player and the to-be-learned content in rich participation structures. (28)*

- *By bounding up disciplinary context within interactive narrative contexts, we have the potential to not only change learners' understanding of the use value of the content and also offer the opportunity for learners to see themselves as capable of meaningfully applying disciplinary content. (29)*

Chapter 3 - *Exploring Cognitive Load in Immersive Educational Games: The SAVE Science Project* (Brian C. Nelson, Diane Jass Ketelhut, & Catherine Schifter)

- *The rich experience enabled by virtual environments contributes to what Mayer and Clark (2007) label the "rich media paradox." The simultaneous presentation of multiple information sources supported by virtual environments raises a learner's cognitive load (the mental effort needed to process all the visual, textual, and audio elements) until (s)he experiences cognitive overload, with the incoming stimuli outstripping the capacity of the learner's memory systems to process the information. (34)*
- *In the SAVE Science project, students have an overall goal of uncovering the likely contributors to a series of problems facing a small virtual town (sick farm animals, weather-related crop failure, and climate-related problems with the town's water)... Upon analyzing final student reports, looking for evidence of understanding of inquiry (e.g., uses data to design hypothesis, experiment is designed to test hypothesis), reports written by students in the River City treatment scored twice that of those written by students in the control treatment. (33)*
- *We are aiming for what we call "essential complexity" of experience—a high level of immersion and embodiment coupled with a reduction in the sense of complexity and associated cognitive load detrimental to completion of assessment tasks. (38)*

Chapter 4 - *Multi-Modal Investigations of Relationship Play in Virtual Worlds* (Yasmin B. Kafai, Deborah Fields, & Kristin A. Searle)

- *We propose a narrative approach that rebuilds the online life of participants by condensing data points into comprehensive accounts. We contend that this approach can reveal particular social practices across online and offline spaces and aspects of individual players' participation not captured otherwise and hence well suited for our focus on anticipatory flirting and dating. We thus applied a new method to analyze logfile data, called qualitative logfile analysis (Kafai & Fields, in press). We then combined the insights gained from qualitative logfile analysis with other data sources to create a fuller picture of anticipatory flirting and dating. (43)*
- *The relatively negative opinions about flirting and dating in Whyville published in The Whyville Times contrasted with the widespread prevalence of these activities...Newer players are more likely to try out widespread flirting while more experienced players tend to develop a preference for particular activities or areas of the virtual world. (47)*

Chapter 5 - *A Next Gen Interface for Embodied Learning: SMALLab and the Geological Layer Cake* (David Birchfield & Mina Johnson-Glenberg)

- *SMALLab is a mixed-reality environment where students collaborate and interact with sonic and visual media using full body movements in an open physical space... This paper presents two experiments pertaining to SMALLab learning in the earth science domain. (51, 53)*

- *Taken together, these two studies offer encouraging evidence that next generation interfaces such as SMALLab are feasible in a classroom context and can have a powerful impact on student learning. (57)*
- *These studies are encouraging and demonstrate that significant learning gains can be made in embodied, mixed-reality environments above and beyond the gains expected from traditional instruction. (59)*

Chapter 6 - *Wee Wii: Preschoolers and Motion-Based Game Play* (J. Alison Bryant, Anna Akerman, & Jordana Drell)

- *There were three key objectives for this research. The first was to understand the range of physical and cognitive abilities of preschoolers in the context of motion-based game play...The second objective was to understand how preschoolers interact with the Wii, specifically how they handle the various forms of play and game mechanics offered by the games currently on the market for this platform. The final objective was to understand the expectations of the parents of preschoolers with regard to these new gaming platforms and the purchase and play contexts within which game play occurs. Our goal was to investigate these considerations in an exploratory manner. (62)*
- *One of the most critical findings is that the Wii was seen by most parents as a gaming "equalizer" – something that everyone in the family, including the preschoolers, could play. It was always set up in the living room as opposed to in the childrens' room, which was more prevalent with other console systems, so that everyone could have access to it. (68)*
- *The critical learning was that preschoolers' movements are grossly exaggerated compared to adult movements, due to a lack of coordination and developing motor skills. In order to effectively create games for them, developers would need to make sure that the "hotspots" (the areas on the screen that would detect Wiimote movement) are sufficiently large and less sensitive than when programmed for adults. (71)*
- *Because young children are still developing their sense of spatial perception, "persistent worlds" and graphics that require them to translate maps in relation to "where they are" in a world were very confusing to them...Another challenge for preschoolers is any form of multi-step or complex game play...A final cognitive aspect of play that was particularly evident with the Wii was the importance of personalization for preschoolers in enjoying their game play. (73)*

Chapter 7 - *Decoupling Aspects in Board Game Modeling* (Fulvio Frapolli, Amos Brocco, Apostolos Malatras, & Béat Hirsbrunner)

- *We propose an extensible and efficient framework called Flexiblerules that aims at taking advantage of both approaches (i.e., physical and digital), by allowing the implementation of board games in a fully flexible and decoupled way. The Flexiblerules framework is comprised of both a conceptual model to design board games and a set of tools, including a domain-specific language and a dedicated compiler, to realize the aforementioned design. (79)*
- *The need to establish standard models for the design and subsequent analysis of games is evident, as it allows for a common understanding and a shared vision among developers and also users. (80)*

- *We recognize two levels of abstraction as far as game modeling is concerned, namely logic and representation, which provide us with an initial separation of concerns. These concerns are modeled separately as logical and representation layers, dealing with a low-level description of game dynamics, and the high-level interface with the real-world (typically a graphical or tangible representation) respectively. Thus, the game model can be viewed as the composition of these two layers. (81)*

- *In this paper we presented the Flexiblerules framework for the modeling of board games. The proposed game model is composed of taxonomy of entities with precise properties and behaviors. In order to simplify the conceptualization of rules, we proposed a decoupling of the game logic into different aspects: laws, behaviors, and side-effects. Consistent with the goals of aspect oriented programming, we believe that such a separation of concerns allows for a more natural way to define the logic behind board games. (95).*

Chapter 8 - *Effects of Playing a History-Simulation Game: Romance of Three Kingdoms* (Kwei Wang)

- *Researchers who study game playing are nearly certain that the more frequently a player plays games, the more confident and the more fluent he or she will be in gaming. (97)*

- *The study reveals that RTK players exhibited higher motivation to access media pertaining to the Three Kingdoms history than did the non-RTKplayers, that the RTK-players were more knowledgeable about the Three Kingdoms history than were the non-RTK players, and that many of the RTK-players were motivated to learn about this period of history by playing RTK. (110)*

- *Game designers who are interested in promoting learning motivation might consider similar strategies to present real historical events and geographical backgrounds of their own history to game players. (111)*

Chapter 9 - *The Design of Virtual Space: Lessons from Videogame Travel* (Steve Guynup)

- *In the world of videogames, designers utilize death as the ultimate penalty and they balance it against constructs that imply success. In a well designed game, all task failures support the user's overall experience and are used to create a sense of value in the completion of game tasks. This leads to some interesting choices in terms of design. (122)*

- *It could be said that invention deals with reality, while convention deals with realism. In virtual space, setting up a design dynamic of realism vs. reality is appealing, but in videogames, much like in film, realism is subordinate to narrative. (124)*

- *Travel, presented in great detail, offers insight into the nature of videogames, virtual space, and the subjects like narrative, realism, usability, motivation, and human computer interaction. The key dynamic within this document is the complex relationship, conflict and harmony between user experience and task completion. (135)*

- *Lastly, if good interfaces are transparent to the task, what does that mean for 3D worlds that strive to be the opposite? The opposite of transparent is immersive, as in the all-surrounding, always present videogame space that guides the users actions as opposed to being the completely interface, wholly subordinate the users wishes. Such questions are difficult to address, but addressed they must be. (139)*

Chapter 10 - *Effects of Built-in Audio versus Unrelated Background Music on Performance in an Adventure Role-Playing Game* (Siu-Lan Tan, John Baxa, & Matthew P. Spackman)

- *As sound design has advanced, the player has taken on an increasingly active role with respect to video game audio. Gamers must decipher cues in the musical score for information about the surrounding environment, and listen for sound effects such as footsteps, which situate the player within the virtual environment. Audio cues alert players to approaching danger, guide them in tracking the moment-to-moment location of enemies, and give immediate feedback on successful execution of actions... Despite video game audio's growing relevance in game design and the wealth of information that it can convey, few empirical studies have examined the role of sound on players' performance and game experience. (143)*
- *Our study compares the effects of (1) built-in video game audio that is contingent on the player's actions and events on the screen (such as sounds of sword slashes, auditory warnings of approaching enemies, and music that signals that one is entering a new territory within the virtual environment), and (2) a musical soundtrack that is unrelated to the player's actions or to events unfolding in the game (therefore referred to as Non-contingent Music). (147)*
- *The findings of our study do not suggest any simple relationships between video game audio and performance or quality of the game experience....what emerged is a picture that is more complex and open to individual variation than we had anticipated. (156)*
- *An unexpected and striking finding of this study was that the highest performance scores were not earned in the conditions with built-in audio, but when playing with background music that was unrelated to the player's actions or events in the game. Specifically, players earned the highest means for total performance score and most performance subscores, and needed the fewest 'continues' in the Non-contingent Music condition. (157)*
- *Among the practical findings that emerged is the discovery that when it comes to video game audio, 'more is not always better' - especially during the initial stages of learning a new game. Further, we discovered that gamers are not a homogeneous group but respond quite differently to the same playing conditions at various stages of a new game. Thus, allowing players to tailor the audio to fit their preferences and the demands of a particular game, as well as the flexibility to modulate these settings as they advance in a game, may lead to optimal performance conditions and the most positive gaming experience. (160)*

Chapter 11 - *Measuring Student Perceptions: Designing an Evidenced Centered Activity Model for a Serious Educational Game Development Software* (Leonard A. Annetta, Shawn Y. Holmes, Meng-Tzu Cheng, & Elizabeth Folta)

- *When students create games with support by teachers in terms of content accuracy, time allowed, and recognition of the work involved and this technology becomes part of the school culture—students become more engaged in the content as well as proficient producers in the digital world. They are thereby simultaneously introduced to modeling and design through immersion in the virtual space. (166)*
- *One main focus to the teacher professional development regarding Serious Educational Game design and infusion into the classroom was the notion of learning becoming stealthy. That is a*

good game would not make students think they were learning but rather they were simply playing in class. (176)

- *What this tells us is that there are clear components of some of these games that met or exceeded the goals of being educational; yet stealthy. Moreover, this informed the research team that this was more of a training delivering issue then it was a software issue. To this end the software is only as good as the training and those using it for educational purposes. (176)*
- *This confirmed that most teachers are not gamers and thus, missed the "fun" of Serious Educational Games. (176)*

Chapter 12 - *Computer-Generated Three-Dimensional Training Environments: The Simulation, User, and Problem-Based Learning (SUPL) Approach* (Michael Garrett & Mark McMahon)

- *The abilities of 3D gaming technologies, in particular the game engines used to power FPS games, have not gone unnoticed, with proponents of computer assisted learning recognising the potential of these technologies to function as simulation environments. This has given rise to the serious games movement, which focuses on the application of gaming technologies and concepts for simulation and learning purposes. (184)*
- *This framework, referred to as the Simulation, User, and Problem-based Learning (SUPL) approach, identifies a series of design factors which guide the learning process and facilitate the transfer of knowledge relative to user, problem-solving task, and 3D simulation environment components. Central to all three components are the aspects of problem-based learning which mediate the learning process. (186)*
- *Simulations and problem-based learning share common goals in that they are both directed towards the application of knowledge and concepts to new situations. Thus, problems can be provided that replicate authentic tasks and enhance the potential for transfer inherent in problem-based learning. (187)*

Chapter 13 - *Friendship, Closeness and Disclosure in Second Life* (Don Heider & Adrienne L. Massanari)

- *Thus, avatars serve an important function within worlds like Second Life – both as expressions of individual identities, and as agents of copresence...So, while some level of fidelity between an individual's offline behavior and her avatar's actions is likely to increase our sense of copresence online, and possibly lead to more meaningful relationships with other players, there is a point at which too much realism actually detracts from an individual's willingness to disclose information more about themselves. (206)*
- *What we're most interested in is that fourth category of self-disclosure. In observations over these four years we noticed a significant difference in people's willingness to self-disclose than in normal everyday real life encounters, and thus, social relationships often have a different quality in Second Life than in a non-virtual world. (208)*
- *Early theory about how computers might affect communication predicted less effective and less meaningful interaction. But we found in some cases, just the opposite, where people in disparate locales formed close relationships in ways that might not occur through face-to-face interactions. (212)*

- *We suggest that anonymity, time compression, lack of physical appearance, and word dependence all contribute to a phenomenon wherein people at a rapid rate get close to other people, a phenomenon we are calling facticius contingo. One thing is clear after spending four years in SL that is these places continue to be important to the people who choose to participate. They are more than places people go to be amused or entertained. People develop social interactions they find meaningful, compelling and gratifying. (212)*

Chapter 14 - *Computer Gaming Scenarios for Product Development Teams* (Andrew J. Wodehouse & William J. Ion)

- *This paper therefore aims to develop theoretical frameworks for improved use of information in progressive concept design approaches by utilizing characteristics of a field where highly engaging and effective information use are essential: computer games. (217)*
- *Computer games have been shown to have a number of potential benefits for team utilization of information during the concept design task. Three key characteristics of computer games are increased motivation of participants, controlled interaction during collaboration, and adding structure to the completion of tasks. (223)*
- *A review of relevant gaming literature as well as an examination of computer gaming genres (including the testing of four titles for illustration) has revealed a number of characteristics in motivation, interaction and structure that are applicable to the design team. (229)*
- *As games developers continue to produce virtual worlds that are visual, information-rich, and engaging it is important that there is a shared awareness of the activities undertaken in traditional industries where games could potentially enhance current practices. (230)*

Chapter 15 - *Adaptive Interactive Narrative Model to Teach Ethics* (Rania Hodhod, Daniel Kudenko, & Paul Cairns)

- *We argue that the development of virtues requires practicing the same way other skills such as reading or writing do. In addition, learning about ethical virtues is different from applying them. (235)*
- *Interactive narrative is an engaging learning medium that allows collaboration of humans and computers in the creation of innovative experiences. Interactive narrative can be seen as an engaging hook where the player feels in control and can see his actions affecting how the story unfolds. (236)*
- *Educational games area gained much attention in the last few decades for its powerful engaging property and the ability of these platforms to deliver learning in various domains. They offer an advantage over traditional schooling, where connection between perception and action that is a highly prototypical form of knowledge, can be represented in the following form of production rules: If this is the current situation, do these. Therefore, immersing the student in a (simulated) environment provides a much richer experience than a worksheet or other homework assignment could. (245)*
- *Different narrative techniques provide various advantages. This paper highlights the synergy of integrating both dynamic narrative and scripted narrative techniques and how a student model can be used to provide an adaptive, interactive narrative model. (245)*

Chapter 16 - *Bio-Affective Computer Interface for Game Interaction* (Jorge Arroyo-Palacios & Daniela M. Romano)

- *Physiological signals offer a promising medium to interact in a natural and intuitive way with the game environment. In addition of being reliable, sensible and provide real time feedback, physiological signals offer an insight into human's physical and mental state which can be used to enrich the game interaction. (249)*
- *There are two important observations from the literature reviewed: i) Most of the emotion recognition systems (ERS) follow an ad hoc strategy (i.e., they provide a solution designed for a specific problem or task, non generalizable, and which is not easily adaptable to other purposes); ii) There are very few multi-category discrimination emotion recognition systems implemented in real-time. All the emotion recognition systems of the games presented in Table 1 are aimed to identify the presence or absence of a particular emotion, or to discriminate among small sets of opposite emotions. (250)*
- *Two machine learning models were trained to recognize the physiological patterns of 4 emotions, having the best results with a PNN with classification accuracy of 84.46% on the training data and 78.38% when it was cross-validated. The two machine learning models were implemented on the system for a real time classification. Finally, a simple application that customizes the desktop wallpaper to the emotional state of the user was developed. The results from our study provide evidence of the feasibility of the use of BAGI as an interface for gaming. (263)*

Chapter 17 - *Evaluating User Experience of Actual and Imagined Movement in BCI Gaming* (Bram van de Laar, Boris Reuderink, Danny Plass-Oude Bos, & Dirk Heylen)

- *While measuring brain activity for detection of movement, whether actual or imagined, other information can be derived from the brain as well, such as the user's mental and emotional state. This could be used to make smarter applications which are more aware of the user. (267)*
- *Results from this study showed that differences in user experience and in performance between actual and imagined movement in BCI gaming do exist. Actual movement produces a more reliable signal while the user stays more alert. On the other hand, imagined movement is more challenging. (276)*
- *Because of the similarities in brain activity between actual and imagined movement and the somewhat lacking of intuitivity for imagined movement one might suggest using actual movement as a training for using imagined movement. The user of the BCI can get accustomed to using movements for communications and at the same time trying to imagine the movement. With the acquired data from the actual movement, the imagined movement could be classified. (278)*

Chapter 18 - *Towards Games for Knowledge Acquisition and Modeling* (Stijn Hoppenbrouwers, Bart Schotten, & Peter Lucas)

- *One idea we are exploring is to look at formal knowledge modelling activities as games (or, more modestly put, 'game-like procedures'), forcing ourselves to look at contextualised, operational modelling in which human factors are inevitably included. Because the way in which we employ games for formal knowledge modelling involves human-computer interactions (HCI), these games-for-modelling systems can best be tested using HCI-like evaluation methods, including existing methods specifically aimed at game evaluation. This combination, games-for-modelling and exploitation of HCI methods for evaluation, is, to the best of our knowledge, new to AI. (282)*

- *Our observations suggest that there is indeed a noticeable difference between players with and without modelling experience. Despite our intentions to make the game playable for players with little or no expertise in modelling, most of those players found it hard to get started. It took them a while to understand what was meant by "task", "step", "ingredient" and "product". It was somewhat of a surprise to us that people by nature do not seem to make a sharp distinction even between actions and objects: sometimes they confuse the name of a step with its products, or describe substeps instead of ingredients. (295)*

- *A further interesting observation is that advanced functions of the game are generally not used. Players simply look for the easiest way to succeed in the game. (296)*

Chapter 19 - *Automated Event Recognition for Football Commentary Generation* (Maliang Zheng & Daniel Kudenko)

- *Most models of events are so complicated that they consist of many rules, for example, ROCCO uses 8 rules to define the ball-transfer event (Voelz et al., 1998). Thus, the generation of reliable models by hand is rather inefficient and may even be infeasible for a large number of more complex events. (301)*

- *In this paper, we present our work on automatically generating commentary rules using inductive learning techniques.Rather than establishing direct relationships between raw data and all commentary concepts, most practices start by extracting fundamental concepts from raw data (Stolarski, 2006), and organizes concepts in a hierarchical way. In other words, the event recognition process can be developed incrementally, and usually commences with modelling the basic actions. Techniques for recognizing the play-byplay events involve state machines, propositional. (313)*

- *rules, and quantitative analysis. We have described an approach to ingame commentary generation, which is based on the mapping of states to commentary concepts. We showed that while some concepts can be produced by hand-coded mappings, other concepts require a more sophisticated approach. Specifically, we propose the application of inductive learning, and the results of our case studies show the feasibility of this approach for the integration of high-level scene analysis and intelligent classification. (313)*

Richard E. Ferdig
Research Center for Educational Technology – Kent State University, USA

Sara de Freitas
Coventry University, UK

Chapter 1
Toward a Theory of Game–Media Literacy:
Playing and Building as Reading and Writing

Idit Harel Caperton
World Wide Workshop Foundation[1], USA

ABSTRACT

This paper discusses varied ideas on games, learning, and digital literacy for 21st-century education as theorized and practiced by the author and James Paul Gee, and their colleagues. With attention to games as means for learning, the author links Gee's theories to the learning sciences tradition (particularly those of the MIT Constructionists) and extending game media literacy to encompass "writing" (producing) as well as "reading" (playing) games. If game-playing is like reading and game-making is like writing, then we must introduce learners to both from a young age. The imagining and writing of web-games fosters the development of many essential skill-sets needed for creativity and innovation, providing an appealing new way for a global computing education, STEM education, for closing achievement gaps. Gee and the author reveal a shared aim to encourage researchers and theorists, as well as policymakers, to investigate gaming with regard to epistemology and cognition.

GAME LITERACY

In order to understand and define game literacy, we must first ask a few big questions: What is the significance of gaming practices for cognitive development and learning? How can games be leveraged as an important component of digital literacy development?

My colleague James Paul Gee and I collaborated at this year's annual meeting of the American Educational Research Association, offering two gaming-based theoretical frameworks for learning and digital literacy. Although we are known

DOI: 10.4018/978-1-4666-0029-4.ch001

to approach these topics ("gaming and learning" and "game literacy") from different perspectives, we attempted to integrate our views regarding 21st-century learners and their preferred learning environments in an effort to arrive at the same focal point.

During the session, we discussed a variety of ideas with examples from our most recent work. We hoped to inspire educational researchers, practitioners, policy makers and funders to deepen their understanding of various "videogame practices," involving 1) commercially-available videogames as learning tools; 2) videogames that teach educational content; 3) games and sims that involve modding and design as a learning environment; 4) game-making systems like GameStar Mechanics, Game Maker, Scratch; and 5) widely-used professional software programming tools like Java or Flash ActionScript.

This AERA session was intended to be a field-building session—a step toward a much larger conversation about the meaning and value of various kinds of game practices and literacies. We sought to shed light on why today's students should become game-literate, and to demonstrate a variety of possible routes that lead to game literacy. We also discussed the role of utilizing games and creating game-media in the learning and cognitive development of today's generation of students and educators.

MULTIPLE TRADITIONS FOR INITIATING AND INTERPRETING GAMING PRACTICES FOR LEARNING

Game literacy is a multidimensional combination of varied practices (e.g., reading, writing, and calculating; textual, visual, and spatial cognition; interactive design, programming, and engineering; multitasking and system understanding; meaning making, storytelling, role playing, perspective taking, and exercising judgment; etc.). Different gaming practices form a whole that has roots in both traditional literacy theories and Constructionist digital literacy. Though seemingly disparate, both traditions attempt to develop methods for describing how players/learners learn and how they construct knowledge in gaming contexts. Both traditions focus on the processes of learning rather than the product (winning the game or the actual game created by a learner/designer). Both traditions struggle with the difficulties of capturing the process of learning (an intersection of individual, context and activity over time within a situated perspective) as a unit of analysis. Despite the challenges that persist in such a dynamic and distributed object of study, educators and researchers continue to explore and refine innovative methodological approaches that capture and track learning as it flourishes within the rich environments of various gaming practices so as to inform instructional practice and design (also known as design-based research, e.g., Brown, 1996; Dede, 2005).

RESEARCH INTO PLAYING VIDEOGAMES

The fascination with and research on the cognitive and learning processes that occurs during videogame play is becoming increasingly prominent—so much so, that a national conference dedicated entirely to this topic was launched by Dr. James Paul Gee in 2004 as a venue for scholarly discourse (Games, Learning and Society, GLS, www.glsconference.org). In this growing field of gaming research, scholars are addressing the nature of cognitive and emotional development, literacy practices, and thinking and learning during gameplay in a range of gaming environments and genres (Barab, 2009; Gee, 2003, 2007; Shaffer, 2006; Squire, 2002, 2006, 2009; Steinkuehler, 2007, 2009a, 2009b). This line of research focuses on assessing different kinds of learning while playing games released commercially for entertainment (e.g., World of Warcraft, Grand Theft Auto, Zelda, Quake, Dance Dance Revolution, Guitar Hero, Rock Band), or edutainment games (e.g., Civilization, Quest Atlantis) in various contexts (mostly out of school, in homes, clubs and afterschool programs).

These scholars claim that videogame players *are* learning—they do not just click the controller or mouse mindlessly or move around randomly. Indeed, players are found to engage in unlocking rich storylines, employing complex problem-solving strategies and mastering the underlying systems of any given game or level. Researchers offer solid evidence that children learn important content, perspectives, and vital 21st-century skills from playing digital games (e.g., Salen, 2007; Lenhart, Kahne, Middaugh, Macgill, Evans, & Vitak, 2008; Thai, Lowenstein, Ching, & Rejeski, 2009). Scholars are also documenting the richness of players' collaborative inquiry, the complexity of play patterns for exploring information and identities and the emergence of complex forms of learning and participation during gameplay. They assert that through playing videogames and participating in videogame worlds, players can develop understandings and dispositions that are difficult to achieve otherwise. It is critical to note that these researchers' key objective is to document and demonstrate that gaming can provide learning experiences, which are rich and difficult (perhaps impossible) to replicate in other circumstances or learning contexts—especially in traditional schools.

RESEARCH INTO MODIFYING AND MAKING GAMES

Simultaneously, a growing number of scholars in the learning sciences, digital media literacy and education fields have researched and/or developed innovative learning programs engaging students in various aspects of game modding and design (see Duncan, 2009; Flanagan & Nissenbaum 2007;

Games, 2008; Hayes, 2008; Hayes et al., 2009; Kafai, 1995, 2006; Klopfer, 2008; Pinkard, 2008; Salen & Zimmerman, 2005; Sheridan, Clark, & Peters, 2009; Squire, 2002, 2005, 2006, 2009a, 2009b). They share the view that modding existing videogames and designing game systems is *itself* essential to digital literacy, as well as to the formation of knowledge and values, scientific thinking and problem solving, self-regulation, and brain development overall.

Some scholars in this group report results about learning environments and tools that utilize game-design platforms (e.g., Gamestar Mechanic, Scratch, Game-Maker, or 3D-engines, Alice, and Maya); others focus on the learning value of modding that can be done within commercial games, by using toolkits that companies make for game players (such as those provided in Civilization or The Sims).

RESEARCH INTO LEARNING GAME MAKING

The research about the learning value of game modding and design connects to Constructionism, a learning theory historically associated with my mentor and colleague Seymour Papert and our colleagues at the MIT Media Lab (www.Papert. org). Since the early 1980s, Constructionist learning theorists and practitioners have emphasized the epistemological value of "MIT-style" computational environments as tools for thinking, tinkering, and learning (Papert, 1980, 1993; Harel, 1988, 1989, 1991; Harel & Papert, 1990, 1991; Kafai & Resnick, 1996). These programmable environments have been designed to facilitate learning and self expression while tinkering with digital media, programming software, and building dynamic models, simulations, computer games, as well as other complex digital artifacts involving robotics. Researchers focused on figuring out how these tools were used as vehicles for driving all kinds of powerful learning and cognition (Harel Caperton, 2005).

Similarly, my colleague John Seely Brown (www.JohnSeelyBrown.com) provides a closely related theory that also advocates the general learning principles of Constructionism. For the past 10 years, he has been emphasizing the value of learning in communities of high-density computer cultures that resemble the ways MIT mathematicians, artists, musicians and engineers collaborate on complex design problems. In his speeches and essays, Brown frequently highlights the importance of learning through tinkering in a studio-like environment, and a "learning-to-be" approach (in contrast to "learning about") to role-taking that emerges from becoming a full participant in a digital learning community (e.g., Brown & Adler, 2008). Moreover, much like the MIT Constructionists (including Seymour Papert and myself), Brown is known for his examples of workshop-style settings, which reinforce the belief that significant global problems are likely to be systemic and can't be addressed by any one specialty. Therefore, students need to feel comfortable working in cross disciplinary teams that encompass multiple ways of knowing and learning.

In 2006, my team at the World Wide Workshop Foundation revitalized this Constructionist tradition through a social-innovation initiative called Globaloria, a global platform or social network and a comprehensive learning program for learning how to create educational web-games and simulations.[2] With a focus on serving (and researching) those who are technologically-underserved and/or economically-underprivileged, the Globaloria networks engage both students and educators to simultaneously master social media technology and learn how to create original web-games with a socially-conscious and/or educational purpose. Breaking away from the typical MIT computational tradition (e.g., the programming languages Logo, Microworlds, StarLogo, NetLogo, Scratch), the Globaloria network participants learn to program in popular, industry-accepted, globally-

employed languages such as Flash ActionScript and MediaWiki (in conjunction with other Google tools and Web2.0 applications) by using an open, yet structured and comprehensive curriculum, and blending in-class with virtual lessons.

Programming games on Globaloria.org (see Figure 1) also engages students in an interest-driven curriculum, allowing them to play games, but also to explore and develop their own games following their individual and situational interests.

Students use computational programming tools and Web2.0 technology to generate a self-determined motivation for learning. In other words, as students engage their curiosity and imagination through teamwork on game construction, they also "learn-to-be," by taking full participation in a networked, software design-based learning community.

A complementary "Research 2.0" agenda[3] has been under conceptualization and development in the past two years to study and assess the effectiveness of this MIT-inspired learning formula. We gradually formed a network of independent researchers who are beginning to observe results indicating the educational value of game making and its contribution to digital literacy and social, emotional and cognitive development especially among low-income students and educators in both rural and urban communities (Harel Caperton, Oliver & Sullivan, 2008, 2009; Knestis, 2008; Nicholson et al., 2009; Harel Caperton & Sullivan, 2009). Globaloria is the largest effort to date to introduce game-media learning and literacy into public schools and public universities (see Figures 2, 3, 4, and 5).

LITERACY AND "GOOD VIDEOGAMES"

James Paul Gee's ideas about the cognitive and learning processes that occur during videogame play are growing in prominence. In 2007, Gee published two seminal books on this topic, *What*

Figure 1. Screen shots of the Globaloria.org platform. It includes a library of web-games to play and evaluate their design and code, integrated with a comprehensive game-making curriculum, tutorials and programming tools and tips – forming a network of online wiki-based design studios and communities-of-practice of project-based Constructionist learning.

Figure 2. Taking Game-Making to School: Building an innovative model to demonstrate the network effect of scaling the Globaloria game-making program over a 5-year Pilot across West Virginia's public school system – middle schools and, high schools, vocational schools, alternative education, community colleges and public universities.

Demonstrating the Network Effect Over 5 Years				
Game Design Pilot Year 1 (2007-08)	Game Design Pilot Year 2 (2008-09)	Game Design Pilot Year 3 (2009-10)	Game Design Pilot Year 4 (2010-11)	Game Design Pilot Year 5 (2011-12)
Participants	Participants	Participants	Participants	Participants
114	325	996	3,000	10,000
7 schools	13 schools	22 schools	37 schools	60 schools
8 groups	24 groups	53 groups	120 groups	300 groups
89 students	291 students	968 students	2,940 students	9,850 students
18 educators	21 educators	36 educators	60 educators	150 educators
7 principals	13 principals	22 principals	37 principals	60 principals
30 games	95 games	300 games	1,000 games	3,000 games

Figure 3. Some students learned science by programming a game they named "Learn the Bones."

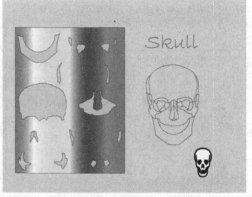

Screen 1. Title screen (when game opens). The Cosmic Energy Team designed two options for the user: Play the game, or learn about the game and how it was made and who made it.

Screen 2. Skull Level. Rolling over the bones with the mouse reveals the scientific name of the bone. Clicking on the bone enables the player to drag it to the picture of the skull. Clicking on the skull graphic in corner enables the player to continue when finished.

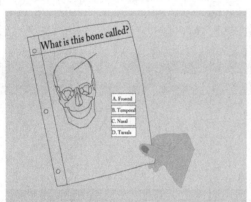

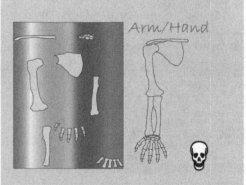

Screen 3. After the player correctly completes the drag-and-drop, they are asked questions related to that level. Right answers score 2 points, and wrong answers lose a point.

Screen 4. Arm-Hand Level: Similar interaction pattern as in Skull Level.

Video Games Have to Teach Us about Learning and Literacy, and *Good Video Games and Good Learning.* In both books, the central theme is that good videogames reflect good principles of learning in their design. Gee focuses on the learning and literacies that develop among players of popular videogames based on learning principles reflected in the game structure itself.

Gee emphasizes an important idea that all literacies must be addressed in relation to specific semiotic domains. He deals with videogames as one such semiotic domain, and explores the processes involved in becoming digitally literate therein. Gee refers to people who play the games as "affinity groups," who, in attaining literacy, are able to situate decoded language, images and other forms of representation within the domains in which they are put to use. Once literacy is established in this contextualized manner, the player is operating in a semiotic domain.[4] Furthermore, Gee (2007b) formulates a number of key learning principles[5] that are intrinsic to the semiotic

Figure 4. Some students learned world history by programming an educational game they named 'Zeit Geist.'

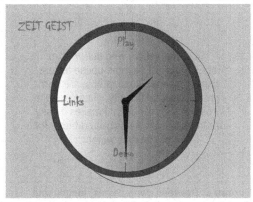

Screen 1. The opening title to the game gives players the options to see a demo, read the rules, look at links (related to the content of the game), or play the game.

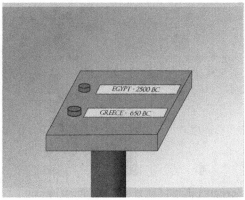

Screen 2. Zeit Geist Game's Menu. Player can choose which country and time period to enter (Egypt or Greece).

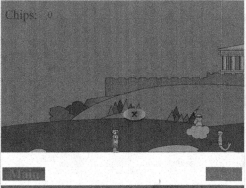

Screen 3. A scene from the Greece level. The main character, the background scenes, as well as the music and sounds effects change depending on the nation and time period.

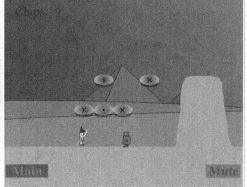

Screen 4. A scene from the Egypt level. Player can see the Chips score (top left), and always select to go back to the main menu, or to mute the music and sound effects (at bottom left and right of screen).

domain of videogames. I have selected five to highlight here:

- **Principle 1:** *Active, Critical Learning:* all aspects of the learning environment are set up to encourage active and critical, not passive, learning.
- **Principle 2:** *Design Principle:* Learning about and coming to appreciate design and design principles is core to the learning experience.
- **Principle 3:** *Semiotic Principle:* Learning about and coming to appreciate inter-correlations within and across multiple sign systems as complex systems is core to the learning experience.
- **Principle 4:** *Semiotic Domains Principle:* Learning involves mastering (at some level) semiotic domains and being able to participate (at some level) in the affinity group or groups connected to them.

Figure 5. Some students examined health-related issues by programming various educational games about healthy eating habits to combat obesity.

Screen 1. Food Fall is a health game where players must control a character moving with a tray trying to catch healthy food and avoid the unhealthy food.

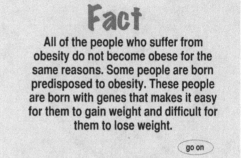

Screen 2. Between game levels, facts about obesity or healthy eating habits are presented. Research was conducted into the topic of obesity in our nation, and what would be a useful interface and play interaction for fostering healthier diet.

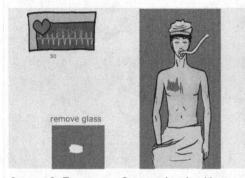

Screen 3. Emergency Surgeon is a health game where players select different medical tools and do surgery. This game includes a health bar and drag-and-drop interaction.

Screen 4. When Zombies Attack is a math game where players must solve sets of mathematical problems to defeat the zombies that have taken over the school. The game includes a timer and a scoring system.

- **Principle 5:** *Meta-level Thinking about Semiotic Domains Principle:* Learning involves active and critical thinking about the relationships between the semiotic domain being learned and other semiotic domains.

These principles address important learning processes that have been built into games by their designers. The above principles (and 25 others listed in his book) suggest that there are in-depth learning-processes at work while playing games. Indeed, game designers learn a great deal as they design game systems and in "good games" some of their learning and system-thinking is transferred to those who play their games.

In his writings, Gee emphasizes how, through good game design, people can leverage deeper learning as a form of pleasure in their everyday lives, without any explicit schooling. He argues that one way to deliver good learning in schools and workplaces would be via games or game-like technologies and calls for making students into full and productive partners in how we design any enterprise in which we use games for learning.

Gee also explores the value of playing games for learning about systems and understanding complex concepts and the way things work in the world. Furthermore, he investigates the potential value of using game engines for knowledge and skill assessment of students learning.

THE IMPORTANCE OF LEARNING TO PROGRAM GAMES TO GAME-MEDIA LITERACY DEVELOPMENT

Despite Gee's important contributions (as well as those from the movement he has inspired), a deeper focus on the potential role of game building, designing and programming in cognition, learning and digital literacy development has been missing from the body of research on "good learning" while playing "good videogames."

The question I am posing to "gameplay researchers" (including Gee) is this: How can players' system-understanding and literacy in the semiotic domain of videogame playing practices be complete without providing them (the players) with the opportunity to learn how videogames are *made* through engagement in the game production process? In other words, while 'systems content' may be more or less present and conveyed through game play, working on game creation arguably conveys understanding of game components and game systems through a more intimate and inter-dependent epistemological context.

At our AERA session, I strongly suggested to Gee that game-playing is like "reading" and game-making is like "writing" in that they must be introduced to learners hand-in-hand from a young age. One learns to read better and more critically by learning creative writing and, conversely learns to write better and more creatively by reading and analyzing the symbolism in books and genres. It does a disservice to the aim of any literacy education (game literacy included) to overlook the mutually constitutive relationship between reading and writing.

LINKING GAME-MAKING PRACTICES TO CONSTRUCTIONISM

In the 1980s and early 1990s, when videogames were still a burgeoning industry, my research focused on children's creation of instructional software games about mathematical concepts related to rational numbers and fractions (Harel, 1988, 1989, 1991; Harel & Papert, 1990). I found that the meta-cognitive process of representation while designing software games requires the designer to go beyond a mechanical interaction with an existing mathematical game and to develop ideas and knowledge in a symbolic form through programming. In my early research in this area, young students used a programming language to represent and teach fractions in a complex set of visual multimedia symbols by coding the design and interactivity in Logo. With my then graduate student, Yasmin Kafai, we found that engaging students in making instructional games to teach younger students about the subject material (vs. creating non-instructional games) cultivated deep epistemological thinking, providing them with opportunities for *learning how to learn*. It has been theorized (and subsequently proven) over decades of research that learners' conscious construction of representational and/or instructional computational artifacts, or a computational model as a technologically-mediated public entity, is highly effective in building knowledge and meaning for the learner and his/her peers (e.g., Harel & Papert, 1990, 1991; Wilensky, 2003). This has led to a wide-spread conclusion that the act of programming (even at a beginner level) is an essential element toward becoming digitally literate.[6]

In the mid 1990s, I took my vision to the Internet and launched MaMaMedia.com, an award-winning website for children. MaMaMedia Inc. was founded during Web1.0 or "old Internet era" and in 1995 was envisioning and pioneering the many participatory media-making-and-sharing principles we now use in the "new Internet era" (Harel, 1996, 1997, 1999). In three years it reached over 50 million children, parents and teachers from 36 countries. At the end of the 20th century, in response to the need for all children to develop new learning skills and digital literacies for the coming millennium, I firmly linked the "3 Rs" of traditional education, Reading, wRiting, and aRithmetic, with the "3Xs": eXploring, eXpressing and eXchanging ideas of new digital media. I brought computational creativity and self-expression together with media technology via browsers to millions of children worldwide, driven by the belief that becoming digitally literate was about actively designing and realizing digital media and not just passively consuming it (Harel, 2002).

As the second decade of 21st century begins, we stand at a pivotal moment in the advancement of videogames, web-games, and web technologies. The computational, social and collaborative principles inherent in the Constructionist framework can now be applied in the context of collaborative game–making projects online. Web2.0 tools allow for learners' conscious construction of a computational public entity to extend beyond their ongoing face-to-face interactions and pre-internet desktop computers into the realm of global networks founded in collaboration and peer-production online.

Much like MaMaMedia, with the invention of Globaloria, Constructionism has influenced the design of program components that engage participants in experiential, project-based design, programming and collaborative experiences within high-density computer environments in the design-studio style. I hypothesize that the Globaloria activities of game design and programming, wiki-based teamwork and Web2.0 communication, collaboration, and project management are particularly powerful in cultivating *transferable* contemporary learning abilities and encouraging game-media digital literacies in participants (see Figure 6).

THE SIX CONTEMPORARY LEARNING ABILITIES: A THEORY-IN-THE-MAKING

The theoretical framework utilized by the World Wide Workshop Foundation to guide the Globaloria program's research is called the "Six Contemporary Learning Abilities with Technology" (6-CLAs) (Reynolds & Harel Caperton, 2009a, 2009b; Knesis, 2008). It is centered on connecting today's youth to computational thinking by making and playing games and thus becoming game-media literate. The World Wide Workshop Foundation believes that the six stipulated Constructionist game-media literacies and competencies are necessary for effective learning and working in today's technology-driven landscape and global workplace. The Six Contemporary Learning Abilities (6-CLAs) are:

- CLA-1. Invention, progression and completion of an original project idea (educational game or simulation system)
- CLA-2. Project-based learning and project management (managing game production in wiki-based networked environment)
- CLA-3. Posting, publishing and distribution of digital media (game designs, video prototypes, graphics and design notes)
- CLA-4. Social-based learning, participation and exchange (sharing game ideas, process notes and code)
- CLA-5. Information-based learning and research (purposeful search and exploration related to game topics and programming)
- CLA-6. Surfing and analyzing websites and web applications (for game code and tips)

This framework is the first to propose integrating Constructionist literacy elements into the domain of gaming and applied digital literacy typologies. We hypothesize that game-making is key to developing the above core competencies.

Figure 6. The Globaloria Learning Formula: Situating game design in a studio-based networked learning for cultivating game-media literacy knowledge and skills that includes both reading and writing games and content learning too. Students and educators work in class as well as virtually, individually and collaboratively, with the transparent help of peers, educators, or experts, on demand.

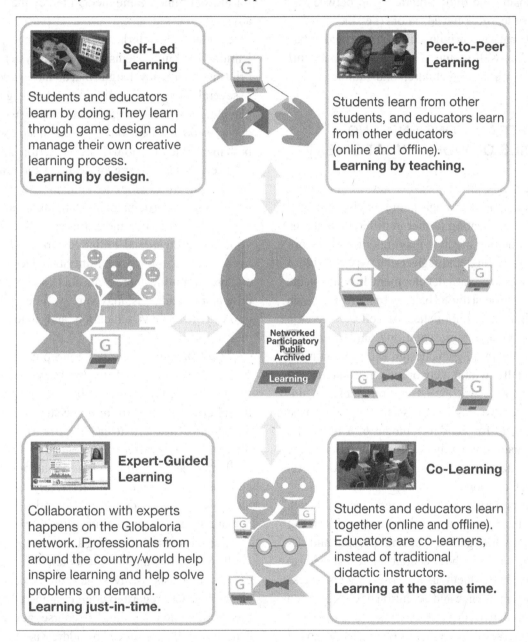

Moreover, by developing these competencies, students cultivate a variation of Constructionist digital literacy, which provides new opportunities for closing the digital-literacy gap between all types of learners and educators (i.e., the "haves:" digital natives, privileged suburban and urban youth, as well as the "have-nots:" low-income inner-city and rural children and adults).[7]

TWO TRADITIONS AND TWO BODIES OF WORK: WHAT'S NEXT?

While Gee's theories on the key learning principles acquired through game-playing are well worth investigating further in different contexts, his privileging of game-playing orients his work toward "reading" and neglects the "writing" side of game media literacy development. In contrast, the Constructionist digital literacy framework, which highlights the importance of self-construction of knowledge representations, and even *prioritizes* learning game design and programming (especially within networked, transparent and collaborative wiki-based environments); it underscores "writing" as an essential project-based component for the development of a fuller and richer game-media literacy, with attention to the Six Contemporary Learning Abilities (6-CLAs) (Harel Caperton et al., 2008).

Despite relevant differences, Gee and I both stress the importance of the process of learning to learn while gaming (in both playing and designing) and we both encourage researchers to identify better methods for observing and tracking the emergence and evolution of concepts and artifacts that occur across extended time frames of game literacy development. Gee and I believe that a learner's understanding of any issue, concept, or system is facilitated and distributed across the network (Globaloria.org) or community (of a commercial videogame players) and that cognition is situated and distributed in both a gameplay and/

or game-making activities. Therefore, capturing learning-in-the-making while playing/reading and/or designing/writing is necessary in order for this combined game media literacy theory to advance.

Similar to the interlaced relationship between learning reading systems and writing systems in print-media literacy, I argue that an integrated set of several game-media activities (including game-playing, game-modding and game-making) should occur *in parallel* in today's Web2.0 landscape both in and out of school (Harel Caperton, 2009).

There is also an urgent need (in the United States and worldwide) to cultivate the desire in youths to participate in computational and engineering thinking and learning of their own volition. Motivational initiatives are especially needed amongst girls and minorities. Designing and programming games and sims, or even modding games and sims, may very well be a useful gateway to STEM education and innovation development.

These broader, integrated conceptualizations by both Gee and myself suggest a new necessity for youths to play games of different genres for the sake of engaged learning and system-thinking. This necessity extends to the design and programming of games in different genres and on different topics in order to yield transferable outcomes and competencies essential to effectively navigate today's technology-driven world and a highly-demanding participatory citizenship in our society – which requires both reading and writing games. Collectively, our aim is to encourage researchers and theorists to investigate the importance of gaming with regard to cognition and advance the gaming and learning discourse generally. This goal will be achieved by addressing the key significance of both game-playing and student-centered game-production experiences in learning and in the successful acquisition of comprehensive game-media literacy.

In closing, readers are invited to continue the dialogue I had with Jim Gee and our moderator Betty Hayes and our audience at AERA, and link their minds to the vision that is spelled out in this essay. While most of the basic parameters are laid out here and in the mentioned literature, a great deal of work on a much larger scale is needed on the ground, especially in these far away corners inside the failing public schools of urban and rural low-income communities. In our session, Gee expressed his rather strong skeptic views about our ability to transform failing schools with good videogames or game-making programs. However, I strongly believe that it is possible and necessary to do so. How else can we help those who are not yet connected regularly to high-speed Internet, who cannot afford or are not yet fluent with videogames and Web 2.0, and never experiences design-based learning projects and Constructionist learning? We can't lose time. We need to reach them in schools. I personally have a strong sense of urgency to move the conversation (and practice and research) from a single focus on assessing 'playing games' in informal settings (homes., afterschool clubs) into 'making games' on purposeful content in and out of school -- mainly because it embodies the essence of what good contemporary learning is all about (I call it STEM-Square) and some kids can only do this in their schools.

This essay is therefore a call to action for my fellow educational researchers, social entrepreneurs, developers and game designers: In a world in which the ability to imagine, represent and create, not just consume, digital media will define citizenship, measure productivity, and enable success, students can afford no less.

ACKNOWLEDGMENT

Special thanks to Jim Gee and Betty Hayes for collaborating on a great panel at AERA-2009. I thank Rebecca Reynolds, Rachel Rosenfelt, Laura Minnigerode, and Bobbi Nicholson for their contributions in turning this AERA panel presentation to a publishable essay. I am deeply thankful for Lisa Dawley's and Jonathon Richter's invitation to participate in their special issue, with additional thanks to Jonathon for his valuable editorial suggestions. I would like to recognize the spectacular World Wide Workshop Foundation's team, as well as our partners and funders for their support of the Globaloria program and long-term vision for transforming education; in particular I thank the West Virginia Governor and First Lady Joe and Gayle Manchin; the West Virginia Department of Education's Dr. Steve Paine, Dr. Jorea Marple and Monica Beane; the West Virginia Center for Professional Development; the Claude Worthington Benedum Foundation; Verizon Foundation; the John S. and James L. Knight Foundation; Advanced Micro Devices; and the Caperton Fund. Finally, I offer my sincere thanks to 1500 Globaloria students and educators who have been pioneering our invention with passion and commitment, quite often working outside of their comfort zone, and teaching us daily through their learning-by-doing how to improve our ideas and designs in order to expand this innovation nationally and globally. Because of them we know it's possible.

REFERENCES

Barab, S. A. (2009, June). *Transformational Play: Why Educators Should Care About Games*. Paper presented at Games, Learning and Society, Madison, WI.

Brown, A. L. (1996). Design experiments: Theoretical and methodological challenges in creating complex interventions in classroom settings. *Journal of the Learning Sciences, 2*(2), 141–178. doi:10.1207/s15327809jls0202_2

Clark, K. A., & Sheridan, K. (2009, April). *Game Design Communities: Exploring a Model for Underserved Students*. Paper presented at the Annual Conference of the American Education Research Association, San Diego, CA.

Dede, C. (2005). Why design-based research is both important and difficult. *Educational Technology*, *45*(1), 5–8.

Duncan, S. (2009, June). *"Here's My Shootorial!":The Scaffolding of Game Design on Kongregate*. Paper presented at Games, Learning and Society, Madison, WI.

Flanagan, M., & Nissenbaum, H. (2007). <u>A Game Design Methodology to Incorporate Social Activist Themes.</u> In *Proceedings of CHI 2007* (pp. 181-190). New York: ACM Press.

Games, A. (2008). *Assessing Game-Based Literacies: The Role of Task Constraints on Strategic Meaning Making Within Gamestar Mechanic*. Paper presented at Games, Learning and Society, Madison, WI.

Gee, J. P. (2003). *What video games have to teach us about learning and literacy*. New York: Palgrave Macmillan.

Gee, J. P. (2007). *Good video games + good learning*. New York: Peter Lang.

Harel, I. (1988). *Software design for learning: Children's learning fractions and Logo programming through instructional software design*. Unpublished doctoral dissertation, MIT Media Laboratory.

Harel, I. (1989, September). Learning About Learning. *Newsweek*.

Harel, I. (1991). *Children Designers: Interdisciplinary constructions for learning and knowing mathematics in a computer-rich school*. Norwood, NJ: Ablex.

Harel, I. (1996). Learning Skills for the New Millennium: The three X's. In *21st-Century Learning*, MaMaMedia.com.

Harel, I. (1997). Clickerati kids, who are they? *21st Century Learning*. Retrieved from http://www.mamamedia.com

Harel, I. (1999). And a Child Shall Lead Them: Young kids show the benefits of a new affinity with technology. *CONTEXT: Man & Machine*.

Harel, I. (2002). Learning new-media literacy: A new necessity for the Clickerati Generation. *Telemedium Journal of Media Literacy*.

Harel, I., Oliver, A., & Sullivan, S. (2008). *Implementing Globaloria in West Virginia: Results from Pilot Year-1*. New York: World Wide Workshop Foundation. Retrieved from http://www.worldwideworkshop.org/reports

Harel, I., & Papert, S. (1990). Software design as a learning environment. *Interactive Learning Environments*, *1*(1), 1–32. doi:10.1080/1049482900010102

Harel, I., & Papert, S. (1991). (Eds.). *Constructionism*. Norwood, NJ: Ablex.

Harel Caperton, I. (2005). "Hard fun:" The essence of good games AND good education. *Telemedium Journal of Media Literacy*.

Harel Caperton, I. (2009). The New Literacy is Game Literacy. In *Proceedings of TEDGlobal*, Oxford, UK. Retrieved from http://www.worldwideworkshop.org/pdfs/Idit_Ted_Lecture.pdf

Harel Caperton, I., Kraus, L., Sullivan, S., & Reynolds, R. (2008). *Globaloria: Social Media Networks for Learning Through Game Production With a Social Purpose*. Paper presented at Games, Learning and Society, Madison, WI.

Harel Caperton, I., Oliver, A., & Sullivan, S. (2009). *Globaloria in West Virginia: Empowering students with 21st-century digital literacy though a game-making learning network*. New York: World Wide Workshop Foundation. Retrieved from http://WorldWideWorkshop.org/reports

Harel Caperton, I., & Sullivan, S. (2009, June). *Students' Development of Contemporary Core Competencies through Making Educational Web Games*. Paper presented at Games, Learning and Society, Madison, WI.

Hayes, E. (2008). Game content creation and IT proficiency: An exploratory study. *Computers & Education, 51*(1), 97–108. doi:10.1016/j.compedu.2007.04.002

Hayes, E., Johnson, B. Z., Lammers, J. C., & Lee, Y. (2009, April). *Taking the SIMS Seriously: Play, Identity, and Girls' IT Learning*. Paper presented at the Annual Conference of the American Education Research Association, San Diego, CA.

Kafai, Y. B. (1995). *Minds in Play: Computer game design as a context for children's learning*. Hillsdale, NJ: Lawrence Erlbaum Associates.

Kafai, Y. B. (2006). Playing and making games for learning: Instructionist and constructionist perspectives for game studies. *Games and Culture, 1*(1), 36–40. doi:10.1177/1555412005281767

Kafai, Y. B., & Resnick, M. (Eds.). (1996). *Constructionism in Practice: Designing, thinking, and learning in a digital world*. Mahwah, NJ: Lawrence Erlbaum Associates.

Klopfer, E. (2008). *Augmented learning: Research and design of mobile educational games*. Cambridge, MA: MIT Press.

Knestis, K. (2008). *Understanding Globaloria as the subject of research: An agenda for future study*. Charleston, WV: Edvantia, Inc.

Lenhart, A., Kahne, J., Middaugh, E., Macgill, A. R., Evans, C., & Vitak, J. (2008). *Teens, Video Games and Civics: Teens' gaming experiences are diverse and include significant social interaction and civic engagement*. Washington, DC: Pew Internet and American Life Project. Nicholson, B., Alley, R., Green, J., & Lawson, D. (2009). *An Analysis of the Effects of a Technology Program on Students' Academic Performance: Are These Vygotsky's Children?* Huntington, WV: Marshall University.

Papert, S. (1980). *Mindstorms: Children, computers and powerful ideas*. New York: Basic Books.

Papert, S. (1993). *The children's machine: Rethinking schools in the age of the computer*. New York: Basic Books.

Pinkard, N. (2009). *Preparing Urban Youth to be Multiliterate*. Chicago: University of Chicago, Center for Urban School Improvement. Retrieved from http://iremix.org/3-research/pages/33-research-overview

Reynolds, R., & Harel Caperton, I. (2009a, June). *Development of Students' Six Contemporary Learning Abilities in Globaloria*. Paper presented at the Annual Conference of the American Educational Research Association, San Diego, CA.

Reynolds, R., & Harel Caperton, I. (2009b, June). *Development of High School and Community College Students' Contemporary Learning Abilities in Globaloria*. Paper presented at the Annual Conference of the American Educational Research Association, San Diego, CA.

Salen, K. (Ed.). (2007). *The Ecology of Games: Connecting Youth, Games, and Learning*. Chicago: John D. and Catherine T. MacArthur Foundation.

Salen, K., & Zimmerman, E. (2006). *The game design reader: A rules of play anthology*. Cambridge, MA: MIT Press.

Seely Brown, J., & Adler, R. P. (2008). Minds on Fire: Open Education, the Long Tail, and Learning 2.0. *Educause Review*.

Shaffer, D. W. (2006). *How computer games help children learn*. New York: Palgrave Macmillan.

Squire, K. (2002). Rethinking the role of games in education. *Game Studies, 2*(1).

Squire, K. (2005). Educating the fighter. *Horizon, 13*(2), 75–88. doi:10.1108/10748120510608106

Squire, K. (2006). From content to context: Videogames as designed experience. *Educational Researcher, 35*(8), 19–29. doi:10.3102/0013189X035008019

Squire, K. (2009a). Designing Educational Systems for a Participatory Media Age. Presented at the *Annual Conference of the American Education Research Association*. San Diego, CA.

Squire, K. (2009b). What Happens When a Game Is a Curriculum? Lessons Learned From a Game-Based Curriculum. Presented at the *Annual Conference of the American Education Research Association*, San Diego, CA.

Steinkeuhler, C. (2009a, April). *Digital Literacies for the Disengaged: Creating After-School Online Game-Based Learning Environments for Boys*. Presented at the Annual Conference of the American Education Research Association, San Diego, CA.

Steinkeuhler, C. (2009b, April). *A Topology of Literacy Practices in Virtual Worlds*. Presented at the Annual Conference of the American Education Research Association, San Diego, CA.

Steinkuehler, C. (2007). Massively multiplayer online gaming as a constellation of literacy practices. *E-learning, 4*(3), 297–318. doi:10.2304/elea.2007.4.3.297

Thai, A. M., Lowenstein, D., Ching, D., & Rejeski, D. (2009). *Game Changer: Investing in Digital Play to Advance Children's Learning and Health*. New York: Joan Ganz Cooney Center at Sesame Workshop.

Whitehouse, P., Reynolds, R., & Harel Caperton, I. (2008). *The Development of a Research Framework to Examine Teacher Professional Development and Educator Experiences in Globaloria, Pilot Year 1*. West Virginia University and World Wide Workshop. Retrieved from http://www.WorldWideWorkshop.org/Reports

Wilensky, U. (2003). Statistical mechanics for secondary school: The GasLab modeling toolkit. *International Journal of Computers for Mathematical Learning, 8*(1), 1–41. doi:10.1023/A:1025651502936

ENDNOTES

[1]   This is a summary of a paper I presented on a panel with **Prof. James Paul Gee** (James.Gee@asu.edu) at the 2009 Annual Meeting of the American Education Research Association (AERA) in San Diego, Interactive Symposium of the SIG Applied Research in Virtual Environments for Learning. Jim Gee is professor at Arizona State University and a member of the National Academy of Education. His book *Sociolinguistics and Literacies* was one of the founding documents in the formation of New Literacy Studies, a field devoted to studying language, learning, and literacy. Professor Gee's most recent work deals with videogames, language, and learning; he shows how they can help us think about "good learning" and the reform of schools.

[2]   See: www.WorldWideWorkshop.org and www.Globaloria.org.

3   See: www.WorldWideWorkshop.org/Reports

4   Semiotics is defined as the study of signs and symbols and how people construct meanings from those signs and symbols. There is the *signifier* (what the word/text/artifact is called, an arbitrary designation – book, film, game) and the *signified* (what it is interpreted to mean). The key is that once the signifier is made public (in a published videogame for instance), the writer/developer no longer has control over how it is received or understood by those who read/play/watch it.

5   See Appendix of Gee's book *What Video Games Have to Teach Us About Learning and Literacy, 2007.*

6   In the past three decades, Constructionist scholars (myself included) were often challenged regarding whether or not Constructionist learning must always include programming to qualify. Is video production considered Constructionist? Is building in Second Life without any programming knowledge, by simply combining prims and dropping in a pre-programmed scripts purchased from somewhere else considered Constructionist? Is using templated environments for building digital media artifacts considered Constructionist? My personal response is: Why not? I am not as 'pure' as many of my colleagues. I believe in the power and value of representing knowledge through programming (as expressed in Globaloria) but I also believe in the value of media making for learning (as expressed in MaMaMedia). Constructionist learning comes in many forms – from Tinker toys, to Logo, to Mindstroms robotics, to Game Maker, to Flash. One thing is sure: all these tools and environments exist on the "writing side" of the literacy equation.

7   In another AERA paper (with Rebecca Reynolds, 2009) we describe the 6-CLAs as an early-stage conceptual framework and we are currently forming goals to establish a criterion for success. Theories have two central properties: they must be falsifiable and have a sense of process (theories are scientific, and must be tested). The CLAs adhere to these theoretical properties in asserting our goal: *the mastery of the CLAs will lead to closing the digital literacy gap*, including the game literacy gap. Globaloria maintains a sense of process in its implementation, and the World Wide Workshop Foundation and its research affiliates are implementing and testing methods for assessing the success of Globaloria in cultivating Constructionist digital literacy. For more on how Globaloria supports 6CLAs literacy in educators, see The Development of a Research Framework to Examine Teacher Professional Development and Educator Experiences (Harel Caperton, Reynolds & Whitehouse, 2008).

This work was previously published in International Journal of Gaming and Computer-Mediated Simulations, Volume 2, Issue 1, edited by Richard E. Ferdig, pp. 1-16, copyright 2010 by IGI Publishing (an imprint of IGI Global).

Chapter 2
Narratizing Disciplines and Disciplinizing Narratives:
Games as 21st Century Curriculum

Sasha A. Barab
Indiana University, USA

Melissa Gresalfi
Indiana University, USA

Tyler Dodge
Indiana University, USA

Adam Ingram-Goble
Indiana University, USA

ABSTRACT

Education is about revealing possibility and exciting passions, empowering learners with the disciplinary expertise to meaningfully act on problematic contexts in which applying disciplinary knowledge is important. Toward this end, we have been using gaming methodologies and technologies to design curricular dramas that position students as active change agents who use knowledge to inquire into particular circumstances and, through their actions, transform the problematic situation into a known. Unlike more traditional textbooks designed to transmit facts or micro-stories, our focus is on building interactive experiences in which understanding core concepts, such as erosion or the idea of metaphor, and seeing oneself as a person who uses these to address personally meaningful and socially significant problems is valued. It is the explicit goal of this manuscript to communicate this power of educational videogames, as well as the design steps that we have been using to make this happen.

DOI: 10.4018/978-1-4666-0029-4.ch002

INTRODUCTION

In many American classrooms, students have opportunities to remember and record decontextualized disciplinary information in ways that all too often contribute to inert understandings. Such positioning of disciplinary content often undermines student appreciation of the potential value of academic content for solving personally meaningful and situationally significant problems. Theoretically, we are arguing for the need to reconnect disciplinary understandings with contexts in which such understandings are useful, specifically by *narratizing disciplines* and, at the same time, to empower youth to *disciplinize narratives*. In realizing this vision, a central goal in our design is to develop play spaces in which the learner has a goal or intention and makes choices in a dynamic environment/storyline that change in relation to these choices. From a design focus, our interest is in (1) legitimizing the key disciplinary content to be learned; (2) positioning the person as an individual with an intention to transform the content; and (3) designing the learning environment as a context in which actions are consequential. The challenge underlying our work is how to use videogames to connect disciplinary content with those situations in which it has personal and functional value.

Toward this end, and as part of our design of a multiuser virtual environment called Quest Atlantis (see http://QuestAtlantis.Org), we have developed a theory around the power of *transformational play*. Playing transformationally involves taking on the role of a protagonist who must employ conceptual understandings to understand and, ultimately, make choices that have the potential to transform a problematic context. For example, in one of our extensively researched designed worlds, a student becomes a scientist, examining the water quality of the green, murky water in a virtual river (Barab, Sadler, Heiselt, Hickey, & Zuiker, 2007; Barab, Zuiker, et al., 2007). In another context, a student becomes a statistician using measures of center to analyze

various choices and help a mayor make the best choices (Gresafli, Barab, Siyahhan, & Christensen, 2009). In still another context, the player becomes an investigative reporter, assembling evidence by talking to game characters to build a persuasive argument for the town newspaper (Barab et al., 2009).

Elsewhere, we have discussed the role of transformational play in supporting learning and, in particular, how our designs support transformational play (Barab, Gresalfi, & Ingram-Goble, 2009; Barab, Gresalfi, & Arici, in press). Here, we focus more specifically on how educational games can be disciplinary worlds, and game play can become a way of *disciplinizing* the world (cf. Roth, 1994; Hoyles, Noss, & Pozzi, 1999)—using disciplinary content as a tool to understand and take actions on problems in the world. The goal of this manuscript is to elaborate on this theoretical stance and to share design strategies that have usefully guided the worlds we have created and have been used in hundreds of 4th-8th grade classrooms worldwide.

THEORETICAL FRAMING

Games as Disciplinary Worlds (Narratizing Disciplines)

Our work entails the use of videogame technologies to establish prototypical situations as exemplars, which serve as the referent that, for the learner, makes visible and valuable the to-be-learned concept. Such work has resonance with simulations and other work designed to *situate* academic concepts (Cognition and Technology Group at Vanderbilt, 1991), but extends further in that we are concerned with situating contexts such that they are responsive to learner actions. In other words, while some have argued for the importance of the framing context in co-determining the meaning of particular content, games allows us to additionally situate the person as the central protagonist who makes key decisions. To elaborate, while in some of our work one can perceptually see a disciplinary concept (e.g., witnessing an algae bloom by examining the green, murky water in a particular location in a virtual river), we are primarily interested in the learner having the experience of *being in* a scenario wherein applying one's understanding of a disciplinary concept has impact on the (virtual) situation—a situation in which the learner has a significant role and which is semantically revealing, thereby helping learners appreciate the meaningfulness of the concept (its use value) for transforming problematic situations (Barab, Zuiker, et al., 2007).

In this manner, our work involves allowing the meaning of concepts to come from their functional value in the world, with the design goal being to create a virtual environment that enables learners to use disciplinary concepts to meaningfully act on this fictional scenario. To further clarify the goal, Gee (2003) has discussed the example of trying to read a game manual without playing the game—a task one finds tedious, uninteresting, and conceptually challenging. However, once one engages the game itself, the manual content becomes clear, interesting to the player, and even valuable for improving one's performance in the game. Extending this thinking to educational settings, it might be argued that schools too often provide learners with the manual and rarely engage them in playing the game. But more than making the concepts meaningful, our goal is to support learners in perceiving themselves as people who can use the content toward meaningful ends with the expectation of allowing them to try on new ways of being in the world. Said another way, in our games, one is not simply playing the game, but playing out the self, as they are stretched into another world and another self (Gadamer, 1989).

So, for example, usefully applying one's understanding of algae blooms to identify a particular cause and generate a solution has the potential of changing one's understanding of self as an individual who uses science to improve the world.

Importantly, the disciplinary worlds in which our game play is situated are fictional, allowing such an opportunity for players who might otherwise never see themselves as able to take on such an identity and meaningfully use disciplinary content. The fictional and sometimes fantastical nature of the stories, we argue, is in part what makes it possible for the player to leave the "real" world and meaningfully enter the virtual one—a world in which they can become a scientist, a historian, a reporter—and in this role of an evolving expert, they address problems that are personally engaging and situationally important. Lastly, a disciplinary world involves more than a framing of possible uses of content, but actually establishes a world in which the only way to succeed is to meaningfully leverage disciplinary content to interpret and to make meaningful game play choices. Just as the storyline *narratizes* the to-be-learned content, the relationship among conditions, actions, and outcomes—the anatomy of player choices—ensures that our designed game play involves *disciplinizing* the narrative; that is, to make useful game play decisions the player must leverage disciplinary understandings to make meaningful play choices.

Game play as disciplinizing a world (disciplinizing narratives). Vygotsky (1933, 1978), a renowned developmental psychologist, argued that "the influence of play on a child's development is enormous … [allowing him or her to act] a head above himself" (pp. 94–95). Through play the child is able to engage in forms of communication, in rule structures, in understandings, and even in identities that are unreachable in more explicit contexts (Barab & Jackson, 2006). It is through play that a child can take on identities and experiment with actions even before she appreciates the meanings associated with these actions. For philosopher Hans-Georg Gadamer (1975), play is serious, structured, and involves the suspension of belief versus pretense, reality versus unreality. We play games again and again, experiencing new paths with a palpable set of constraints. We play with ideas, piecing together seemingly useless sets of understanding, sometimes weaving our way into creative contributions. We play roles not to step into the life of some imagined Other but to stretch ourselves into another being (character) that can act with that Other. And in the games we design, we design storylines that require one to step into the role of a scientist, a historian, a reporter, a statistician—one who learns not only about disciplinary content but also about themselves as individuals who use content and about which contexts benefit from the application of content understandings.

We understand play as both a kind of activity and a kind of freedom within constraints, that is, a quality embodied to greater or lesser degrees in an immediate environment (i.e., a virtual world). The challenge is in building a virtual world that is not overburdened by rules but that affords opportunities for the player–character to apply disciplinary understandings to make sense of and, ultimately, transform the virtual world in productive ways. In our work, disciplinary concepts come to define the boundaries for what actions are reasonable and which actions fail to meaningfully impact the virtual world—and it is these types of constraints that determine the value of different player actions in a conceptual play space. More than a simple narrative cover-story, the play spaces we design afford intense interactivity, allowing the player to test conjectures, act upon them, and witness the consequences within the context of that narrative. Accordingly, a player can bring about a particular chemical reaction or even act as a fictional newspaper editor who approves a particular story and then witnesses the effects of that decision. This sort of consequential engagement is very difficult to accomplish in schools and even in non-interactive media. Teachers can describe a situation, share a book, or even show a movie but not establish a proxy character and setting that the learner can enlist and act upon.

Game designers, on the other hand, can embed a learner within a story, not simply as an observer but as a first-person protagonist who experiences

intentionality, legitimacy, and *consequentiality* (see Figure 1) (Barab, Gresalfi, & Ingram-Goble, 2009). Said another way, we view games as spaces for positioning the person with intentionality, for positioning content with legitimacy, and for positioning context with consequentiality. Some might argue that the ability to test the water quality in a virtual world and even examine the outcome of different choices remains simply a simulation, conceptually powerful but not personally transformational. However, we argue that a well-designed digital game offers something beyond the traditional simulation: it creates a potential for a player to leverage their understanding a concept (*content*) to actually transform a storyline (*context*), thus creating opportunities for one to reflect on one's in-game identity (*person*) as the type of person who uses content to change contexts. In other words, as game play unfolds, the narrative *context* evolves and changes based on the player's efforts and decisions. At the same time, the *player* herself also evolves, because she is treated differently by other in-game characters and real-world players based on her accomplishments and decisions. Finally, her actual tasks in the game require increasingly sophisticated *content* usage, as the game-world dilemmas become more complex over time.

The idea is that through participation one becomes bound up as part of a context in which he or she experiences the consequences of particular understandings, resulting actions, and environmental consequences. Dewey and Bentley (1949) introduced the transactional perspective to characterize the inseparable and mutually constitutive nature of subject and object. Transaction, according to the Merriam-Webster dictionary, is "a communicative action or activity involving two parties or things that reciprocally affect or influence each other." It is the adoption of an intention that is tightly coupled to, and helps to knowledgeably act upon, the environment or situation that allows for the dynamic (transactional) unity of individual, concept, and the en-

Figure 1. Elements of transformational play

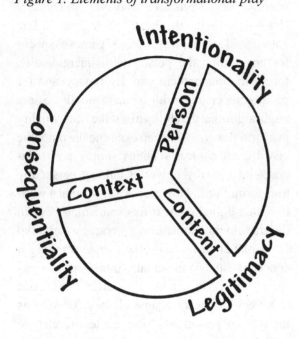

vironment (Barab, Cherkes-Julkowski, Swenson, Garrett, Shaw, & Young, 1999). The goal from a curricular design perspective is to establish a context upon which the learner can perform knowledgeable actions that, if properly understood, result in productive world changes. Such a positioning, one in which the learner enters a situation and as a virtual character applies disciplinary content in useful ways, has the potential to transform the textbook as we know it.

Designing Transformational Play Spaces

Beyond a theoretical argument, we have been translating these ideas into dozens of games nested in the Quest Atlantis (QA) learning and teaching project. QA is an international learning and teaching project that uses a 3D multi-user environment to immerse children, ages 9–15, in educational tasks (see Figure 2); currently we have over 20,000 members distributed across the world on four continents. QA combines strategies used in the commercial gaming environment with

lessons from educational research on learning and motivation. The core elements of QA are (1) a 3D multi-user virtual environment, (2) a scripting engine for creating interactive stories and objects, (3) inquiry learning Quests, assessments, and missions, (4) a meta-storyline as well as nested storylines associated with various game worlds, (5) a teacher toolkit for managing students and their work, and (6) a globally-distributed community of participants (Barab, Arici, & Jackson, 2005; Barab, Thomas, Dodge, Squire, & Newell, 2004). QA was designed to foster inter-subjective experiences through structuring interactions, toward helping children to realize that there are issues in the world upon which they can take action. Through QA, players can travel to virtual places to perform various educational activities, talk with other users and mentors, and build virtual personae.

The QA virtual environment, storyline, associated structures, explicit social commitments, and social policies constitute what is referred to as a meta-game context, a genre of play in which an overarching structure lends form, cohesion, and meaning to a collection of nested activities, each with its own identifiable rules and challenges (Salen & Zimmerman, 2004). As students complete these various activities, their game character visibly "luminates" on core social commitments (e.g., environmental awareness, diversity affirmation, etc.), representing an increased functionality (i.e., their game character can perform previously inaccessible behaviors) and characterizing participation in terms of the foundational storyline (Barab, Dodge, Tuzun, et al., 2007). Further, within constraints assigned by one's teacher, each player can evolve her character based on personal interests and priorities such that after two months of participation, players rarely have similar game experiences and character profiles. Also, because of the program's multi-user nature, finding players with particular profiles becomes a useful means for completing collaborative activities and advancing the unfolding narrative.

Figure 2. Screenshot of the Quest Atlantis gaming project

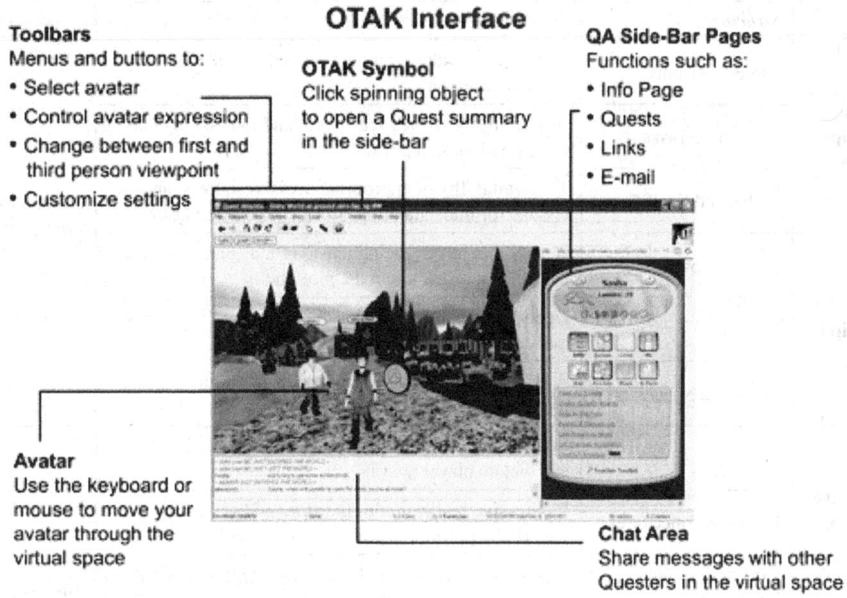

Within this meta-game context, we have developed numerous worlds, and through research we revise these designs in response to classroom implementations, allowing us to evolve theoretical claims in terms of teaching and learning and the possible value of games for supporting this process.

While there are numerous worlds, each with its own narrative frame and targeted to support particular conceptual understandings, all designs have been informed by the design assumptions and the transformational play theory discussed here. When designing for the experience of transformational play, we have found it necessary to weave together particular design threads to form what we refer to as substantive, immersive, impactive, and reflexive participation (see Table 1). Briefly, substantive participation involves students enlisting target concepts in the service of solving a particular task. Immersive participation involves situating tasks in the context of a larger dramatic storyline that creates a legitimate reason and context for disciplinary engagement. Impactive participation occurs when a player's actions affect a situation and, at the same time, reflexively

impact the actor, positioning the self in terms of the virtual world. Finally, reflexive participation involves examining how one's own participation changed the environment and then using this understanding to interrogate the dynamics of the environment as well as their role in influencing such dynamics.

Collectively, when properly integrated, these design braids form a curricular drama in which the disciplinary content is narratized, while simultaneously requiring the player to use academic content to productively discipline and transform the narrative. Whereas the former illuminates why academic content is important, the latter illuminates what is the academic content, and when experienced as part of transformational play, they establish the player as someone who knows how to use academic content to achieve useful ends. Specifically, the substantive and immersive braids constitute the disciplinary and narrative content with which students engage, while the impactive and reflexive braids create the rules and structures that support such forms of engagement. While narratizing or contextual-

Table 1. Braids of transformational play

	States	Structures	Description		
Trans-active States	**Substantive Participation**	Target Concepts	Core understandings and practices that students are expected to learn	*Narratizing Disciplines*	**Game Structures**
		Legitimate Tasks	Increasingly complex real-world and fantastical challenges with nested goals		
		Embedded Scaffolds	The availability of appropriate tools, resources, and lessons for understanding and accomplishing tasks		
	Immersive Participation	Dramatic Storyline	A story that has engaging tensions and characters who have motives that affect the plot line		
		Role Play	Opportunities and identities that players enlist as they transform the story and tasks		
		Contested Space	A physical or perceptual environment within which player actions and the storyline takes place		
	Impactive Participation	Interactive Rules	Logical and accumulative structures that respond to and dictate player actions	*Disciplinizing Narratives*	
		Leveling Trajectories	Progressive realization of the story and nested goals as well as the player's position and potentialities		
		Critical Decision Points	Significant junctions in the storyline dependent on the player's choices and actions		
	Reflexive Participation	Feedback Episodes	Game structures that provide feedback to the player of their choices and submissions		
		Character Evolutions	Stages in which understandings, commitments, and achievements become reified in the player character		
		Transfer Challenges	Opportunities to engage emergent abilities and understandings to transform other related contexts		

izing content is consistent with many other project-based design efforts, the latter two braids capture the transactive nature of the experience, in which during transformational play the game world itself changes based on player choices, thereby having the potential to change the player's appreciation of themselves as someone who can used (and has used) disciplinary content to bring about desired ends.

Substantive Participation

Substantive participation refers to one's potential to usefully engage in meaningful tasks. It begins with being immersed in a particular context that frames meaningful challenges that require students to engage in problem solving and inquiry (Savery & Duffy, 1998). The types of challenges

that interest us require students to make choices about how disciplinary information relates to real-world contexts, thus illuminating more than one meaning for conceptual understandings. For example, instead of teaching students about water quality to pass a science test, we are interested in engaging children in scenarios (Barab et al., in press) that require *leveraging* what they know about water quality to better understand a problem and pose a solution. These scenarios have either participatory authenticity, in that they occur in a real-world context, or simulatory authenticity, in that they involve solving authentic activities but in fictional scenarios (Barab, Squire, & Dueber, 2000). It is in this way that learner actions bear legitimacy. The contextualized challenges are designed such that, in order to solve them, the participant must locate and employ tools and resources—pedagogical scaffolds that they access through their participation in the transformative play space.

Immersive Participation

Once the designer has identified targeted core concepts and those contexts in which they find functional value, the next step is to establish an overarching immersive framework—usually one that involves a narrative. More than a simple context, an overarching framework creates a tension which involves a balance among particulars, including setting, characters, and plot. More elaborately, Bruner (2002) describes Burke's (1945) dramatic Pentad, or narrative grammar, as consisting of "an Agent who performs an Action to achieve a Goal in a recognizable Setting by the use of certain Means" (p. 34; cf. Aristotle, 1992). This conflict involves some sort of story complication to which there is also a turning point, reversal of the problematic situation, and ultimately a resolution of balance. Whereas a particular narrative affords engagement, perspective taking, and projective identification with plotlines that potentially resonate with other situations (cf. Bruner's 1992 notion of "metaphorical loft"), videogames additionally reposition the audience such that they experience a sense of agency and consequentiality with respect to their engagement with the narrative (Gee, 2003). The aspects of our designs which support these active forms of engagement are described in the two design braids described below.

Impactive Participation

In our designs, we work not to simply narrate a story but to position learners within the story so that their actions affect its progress (Sheldon, 2004). This involves not only establishing a context in which the learner finds an important role but, further, building an environment in which this role has consequence for the unfolding of the story. That is, as the player makes choices and interacts with different game features, her achievements affect the ongoing narrative, and underlying tensions and possible resolutions are progressively revealed. The design of the learning space affords this sense of interactivity through sets of logical rules and networks of narrative trajectories that position the player as a protagonist who determines, within designed parameters, how the story will unfold. As such, properly designed conceptual play spaces position the player as protagonist in a *contested space* in which one finds a spatially-bound problem that changes over time, based on player decisions as one navigates the game environment (Lee, Park, & Jin, 2006; Squire & Jan, 2007). Experiencing the drama, then, means not simply witnessing but participating in its realization in a transactional relation diffusing the conventional distinction between subject and object (Dewey & Bentley, 1949). That is, no drama—indeed, no content, not even domain-related concepts—exists per se apart from the player's activity; it is occasioned by the interplay between the user and the system as the former navigates and negotiates the branches and decision points that bear critical consequence on the narrative that ensues.

Reflexive Participation

Just as a game narrative is shaped only through the virtual actions of one's game character, a player's identity is also formed through the actions she takes. To begin, over time the actions a player performs serve to evolve the functionality and talents of the in-game character. More than a merely symbolic act, the evolution of the game character changes possibilities for in-game actions, as the player can engage in activities unavailable to lower-level players or players who have evolved with different profiles. Moreover, one's actions and choices contribute to one's sense of self. In our designs, such reflexive participation is supported by allowing students to evolve their avatars in ways that are reflective of the decisions they have made in the game. The opportunities that players realize and the challenges they successfully resolve represent not simply accomplishments but advancements of themselves, as one increasingly identifies with the world of those practices. Thus, as players make choices that demonstrate their commitment to and understanding of the environment, for example, their character develops, and the interactions they have with other players and non-player characters change and respond to their new status and accomplishments. Importantly, there are three areas in which we work to facilitate reflexive relations to one's play: reflecting on how content understanding is what allowed them to transform the context in productive ways, what their particular choices say about them and their potential to meaningfully use academic content, and what features of the content lend themselves to transformational acts.

Design Braids in Practice

The unit Saving the Black Rhino, as one example of an environment designed to support transformational play, consists of both a series of standards-based curricular activities and a virtual environment resembling a factual game reserve located in the East African country of Tanzania. Specifically, the unit plan, which takes from six to ten class periods to complete, contains seven learning components targeted to engage students in developing an appreciation of endangered species, ecotourism, relative scale, and multiple perspectives. Students are asked to help determine how to best manage the game reserve, and the unit is designed to support their understanding of ecology, geography, politics, medicine, and economics, all of which they leverage to address the problem. The unit was designed to establish the design braids advanced in this manuscript (see Table 2). Indeed, because of its factual grounding in the people, places, and issues relating to the

game reserve, the unit weaves together the four braids in an elegant and engaging result.

To support substantive participation, the activities progress from a general introduction to the topic of extinction, to a detailed investigation of issues relating to maintaining the game reserve, to addressing the balance of social and environmental priorities through ecotourism, and finally to examining similar issues in students' own communities. Toward understanding these issues, students have to learn about the biology of animals and how different ecological niches can best support the needs of particular animals. They also learn history as they evaluate the appropriateness of government land in Tanzania being managed by a foreigner, an issue that brings with it a host of tensions related to imperialism and the relations between Africa and other nations. Lastly, players struggle with economics as they determine how to financially support the reserve and must understand concepts of relative scale as they relate the virtual locations to their design of a physical map. They then use this map to measure distances and provide recommendations of tour routes that, depending on their accuracy, result in low or high game scores and feedback from virtual tourists. Importantly, more than simply conceptual struggling with the academic content, they must also engage their personal values as they make decisions based on moral judgment that have economic, political, and imperialistic consequences.

In order to support immersive participation, the Black Rhino unit takes place in a virtual world that becomes a contested space for experience and learning and involves multiple nested storylines, each one framed as a different mission. However, more than just a fictional storyline, this unit is based on actual people, places, and issues. This real-world connection has proven to be of compelling interest to students who have completed the unit: one student explained, "I actually feel like I'm halfway around the world," and another added, "I think it is cool that all these people are

Table 2. Alignment between the design braids and the Saving the Black Rhino curricular unit

Braid	Description
Substantive Participation	The academic content involves a cluster of related topics, including extinction and endangered species (target concepts). Students investigate the park in order to develop a recommendation of how the land should be used (legitimate tasks). Students are given planning documents from game characters to learn about ecotourism and historical problems that prevent simple solutions from working (pedagogical scaffolds).
Immersive Participation	The unit centers on a representation of a factual game reserve in Tanzania and involves students in the perspectives of the various stakeholders (dramatic storyline). Students freely wander through the virtual game reserve, interviewing characters in order to develop their own perspectives on the situation (participation roles). Students interact with people, animals, and natural and man-made structures in order to develop a viable ecotourism scenario (contested space).
Impactive Participation	The virtual environment functions interactively: for example, characters present text pages stating their understandings of the situation, and these statements change based on student experiences and choices (interactive rules). Students progressively negotiate the different perspectives to develop their own informed and supported opinions relating to the game reserve (leveling trajectories). Arriving at individual conclusions involves adopting various perspectives and committing to difficult choices (critical decision points).
Critical Participation	As students receive feedback from teaches and from the game itself in terms of consequences to their actions, they are able to develop increasingly sophisticated conceptual understandings and make more informed decisions (feedback structures). More than simply understanding content, they are also positioned differently as players who have different levels of expertise and subsequent choices (character evolution). Students are also asked to apply what they are learning to different contexts, both in the Rhino world and as they engage in side missions and on other storylines (transfer challenges).

real and actually living in Africa right now, talking about these issues."

To support impactive participation, as students move through the experience, the interactive links change such that the same people over time provide new information, depending upon which trajectory students choose to pursue. For example, as students initially work to discover people's opinions and earn the trust of the park's population, most of the information is relatively informal. However, as it becomes known that students are engaged in a different trajectory, namely building a scientific-economic report, the characters begin to provide richer information that requires deeper inquiry on the part of the students and that may even be integrated into their final reports. Further, depending on student choices, the information they receive varies so that different students end up with slightly different stories—with the information changing more drastically at critical decision points where students align themselves with particular views.

Finally, reflexive participation can be seen through the actions that students took as they

worked through the unit to understand contrasting points of view, effectively adopting the concerns, values, and opinions of a variety of stakeholders and ultimately developing an ecotourism scenario to balance and improve conditions for both the animals and humans of the area. That is, because the students are involved in real-world dilemmas and informed by factual details, their efforts bear value and consequence. Significantly, the students reflect on this impact with clarity: one noted, "I think this unit was important so we could learn to save an environment in a virtual world, so we would know how to do it in the real world." And another, "I feel proud of the work I have done.... This unit changed me because now I look at things in a different way, and now I have more perspectives."

Through affording a more richly contextualized experience, the designed space creates opportunities for engaged and meaningful learning. Indeed, teachers continually commented how useful they found it to take this "virtual fieldtrip," thereby situating children in the Tanzanian context. One California teacher stated,

It was a shining example of what great things can come from students if you engage them in learning not just curriculum ... because the students really cared about the Black Rhino, the Maasai Tribe, or the farmers. They were motivated to really understand these perspectives in order to discuss and debate the perspectives of the poachers and government officials.

As example of the types of changes occurring over the duration of the unit, the following shows a sixth grader's movement from a superficial description to one of more depth on the transfer scenario tasks.

Pre-test response: The trade of illegal drugs is an important issue. Poor farming families know they can make money off of selling illegal substances. Drug usage is dangerous and this is an important issue.

Post-test Response: In many countries, rainforest logging is a major issue. People from wealthy countries such as our own might protest it because it kills so much of our beautiful environment, but in a country where fine rainforest wood is a major industry and especially if the countries economy is weak, it's not really fair to say they can't do it anymore. This is a very controversial issue, because we are basically weighing human life and animal life, two things that depend on each other.

While the pre-test response shows an attempt to address a factual issue, it lacks the depth and complexity of that of the post-test, which demonstrates multiple perspectives, considers economic and societal issues, and weighs contradicting factors. More generally, we examined student learning in four classrooms, and in all four classrooms, we found significant learning gains from pre-test to post-test: the New York site (Pre$M$ = 12.14, Post$M$ = 18.74; $t(27)$ = 12.17, p <.01), the Indiana site (Pre$M$ = 6.82, Post$M$ = 13.65; $t(16)$ = 9.23, p <.01), the California site (Pre$M$ = 2.66, Post$M$ = 11.27; $t(29)$ = 12.66, p <.01), and the Indiana after-school site (Pre$M$ = 6.12, Post$M$ = 11.38; $t(7)$ = 10.45, p <.05).

The design process involved understanding the perspectives of the various stakeholders, collecting authentic resources such as historical documents, and developing an immersive, interactive virtual space. All of this also had to be considered in terms of the utility it would bring to the lessons as well as the appeal it would bear for the children. In the end, the designed space served to provide an engaging context for students to experience the curriculum. Specifically, it was clear that students were able to *narratize* the content of the unit by understanding formalisms in the context of the storyline. Likewise, students were able to *disciplinze* their narrative experience by looking for and leveraging disciplinary ideas to make sense of and change the storyline of the game.

CONCLUSION

We began this manuscript with the premise that all too often classroom learning overemphasizes disciplinary content (universals) and underrepresents the contexts (particulars) for which this content has value. In highlighting this problem, we return to Gee's (2003) example of reading a game manual without playing the game: removed from its context and purpose, the manual seems uninteresting, but in relation to the game itself, its content becomes meaningful, even valuable. Likewise, learning in classroom contexts is often removed from its contexts of practice. Such learning can be both conceptually impoverished and also motivationally monotonous; degrading disciplinary knowledge from a useful tool to a set of facts or disembodied rules to be memorized. Therefore, curriculum designers might benefit from an examination of how gaming methodologies and technologies situively embody the player and the to-be-learned content in rich participation structures. In particular, the digital age has established entirely new possibilities and even extended identities that challenge traditional ontological conceptions of what is self, what is real, what is valued, and what is knowing.

Capitalizing on this affordance of videogame technologies, we have advanced a transactive perspective that involves positioning concepts and learners within rich, interactive contexts that elevate concepts from abstracted facts to conceptual tools that operate and transform those very same narratives that imbued the concepts with worth—simultaneously *narratizing disciplinary content* at the same time learners use their conceptual understandings to usefully *disciplinize narrative contexts*. Transformational play, as a goal for designing curriculum, offers much in terms of curing the crises of meaning that many youth are experiencing when it comes to academic content. To restate, our interest is not simply in making the abstract concrete (that is, providing a perceptual instantiation of an academic concept) but making the abstract consequential as one uses it to make sense of and transform particular storylines. By bounding up disciplinary context within interactive narrative contexts, we have the potential to not only change learners' understanding of the use value of the content and also offer the opportunity for learners to see themselves as capable of meaningfully applying disciplinary content. Many commercial games, and especially the transformational play spaces that we have been designing, provide learners with a sense of legitimacy, intentionality, and consequentiality in ways that are different to achieve in many school-based lessons.

Our hope for the future is that school curriculum can focus more on engaging students in the game (narrative particulars) and less on providing them the manual (disembodied universals). This is not to argue against there being a place for lectures or explicit content presentation. Certainly, for those who already have an appreciation of the real and problematic situations that disciplinary content can help address, listening to well-organized presentation of information can be very informative.

Their intentions have been established; they arrive at a situation with an appreciation of its use; for them, the content is already situated. This situation is not usually the case for most young learners, especially those being left behind by our school system—and we don't see increasing accountability measures as the solution. Our interest is to ensure that all children understand and care about big ideas, and to supporting teachers in making classrooms places that excite interest and passion for learning. Specifically, we have argued that the transformational potential of videogames creates opportunities for children to play scientists, historians, lawyers, accountants doctors, etc. who use domain knowledge to address personally engaging and situationally important problems. It is for this reason that we regard games as offering a new pedagogy for the 21st century, one that has the potential to not merely fill individual minds, but empower whole persons, and to transform learning from a rote acquisitional process to a transactive one in which conceptual understandings have transformational significance.

ACKNOWLEDGMENT

The work reported in this manuscript was supported by the National Science Foundation (Grant # 9980081 and 0092831) and by the John D. and Catherine T. MacArthur Foundation (Grant # 06-88658-000-HCD). Also, special thanks to Anna Arici for supporting the implementation and data collection of Rhino World, and for OPEN in securing funds to design the world.

REFERENCES

Aristotle. (1992). Poetics (S. H. Butcher, Trans.). In H. Adams (Ed.), *Critical theory since Plato* (pp. 49-66). Fort Worth, TX: Harcourt Brace Jovanovich College Publishers.

Barab, S., Dodge, T., Tuzun, H., Job-Sluder, K., Jackson, C., Arici, A., et al. (2007). The Quest Atlantis Project: A socially-responsive play space for learning. In B. E. Shelton & D. A. Wiley (Eds.), *The educational design and use of simulation computer games* (pp. 159-186). Rotterdam, The Netherlands: Sense Publishers.

Barab, S., & Jackson, C. (2006). From Plato's Republic to Quest Atlantis: The role of the philosopher-king. *Technology, Humanities, Education, Narrative [THEN] Journal, 2.*

Barab, S., Sadler, T., Heiselt, C., Hickey, D., & Zuiker, S. (2007). Relating Narrative, Inquiry, and Inscriptions: A Framework for Socio-Scientific Inquiry. *Journal of Science Education and Technology, 16*(1), 59–82. doi:10.1007/s10956-006-9033-3

Barab, S., Thomas, M., Dodge, T., Carteaux, R., & Tuzun, H. (2005). Making learning fun: Quest Atlantis, a game without guns. *Educational Technology Research and Development, 53*(1), 86–108. doi:10.1007/BF02504859

Barab, S., Thomas, M., Dodge, T., Squire, K., & Newell, M. (2004). Critical design ethnography: Designing for change. *Anthropology & Education Quarterly, 35*(2), 254–268. doi:10.1525/aeq.2004.35.2.254

Barab, S., Zuiker, S., Warren, S., Hickey, D., Ingram-Goble, A., & Kwon, E.-J. (2007). Situationally embodied curriculum: Relating formalisms and contexts. *Science Education, 91*(5), 750–782. doi:10.1002/sce.20217

Barab, S. A., Arici, A., & Jackson, C. (2005). Eat your vegetables and do your homework: A design-based investigation of enjoyment and meaning in learning. *Educational Technology, 65*(1), 15–21.

Barab, S. A., Cherkes-Julkowski, M., Swenson, R., Garrett, S., Shaw, R. E., & Young, M. (1999). Principles of self-organization: Ecologizing the learner-facilitator system. *Journal of the Learning Sciences, 8*(3-4), 349–390. doi:10.1207/s15327809jls0803&4_2

Barab, S. A., Dodge, T., Ingram-Goble, A., Volk, C., & Peppler, K. (2009). *Pedagogical dramas and transformational play: Narratively-rich games for learning.* Manuscript submitted for publication.

Bransford, J. D., Brown, A. L., & Cocking, R. R. (Eds.). (2000). *How people learn: Brain, mind, experience, and school.* Washington, DC: National Academy Press.

Bruner, J. (2002). *Making stories: Law, literature, life.* New York: Farrar, Straus and Giroux.

Dewey, J., & Bentley, A. F. (1949). *Knowing and the known.* Boston: Beacon.

Gee, J. P. (2003). *What video games have to teach us about learning.* New York: Palgrave.

Gresalfi, M., Barab, S. A., Siyahhan, S., & Christensen, T. (2009). Virtual worlds, conceptual understanding, and me: Designing for consequential engagement. *Horizon, 17*(1), 21–34. doi:10.1108/10748120910936126

Lee, K. M., Park, N., & Jin, S.-A. (2006). Narrative and interactivity in computer games. In P. Vorderer & J. Bryant (Eds.), *Playing video games: Motives, responses, and consequences* (pp. 259-274). Mahwah, NJ: Lawrence Erlbaum Associates.

Rosenblatt, L. M. (1995). *Literature as exploration* (5th ed.). New York: Modern Language Association of America.

Ryan, M.-L. (2001). *Narrative as virtual reality: Immersion and interactivity in literature and electronic media.* Baltimore: Johns Hopkins University Press.

Salen, K., & Zimmerman, E. (2004). *Rules of play.* Cambridge, MA: MIT Press.

Sheldon, L. (2004). *Character development and storytelling for games.* Boston: Thomson Course Technology.

Squire, K. D., & Jan, M. (2007). Mad City Mystery: Developing scientific argumentation skills with a place-based augmented reality game on handheld computers. *Journal of Science Education and Technology, 16*(1), 5–29. doi:10.1007/s10956-006-9037-z

Tamborini, R., & Skalski, P. (2006). The role of presence in the experience of electronic games. In P. Vorderer & J. Bryant (Eds.), *Playing video games: Motives, responses, and consequences* (pp. 225-240). Mahwah, NJ: Lawrence Erlbaum Associates.

This work was previously published in International Journal of Gaming and Computer-Mediated Simulations, Volume 2, Issue 1, edited by Richard E. Ferdig, pp.17-30 , copyright 2010 by IGI Publishing (an imprint of IGI Global).

Chapter 3
Exploring Cognitive Load in Immersive Educational Games:
The SAVE Science Project

Brian C. Nelson
Arizona State University, USA

Diane Jass Ketelhut
Temple University, USA

Catherine Schifter
Temple University, USA

ABSTRACT

SAVE Science is a research project focused on creating an innovative model for assessment of learning in STEM. In SAVE Science, we are implementing game-like modules for evaluating science content and inquiry in grades 7-8, using an assessment rubric of student interactions in a virtual environment designed to capture evolving patterns of scientific understanding among students. We are also investigating two "conditions for success" for virtual environment-based assessment: managing the effects of cognitive load students experience in complex virtual environments, and helping teachers integrate technology into their pedagogy. In this paper, we provide an overview of our design approaches aimed at helping students manage the high levels of cognitive load they report experiencing in virtual environments. By reducing the perceived complexity of virtual environment-based assessments, we hypothesize that learners will be better able to attend to the processes associated with the assessments, leading to more accurate evidentiary data.

BACKGROUND

Educational virtual environments have emerged in recent years as a platform for hosting science curricula centered on inquiry situated in realistic simulations of the visual contexts and functional processes found in the real world (Nelson & Ketelhut, 2007; Slator, Hill, & Del Val, 2004; Zacharia, 2007). For example, students can view books in a digital library, talk to computer-based residents of virtual towns, and test the water quality of rivers and lakes. Importantly for educational purposes, students in virtual environments can also conduct

DOI: 10.4018/978-1-4666-0029-4.ch003

realistic inquiry activities and seek solutions to complex problems modeled in the game-like environments. In the *SAVE Science* project, students have an overall goal of uncovering the likely contributors to a series of problems facing a small virtual town (sick farm animals, weather-related crop failure, and climate-related problems with the town's water). To accomplish the overall goal, students need to apply knowledge and skills learned in their classroom-based science curricula through a series of assessment quests embedded in the *SAVE Science* virtual world. Students enter the *SAVE Science* world multiple times over the course of a school year, conducting a new inquiry quest on each visit.

The *SAVE Science* project makes use of an educational virtual world called Scientopolis that we have developed. Our virtual environment has been designed to incorporate and build upon findings from our extensive previous research with the River City Project. The River City curriculum is centered on scientific inquiry skills, particularly of hypothesis formation and experimental design. The main learning goal for students exploring River City is to discover why residents of the virtual town are getting sick (Nelson, Ketelhut, Clarke, Bowman, & Dede, 2005). The River City virtual world is set in the late 1800's, and named for the river that runs through most of the town. River City includes a main street with shops, a library, and elementary school, along with institutions such as a hospital, university, and city hall. Upon entering the city, students can investigate why town residents are sick by interacting with computer-based city residents, explore possible contamination sites such as muddy streets or an insect-filled bog, and encounter auditory stimuli such as the sounds of coughing town residents that provide tacit clues as to possible causes of illness. Students work in small teams to develop and test hypotheses about why residents are ill. Three different illnesses (water-borne, air-borne, and insect-borne) are integrated with historical, social and geographical content, allowing students

to develop and practice the inquiry skills involved in disentangling multi-causal problems embedded within a complex environment (Ketelhut, 2007).

A series of studies have been conducted investigating the viability of the River City virtual environment and curriculum to motivate students to learn science and improve science learning. A subset of the results from a series of controlled implementations of the River City virtual environment are listed below:

- Upon analyzing final student reports, looking for evidence of understanding of inquiry (e.g., uses data to design hypothesis, experiment is designed to test hypothesis), reports written by students in the River City treatment scored twice that of those written by students in the control treatment (p<.05; n=173; Ketelhut, Dede, Clarke, & Nelson, 2007);
- Use of an embedded individualized guidance system led to significantly higher scores from pre- to post-tests on scientific inquiry skills and disease transmission knowledge for both boys and girls (p <.05; n=272; Nelson, 2007);
- River City girls outperform all students in either treatment on learning scientific inquiry skills (p<.05; n=449; Nelson & Ketelhut, 2007).

Although studies into learning and engagement with the River City environment have been largely positive, evidence gained through classroom observations, student interviews, and surveys indicates that many learners in River City struggle to cope with the complexity of the virtual worlds. Students often report not knowing where to focus their attention in the environment, and difficulty in keeping track of the many sources of information encountered while exploring the virtual worlds (Nelson, 2007). For example, roughly a quarter of the students in the embedded guidance system study with access to guidance messages did not view any of them. When a random sub-set of students were interviewed about their use (or lack thereof) of the guidance system, their responses fell into two categories: (a) they didn't notice the guidance tool because their attention was centered on the 3-D environment, or (b) there were so many sources of information to keep track of simultaneously on-screen that students gave up on trying to pay attention to all of them (Nelson, 2007). Thus, while the overall results from the studies in River City are encouraging, it is interesting to speculate how much more positive they might have been if the virtual environments had been designed in a way that better supported students' interactions within them.

VIRTUAL ENVIRONMENTS AND COGNITIVE LOAD

From a cognitive processing viewpoint, the difficulties reported by students exploring educational virtual environment-based games are not surprising. The rich experience enabled by virtual environments contributes to what Mayer and Clark (2007) label the "rich media paradox." The simultaneous presentation of multiple information sources supported by virtual environments raises a learner's cognitive load (the mental effort needed to process all the visual, textual, and audio elements) until (s)he experiences cognitive overload, with the incoming stimuli outstripping the capacity of the learner's memory systems to process the information. Research has shown that multimedia messages designed in manner supportive of how the human mind is thought to operate are more likely to lead to meaningful learning than those that are not (Mayer & Moreno, 2003). Similarly, by approaching the design of information presented in educational virtual environments from a cognitive processing framework, more meaningful learning may occur. The challenge for designers of these environments is to create virtual worlds that don't overwhelm learners in terms of complexity,

while not stripping away the situated embodiment and immersion that is the hallmark of virtual environment-based inquiry games.

In SAVE Science, we are investigating approaches that may help address this challenge, by incorporating and evaluating multimedia design principles adapted from cognitive processing literature.

MULTIMEDIA PRINCIPLES AND GAME-BASED INQUIRY ENVIRONMENTS

Mayer and Moreno (2003) describe multimedia learning as learning from words and pictures, and multimedia instruction as the presentation of words and pictures in a way that fosters learning by helping people create mental representations of incoming information. To process information, humans possess two "channels": one for words and one for pictures (Paivio, 1986, 1991). Each of these two channels has a limited processing capacity at any given time (Sweller, 1999). In other words, people are able to process a very limited amount of information at a given time before experiencing "cognitive overload"—i.e. an overload of information resulting in diminished ability to process (Mayer, 2005).

Researchers into the design of computer-based instructional materials propose a number of design principles to address these issues. The most basic of these is the Multimedia Principle. This principle states that people learn better from words and pictures together than from words alone (Fletcher & Tobias, 2005; Mayer, 1997). Other multimedia principles build on this basic idea by offering approaches for organizing and presenting visual and verbal information to learners. The multimedia principles are concerned with how multimodal elements (text, pictures, sounds, animations, etc.) can be arranged to assist learners in managing cognitive load, which in turn allows them to focus the maximum amount of available short-term memory to dealing with new incoming information.

In investigating the effectiveness of these principles for reducing cognitive load and supporting learning, researchers have focused their attention primarily on what might be called "traditional" computer-based instruction environments. By this we mean presentational learning environments in which learners move from screen to screen of content in a sequence. To date, little research has been done on the usefulness of multimedia design principles in the creation of complex 3-D situated inquiry games such as educational virtual environments (Nelson & Erlandson, 2008).

To investigate the challenges educational students report in managing information while performing learning and assessment activities in the environments, we conducted a design case study of the River City virtual environment (Nelson & Erlandson, 2008). Through our study, we identified a set of design approaches for creating educational virtual environments for science inquiry that we posit may reduce learner cognitive load while maintaining a high level of immersion. A subset of the approaches most relevant to the discussion here is summarized in Table 1.

Building on our design case study, we conducted an investigation of the cognitive load impact of an educational virtual environment that incorporates one of the principles identified in our case study: the Modality Principle. This principle states that cognitive load can be reduced when the words contained in multimedia environments are spoken rather than printed (Mousavi, Low, & Sweller, 1995). This is based on an assumption that use of spoken words in conjunction with visuals allows more information to be processed in working memory.

In our first design principles study, conducted in fall 2007, we implemented the modality principle in a virtual environment through the use of a voice-based chat system used for student team member communication while completing the curriculum. In a quasi-experimental control-treatment study, we compared self-reported cognitive load levels between students communicating by voice to those communicating through the use of a text-based chat tool embedded in the virtual environment. Findings from the study showed that students using a virtual environment with a communication system incorporating the modality principle reported significantly lower overall cognitive load ($p<.05$), lower levels of cognitive load related to team communication ($p<.01$), and greater engagement with the learning environment ($p<.05$). In addition, students in the "modality virtual environment" were more likely to report that they "felt like a scientist" ($p<.05$) while completing the curriculum than those in the virtual environment with the text-based communication system (Erlandson & Nelson, 2008).

Table 1. Design approaches to reduce perceived complexity in immersive games

Virtual Environment Cognitive Load Issues	Redesign Approaches
Visual information related to the learning/assessment tasks is present in multiple locations simultaneously	• **Modality Principle:** Replace printed text with narration when possible: Interactions with in-world characters should be via narration (with optional printed transcripts). Users should be able to pause/replay/store narration • **Modality Principle:** Replace text-based learner-to-learner chat system with a voice-based system. • **Spatial Contiguity Principle:** Keep in-world interactions in the 3-D world: reduce split attention by enabling learners to examine objects in the world itself rather than in a visually separate location.
Large amounts of extraneous or redundant information is presented along with information related to the learning/assessment tasks	• **Signaling Principle:** use visual and/or auditory signaling cues to draw learner attention to objects and locations in the 3-D world that are related to the learning/assessment activities and goals.

DESIGN APPROACHES IN SAVE SCIENCE

As a sub-study within the overall goals of SAVE Science, we are currently investigating a design approach identified in our earlier case study as having potential impact on perceived cognitive load in game-based assessments: the Signaling Principle. This principle states that perception of extraneous cognitive load can be reduced and learning can be better supported when visual and/or auditory cues highlight and draw learner attention to material central to the assessment tasks. In SAVE Science, we are incorporating this principle through two approaches: the use of "pointers" and tacit guidance.

Embedded visual and audio "pointers" in the *SAVE Science* virtual world are being used to indicate to the learner which objects encountered in the world contain information germane to the assessment tasks. For example, our first assessment quest "Sheep Trouble" centers on an embedded assessment of student understanding of adaptation of an organism to a given environment over time. In the quest, students enter a virtual farmstead set in a mythical medieval setting. They are asked to gather evidence for why a recently imported herd of sheep is becoming sickly and weak, while

'native' sheep are healthy. In gathering evidence, students are given the opportunity to demonstrate both competency at conducting scientific inquiry and their understanding of the relationship between specific physical adaptations and a given environment. As students conduct their assessment quest, data are automatically collected about their level of understanding and application of the science concepts the quest is designed to assess. To support their activities, and subtly guide them toward objects and interactions in the virtual world that contain information relevant to the assessment, we have incorporated visual signaling techniques. Objects in the world containing information related to the assessment tasks visually "glow" as students approach (Figure 1).

For the second approach to the application of the signaling principle, we have designed the virtual environment itself in a way that subtly guides students toward objects and areas containing information that is central to the assessment. For example, students will be able to walk through a neighborhood of homes, most of which will be locked, with shades drawn. However, a small subset of homes containing germane information will be visibly open, with a house resident standing near the doorway (Figure 2).

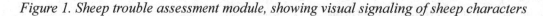

Figure 1. Sheep trouble assessment module, showing visual signaling of sheep characters

Figure 2. Visual signaling on a Non-Player Character (NPC)

RESEARCH APPROACH

In our investigation of the viability and effectiveness of these signaling techniques, we are asking the following specific research questions:

1. In terms of perceived student cognitive load, how does the use of visual and auditory signaling techniques incorporated into a virtual environment-based assessment compare to a version of the assessment activity not explicitly designed to incorporate these principles?
2. How does a virtual environment-based assessment designed to reduce learner perception of cognitive load through use of signaling principles impact student scores on a game-based assessment of science content and inquiry skills compared to a version of the environment not explicitly designed to incorporate these principles?
3. To what extent does the use of visual and auditory signaling techniques impact the "efficiency" of assessment activities embedded in a virtual environment. Do students completing assessments in an environment incorporating signaling techniques conduct a larger proportion of 'on-task' assessment activities than those in a version of the environment without these design methods?

To investigate these questions, *SAVE Science* will be implemented in 7th and 8th grade science classes in a large urban school district beginning in fall 2009. Teacher volunteers will be solicited from within this pool to implement *SAVE Science* in their classes. Participating students will be randomly assigned to one of two conditions, SIGNALING and control. The assessment tasks and story line presented in the virtual worlds of each condition will be identical. In the SIGNALING condition, the world will include the visual and auditory signaling methods described earlier. Students will work through the assessment activities individually, with each session lasting approximately 45 minutes. All teachers will participate in professional development to improve their understanding of the science being assessed and the value of virtual environments in the classroom.

In investigating the cognitive load impact of the signaling principle applied to educational virtual environments, we will utilize a rubric for measuring cognitive load that combines subjective and direct measurement approaches. *Subjective cognitive load* will be assessed via modified version of the NASA-TLX (Hart & Staveland, 1988). This will enable us to directly test assumptions concerning different aspects of cognitive load as has been predicted from a cognitive perspective. The modified version of the NASA-TLX has been proven very useful to distinguish between cognitive load caused by the need to interact with the learning environment (e.g., selecting materials) and load directly associated with the process of learning itself. *Direct Cognitive load* will be assessed via an eye-tracking system, which will be used to detect and collect eye-gaze data during completion of the assessment activities. A small subset (10% of the experiment's overall number) of the participants within each condition will be randomly selected to participate in this aspect of the data collection. The software accompanying the eye-tracking system will be used to examine the learner's eye-movements by means of a post-hoc analysis of visual fixations falling within different areas of the virtual environment. Specifically, captured images of the environment will be manually divided into natural segments of interface real estate (e.g., the 3-D world, menu bar, and GUI overlays).

To assess whether the use of signaling design techniques impacts assessment outcomes, we will use a combination of three data sources:

Automatically recorded in-world behaviors: students problem-solving behaviors will be recorded in the database that connects to *SAVE Science* with a location and time-stamp. By coding these behaviors based on content expert analysis, we will score students' process in solving the posed problems.

Embedded questions: while automatically recorded process data will help us assess students' tacit understandings of material and concepts in the virtual world, it is important to assess students' ability to articulate and apply what they have learned. Therefore, each assessment quest will conclude with a series of embedded questions about what students conclude and the evidence for that conclusion.

Benchmark questions: the school district that we are working with has several different standardized assessments of their curriculum which students are required to take. Using questions from both assessments, we have designed the quests to clearly show, either in behaviors, articulation or both, whether they can answer those questions.

IMPORTANCE OF THE STUDY

Through our research in SAVE Science, we hope to contribute to the burgeoning field of game-based STEM education by producing recommendations for how researchers can design situated, virtual environment-based assessments with rich immersion in authentic inquiry practices coupled with manageable complexity. Through our investigation into the role of perceived cognitive load in game-based assessments, and into the impact of design approaches employed to produce more meaningful data from in-game assessment activities by managing learner perceived cognitive load, we hope to disentangle the theoretical dissonance between complex experiences found in immersive game-based educational learning and assessment environments and the simplified experiences typically found in more traditional forms of assessment. In addition, we are interested in discovering if use of such techniques reduces the sense of situated embodiment in virtual space. We expressly do NOT want to reduce the feeling of immersion that is the hallmark of virtual environments. Rather, we are aiming for what we call "essential complexity" of experience—a high level of immersion and embodiment coupled with a reduction in the sense of complexity and associated cognitive load detrimental to completion of assessment tasks.

REFERENCES

Erlandson, B., & Nelson, B. (2008). *The Effect of Collaboration Modality on Cognitive Load in a Situated Inquiry Environment.* Paper presented at the American Educational Communication and Technology Conference, Orlando, FL.

Fletcher, J. D., & Tobias, S. (2005). The Multimedia Principle. In R. E. Mayer (Ed.), *The Cambridge Handbook of Multimedia Learning* (pp. 117-133). New York: Cambridge University Press.

Hart, S. G., & Staveland, L. E. (1988). Development of a multi-dimensional workload rating scale: Results of empirical and theoretical research. In P. A. Hancock & N. Meshkati (Eds.), *Human mental workload,* (pp.139-183). Amsterdam, The Netherlands: Elsevier.

Ketelhut, D. J. (2007). The Impact of Student Self-Efficacy on Scientific Inquiry Skills: An Exploratory Investigation in River City, a Multi-User Virtual Environment. *Journal of Science Education and Technology, 16*(1), 99–111. doi:10.1007/s10956-006-9038-y

Ketelhut, D. J., Dede, C., Clarke, J., & Nelson, B. (2007). Studying Situated Learning in a Multi-User Virtual Environment. In E. Baker, J. Dickieson, W. Wulfeck & H. O'Neil (Eds.), *Assessment of Problem Solving Using Simulations* (pp. 37-58). New York: Lawrence Erlbaum Associates.

Mayer, R. E. (1997). Multimedia learning: Are we asking the right questions? *Educational Psychologist, 32*(1), 1–19. doi:10.1207/s15326985ep3201_1

Mayer, R. E. (2005). Cognitive Theory of Multimedia Learning. In R. E. Mayer (Ed.), *The Cambridge Handbook of Multimedia Learning* (pp. 31-48). New York: Cambridge University Press.

Mayer, R. E., & Clark, R. C. (2007). Using Rich Media Wisely. In R. A. Reiser & J. V. Dempsey (Eds.) *Trends and Issues in Instructional Design and Technology* (pp. 311-322). Upper Saddle River, NJ: Pearson Education Inc.

Mayer, R. E., & Moreno, R. (2003). Nine Ways to Reduce Cognitive Load in Multimedia Learning. *Educational Psychologist, 38*(1), 43–52. doi:10.1207/S15326985EP3801_6

Mousavi, S., Low, R., & Sweller, J. (1995). Reducing cognitive load by mixing auditory and visual presentation modes. *Journal of Educational Psychology, 87,* 319–334. doi:10.1037/0022-0663.87.2.319

Nelson, B. (2007). Exploring the use of individualized, reflective guidance in an educational multi-user virtual environment. *Journal of Science Education and Technology, 16*(1), 83–97. doi:10.1007/s10956-006-9039-x

Nelson, B., & Erlandson, B. (2008). Managing Cognitive Load in Educational Multi User Virtual Environments: Reflection on Design Practice. *Educational Technology Research and Development, 56,* 619–641. doi:10.1007/s11423-007-9082-1

Nelson, B., & Ketelhut, D. J. (2007). Designing for Real-World Inquiry in Virtual Environments. *Educational Psychology Review, 19*(3), 265–283. doi:10.1007/s10648-007-9048-1

Nelson, B., Ketelhut, D. J., Clarke, J., Bowman, C., & Dede, C. (2005). Design-based research strategies for developing a scientific inquiry curriculum in a multi-user virtual enviroment. *Educational Technology, 45*(1), 21–27.

Paivio, A. (1986). *Mental Representations.* New York: Oxford University Press.

Paivio, A. (1991). Dual Coding Theory: Retrospect and Current Status. *Canadian Journal of Psychology, 45,* 255–287. doi:10.1037/h0084295

Slator, B. M., Hill, C., & Del Val, D. (2004). Teaching Computer Science with Virtual Worlds. *IEEE Transactions on Education, 47*(2), 269–275. doi:10.1109/TE.2004.825513

Sweller, J. (1999). *Instructional design in technical areas.* Camberwell, Australia: ACER Press.

Zacharia, Z. C. (2007). Comparing and combining real and virtual experimentation: an effort to enhance students' conceptual understanding of electric circuits. *Journal of Computer Assisted Learning, 23*, 120–132. doi:10.1111/j.1365-2729.2006.00215.x

This work was previously published in International Journal of Gaming and Computer-Mediated Simulations, Volume 2, Issue 1, edited by Richard E. Ferdig, pp. 31-39, copyright 2010 by IGI Publishing (an imprint of IGI Global).

Chapter 4
Multi–Modal Investigations of Relationship Play in Virtual Worlds

Yasmin B. Kafai
University of Pennsylvania, USA

Deborah Fields
University of California, Los Angeles, USA

Kristin A. Searle
University of Pennsylvania, USA

ABSTRACT

Millions of youth have joined virtual worlds to hang out with each other. However, capturing their interactions is no easy feat given the complexity of virtual worlds, their 24/7 availability, and distributed access from different places. In this paper, we illustrate what different methods can reveal about the dating and flirting practices of tweens in Whyville.net, a virtual world with over 1.5 million registered players in 2005 between the ages 8-16 years old. We compare findings from analyses of tweens' newspaper writings, chat records, and logfile data. Our analysis demonstrates the mixed attitudes toward flirting on Whyville and the pervasiveness of flirting as a whole, as well as the breadth and selectivity of tweens' adoption of flirting practices. We discuss how our multi-modal investigation reveals individual variation and development across practices and suggests that player expertise might contribute to the striking contrast between formal writing about dating and the frequency of it on the site. Finally, we discuss the limitations of our methodological approaches and suggest that our findings are limited to a particular space and time in the existence of Whyville and the tweens who populate it.

DOI: 10.4018/978-1-4666-0029-4.ch004

INTRODUCTION

To date, most studies of virtual social spaces have focused on college youth and adults while largely ignoring younger players. Yet teens have rapidly adopted social networking sites like MySpace and Friendster as their own for continuing friendships and developing casual relationships (Buckingham & Wilett, 2006; Mazarella, 2005). Further, many online spaces have opened up for even younger players than in the previous decade. Toontown, Club Penguin, Neopets—to name but a few—are aimed at younger players, called tweens, and millions of them have joined these places to hang out with each other. Researcher Danah Boyd (2008) suggests that one attraction of these sites is that they "provid[e] teens with a space to work out identity and status, make sense of cultural cues, and negotiate public life" (p. 120). As tweens move from childhood into adolescence they try out various ways to begin relationships that they anticipate engaging in. While such relationship-play is an important steppingstone in tweens' social development (Thorne, 1993) it often takes place outside adult-supervised spaces and might explain the increasing prominence of virtual worlds. Studying such social interactions in virtual worlds is difficult given the complexity of virtual environments, their 24/7 availability, and distributed access from different places. The study of tween flirting and dating in virtual worlds so far has received little attention and will be the focus of this paper.

In this paper, we want to illustrate what different methods can reveal about a particular set of social practices, namely dating and flirting, of tweens in Whyville.net, a virtual world with over 1.5 million registered players in 2005 between the ages 8-16 years old. In Whyville, citizens play casual science games in order to earn a virtual salary (in 'clams'), which they can then spend on buying and designing parts for their avatars (virtual characters), projectiles to throw at other users, and other goods. The general consensus among Whyvillians (the citizens of the virtual community of Whyville) is that earning a good salary and thus procuring a large number of clams to spend on face parts or other goods is essential for the primary desire of Whyvillians, developing relationships (Kafai & Giang, 2007). From our previous research on Whyville, we know that tweens spend most of their time in virtual worlds socializing with one another and engaged in identity play with their avatars as a vehicle for these explorations (Feldon & Kafai, 2008; Fields & Kafai, in press). Beyond these central activities, players develop niches depending on their interests and levels of expertise. Often girls and boys play in same-sex groupings, but sometimes come together, as evidenced in the diffusion of teleporting and projectile throwing practices through the after school gaming club (Fields & Kafai, 2009; Fields & Kafai, 2008; Kafai, 2008). Our studies of these practices were very focused, looking closely at how club members learned from each other how to teleport and how to throw projectiles. To do this we searched logfiles selectively and drew on observations from the club to put together a larger picture of the diffusion of these practices (Kafai & Fields, in press).

Capturing flirting and dating proved to be difficult because the practices were more complicated, not being limited to particular commands but being much more dependent on context. Additionally, field observations in the after-school gaming club provided limited evidence that boys flirted in Whyville yet we had hints from the logfiles that the girls flirted without advertising it in the club (Kafai, 2008; Fields & Kafai, 2008). These initial observations suggested discrepancies between online and offline activity in regard to flirting. In the following sections, we describe our efforts to engage other methods that captured what tweens did and how they talked about flirting and dating, starting with a content analysis of the newspaper writings about flirting and dating in *The Whyville Times*, the weekly online newspaper, followed by a word frequency search of chat records. Only by analyzing logfiles to develop case studies that provided detailed context of flirting, were we able to capture the richness and nuances in flirting and dating that were not visible or documented in other data sources.

BACKGROUND

Researchers of virtual worlds have employed various methods to understand dimensions of social activity: extensive ethnographies to capture detail and richness of interactions over time (e.g., Boellstorff, 2008; Taylor, 2006), surveys to capture the range of interests and experiences of the massive number of participating players (Williams, Yee & Caplan, 2008), field observations to capture play in the virtual and the real as integrated aspects of play in virtual communities (Castronova, 2005; Jenkins, 2006; Kafai, 2008; Leander & Lovvorn, 2006), logfiles for revealing trends and patterns (Bruckman, 2006; Williams, Consalvo Caplan, & Yee, in press), and content analyses of discussion boards to capture players' thoughts and strategy formation about the virtual world (Steinkuehler & Duncan, 2008).

While each of these methods reveals valid aspects of online life, tracking data in the form of logfiles and chat can provide a promising avenue to capture the private nature of relationship play that might often take place outside public view. Traditionally, researchers have conducted extensive quantitative analysis of logfiles to capture patterns over a large number of people over a long period of time (e.g., Williams et al., 2008), analyze social networks (Duchenaut, Yee, Nickell, & Moore, 2006) or combine multiple data sources (Feldon & Kafai, 2008). While these quantitative approaches reveal trends and patterns, they might also leave aside some of the more subtle cues employed in social interactions. Some researchers have used logfiles qualitatively over a short period of time, for instance two girls over a few days (Bruckman, 2000), a small group during a

few class periods (Clarke & Dede, 2007), or local chat interactions (Nardi, Ly, & Harris, 2007).

Here we propose a narrative approach that rebuilds the online life of participants by condensing data points into comprehensive accounts. We contend that this approach can reveal particular social practices across online and offline spaces and aspects of individual players' participation not captured otherwise and hence well suited for our focus on anticipatory flirting and dating. We thus applied a new method to analyze logfile data, called qualitative logfile analysis (Kafai & Fields, in press). We then combined the insights gained from qualitative logfile analysis with other data sources to create a fuller picture of anticipatory flirting and dating.

CONTEXT, METHODS, AND PARTICIPANTS

The data for our study come from three primary sources: (1) articles from the archives of the weekly Whyville newspaper, *The Whyville Times*; and (2) chat records of 595 participants over six months participation in Whyville from January to June 2005; and (3) logfiles and chat of 595 participants over six months participation in Whyville from January to June 2005. Our analyses are supplemented by hundreds of hours of play on Whyville ourselves over the past several years.

Online Content Analysis

To illuminate players' reflections on flirting, we searched the archive of Whyville's weekly, player-written newspaper, *The Whyville Times*, which contains over 9,000 articles. Using the word "dating" as a search term, we found 129 articles published from October 26, 2000 through June 1, 2008. After reading the articles, we determined 51 to be relevant to dating on Whyville and further analyzed them to determine their stance on Whydating and Whymarriage.

Online Chat Analysis

To substantiate the findings from the case studies, we conducted a word frequency count of the chat and whisper texts by all 595 participants over six months using Mathematica (by Wolfram). From the database of over 4.7 million lines of chat and whisper we sorted out various terms associated with discourses of flirting and romance identified in the case study analysis.

Online Interaction Analysis

To identify flirting practices amongst tweens on Whyville, we began by choosing six tweens from the after school club based on their participation profiles to capture a broad range of online players. We isolated their logfiles then sampled the days these players were on Whyville. Each line of the logfiles contained a username, time stamp (year-month-day-hour-minute-second), location in Whyville, and if applicable, chat or whisper text. Selecting their first seven days on Whyville then alternating every five or six days to ensure breadth of days of the week in our sample, we went click by click through the logfile data in order to create minute-by-minute summaries of the players' Whyville activities. We then condensed these into short daily narratives that noted patterns and changes in participation over time. In all we analyzed about 30 days during their six months on Whyville from January 11 to June 5, 2005.

FINDINGS

In order to highlight the affordances and limitations of each aspect of our data collection and analysis, we briefly report what we knew about flirting and dating from our study of an after school club where tween members played on Whyville, then show how each aspect of our methods provided

a different angle on flirting and dating, from the content analysis of the online newspaper, to the chat frequency count, to the click-by-click case studies. Our analysis demonstrates the mixed attitudes toward flirting on Whyville and the pervasiveness of flirting as a whole, as well as the breadth and selectivity of tweens' adoption of flirting practices.

After School Club

In the after school club, boys talked loudly about flirting with people on Whyville, generally done by complimenting girl avatars on their looks or giving girlfriends gifts. However we found no evidence of girls participating in these activities from the observations that took place in the club based on field notes, video, and interviews (Fields & Kafai, 2008; Kafai, 2008). As we will demonstrate later, girls did participate in flirting on Whyville, and this difference between public and private activity is intriguing.

Whyville Times Content Analysis

Many online virtual worlds have forums where players can express their opinions publicly. In contrast to data sources where our perspective as researchers is central, these forums provide a way to grasp the range in player opinion about a given topic at a particular moment in time and across longer expanses of time (Dibbell, 1998; Ludlow & Wallace, 2007; Suzuki & Calzo, 2004). In order to better comprehend public opinion about and understanding of flirting and dating in Whyville we turned to a set of 51 articles dealing with "dating" that were published in *The Whyville Times* between 1999 and 2008. These articles highlighted that tweens have a range of opinions about flirting and dating practices in Whyville, from initial flirtations through getting serious and even considering Whymarriage and Whybabies.

Overall, only a few articles (12) took a pro-dating stance. The majority (33) was against dating in Whyville. Only six articles took a neutral stance towards the issue. Key themes included how to distinguish between real-life and virtual dating practices, the importance of avatar appearance, and how to deal with inappropriate behavior online. For instance, most authors stressed that an individual's level of comfort with flirting and dating practices in real life should guide his or her flirting and dating practices in Whyville. At the same time, some authors highlighted the potential benefits of dating in Whyville and saw it as a relatively low-risk space in which to try out flirting and dating. Even XKaileeX (2003), who titled her article "Anti-Virtual Dating," conceded that "it is easier to ask [someone out] online because you're not really there to experience it and if you get turned down, it isn't that embarrassing, since not everyone knows and not everyone cares." These comments suggest that tweens view virtual worlds like Whyville as a relatively safe space for initial forays into flirting and dating but also observe particular etiquette standards. This also supports findings described below about the frequency of flirtatious solicitations (such as pick-up lines) and the relative infrequency of dating relationships in Whyville.

Chat Content Analysis

Despite most of the opinions discussed in *The Whyville Times*, our chat frequency count demonstrates the pervasiveness of flirting as a practice on Whyville. To put the frequencies in perspective, the most common word, "u," had a frequency of 333,603. Other common words included "lol" (156,170), "hi" (70,819), and "but" (54,555). Though less common than these everyday parts of virtual text and speech, words with romantic connotations were common enough to demonstrate their relative frequency, including "love/luv"

(19,926), "hot/hott/hottie/hot!" (12,522), "single" (8881), "asl" or "a/s/l" (6914), "kiss/kisses" (5,691), "heart/hearts" (5,431), "gf" [girlfriend] (3,793), "bf" [boyfriend] (3597), "m/o" or "mo" [make-out] (3448), and "sessy/sesky" (3024). The frequency of these terms is comparable to words such as "about" (19224), "friends" (5629), and "thx" [thanks] (3390). While demonstrating that flirting terms were used quite often, this analysis lacks the contextualized portrait provided by our qualitative analysis of logfile data. Without context it is difficult to say how these terms were used.

Observations of Online Flirting and Dating

The six case studies we developed through a qualitative analysis of logfile data indicate that tweens engaged in some common practices of flirting and dating with varying intensity during their first six months on Whyville. There were also some practices that were less common amongst the case studies as well as different styles of engaging in flirting practices. Below we describe some of the common practices as well as the divergences amongst the case studies.

Frequent flirting practices involved soliciting relationships with the opposite sex and were common across all of the case studies. These solicitations took two main forms: publicly stating an interest in finding a dating relationship and privately expressing interest. Both were usually done in crowded, populated areas of Whyville such as the Beach or Sector Y. Public, large group solicitation usually involved asking players to respond to a question by giving a specific three-number response, such as "123 if ur single," or "555 if im hot." Players responded to this by saying "123" or whatever 3-digit number was said. Another tactic was to say "a/s/l" (age/sex/location) (see also Subramahayan et al., 2004). Players responded by giving their age, gender, and general area where they lived (large city, state, or country), as in: 12/F/LA or 13/M/USA. Often our case studies lied about their age, giving ages of 13+. Apparently being a teenager is seen as more acceptable for dating than being of ages 9-12. This finding was confirmed by our content analysis of dating related articles published in *The Whyville Times*. Private, individual solicitations also tended to focus on singleness and looks. Common pick-up lines included "r u single" or "u r hot" (or "cute"). The chat frequency count supports this finding based on the frequency of words like "single" and variations of "hot."

Less common flirting practices, for instance, involved throwing a projectile such as a heart or kiss at a desired avatar (see Fields & Kafai, 2008). Alternatively sometimes girls or boys offered money (clams) if someone would become their girlfriend or boyfriend. Though most flirting on Whyville consisted of soliciting relationships, sometimes Whyvillians followed-up on a solicitation beginning by replying to the initial question about being single or saying one's age/sex/ location (a/s/l). Then the couple left the crowded, populated area for a more private place – often a planetary location such as the Moon, Mars, or Saturn. Talking about common interests, expressing affection ("i love u"), or even saying "i really like u" might be said during the conversation, especially at the end. Sometimes at the end of the conversation one person might ask "r we bf/ gf" or "r u my bf?" to confirm the status of the relationship. If these statements of affection were well received, then there might be an extension to the flirtation/relationship. Sometimes the couple will stand next to each other—their avatars overlapping—in a manner that is akin to cuddling or holding hands. There is sometimes talk about "mo" or "m/o"—making out. If they decide to kiss, this is what it looks like—avatars so close to each other that they overlap. Though making out is something the couple may "do," it is not usually explored more than avatars standing next

to each other—Whyvillians do not tend to role-play. Notably, while tweens have various strategies for soliciting relationships in large groups and following up on them, we did not see many relationships last beyond a few days.

Individual variations were observed in the six tweens we studied in how much they took up flirting practices, though they all solicited relationships with pick-up lines. A few started flirting within days of joining Whyville and continued it for about a month, dropping the practice almost entirely for several months. One boy (Brad/Vulcan61) started flirting only after he had already spent an entire month on Whyville, did it for a few weeks, then stopped. In contrast, flirting was consistently a central activity for another boy (Aidan/Masher47), but he never moved beyond the initial stages of forming a relationship. Amongst the girls, two pursued flirting and dating beyond the initial solicitation of relationships. For one of these girls (Isabel/Ivy06), flirting became her primary pattern of interacting with others, whether she way playing in the after school gaming club or at home. Conducting a qualitative analysis of the logfile data allowed us to observe these shifts in participation across time and space and provided us with a more nuanced portrait of tween players flirting and dating practices. In other words, we were able to observe flirting and dating practices that were fairly common among all Whyvillians as well as the nuanced ways in which players adopt these practices as their own.

DISCUSSION

Using a multi-modal investigation, we sought first to understand and confirm the prevalence of flirting and dating interactions in Whyville by triangulating our data in a traditional way. Furthermore, we aimed to broaden our perspective on the range of anticipatory flirting and dating practices that had not been observed before in virtual worlds. Our investigations of tween flirting and dating practices revealed nuances and diversity in how much, in what ways, and for how long tweens flirted in Whyville. Most interestingly our analyses revealed differences between the presence of flirting and the ways it is discussed in public forums. These findings alone provide rich material for discussion for those interested in tween development in online spaces, something beyond the scope of this paper. Here we will briefly discuss some of the discrepancies we observed in flirting and dating interactions and address some of the challenges we observed in using a multi-modal investigation.

The relatively negative opinions about flirting and dating in Whyville published in *The Whyville Times* contrasted with the widespread prevalence of these activities. We suspect that part of this has to do with player expertise (Stevens, Satwicz, & McCarthy, 2008). In other words, as we saw in most of the case studies, newer players are more likely to try out widespread flirting while more experienced players tend to develop a preference for particular activities or areas of the virtual world. For instance, one of the most experienced boys became a dealer of hard-to-find face parts on Whyville and spent most of his time at the trading post completing financial transactions. Our multi-modal approach allowed us to observe not only that tweens did one thing and said another in the pages of *The Whyville Times*, but also that variables such as player expertise are important. Thus, we can qualify our observation that flirting and dating are relatively common practices on Whyville by saying that this is true mostly for newer players and usually for a short period of time before they become engaged in more substantive aspects of game play in Whyville.

While multiple methods served us well in beginning to understand anticipatory flirting and dating of tweens, we also need to acknowledge some limitations. Regarding our analyses of some of the more formal discourse concerning flirting reported in *The Whyville Times*, articles are submit-

ted by Whyvillians and selected for publication by the paper's editor, an employee of the company that owns Whyville. So while published articles represent a wide variety of opinions on most subjects, we cannot assume that the articles selected for publication are perfectly representative of Whyvillians' views because we do not know all the selection criteria that influence what is published in *The Whyville Times*. Furthermore, we used logfile data to capture the "who, when, how and where" but supplemented this with information available from field notes, video records, and interviews. Making sense of logfiles qualitatively, especially longitudinally following one person over several months, is challenging and unusual. We did not have room in this paper to detail the case studies that provided the foundation for our summaries of flirting and dating. The six boys and girls, ranging in their virtual world participation from core to peripheral players, displayed considerable variety in their explorations of romance. In some cases, we found evidence of only light and infrequent flirting while in others it permeated nearly all their online interactions with others. These variations should not come as a surprise given the transitional status of our tween players moving from childhood into adolescence. In the end, we understand that even adding more data sources will not solve a fundamental conundrum of all research—to account as fully as possible about events, activities, and players in online and offline communities.

ACKNOWLEDGMENT

The data collection for this research was supported by a grant of the National Science Foundation (NSF-0411814) to the first author while the analyses and writings were supported by a grant of the MacArthur Foundation to Douglas Thomas and the first author. The views expressed are those of the authors and do not necessarily represent the views of the National Science Foundation, MacArthur Foundation, the University of Pennsylvania, the University of California, Los Angeles, the University of Southern California, or Numedeon, Inc. Numedeon, the company that owns and hosts Whyville.net, has no control over the publication of the results. The authors have no financial interest or any other official relationship with Numedeon. We appreciate Numedeon's willingness to cooperate in the research studies and to provide access to their logfile data. Special thanks also to Jason Fields who developed and conducted the analysis of the chat records in Mathematica and to Cameron Aroz who assisted in reducing the clicks and chat to first minute-by-minute and finally daily summaries.

REFERENCES

Boellstorff, T. (2008). *Coming of age in Second Life: An anthropologist explores the virtually human*. Princeton, NJ: Princeton University Press.

Boyd, D. (2008). Why youth "heart" social network sites: The role of networked publics in teenage social life. In D. Buckingham (Ed.), *Youth, identity, and digital media* (pp. 119-142). Cambridge, MA: MIT Press.

Bruckman, A. (2000). Situated support for learning: Storm's weekend with Rachael. *Journal of the Learning Sciences, 9*(3), 329–372. doi:10.1207/S15327809JLS0903_4

Bruckman, A. (2006). Analysis of log file data to understand behavior and learning in an online community. In J. Weiss, J. Nolan, J. Hunsinger, & P. Trifonas (Eds.), *The International handbook of virtual learning environments* (pp. 1449-1465). New York: Springer.

Buckingham, D., & Willett, R. (2006). *Digital generations: Children, young people, and new media*. Mahwah, NJ: Lawrence Erlbaum Associates.

Castronova, E. (2005). *Synthetic worlds: The business and pleasure of gaming*. Chicago: University of Chicago Press.

Clarke, J., & Dede, C. (2007). MUVEs as a powerful means to study situated learning. In C. Chinn, G. Erkins, and S. Puntambekar (Eds.), *Proceedings of CSCL 2007: Of mice, minds and society*, New Brunswick, NJ (pp. 144-147).

Dibbell, J. (1998). *My tiny life: Crime and passion in a virtual world*. New York: Henry Holt and Company.

Ducheneaut, N., Yee, N., Nickell, E., & Moore, R. (2006). Building an MMO with Mass Appeal: A Look at Gameplay in World of Warcraft. *Games and Culture, 1*(4), 281–317. doi:10.1177/1555412006292613

Feldon, D. F., & Kafai, Y. B. (2008). Mixed methods for mixed reality: Understanding users' avatar activities in virtual worlds. *Educational Technology Research and Development, 56*, 575–593. doi:10.1007/s11423-007-9081-2

Fields, D. A., & Kafai, Y. B. (2008). Knowing and throwing mudballs, hearts, pies, and flowers: A connective ethnography of gaming practices. In V. Jonker, A. Lazonder, & C. Hoadley (Eds.), *Proceedings of the Eighth International Conference of the Learning Sciences*, Utrecht, The Netherlands.

Fields, D. A., & Kafai, Y. B. (2009). A connective ethnography of peer knowledge sharing and diffusion in a tween virtual world. *International Journal of Computer-Supported Collaborative Learning, 4*(1), 47–68. doi:10.1007/s11412-008-9057-1

Fields, D. A., & Kafai, Y. B. (in press). Navigating life as an avatar: The shifting identities-in-practice of a girl player in a tween virtual world. In C. C. Ching & B. Foley (Eds.), *Constructing identity in a digital world*. Cambridge, UK: Cambridge University Press.

Fields, D. A., & Kafai, Y. B. (in press). Understanding Player Participation and Practices in Virtual Worlds: A Proposal for Qualitative Analyses of Log File Data. In D. Thomas (Ed.), *Research methods in virtual worlds*. Cambridge, MA: MIT Press.

Gee, J. P. (2003). *What video games have to teach us about learning and literacy*. New York: Palgrave MacMillan.

Jenkins, H. (2006). *Convergence culture: Where old and new media collide*. New York: New York University Press.

Kafai, Y. B. (2008). Gender play in a tween gaming club. In Y. B. Kafai, C. Heeter, J. Denner, & J. Sun (Eds.), *Beyond Barbie & Mortal Kombat: New perspectives on gender and gaming* (pp. 111-124). Cambridge, MA: MIT Press.

Kafai, Y. B., Feldon, D., Fields, D. A., Giang, M., & Quintero, M. (2007). Life in the times of Whypox: A virtual epidemic as a community event. In C. Steinfield, B. Pentland, M. Ackerman, & N. Contractor (Eds.), *Proceedings of the Eighth Conference of Computer Supported Collaborative Learning*, New Brunswick, NJ (pp. 196-205).

Kafai, Y. B., & Giang, M. (2007). Virtual playgrounds: Children's multi-user virtual environments for playing and learning with science. In T. Willoughby & E. Wood (Eds.), *Children's Learning in a Digital World* (pp. 196-217). Oxford, UK: Blackwell Publishing.

Leander, K. M., & Lovvorn, J. F. (2006). Literacy networks: Following the circulation of texts, bodies, and objects in the schooling and online gaming of one youth. *Cognition and Instruction, 24*(3), 291–340. doi:10.1207/s1532690xci2403_1

Ludlow, P., & Wallace, M. (2007). *The Second Life Herald: The Virtual Tabloid that Witnessed the Dawn of the Metaverse*. Cambridge, MA: MIT Press.

Mazzarella, S. R. (2005). *Girl wide web: Girls, the internet, and the negotiation of identity*. New York: Peter Lang.

Nardi, B., Ly, S., & Harris, J. (2007). Learning conversations in World of Warcraft. In *Proceedings of the 2007 Hawaii International Conference on Systems Science* (pp. 79). Washington, DC: IEEE Computer Society.

Steinkuehler, C. A., & Duncan, S. (2009). Scientific habits of mind in virtual worlds. *Journal of Science Education and Technology, 17*(6), 530–543. doi:10.1007/s10956-008-9120-8

Stevens, R., Satwicz, T., & McCarthy, L. (2008). In-Game, In-Room, In-World: Reconnecting video game play to the rest of kids' lives. In K. Salen (Ed.), *The ecology of games: Connecting youth, games, and learning* (pp. 41-66). Cambridge, MA: MIT Press.

Subrahmanyam, K., Greenfield, P. M., & Tynes, B. (2004). Constructing sexuality and identity in an internet teen chatroom. *Journal of Applied Developmental Psychology, 25*, 651–666. doi:10.1016/j.appdev.2004.09.007

Suzuki, L. K., & Calzo, J. P. (2004). The search for peer advice in cyberspace: An examination of online teen bulletin boards about health and sexuality. *Journal of Applied Developmental Psychology, 25*, 685–698. doi:10.1016/j.appdev.2004.09.002

Taylor, T. L. (2006). *Play between worlds: Exploring online game culture.* Cambridge, MA: MIT Press.

Thorne, B. (1993). *Gender play: Girls and boys in school.* New Brunswick, NJ: Rutgers University Press.

Williams, D., Consalvo, M., Caplan, S., & Yee, N. (in press). Looking for gender (LFG): Gender roles and behaviors among online gamers. *The Journal of Communication.*

Williams, D., Yee, N., & Caplan, S. (2008). Who Plays, How Much, and Why? A Behavioral Player Census of Virtual World. *Journal of Computer-Mediated Communication, 13,* 993–1018. doi:10.1111/j.1083-6101.2008.00428.x

XKaileeX. (2003). Anti-virtual dating. *The Whyville Times.* Retrieved November 2, 2008, from Whyville.net.

This work was previously published in International Journal of Gaming and Computer-Mediated Simulations, Volume 2, Issue 1, edited by Richard E. Ferdig, pp. 40-48, copyright 2010 by IGI Publishing (an imprint of IGI Global).

Chapter 5
A Next Gen Interface for Embodied Learning:
SMALLab and the Geological Layer Cake

David Birchfield
Arizona State University, USA

Mina Johnson-Glenberg
Arizona State University, USA

ABSTRACT

Emerging research from the learning sciences and human-computer interaction supports the premise that learning is effective when it is embodied, collaborative, and multimodal. In response, we have developed a mixed-reality environment called the Situated Multimedia Arts Learning Laboratory (SMALLab). SMALLab enables multiple students to interact with one another and digitally mediated elements via 3D movements and gestures in real physical space. It uses 3D object tracking, real time graphics, and surround-sound to enhance learning. We present two studies from the earth science domain that address questions regarding the feasibility and efficacy of SMALLab in a classroom context. We present data demonstrating that students learn more during a recent SMALLab intervention compared to regular classroom instruction. We contend that well-designed, mixed-reality environments have much to offer STEM learners, and that the learning gains transcend those that can be expected from more traditional classroom procedures.

INTRODUCTION

SMALLab is a mixed-reality environment where students collaborate and interact with sonic and visual media using full body movements in an open physical space. This represents a new breed of a technology-based student-centered learning environment (Bransford, Brown, & Cocking, 2000), one that incorporates multimodal sensing, modeling, and feedback while still addressing the financial and logistical constraints of a real world classroom. Physically, *SMALLab* is a cubic space that measures 15-feet wide x 15 feet wide x 12

DOI: 10.4018/978-1-4666-0029-4.ch005

feet high. It includes a vision-based tracking object tracking system, a top-mounted video projector providing real time visual feedback (typically projected onto the floor), four audio speakers for surround-sound feedback, and an array of tracked physical objects called glowballs (Birchfield et al., 2006). In addition, a set of common wireless video game interfaces (e.g., gamepad, Wii Remote, see Shirai, Geslin, & Richir, 2007) can be added. The glowballs are handheld, lit from within, and are the size of grapefruits. Students move freely in the space - they are not dragging wires or attaching sensing equipment to their bodies or clothes. They are able to immediately SEE the impact of their movements, FEEL the results kinesthetically, and HEAR immersive sound as they engage elements of the feedback apparatus. All of this is done in a collaborative manner with all students in a typical classroom participating. Video documentation of student learning in *SMALLab* is available at: http://ame2.asu.edu/projects/emlearning. See Figure 1 for an example of a typical classroom layout.

A growing body of evidence supports the theory that cognition is "embodied" and grounded in the sensorimotor system (Barsalou, 2008; Fauconnier & Turner, 2002; Glenberg, Gutierrez,

Levin, Japuntich, & Kaschak, 2004; Hestenes, 2006; Hutchins, 1995). This research posits that the way we think is a function of our body, its physical and temporal location, and our interactions with the world around us. In the domains of interactive media and digital learning, the concept of embodiment has been applied in a numerous ways. The *River City* virtual environment exemplifies one conception of embodiment (Dede & Ketelhut, 2003; Dede, Ketelhut, & Ruess, 2002; Ketelhut, 2007; Nelson et al., 2007). In *River City*, student actions and observations are embodied as virtual avatars in a virtual world. Dourish (2001) offers another conception of embodiment that is grounded in the domain of social and tangible computing. He writes, "embodied phenomena are those that by their very nature occur in real time and real space." Our work draws upon both of these concepts of virtual and physical embodiment to generate learning experiences that directly couple physical action with interactive digital media. By embodiment in *SMALLab* we mean interaction that engages students both in mind and in body, encouraging them to physically explore concepts and systems by moving within and acting upon a mediated environment. Impor-

Figure 1. Students construct a layer cake structure in SMALLab

tantly, this interaction is multimodal. It engages the full visual, sonic, and kinesthetic capabilities of students.

This paper presents two experiments pertaining to *SMALLab* learning in the earth science domain. For the first pilot study, we wanted to know *can SMALLab be effectively integrated into a conventional high school context and is there preliminary evidence of student learning?* In the second controlled experiment we wanted to look more closely at student achievement and address the question, *does the SMALLab learning experience yield greater student gains than regular classroom instruction?*

RESEARCH CONTEXT

SMALLab has been permanently installed in a classroom in a large urban public High School in the southwest United States. Over half of the students at the school are on free or reduced lunch—an indication of low socio-economic status—and 89% of them speak Spanish at home. Our researchers, along with teachers and students, work collectively to design learning scenarios in *SMALLab* using a custom set of authoring tools. At present the library consists of over thirty such learning scenarios, and, having participated in the design process, our partner-teachers take great ownership over them. A partner earth science teacher and his ninth-grade students from multiple classes were recruited. All students were enrolled in a program for at-risk students. Students were identified as at-risk because they were reading at least two levels below their grade, and were recommended by teachers and counselors.

Geological evolution is an important area of study for high school students because it provides a context for the exploration of systems-thinking (Chen & Stroup, 1993) that touches upon a wide array of earth science topics. Despite the nature of this complex, dynamic process, geological evolution is often studied in a very static manner. In a typical learning activity, students are provided with an image of the cross-section of the earth's crust. Due to the layered structure of the rock formations, this is sometimes called a *geological layer cake*. Students are asked to annotate the image by labeling the rock layer names, order the layers according to which were deposited first, and identify evidence of uplift and erosion, and note the presence of index fossils (Lutgens, Tarbuck, & Tasa, 2004). Traditionally, it is rare that students are offered a hands-on learning experience that captures the dynamic process of geological evolution.

Our partner teacher, an experienced earth science educator, identified a deficiency of the traditional instructional approach: when students do not actively engage geological evolution as a time-based, generative process, they often fail to conceptualize the artifacts (i.e., cross-sections of the earth's surface) as interconnected products of a complex, dynamic system. They often do not actively conceptualize geological evolution and the layering process as a time-based, generative construct. They rarely understand that the cross-sections of the earth's surface represent the products of a complex, dynamic system. As a consequence, they struggle to develop robust conceptual models during the study of geological structures and strata formation. For six-weeks we collaborated with our partner teacher, using the *SMALLab* authoring tools to realize an interactive mixed-reality simulation of the layer cake formation process. Working in *SMALLab*, we sought to leverage the powerful capabilities of digital games and simulations to aid learning in new ways, while fostering face-to-face collaboration among students and teachers that is only possible in real physical space.

METHOD

I. Layer Cake Builder Simulation

As shown in Figure 1, during the learning activities, all students are co-present in the space. Figure 2 shows the visual scene that is projected onto the floor of *SMALLab*. Within the visual display, the center portion is the layer cake construction area where students deposit sediment layers and fossils. Shown here is a partially built layer cake structure. Along the edges, students see three sets of images. Along one edge they see depictions of depositional environments. Along another edge are images that represent sedimentary layers. Along a third edge they see an array of plant and animal images that represent the fossil record. Each perimeter image is an interactive element that can be selected by students and inserted into the layer cake structure. The images are iconic forms that

students encounter in their earth science studies outside of *SMALLab*.

Sediment. Along the top edge of the display are the five types of sediment: coal, shale, limestone, conglomerate, and sandstone.

Depositional Environment. A standard wireless gamepad controller is used to select a depositional environment from among the five options that are pictured along the bottom edge. The five environments are a swamp, a mountain stream, a delta, a desert, and a shallow ocean. When a student makes a selection, they will *see* the image of the environment and *hear* a corresponding ambient soundfile. For example, if a student selects the fast moving mountain stream environment, students hear the sound of rushing water. After one student selects a depositional environment, a second student holds a glowball, using it to grab a sediment layer and drop it onto the layer cake structure in the center of the space. This action inserts the layer into the

Figure 2. Screen capture of Layer Cake after a fault has been activated

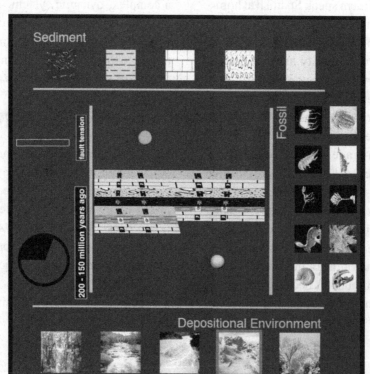

layer cake structure at the level that corresponds with the current time period.

Fossils. A third student uses his or her glowball to grab a fossil from among ten options and drop it onto the structure. This action embeds the fossil in the current sediment layer. The set of fossils include multiple species that are present in different geological epochs and depositional environments such as a fern, trilobite, jellyfish, whale, dinosaur, and rabbit.

Geological Time and Fault Tension. On the left side of the display, students see an interactive clock with geological time advancing to increment each new period. Three buttons on a wireless pointer device are used to pause, play, and reset geological time. A bar graph displays the current fault tension value in real time. Students use a Wii Remote game controller with embedded accelerometers, to generate fault events. The more vigorously that they shake the device, the more the fault tension will increase. Holding the device still will decrease the fault tension. When a tension threshold is exceeded, a fault event (i.e., earthquake) will occur, resulting in uplift in the layer cake structure. Fault events can be generated at any time during the building process. Subsequently erosion occurs to the uplifted portion of the structure.

Student participation framework. The process of constructing a layer cake involves four lead roles for students: (1) the depositional environment selector uses the gamepad controller, (2) the sediment layer selector uses a glowball, (3) the fossil record selector uses a second glowball, and (4) the fault event generator uses the Wii remote. The teacher typically assumes the role of geological time controller, using a wireless pointer device. The computer interfaces define clear roles for multiple participants, and their success depends upon careful timing and execution of a collaborative choreography of action.

In the classroom, approximately fifteen to twenty students are divided into four teams of five or six students each. Three teams are in active

rotation during the build process, such that they take turns serving as the action lead with each cycle of the geological clock. These teams are the (1) depositional environment team and fault event team, (2) the sediment layer team, and (3) the fossil team. The remaining students constitute the evaluation team. These "evaluator" students are tasked to monitor the build process, record the activities of action leads, and to steer the discussion during the reflection process. Students from all teams are encouraged to verbally coach their teammates during the process. Thus, all students are engaged via role play.

Curriculum. The three-day curriculum features intense collaboration and a repeating cycle of alternating hands-on episodes and reflection episodes. From a modeling instruction perspective (Hestenes, 1992, 1996), this cycle supports critical cognitive processes and results in knowledge construction and consolidation. During the hands-on episodes, students devise conceptual models about the subject matter and underlying systems. Working in teams, they are continuously forming, testing, and revising their conceptual models together. During the reflection episodes, students discuss activities, analyze any faults in decision-making, ask questions about various aspects of the structure, and challenge one another to justify their decisions and actions.

II. Pilot Study

In this first study we wanted to know, *can SMAL-Lab be effectively integrated into a conventional high school context* and *is there preliminary evidence of student learning?* The first part of this question is intended to assess the design of the described university/K-12 partnership and the efficacy of the scenario co-design process. To assess individual students' content learning gains, a ten-item hard copy test was designed to assess knowledge of earth science topics relating to geological evolution. Each item included a multiple-choice concept question followed by an open-ended question eliciting an explanation or justification. All test concepts were covered in the teacher's classroom using traditional instructional methods in the weeks leading up to the experiment. Thus, at the time of the pretest, students had been exposed to all of the test material. The pretest actually served as a measure of what students learn after traditional instruction measures. The three-day experiment did not introduce any new concepts, but rather reinforced and reviewed previously studied topics. The concept test was administered one day before and then one day after the intervention. We did not collect data from an untreated control group in this pilot study.

Results. Table 1 lists the results of the concept test. A gain of 23.5% was seen in the free response section that scored the students answers to the open-ended questions. Answers were rated on a 0 - 2 scale. Gains are presented as Hake gains, the actual percent gain divided by the maximum possible gain (Hake, 1998). Participants achieved a 22.6% overall percent increase on their multiple choice question scores, and a Hake gain of 48% (SD=1.90), Effect Size (ES) =.81. Participants achieved a 40.4% overall percent increase in their justification scores, and a Hake gain of 23.5% (SD = 2.8), ES =.53

III. Controlled Study

To build upon the results of the pilot study in the subsequent academic year (2009), we designed a second study to focus on the question: *does SMALLab learning yield greater student gains than typical classroom instruction?* Here, seventy-one ninth-graders from five earth science classes at the same school participated. We collaborated with the same classroom teacher as in the pilot study.

This study represents a mixed design with three measurement time points. The teacher taught five geology classes throughout the day. The classes were randomly assigned to condition (group). Group 1 received three days of regular classroom instruction and then three days of *SMALLab*. For Group 2 the order of intervention was switched; Group 2 first received the *SMALLab* intervention and then the three days of regular classroom instruction. In this manner, Group 1 served as a "waitlist control". During the *SMALLab* treatment, students were exposed to the same set of learning activities as described in the pilot study. These activities were framed as a context in which students can apply their understanding of the fundamental concepts. The regular classroom intervention mixed instructional lectures and hands-on activities (e.g., students created geological timelines) that—similar to the *SMALLab* condition—challenged students to apply their understanding of the

Table 1. Summary of mean pre- and post-treatment scores

		Mean Scores
Multiple choice test items (n=72)	Pre-treatment multiple choice average score	6.82
	Post-treatment multiple choice average score	8.36
	% increase	23%
	Hake gain	48%
Free-response justifications (n=72)	Pre-treatment explanation average score	3.68
	Post-treatment explanation average score	5.17
	% increase	40%
	Hake gain	24%

inter-dependent relationships between geological forces over time.

Each participant took an invariant knowledge test three times. They took a pretest immediately before the first intervention, a midtest after the first three-day intervention, and a posttest immediately after the second intervention. This measure was a revision of the test used the previous year. It included thirteen items. It was primarily created by the geology teacher. Six of the items on the test were constructed response "how" and "why" questions that prompted participants to explain their choices. The maximum score was 100.

Results. Table 2 lists the descriptive statistics from the Layer Cake geology study. Groups 1 and 2 were matched at pretest, even after adjusting for significantly different variances between the groups, $t < .50$.

Group 1. Paired t test analyses revealed that the gain for Group 1 from pretest to midtest was just significant, $t_{(28)} = 2.03$, $p = .05$. The gain from midtest to posttest for Group 1 was highly significant, $t_{(32)} = 7.48$, $p < .001$.

Group 2. Paired t test analyses revealed that the gain for Group 2 from pretest to midtest was highly significant, $t_{(36)} = 8.52$, $p < .001$. The gain from midtest to posttest was not significant. That is, after SMALLab, the group did not gain significantly more knowledge from the three days of lecture.

An ANOVA comparing the TOTAL gains between the experimental groups (conceived of as posttest minus pretest) was significant, Group

$1 = 22.87 (14.93)$; Group $2 = 16.37 (11.64)$; $F_{(1, 64)} = 3.94$, $p = .05$. These results reveal that receiving regular instruction before exposure to *SMALLab* significantly affects overall learning of content, at least for this sample, average comparative 6.50% gain for Group 1. Figure 3 illustrates these gains over time. A repeated measures analysis on the data revealed that the interaction of time by condition was highly significant with an F value greater than 52.

DISCUSSION AND CONCLUSION

We have presented a next generation interface for learning called *SMALLab*, a mixed-reality environment created using the latest theories in the learning sciences. We have described the implementation of a new earth science learning scenario, and have presented quantitative data regarding two studies of student learning gains. Taken together, these two studies offer encouraging evidence that next generation interfaces such as *SMALLab* are feasible in a classroom context and can have a powerful impact on student learning. In this context, there are important related questions with regard to how any new technology can be successfully integrated with existing curricula and instructional methods. We contend that both studies support the notion that *SMALLab* learning can complement and enrich existing school practices. Results from the pilot study show that *SMALLab* can facilitate new learning, even

Table 2. Means, SDs (in parentheses), and effect sizes for groups in Layer Cake study

Group	Pretest	Intervention	Midtest	Gain	Intervention	Posttest	Gain
1 max[a] n = 34	49.03 (13.60)	Regular Classroom Instruction	52.69 (16.52)	3.65[b] *ES =.38	*SMALLab*	72.03 (19.42)	**19.42 ***** ES= 1.34
2 max n = 37	46.97 (18.21)	*SMALLAb*	63.97 (22.48)	**18.00 ***** ES =1.44	Regular Classroom Instruction	62.41 (20.88)	**-1.56** ES= -.09

Notes. [a] At the test time point Means are for all students who took the test at that point. Analyses include only students who took all three tests.

* = p value less than.05, *** = p value less than.001.

Figure 3. Graph of mean scores for both groups, solid line represents RegularInstruct/SMALLab

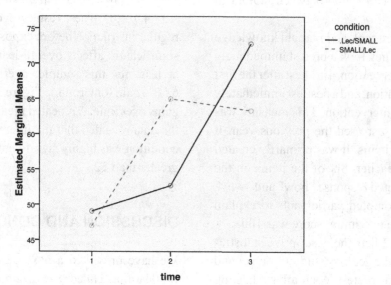

when following extensive classroom instruction. This result is replicated in the comparison study. Moreover, in keeping with a preparation for learning paradigm, the controlled study indicates that the order of learning activities is crucial. In this instance, regular classroom instruction, followed by *SMALLab* is demonstrated to be optimal for student achievement.

At this juncture we cannot yet say which components lead to the increase in student learning. *SMALLab* incorporates at least three powerful learning constructs.

1. *Embodiment Interaction and Multimodal Feedback.* All scenarios are designed so that students move their corporal bodies and use multiple senses. We try to engage modalities that are typically not stimulated during regular instruction. For example, while the earthquake is occurring the image on the floor shakes vigorously and probably engages the vestibular system. By hearing the different water sounds associated with the depositional environments, we posit that more complex memory traces are being laid down in the students' brains, and these

should reinforce concept learning. We also believe that just moving the physical body through real space and manipulating the icons is novel.

2. *Collaboration.* All students in the class are engaged in tasks and play a role. Because they have a responsibility, even as note takers on the sidelines when not in the space, they stay attuned. These game-style Communities of Practice are powerful predictors of learning and aid in leading users on the pathway to expertise (Gee, 2007).

3. *Novelty.* We know via animal models that novelty (and the perception of novelty) is extremely important for learning information and maintaining attention. Giving students opportunities to experience content in a novel manner turns on the limbic rewards system (McCoulough, Bernstein, & Conrad, in press). Observationally we would say that our students stay engaged through the fifty-five minute class period. Novelty does not merely affect the students. The teachers are also engaged in a manner that is atypical. *SMALLab* teachers self-select to be part of this process. These are generally the more

creative and tech-savvy teachers at a school. They are paid a small stipendium throughout the year They seem energized by the process of co-creating and while demonstrating the scenarios to their students, they too must be up and moving. Surely this is more kinesthetic than the blackboard lecture.

Future studies should pull these components apart and try to ascertain which one - or combination - is responsible for the increased learning gains. To that end, we have studies underway that vary the amount of collaboration (e.g., one-on-one physics learning in the *SMALLab* space), and amount of embodiment (e.g., the floor projection is now the screen on a desktop computer and the mouse is used to manipulate the glowball). Perhaps with passing years, teaching in *SMALLab* will no longer be so novel for our partner teachers. In sum, these studies are encouraging and demonstrate that significant learning gains can be made in embodied, mixed-reality environments above and beyond the gains expected from traditional instruction.

ACKNOWLEDGMENT

This work has been supported by the MacArthur Foundation under a grant titled *Gaming SMALLab*; by the Intel Corporation under a grant titled *Gaming SMALLab*; and by the National Science Foundation CISE Infrastructure grant under Grant No. 0403428 and IGERT Grant No. 050464. Portions of this research were first presented at American Educational Research Association in San Diego, CA, April 2009.

REFERENCES

Barsalou, L. W. (2008). Grounded Cognition. *Annual Review of Psychology*, *59*, 617–645. doi:10.1146/annurev.psych.59.103006.093639

Birchfield, D., Ciufo, T., Minyard, G., Qian, G., Savenye, W., Sundaram, H., et al. (2006). *SMALLab: A Mediated Platform for Education*. Paper presented at ACM SIGGRAPH, Boston.

Bransford, J. D., Brown, A. L., & Cocking, R. R. (Eds.). (2000). *How People Learn: Brain, Mind, Experience, and School*. Washington, DC: National Academy Press.

Chen, D., & Stroup, W. (1993). General Systems Theory: Toward a Conceptual Framework for Science and Technology Education for All. *Journal of Science Education and Technology, 2*(3), 447–459. doi:10.1007/BF00694427

Dede, C., & Ketelhut, D. J. (2003). *Designing for motivation and usability in a museum-based multi-user virtual environment*. Paper presented at the American Educational Research Association Conference, Chicago.

Dede, C., Ketelhut, D. J., & Ruess, K. (2002). *Motivation, usability and learning outcomes in a prototype museum-based multi-user virtual environment*. Paper presented at the 5th International Conference of the Learning Sciences, Seattle, WA.

Dourish, P. (2001). *Where the action is: The foundations of embodied interaction*. Cambridge, MA: MIT Press.

Fauconnier, G., & Turner, M. (2002). *The Way We Think: Conceptual Blending and the Mind's Hidden Complexities*. New York: Basic Books.

Gee, J. P. (2007). *Good Video Games and Good Learning: Collected Essays on Video Games, Learning and Literacy*. New York: Peter Lang Publishing.

Glenberg, A. M., Gutierrez, T., Levin, J., Japuntich, S., & Kaschak, M. P. (2004). Activity and Imagined Activity Can Enhance Young Children's Reading Comprehension. *Journal of Educational Psychology, 96*(3), 424–436. doi:10.1037/0022-0663.96.3.424

Hake, R. R. (1998). Interactive-engagement vs Traditional Methods: A Six-Thousand-Student Survey of Mechanics Test Data for Introductory Physics Courses. *American Journal of Physics*, *66*, 64–74. doi:10.1119/1.18809

Hestenes, D. (1992). Modeling Games in the Newtonian World. *American Journal of Physics*, *60*, 732–748. doi:10.1119/1.17080

Hestenes, D. (1996). *Modeling Methodology for Physics Teachers*. Paper presented at the International Conference on Undergraduate Physics, College Park, MD.

Hestenes, D. (2006). *Notes for a Modeling Theory of Science Cognition and Instruction*. Paper presented at the GIREP Conrerence, Modeling and Physics and Physics Education.

Hutchins, E. (1995). *Cognition in the Wild* (Vol. 1). Cambridge, MA: MIT Press.

Ketelhut, D. J. (2007). The impact of student self-efficacy on scientific inquiry skills: An exploratory investigation in River City, a multi-user virtual environment. *Journal of Science Education and Technology*, *16*(1), 99–111. doi:10.1007/s10956-006-9038-y

Lutgens, F., Tarbuck, E., & Tasa, D. (2004). *Foundations of Earth Science* (4th ed.). Upper Saddle River, NJ: Prentice Hall.

Nelson, B., Ketelhut, D. J., Clarke, J., Dieterle, E., Dede, C., & Erlandson, B. (2007). Robust design strategies for scaling educational innovations: The River City MUVE case study. In B. E. Shelton & D. A. Wiley (Eds.), *The Educational Design and Use of Computer Simulation*.

Shirai, A., Geslin, E., & Richir, S. (2007). *Wi-iMedia: Motion Analysis Methods and Applications Using a Consumer Video Game Controller*. Paper presented at the Sandbox: ACM Siggraph Symposium on Video Games, San Diego, CA.

This work was previously published in International Journal of Gaming and Computer-Mediated Simulations, Volume 2, Issue 1, edited by Richard E. Ferdig, pp. 49-58, copyright 2010 by IGI Publishing (an imprint of IGI Global).

Chapter 6
Wee Wii:
Preschoolers and Motion–Based Game Play

J. Alison Bryant
Consultant, USA

Anna Akerman
Adelphi University, USA

Jordana Drell
Nickelodeon/MTV Networks, USA

ABSTRACT

In this paper, the authors specifically focus on the opportunities and challenges presented by the Nintendo Wii to preschoolers in context to three key objectives in order to facilitate game development: First, to understand the range of physical and cognitive abilities of preschoolers in motion-based game play; Second, to understand how preschoolers interact with the Wii; Third, to understand the expectations of the parents of preschoolers with regard to these new gaming platforms and the purchase and play contexts within which game play occurs. In addition to reporting challenges and advantages of the motion-based play for preschoolers, the authors also discuss how the findings of this research were then implemented by the game producers to develop the first preschool-targeted game on the market in the United States.

INTRODUCTION

Both traditional and newer media are an increasingly integral part of daily life for families around the world. For example, in the U.S., the average family home comes fully equipped with innumerable electronic and digital choices including televisions, video game consoles, personal computers and mp3 players (Rideout & Hamel, 2006), often to the delight of the household's youngest members who are eager to explore novel forms of entertainment and play. Media use is no longer an option; it is an integral part of everyday life for these families. As the media landscape becomes increasingly varied due to the infiltration of innovative technologies, it is crucial to evaluate how new household adoptions affect the lives of those who consume them. Even when new purchases are made for adult family members, the children are often affected – be it via mere exposure or

DOI: 10.4018/978-1-4666-0029-4.ch006

active investigation. Such is particularly true of gaming devices. Given that, over a third (36%) of four to five year-olds in the U.S. have played console video games and almost a quarter have played handheld games (NPD, 2008), it becomes important to assess further the context for pre-schoolers' play, particularly since the majority of gaming equipment is designed for a much older target audience.

In this article, we examine a specific video game console: Nintendo's Wii. Unlike past systems, this gaming device relies on real-time physical movements to dictate on-screen activity. Released in North and South America in November 2006, the Wii has been extremely successful, outselling competitors like Microsoft's Xbox 360 and Sony's PlayStation 3, prompting its declaration as "the world's best-selling next-generation games console" (Sanchanta, 2007). Since its release, sales have remained relatively constant -- a rare feat in the fast-changing consumer electronics space (SlashGear.com, 2009). The Wii's success has been partly attributed to its ability to attract non-traditional gamers, such as children, mothers, and senior citizens, as opposed to the narrower segment of more traditional or hard-core gamers.

Unlike most traditional academic research, the research reported here grew out of a concrete commercial need. The game and digital product production team for Nick Jr., the preschool arm of Nickelodeon, recognized the possible business opportunity in the preschool space created by the advent of a motion-based gaming platform. They saw the Wii as having special potential for their audience, but also realized that in order to create a game that would both engage their audience and be developmentally appropriate they needed to understand how preschoolers were already interacting with the platform as well as what boundaries would be set on their creative direction due to the developing physical, motor, and cognitive abilities of 3-5 year olds. Moreover, they were also interested in understanding the potential for creating games for preschoolers on

other platforms, particularly the PlayStation 2, Nintendo DS and mobile phones. To better understand this potential consumer group and their needs and motivations for playing games, they turned to the Nickelodeon Kids & Family Group Consumer Insights research team.

In many respects, the investigation that grew out of this business decision turned traditional game creation and research on its head. Most game developers create games first and then test them with the consumer later to see if the user experience is of sufficient quality for release. In this case, however, the game producers started with understanding the consumer (preschoolers and their families) and then created the game around their abilities, interests, and preferences, engaging in both exploratory research before the game was designed and formative research during the design process.

There were three key objectives for this research. The first was to understand the range of physical and cognitive abilities of preschoolers in the context of motion-based game play. Knowing that a 3 year old may differ greatly in his/her game play abilities when compared to a 5 year old suggests that some game functionalities may be better for younger children than others. In addition, extensive previous internal user experience research at Nickelodeon in the area of preschoolers and gaming had shown us that there are other critical factors, such as gender or birth order, that affect preschoolers' adoption of gaming technologies and their subsequent performance with the games. The second objective was to understand how preschoolers interact with the Wii, specifically how they handle the various forms of play and game mechanics offered by the games currently on the market for this platform. The final objective was to understand the expectations of the parents of preschoolers with regard to these new gaming platforms and the purchase and play contexts within which game play occurs. Our goal was to investigate these considerations in an exploratory manner.

In this article we will discuss previous research that has been done with preschoolers looking at their physical, motor and cognitive development in the context of gaming; outline and report on the research project designed to better understand the challenges and advantages of the motion-based play for preschoolers; and then discuss how the findings of this research were then implemented by the game producers. We will also mention research done to test the Wii game that was developed out of this exploratory study in order to assess whether this initial and highly preliminary study provided effective information for our game producers and developers.

LITERATURE REVIEW

Motor and Physical Development in Preschoolers

Children's motor and physical abilities change dramatically, particularly during the early years. As Gallahue and Ozmun (1995) explain, the initial forms of movement, beginning with the fetus, are entirely reflexive, and thus involuntary. The first voluntary movements, which begin in infancy and dominate until approximately 2 years of age, are referred to as the rudimentary movement phase. By preschool, children are typically thought to be in the *fundamental movement phase* of motor development (see also, Benelli & Young, 1995). This is described by Gallahue and Ozmun (1995) as, "a time in which young children are actively exploring and experimenting with the movement capabilities of their bodies" (p. 86).

According to Wang (2004), the development of skill efficiency in three specific areas of motor development is particularly critical during the preschool years. These are: gross motor locomotion, posture and balance control, and object manipulation. Their significance may relate to the idea that, as Gallahue and Ozmun (1995) explain, all observable movements can be grouped as belonging to one, or some combination of, these three basic categories, which they coin: locomotor, stability, and manipulative movements. Gross motor patterns of locomotion are typified by movements that involve change in location. Clear examples of such would be: crawling, walking, and running. Posture and balance control, which Wang (2004) describes simply as "good body mechanics and movement efficiency" (p. 35), involves, fundamentally, the ability to maintain equilibrium. Movements like standing, twisting, and sitting are commonly cited instances. Finally, object manipulation, which involves fine motor movements, entails directing control over objects in one's immediate environment. As Wang (2004) explains, this entails not only locating something visually and/or aurally, but making contact with it and identifying it tactilely too. Eating and drawing are examples.

The preschool years represent a time of dramatic change in gross motor control, which improves significantly (Gallahue & Ozmun, 1995). While fine motor skills lag behind gross motor abilities, strides are certainly being made in the former category too. Generally speaking, as motor activities become increasingly refined with the help of age, practice and experience they also grow more efficient, coordinated and deliberate (Bukatko & Daheler, 2001). Essentially, preschoolers become better able to *control* both large and small muscles (Needlman, 1996).

While motor growth and development has historically been characterized as a series of behavioral milestones that children traverse in a predictable, systematic and universal fashion, most notably by Gesell (as cited in Thelen, 1995), more modern approaches have emphasized the role of the physical and social environment in influencing developmental trajectories too (Needlman, 1996). According to Thelen (1995),

Movements are always a product of not only the central nervous system but also of the biochemical and energetic properties of the body, the environ-

mental support, and the specific (and sometimes changing) demands of the particular task (p. 81).

Unlike traditional accounts of motor development that privilege the role of biological maturation and endogenous differences in propagating change, advocates of this alternative view focus additionally on the contextual factors that influence behavioral changes, including, ultimately, motor milestones. Roesengren, Savelsbergh, and van der Kamp (2003) argue that to understand emerging motor behaviors in the early years of life requires an analysis of both the tasks children are confronted with as well as the corresponding goals they are trying to achieve. Within their conceptualization, "tasks" are defined as "the particular problems the child faces over the course of his or her life" (Roesengren, Savelsbergh, and van der Kamp, 2003, p. 484) and include such examples as working one's body to eat, escape, and explore, namely in the interest of survival.

As the media landscape changes, so too does the context in which children develop and, as a result, the "tasks" which they encounter. Consistent with the literature reviewed above, Gallahue and Ozmun (1995) similarly maintain that a child's developmental status is fundamentally affected not only by biological influences but by environmental ones as well. If we accept this framework, it becomes critical to understand new tasks and demands as they emerge in children's constantly evolving surroundings. New technologies are rapidly entering children's homes. As a result, preschoolers are increasingly being exposed to diverse media that were not necessarily created for their use. Given this reality, it is crucial to evaluate how these latest media innovations are received – especially by the youngest members of society (Wartella & Robb, 2007).

Given the extent to which even motor development is influenced by one's environmental surrounds, it is important to examine new gaming platforms to evaluate not only whether (and, how) they will be adopted by preschoolers but, beyond

that, if playing with these latest technologies might influence subsequent behavior. Caregivers are a fundamental social force with the power to further develop children's natural movement impulses by encouraging them to engage in activities and with materials that are appropriately challenging; they have the unique ability to keep children motivated to move (Wang, 2004). Can video game play be an activity that caregivers would feel comfortable promoting for physical activity? Though typically, such game play is sedentary, new platforms like the Nintendo Wii defy this model and present players with the possibility to engage in motion-based, interactive play. While this kind of activity clearly has implications for gross motor development, the various game mechanics currently integrated into these games also require significant cognitive and fine motor skills. Given that preschoolers are still developing these skills, one might speculate that fine motor and perhaps even cognitive development could, in fact, be furthered through the encouragement of these gaming platforms.

Though we are far from understanding how this innovative kind of motion-based video game play interacts with motor (as well as social and cognitive) development, these are certainly platforms that present new challenges or "tasks" and ones which younger and younger children are highly motivated to achieve. Because motor activity is associated with positive self-concept and successful social integration with peers (Benelli & Yongue, 1995), this begs the question: can new gaming platforms represent a positive force by which motor activity can be encouraged, and subsequently represent a positive influence in developmental trajectories?

Play, Video Games, Mapping and Preschooler Cognition: Towards Greater Realism

Most of preschoolers' waking hours are spent playing. Indeed, as Needlman (1996) points out preschool represents a time when physical energy peaks and the number of required hours for sleep in fact decreases. Play is a fundamental mechanism by which children can learn about their bodies and their movement capabilities (Gallahue & Ozmun, 1995). As such, physical play is known to assist children's development of numerous skill sets, including fine and gross motor skills.

While recreation of a physical nature has traditionally been enacted by young children in a non-mediated context, as indicated earlier, such is no longer the case. A new increasingly popular category of electronic games requires physical movement for game play (Papastergiou, 2009). One of the first "exergames" to be brought into the home via a gaming console was the dance simulation game, *Dance Dance Revolution*. With the motion capabilities of the Wii, we have seen more active video game play entering the living room (although it should be noted that at the time of this research, shortly after the release of the system, there were not many of these games on the market). With the Wii, players' movements in real space similarly dictate what happens on screen. This occurs via a hand-held wand-like controller, which is used instead of more historically conventional input controllers that have relied on buttons and keys or joysticks to translate user's gaming intentions into on-screen actions.

One perceived advantage of this new system is that it allows gamers to experience more cybernetic realism while playing (Skalski, Lange, Tamborini, & Shelton, 2007). In achieving this realism, Tamborini and Skalski (2006) cite the importance of mapping which they define as "how closely actions represented in the virtual environment match the natural actions used to change a real environment" (p. 228). Research with adults suggests that mapping of natural body actions to on-screen behavior results in more vividness and interactivity while gaming, and, by extension, a greater sensation of presence – or, as Tamborini and Skalski (2006) describe it "a sense of 'being there' inside the game world…" (p. 225). After

all, rather than pressing buttons, players are now able to simply simulate physically what they wish to see and do on-screen. The Wii thus provides players with an unprecedented level of mapping since unlike most prior game controllers, which required button-pressing and joystick manipulations to perform on-screen action, this system allows natural movements to be represented virtually. Players' hand and arm movements in their living room directly dictate their on-screen behavior – be it swinging a tennis racket or sword-fighting an enemy.[1]

While the greater presence afforded by new technologies is generally conceptualized as positive and enjoyment-inducing for adults, might the same be true of child users? Revelle and Medoff (2002) consider mapping a major cognitive stumbling block for pre-school adoption of adult gaming systems. Preschoolers' level of cognitive development limits their capacity to understand screen-based representation, as well as traditional mapping systems where real life movements do *not* translate into game-based activity (Revelle & Medoff, 2002). Thus, heightened realism and natural mapping could presumably make game play more accessible for this age group.

Clearly, cognitive development raises certain important considerations when it comes to game design and play. According to Piaget, 3-5 year olds fall into the preoperational developmental stage, characterized mainly by their limited abilities to perspective-take or entertain multiple concepts simultaneously (Siegler, 1991). Mental manipulations as well as symbolic and abstract thinking can be quite difficult for children of this age. Preschoolers frequently delegate their attention to a single feature of the perceptual space – that which is most salient – to the exception of others. Not surprisingly, these cognitive constraints affect the manner in which play is enacted, with video gaming posing no exception. On the other hand, the Wii could conceivably eliminate some of this difficulty since its most dramatic departure from prior gaming models is that users' actions off-screen are fundamentally connected to those occurring on-screen.

Though limited, some research exists on preschoolers' usage on earlier interactive gaming technologies. Revelle and Medoff (2002) note that, for reasons described above, many conventional input devices, which are typically designed for adult use, can be quite challenging for young children. Yet, surmounting evidence suggests that even the youngest members of the household play with the console game systems found in their family rooms, and sometimes, even, their bedrooms (Rideout, Vanderwater, & Wartella, 2003). Not surprisingly, many of the difficulties preschoolers face when trying to use systems created for the adult world result from their level of cognitive and motor development. After all, most preschoolers lack fine motor control, cognitive understanding of the mapping between controller use and on screen activities, and, the kinds of abstract thinking skills required to understand the representational nature of concepts, in this case those taking place on screen (Revelle & Medoff, 2002).

The Nintendo Wii poses an interesting situation. Unlike other game consoles, the Wii was created to engage not only hard-core, adult gamers, but also non-traditional gamers, therefore increasing the potential market. In households with children, the system was and continues to be increasingly taken up by the preschoolers (NPD, 2009). And yet, academic research related to preschoolers' adoption of the latest gaming technology is scarce. Papastergiou (2009) provides a review of the recently published scientific literature examining the potential of new electronic games, like exergames, for health and physical education. In her report, half of the studies that looked at physical education did so with an adult (mostly college-aged) sample. Of the studies conducted with youth, none examined children under nine years old. Notably, the only research that examined how playing might impact motor skill acquisition did so with an adult sample. Our purview here differs from these studies in that the scope of this

research was not focused on certain pre-defined educational goals of the game. Instead, our key objective was to take a step back to understand fundamentally the user experience with the platform. After all, before we can truly grasp how the Nintendo Wii might influence preschoolers' cognitive and motor development, we must first examine how they interact with the system.

METHODOLOGY

Although the Wii was the primary platform of interest for this exploratory research, this study also incorporated 3 other gaming platforms of interest to the game producers: the Sony Playstation 2, the Nintendo DS, and mobile phones. In reference to the Wii, these platforms provided critical comparisons by which we could assess the physical and cognitive abilities of the preschoolers and the general family game play. Since these platforms were part of the methodology, they will be mentioned in this section, but will not be part of the subsequent discussion.

Method: In-Home Interview

In order to examine preschoolers in a natural setting, as well as to garner information about their home ecology, 26 in-home interviews were conducted in 3 U.S. locations (a West coast urban/suburban area, a Midwest suburban/rural area, and an East coast urban/suburban area). Each of these interviews lasted between one and two hours and included the preschooler, at least one parent, and often siblings and another parent or caregiver. All interviews were videotaped. Notes were made by a research assistant during the game play, and afterwards the videotapes were reviewed again.

Because of the wealth and depth of data presented, and the lack of previous research in this area, we took a *grounded theory* approach to analyzing the data (Glaser, 1998). Grounded theory allows us to look at the data through abductive reasoning. Patterns in the interviews were noted through review of the videos by the research team, and the findings were compiled based on those patterns and with researcher agreement.

During each interview three types of information were gathered. From the parents and any older siblings that were available we collected information about: the purchase decisions surrounding game systems in the household, the family's typical game play patterns, levels of parental moderation with regard to gaming, and favorite games played by various family members. Because these interviews were in-home, we were also able to understand the ecology of gaming in their home: what types of spaces (communal or private) were used for game play, how the systems were set up (in particular, where was the sensor for the Wii placed), and the number and type of games and game systems owned. Finally, and most importantly, we gathered the game play data for each child on at least 3 gaming platforms: the Nintendo Wii or the Sony Playstation 2, the Nintendo DS, and a mobile phone (a Motorola RAZR). Only findings concerning the Nintendo Wii system are presented here.

With regard to the interview format, each interview followed a detailed discussion guide that outlined the home ecology issues and the various games, mechanics, and corresponding motor and cognitive skills that the researcher needed to observe. Prior to the interviews, the research team had worked with the game producers to create a list of game mechanics and issues tied to preschoolers' motor and cognitive abilities that were critical for them to understand before developing the games. These ranged from more general dexterity issues related to game controllers, to the effectiveness of in-game instructions, to specific mechanics in current games that the producers were interested in implementing in future preschool titles. Each game selected for the in-home research was tied to specific motor or cognitive abilities; and those were all outlined in the discussion guide.

As the researcher moderated the interview, he/she referred to the discussion guide, which clearly laid out which games to have the child play and which motor or cognitive abilities should be observed. In addition, the researcher was guided to make general observations about the child's play patterns and parent-child interaction. Since this was exploratory research, the expectation was that insights would arise that had not been strictly defined a priori.

The moderator began the interviews by observing the preschoolers in their usual gaming activities, talking with both the child and his/her parent about typical usage habits, abilities, likes and dislikes. The moderator guided the preschooler though the series of games, so that he/she could observe the interaction and probe both the preschooler and his/her parent on feelings, attitudes, and frustrations that arose in the various circumstances observed. Because of the still-developing social and communication skills of the preschoolers, much of the data was gathered through observing the child's physical and emotional interactions with the game. In addition, parents would often make comments during the child's play that compared it to other game or entertainment experiences their child normally has, which gave the researcher an indication of difficulty and enjoyment.

If the child had previous experience with the game system, he/she was first asked to play his/her favorite game on that system. For all Wii adopters, the *Wii Sports* gaming suite, which is included in the initial system purchase, was their choice. *Wii Sports* includes *Tennis, Baseball, Bowling, Golf,* and *Boxing*; and the specific sports played varied across the preschoolers.[2] After playing their game-of-choice, preschoolers were then asked to play specific games that were part of the *Wii Play* gaming suite (including *Table Tennis, Laser Hockey, Fishing, Find Mii, Pose Mii, Shooting Range, Billiards, Charge!,* and *Tanks!*), chosen by the moderator based on the list of pre-defined mechanics targeting various levels of motor development and cognitive understanding of game rules and play. Parents and older siblings were instructed to interact with the preschooler during game play only if that interaction was a normal part of their game play.

Sample

The preschoolers in this study included 11 boys and 15 girls ranging in age from 3 years & 3 months to 5 years & 11 months. In addition, because previous internal research had shown the effects of older siblings on game play, such as more advanced motor coordination when using a computer mouse, households were recruited to have a combination of preschoolers with older siblings and without. Families were recruited based on the console game systems they owned, with 13 owning a Wii and 18 owning the PS2. Every preschooler in the study, therefore, had some experience with the console game system. In addition, 13 families had at least one Nintendo DS. For those households that did not own a DS, one was brought to the interview for the child to play. Finally, a Verizon Motorola RAZR phone was brought to each household, so that the child could try two mobile phone games.

Because we were looking for both the innate movements the preschoolers employed in game play and those mechanics that were most quickly and easily learned, a combination of naïve players (those who had played with the console system for less than 3 months) and more experienced players (those who had played for greater than 3 months) were part of the sample, with 13 of each included. This allowed us to see both the instinctive movements of the new players (and of the more experienced players when playing new games), as well as those aspects of game play that had been learned through experiences with the more experienced players. Moreover, by requiring at least minimal experience with the platforms, we were able to avoid high frustration

levels in the preschoolers during the play portion of the interview, which often comes with having them interact with an unknown platform, and allow them to feel as though they were showing mastery of their gaming skills. This made both the child and the parent feel more comfortable and forthcoming during the research process.

FINDINGS

Families and the Wii

Although the primary thrust of this project was to assess the physical and cognitive abilities of preschoolers in relation to the Wii, there are some more general findings about how families interact with this new gaming platform which we found both critical to game development and which provide the context within which the preschoolers' play must be understood. Therefore, we will briefly outline some of those findings first.

One of the most critical findings is that the Wii was seen by most parents as a gaming "equalizer" – something that everyone in the family, including the preschoolers, could play. It was always set up in the living room as opposed to in the childrens' room, which was more prevalent with other console systems, so that everyone could have access to it. Parents discussed (often unaided) the fact that the Wii differed from other systems in the household from both a play and a purchase perspective. Because everyone (or almost everyone) played with it, and it was often purchased with the whole family in mind, it was located more centrally.

Interestingly, this family-oriented setup seems to have one major drawback for preschooler game play – the Wii-sensor was often placed too high for the sensor to recognize their movements, either on a mantle or on top of a TV. None of the parents in the study recognized this issue, but, as a result, the children would modify their play (e.g., by standing on a stool while playing).

The Wii and the games were usually bought with the entire family in mind, and family members played together in various combinations: siblings, parents with their children, and parents with each other. In addition, as has been highly touted in the press, non-traditional gamers like moms, preschoolers, and even grandparents are just as likely to play with the Wii as the heavier gamers in the family (Vorhaus, 2008). In very heavy gaming households, which tended to correspond to those with younger parents, we found that this family-oriented Wii play was beginning to take the place of more traditional media (e.g., television) as a space for family interaction.

The element of cooperative play is particularly important in the context of studying preschooler play because we saw that there tended to be more supervised play on this system than the others studied or mentioned, since parents or older siblings were almost always playing with the young child. These co-players provided both verbal and physical directions to the child, such as help holding the controller and changing positions. Older siblings taught and guided younger ones, engaging in complex interactions that combined both cooperation and competition.

The parents in this study clearly saw the Wii as a fundamentally different gaming platform, and often talked, unprompted, about why they preferred it to other platforms, both for their preschooler as well as for themselves. Parents praised the Wii for offering their children an opportunity to engage in physical activity, and cited examples of games that they felt required physical exertion or pointed out how hard their child was working during the interview. Interestingly, parents did not perceive the Wii games, in particular the sports games, as reinforcing a child's skills in the real-life counterpart games. For example, they did not think that playing baseball with *Wii Sports* would help their child make the varsity team. But, parents did feel that playing these games helped their child to learn the various rules and terms for the sports. Although preschoolers playing with the PS2 also played sports games, such as *Madden NFL*, this type of rule-learning was not mentioned by the parents of those children.

Preschoolers and the Wii

Physical Interactions

Watching preschoolers play with the Wii reinforced our understanding of the unique challenges they face in console game play due to their ongoing motor development. Basic Wii remote (Wiimote) use is hindered by the fact that their hands are not large enough to effectively use the device. For example, preschoolers could not simultaneously press the A and B buttons, which is the current industry norm to start game play (see Figure 1 for a picture of the Wiimote).

In tandem with proprietary internal research that we've done on other platforms, there is considerable difference in adeptness with the Wiimote between preschoolers who are only or eldest children and those who have older siblings. This seems to be attributed to the fact that older siblings provide models for the younger siblings to mimic, and then adopt as their own. This is in line with ongoing research by our team on computer game play, which finds that preschoolers with older siblings tend to adopt the traditional "adult" grip on the mouse with the index finger clicking the left mouse button, whereas only children and preschoolers who are the oldest child tend to maintain a modified grip, with the hand rotated 90° clockwise, so that they use their thumb to click the left mouse button.

In addition, there were several specific game mechanics that consistently proved difficult for the motor skills of 3-5 year olds (see Figure 2 for screenshots from the various Wii games mentioned below). These were mechanics that the preschooler

Figure 1. The Wiimote

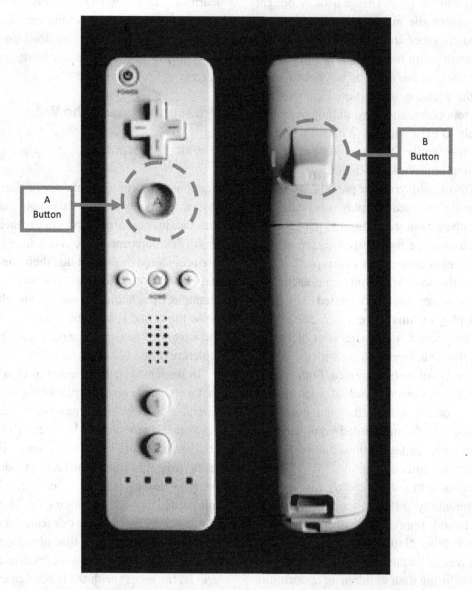

either needed help multiple times from the parent or that they never mastered during the research session. These fell into 3 categories:

- *Fine motor skill issues*, such as angling the Wiimote in slight degrees to move an item (*Laser Hockey*, *Pose Mii)* and making small, controlled movements (*Fishing*, *Pose Mii*)

- *Conceptually difficult moves*, such as tilting the Wiimote forward (while holding it horizontally) so that your character moves faster and tilting it back so the character move slower (*Charge!*); having to understand spatial dimensions when pulling back on the Wiimote and then moving forward to hit an object (*Billiards*); or holding the Wiimote vertically and using the end of

Figure 2. Screenshots from Wii Sports and Wii Play games

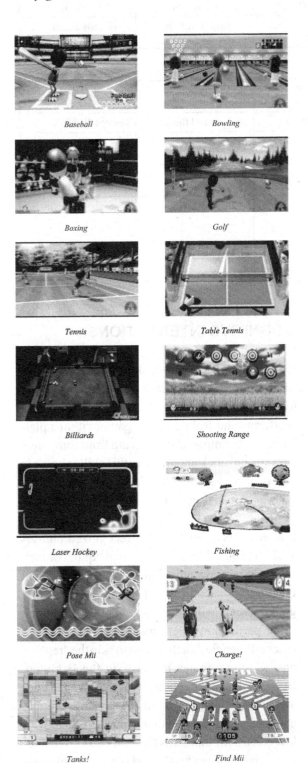

Baseball

Bowling

Boxing

Golf

Tennis

Table Tennis

Billiards

Shooting Range

Laser Hockey

Fishing

Pose Mii

Charge!

Tanks!

Find Mii

the Wiimote, which is normally pointed toward you, to move an item (*Table Tennis*)

- *Complex or multi-step movements*, such as holding down a button and then releasing it midway through an arm movement (*Bowling, Golf, Billiards*) or having to consider multiple factors simultaneously, such as aiming, shooting and dodging bullets (*Tanks*)

Even for those preschoolers who had played the Wii extensively these were recurring difficulties. Of course, there were significant differences in the level of difficulty experienced by the preschooler as related to their age. Table 1 highlights the age differences for each of these game mechanics.

On the other hand, games based on mechanics that did not require complex or fine motor skills, such as *Tennis, Baseball* and *Boxing* were both easy for preschoolers to play and were also often mentioned as their favorite games. For those games, the critical learning was that preschoolers' movements are grossly exaggerated compared to adult movements, due to a lack of coordination and developing motor skills. In order to effectively create games for them, developers would need to make sure that the "hotspots" (the areas on the screen that would detect Wiimote movement) are sufficiently large and less sensitive than when programmed for adults. So, if a preschooler is just moving his/her Wiimote back and forth when playing *Tennis*, the game will pick up that movement as a legitimate swing.

In addition to these more general motor development-related findings, there were also a couple of interesting findings with regard to preschoolers' physical interactions with the Wii. The first is how they intuitively expected the Wiimote to work when they were confronted with a new game. The clearest example of this came when preschoolers were confronted with the need to "go faster" in a game. Almost every time, the first response of the preschooler was to tilt the Wiimote back and forth (like a see-saw).

Table 1. Relation of game mechanic to level of difficulty by age

Game Mechanic	Associated Games	3 Year Olds	4 Year Olds	5 Year Olds
Hold down a key and release on time/ multi-step	Bowling, Fishing, Billiards	Very difficult	Moderately difficult	Moderately difficult
Hold down two keys (A & B)	Multiple games	Very difficult	Moderately difficult	Moderately difficult
Tilt forward and backward	Charge!	Moderately difficult	Moderately difficult	Easy
Angle the paddle	Laser Hockey	Moderately difficult	Moderately difficult	Moderately difficult
Point the end of controller at the screen	Table Tennis	Moderately difficult	Easy	Easy
Small movements	Fishing, Pose Mii	Very difficult	Moderately difficult	Moderately difficult (easier for girls)
Perpendicular movements (like pulling back, away from the screen)	Billiards	Very difficult	Moderately difficult	Moderately difficult
Consider multiple factors, such as aiming, shooting, dodging bullets	Tanks	Very difficult	Moderately difficult	Moderately difficult

After probing as to why they did this, it became clear that this motion to them mimicked running. A second interesting finding was the level of help needed for preschoolers to switch back and forth between different Wiimote stances. One of the great things about motion-based play is that game developers can incorporate a variety of motions and keep things interesting and challenging for the player. The instruction screens provided by current games on the market, however, are very text-heavy and include static illustrations. The younger preschoolers, therefore, had a hard time positioning their hands, as well as remembering which Wiimote stance corresponded with which game; in almost every case they needed parent or older sibling help to move between the different stances. For example, if they were holding the Wii-mote horizontally to race the cow in *Charge!* and then switched to *Bowling*, in which they need to hold the Wii-mote vertically, the parent usually needed to assist them in making that switch. Like several of the challenges mentioned in this section, this is both a physical and cognitive challenge.

COGNITIVE INTERACTIONS

Children, even those as young as the 3-5 year olds in this study, quickly learn a digital language of symbols, actions, icons etc. which carries across platforms and from game to game within a platform. For example, children learn from computers to point and click and transfer this skill to console and handheld games. In addition, even children who can't read learn to recognize recurring words or memorize the location of particular buttons on a screen. For example, they recognized phrases such as "enter," "play again," and "quit," or they learned from watching their older sibling that clicking the second button from the right on a game screen will save their game. Moreover, some participants were aware of shortcuts and other efficiencies, such as how to skip the "replay" on the sports games by pushing the B button. Because they are dependent on these visual cues and standard game mechanisms for game play and navigation, it is critical that game developers follow consistent standards for icons, color schemes (e.g., green means "go"), and placement of items on the screen. These visual cues and cognitive shortcuts were consistently used by preschoolers in this study, either when playing games they were already familiar with or figuring out game play in new games.

Although preschoolers adapt quickly to these gaming environments, there are also limits to their cognitive interactions with the games. For example, because young children are still developing their sense of spatial perception, "persistent worlds" and graphics that require them to translate maps in relation to "where they are" in a world were very confusing to them. For example, in *Golf* players are shown a 2-D map in the top corner of their screen in order to help them aim their shot. None of the preschoolers who played the game in this study understood the purpose of the map, even with their parents persistently trying to explain it to them. In other Wii games, and in a persistent world game that the PS2 users played, even children who listened to and viewed instructions providing an overview of the terrain got lost, wandered aimlessly, and failed to recognize that they were returning to a place they had already been.

Another challenge for preschoolers is any form of multi-step or complex game play. Games where you have to first move your Wiimote to aim, subsequently press a button to lock your direction, and then make your action motion were very difficult for most preschoolers. For example, in *Bowling* players have to first aim their ball and then roll it and in *Baseball* they can change the pitching style by pushing buttons. For a few of the older, heavier gamers, who consistently played the Wii and watched and mimicked others, these multi-step movements could eventually be learned; but, for most of the participants this more advanced play was lost on them.

On the other hand, although preschoolers found some of these cognitively complex games challenging, their response to these games was positive (e.g., laughing while playing, asking to play over and over again, or saying "This is fun!"),

even if they did not perform the tasks required by the game to win. Hitting the ball out of bounds in *Golf* or mowing down trees instead of scarecrows in *Charge!* was often just as satisfying to them (and sometimes more satisfying) than accomplishing the goals set out in the game. This speaks to an important criterion for games targeting this age group. Young children in this study, particularly 3 and 4 year olds, needed to feel some sense of accomplishment when playing a game. For the most part, children this young are not motivated by scoring, often because they are still relatively unfamiliar with the high numbers used to score in most video games; they are, however, motivated by other measures of success, such as collecting items that then show up on their screen. In addition, accepting failure is difficult for this age group, which is constantly trying to learn and succeed, so messages such as "You lose" or "Loser" are often taken much more viscerally. When the failure is comical, however, children tend to accept it much more willingly.

A final cognitive aspect of play that was particularly evident with the Wii was the importance of personalization for preschoolers in enjoying their game play. With the Wii, players can create Miis (avatars) to play with. For preschoolers, who are in the process of learning about who they are and are just beginning to develop a sense of self, the ability to create a virtual representation of themselves and the people they know was incredibly engaging. They always chose to play with "their" Mii and when Miis that represented other people that they know were on screen they would refer to them by name (e.g., "That's Uncle Ned."). Their attachment to these personalized avatars was so strong that several preschoolers refused to play with the Wii if they could not play with their Mii.

Implementation

The findings from this research became the foundation for the way in which the game producers in the entertainment company then designed their first Wii game for preschoolers, *Go! Diego Go! Safari Rescue*. Most of the findings affected the game mechanics themselves, but a few were useful outside of the game context. Most notably, the realization that Wii-sensors are often being placed too high for preschoolers altered the packaging for the preschool games developed, so that it now includes a note to the parents reminding them to lower their Wii-sensor when their preschoolers are playing.

Another piece of family-oriented learning from the research that affected the game itself was the recognition that one of the most striking differences between the Wii and other platforms is that parents (and older siblings) chose to stay in the room and participate in game play rather than leaving the child alone to play. In designing the *Go! Diego Go! Safari Rescue* game for the Wii it seemed crucial to capitalize on the presence of a parent or older siblings as a vehicle to further enhance the preschool user's gaming experience. Therefore cooperative-play (co-play) features were incorporated throughout the game, allowing a second player to help during the motion-based mini-games, such as helping Diego blow up a hot air balloon to get over a mountain by pumping up and down, or digging in the dirt to help an elephant find a magic drum. These "mini-games" can be played and enjoyed when the child is playing by him/herself, but games are enhanced with speed and vibrant animations when a second player (i.e., the parent or older sibling) picks up the second Wiimote and assists the younger child. In order to alert the preschooler and the other person playing that co-play is possible at that point during the game, an icon appears on-screen.

In addition, based on the findings related to the effect of preschoolers' physical and cognitive interactions with Wii games and the Wiimote, the game developers adapted the overall game play mechanics in the game. First, after seeing preschoolers struggle with spatial perception across platforms in the research, the game developers settled on a side-scroll game (like *Super Mario*

Bros.) that has subtle dimension provided by "2 1/2-D" game graphics. Players can move forward and back, but are consistently pointed in the correct direction to continue on their adventure by arrows and clearly defined paths.

Second, the game developers decided to use the preschoolers' natural mapping seen in the research as a guide to develop the game controls. Because it was clear from the research that the intuitive movement for running was tilting the Wiimote back and forth and that the fine motor skills needed to make small movements, such as pointing and clicking on a particular object, are not sufficiently developed in most preschoolers, the developers limited the main Wiimote actions to two main play elements: 1) players hold the Wiimote horizontally and tilt it to the right to go forward and left to go backward (tilting it further makes you go faster) and, 2) players can push any button on the Wiimote to activate an element that they pass by (such as searching in a bush) or to jump.

In addition to these to main play mechanics, based on the research the game development team created thirteen intuitive Wii-centric motions that were included and incorporated into game play for the *Go! Diego Go! Safari Rescue* game. Preschoolers can drum along with Diego by holding the Wii remote in one hand and moving their hands up and down as if beating a drum. They can paint the stripes back on a zebra by holding the Wii remote in one hand and moving their arm up and down as if using a paint brush. They can also help the characters swim by holding the Wii remote in one hand and moving their arms in a swimming-like motion, climb a ladder by tilting the Wiimote left and right as if reaching for the next rung on the ladder, or pump up a balloon by moving their hands up and down as if using a bicycle pump.

Moreover, because it was clear that preschoolers lack the cognitive capacity and motor memory to remember which movements they should be doing at a particular time during the game, animated icons were designed to appear on-screen and show the player what to do. The icons are cleanly designed and clearly communicate what motions need to be done with the Wii remote and one's body. In addition, the game sensors are very accommodating so that if the child is not doing the motion exactly as the icon is demonstrating, he/she will still be able to achieve the goal, feel accomplishment, and continue with the game. This adjustment in the motion detection is seamless and is never apparent to the player.

After implementing these design decisions based on the initial research, subsequent usability testing on the game was conducted in order to confirm that the game mechanics were both intuitive and simple for preschoolers, yet engaging for all members of the family in order to promote cooperative play. Although, presentation of the specific findings of that research is outside of the scope of this article, there are a few key results that are useful as markers of the success of this research.

With regard to the success of implementing intuitive and simple Wiimote movements into the game, none of the preschoolers in the follow-up testing (or their family members) had any difficulty in adopting the movements; all were able to fully engage in both the movement and action aspects of game play within the first minute of playing. In addition, the parents and children both found the game play engaging and often older siblings quickly wanted to have a turn at trying out the game. Tellingly, many of the children (and a few of their much-older siblings) said that they would want to play the game again, even though they did not have high affinity for the character Diego.

CONCLUSION

Because of the perceived success of this integrative research-production process, this method has become the model for preschool game development within Nickelodeon. Although the up-front time and costs were additional, the time and money

that would have been spent on the back-end of game production would have been considerably more. But, most importantly, the final product that children and parents will have a chance to play on their Wii console at home will be more engaging, more developmentally appropriate, and (hopefully) more fun than if research had not been part of the process.

From a business standpoint, the success of this Diego game in the marketplace and the rave reviews (and awards) that it won changed the perception of the viability of games created for preschoolers. Nickelodeon has since released four more preschool games for the Wii, and has more in development. Other preschool targeted properties, like Knowledge Adventures and *Sesame Street* have released Wii games and/or have a slate in development. For the most part, these competitors are also including research as part of the production process.

In addition, the preschool-targeted success of these games for the Wii has opened the door for preschool-targeted games on other gaming platforms and systems. In particular, Microsoft's upcoming extension to its Xbox 360 system (currently being called Project Natal) which provides for controller-less motion-based play, is already creating excitement in the game development community when it comes to creating for preschool consumers and their families. In addition, handheld platforms, and in particular the Nintendo DS, have seen dramatic uptake from preschoolers (see Bryant, Akerman, and Drell, in press, for more on developing for the DS). Finally, mobile platforms, like the iPhone, which allow for simple touch screen interface play, have become more popular preschool gaming platforms (Nickelodeon, 2009). In addition to several independent developer applications, both Nick Jr. and *Sesame Street* have recently released iPhone applications.

Though the nature of the study outlined above was exploratory, we see it as a useful model that could potentially serve as a case study for other endeavors that involve entering new terrain – in our case, the world of preschoolers. As mentioned at the beginning of this article, most game platform and software development is done with minimal research, which often happens towards the end of the development cycle. Conducting more exploratory research beforehand is useful as fuel for the creative process, and can also help identify "non-starter" ideas earlier.

For the academic community, this research points to a further need to get the research being done on university campuses out to the game community in a timely manner. It also highlights the potential benefits of academic-industry partnerships.

Although this research and discussion has primarily focused on preschoolers, there is plenty of opportunity for incorporating exploratory and development research with other user groups. In particular, the very general consumer group of "casual gamers," basically defined as anyone who is not a hard core game player, needs to be further researched as to their motivations for game play. And, of course, this type of research agenda is relevant not just for gaming, but for any other entertainment media. We sincerely hope to see even more of this type of research in both the industry and academia.

REFERENCES

Benelli, C., & Yongue, B. (1995). Supporting young children's motor skills. *Childhood Education, 71*(4), 217–220.

Bryant, J. A., Akerman, A., & Drell, J. (in press). Diminutive subjects, design strategy, and driving sales: Preschoolers and the Nintendo DS. *Game Studies*.

Bukatko, D., & Daehler, M. W. (2001). *Child Development: A thematic approach* (4th ed.). Boston: Houghton Mifflin.

Gallahue, D. L., & Ozmun, J. C. (1995). *Understanding motor development: Infants, children, adolescents, adults* (3rd ed.). Madison, WI: Brown and Benchmark Publishers.

Glaser, B. G. (1998). *Doing grounded theory: Issues and discussions*. Mill Valley, CA: Sociology Press.

Needlman, A. R. D. (1996). Growth and development. In R. E. Behrman, R. M. Kliegman, & M. Arvin (Eds.), *Nelson textbook of pediatrics* (15th ed., pp. 30-72). Philadelphia: Saunders.

Nickelodeon. (2009). *iPhone & iPod Touch Consumer Research*. New York: Internal Data.

NPD. (2008). *Kids & Consumer Electronics (Rep.)*. NY: Port Washington.

NPD. (2009). *Kids & Gaming (Rep.)*. NY: Port Washington.

Papastergiou, M. (2009). Exploring the potential of computer and video games for health and physical education: A literature review. *Computers & Education, 53*, 603–622. doi:10.1016/j.compedu.2009.04.001

Revelle, G. L., & Medoff, L. (2002). Interface design and research process for studying the usability of interactive home-entertainment systems by young children. *Early Education and Development, 13*(4), 423–434. doi:10.1207/s15566935eed1304_6

Rideout, V., & Hamel, E. (2006). *The media family: Electronic media in the lives of infants, toddlers, preschoolers and their parents*. Menlo Park, CA: Henry J. Kaiser Family Foundation.

Rideout, V. J., Vanderwater, E. A., & Wartella, E. A. (2003). *Zero to Six: Electronic Media in the Lives of Infants, Toddlers and Preschoolers*. Menlo Park, CA: Henry J. Kaiser Family Foundation.

Roesengren, K. S., Savelsbergh, G. J. P., & van der Kamp, J. (2003). Development and learning: A TASC-based perspective of the acquisition of perceptual-motor behaviors. *Infant Behavior and Development, 26*, 473–494. doi:10.1016/j.infbeh.2003.08.001

Sanchanta, M. (2007, September 7). Nintendo's Wii takes console lead. *The Financial Times*. Retrieved October 29, 2001, from http://www.ft.com/home/us

Siegler, R. (1991). *Children's Thinking* (2nd ed.). Englewood Cliffs, NJ: Prentice Hall.

Skalski, P., Lange, R. L., Tamborini, R., & Shelton, A. K. (2007). *Mapping the road to fun: Natural video game controllers, presence and game enjoyment*. Paper presented at the International Communication Association Conference, San Francisco, CA.

SlashGear.com. (2009, January 16). *Nintendo Wii sales set new industry record*. Retrieved from http://www.slashgear.com/nintendo-wii-sales-set-new-industry-records-1630867/

Tamborini, R., & Skalski, P. (2006). The role of presence in the experience of electronic games. In Vorderer, P., & Bryant, J. (Eds.), *Playing video games: Motives, responses, and consequences* (pp. 225–240). Mahwah, NJ: Lawrence Erlbaum Associates.

Thelen, E. (1995). Motor development: A new synthesis. *The American Psychologist, 50*(2), 79–95. doi:10.1037/0003-066X.50.2.79

Vorhaus, M. (2008). From gathering around TV to gathering around Wii. *Advertising Age, 79*(27), 18.

Wang, J. H. T. (2004). A study on gross motor skills of preschool children. *Journal of Research in Childhood Education, 19*(1), 32–43.

Wartella, E., & Robb, M. (2007). Young children, new media. *Journal of children and media, 1*(1), 35-44.

ENDNOTES

[1] This realism has recently come under fire, especially in the context of extremely violent video games which now have players enacting movements such as slitting the throat of or ruthlessly punching one's virtual opponent.

[2] The PS2 players played a wide variety of games, including *Frogger, Guitar Hero, Grand Theft Auto, Bratz, SpongeBob SquarePants, Harry Potter, Tony Hawk*, and *Pirates of the Caribbean*. The Nintendo DS selections were similarly broad, including *Nintendogs, Super Mario Bros., Tony Hawk*, and *Sonic Rush*. None of the children had previous experience with playing games on the mobile phone, an interesting finding in and of itself that stemmed from parents' fear of giving their preschoolers their mobile phones to play on.

This work was previously published in International Journal of Gaming and Computer-Mediated Simulations, Volume 2, Issue 2, edited by Richard E. Ferdig, pp. 1-17, copyright 2010 by IGI Publishing (an imprint of IGI Global).

Chapter 7
Decoupling Aspects in Board Game Modeling

Fulvio Frapolli
University of Fribourg, Switzerland

Amos Brocco
University of Fribourg, Switzerland

Apostolos Malatras
University of Fribourg, Switzerland

Béat Hirsbrunner
University of Fribourg, Switzerland

ABSTRACT

Existing research on computer enhanced board games is mainly focused on user interaction issues and look-and-feel, however, this overlooks the flexibility of traditional board games when it comes to game rule handling. In this respect, the authors argue that successful game designs need to exploit the advantages of the digital world as well as retaining such flexibility. To achieve this goal, both the rules of the game and the graphical representation should be simple to define at the design stage, and easy to change before or even during a game session. For that reason, the authors propose a framework allowing the implementation of all aspects of a board game in a fully flexible and decoupled way. This paper will describe the FLEXIBLERULES approach, which combines both a model driven and an aspect oriented design of computer enhanced board games. The benefits of this approach are discussed and illustrated in the case of three different board games.

INTRODUCTION

Recent research in the domain of multi-user interaction, such as multi-touch interactive tables (Loenen et al., 2007; Mazalek, Reynolds, & Davenport, 2007), opened a broad range of new

possibilities redefining the concept of human computer interaction. Noteworthy applications of these devices are computer enhanced games, which take advantage of both the physical and the digital worlds in order to improve the user experience. Our research is focused on computer enhanced board games, aiming at improving user experience by mixing the full flexibility of traditional board

DOI: 10.4018/978-1-4666-0029-4.ch007

games played around a table with computational functionalities from the digital world.

Games benefit from the features offered by digital environments, such as the high degree of dynamicity that can be introduced by means of advanced visual and audio effects. These further promote improvements in the immersive experience (Amory & Adams, 1999), and the interactivity of the game-play (Malone, 1981). It is evident that a significant amount of benefit can be gained by transferring the concepts and the games themselves from the physical to the digital world. Advanced visualization capabilities spur the development of innovative and sophisticated representations of game graphics and computer support can also help ease complex game tasks or situations, for instance by calculating intricate winning conditions, or by performing mundane tasks such as card shuffling or point distribution. However, the rules that guide the game-play are typically handled by the game software and are tightly intertwined with it, with their implementation hidden and inaccessible during game-play.

While the porting of physical board games to their computer-enhanced counterparts has been to a large extent successful, there exist certain aspects of traditional game- play that are not inherently supported to date. These deficits diminish the merits of computer-enhanced board games and lead to players registering a smaller degree of game satisfaction. As pointed out in (DeKoven, 1978; Salen & Zimmerman, 2003), the ability to modify the rules should not be considered just as an additional feature of the game, but as a central aspect of it that should not be neglected. It empowers the players by giving them overall control of the game and its features, while at the same time enabling them to modify the level of difficulty of the game or even its winning conditions. One additional advantage of being able to dynamically update the game rules and logic is the ability to extend the game-play and incorporate or update specific options and parameters that are usually hard-coded in the game software. Unfortunately, traditional approaches to game software development fail to support this vision, and represent a high barrier for both casual and experienced players without any programming skills, wanting to modify some rule of the game. Furthermore, depending on how the game is implemented, it could be difficult even for a programmer to add a certain rule without having to modify large portions of the code. In contrast, physical games allow the redefinition of rules by means of social agreement between players at any time during game-play.

In this paper we propose an extensible and efficient framework called FLEXIBLERULES that aims at taking advantage of both approaches (i.e., physical and digital), by allowing the implementation of board games in a fully flexible and decoupled way. The FLEXIBLERULES framework is comprised of both a conceptual model to design board games and a set of tools, including a domain-specific language and a dedicated compiler, to realize the aforementioned design. The different aspects of the game, such as the logical behavior of the different game objects, their representation, and the outcome of each action are modeled separately and can be freely modified during game-play. The main goal is to promote modularity and clarity: the user should be able to quickly identify what is to be modified and where, in order to change something in the game. Another requirement that was taken into consideration was simplicity of use, as it is not to be expected that all users will be skilled developers. To this end, the FLEXIBLERULES framework employs a user-friendly, Lisp-inspired language to implement its functionality. Another important aspect is providing the user with full control of the degree of automation: game rules can either be enforced by the system, or left to a human referee. Additionally, the framework aims at providing game designers with tools to support the modeling of a game and allowing the creation of prototypes that can be tested and fine tuned.

The rest of this paper is organized as follows. The next section discusses and reviews related work in the field of aspect oriented development and games. We then present the conceptual model that lies behind the FLEXIBLERULES framework, followed by a detailed description of the basics of the game definition language. The development environment that enables the implementation of actual board games based on the aforementioned model and language is subsequently described. In the section concerning the FLEXIBLERULES examples, we review the implementation of three different games, illustrating their differences in the light of the FLEXIBLERULES framework. Finally, we provide some conclusions on the presented work and insights on future work, having first discussed relevant implications in research, development and practice.

RELATED WORK

The motivation behind this research work has been to fully support the conveying of physical board games into the digital environment. The main deficit of existing digital board games is that they take into account the graphical representation of the game and its rules of play, but neglect the social interactions that occur during traditional sessions of game-play. One aspect of this is the freedom of letting players define house rules to make the game more enjoyable and suited to their standards. It has been well-established (DeKoven, 1978; Salen & Zimmerman, 2003) that this ability constitutes a focal point of any successful game design. In order for the game to have any degree of flexibility, interactivity and to be enjoyable to play, the support for house rules (Mandryk & Maranan, 2002) is a necessity, since amongst other things it promotes a much desired level of human-to-human interaction. In this respect, we present a holistic framework, called FLEXIBLER-ULES, to address the aforementioned issues at the game modeling level.

The need to establish standard models for the design and subsequent analysis of games is evident, as it allows for a common understanding and a shared vision among developers and also users (Bjork & Holopainen, 2004). Modeling a board game requires a deep understanding of all the objects involved, their behaviors and interactions, as well as the laws that govern the game world (i.e. rules that define al- lowed actions during game-play) and the winning conditions (Sanchez-Crespo, 2003). A first effort to simplify the modeling of a problem can be achieved through object orientation, and the definition of objects roles (Steimann, 2000). By recognizing the different entities composing the game, along with their relationships and roles, it is possible to create a model in a more natural way. Additionally, by separating different functional concerns encompassing single entities, as done with Aspect Oriented Programming (AOP) (Kiczales et al., 1997), the logic behind each object can be further simplified. Whereas (Steimann, 2005) considers aspects only as concerns of programming, there are many examples presenting them as core functional parts of a system (Rashid & Moreira, 2006), and as useful abstraction mechanisms which help express computer programs in a more natural way (Lopes, Dourish, Lorenz, & Lieberherr, 2003). In the same spirit, we want to promote aspects as a central functional part of modeling, and argue that an advanced separation of concerns will not only ease the modeling and implementation phases (Miller, 2001), but also effectively help end-users better understand the logic of the game.

A first step in this direction was taken by (Reese, Duvigneau, Köhler, Moldt, & Rölke, 2003), who divided the logic behind the game in terms of states, behaviors and rules. Different aspects of the game Settlers Of Catan ™ are distributed between two types of agents: administrative agents and players. Administrative agents are in charge of controlling the game board state, monitoring the enforcement of the game rules, and the resources owned by player agents, while player agents represent both the computer controlled player and the human counterpart. (Järvinen, 2003) proposes an approach for describing game rules as different aspects. The authors point out that game rules can be divided into five types: rules governing the game components and their function, rules governing relations between elements, rules that define game environments (i.e., the physical boundaries of components), rules that define the theme and rules for the user interactions.

Building on the aforementioned concepts and ideas we plan to extend current approaches and distribute all of the game logic within the game entities, as well as dividing it into different aspects; by clearly separating concerns of the game, we aim at simplifying the logic, and easing its comprehension by users, while catering for the full support of flexibility that traditional board games exhibit.

FLEXIBLERULES MODEL

FLEXIBLERULES is a framework for modeling and implementing board games around their atomic elements, the game entities, aiming at a simplified functional description of the game logic and its graphical representation. This section details all the elements that conceptually define the game model, both from a structural and a functional point of view. The game definition language presented in the following section comprises the infrastructure for developers to implement their games based on the proposed conceptual model.

We recognize two levels of abstraction as far as game modeling is concerned, namely logic and representation, which provide us with an initial separation of concerns. These concerns are modeled separately as logical and representation layers, dealing with a low-level description of game dynamics, and the high-level interface with the real-world (typically a graphical or tangible representation) respectively. Thus, the game model can be viewed as the composition of these two layers.

LOGIC LAYER

The Logic Layer is comprised of entities, which are the building blocks that define the functional core of a game. We distinguish between two types of logic entities: active (such as human or computer players) and reactive (such as the pawn or the board). Reactive entities behave in response to events originating from active ones. Because the FLEXIBLERULES framework is not concerned with modeling real or artificial intelligence players, the proposed model only focuses on reactive entities, and for the rest of this paper we will use the term entity as referring only to reactive ones. Extending the proposed model to encompass active entities will be considered in our future research. An overview of the elements of the FLEXIBLERULES model concerning the logic layer and the interactions between these elements is shown in Figure 1.

An entity is characterized by a functional behavior and a set of private properties, which can be accessed and modified only by the entity itself. Coordination and communication between entities is performed through the use of messages. Messages are information containers that are exchanged between entities during execution. Each message is identified by a label, which is used to dispatch it. All game actions are triggered by information exchanged between entities through message passing. Upon reception of a message, an entity triggers a certain internal reaction, its behavior, according not only to the received information, but also to its current internal state. The latter is stored as a specific state property in each entity. This allows the implementation of separate behaviors for the same message type for different states. The execution mechanism is thus similar to a finite automaton, such that actions executed by an entity are univocally defined by the input triple entity, state, message label.

Figure 1. Overview of the FLEXIBLERULES model

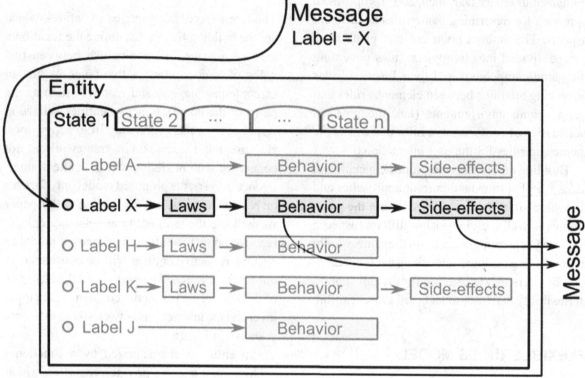

Semantic Aspects

The behavior of an entity describes how it should act in a certain situation, without being concerned with game rules that might disallow that particular behavior or make it produce some secondary outcome. These additional aspects of the game, referred to respectively as laws and side-effects, are modeled separately as *around* and *after* returning advices.

Laws. The join point (a join point is the aspect-oriented programming term for an interaction point with the rest of the system (Elrad, Filman, & Bader, 2001)) for laws is before the execution of a particular behavior: according to the current state of the entity, and the values in the incoming message,

preconditions for the execution of the behavior are checked. If pre-conditions are not met, a law advice can prevent the execution of the behavior. Laws also typically prevent the game from reaching an invalid situation, and can perform a rollback to restore the last valid situation (for example, the status just before an invalid player move). In order to analyze the actual global situation, laws can access all properties defined by all the entities of the game.

Side-Effects. The join point for side-effects is after the execution of a behavior. Side-effects define secondary outcomes of a behavior (for example, assigning points to the players after the successful completion of a complete round in a turn-based board game). Within a side-effect, it is possible to query attributes of each game entity, perform rollbacks, and send messages to other entities (for example, to inform them about the points earned by the player in the current turn). Finally, side-effects can also be used to determine whether winning conditions have been reached, thus ending the game session.

REPRESENTATION LAYER

Having defined the logic layer and the semantic aspects of the entities that comprise it, we present in this section the second level of abstraction that we have previously introduced, namely that of representation. Logic entities may have a dual in the representation layer, commonly referred to as their representation. Different forms of representation can exist, such as graphical or tangible. On a computer interface, a representation is typically composed of some graphical elements that decorate the game world and provide a visual feedback of the actual situation in the game. At any time during the game-play, a representation should reflect the internal state of its logical counterpart, by accessing its properties and executing any appropriate update procedures to mirror any potential changes in the background logic. Moreover, representations can also define representational properties, typically for storing graphical aspects such as their color, size or their position on the screen. To retain consistency with the proposed aspect-oriented approach throughout the FLEXIBLERULES framework, updates to the representations are also modeled as separate aspects in the form of *before* or *after* advices.

Representation Updates. Join points for representation updates are placed before or after changes to internal properties of a logical entity. In this respect, the behavior of the representation layer is to observe the logical layer and respond to any modifications by appropriately reformatting the graphical representation of the game. Update procedures can access both the value before and after the property change, therefore allowing the implementation of advanced graphical transitions.

USER INTERACTION

A game is a system that often requires mixed user interaction. On one hand the user should be able to interact explicitly with the game by manipulating representations (Intentional User Interaction), e.g., to move pawns around a checkerboard; on the other hand an entity may request user intervention in order to perform a certain operation (Forced User Interaction), e.g. information cards presented to the users to notify them about game state. These two different aspects of user interaction concern both the logical and the representation layers: logic entities may trigger forced inter- action, whereas representations may be the starting point for intentional interaction.

Intentional User Interaction. The representation becomes an interface that allows the user to communicate with game entities. During the game process, a representation can send messages to its logical counterpart, and can also provide a visual feedback by modifying its appearance.

Forced User Interaction. Interactions with the user can be necessary to determine the sequence of events to be executed in the game. Thus, the execution of a behavior may temporarily stop to allow interaction with the user, and then continue accordingly. Forced user interaction can be compared to modal message dialogs shown by computer applications.

GAME DEFINITION LANGUAGE

The core of the FLEXIBLERULES framework is the domain-specific programming language for representing and subsequently developing board games, based on the conceptual model that we have presented. The language exposes all the previously presented abstractions and allows the full implementation of different kinds of board games using the FLEXIBLERULES development environment that will be presented in the following section.

LANGUAGE BASICS

The language syntax is inspired by Lisp: expressions are written using a prefix notation, and are enclosed within parentheses. It is noteworthy to mention that we have also implemented a compiler for the language we defined. The need to introduce a novel language is spurred by the observation that current scripting languages have a general scope, while we wished to express the semantics of the FLEXIBLERULES model and hence defined this domain-specific language specifically targeted at board game design.

The language uses dynamic typing, and recognizes six different data types: numbers (either integer or float values), strings, lists, dictionaries (hashtables mapping string keys to data values), messages and *nil* (equivalent to Boolean false). Common operators to manipulate these data types are available. Local temporary variables, with scope limited to the current behavior, can be defined using the **var** statement:

```
(var <identifier> <value>)
```

Flow control can be managed both by using conditional statements, as well as by means of loop statements:

```
(if <condition> <body> else <body>)
(switch <identifier>
```

```
(case <value> <body>)
...
(case <value> <body>))
(foreach <identifier> in <list>
<body>)
(while <condition> <body>)
```

The body element shown in the previous examples represents only a single statement. To define sequences of multiple statements the following expression can be used:

```
(do <statement>... <statement>end)
```

ENTITY DEFINITION

Entities are composed of behaviors and properties. For each possible state, we can define the behavior to be executed upon receiving a message with the specified label as follows:

```
#state<name>#onMessage<name>
<behavior>
...
#onMessage<label>
<behavior>
```

An entity can modify its state at any time by means of the **changeState** function. Properties can be defined and initialized from within a behavior using the following statement:

```
(new property<name>as<value>)
```

Values associated with properties can be retrieved using the **property** function, and changed with the **update property** function as follows:

```
(property<name>)
(update property<name>to<value>)
```

Notice that the **property** function does not return a reference to the property but just its value. To manipulate property values it is thus often necessary to use a temporary variable and update the property afterwards.

MESSAGING

Entities can communicate by exchanging messages, which carry key-value pairs called *attributes*. Messages are identified by a label, which is itself an attribute associated with the key *label*. The primitive for sending messages along with their attributes is the following:

```
(send new message <label>to
<recipient>with
<attribute name> <value>
...
<attribute name> <value>)
```

It is also possible to change some values of the received message and then forward it:

```
(update message attribute <key>to
<value>)
(forward message to <recipient>)
```

The sending or forwarding of messages is a blocking operation, i.e., the current behavior is halted until the recipient completes its execution. An entity waiting on a send or forward operation can nonetheless accept and process incoming messages.

LAWS AND SIDE-EFFECTS

Law and Side-Effect advices are defined using the same syntax as behaviors, i.e., the aforementioned language statements. To bind them with an entity, the following directives are used:

```
#law on<label>to<entity>in<state>is<l
aw>#sideeffect on<label>to<entity>in<
state>is<se>
```

Assuming that laws and side-effects are stored in different files, these directives bind the law specified in file *law*, respectively the side-effect in file *se*, to entity *entity*. In particular, the law is applied upon receiving a message with label *label* in state *state*, whereas the side-effect executes after the corresponding behavior. If multiple laws and side-effects match a specified join-point, they are executed sequentially following the order of the definitions. It is possible to refer to generic pointcuts by replacing either *label* or *state* with the wildcard character *. For example,

```
#law on * to<entity>in "default"
is<law>
```

inserts a law advice before every behavior in state default. Laws and side-effects can also cancel a player's move by performing a rollback. In order to perform a rollback, an entity must first create a checkpoint to save the actual status of the game:

```
(open checkpoint)
```

A rollback can then be invoked to restore the status up to the last checkpoint:

```
(rollback<reason>)
```

The reason argument allows specifying a text message to be shown to the user explaining the reason for the rollback.

REPRESENTATIONS

Representations are the entities' interface to the real world. Since actual implementation just focuses on 2D representations, we restrict the world to a 2-dimensional plane displayed on a computer screen, but other kinds of interfaces could be easily implemented. Thus, the representation of an entity consists of one or more graphical objects, each one characterized by some *physical* attributes, such as size, position on the canvas, color, etc. According to the FLEXIBLERULES model, a representation must reflect the status of the corresponding logical entity at all times. Each representation therefore, as we have already described, defines update procedures that are executed upon modification of any of the observed properties of the underlying logical entity. Additionally, representations can also define private properties not tied to their *physical* appearance, in order to keep persistent information across updates.

A representation is modeled similarly to an entity; nonetheless some important differences exist:

- Representations can instantiate and manipulate graphical objects, whereas entities cannot;
- Representations can only send messages to the underlying entity (for user interaction purposes).

The latter difference results in a tight relationship between the representation and the corresponding logical entity.

Graphical Objects

Representations can create simple graphical objects on the representation canvas, which can be identified by means of a unique name. These objects can only be modified or destroyed by the representation. To create a new graphical object, the **new graphic** function is used in the following manner:

```
(new graphic<id>)
(new graphic<id>with
<attribute name> <value>
...
<attribute name> <value>)
```

Attributes of the graphical object can be specified at construction time (using **with** <*attributes*>), as well as modified at runtime as follows:

```
(update graphic<id>attribute<attribute>to<value>)
```

Finally, it is possible to delete a graphical object using the **delete graphic** function.

Representation Updates

One noteworthy element of the language is the coupling of the representation layer to the logical one. Representations can define observers on properties defined by their logical counterpart. Observers are triggered when the corresponding property is updated, and can be effectively set up by the representation as follows:

```
(observe<property>notify<label>)
```

Before the observed property is updated to a new value, the representation receives a notification message labeled *label* along with the new value.

USER INTERACTION

User interaction with graphical objects can be distinguished as signals and messages. On one side, Intentional User Interaction is accomplished by hooking interaction events generated by graphical objects to the delivery of predefined messages that are dispatched to the representation. As an example, to deliver the message *message* when the user clicks on the object *id*, the syntax is:

```
(on<id>clicked notify<message>)
```

Notice that the message must be constructed in advance, and can carry additional user-defined attributes. On the other side, Forced User Interaction is achieved with signals. Signals are generated by graphical objects in response to some user action; an entity waits for a signal using the **wait signal** primitive, stopping its execution until the signal is emitted by some representation.

```
(on<id>clicked emit<signal>with<tag>)
(wait signal<signal>)
```

Upon hooking an event with a signal, a string tag value may be specified: when the corresponding wait function intercepts the signal, this value will be set as the return value.

DEVELOPMENT ENVIRONMENT

The FLEXIBLERULES framework is founded on the aforementioned well-defined conceptual model and additionally provides a development environment taking into account the separation of concerns and enabling rapid implementation of computer enhanced board games. The implementation of board games using the development environment is a two step process. The first step involves the *Logic Editor* tool that allows high-level design of the game building on the principles of the model, namely defining the corresponding entities, their properties and relations in a visual manner. During the second step the actual implementation of the game functionalities takes place through the *Code Editor*.

The *Logic Editor* (Figure 2) is used to visually define game entities along with their properties and relationships, allowing therefore for a user-friendly modeling of the logical structure of the game. In the editor, relationships among entities are represented by means of edges of a directed graph, the nodes of which are the game entities. Moreover, the designer is given the option to define a hierarchy of entities, thus enabling inheritance of entities' characteristics and their local properties. This creates the abstract outline of the logical part of the entities. Concrete implementation

of the game itself is achieved by implementing entities' functionalities, such as the specification of *behaviors*, *laws* and *side-effects*. The latter is performed using the *Code Editor*, which is based on the open source Gedit[1] text editor that has been enhanced with custom plug-ins, such as syntax highlighting of the Game Definition Language. As depicted in Figure 3, the left side of the *Code Editor* enables the browsing of code, while in parallel maintaining an overview of its structure. Furthermore, in the lower part a pane displaying the order of *laws* and *side-effects* attached to a specific *behavior* is presented.

FLEXIBLERULES GAME EXAMPLES

We have presented the conceptual model of the FLEXIBLERULES framework and explained the Game Definition Language that we have implemented along with the two visual tools composing the framework, namely the *Logic Editor* and the *Code Editor*. The Java programming language was used to implement the tools in order to take advantage of its portability and interoperability across diverse platforms. The latter constituted an important requirement for our design, as we envisage that the developed board games will be deployed on a multitude of hardware infrastructures, such as PCs, interactive tables, PDAs, etc. In the following we present some of the games that have been implemented to validate the FLEXIBLERULES framework approach. In particular, we strive to highlight the major conceptual differences between these games, and thus the different aspects involved in their modeling. Table 1 provides a summary of these characteristics.

The games that we chose to illustrate as proof-of-concepts, available to play online at the FLEXIBLERULES website[2], are Awele, Go and Himalaya™. Awele is one of the games with the biggest number of known variants in the world, which validates the need to have a framework like the one proposed in order to allow for the

Figure 2. Logic Editor

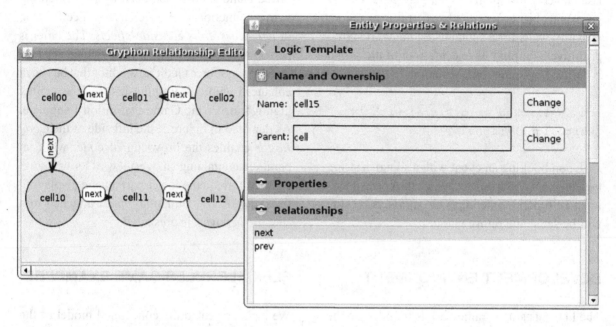

Figure 3. Code Editor

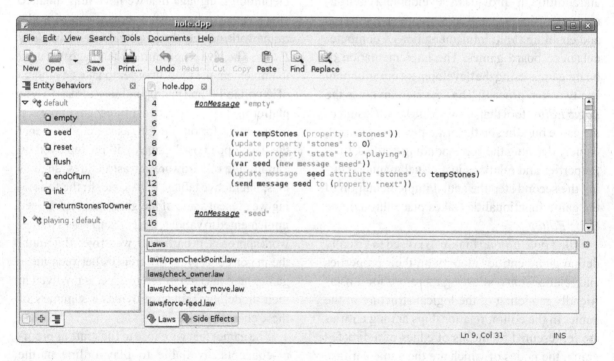

modification of rules and thus cater for multiple variants. The difficulties in designing Go in a fully distributed manner, make it a great candidate to exhibit the capabilities of our framework in

this respect. The game logic and ruleset of Himalaya™ have a higher degree of complexity compared to the other two games. Taken together, the implementation of these three games serves as

Table 1. Game models characteristics comparison

	Awele	Go	Himalaya™
Types of Entities	few	few	many
Board Topology	Ring	Grid	Free
User Interfaces	single (public)	single (public)	multiple (public, private)
Number of Players	2	2	3 to 6
Mundane Tasks	None	None	Many
Game-play and Rules Complexity	Simple	Medium	Hard
User Interaction	Start of turn	Start of turn	Continous
Game Variants	Many	Few	Few

evidence that the FLEXIBLERULES framework can be equally successfully used for different types of board games.

AWELE

Awele (also known as Oware) is an African turn-based game (Figure 4). It is an interesting example because in contrast to other popular games, there exist hundreds of different variants. We recognize very few entities in the game model, namely *hole* (which manages its seeds and the actual game-play) and *game* (which manages player turns

and players' points earned during the game). The basic behavior of each entity is easily modeled, and most of the different variants of the game can be implemented by just adding or removing laws and side-effects. Since many *laws* and *side-effects* require a deep knowledge of the underlying structure of the game, in the following we will discuss only a simple example of both a law and a side effect regarding allowed moves and winning conditions. Table 2 summarizes all the *laws* and *side-effects* attached to the entities *hole* and *game*.

The most recurrent rule in turn-based games such as Awele dictates that a player cannot play unless it is her turn (Figure 5). The implementa-

Table 2. Awele laws and side-effects

Law	Entity	Behavior	State
Allow Only Current Player	Hole	startSeeding	default
Allow Only Non Empty Hole	Hole	startSeeding	default
Let The Opponent Play	Hole	startSeeding	default
Open Check-point	Hole	startSeeding	default
Stones' Capturing	Hole	giveStones	default/lastSeed
Side-effect	**Entity**	**Behavior**	**State**
End Of Turn	Hole	startSeeding	default
Last Seed	Hole	seed	default
Chain Reaction	Hole	giveStones	default
Chain Reaction Avoiding GrandSlam	Hole	giveStones	lastSeed
Game Over	Game	endOfTurn	default
Check Winning Condition	Game	giveStonesToCurrentPlayer	default

Figure 4. Awele game

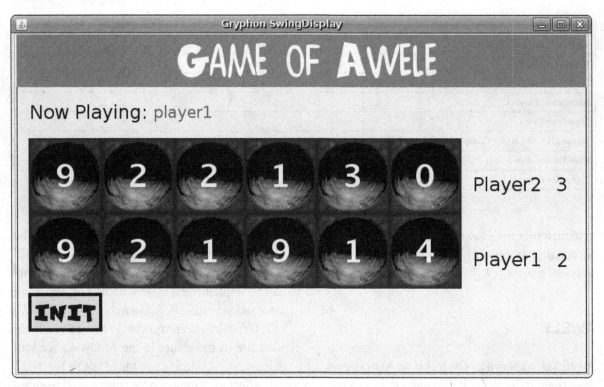

Figure 5. Law: Allow only current player

```
(var currentPlayer (first (property "players" of "game")))

(if (!= (property "owner") currentPlayer)
        (return))
```

Figure 6. Side-effect: Check winning condition

```
(var currentPlayer (first (property "players")))
(var CurrentPlayerStones (match currentPlayer in (property "playerStones")))

(if (> CurrentPlayerStones 24) (do
        (send new message "gameover" to "game" with
                "winner" currentPlayer)
end))
```

Figure 7. Go game

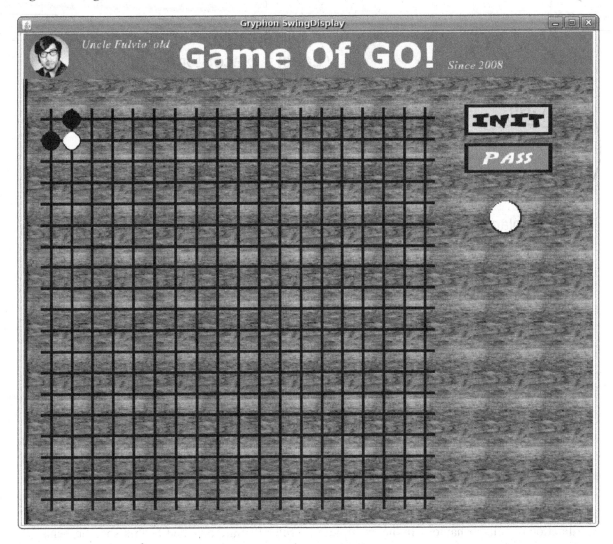

tion just compares the current player property stored by the *game* entity with the identifier of the player executing the move.

A side-effect that can be easily changed is the number of points required to win the game. Commonly a player wins by collecting at least 25 stones. The validity of this condition is checked every time a hole sends its stones to the game by the *Check Winning Condition* side-effect (Figure 6). A potential variant of the game would just require a change in the value being tested.

It is interesting to note that this winning condition is completely separated from the behavior of the entities. In fact, it could be possible to completely remove this side effect, thus letting the users continue their game.

GO

Go (Figure 7) falls into the category of checkerboard games and is probably one of the most interesting games that we have chosen to model and implement with the FLEXIBLERULES framework. First, different game variants exist. Secondly, the complexity of interactions between game entities

Figure 8. Go modeled using FLEXIBLERULES

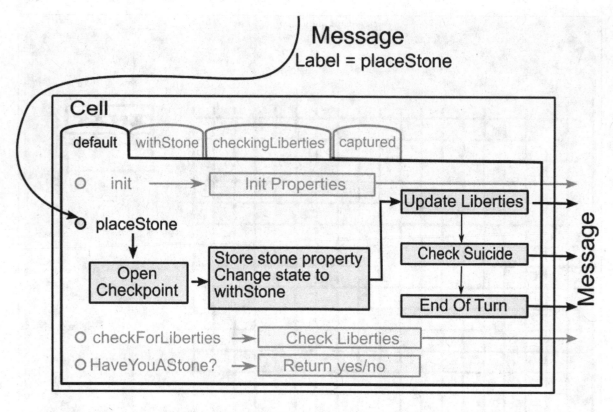

is certainly higher than in Awele. The modeling of the game is challenging and game-play rules can be implemented by the cells themselves. Since each cell is only aware of its local neighbors, many steps of the game-play require the coordination of cells' behaviors. In the example of Figure 8 we illustrate the logical modeling of a cell and the execution flow occurring when a new stone is placed on it by means of a message labeled "placeStone".

At any time in the game a cell can be in one of four different internal states. Empty cells are in state *default*, while cells hosting a stone are in state *withStone*. During the game, cells have to recognize in a distributed way whether they have liberties or not; hence two additional intermediate states are needed, namely *checkingLiberties* to underline that a cell cannot infer its liberties

without the help of its neighbors and *captured* for cells that have established that they do not have any liberties. The behavior of a cell when a new stone is placed on it consists in changing its state to *withStone* and storing the stone's color. The rules that are attached to this specific behavior include a *law* and three *side-effects*, as shown in Figure 8. Certain moves are forbidden in Go (e.g., a stone cannot commit "suicide") thus a checkpoint should be opened allowing for a rollback, if such a forbidden situation is reached. Moreover, the *updateLiberties* side-effect sends messages to the neighbors to trigger the update of their liberties, as the newly placed stone may have removed the last liberty of some opponent's stones and therefore led to their removal from the game. Subsequently, the *checkSuicide* side-effect checks whether the newly placed stone is situated in a

Figure 9. Himalaya™ game

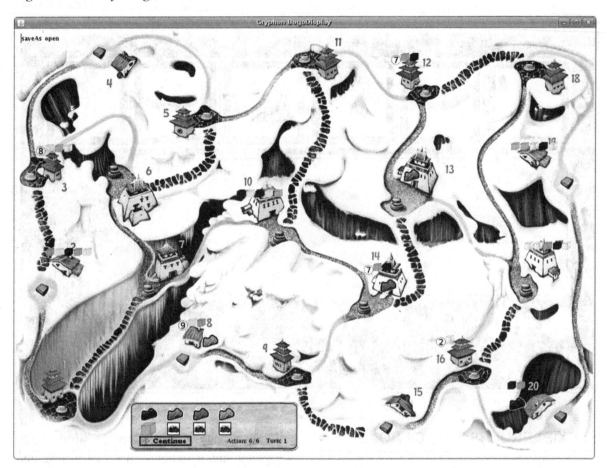

cell without liberties. If this is the case the suicide rule has been broken and a rollback to the last valid checkpoint (stored by the law) has to be performed. Otherwise, the final side-effect *end-OfTurn* is executed informing all interested entities that the turn is over.

HIMALAYA™

Himalaya™ is a board game characterized by the complexity of its rules. In contrast to Awele and Go, the game can be played by 3 to 6 players, and interactions between the user and the game are continuous. In fact, each player secretly chooses her moves (typically 6) at the beginning of each turn. Once all the players have made their choices,

the game proceeds by executing one move per player. During game-play some actions require user intervention, for example to let the user choose where to place some objects on the board; thus, Himalaya™ also served as a validation testbed for Forced User Interaction, as conceived within the FLEXIBLERULES framework.

The implementation makes use of different separate displays: a public one, and personal ones for each player. The public display (pictured in Figure 9) serves as the gameboard, which provides visual feedback of the game situation and of players' actions. Each personal display (Figure 10) shows private information and enables players to secretly interact with the game while choosing their moves and actions.

Figure 10. Himalaya™ player view

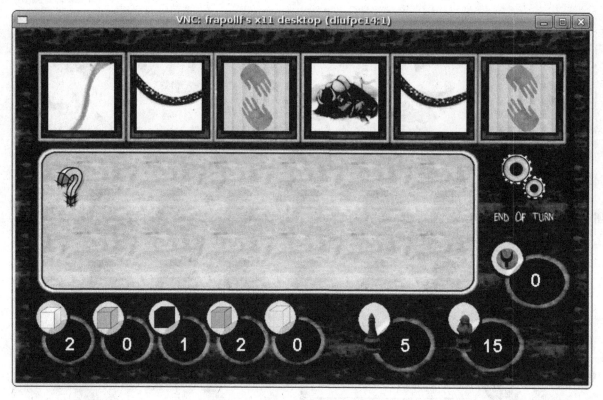

FLEXIBLERULES IMPLICATIONS

The FLEXIBLERULES framework makes it easier for game designers and casual gamers to develop new board games or modify existing ones. Regarding game designers, the aforementioned advanced features of FLEXIBLERULES enable rapid prototyping and beta testing of digital board games, having therefore a noteworthy impact on the time and effort required to find the best possible game balance. Contrariwise, casual gamers gain an increased level of satisfaction and enjoyability, as they have overall control of the game and its features.

Furthermore, FLEXIBLERULES has implications on the educational domain as it can be used to stimulate the programming learning process through its user friendly intuitive environment. IT students profit from and are motivated by a game-oriented development environment, which effectively makes the interactive learning of basic programming paradigms more enjoyable and hence successful. Moreover, it is evident that the direct involvement of the end-user in the game development process will lead to enhanced and more widely accepted digital board games.

CONCLUSION AND FUTURE WORK

The facilitation of board game development efforts and support for the complete set of features that traditional physical board games exhibit, most importantly the high degree of flexibility in player actions, has been the motivation of our work. In this respect, we deem it necessary to have a well-established model for board game modeling, taking into account their inherent characteristics and avoiding the rigid-ness of current implementations. Additionally, developers of games should be provided with useful tools to make their task easier and to allow for game-specific patterns to be employed.

In this paper we presented the FLEXIBLERULES framework for the modeling of board games. The proposed game model is composed of taxonomy of entities with precise properties and behaviors. In order to simplify the conceptualization of rules, we proposed a decoupling of the game logic into different aspects: laws, behaviors, and side-effects. Consistent with the goals of aspect oriented programming, we believe that such a separation of concerns allows for a more natural way to define the logic behind board games. The framework has been validated through the implementation of three games, i.e., Awele, Go and Himalaya™.

Future work will include the improvement of existing tools and the implementation of an integrated visual game development environment. Additionally, both a qualitative and a quantitative user evaluation of the framework will be carried out. The former aims at assessing the game-play enjoyment compared to traditional physical games, while the latter will focus on the usability of the game modeling language and tools, which will give us indications about the effort put in by inexperienced users to do the modeling.

ACKNOWLEDGMENT

The authors would like to thank Dr Agnes Lisowska for her invaluable help and useful comments.

REFERENCES

Amory, A. N. K. V. J., & Adams, C. (1999). The use of computer games as an educational tool: identification of appropriate game types and game elements. *British Journal of Educational Technology, 30*(4), 311–321. doi:10.1111/1467-8535.00121

Bjork, S., & Holopainen, J. (2004). *Patterns in game design (game development series)*. Boston: Charles River Media.

DeKoven, B. D. (1978). *The well-played game: A player's philosophy*. New York: Anchor Books.

Elrad, T., Filman, R. E., & Bader, A. (2001). Aspect-oriented programming: Introduction. *Communications of the ACM, 44*(10), 29–32. doi:10.1145/383845.383853

Järvinen, A. (2003, November). Making and breaking games: a typology of rules. In C. Marinka & R. Joost (Eds.), Level up conference proceedings (pp. 68–79). Utrecht, The Netherlands: University of Utrecht.

Kiczales, G., Lamping, J., Mendhekar, A., Maeda, C., Lopes, C., Loingtier, J.-M., et al. (1997). Aspect-oriented programming. In *Proceedings of Ecoop'97 object-oriented programming* (pp. 220-242).

Loenen, E. van, Bergman, T., Buil, V., Gelder, K., van, Groten, M., Hollemans, G., et al. (2007). Entertaible: A solution for social gaming experiences. In *Proceedings of Tangible play workshop, IUI conference*.

Lopes, C. V., Dourish, P., Lorenz, D. H., & Lieberherr, K. (2003). Beyond aop: toward naturalistic programming. In *Proceedings of the Companion of the 18th annual ACM SIGPLAN conference on object-oriented programming, systems, languages, and applications (Oopsla'03)* (pp. 198-207). New York: ACM.

Malone, T. W. (1981). Toward a theory of intrinsically motivating instruction. *Cognitive Science, 5*(4), 333–369. doi:10.1207/s15516709cog0504_2

Mandryk, R. L., & Maranan, D. S. (2002). False prophets: exploring hybrid board/video games. In *Proceedings of Chi '02 extended abstracts on human factors in computing systems* (pp. 640–641). New York: ACM.

Mazalek, A., Reynolds, M., & Davenport, G. (2007, October). The tviews table in the home. In *Proceedings of the Second Annual IEEE International Workshop on Horizontal Interactive Human- Computer Systems (TABLETOP '07)* (pp. 52-59).

Miller, S. (2001). Aspect-oriented programming takes aim at software complexity. *IEEE Computer*, *34*(4), 18–21.

Rashid, A., & Moreira, A. (2006). Domain models are not aspect free. In *Proceedings of Model Driven Engineering Languages and Systems* (pp. 155-169).

Reese, C., Duvigneau, M., Köhler, M., Moldt, D., & Rölke, H. (2003, February). Agent based settler game. In *Proceedings of agentcities agent technology competition (ATC03)*, Barcelona, Spain. Agentcities.NET.

Salen, K., & Zimmerman, E. (2003). *Rules of play: Game design fundamentals*. Cambridge, MA: MIT Press.

Sanchez-Crespo, D. (2003). *Core techniques and algorithms in game programming*. New Riders Games.

Steimann, F. (2000). On the representation of roles in object- oriented and conceptual modelling. *Data & Knowledge Engineering, 35*(1), 83–106. doi:10.1016/S0169-023X(00)00023-9

Steimann, F. (2005). Domain models are aspect free. In Briand, L. C., & Williams, C. (Eds.), *Models* (pp. 171–185). New York: Springer.

ENDNOTES

[1]   http://projects.gnome.org/gedit/
[2]   http://diuf.unifr.ch/pai/flexiblerules/

This work was previously published in International Journal of Gaming and Computer-Mediated Simulations, Volume 2, Issue 2, edited by Richard E. Ferdig, pp. 18-35, copyright 2010 by IGI Publishing (an imprint of IGI Global).

Chapter 8
Effects of Playing a History– Simulation Game:
Romance of Three Kingdoms

Shiang-Kwei Wang
New York Institute of Technology, USA

ABSTRACT

Studies on game-based learning usually investigate at least one of three subjects: the effects of gaming on learning performance, the effects of gaming on cognitive skills and attitudes, and learners' game-design experiences. Whether gaming relates positively to learning outcomes is still under investigation. This study examines the components contributing to the development of a literate game player and how players could cognitively grasp the design of a game scenario based on real history (namely, the game Romance of the Three Kingdoms). This study surveyed 497 participants in Taiwan on their knowledge of Chinese history (the Three Kingdoms period). The participants constituted two groups: participants who had years of gaming experience and participants who did not. The study examined test performance by using an independent sample t-test and one-way ANOVA and Pearson-correlation methods. The results revealed that the game players were more knowledgeable about the history of the Three Kingdoms period, had greater motivation to learn history, and were more motivated to learn history by playing the game than was the case with the non-game players.

PURPOSE OF THE STUDY

The effects of game-based learning on cognitive gains are still being investigated (Connolly, Stansfield, & Hainey, 2007; de Jong & van Joolingen, 1998; Washbush & Gosen, 2001). However,

researchers who study game playing are nearly certain that the more frequently a player plays games, the more confident and the more fluent he or she will be in gaming (Bonanno & Kommers, 2008). So, would game players learn more about a subject if the game concerned real history and if knowledge of the history were part of the gaming

DOI: 10.4018/978-1-4666-0029-4.ch008

literacy? To further explore whether a game concerning real history can affect players' spontaneous motivation to learn and players' knowledge of history, this study surveyed Taiwan game players familiar with a history-simulation game that is popular in Asia and that was developed by the Japanese KOEI company. The game is *Romance of the Three Kingdoms (RTK)*. The purpose of this study is to investigate if there is any association between playing *RTK* and players' knowledge of the events in this historical period, the part of the *RTK* gaming literacy.

LITERATURE REVIEW

Game-Based Learning

Almost every teacher incorporates some type of game into teaching (e.g., puzzles and chain reactions) because playing games is fun and engages students (Berrenberg & Prosser, 1991). With the advancement of computers, networks, and entertainment technology, more and more students in recent generations have engaged in playing computer video games outside the classroom to enjoy the state of flow described by Csikszentmihalyi (1985). Many educators and researchers, such as Gee (2007), Squire (2006), Salen and Zimmerman (2005), and Salen (2007), have deemed computer video games a new media that educators should integrate into learning. There are also voices advocating that educators trigger learners' motivation and improve their learning outcomes by having them play games whose features pair with specific instructional content (Garris, Ahlers, & Driskell, 2002).

Usually, three types of games are discussed in the educational context: commercial games, educational games, and simulation games. Commercial games are designed for entertainment and include, for example, *Diablo* and *World of War Craft* (produced by Blizzard). Players have

to unravel the goals, rules, and operations of the game, and figure out strategies to win battles with allied online players. Educational games are gaming systems that incorporate gaming elements (goals, rules) and intrinsic motivational determinants (challenge, curiosity, control, and fantasy, suggested by Malone & Lepper, 1987) into the game design to encourage learners to complete drill-and-practice exercises or multiple-choice questions pertaining to an academic area. *Where in the World Is Carmen San Diego* is one of the representative educational games. Simulation games provide near-real environments to enrich learners' experience. Simulation games combine various input and output parameters to allow learners to manipulate and observe how combinations of these factors influence the simulation consequences of a complex system and the underlying rules. *SimCity* is one of the most discussed simulation games in the educational context.

Studies on gaming and learning have been taking various approaches owing to the distinct features of these games and of the target learners. The first task that researchers undertook is to study the effects of gaming on learners' cognitive skills and attitude (Bonanno & Kommers, 2008; Bottino, Ferlino, Ott, & Tavella, 2007; Childress & Braswell, 2006; Henderson, Klemes, & Eshet, 2000); the second task is to investigate the effects of game-based learning on learning outcomes and training performance (Faria & Wellington, 2004; Parchman, Ellis, Christinaz, & Vogel, 2000; Washbush & Gosen, 2001); last is to present learners' experiences in relation to game designers (Childress & Braswell, 2006; Connolly, Stansfield, & Hainey, 2007; Robertson & Howells, 2008). A majority of research on gaming and playing focuses on the medical-education domain and the business-management domain, whereas most research on the use of gaming in K-12 education is in the form of case studies (Wideman et al., 2007).

Although researchers have extensively studied the effects of playing games on learning, several researchers' extensive literature reviews found that there is no confirmed conclusion regarding the effects of playing on learning outcomes. Connolly, Stansfield, and Hainey (2007) examined a series of studies focusing on the use of games to facilitate learners' learning of software engineering in higher education, and they found out that the evaluation of the effects of games-based learning is limited and that more longitudinal studies are needed. Washbush and Gosen (2001) reported that playing simulation games is not associated with learning performance in the business-marketing domain, and this finding agrees with de Jong and van Joolingen's (1998) conclusion drawn from their review of numerous simulation-game studies. Vogel et al. (2006) conducted a meta-analysis of 32 interdisciplinary game studies and reported a different finding: learners' attitudes toward learning were better than, and cognitive gains were higher than, those attributable to traditional teaching methods; however, this 2006 study also admitted that more studies without design flaws are needed to accurately analyze the effects of games-based learning. Egenfeldt-Nielsen (2007) examined game-based learning studies in K-12 contexts and concluded that learners' learning outcomes improved through learners' playing of games; however, playing games is only one form of learning, and thus, the researchers could not conclude that gaming is more valuable or more effective than other media or teaching styles. Overall, most of these game-based studies did not yield convincing evidence to connect game playing with learning outcomes because of the following "research design"-related issues: short gaming-exposure time, lack of a control group, experiment groups' insufficient game-playing time, researchers' bias, reliance on learners' self-reports of perceptions of games, lack of longitudinal studies, and small sample size (Connolly, Stansfield, & Hainey, 2007; Egenfeldt-Nielsen, 2007; Vogel et al., 2006; Wideman et al., 2007).

Gaming Literacy

Definition

To further explore the effects of gaming on learning, in addition to learning performance, many researchers study (or advocate studying) the effects of gaming on motivation, cognitive skills, attitudes, communication, and system operation rather than learning outcomes (Gee, 2003; O'Neil, Wainess, & Baker, 2005; Wideman et al., 2007). In order to better identify the effects of playing games on learning, researchers have started to define games from a literacy perspective (Buckingham & Burn, 2007; Salen, 2007). The definition of literacy has evolved owing to the advancement of technologies that mediate between reading and writing behaviors. Leu, Kinzer, Coiro, and Cammack (2004) first described new literacies as uses of information communication and of technology tools that enable people to "identify important questions, locate information, critically evaluate the usefulness of the information, synthesize information to answer those questions, and then communicate the answers to others" (p. 1,572). Gee (2006) states that video games exemplify a technology that enables players to decode and produce meanings by using symbols (p. 5). Therefore, the definition of gaming literacies has arisen from both "reading" and "writing" perspectives to illustrate the multi-mode learning that might be promoted through playing and designing games: "Gaming literacies refer to a set of skills, tools, and experiential dispositions that come from the design, culture, and play of games" (Institute of Play, 2007; Salen, 2007; Gee, 2007). There are studies claiming that, from the process of designing a game, game designers learn how to collaborate, solve problems, polish "media content"-production skills, and express creativity (Buckingham & Burn, 2007; Hutchison, 2007; Robertson & Good, 2005; Robertson & Howells, 2008; Salen, 2007; Squire, 2006).

A Literate Game Player

From the game playing (read game) perspective, to become a literate game player means to possess skills and abilities in operating game-related technology, in navigating fluently within the game environment, in understanding the meaning of a particular game environment's multi-modal elements, in recognizing the goals and the rules of a game, and in coming up with winning strategies (Buckingham & Burn, 2007; Gee, 2003; Hsu & Wang, in press; Reese, 2007; Wideman et al., 2007). A different game requires a different set of gaming-literacy elements. Squire (2005) described the difficulty he encountered when introducing the strategic game *Civilization* into a K-12 classroom. Players had to master the operations of the game, understand the concepts of the game, and learn the survival strategies corresponding to the selected civilization—a set of tasks that was sometimes too complicated for some game players to master. Therefore, in general, one must acquire gaming literacy required for a particular game in order to be considered as a literate game player,

One component should be scrutinized in the definition of a literate game player in order to identify its impact on game players: familiarization with a game's context design. There are three types of context design of a game. The type 1 game is a "game without any context design": for example, *TETRIS* (a puzzle game). The purpose of playing such a game is to achieve higher scores by advancing one's skills.

The type 2 game has a scenario design, whose purpose is to embellish the storyline, attract different groups of target players, and improve players' playing motivation. Game players' understanding of the scenario does not affect their gaming performance. *Diablo* (a massively multiplayer online game, MMOG) and *Civilization* are examples of type 2 games. The scenario of *Diablo* is a fantastic world created by a game designer. There are studies that adopt type 2 games to in-

vestigate how players' game playing affects the players' attitude changes or cognitive processes (Bonanno & Kommers, 2008; Inal & Cagiltay, 2007; Williams, 2006). Since these games are not designed for educational purposes, studies on how this type of games contribute to learning of a particular subject are rarely reported.

Context design of the type 3 game is integrated with background knowledge. Game players' familiarization with background knowledge does affect their gaming performance, because the purpose of playing games is to learn the content. To win the game, players have to gain knowledge and skills relative to a particular topic. Many game-based learning studies adopt this type of game to investigate whether or not game playing affects learners' knowledge acquisition of a particular topic (Brozik & Zapalska, 2000; Ke, 2008; Lainema & Makkonen, 2003; Silk et al., 2008; Wiebe & Martin, 1994). For example, one needs to be familiar with the geographical information of the major cities in the world in order to score high in the game *Where in the World is Carmen San Diego*? Another example is that the players have to be familiar with the process and strategies to manage and operate the restaurant business in order to win in the *Restaurant Game* (Brozik & Zapalska, 2000).

This study adopts a type 2 game (*RTK*) described in the literature review, a game designed for entertaining, not educational purpose. *RTK* has a scenario design based on real history; however, game players can enjoy the game and have a great gaming performance without understanding this period of history at all. There is little research focusing on how a game's scenario design affects game players' motivation to learn a topic related to the game's scenario, and on the effect of playing entertaining games on learning. The purpose of this study is to explore whether playing this type of game correlates with players' motivation to learn more about the scenario design—the real history. The study examines a history-simulation game as it has existed and evolved over two decades, and the study does not treat the game as a learning medium that intervenes in a formal school environment.

THREE KINGDOMS HISTORY

To better understand details of this game and its extensive influence on Asian game players, readers should grasp the background of the Three Kingdoms history and of the two crucial books documenting this period.

In A.D. 220, a year in which the Roman Empire continued its decline, China was just entering one of the bloodiest periods in Chinese history some 4,400 miles away. During the Three Kingdoms period, three emperors separately claimed that they, individually, were the legitimate successors of the previous Han Dynasty. Millions of people died because of these claimants ambitions to unite the country (de Crespigny, 2003). This period in history was short-lived (about 60 years) yet complicated, and gave rise to hundreds of heroes who have since then been worshiped, an idea of brotherhood that has been praised, and wars that have been remembered and have been discussed often during daily life even for now. Chen Shou documented the history in the book *Records of the Three Kingdoms*, written in literary Chinese. *Records of the Three Kingdoms* is an important historical document for both ancient Chinese history and ancient Japanese history. It provided extensive materials for the more popular novel *Romance of the Three Kingdoms*, written by Luo Guanzhong in the fourteenth century. *Romance of the Three Kingdoms* has been deemed one of the four greatest classical novels of Chinese literature, containing 800,000 words, approximately double the length of the French novel *The Count of Monte Cristo*. About seventy percent of *Romance of the Three Kingdoms* was written on the basis of historical facts, and the rest of the novel contained the author's fabrications and embellishments. It

has had a significant influence on Chinese popular culture, stimulating the production of numerous movies, comic books, other works of literature, and TV dramas. Most of these productions depict only limited events or select heroes of this period; thus, the two books still constitute the principal knowledge source regarding the period.

These two books provide readers a body of knowledge pertaining to various longitudinal dimensions of Chinese culture. If read through and understood, the books could increase readers' knowledge of the ancient government system, stimulate a sense of continuity, encourage historical thinking, and promote cultural awareness, which are outcomes consistent with curriculum standards for Taiwan's high school history education (Taiwan Ministry of Education, 2008) and which are very similar to the curriculum standards for U.S. social studies (NCSS, 1994). However, the underlying issue is how to encourage learners to start reading these lengthy, sometimes arcane books.

Game Background

On the basis of the novel, a Japanese computer-game company, KOEI, designed an off-line strategy game (a historic-battle simulation) named *Romance of the Three Kingdoms* (*RTK*), see Figure 1. The first edition was announced in 1985, and ever since, the production of eleven evolving editions has been attracting millions of game players in Asia. The game design is similar to the popular strategy game *Age of Empires*, developed by Microsoft. In *RTK*, the player plays the role of an emperor in the Three Kingdoms period, manages the economy, commands the military forces of his or her governed cities, summons military counselors and generals, and expands his or her territory by fighting with other emperors. If a player is more familiar with the particularities of each character and of each surrounding terrain, the player could be able to win the war more efficiently by deploying appropriate strategies. The

Figure 1. Screenshot of the game Romance of the Three Kingdoms. (Permission to use the screenshot has been granted by KOEI)

game displays historical events depending on the period and the emperor that the user selects. In this way, circumstances and conditions reflect a given historical context. RTK players can still enjoy the game and achieve the goal (to unite the kingdom) without having the abovementioned knowledge.

RESEARCH QUESTIONS AND HYPOTHESES

To explore the effects of playing *RTK* on game players' motivation to learn and their knowledge (scenario design of the game) of the Three Kingdoms history, the current study tested the following research questions and hypotheses.

RQ1: Do *RTK* players exhibit higher motivation to access media on the Three Kingdoms history than do non-*RTK* players?

RQ2: Is there any relationship between *RTK*-playing experience and test performance (dependent measure) on the Three Kingdoms history?

- H1: *RTK* players' test scores regarding the Three Kingdoms history are better than non-*RTK* players' corresponding test scores.

- H2: *RTK* players' test performance relates to either game-playing history or duration of game playing.

○ H3: Among the *RTK* players, greater duration of playing *RTK* results in higher test performance.

RQ3: What are *RTK* players' perceptions of the *RTK* game?

RQ4: How does playing *RTK* affect players' interests and motivation in learning the Three Kingdoms history?

METHOD

Participants

The survey data were collected from the largest terminal-based system in the world, Professional Technology Temple (aka PTT), sponsored by National Taiwan University (Wikipedia, 2008). The PTT system can handle up to 120,000 visitors online at a time, with over a million registered users (most are Taiwanese), which is a large portion of the total Taiwan population (23 million). Users discuss numerous topics from popular culture to academic subjects in more than 500 boards on PTT. KOEI is a board that allows users to discuss their experiences of playing KOEI games, and it became the chief source for the current study's recruitment of *RTK* players. The study recruited 497 PTT users to complete the online survey. Herein, a game player was a participant who has been playing the latest version of the game *RTK* (n=304). A person who had never or had not played the game in five years is defined here as a non-game player (n=193). Each participant was provided with virtual PTT currency (valued at 50 units) as incentive for taking part in the survey.

Instrument

The instrument "My understanding of the history of the Three Kingdoms period and my perception of *RTK*" comprises three categories: demographic factors (age, gender, education, marital status, city born in, and years of playing *RTK*) test questions (11 multiple-choice items and 3 short-answer items, most of the questions were modified from the Taiwan high school test banks), and perception of *RTK* (13 items) (Appendix 1). *RTK* players completed items in all three categories whereas non-*RTK* players completed items in only the first two categories. Many of the test questions were designed according to high school history exams, which are not related to the game's operation or environment. In other words, test questions were used to examine participants' knowledge of the Three Kingdoms history, not of the *RTK* game (with the exception of one item; see Appendix, note 18). Participants received 1 point for every selection of a correct answer. The three short-answer items were designed to test whether or not the participants could identify the right answers despite other media's presentation of misleading information (for an example, see Appendix, note 20). The short-answer items were rated according to the given answer's level of depth, 1 would correspond to an answer that is commonly known by means of in-school education or mass media whereas 2 would correspond to an answer exhibiting obvious familiarity with the real history of the Three Kingdoms period. The sum of the correct answers of all test questions is 17 points (11 multiple-choice items and 3 short-answer items), which is the dependent measure.

The study adopted item analysis (Edwards, 1957) to determine the reliability of the 14 test items to confirm whether or not items were too difficult or too easy. Two groups were arranged into pre-27% and post-27% groups in terms of total grades. The critical ratio was calculated for each item. The critical ratio of all items is at a .01 significance level or better, which indicates that these test items can discriminate between the higher- and lower-grade groups. Furthermore, the present study calculated the Pearson correlation coefficient to examine the correlation of all items with the total grade. All items were correlated with the total grade at a 0.1 significance level or better. The present study adopted Cronbach's alpha

Table 1. demographic data of gender, age, and educational level

	Frequency	Percentage
Gender		
Male	336	67.6%
Female	157	31.6%
Age		
Below 20	68	13.7%
21-25	293	59%
26-30	111	22.3%
Above 31	22	4.4%
Educational level (including in the process of obtaining the degree)		
Below college	12	2.4%
College	333	67%
Graduate school	137	27.6%
Doctor	13	2.6%

Gender, Age and Educational Level of the Respondents (n=497)

(Cronbach, 1951) to measure the internal consistency for both the test-question category and the *RTK*-perception category. The Cronbach's alpha of the test-question category was 0.865, while that of the *RTK*-perception category was 0.751. Both are above 0.7, which is an acceptable reliability coefficient according to Nunnaly (1978).

RESULTS

Demographic Data

The present study adopted the crosstab analysis method to examine the relationship between the demographic variables and preference for playing *RTK*. Table 2 shows the crosstab regarding the relationship between the gender and preference for playing *RTK*. A 2 x 2 Chi-square test for independence revealed a significant difference $\chi^2(1, N = 497) = 244.40, p = .000$, suggesting that the number of male *RTK* players are significantly greater than females.

Crosstab analysis also revealed that the preference for playing the *RTK* game related significantly neither to age ($\chi^2(3, N = 494) = 1.63, p > .05$) nor to educational level ($\chi^2(3, N = 495) = 0.55, p > .05$). This means that the percentage of *RTK* game players is equal among all age and educational levels.

The datum "first edition of the *RTK* played" represented players' experience with playing the *RTK* game. The first edition of *RTK* was published in 1985, and the most recent edition (eleventh) was published in 2006. Figure 2 shows that 94% of the *RTK* players started to play *RTK* either before or beginning with the seventh edition (published in 2000), which means that the majority of the *RTK* players started playing the *RTK* at least 8 years ago.

Table 2. RTK game playing preference and gender crosstab analysis

			Gender		Total
			Male	Female	
Game preference	Play RTK	Count	284	17	301
		% within gender	84.5%	10.8%	61.1%
		% of Total	57.6%	3.4%	61.1%
	Do not play RTK	Count	52	140	192
		% within gender	15.5%	89.2%	38.9%
		% of Total	10.5%	28.4%	38.9%
Total		Count	336	157	493
		% of Total	68.2%	31.8%	100.0%

(n=497)

Media Influence on Perceptions of the Three Kingdoms History

As mentioned above, the Three Kingdoms history has been depicted by numerous media, even though most of the media could cover only a small part of the sprawling, intricate history. Table 3 provides an overview of participants' preferences for accessing media that describe the Three Kingdoms history. This section reports the results in regards to RQ1: do *RTK* players exhibit higher motivation to access media treatment of the Three Kingdoms history than do non-*RTK* players?

For both the *RTK* players and the non-*RTK* players, TV dramas (85.1% for *RTK* players, 73.9% for non-*RTK* players) and books (96% for *RTK* players, 84% for non-*RTK* players) were the major sources of information regarding the Three Kingdoms history. Non-*RTK* players pointed out that school education (57.4%) was the third major

source of information from which they had learned about the Three Kingdoms history. *RTK* players showed higher motivation and higher interest in accessing media content pertaining to the Three Kingdoms history: *RTK* players' attraction to the media of comic books (83.5%), games (96.4%), and movies (65%) was higher than non-*RTK* players' attraction to those media (42%, 6.4%, 41.5%, respectively).

Knowledge About the Three Kingdoms History

RQ2 investigates the relationship between *RTK*-playing experience and the test performance on the Three Kingdoms history. Table 4 displays independent sample t-test results comparing the mean test scores of the *RTK* players with the mean test scores of the non-*RTK* players.

Figure 2. First started playing RTK game edition of the RTK players (n=304)

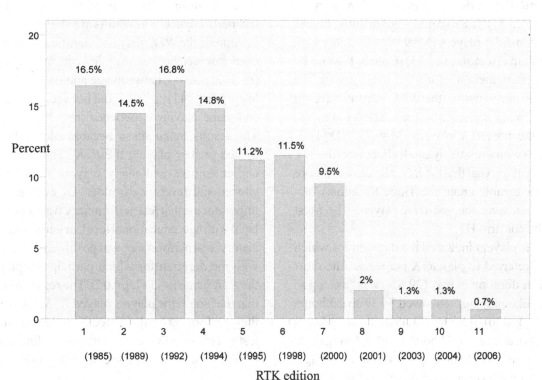

Table 3. Access to the Three Kingdoms history media

			media1(a)							Total
			TV	Book	Comic	Game	Movie	School	Friend	Total
RTK players	Count		258	291	253	292	197	139	124	303
	% within game		85.1%	96.0%	83.5%	96.4%	65.0%	45.9%	40.9%	
	% within $media1		65.0%	64.8%	76.2%	96.1%	71.6%	56.3%	85.5%	
	% of Total		52.5%	59.3%	51.5%	59.5%	40.1%	28.3%	25.3%	61.7%
Non-RTK players	Count		139	158	79	12	78	108	21	188
	% within game		73.9%	84.0%	42.0%	6.4%	41.5%	57.4%	11.2%	
	% within $media1		35.0%	35.2%	23.8%	3.9%	28.4%	43.7%	14.5%	
	% of Total		28.3%	32.2%	16.1%	2.4%	15.9%	22.0%	4.3%	38.3%
Total	Count		397	449	332	304	275	247	145	491
	% of Total		80.9%	91.4%	67.6%	61.9%	56.0%	50.3%	29.5%	100.0%

(n=491)

Percentages and totals are based on respondents.

a Dichotomy group tabulated at value 1.

*Note: shading cells indicate that the respondents are over 50%.

Overall, male participants earned higher grades (M=13.5) than female participants (M=7.1). Among the male participants, *RTK* players (M=14.2, SD=2.8) scored significantly higher than non-*RTK* players (M=9.96, SD=4.96) with a medium effect size (d=.43) (Cohen, 1988). The same phenomenon expressed itself among the female participants, the *RTK* players scoring significantly higher (M=10.65, SD=5.6, t=5.98) than the non-*RTK* players (M=6.71, SD=4.13, t=3.55) with a relatively small effect size (d=.27). The results reveal that the *RTK* players were more knowledgeable about the Three Kingdoms history than were the non-*RTK* players. The t-test results confirm H1.

RTK players indicated the duration for which they preferred to play *RTK* per week. The most popular duration of play (29.6%) was "as long as I feel like playing," followed by 11 to 20 hours (28.3%), 0 to 10 hours (23.4%), 21 to 30 hours (11.2%), and above 31 hours (7.6%). Using these data, plus the demographic variables of age, educational level, and game-playing history (first edition of the *RTK* played), the current study conducted a Pearson correlation analysis to observe the relationship between these measures and the test performance. The results are shown in Table 5. Among the *RTK* players, significant correlations emerged between age and educational level (r=.372, p <.01), between age and game-playing history (r= -.431, p<.01), and between education and game-playing experience (r= -.215, p<.01). The results make sense because older players tended to start playing the *RTK* game from the earlier edition, and many players with higher educational levels were older. Of even greater importance is that test performance was not correlated with age, educational level, or game-playing history. Test performance was positively correlated with the duration for which participants played the *RTK* game (r=.117, p<.05). The result implies that the longer the players played *RTK*, the better they performed on the Three Kingdoms history test questions. H2 was accepted according to the results of the Pearson correlation analysis.

Table 4. Test analysis of RTK game playing preference

	Whole sample		RTK player			Non-player					
	M [a]	SD	M	SD	n	M	SD	n	t	d [d]	p
Male	13.5	3.56	14.2	2.8	284	9.96	4.96	52	5.98[b]	.43	.000
Female	7.1	4.47	10.65	5.6	17	6.71	4.13	140	3.55[c]	.27	.001

(n=493)

(*a*) Mean of Three Kingdoms test questions, total grade is between 0 to 17.

(*b*) Unequal variances, df=57. Adjusted t-values and degrees of freedom (df) were used to determine statistical significance due to the violation of the homogeneity of variance assumption.

(*c*) Equal variances, df=155.

(*d*) d = eta, the measure of effect size.

However, game-playing experience was not correlated with test-question performance. One explanation is that the players who had started playing *RTK* years earlier had stopped playing *RTK* consistently at some point afterward, so that these players seemed to have possessed significant earlier gaming experience but, in fact, had not translated that experience into retainable gaming skills.

The present study performed a one-way ANOVA test to identify test-performance differences among the five different duration-of-*RTK*-playing groups. Test performance differed significantly across some of the duration groups, $F_{(4, 299)} = 4.203$, p<.05. Tukey post-hoc comparisons of the five groups indicate that the scores for the groups playing 11-20 hours (M=14.4), 21-30 hours (M=14.94), over 31 hours (M=14.435), and "as long as I feel like playing" (M=14.11) were significantly higher than the scores for the group playing 0 to 10 hours (M=12.79). Comparisons between other groups were not statistically significant at p <.05. The effect remains the same after playing over 20 hours. Those groups playing more than 20 hours had performance outcomes not significantly different from the performance outcomes attributable to the group playing between 11 and 20 hours. Hence, the one-way ANOVA analysis results confirm H3.

Table 5. Zero-order Pearson correlations between measures of RTK game preference

	Education	Generation	Hours of playing RTK a week	Test performance
Age	.372(**)	-.431(**)	.005	.100
Education		-.215(**)	-.113(*)	.075
Generation			-.060	-.013
Hours of playing RTK a week				.117(*)

(n=304)

** p <.01.

* p<.05.

Players' Perception of Why They Liked to Play RTK

RQ3 investigates *RTK* players' perceptions of the game. *RTK* players indicated reasons for their enjoyment of playing this particular off-line game. Among the 301 game players, only 4 (1.3%) stated that they liked to play *RTK* owing to the influence of their friends. A much larger number, 243 players (80.7%), pointed out that they liked to play *RTK* because they loved this version of the history of the Three Kingdoms period. A similarly large number (202, 67.1%) attributed their enjoyment of playing *RTK* to their enjoyment of uniting the country, and 127 participants (42.2%) stated that they liked the feeling of defeating the computer's artificial intelligence. Significantly fewer participants (105, 34.9%) enjoyed playing the game owing to its fancy multimedia design.

Although *RTK* players can choose approximately ten different sovereigns in the *RTK* game or create a new, originally named sovereign, almost half of the players (45.7%) preferred to play as Emperor Liu Bei, followed by Cao Cao (28%) and Sun Chun (9.5%), who were the three emperors constituting the Three Kingdoms. Only 7.2% of the *RTK* players chose to create a new sovereign. The book *Romance of the Three Kingdoms* depicted Liu Bei (emperor of the Kingdom of Shu) as the emperor who was moral, cared about his people, respected his generals, and had great loyalty and compassion. He has been praised in novels, traditional operas, and TV dramas. Cao Cao (emperor of the Kingdom of Wei), who was portrayed as a merciless and disloyal tyrant in the novel, actually was a versatile, knowledgeable, and ambitious hero. However, a negative image of him has long been penetrating into Chinese people's mindset. Sun Chun (emperor of the Kingdom of Wu) received a less lengthy description in the novel, but he also led many skilled and talented generals to help him reign over his kingdom. *RTK* players' impression of the three emperors

greatly influenced the players' preference for a particular sovereign.

Of the 304 *RTK* players, 87.5% agreed or strongly agreed that they played the *RTK* game over and over again even after they had united the country. Moreover, there are many different strategies to win the game. The fun of playing the *RTK* game varied according to both the emperor and the period that the player would choose because players could control different heroes, oppose different emperors, and observe different events.

An Association between Playing RTK and Motivation to Learn the Three Kingdoms History

RQ4 investigates how playing *RTK* affects players' interests in learning, and players' motivation to learn, the Three Kingdoms history. In addition to the evidence, mentioned above, that the *RTK* players outperformed the non-*RTK* players regarding the history-test performance (*RTK* players scored higher than non-*RTK* players, duration of game playing positively related to performance), more evidence provides in-depth descriptions of how playing *RTK* influenced *RTK* players' motivation to learn history.

Among the 304 *RTK* players, 195 (64.1%) pointed out that they had been familiar with the Three Kingdoms history before first playing the *RTK* game; 98 players (32.2%) indicated that they had first played the *RTK* game and, then, grown intrigued with learning more about the history behind *RTK*. Motivation to study the history and motivation to play the game perhaps influenced each other, but there is no doubt that playing *RTK* was a catalyst in encouraging players to learn more about the history. Table 6 provides more evidence describing how *RTK* players' playing the game encouraged them to learn the referenced history.

Almost every player (97.4%) agreed or strongly agreed that it is more fun to play *RTK* if the player is familiar with the history of the Three Kingdoms. Knowing the background of a par-

Table 6. RTK players' perception toward playing RTK and motivation

	SD	D	N	A	SA
I enjoy playing the game over and over even after I unite the country.	0	3.3%	8.9%	44.1%	43.4%
It is more fun to play the RTK game if you are familiar with the history of Three Kingdoms.	0	0.3%	2.3%	26.3%	71.1%
I read the history books to understand the events occurred in the RTK game.	0.3%	3.3%	9.5%	42.4%	43.4%
I know at least 70% of the characters and events of the RTK game.	0	2.3%	5.9%	39.8%	52%
The map of the RTK game is very helpful to let me image the geography of the Three Kingdoms period when I read history books.	3.7%	3.3%	9.2%	42.1%	41.8%
I believe that playing the RTK game helps players get familiar with the Three Kingdoms history.	0	2.3%	7.2%	47.4%	42.8%

(n=304)

*SD= strong disagree, D=disagree, N=neutral, A=agree, SA=strong agree.

ticular emperor, hero, city, and event was an important component of gaming literacy with which *RTK* players strove to equip themselves. Because this gaming literacy was so important for players' enjoyment of the game, 85.8% of the players read pertinent history books to equip themselves knowledge of the Three Kingdoms history. And 91.8% of the players agreed or strongly agreed that they should know at least seventy percent of the characters and events occurring in the game. Another 59.5% of the *RTK* players indicated that, when playing *RTK*, they would intentionally trigger events, and the design of *RTK* events rests on the Three Kingdoms history. Here is an example of one such *RTK* event: if a player chooses the game period A.D. 196, chooses the emperor Liu Bei, reigns over the two cities Xia Pei and Xiao Pei, and possesses the character Mi Zhu, and if Mi Zhu's loyalty sufficient, a specific event occurs (Mi Zhu's sister marries Liu Bei), resulting in the improvement of Liu Bei's skills. Therefore, the players' preference to play RTK by choosing actual sovereigns, and their intention to trigger historical events during the play strongly suggests that *RTK* players preferred to play in a near-real history environment, which would appear to slip deeply into fiction were players to create fictitious emperors; in other words, the preference was not to create

a new sovereign so as to enjoy simply the fun, history-independent elements of gaming.

One of the difficulties of reading *Records of the Three Kingdoms* and *Romance of the Three Kingdoms* is that many readers lack even a passing familiarity with numerous cities, gateways, and harbors mentioned in these books, many of which have different names nowadays. In this regard, 83.9% of the *RTK* players pointed out that the map of the *RTK* game greatly helps them to visualize the geography of the Three Kingdoms period when reading history books. Lastly, 90.2% of the *RTK* players expressed the belief that playing the *RTK* game helps players familiarize themselves with the Three Kingdoms history.

Some might still be suspicious of the motivating effect that playing *RTK* seems to have had on players' efforts to learn history. Indeed, these players might have already been interested in the Three Kingdoms history and, for that reason, happened to love playing *RTK*, or their interests might have been triggered by media other than the game; however, *RTK* players' responses to survey item 17 and 18 confirmed that, after playing history-simulation games, many players were motivated to learn about a brand new subject by reading up on it. KOEI has invented history-simulation games in addition to *RTK*. One of these is *Nobunaga's Ambition*. Oda Nobunaga was a warlord during the Sengoku period of feudal Japan and eventually united Japan in the later sixteenth century after nearly a hundred years of disorder. In Taiwan, neither social-studies curriculum nor other pertinent media have sufficiently treated this critical period of Japanese history, and Taiwanese are rarely familiar with the story. Of the 304 *RTK* players, 178 (58.6%) pointed out that they had played the game *Nobunaga's Ambition*. Of the 178 players, 91 (49.7%) indicated that playing the game had triggered their interest in learning about the history of Nobunaga's period, and they translated the motivation into action by searching for lots of information pertaining to Nobunaga; indeed, 78 of these players (42.6%) researched information about this historical period in order to strengthen their understanding of the game. Therefore, the current study concludes that players are willing to spend time learning history and internalizing the knowledge so that it becomes part of their gaming literacy, which can, in turn, enhance the players' enjoyment of game-playing.

CONCLUSION

The study reveals that *RTK* players exhibited higher motivation to access media pertaining to the Three Kingdoms history than did the non-*RTK* players, that the *RTK*-players were more knowledgeable about the Three Kingdoms history than were the non-*RTK* players, and that many of the *RTK*-players were motivated to learn about this period of history by playing *RTK*. *RTK* is not an online multiple-players game, nor does it have a vivid 3D environment or fancy multimedia elements as do other popular games (e.g., Guild Wars, Postal). However, several generations of game players have been attracted to *RTK*. What elements have contributed to the success of the *RTK* game? First, *RTK* has been built on rich historical materials. The geographical descriptions in RTK are compellingly authentic, as are the gaming situations and the events, and even the looks

of the heroes stem from precise descriptions in historical works. Playing *RTK* is like experiencing the history of the Three Kingdoms centuries after it occurred. Second, *RTK* does not "sugar-coat" the "learning materials" with gaming elements as do many educational games (namely, the type 3 game described in the literature review), which are disliked by genuine learners in comparison with "real games" (Mitchell & Savill-Smith, 2004, p. 44). *RTK* contrasts with flashy style-over-substance games by being an easily addictive, fun-to-play game that uses real history as the core content of the game. Once players start playing the game, they feel that they learn more about the game, more about the historical period, and more about their own desire to research the period by means of various media. One wonders whether or not these same outcomes would be as pronounced or even present in the majority of the "history-based" games, whose stories rest on fictitious stories or fictional scenarios. Players who recognize the superficiality of these stories might, for this very reason, lose interest in the game as a "history-based" game. With *RTK*, players have to learn the background stories of each character in order to win and enjoy the game. In turn, successful players' sense of accomplishment—their self-identification as "experts" of the Three Kingdoms history—can improve their intrinsic motivation to learn yet more about the historical period. Csikszentmihalyi and Hermanson (1999) described that intrinsic motivation to learn refers to the spontaneous learning The example they provided was to watch children play. Children pay attention to the gaming process because the information is interesting and important to its own right (p. 147). In this study, RTK players exhibit the same spontaneous motivation to learn. RTK not only triggers players' motivation to play, but also triggers players' spontaneous motivation to further learn extensive materials related to the historical period embedded in RTK to enhance the fun.

IMPLICATION

The nature of the argument over whether game-based learning is associated with learning outcomes is the same as the classic debate between Clark and Kozma regarding media effects (Clark, 1983, 1994; Kozma, 1991, 1994). Games constitute a type of media. To maximize its learning effect, educators could analyze games and select one that features a curriculum-related scenario design, and could introduce the game at the right time and in the right way to trigger learners' learning motivation to learn the subject, not just the motivation to play games. The process of playing games might promote players' gaming literacy and might, in turn, promote their familiarization with the curriculum-related scenario. More studies should address this area to yield advice for educators, specifically introducing them to various games and the pairing pedagogy in a particular subject area so that the educators can improve learners' intrinsic motivation to learn. This approach corresponds with what Egenfeldt-Nielsen (2007) advocated regarding "the third generation educational use of games," which should help teachers become facilitators of balancing the gaming experience and the learning content. Game designers who are interested in promoting learning motivation might consider similar strategies to present real historical events and geographical backgrounds of their own history to game players. Western culture is replete with rich historical materials that can be incorporated into game design and that can stimulate cultural awareness and learning interests. However, an educational game that successfully attracts game players into the world of substantive educational games must rest on a design featuring unique gaming elements that distinguish the game from already existing and popular—but less substantive—games.

ACKNOWLEDGMENT

The author would like to acknowledge the following sources of support for this research: Dr. Hui-Yin Hsu provided her insights and opinions to improve the quality of this paper, Chia-Yi Cheng provided virtual PTT currency to compensate the participants for their participation in this study's survey, and Hui-Ling Wang's assistance to help conduct this study.

REFERENCES

Berrenberg, J. L., & Prosser, A. (1991). The create-a-game exam: a method to facilitate student interest and learning. *Teaching of Psychology, 18*(3), 167–167. doi:10.1207/s15328023top1803_9

Bonanno, P., & Kommers, P. A. M. (2008). Exploring the influence of gender and gaming competence on attitudes towards using instructional games. *British Journal of Educational Technology, 39*(1), 97–109.

Bottino, R. M., Ferlino, L., Ott, M., & Tavella, M. (2007). Developing strategic and reasoning abilities with computer games at primary school level. *Computers & Education, 49*, 1272–1286. doi:10.1016/j.compedu.2006.02.003

Brozik, D., & Zapalska, A. (2000). The restaurant game. *Simulation & Gaming, 31*(3), 407–416. doi:10.1177/104687810003100305

Buckingham, D., & Burn, A. (2007). Game literacy in theory and practice. *Journal of Educational Multimedia and Hypermedia, 16*(3), 323–349.

Childress, M. D., & Braswell, R. (2006). Using massively multiplayer online role-playing games for online learning. *Distance Education, 27*(2), 187–196. doi:10.1080/01587910600789522

Clark, R. E. (1983). Reconsidering research on learning from media. *Review of Educational Research, 53*, 445–459.

Clark, R. E. (1994). Media will never influence learning. *Educational Technology Research and Development*, *42*(2), 21–29. doi:10.1007/BF02299088

Cohen, J. (1988). *Statistical power and analysis for the behavioral sciences* (2nd ed.). Hillsdale, NJ: Lawrence Erlbaum Associates.

Connolly, T. M., Stansfield, M., & Hainey, T. (2007). An application of games-based learning within software engineering. *British Journal of Educational Technology*, *38*(3), 416–428. doi:10.1111/j.1467-8535.2007.00706.x

Cronbach, L. J. (1951). Coefficient alpha and the internal structure of tests. *Psychometrika*, *16*(3), 297–334. doi:10.1007/BF02310555

Csikszentmihalyi, M. (1985). Emergent motivation and the evolution of the self. In Kleiber, D. A., & Maehr, M. (Eds.), *Advances in motivation and achievement* (*Vol. 4*, pp. 93–119). Greenwich, CT: JAI Press.

Csikszentmihalyi, M., & Hermanson, K. (1999). Intrinsic motivation in museums: why does one want to learn? In Hooper-Greenhill, E. (Ed.), *The educational role of the museum* (2nd ed., pp. 146–160). New York: Routledge.

De Crespigny, R. (2003). The Three Kingdoms and western Jin: A history of China in the third century AD. *Faculty of Asian Studies, 1*, 1-36. Retrieved July 18, 2008, from http://www.anu.edu.au/asianstudies/decrespigny/3KWJin.html

De Jong, T., & van Joolingen, W. R. (1998). Scientific discovery learning with computer simulations of conceptual domains. *Review of Educational Research*, *68*(2), 179–201.

Edwards, A. L. (1957). *Techniques of attitude scale construction*. New York: Appleton-Century Crofts.

Egenfeldt-Nielsen, S. (2007). Third generation educational use of computer games. *Journal of Educational Multimedia and Hypermedia*, *16*(3), 263–281.

Faria, A. J., & Wellington, W. J. (2004). A survey of simulation game users, former-users, and never-users. *Simulation & Gaming*, *35*(2), 178–207. doi:10.1177/1046878104263543

Garris, R., Ahlers, R., & Driskell, J. E. (2002). Games, motivation, and learning: A research and practice model. *Simulation & Gaming*, *33*(4), 441–467. doi:10.1177/1046878102238607

Gee, J. P. (2003). *What video games have to teach us about learning and literacy*. New York: Palgrave Macmillan.

Gee, J. P. (2006). *Games and Learning: Issues, Perils, and Potentials. A Report to the Spencer Foundation*. Retrieved August 2, 2008, from http://iop.onearmedman.com/content/Gee_Spencer_report_2006.pdf

Gee, J. P. (2007). *Good video games and good learning: Collected essays on video games, learning and literacy*. New York: Peter Lang.

Henderson, L., Klemes, J., & Eshet, Y. (2000). Just playing a game? Educational simulation software and cognitive outcomes. *Journal of Educational Computing Research*, *22*(1), 105–129. doi:10.2190/EPJT-AHYQ-1LAJ-U8WK

Hsu, H.-Y., & Wang, S.-K. (in press). Using gaming literacies to cultivate new literacies. *Simulation & Gaming*.

Hutchison, D. (2007). Video games and the pedagogy of place. *Social Studies*, *98*(1), 35–40. doi:10.3200/TSSS.98.1.35-40

Inal, Y., & Cagiltay, K. (2007). Flow experiences of children in an interactive social game environment. *British Journal of Educational Technology*, *38*(3), 455–464. doi:10.1111/j.1467-8535.2007.00709.x

Institute of Play. (2007). *What are gaming literacies*? Retrieved November 15, 2008, from http://www.instituteofplay.com/node/71

Ke, F. (2008). A case study of computer gaming for math: Engaged learning from gameplay? *Computers & Education, 51*(4), 1609–1620. doi:10.1016/j.compedu.2008.03.003

Kozma, R. B. (1991). Learning with media. *Review of Educational Research, 61*, 179–211.

Kozma, R. B. (1994). The Influence of Media on Learning: The Debate Continues. *School Library Media Research, 22*(4). Retrieved July 29, 2008, from http://www.ala.org/ala/aasl/aaslpubsandjournals/slmrb/editorschoiceb/infopower/ALA_print_layout_1_202756_202756.cfm

Lainema, T., & Makkonen, P. (2003). Applying constructivist approach to educational business games: Case REALGAME. *Simulation & Gaming, 34*(1), 131–149. doi:10.1177/1046878102250601

Leu, D. J. Jr, Kinzer, C. K., Coiro, J., & Cammack, D. (2004). Toward a theory of new literacies emerging from the Internet and other information and communication technologies. In Ruddell, R. B., & Unrau, N. (Eds.), *Theoretical models and processes of reading* (5th ed., pp. 1568–1611). Newark, DE: International Reading Association.

Malone, M. R., & Lepper, M. R. (1987). Making learning fun. In R. E. Snow & M. J. Farr (Series Eds.) and R. E. Snow & J. F. Marshall (Vol. Eds.), *Aptitude, learning, and instruction: Vol.4 Conative and affective process analyses* (pp. 223-253). Hillsdale, NJ: Lawrence Erlbaum Associates.

Mitchell, A., & Savill-Smith, C. (2004). *The use of computer and videogames for learning: A review of the literature*. London: Learning and Skills Development Agency. Retrieved July 31, 2008, from http://www.lsda.org.uk/files/PDF/1529.pdf

National Council for the Social Studies. (1994). *The curriculum standards for Social Studies*. Retrieved July 18, 2008, from http://www.social-studies.org/standards/

Nunnaly, J. (1978). *Psychometric theory*. New York: McGraw-Hill.

O'Neil, H. F., Wainess, R., & Baker, E. L. (2005). Classification of learning outcomes: Evidence from the computer games literature. *Curriculum Journal, 16*(4), 455–474. doi:10.1080/09585170500384529

Parchman, S. W., Ellis, J. A., Christinaz, D., & Vogel, M. (2000). An evaluation of three computer-based instructional strategies in basic electricity and electronics training. *Military Psychology, 12*(1), 73–87. doi:10.1207/S15327876MP1201_4

Professional Technology Temple. *Wikipedia*. Retrieved July 18, 2008, from http://en.wikipedia.org/wiki/Professional_Technology_Temple

Reese, D. D. (2007). First steps and beyond: Series games as preparation for future learning. *Journal of Educational Multimedia and Hypermedia, 16*(3), 283–300.

Robertson, J., & Good, J. (2005). Children's narrative development through computer game authoring. *TechTrend, 49*(5), 43–59. doi:10.1007/BF02763689

Robertson, J., & Howells, C. (2008). Computer game design: Opportunities for successful learning. *Computers & Education, 50*, 559–578. doi:10.1016/j.compedu.2007.09.020

Salen, K. (2007). Gaming literacies: A game design study in action. *Journal of Educational Multimedia and Hypermedia, 16*(3), 301–322.

Salen, K., & Zimmerman, E. (2005). *The game design reader: A rules of play anthology*. Cambridge, MA: MIT Press.

Silk, K. J., Sherry, J., Winn, B., Keesecker, N., Horodynski, M. A., & Sayir, A. (2008). Increasing nutrition literacy: Testing the effectiveness of print, web site, and game modalities. *Journal of Nutrition Education and Behavior, 40*(1), 3–10. doi:10.1016/j.jneb.2007.08.012

Squire, K. (2005). Changing the game: What happens when video games enter the classroom. *Innovate: Journal of Online Education, 1*(6). Retrieved July 28, 2008, from http://www.academiccolab.org/resources/documents/Changing%20The%20Game-final_2.pdf

Squire, K. (2006). From content to context: Videogames as designed experience. *Educational Researcher, 35*(8), 19–29. doi:10.3102/0013189X035008019

Taiwan Ministry of Education. (2008). *The curriculum standards for senior high school history study.* Retrieved July 18, 2008, from http://203.68.236.92/95course/content/98-01.pdf

Vogel, J. J., Vogel, D. S., Cannon-Browers, J., Bowers, C. A., Muse, K., & Wright, M. (2006). Computer gaming and interactive simulations for learning: A meta-analysis. *Journal of Educational Computing Research, 34*(3), 229–243. doi:10.2190/FLHV-K4WA-WPVQ-H0YM

Washbush, J., & Gosen, J. (2001). An exploration of game-derived learning in total enterprise simulations. *Simulation & Gaming, 32*(3), 281–296. doi:10.1177/104687810103200301

Wiebe, J., & Martin, N. J. (1994). The impact of computer-based adventure game achievement and attitudes in geography. *Journal of Computing in Childhood Education, 5*(1), 61–71.

Wildeman, H. H., Owston, R. D., Brown, C., Kushniruk, A., Ho, F., & Pitts, K. C. (2007). Unpacking the potential of educational gaming: A new tool for gaming research. *Simulation & Gaming, 38*(1), 10–30. doi:10.1177/1046878106297650

Williams, D. (2006). Groups and Goblins: The social and civic impact of an online game. *Journal of Broadcasting & Electronic Media, 50*(4), 651–670. doi:10.1207/s15506878jobem5004_5

ENDNOTES

Zhou Yu: a famous military strategist who served the emperor Sun Chun. The book *Romance of the Three Kingdoms* portrays him as a conceited person who covets the intelligence of Zhuge Liang, the counselor of the emperor Liu Bei. In the novel, Zhou Yu often tries to place Zhuge Liang in a deadly trap; however, this scenario did not occur in real history. The fabricated scenario is so famous that most people believe it is true. This short-answer item could test whether or not players really knew the true history.

Zhuge Liang: he has been portrayed as the most intelligent man in Chinese history and as a man who, with a handful of soldiers, defeated opponents possessing much larger military forces. He was not only a military strategist, but also a politician and an inventor. His nickname was "The Crouching Dragon," and he successfully predicted the state of the Three Kingdoms before the status of disorder was clear.

Battle of Guandu: The Battle of Guandu was a crucial event for Cao Cao in his efforts to become one of the emperors in the Three Kingdoms history. Yuan Shao, who was another warlord and a major opponent of Cao Cao at that time, was defeated by Cao Cao because Yuan Shao had failed to take advice from his counselors who warned of securing the grains that were in Crow's Nest and that the soldiers needed. This war has been remembered as a symbol of the following maxim: greater numbers do not always translate into victory. In the 11th edition of the *RTK* game, KOEI incorporated this battle into a short scenario game to test whether or not players could defeat Yuan Shao by using Cao Cao's historically accurate strategy.

Battle of Red Cliff: Cao Cao won the Battle of Guandu, but ironically he failed in the Baltle of Red Cliff because of the same cause. Cao Cao united the northern area and wanted to invade the southern allied forces between Liu Bei and Sun Chun. Huang Gai, Sun Chun's general, sent a letter to Cao Cao feigning surrender, triggering a series of strategies that eventually led to the defeat of Cao Cao.

Baidi City: the city in which Liu Bei died.

Mai City: Mai City is where Guan Yu, Liu Bei's general, died. Chinese people have long worshipped Guan Yu, who is referred to as the God of War. In the novel, Guan Yu swore to be brothers with Liu Bei and Zhang Fei, and left a legendary oath "dying on the selfsame day."

Wuzhang Plains: Zhuge Liang died of overwork and illness during the Battle of Wuzhang Plains.

Luoyang City: The capital of China during the pre-Three Kingdoms history. The Emperor Ling of the Han dynasty was captured by one of the powerful warlords, Dong Zhuo, in Luoyang City. To avoid the coalition of warlords opposing him, Dong Zhuo moved the capital from Luoyang City to Chang'an and killed many civilians.

Liu Shan: son of Liu Bei, the last emperor of the Kingdom of Shu. Liu Shan was portrayed as an incompetent, even retarded emperor in the novel. He was captured by Sima Zhao, whose son united Three Kingdoms and established the Jin Dynasty. When Sima Zhao asked Liu Shan whether or not he missed his former kingdom, he replied, "I am too happy here to think of Shu at all."

This phrase became a Chinese idiom meaning "too happy to think of home."

Jiang Wei: a military general serving the Kingdom of Shu. He was the successor of Zhuge Liang. Along with Fei Yi, an official of the Kingdom of Shu, Jiang Wei tried to attack the Kingdom of Wei and to revive Zhuge Liang's unfulfilled wish.

Emperor Xian: Emperor Xian of Han was captured and controlled by Dong Zhuo and then by Cao Cao. He had no political power at all.

Wooden ox and floating horse: an efficient automatic transportation device invented by Zhuge Liang to transfer grain for his military forces.

Wooden master: the wooden master was a fictitious tool invented by KOEI as a device to attack city walls in the *RTK* game.

Lu Bu: Lu Bu was a warlord during the late Eastern Han Dynasty, known as the Flying General. He has been recognized as the most powerful warrior in the history of China because of the description of him in the novel. He has also been known as a traitor who betrayed two of his masters, including his adoptive father Dong Zhuo.

Guo Jia: military strategist of Cao Cao who was brilliant and loyal to his master.

Pang Tong: counselor of Liu Bei. His nickname was "The Young Phoenix." He and "The Crouching Dragon" have been considered the most brilliant strategists during the Three Kingdoms period.

Xu Shu: Xu Shu was a counselor of Liu Bei. Cao Cao admired Xu Shu's intelligence, captured his mother, and hoped that Xu Shu could betray Liu Bei and join Cao Cao's forces. Xu Shu went to Cao Cao to save his mother, but she hung herself because she thought that Cao Cao was not a righteous master and that her son Xu Shu should never have left Liu Bei.

Huang Yueying: Huang Yueying was a fictitious name invented by KOEI. Referred to as Ms. Huang in the history books, Huang Yueying had a real name that was never revealed during the historical period in question. The current study used this item to test whether or not the given *RTK* player was a serious game player or just an occasional player. Only a serious game player would realize that the character is the wife of Zhuge Liang.

Zhao Yun: a military general of Liu Bei. The novel portrayed him as a brave, loyal, powerful general. He saved Liu Shan when

the latter as an infant during wartime and when Zhao Yun was in a dangerous situation. He died owing to illness.

Cao Ying: a fictitious character invented by a recent movie portraying the life of Zhao Yun. In this movie, Cao Ying was Cao Cao's granddaughter and killed Zhao Yun. The current study used this item to test how many participants had been influenced by the movie in regards to their perception of the Three Kingdoms history.

APPENDIX

Gender:	□Male	□Female				
Age:	□under 10	□11-15	□16-20	□21-25	□26-30	□over 30

Your PTT ID: _____ (for distributing the PTT currency)

Education (including in the process of obtaining a degree):				
□Elementary and middle school	□High school	□College	□Graduate school	□Doctoral degree

What sources have you ever accessed to learn about the Three Kingdoms history?						
□TV dramas	□Historical books	□Comic books	□Games	□Movies	□Schools	□Friends
□None	□Other					

Name the last media you have accessed in regards to the Three Kingdoms history.
_____

Have you ever played the *Romance of the Three Kingdoms* game developed by KOEI?	
□Yes	□No (or not in the last 5 yrs): skip to item 19

Which edition of *RTK* did you start playing? (indicate one between edition 1 and 11)

Which of the following statements best represents your situation?
□ You knew the history of the Three Kingdoms before you started playing the *RTK* game.
□ You played the *RTK* game before you knew the history of the Three Kingdoms.
□ You don't remember.

Please indicate your agreement with the following statements.				

I can repeatedly play *RTK* over and over again, even after uniting the country.				
□Strongly disagree	□Disagree	□Neutral	□Agree	□Strongly agree

It is more fun to play *RTK* if you know the Three Kingdoms history well.				
□Strongly disagree	□Disagree	□Neutral	□Agree	□Strongly agree

I read either *Records of the Three Kingdoms* or *Romance of the Three Kingdoms* to understand the events that would occur during the *RTK* game.				
□Strongly disagree	□Disagree	□Neutral	□Agree	□Strongly agree

I know at least seventy percent of the characters and events that occur in the *RTK* game.				
□Strongly disagree	□Disagree	□Neutral	□Agree	□Strongly agree

The *RTK* game map greatly helped me read the historical book *Romance of the Three Kingdoms*.				
□Strongly disagree	□Disagree	□Neutral	□Agree	□Strongly agree

I read the bios of the heroes designed by the *RTK* when I play the game.				
□Strongly disagree	□Disagree	□Neutral	□Agree	□Strongly agree

continued on following page

Appendix Continued

Playing the *RTK* game can help players know the history of the Three Kingdoms period.				
□Strongly disagree	□Disagree	□Neutral	□Agree	□Strongly agree

I prefer to play a particular hero when I play *RTK*.			
□Liu Bei	□Sun Chun	□Cao Cao	□Other

During the summer or winter vacation, I have often spent ____hours playing *RTK* every week.				
□ 0-10	□11-20	□21-30	□above 31	□as long as I feel like playing

Why do you like to play *RTK*? (choose all that match)
□My friends play *RTK*, so I want to play too.
□I like the history of the Three Kingdoms period.
□I like the feeling of uniting the country.
□I like the graphics and sound design of the game.
□I like to compete with the computer's artificial intelligence.
□Other.

Would you intentionally trigger an event when you play *RTK*?					
□Yes	□No				

Have you played the game Nobunaga's Ambition designed by KOEI?					
□Yes	□No (Skip to item 19)				

Did playing Nobunaga's Ambition trigger your interest in learning that period of Japanese history?
□Yes. I looked for lots of materials about that period of Japanese history.
□Yes. I looked for brief summaries of that period of Japanese history.
□Not at all.

Short-answer questions
What was the most impressive story in the Three Kingdoms period for you?
Why did Zhou Yu[1] want to kill Zhuge Liang[2]?
During the Battle of Guandu,[3] why did Yuan Shao (who had a greater numbers of soldiers) lose the battle to Cao Cao?

Multiple-choice questions				
Who surrendered to Cao Cao during the Battle of Red Cliff[4]?				
□ Huang Gai	□Huang Zhong	□Kan Ze	□Gan Ning	□Don't know or don't remember
Where did Zhuge Liang die during his last northern expedition?				
□ Baidi City[5]	□Mai City[6]	□Wuzhang Plains[7]	□Mount Qi	□Don't know or don't remember

continued on following page

Appendix Continued

Where did Yuan Shao reserve the grains for soldiers during the Battle of Guandu?				
□Mount Jutie	□Crow's Nest	□Three Rivers	□Luoyang City[8]	□Don't know or don't remember

Who was the successor of Zhuge Liang after he died in the Kingdom of Shu?				
□Liu Shan[9]	□Ma Zhong	□Deng Zhi	□Jiang Wei[10]	□Don't know or don't remember

Cao Cao held the emperor hostage to control the warlords. Who was the Emperor?				
□Emperor Xian[11]	□Emperor Huan	□Emperor Ling	□Emperor Zhang	□Don't know or don't remember

What was the automatic transportation device invented by Zhuge Liang?				
□Waterwheel with dragon bone	□Wooden ox and floating horse[12]	□Wooden master[13]	□Throwing stone wheel	□Don't know or don't remember

Who was the present hero Cao Cao referred to when drinking wine with Liu Bei?				
□ Sun Chun	□ Lu Bu[14]	□ Yuan Shao	□Liu Bei	□Don't know or don't remember

Who was the Young Phoenix?				
□Guo Jia[15]	□Pang Tong[16]	□Xu Shu[17]	□Zhou Yu	□Don't know or don't remember

Huang Yueying was whose wife? [18]				
□Zhuge Liang	□Ma Chao	□ Zhou Yu	□ Liu Bei	□Don't know or don't remember

How did Zhao Yun[19] die?
□Killed by Han De
□ Killed by Cao Cao's granddaughter Cao Ying on Mount Feng Ming. [20]
□Of illness.
□ By Sima Yi's strategy.
□Don't know or don't remember

The Three Kingdoms was in between which two united dynasties?
□Western Han Dynasty – Eastern Han Dynasty
□Eastern Han Dynasty – Western Jin Dynasty
□Western Jin Dynasty – Eastern Jin Dynasty
□Eastern Jin Dynasty – Sui Dynasty

Do you have anything else to say about the Three Kingdoms history or the *RTK* game?

This work was previously published in International Journal of Gaming and Computer-Mediated Simulations, Volume 2, Issue 2, edited by Richard E. Ferdig, pp. 36-56, copyright 2010 by IGI Publishing (an imprint of IGI Global).

Chapter 9
The Design of Virtual Space:
Lessons from Videogame Travel[1]

Steve Guynup
Art Institute of Pittsburgh - Online Division, USA

ABSTRACT

Videogames are the starting point for the general understanding of virtual space. (Grove & Williams, 1998). Academics use videogames to describe virtual space (Murray, 1997; Nitsche, 2009). Others argue that there is no understanding of virtual space, only a loose collection of articles connected by the issue of realism in rendering or behavior (Manovich, 2001). These statements point to a lack of understanding of virtual space on its own terms and set the stage for this document. This is a design document, written by a designer of virtual spaces. Its purpose is to provocatively explore user experience and task completion as forces that influence the design of virtual space. This is not a conventional research paper. The complex relationships of narrative, realism, motivation, usability, and human computer interaction (HCI) are unpacked in the videogame World of Warcraft through a detailed examination of travel. It is proposed that the exploration of travel in a videogame can provide a toolkit of ideas for the application of narrative, realism, motivation, and usability in virtual space. Travel can inform designers on issues of user experience and task completion in virtual spaces

OVERVIEW AND BACK-STORY, THE WISDOM OF WARCRAFT

Overview and Terms

Virtual space in this document is defined as a computer generated, visually dimensional environment traversable by a user. Virtual space is capable of supporting both work and play. Work

and play place different design objectives upon a virtual space. In this document, work takes on the functional imperative of efficient task completion. Play is loosely translated interactions outside the domain of work and is expressed as user experience. Videogames are seen as a subset of virtual space. The key difference in this document is that while virtual space allows for task failure, videogames actively prioritize user experience over efficient task completion. They expect and utilize

DOI: 10.4018/978-1-4666-0029-4.ch009

task failure. This simple change of priorities, a promoting of user experience over task completion, turns even basic behaviors like falling down, into very complex interactions.

The virtual design forces discussed here, user experience and task completion, should be in harmony. Harmony however, is not a magical occurrence. It takes effort and understanding to balance these forces and meet the needs of the user. In this document, task completion is further understood through the computer science domain of human computer interaction (HCI) and its subset usability. Usability is narrowly defined as the software's ability help accomplish productive tasks effectively and efficiently (Hackos & Redish, 1998). Example productive tasks are image manipulation in Adobe Photoshop and text editing in Microsoft Word. The idea of a productive task and task completion in virtual space, in this document, is held to that same practical standard.

User experience could be addressed through HCI studies, but given the need to understand user experience as separate and possibly in conflict with task completion, user experience is addressed through narrative and film studies. The use of storytelling and narrative in games is well known (Murray, 1996). Linking narrative to representation, or realism is common in film studies (Bordwell, 1985). Manovich's statement that virtual space is understood through realism in rendering or behavior, demonstrates the deep and often hidden role narrative plays in design as narrative is linked to realism.

The idea of conflict between user experience and task completion, as narrowly defined above, is straightforward in software like Microsoft Word. Users of Microsoft Word, don't wish to slay dragons to edit a line of text, find hidden treasure behind a magic keystroke, or lose themselves in a complex immersive interface. Connecting this definition of task completion to virtual space is awkward. This awkwardness may be due to the common conception of virtual space as a video-

game, a place where you are in fact tasked to slay dragons and find treasure.

To smooth this awkwardness, the idea of an avatar as a network cursor (Heim, 1998) may be helpful. Rather than view a user's avatar as a faux human mask for role-playing (Laurel, 1994), an avatar can be seen as a point from which a user accesses, manipulates and shares data (Carlson & Guynup, 2002). Like the cursor in Microsoft Word, avatars move and generate actions within a digital interface. This simple analogy does connect travel in virtual space to conventional usability two dimensional interface practices, and should be kept in mind throughout this document. This analogy of avatar as a network cursor can highlight the exponential impact of narrative and motivation on virtual design. It also highlights the impact of going from two to three dimensions in terms of usability. The next section steps into the specifics of the design forces in videogame based virtual spaces and offers an example of one particular cursor-avatar.

While Traveling on a Zeppelin … A Cursor Story

It was early Sunday afternoon, and I was riding the zeppelin to the Undercity. A woman was standing uncomfortably close to the edge of the gondola. Before we reached the city's sky tower platform, she leapt from the zeppelin. Silently she fell. She died on impact. With the knowledge of her death, a word crossed my mind—Noob.[2]

This *World of Warcraft* player tried to cut a corner. She tried to make her travel task shorter by not waiting for the zeppelin's designated stop at the sky tower. Yet, she misjudged the safeness of the height from which she jumped and died. This player was now running back from the graveyard to retrieve her body. Luckily, videogame death is not permanent; it is merely a delay in task completion. *World of Warcraft* teleports you to the region's graveyard and forces the player/user, in a ghost form, to run back to their body. While dead, the player/user cannot speak with other players or interact with the world in any way. The player/user must reach their body in 6 minutes and accept resurrection, or additional game related penalties will be assessed.

Once alive, she would resume her original game-related task of travel to the Undercity—a task delayed by a meaningless death. Having died in *World of Warcraft* in equally ignoble fashions, I pondered her loss. As a designer of virtual space, I pondered the role the designers of *Warcraft* had in shaping her fate. Was her death truly meaningless?

Falling as Travel Technique, Death as Task Failure

Death is the ultimate failure of a task. In the real world, designers go to great lengths to avoid any chance that a user may die. Games are different; death is part of the game (Rouse, 2001). In the real, physical world, death is an extreme example of task failure, but a useful one here. In the revivable, re-playable, and fictional world of videogames, death is only a temporary setback. The point of a comparison of real, physical death and fictional game death is to lay a foundation to break virtual space away from goals of realism, and more importantly, draw out the design factors of user experience and task completion.

In the world of videogames, designers utilize death as the ultimate penalty and they balance it against constructs that imply success. In a well designed game, all task failures support the user's overall experience and are used to create a sense of value in the completion of game tasks. This leads to some interesting choices in terms of design. The HCI issues surrounding our simple fall from a zeppelin are very complex. It is the failure of a travel task, through an unusual, optional, yet completely reasonable travel mode in games called falling—a travel mode that stretches the core of the earlier idea of avatar as network cursor (Heim, 1998).

Falling, travel, and death are a specific example set. To connect this and other videogame practices to conventional HCI principles, such as those that guide the use of a cursor, a range of larger issues must be addressed. It is well known that videogames utilize less than optimal methods for completing tasks. The initial key is how prioritizing user experience above task completion in videogames opens the door to a cascade of design options and issues to be understood. The interplay of narrative and interactivity takes on new and far reaching significance and the larger issue of narrative in virtual space begins to shape.

The simplified list of game design and HCI issues includes:

Failure: its use by videogames allows less than optimal HCI practices to be employed, if justified by narrative or motivational needs.

Narrative: positions the user/player's concept of task success/failure.

Aesthetics: bridge the gap between the purely usable/HCI-driven space, and the immersive narrative/story in which the user/player plays.

Motivation: the need to keep the user/player playing.

Our best option for connecting the list of ideas above to standard HCI/usability practices is in the well-studied domain of virtual travel and speed. Videogames like *World of Warcraft* employ numerous travel techniques. The first issue in our list above is, in a sense, broken down into the three issues that follow it. It should be noted that it is wrong to declare that poor HCI practices (nonfunctional buttons, overly complex displays, or hidden features) are appropriate in designing videogames. It is the ties to narrative and motivation that justify the possibility of failure and define success. This narrative justification of task success and failure is discussed in detail later in the paper, when HCI virtual travel taxonomies are directly tied to *World of Warcraft* practices.

Videogames are complex sets of rules and fiction (Juul, 2005) geared to create play and the desire for play. This divide between rules and fiction (also known as ludic and narrative) is the basis for the use of terms narrative and motivation within this paper. Both terms, narrative and motivation, seem necessary to incorporate failure into a domain of rules and fiction. Games are also autotelic (Csikszentmihalyi, 2001); all the activity in the videogame serves some purpose within the videogame. Every task and subtask has value and can be linked to issues of success and failure.

Even when a player/user is dead, motivational value can occur. In *World of Warcraft,* this comes from the fact that once you are dead—you cannot die. While running back from the graveyard area to their body, players may now fall from any height and survive. In an area called the Charred Veil, many dead players retrieve a small pleasure in their death by leaping over the edge of the high cliffs. This travel method offers both a shortcut to their body and the unique, previously not survivable, thrill of scenic downward travel.

Convention and Invention, Narrative Impact

Before addressing complexity of travel modes in *World of Warcraft* and connecting them to HCI taxonomies of virtual travel, it would be helpful to first provide one detailed example of the impact of narrative and narrative aesthetics on travel. Since falling as a travel mode has already been cited, it seems the most appropriate starting position. In a formal sense, the falling (or jumping) off a building often allows the player the quickest path to the ground. Therefore, falling could be seen as an efficient travel mode. It also requires little, if any, training (the basic concept of falling is well known to all human beings). This ease of understanding allows falling as an act of virtual travel and is utilized by players in many types of videogames. From a usability perspective, falling allows for a more efficient method of movement

when compared to common alternative presented in the virtual space—the walking down of a long, narrow, often winding, set of stairs or path. In a virtual space, falling to one's death can be completely removed. Unlike a videogame, is no need for that level of task failure or to tie falling to a narrative outcome like death.

The impact of falling as a travel mode on the design of a virtual space can still be uncovered by juxtaposing a videogame world, with the real, physical world. Consider the following thought experiment. If our ability to fall and survive occurred in reality, if human beings could literally survive falls of great heights, real world architects would invent different structures. These new buildings would exploit our ability to fall. These new buildings would become more usable. While it is unclear what these buildings would look like, any advantageous design modification in support of our new found ability to fall would certainly be utilized. Architects would invent a new element to add to their buildings, one that incorporates the real world ability to be uninjured by great falls. The design of stairs, elevators, railings, balconies, and rooftops would evolve. Places for people to land would be created by architects seeking to maximize this new ability to complete travel tasks more effectively. Like architects, many HCI scholars champion the following of such real world forces over metaphors that simulate past designs in the creation of interfaces (Gentner & Nielson, 1996).

Since videogames do support falling as a travel mode, it would seem plausible that their architecture, buildings, and landscapes would reflect and invent new elements to support falling. The casual observer is unlikely to notice these changes in architectural style that allow for failing as travel mode. Yet, in videogames, like *World of Warcraft*, these elements and design styles do exist, but are not be readily visible. The answer to this invisibility of design lies in narrative and its impact on aesthetics. To understand the role of narrative and narrative aesthetics we must now leave both reality and the videogame world behind. Film studies offer a design space driven by narrative and narrative aesthetics. The survivability of a fall, in a Hollywood movie, requires narrative intervention. A well placed awning or swimming pool to break the fall, some superpower, or a timely act of god. Examples are commonly found in blockbuster movies such as *Indiana Jones, Temple of Doom* (awnings), *James Bond, Thunderball* (swimming pool), and *Superman* (superpowers). In videogames the changes in style are hidden by the narrative, or more appropriately, the changes in architectural style are made to feel acceptable to the user/player.

Hiding an architectural style that supports falling as a travel mode is only the beginning of the relationship between narrative and user tasks. In film, buildings have no direct connection to real world forces. In fact, many structures are complete fake. Flat storefronts make a town, small scale models or digital creations make whole cities. The rooftops of filmic buildings may not keep out the rain; filmic doors will not keep out trespassers. Some doors will not even open. The force that guides their entire presence and whole of their design is narrative. Is the building modern or ancient Greek? Is the building clean or is it dirty and run down? These factors are driven by narrative and are determined not by invention, but by narrative convention (Carroll, 1992).

It could be said that invention deals with reality, while convention deals with realism. In virtual space, setting up a design dynamic of realism vs. reality is appealing, but in videogames, much like in film, realism is subordinate to narrative (Bazin, 1971, Bordwell, 1985). Proof can be found in the fact that films are often most immersive, most powerful when they break the rules of reality. From the slow motion spin effect highlighted in the Matrix movies, to the jump cuts used for two people in conversation on a television screen, unreal montage heightens the narrative power of the media.

A second takeaway from the preceding paragraph is that realism is not an end goal, but tool used to shape user, viewer or player behavior and understanding. Narrative is key to being able to apply realism effectively or to break from realism effectively with both videogames and virtual spaces. Film studies offer deep insight into realism and rearranging realism though montage to create more powerful, compelling outcomes. The cutting and pasting of virtual space, like cutting pieces of film may allow for more efficient scenes to be produced. The new factor in manipulating realism is usability and in fact usability may override narrative in virtual spaces that lack overarching storylines. Regardless of future hierarchies, a starting point lies in understanding narrative, narrative convention, and user experience in videogames.

Film highlights the impact of narrative and narrative conventions. Film is a domain dedicated to generating powerful user experiences. The clarity between film conventions and real world invention is shattered in the domain of videogames. The videogame designer's desire for immersion in a storybook reality is balanced with the rules, the play, and the mechanics of task completion. Suspension of disbelief is balanced against the player/users desire for maximum efficiency in task completion (usability). Task efficiency within the boundaries of user acceptance (or the suspension of disbelief in games spaces), equals a sense of great power in the digital domain.

In *World of Warcraft*, travel modes not only use narrative conventions with ties to magic, myths, and science fiction, but they also extend and interweave with the design of buildings and landscapes themselves. Buildings and landscapes are not simply following realistic conventions in order to support the suspension of disbelief, they actively determine travel modes, user tasks, and end goals. Hidden behind the realistic conventions, the forces of invention, HCI, and usability are active. In the *World of Warcraft*, roofs and doors are designed in accordance both the game's narrative and its usability needs. The lines between invention and convention blur. A videogame and possible virtual space design aesthetic emerges.

Convention and Invention, Addition and Subtraction

Returning to videogames, new travel modes, like falling great distances, should have an impact on design of environment in which the player/user inhabits. In *World of Warcraft*, buildings however do not reflect any new architectural developments that explicitly demand the leaping of users to the ground. Beyond a graphic novel, fantasy feeling, the buildings in *World of Warcraft* visually reflect traditional conventions of falling equals death. Note the term visual, for there are in fact great changes afoot, but they are often hidden or not seen as additions, but rather simple things that are missing or whose function is subtly transformed.

A primary reason that the architecture of *World of Warcraft* does not directly alter itself to exploit the fullest potential of virtual space, including the survivability of great falls, is narrative. *World of Warcraft* is a storybook world, a world dependent on the suspended disbelief of the player. To visually acknowledge and design for this digital survivability of great falls, would remind the user of their own digital fakeness. The entirety of the *World of Warcraft* paradigm is wrapped in a magical story. Magic powers and mythic beasts are used to justify the player/user tasks and abilities, as well as the design of the videogame world itself.

It would be easy to declare that all new design possibilities that enhance usability simply reach back to narrative domains and the addition of magic, mythos, or science fictions for justification. That justification is false, as upon deeper study a second hidden path for innovation design emerges. Since to invent new elements solely by utilizing the affordances of virtual space, and therefore ignore the game's narrative is not allowed, *World of Warcraft*, rather than add conspicuous architectural elements to support the survivability of great falls,

World of Warcraft subtracts. Innovative design is not always the conceptually new, but can also come from the removal of the old and unneeded.

In the case of supporting jumps from places, railings are removed. In *World of Warcraft* cities like *Orgimmar*, caves in *Un'goro Crater*, and the Elven buildings in *Ghostwood*, structures support the leaping down of players/users and help speed them back into game play rather than require players/users to backtrack down paths they have little to gain from. In *Orgimmar*, falling allows travel across rooftops. The functionality of rooftops is no longer the reality based need to keep out rain, but is now tied to travel and allowing (or stopping) players/users from traversing them.

Other *World of Warcraft* omissions include rooms, especially in instances. Instances are special game play centered areas that focus on specific missions rather than support multiple general play tasks. Rather than utilize the square footage and construction costs to build compartments the way a real world architect would, instances tend to be a series of winding paths that connect with occasional larger spaces in which battles occur. This path-like approach to game architecture allows play to flow through the virtual space. From rooms we move to doors. Doors, which open and close in *World of Warcraft*, are largely removed. To enter most buildings, players/users travel through open archways and complete their tasks without the interruption of having to stop and open a door. When doors do appear in *World of Warcraft*, a sense of narrative need also appears. Doors segment game events, act as structural chapter or paragraph headings which serve notice that a new event will be coming. Doors, once an invention are now a videogame convention.

World of Warcraft, architecture does support the act of falling as a travel technique. Defining downward travel through the term falling, allows consideration of both intentional and unintentional acts, which is important as videogames support and utilize both task success and task failure. Falling can be a short-cut or it can bring death and so allow great heights to act as walls, boundaries that guide the player's actions and their knowledge of the world. The player/user can also fall into a pit of monsters, which, depending on the player/user's level, may be fatal or may be a short cut accessible by only higher level player/users. Falling is also unidirectional, so it affords a linear design element. Videogame level designers use space, through elements like falling to negotiate time (and therefore narrative) with the player/user. All of these past statements tie falling and its architectural impact not to the world of real world physical architecture, but the narrative aspects of videogame play.

Through this one example of falling as travel technique, it has been shown that narrative operates in a complex, flexible space, and is difficult to contain or cleanly evaluate. Even videogames like *Tetris*, which were created without narrative caveats, can find themselves having narratives mapped on to them by the player/user (Juul, 2005). In a sense, all videogames contain narratives, but "some narratives will be more discernable than others" (Juul, 2005). Juul's work addresses the ludic and narrative divide (reshaped in videogames as sets of rules and fictions). This confirms the idea that narrative is always present, but is never is a complete explanation for the design of virtual space. A second related avenue previously described as motivation, warrants further HCI study. Motivation, like narrative, addresses user experience but not necessarily task completion.

Modes and Motivation, Becoming More Usable

"Players expect to fail" (Rouse, 2001). This simple statement underpins the division between the domain of usability and that of videogames. With failure not only an option, but a design necessity, interactive methods that usability scholars shun are suddenly given new life. The concept of modes is a major example. Despite their proven usability problems in interfaces and task completion

(Sutcliffe, Ryan, Doubleday, & Springet, 2000), modes are commonly found in games. Modes including stealth, berserker, shadowform, and dozens of travel options and effects are found in *World of Warcraft*. The reason modes are acceptable in games is simple but multilayered. Videogame modes are tied to motivational (and narrative) forces.

During successful play, users gain new modes. The new modes empower the user to complete larger game tasks. In a sense, games become more usable over time. New modes are granted which increase the speed or killing power of the player/user, and allow for the more prompt completion of fictional tasks. This gaining of power also leads to another note on modes. Modes intertwine with the motivational needs of game design. Gaining modes that are more powerful is a strong motivator for continued game play.

The use of modes and the failure of some game designers in addressing basic tasks like travel open the door to a common ground with general usability principles. The preceding pages addressed a range of issues. The common use of falling as a kind of short-term travel mode in videogames underscored the complexity of the domain. The role of narrative in defining forms of user ability, such as adding magic or subtracting doors, and the use of practices that cause failure, such as modes, shift videogames away from standard HCI/usability principles used to design interfaces and non-game software.

To more deeply address the divide between game design and standard usability and see how usability is applied to generating user experiences within the videogame world common ground must be found. Speed and travel are issues found in both videogame and non-videogame spaces. The latter portion of this paper goes into detail on the practices found in *World of Warcraft*. In that latter discussion, videogame practices of modes and narrative will play a key role, alongside current computer science and HCI scholarship on virtual navigation. Before merging narrative and motivation into past HCI scholarship on videogames and virtual travel, the limited nature of past scholarship and the differently purposed research of virtual travel, must be addressed. It is far too easy to assume that much of what has been written here has been addressed by others. A sense of past scholarship, blended with the preceding text past, lends a new context for interpreting studies of virtual worlds, and allows the continued use travel/navigation example in making a larger case for usability in virtual space and the real lessons of game design.

USABILITY AND GAMES

Historical Separation

Early HCI scholarship on the usability of videogames viewed them in simplified terms. It placed videogames under the comfortable rubrics of its own academic domain "All video games are interfaces between the child and an elaborate scoring system" (Pausch, 1994). Although the whole of a game could be seen in the light of an interface tied to a scoring system, this approach clearly overlooks the roles of narrative and ludic demands in game design. The use of the term "child" to describe the player/user carries its own implications as to how HCI scholars once viewed this design domain.

This narrow focus of HCI scholars on videogames as interfaces allowed them to apply standard usability principles in regards to videogames as a whole, yet it kept them from approaching a broad range of game design issues. Past papers like Steve Cornett's "The Usability of Massively Multiplayer Online Role-playing Games: Designing for New Users" (2004) does an excellent job of applying standard principles and practices to videogame interface evaluation. Measurements of success and failure were limited to a 2D interface. Acts of play—tasks within the 3D environment—were untouched. In the end, despite the common ground

of humans, computers, and shared interest in the user's needs and interaction, HCI and videogame design are most often kept separate.

A generic feature of the two fields is the dedication to providing users what they want, but nevertheless there has been very little interaction between them (Jorgensen, 2004)

This relationship between theories of game design and traditional HCI evaluation methods has yet to be defined but definitely yields an exciting future (Pagulayan, Kekker, Wixon, Romero, & Fuller, 2003)

Falling from a building may not be the best example to tie game activity and usability together. There is little usability and architectural scholarship on the design of buildings in virtual spaces. Much of the work consists of general statements, such as limiting user behavior and aligning structures for easier searches (Shneiderman, 2003) or that realism may not always be the best approach (Poupyrev, 2000). The most specific virtual research that has been done seems only indirectly applicable, largely because interest has been directed at novel input devices or travel/navigation techniques that overlook screen-based, mouse driven worlds (Bowman, Krufijff, LaViola, & Poupyrev, 2000; Poupyrev, 2000). Although the act of falling is a valuable travel technique in videogames, HCI scholars of virtual space have not researched the value of falling. Comically, it appears to be a technique they wished to avoid.

The larger issue of travel however may hold enough overlap for our discussion. many HCI papers have been written concerning virtual navigation. The general focus of all of these papers relates to the improvement of travel and interaction in virtual space. Given the novel techniques, range of possible behaviors, and variety of goals, it becomes necessary to pare down the issue of travel further. Velocity—the issue of speed can be connected to travel in videogames, virtual spaces and two dimensional interfaces. In broad sense speed, the ability to optimally across a digital space, reconnects with the idea of avatar as cursor.

Avatar-Cursor Velocity (Full Speed Ahead)

Velocity is a design issue confronted by HCI scholars (Bowman, Kruijiff, Laviola, & Poupyrev, 2000). Designers of virtual space control the speeds afforded to the user in traveling through the space. Choice of speed or range of speeds can be a difficult task. Too slow and users will be unnecessarily delayed. Too fast and users may find navigation difficult to control, especially for short precise tasks. A range of speed can be offered by modes or continuous control. Yet, the use of continuous control places an additional cognitive burden on the user that may influence other tasks undertaken while moving. A number of specific speed modes can be used, but in general, HCI scholars have discourage the use of modes as they can confuse and frustrate the user (Hackos & Redish, 1998).

Videogames break from HCI efforts and may support either continuous control when play is of a racing nature and the added cognitive control issue is factored into the balancing of task failure and task success. In contrast, RPG videogames like *World of Warcraft* use travel modes. As *Warcraft* is the example of this paper and it uses a variety of videogame travel modes, a HCI driven taxonomical review built upon the research of Bowman, Krufijff, LaViola and Poupyrev seems appropriate.

Starting in the domain of past HCI studies of virtual travel, the factors that influence optimal travel speed in any given virtual space are linked to the following:

User Experience: User skill in managing speeds includes benefits of practice and physical reaction time.

Demands of Task: Straight line, avoiding targets, gathering objects, gathering information, and/or interacting with fellow users.

Demands of the Space: An open field, a maze, rooms of a building, and/or a series of pits to leap across or vines to grasp.

Input/Output Devices: Joysticks, thumbsticks, mice, steering wheels, monitor, goggles, caves.

Technical Affordances: Processor speed, rendering speed, frame rate, internet connection (online game play only)

Software Affordances: Variable speed control, instant speed boosts, teleportation, guided navigation.

The factors above represent a methodology for describing the larger factors influencing how users manage velocity. Some are constant, such as Input/Output Devices and Technical Affordances. They do not change while the user is interacting. In contrast, User Experience is generally seen as a linear progression allowing for greater speed and diversity of behaviors. The Demands of Task, Demands of the Space, and Software Affordances can vary greatly within the space. Fortunately it is also these latter three that designers of virtual space have the greatest influence over.

On the matter of velocity, the subtask taxonomies of Exploring, Searching, and Inspecting do not have a direct influence. Given the great diversity of application and cognitive processing, the subtasks of Exploring and Inspecting are not an optimal starting point for connecting videogames to HCI/usability practices. Travel to a known location factors out the cognitive load of users' issues of having to interpret their surroundings. Focus on travel will be limited to Searching—travel between known points.

Under Input/Output Devices, the question of Immersive, Semi-Immersive, and Non Immersive can be raised. Given that most games are screen-based, we can look to what is seen as, in an ACM context, as Non-Immersive work. Unfortunately, most of the computer science research has focused on Immersive and Semi-Immersive domains, which is due, in part, to a focus on phenomicologically driven realism (Manovich, 2001).

The last major taxonomy involves the manner by which users control navigation and speed. Five categories of interaction techniques can describe the means by which travel is controlled (Bowman et al., 2000). These techniques differ from the factors above in that they deal with the actual user input.

Physical Movement: Walking, treadmills, stationary bicycles.

Manual Viewpoint Manipulation: Grabbing and pulling, leaning one's body to control both direction and speed.

Steering: Continuous specification of direction. Motion itself is automatic and speed is typically constant.

Steering Automatic: User specifies direction, but does not require cognitive or physical effort maintaining direction. Motion itself is automatic and speed is typically constant.

Target-Based Travel: User specifies a destination, system handles details. With or without transitional travel (i.e., teleportation)

Route Planning: User specifies a path to follow. The user retains the ability to adjust travel or destination while in transit.

Each of the preceding lists of taxonomies highlights the complexity of virtual space and the seemingly simple act of travel. These taxonomies need to be understood and defined prior to a direct review of videogame interactions and their possible use in non-videogame spaces. For the purpose of usability evaluation, travel in *World of Warcraft* appears to be an ideal candidate for a number of reasons. *World of Warcraft* uses the standard interface input and output devices of mouse, keyboard and screen (not a game controller). Unlike a racing game, the task of travel in *Warcraft* is not a goal in and of itself. Speed

varies, but is not under continuous control (racing game). It uses dozens of modes instigated in a number of ways. Travel tasks in this paper are further limited to being a subtask of Searching, as in traveling between known points. Searching is a common task, one that also raises the importance of task completion in relation to user experience. In a sense player/users travel to places to begin missions, to play and generate user experiences. Searching therefore becomes more inherently connected to past standard HCI concerns of task completion than Exploring or Inspecting. Lastly, *World of Warcraft* also utilizes both Steering and Target-Based control techniques.

The next section enters into a more direct drawing of usability practices out of the *World of Warcraft* videogame. It is worth restating that videogames are not an interface connected to a complex scoring system. Videogames are complex environments centered on generating unique user experiences. Videogames incorporate task failure and become more usable over time. As shown in the detailed example of falling as travel technique, a range of design issues tied to narrative and motivation are present in videogames.

The larger benefit is not necessarily the application of usability principles to videogame design, but rather how practices in videogames are formed. From that, foundational principles applicable in non-videogame related virtual spaces may emerge.

USABILITY AND TRAVEL IN WARCRAFT

General Connections

The preceding section offered a detailed description of travel methods in virtual space. These travel methods show the complex web of options available to designers for an avatar-cursor. Missing from the previous section was the issue of player/user experience. Videogames and virtual spaces hold narrative and motivational elements that greatly impact player/user experience (Murray, 1997). *World of Warcraft,* has already been shown to hide and/or alter the usability of its landscapes and architecture through narrative and/or motivational forces. Travel in *World of Warcraft* also overflows with hidden connections to user experience, narrative, and motivation. These connections, presented in full detail here, serve to underscore the role of narrative and motivation in game design and highlight the possible design differences between videogames and virtual non-game spaces.

World of Warcraft offers 70 experience-based levels. Players start at level 1. By completing missions and slaying monsters, they rise in level. At certain levels, players gain new travel modes. Without exception, these new travel capabilities always afford an increase in velocity. From a pure game play perspective, the link to increased velocity in the new travel modes is a motivational carrot for users. After the initial task of Exploration comes Search directed travel. *World of Warcraft* game tasks, or quests, typically require repeated Search directed travel to known and often distant destinations.

Greater speeds improve the task of Search directed travel. As the gaining of velocity is tied to player level, User Experience is addressed. The player/user gains new travel modes upon proven mastery of past abilities. The player/user gains new travel modes after experiential demands have taken them to ever more distant areas of the game. The stair stepping of modes is tied the growing travel demands of quests. *World of Warcraft* first manufactures a user need for increases in travel speed, and then fulfills that need. It is a simple, but very effective, methodology. Many different modes of travel and sub-variations of travel modes are not only allowed, they are required. As these modes scale up, grow faster, fundamental constructs of usability, limiting of user choices and degrees of freedom become enrobed in narrative and sculpted by the needs of play.

The techniques for travel fall under the headings of Steering and Target Based control. Users start with access to both techniques. Steering begins with two speeds, run and walk. Running, default setting, is used while users engage in a range of interactive tasks. This range includes most travel during combat tasks, travel within instances, and travel to NPCs (Non Player characters, with whom conversations, purchases, repairs can be had). The latter, and often Search directed task of travel to NPCs, requires close proximity to the NPC target before the second task of NPC interaction is allowed by the game mechanics. Running is also used for travel inside of buildings.

A slower walk mode is available, but no lesson in the game teaches its use. It is seldom utilized, as most interaction in the game seems effective with run speed (The exception being players in Stealth Mode). In terms of initial travel modes, one Target-Based Travel mode is also immediately available to the new player/user. This Target-Based Travel is a teleportation mode triggered by a Hearth Stone. Clicking on this object, the user is teleported to their chosen home or Inn, which lies in a town where goods may be purchased and quests completed or initiated. An overall view of velocity and travel modes, in a loose order of availability to the player/user, is:

Steering Based:

Running*: Default, and the most common, used for engaging in other interaction

Walking: Slower than running, available at level 1, seldom used

Buffs: These potions, magic items, or class traits allow for either small increases or short bursts of speed

Travel Forms: At level 20+ some character classes, Shamans, Druids & Hunters get a new ability, a travel mode that allows for 30 to 40% movement

Mounts: At level 30 users can purchase an animal to ride. Speed increase is 60%

Epic Mounts: At level 60 users can gain mounts that offer a 100% increase.

Flying Mounts: At level 70 users can purchase or earn fast mounts that can fly, these are only usable in the new Outland area***

Epic Flying Mounts: At level 70 users can purchase or earn very fast mounts that can fly, these are only usable in the new Outland area***

> * moving requires the holding down a of key or use of the auto run - a toggle key that engages any pre-selected mode and causes the player/user to move. Auto run requires steering

> ** all speed increases are measured as percentages of run speed

> *** flight raises new design issues that the original areas of *World of Warcraft* were unable to cope with, interesting one issue is an attack strategy where a flying player exits flight mode, falls to the ground, and attacks an enemy player by surprise

Target Based:

Hearth Stone: Teleportation to a single pre-chosen destination.

Flight Paths: Guided point to point travel on flying animals.

Portals: An ability gained by magic classes, they can summon other characters to their current location.

Ships and Zeppelins: The domain of *Warcraft*, the world of Azeroth, is currently divided into two "continents." These vehicles allow for travel across this digital distance. Both methods move away from their initial locations, and then teleportation action occurs bringing users in view of the other continent.*

Falling: Short term downward travel.

> * list compiled before the release of Burning Crusade and Wrath of the Lich King More variations on the above themes may now available.

General details of *World of Warcraft* player/ user control of views and perspective are worth noting, as the player/user can adjust their view during Steering based travel. The majority of travel is done in third person perspective. Users can zoom into their character and assume a first person viewpoint. Few seem to do so. Despite the greater sense of presence and immersion, users opt for the more efficient and usable third person view. Third person perspective allows for a higher and more complete view of the user's surroundings. Especially important is that it provides a view of what is behind the player/user. The viewpoint can be separate from the user's avatar, in terms of rotation. Right clicking and rotating allows the player to view his character, the axis of rotation, from any angle. In addition, the third person perspective has a default straightening effect. Forward travel brings the user view parallel to the direction of travel—unless the right mouse button is held. This approach allows for visual exploration without commitment to a travel direction, and conversely easy shifting to a travel direction based on visual exploration.

Lastly, the viewpoint's distance from the player's avatar, while controllable by the thumbwheel, is also limited. Both in general distance, approximately 15 meters, and by any obstruction, the viewpoint may encounter. This includes the inside of roofs, branches, and even high walls. Any obstruction pushes the viewpoint toward the viewer's avatar. This helps maintain the immersion, by not allowing users to see through a structure's geometry in an odd or overly unrealistic manner in addition to keeping the player/user's character visible and more controllable. The usability of third person perspective has driven it to become a part of the aesthetic of videogames. Third person perspective is acceptable not by the literal narrative within the *World of Warcraft*, but by the larger cultural narrative of videogames. It is an example of the blurry line between invention and convention. To address invention and convention from a more stable direction, a review of *World of*

Warcraft's use of narrative in interfacial direction may be helpful.

Narrative Ties, Visual Indication of State

From cursor changes to show state, menu item hotspots that glow on mouseover, to the color and image coding of Web pages that add site location cues and contextual support to the data on the page, interface designers use visual cues to reinforce changes in user position and state. In games is not a question singular indication for a player/users state or mode, but a rich blend of conventional visuals and audio with narrative based visuals and audio. The *World of Warcraft*'s 2D interface positions indicators of state in the upper right menu. As the player/user enters various travel states, a small visual icon of the state is shown.

Beyond the standard menu indication, *World of Warcraft* draws inspiration directly from psychology rather than usability. While *Warcraft* draws on intuitive themes to indicate speed, the field of psychology opens the door to counter intuitive slowing of speed to indicate velocity as seen in the TV show "Six Million Dollar Man." The *Matrix* shows some novel ideas on how to visually relate speed to users (Duvall, 2001).

In *World of Warcraft*, the more common approaches found in Steering Based travel include, the kicking up of dust and debris, motion blur, glowing feet, wind streaking. These are all metaphors for active speed. Typically the latter three (all but the kicking up of dust) are also tied to a narrative of magical enhancement. Target based travel, the act of teleportation, includes a glow—typically from the hands of player/user which move in an preprogrammed act of faux spell casting. All players/users can teleport to one Inn, designated by them. Further Target Based, point to point travel can be done by the warlock class using the Ritual of Summoning. A visual of a portal, an image of the destination embedded in a two meter circular spatial distortion, appears.

The three players needed to support the ritual all auto-animate in a magical gesture at the portal and the distant player being teleported or summoned visually fades into their location. Since the *World of Warcraft* often places player's quests inside of instances and quests within instances typically require a group of players to complete the quest task, special Meeting Stones are placed outside of them. Meeting Stones are part of an in-world interface and can be used to summon other players/users to that instance location. Some travel modes that are tied to magical narrative driven items, utilize cartoon or film-like special effects to steer the user's mind to an association with speed and the acknowledgement of state or mode (Duvall, 2001).

Beyond cartoon speed effects and portals, *World of Warcraft* indicates changes in some travel modes by visually adding objects and elements. One addition is the shape shifting of specific character classes into faster travel forms. The player/user's character literally changes—ghost wolf mode for shamans and cat mode for druids. With the new mode comes a narrative driven visual change highlighting the new mode. At level 30, *Warcraft* characters get mounts. At level 60, faster, and more decorated, "epic" mounts are available. Both mounts and epic mounts are character connected, narrative driven. Some examples include ogres riding wolves, the new mythos of taurens riding kodos (big cow people on the backs of big dinosaurs), humans riding horses, and of course undead humans having undead horses. Target based travel modes include use of ships, zeppelins, gryphons, hippogryphs, bats and wyverns. Each mode has a unique connection with the *Warcraft* storyline, either a classical mythos ogres riding wolves or a new mythos taurens riding kodos. All mythos are accepted by the larger videogame narrative and share a common HCI usability based travel function. Aesthetics merge the diversity of the narrative storylines with the needs of HCI activity.

Limiting Behavior at Greater Speeds, Connecting Dots

There is a common thread among computer scientists and HCI researchers regarding 3D interaction. It is that by removing unneeded user's choices or properly limiting user behavior, they can increase the usability of the interface (Shneiderman, 2003). This can be restated as:

1. Minimize the number of navigation steps, needed to accomplish tasks. This includes treks between points and the subtasks of rotation and repositioning.
2. Avoid unnecessary visual clutter that distracts from or inhibits user tasks.
3. Simplify object movement; use predictable paths and less than 6DOF (Six Degrees of Freedom)

Removing and limiting choices that users would find difficult to manage at higher speeds (and would also adversely affect game play) is a standard practice in videogames. *World of Warcraft*, like other games, places limits on the interactive behavior of users while in higher speed modes. To do this *Warcraft* applies narrative driven rationales for some limits and allows for in-game penalties for others. An example of narrative driven limitation is to allow only the running mode behavior inside of buildings and most instances (these special questing areas are typically indoors, like a dungeon). This limitation is enforced by the software and automatically transforms a mounted player/user character into the un-mounted run mode when building or instances are entered. Trying to mount inside a building and most instances will only bring a message of its unavailability across the center of the player/user's screen.

Players, even those who may not own horses, understand that horses and other mounts are not typically used inside of buildings. By limiting the speed of indoor behavior to essentially one speed

and temporary magic driven increases (also called buffs), *Warcraft* designers can build structures optimal for that speed.

All higher-velocity, steering-based travel modes have limitations. The modes which involve shape shifting (ghost wolf for the Shaman character class, cat for the Druid character class) limit the user from casting magical spells, conversing with NPCs, creating magical items, and number of other, but not all, in-game interactions. In the special player vs. play areas, such as Warsong Gulch, characters in animal formed travel modes can still capture the flag and win the game. They can still attack other players, but in travel form, they typically do less damage.

The target based travel modes (Flight Paths, Ships/Zeppelins, and Portals) each follow three separate methodologies. All three are considerably faster than the steering travel modes. Flight paths are point to point travel, with transitional movement between locations specified by the game designers. Player/users mount a flying beast, a beast who in terms of narrative controls the path and speed while in flight. General interface tasks are allowed, but player/user movement is limited to rotation of viewpoint. Rotation provides a unique interactive-cinematic user experience as the player/user's path is, in part, plotted to be visually dramatic. The larger limitation of *World of Warcraft* Flight Paths is that they require the user to use Exploring based travel to discover where travel end points are. Players/users must find the Flight Master, the NPC character at an end point, before being allowed to use a Flight Path in the future. The requirement of discovery, finding the Flight Master, effectively limits new player/users from having immediate access to the entire *World of Warcraft* continent. High level areas feature monsters that are especially attracted to low level characters (in a radial effect called aggro), and so player/users are limited by level in terms of where they can safely travel. The gaining of new Flight Paths becomes a motivation perk, one that makes the *World of Warcraft* more usable. Low level player/users can however unsafely travel to most locations. The opportunity for failure of travel tasks here is firmly integrated into game play and is a measured part of the user's experience.

In addition to travel, Flight Paths impact usability of the game space in a unique way They help teach users the spatial relationships and distances between points, then allows for quicker travel between them. Players actually fly along these paths seeing all the land below. This reinforces their spatial understanding of the world. Lastly on Flight Paths, this transitional travel, the seeing of the land below, does impact travel time. Despite greater speed, compared to Steering modes, some Flight Path journeys can still take several minutes.

The next highest velocity is found in Ships and Zeppelins. This method is limited to a few locations and is used to span the great ocean between the two digital continents of Azeroth. Unlike Flight Paths, no prior knowledge of the destination is required. Ships and Zeppelins limit the users under the same rules as being inside. Players can fight and create items while on these vessels. The time of travel is brief, once the Ship or Zeppelins arrives and is boarded; only a minute passes before a teleportic transition occurs bringing them in sight of the coast of the other digital continent.

This example highlights a past design statement on subtraction – the bulk of the ocean is removed. The narrative of Ship or Zeppelin travel is placed before users and initiated but unnecessary waiting aboard them while they move over vast spaces is cut out. Users, whose quests lie on the other end of the journey, do not seem to mind this unreal, filmic, jump cut to the other side. The issues of subtraction, touched on here, also cast the third method of Target based travel, Portals and Hearthstones, in a somewhat different category.

Beyond Limits, Enabling Travel Task Failure

Some Steering and Target based travel modes are designed to enable travel task failure in certain,

generally combat related, circumstances. An example of enabling travel task failure in a Steering mode can be seen in the Hunter character class. At level 20, it receives the Aspect of the Cheetah travel mode. *World of Warcraft* limits the Aspect of the Cheetah travel mode's usage by adding a negative behavior. If a player/user in that mode is struck (typically, but not always in combat), the player/user is disoriented. The users travel speed slows to a walk and their defensive ability is lowered. While the higher priority for the game designer may be balancing combat-directed game play, the subtext is that travel Aspect of the Cheetah mode is best suited to Search Based travel.

Hunters also get Aspect of the Pack mode that allows them to share their more speedy travel mode with members of their group. When any member of a group in Aspect of the Pack mode is struck, the entire group is disoriented. Clearly, the speed of Aspect of the Pack mode is not applicable to combat situations. Task failure, tied loosely to narrative titles is again utilized by the *World of Warcraft* designers.

With an eye toward task failure and subtraction, Portals and Hearthstones can now be addressed. Portals and Hearthstones allow for nearly instantaneous travel. In fact, no time is spent in travel, as it is a teleportation mode. In the narrative, it is a magic spell that is cast. The limitations this method has include simple issues such as of time of casting and time between castings. Several seconds pass while the character gestures, visually indicating a process is occurring, and then the travel event happens. In addition, variations on teleportation modes have in game limits such as a recharge time, magic items needed, or in the case of portals—two other characters in addition to the caster to assist the process.

From the usability perspective, teleportation could be instantaneous. All of these modes might be more efficient if made immediate. The time spent casting the Portal spell, could be tied to state change and viewed as narrative-driven transition statement. In a world that exploits failure however, the longer than perhaps needed casting time allows for interruption. Time is not needed for successful action, only for unsuccessful action. Players losing a battle or in a tough situation cannot instantly retreat. Other enemy users (or monsters) get an added shot at killing the teleporting user while the casting time passes by. The software could easily move characters throughout the game world, but by allowing for failure by some, *World of Warcraft* increases the chance of task success for others.

Some portals, as now applied in the *Burning Crusade* expansion, also raise a new and interesting design change in the buildings within *World of Warcraft*. Whereas this article began with falling and its impact on buildings and landscapes, the opposite mode of generally upward travel is found here. The architecture of the *Blood Elves* uses teleportation devices, *Translocation Orbs*. These orbs allow player/users to teleport up and across buildings to gain access to higher floors. Ramps and staircases (much like doors, railings, and rooms) are, occasionally, subtracted from the architecture and replaced by a magical device.

In a sense, *Translocation Orbs*, point to an evolution in the design of buildings within *Warcraft's* videogame aesthetic. Interestingly, while falling holds possible death as complete task failure and narrative outcome, determined by height, use of *Translocation Orbs*, carry no such weight. It is possible that the fictional nature and newness of the *Translocation Orbs* places the narrative depth of its interactive failings at a minimum. It cannot cause death, not because the game designers are unable to encode death, or just because death lacks value, but because the users are unable to immediately shape this travel modes failure into a narrative outcome. Unlike falling, users have only fictional experience with teleportation.

Walking, the Lost Mode

If the future involves a role for *Translocation Orbs* and an associated shift in the design of virtual buildings and landscapes, what about the past?

What is the impact and role of the oldest and most common real world travel mode, walking? Walking is also available, but it rarely used. To push the lost point further, walking is in fact a penalty used to balance the tactical advantage of stealth. (*Rogue* and *Druid* class characters walk in stealth modes). Running is the default game setting in *World of Warcraft*. Interestingly, we could say that *Warcraft* is a world without walking. The most basic of all real world travel modes seems unneeded by the videogame. If videogame design is to influence the design of non-videogame virtual spaces, the concept of walking may need to find a new functionality outside of *Search* based travel.

CONCLUSION

Understanding Virtual Space

This is not a conventional research paper; far too many concepts have been examined and woven loosely together on the preceding pages. Literary sources are sparse, but they are also well established, have historical value, and represent key issues from various academic domains. Presenting a clear picture of virtual space, one able to satisfy these diverse academic domains individually was never seen as plausible. The core audience for this article is designers of virtual spaces, those who can model and code. An audience that wishes to finally do more than build mirror worlds (Gelertner, 1993).

This document is a starting point, one that both uses and breaks from goals of realism and game design. Travel, presented in great detail, offers insight into the nature of videogames, virtual space, and the subjects like narrative, realism, usability, motivation, and human computer interaction. The key dynamic within this document is the complex relationship, conflict and harmony between user experience and task completion.

There are a broad number of statements found in this article. Many ideas, such as the relationship of games and failure, limiting user behavior to gain usability, and HCI discouragement of modes are well known. Interconnecting these ideas becomes the hallmark of this design document. A basic list of conclusions, based on both academic scholarship and the simple personal observations of a designer of virtual spaces is presented. This list is a mix of conjecture and research, it is assumed the reader can pull value from it and link it to their own experience in designing virtual spaces.

1. Virtual space is often seen as a videogame. This may be driven by the popularity of videogames in both public and academic circles.

2. Virtual space is often tied to realism in rendering or behavior. This includes social interactions and cultural studies of users. (Videogames like *Tetris* may lack many of the visual elements of a real world, but even here some scholars like Janet Murray claim that *Tetris* has a narrative based on the fast pace of American culture.)

3. As general observation, unplanned task failure in virtual space seems often associated with a lack of realism in rendering or behavior. The solution seemingly proposed is more realism in rendering or behavior. (Developers seem unaware of their cyclical situation that realism encourages more realism, and that other solutions may allow successful task completion.)

4. Virtual space has no widely accepted understanding beyond videogames and realism. (Other applications of virtual space, such as data visualization exist, but not widely accepted understanding of virtual space in that context appears to be currently available.)

5. Videogames prioritize user experience over task completion. In this document, task completion is defined sole by the speed by which a task can be completed. (Unlike users of Microsoft Word, videogame players often enjoy crashes, provided the crash is accompanied by a colorful explosion.)

6. Prioritizing user experience greatly raises the importance of narrative and motivation.

7. Realism is subordinate to narrative and motivation.

8. Realism is a tool (not a goal) and can be used to shape user behavior and understanding within virtual space.

9. Realism and narrative can create a sense of immersion and presence. Immersion like realism is a tool.

10. A virtual equivalent to filmic montage driven by usability and narrative may exist. (A better description, discussion is beyond the scope of this article.)

11. Narrative functions through conventions. Conventions are often arbitrary ·and require user acceptance and understanding to function.

12. Usability (as narrowly defined in this document) functions through inventions. Inventions do not require user acceptance or understanding to function. (Users do not need programming skill or a background in electronics to operate a computer.)

13. Aesthetics link narrative and usability in virtual space. Done well, aesthetics can hide their usability role. (A house with a slanted roof is seen as normal; it fits our existing narrative of what a house should look like. The use of the slant, to channel rain off the roof is known, but in a virtual space, there is no real rain. In *World of Warcraft*, roofs become tied to travel paths, and a travel mode called Falling.)

14. Because videogames support task failure, interaction methods discouraged by HCI scholarship find new life, like multiple modes.

15. Gaining new modes becomes an integral part of long-term play in some types of videogames (i.e., *World of Warcraft*). They

allow for new and greater challenges (as well as past failures) to be overcome.

16. Granting new modes becomes a motivation tool of videogame designers.

17. Videogames become more usable over time. New modes in videogames allow quicker and larger fictional tasks to be completed.

18. Some interactions, while more efficient if immediate are delayed to give opposing forces time to cause failure (Hearthstones - Teleportation). Some delays are also artificially added to mimic a real-world sense of creation or construction time (Casting of a portal or Summoning Spell - Teleportation).

19. Standard HCI practices of limiting user choices and behaviors become intertwined with modes and narrative concepts (i.e., limiting optimal travel speed by forbidding mounted travel modes inside of buildings).

20. Addition of new elements: In videogame worlds abilities are linked to narrative titles and become conventions, often of magic (Hearthstones) or some in game technology (Zeppelins).

21. Subtraction of elements: Rather than add conspicuous new elements to support new behaviors or improve task completion rates, videogames may opt for a removal of unneeded real world elements (Railings, Rooms, Doors).

22. Maintaining the suspended disbelief of the user/player is an important factor in RPG videogames. This factor helps drive the concept of removing unneeded elements rather than adding new elements.

23. Non-story-based, productive, virtual spaces deal with suspended disbelief differently than RPGs or story-based worlds and may not be as affected by aforementioned narrative issues. They can utilize narrative without being bound by narrative.

The larger lesson to be gained from studying videogames may not lie in efficient task comple-
tion and the inventions that promote task completion, but in experience management and exposing the role of narrative conventions. Videogames seek to manage the difficulty of tasks, rather than remove said difficulty. They incorporate motivational, narrative and user experience into their design. Usability issues are present within the videogame world, but the preceding factors change the nature of their application.

Videogames, via their economic and social dominance, play a major role in the development of non-videogame virtual spaces. New users tend to interpret virtual space as a videogame environment. As users become more sophisticated, more accustomed to the broadening variations of interaction within videogame worlds, the ability of non-videogame spaces to utilize those abilities also grows. Players mature and become users and virtual space breaks the grip of game limitations. What may evolve is an outgrowing of many of the narrative, experiential, and/or motivational limits placed on virtual space by the demands of game design. Much like the modern desktop and its ongoing use of narrative labels applied to elements such as files and folders, the power and functionality underlying these digital constructs far outstrips their narrative labels and implied limitations.

For the moment, the speed of this act of growth is open ended and unknown. Current designers of non-videogame virtual spaces may still need to take into account narrative, experiential, and motivational elements in creating their spaces. Standard usability practices still apply, but in lines of conceptual grey, a blurring of the relationship of user experience and task completion is underway.

Further Study, Experience and Completion Conflict

Improvement makes straight roads, but the crooked roads, without Improvement, are roads of Genius.
- William Blake

One subject deserving more research is the resolving the conflict between task completion and user experience. In successful videogames like *World of Warcraft*, user experience and task completion are in harmony as priority is given to user experience. Failure is part of the videogame world. In successful software tools, like Adobe Photoshop or iTunes, user experience and task completion are in harmony, task completion is prioritized. Failure to manipulate an image or download a song is not encouraged by the software. Yet, in designing innovative virtual spaces that are neither pure videogame nor pure software tool, this conflict between task completion and user experience emerges.

A non-travel example is as follows: In a virtual space, one resembling a home, it may be an innovative idea to encode textures that show wear and tear over time. Faded wallpaper and stains on carpet could add to the user experience and sense of immersion in home. Yet if the home serves an innovative purpose, as an interface to images, music, and texts of the user, is the decay of the interface useful? Owners of Adobe Photoshop software are unlikely to support random stains and gradual fading of text and tool icons in the interface. Aside from the developers of Photoshop smirking over the potential sales of a software Sham-Wow to restore the interface's original luster, it is difficult to envision a harmonic compromise.

An example closer to the issue of travel is the casting time for a teleportation spell. Casting time is described as needed to enhance user experience by allowing for the chance task failure. In any non-videogame interface, the addition of time to a user task would seem absurd. Often usability professionals use GOMs (Goals, Objects, and Methods) analyses and constructs like Fitts Law to reduce task completion times. Whenever possible, steps in a task are removed (Hackos & Redish, 1998). In contrast, user experience often adds steps. It is a fundamental conflict, and every user action, every press of a key and move of a cursor has ties to both user experience and task completion.

Videogames, like *World of Warcraft* deftly use narrative to shape a user's expectations for experience and completion of tasks. This role of narrative in the shaping of user expectations and behaviors remains intact in non-game virtual spaces. How this role takes shape remains to be seen.

In non-game systems, the role of task completion in virtual space rises in importance and the usefulness of failure are dialed back. The question that arises is one of true goals and multiple goals inside a single screen. Is reaching the end the goal (task completion) or is the journey to that goal (user experience) of greater importance. The quote by William Blake at the start of this section sets the tone for just how deep this question truly runs. Standard usability like that of a cursor seeks the straight road, while those concerned with user experience in games run avatars along the crooked path. Designing a virtual space for a cursor-avatar that allows for both, an immediate completion of the journey and a compelling experience on the way to that journey's completion is a hefty conceptual problem.

Despite the obvious nature of the conflict between user experience and task, completion the conflict has been hidden academic labels and presumptive application of 2D and 3D forms. The academic label of a virtual interface focuses on task completion. The academic label of virtual environments focuses on user experience. In academic texts, virtual interfaces and virtual environments are considered separate uses of virtual space. They are discussed as separate ideas in different chapters of the same book (Shneiderman & Plaisant, 2004). The truth that virtual space is both interface and environment is lost.

The second factor hiding the conflict between user experience and task completion is the presumptive application of 2D and 3D forms. 3D forms are seen solely as an environment and 2D forms are seen solely as an interface. In videogames like *World of Warcraft*, the interface is seen as all the 2D elements, the window frame of buttons and pop-up menus that surround a 3D environment centered on the screen. Rules of HCI and usability apply to the 2D interface elements while the rules of narrative/storytelling guide the design of the 3D environment. This 2D interface and 3D environment construct is convenient, but very harmful to innovative design. Declaring that 2D and 3D forms can only play certain functions is to say that form leads function. This is untrue, for all creative designers understand that form follow function. In broad terms then, the focus on realistic forms creates a design perspective that limits possibility functionality. Only functions that fit the realistic forms are deemed acceptable, and worse a cycle of failure leads some individuals to assume that only ever more realistic forms and interactions are the solution. Meanwhile, the power of the digital space and the affordances of mouse, keyboard and screen are discarded in favor of faux realism and the user experience of role-playing rather than task completion.

Lastly, if good interfaces are transparent to the task, what does that mean for 3D worlds that strive to be the opposite? The opposite of transparent is immersive, as in the all-surrounding, always present videogame space that guides the users actions as opposed to being the completely interface, wholly subordinate the users wishes. Such questions are difficult to address, but addressed they must be. Academia seems to have lost its leadership position in the design of virtual space. To move forward, hard questions must be answered and the conceptually cowardly hiding in concepts of realism (Manovich, 2001), simulations, and games (Murray, 1997; Nitsche, 2009) must end. To design virtual space, functionality must be understood. Form must again follow function.

REFERENCES

Bazin, A. (1971a). *What is cinema? Vol I.* (H. Gray, Trans.). Berkeley, CA: University Of California Press. (Original Works Published 1940-1955).

Bazin, A. (1971b). *What is cinema? Vol II.* (H. Gray, Trans.). Berkeley, CA: University Of California Press. (Original Works Published 1940-1955).

Bordwell, D. (1985). *Narration in the fiction film.* Madison, WI: University Of Wisconsin Press.

Bordwell, D., Staiger, J., & Thompson, K. (1985). *The classical Hollywood cinema.* New York: Columbia University Press. doi:10.4324/9780203358818

Bowman, D., Kruijff, E., Laviola, J., & Poupyrev, I. (2000, July 23-28). An introduction to 3d user interface design. Paper presented at SIGGRAPH 2000, New Orleans, Louisiana.

Carlson, K., & Guynup, S. (2002). Avatar as content delivery platform. *Future Generation Computer Systems, 17,* 65–71.

Carroll, N. (1985). The power of movies. *Daedalus, 114,* 79–103.

Comolli, J. (1996). Machines of the visible. In Druckrey, T. (Ed.), *Electronic culture: technology and visual representation* (pp. 109–117). New York: Aperture Books.

Cornett, S. (2004, April 24-29). The usability of massively multiplayer online roleplaying games: Designing for new users. In *Proceedings of the SIGCHI conference on Human factors in computing systems (SIGCHI 2004),* Vienna, Austria (Vol. 6, pp. 703-710). New York: ACM Publishing.

Csikszentmihalyi, M. (2001). *Flow: The psychology of optimal experience.* New York: Harpers & Row.

Gelernter, D. (1993). *Mirror worlds: Or the day software puts the universe in a Shoebox... how it will happen and what it will mean*. Oxford, UK: Oxford University Press.

Gentner, D., & Nielson, J. (1996). The anti-mac interface. *Communications of the ACM, 39*(6), 70–82. doi:10.1145/232014.232032

Grove, J., & Williams, H. (1998). Explorations in virtual history. In Monteith, M. (Ed.), *IT for learning enhancement*. Lisse, The Netherlands: Swets & Zeitlinger.

Heim, M. (1998). *Virtual realism*. Oxford, UK: Oxford University Press.

Heim, M. (2001). The avatar and the power grid. *Mots Pluriels, 19*(2001).

Jorgenson, A. (2004, October 23-27). Marrying HCI/usability and computer games: A preliminary look. In *Proceedings of the third Nordic conference on Human-computer interaction (NordiCHI 2004)*, Tampere, Finland (Vol. 82, pp. 393-396). New York: ACM Publishing.

Juul, J. (2005). *Half real*. Boston: MIT Press.

Laurel, B. (1994). Placeholder: Landscape and narrative in virtual environments. *ACM Computer Graphics Quarterly, 28*(2), 118–126. doi:10.1145/178951.178967

Manovich, L. (2001). *The language of new media*. Boston: MIT Press.

Murray, J. (1997). *Hamlet on the holodeck: The future of narrative in cyberspace*. Boston: MIT Press.

Nitsche, M. (2009). *Video game spaces: Image, play, and structure in 3d worlds*. Boston: MIT Press.

Pagulayan, R. J., Keeker, K., Wixon, D., Romero, R., & Fuller, T. (2003). User-centered design in games. In Jacko, J., & Sears, A. (Eds.), *Handbook for human-computer interaction in interactive systems* (pp. 883–906). Hillsdale, NJ: Erlbaum.

Pausch, R. (1994, April). What HCI designers can learn from video game designers. In *Proceedings of the Conference on Human Factors in Computing Systems (SIGCHI 1994)*. Boston, MA (pp.177-178). New York: ACM Publishers.

Poupyrev, I. (2000, July 23-28). 3D manipulation techniques. In the *Course Notes of the 27th International Conference on Computer Graphics and Interactive Technologies (SIGGRAPH 2000)*, New Orleans, LA.

Rouse, R. (2001). *Game design–theory and practice*. Sudbury, MA: Jones and Bartlett.

Shneiderman, B. (2003). Why not make interfaces better than 3D reality? *IEEE Computer Graphics and Applications, 23*(6), 12–15. doi:10.1109/MCG.2003.1242376

Shneiderman, B., & Plaisant, C. (2004). *Designing the user interface: Strategies for effective human-computer interaction*. Reading, MA: Addison Wesley.

Sutcliffe, A., Ryan, M., Doubleday, A., & Springet, M. (2000). Model mismatch analysis: Towards a deeper explanation of users' usability problems. *Behaviour & Information Technology, 19*(1), 43–55. doi:10.1080/014492900118786

Tan, D., Robertson, G., & Czerwinski, M. (2001). Exploring 3D navigation: Combining speed-coupled flying with orbiting. *SIGCHI'01, 3*(1), 418-425.

ENDNOTE

1. Additional support provided by Vizzini, Goonie, and members of my *World of Warcraft* guild, Corrupted Destiny on Skywall Server. A short discussion of a early draft of this paper can be found at http://corrupted-destiny.guildportal.com.

2. *Noob* or *Newbie*. Any player new to the game. Some players consider it an insulting term (*World of Warcraft* Game Manual, Blizzard Entertainment, 2006).

This work was previously published in International Journal of Gaming and Computer-Mediated Simulations, Volume 2, Issue 2, edited by Richard E. Ferdig, pp. 57-76, copyright 2010 by IGI Publishing (an imprint of IGI Global).

Chapter 10
Effects of Built-in Audio versus Unrelated Background Music on Performance in an Adventure Role-Playing Game

Siu-Lan Tan
Kalamazoo College, USA

John Baxa
Kalamazoo College, USA

Matthew P. Spackman
Brigham Young University, USA

ABSTRACT

This article presents an empirical study of the role of video game audio on performance. Twenty participants played The Legend of Zelda: Twilight Princess on the Wii console for a 45-minute session on five consecutive days. Employing a repeated measures design, the authors exposed players to one orientation session and four sound conditions, i.e., silence, remote control sounds, remote control and screen sounds, and unrelated music played on a boom-box, in a counterbalanced order. Performance was weakest when playing without sound, increasingly stronger with audio emitted by remote control only, and by remote-and-screen respectively. Surprisingly, the highest scores were earned when playing with music that was unrelated to players' actions or events unfolding on screen. These findings point to the challenges of processing multisensory cues during the initial stages of an elaborate role-playing game, and suggest that the most effective players swiftly develop strategies incorporating task-relevant information conveyed by both sound and images.

DOI: 10.4018/978-1-4666-0029-4.ch010

INTRODUCTION

Video game audio has come a long way since the bleeps and blips of pioneering games such as *Pong* (Atari, 1972). In particular, as sound design has advanced, the player has taken on an increasingly active role with respect to video game audio. Gamers must decipher cues in the musical score for information about the surrounding environment, and listen for sound effects such as footsteps, which situate the player within the virtual environment. Audio cues alert players to approaching danger, guide them in tracking the moment-to-moment location of enemies, and give immediate feedback on successful execution of actions. Sound can be used to communicate aspects of the narrative, enhance immersion, and convey emotion (Zehnder & Lipscomb, 2006). An increasing number of consoles and games also allow players to select from various musical soundtracks (e.g., *de Blob*, Blue Tongue Entertainment, 2008) or to incorporate music entirely of their own choice into the gameplay (e.g., *Project Gotham Racing 4*, Bizarre Creations, 2007). This introduces another sort of control of sound by the player, though this music is not linked to the player's actions or events occurring in the game.

Despite video game audio's growing relevance in game design and the wealth of information that it can convey, few empirical studies have examined the role of sound on players' performance and game experience (Collins, 2007; Hébert, Béland, Dionne-Fournelle, Crête, & Lupien, 2005; Tafalla, 2007). In order to address this important gap in the empirical literature, the present study explores the effects of built-in video game audio and unrelated background music on players' performance and quality of gaming experience in *Twilight Princess* for the Wii console.

The Wii Console and 'The Legend of Zelda'

The Nintendo Wii console was first released in 2006 and gained immediate and widespread popularity. The Wii console's use of a simplified interface capitalized on a market saturated with sophisticated, but specialized, consoles. In turn, it has allowed many players to access games previously perceived as too difficult to play.

A unique feature of the Wii console's interface is that its controller relies on kinetic-gestural movements for input. Moving the controller a certain way seems to cause the avatar on the screen to enact the same motion. For instance, in *The Legend of Zelda: Twilight Princess* (Nintendo, 2006), the player moves the Wii remote as if it were a sword - compared to previous gaming consoles, which relied exclusively on button input. The Wii remote also features a small speaker, which can emit a variety of sounds that are linked to the kinetic gestures of the player – such as 'swooshes' and 'slashes' when handling the remote as a sword. This extends the interactive element of the Wii remote to include both movement and sound.

The Nintendo Wii console hosts one of the latest installments of *The Legend of Zelda*, a widely popular game series. *The Legend of Zelda* series debuted in 1986, and introduced a novel gaming experience. The series features non-linear explorative play focusing on puzzles and problem-solving, rather than a strict point-based system. The player moves about freely in the environment along any routes and can accumulate any of a wide selection of items along the way. The game series' creator, Shigeru Miyamoto, wanted to create an experience in which players try to complete an adventure rather than simply aim to earn the highest possible score (Vestal, O'Neill, & Shoemaker, 2008). The original game provided a template for other non-linear games and has been credited as one of the inspirations for the creation of the genre of Role-Playing Games or RPGs (Long, 2000).

Another defining characteristic of the series is its pervasive use of music and especially the inclusion of music into its game play, for example as audio cues for the player. In particular, one of the later games in the series - *The Legend of Zelda: Ocarina of Time* (Nintendo, 1998) – was the first non-music game to significantly incorporate music-making into its structure (McDonald, 2008). In addition to its use of sound effects and music to convey meaning to the player, the game also uses distinctive musical ideas as a tool for solving puzzles. Characters in the game are linked to specific themes, and players must recognize these characters' musical themes (*leitmotifs*) to successfully interact with the virtual environment. Specific regions of the virtual world also have their own *leitmotifs*, and musical ideas similar to them are associated with characters belonging to those regions. In one puzzle, for instance, players have to navigate a forest maze by following the melody played by a character hidden at the end of the maze. The melody serves not only as the *leitmotif* for this character, but is interwoven into the bass line of the overarching theme for the forest area. By using music in both a cinematic and interactive fashion, *Ocarina of Time* broke ground for non-music games, and cemented the central role of music in the series.

Music and other sounds are also richly incorporated into *The Legend of Zelda: Twilight Princess* (Nintendo, 2006), the game used in the present study. The most recent in *The Legend of Zelda* series at the time of this study, *Twilight Princess* incorporates two forms of dynamic sound in video games (interactive audio and adaptive audio), as described by Collins (2007). Specifically, the musical cues that signify that the player has accomplished an important goal (as opposed to a more ordinary task), and the rising pitch and loudness of the sounds of successful sword attacks on an enemy (compared to the dull 'thuds' a player hears for unsuccessful attacks) are examples of *interactive audio* (i.e., sounds in response to the actions of the player). The interactive audio in this game ranges from localized sound effects (e.g., digging a hole, locking onto an enemy with one's targeting system) to global shifts of mood and intensity in the musical score as the avatar moves through the virtual environment. There is also the use of *adaptive audio*, triggered by changes within the game. For instance, the dawning of a new day (within the world of *Twilight Princess*) is always accompanied by the main musical theme. In addition, the motion-sensitive Wii remote also incorporates *kinetic-gestural audio interaction* into the game play, in which the player "bodily participates with the sound" (Collins, 2007, p. 268). For example, when a player uses specific items (such as a sword, a bow and arrow, or a bottle) or attacks as a wolf, the remote will emit sounds corresponding with the actions the player performs with it. Table 1 provides many examples of audio cues that can aid the player in completion of tasks and successful navigation of the virtual environment of a few levels of *Twilight Princess*.

Clearly, there are numerous sources and functions of sound in video games (see Collins, 2007; Stockburger, 2003 for useful typologies). Interpreting these dynamic cues while in the flow of an unfamiliar game can be a demanding task. Further, following a 'situation-oriented' view of auditory processing, "auditory comprehension is oriented towards interpreting sounds in terms of *events* instead of in terms of *objects*" (Jørgensen, 2008b, p. 3, emphases added). Thus, particularly in the elaborate fictional world of the adventure RPG, most sounds cannot be interpreted in isolation but only with the *intrinsic knowledge* gained from experience within the 'world' of a particular game (Rollings & Adams, 2003). Some changes in sound, such as the difference between successful or unsuccessful sword strikes, give players feedback that can help fine-tune their actions in an intuitive fashion as they draw on *extrinsic knowledge* outside the world of the game. However, the ability to distinguish between an auditory cue signaling the arrival of an enemy or ally, or to recognize the *leitmotif* for a character or a

Table 1. Examples of Audio Cues in Selected Levels of 'Twilight Princess'

Levels and Tasks	Description of Sound/Facilitation of Task Completion
Forest Temple: (Episode 1 in study)	Monkey claps/squeaks near correct path Enemies' movements make sounds alerting players to presence Non-diegetic music changes with the presence of an enemy and when player enters battle Successful attacks on enemies sound different than unsuccessful ones Midna giggles near altar to alert player to in-game hint Monkey squeaks in fear near enemies Captured monkeys squeak to alert player to their location Sound of bomb's fuse increases in speed when bomb is close to exploding Ook's weapon makes sound when it is headed towards player Ook's weapon makes sound when it allows smaller enemies to attack player Music changes to 'Heroes' Theme' when Ook is in vulnerable state
Eldin Province: (Episode 2 in study)	Enemies' movements make sounds alerting players to presence Non-diegetic music changes with the presence of an enemy and when player enters battle If player leaves one Twilit Messenger alive, then the Messenger shrieks, bringing others back to life Enemies' movements make sounds alerting players to presence – despite being invisible Midna giggles near areas of interest, allowing them to access important areas When house is on fire, non-diegetic music turns frantic, suggesting danger by staying in the house Sound of horse grows louder as horse draws near As horse's strength returns, sound accompanies visual cues
Goron Mines: (Episode 3 in study)	Lava pillars make sound as they rise, allowing players to dodge/time attempts to jump Switches have timers that increase in speed as switch is about to turn off Successful attacks on enemies sound different than unsuccessful ones Stone slab makes sound as it moves, allowing players to see if they have time to get past it Sound of Iron Boot footsteps change when on magnetic surfaces, helping player recognize they are successfully attached Sound of crane's movement alerts player to its approach Switches have timers that increase in speed as door is about to close Before Beamos attack, they make a sound, allowing player to dodge Enemies' movements and attacks make sounds alerting players to presence
Sacred Grove: (Episode 4 in study)	Z-Targeting makes 'lock sound' onto appropriate part of bridge Skull Kid plays melody from a horn, and this melody can be heard in the rooms the Skull Kid is in Skull Kid's horn blares when he summons enemies to attack you Enemies' movements and attacks make sounds alerting players to presence Non-diegetic music changes with the presence of an enemy and when player enters battle If player leaves one Twilit Messenger alive, then the Messenger shrieks, bringing others back to life Successful attacks on enemies sound different than unsuccessful ones

zone, for instance, is highly contextualized within the game's matrix. It requires great skill to detect fine changes and decipher their meanings while solving lateral-thinking puzzles – especially if these 'clues' are not also provided visually.

Video Game Audio and Performance

The sparse empirical research on the effects of video game audio on performance and various aspects of the game experience has yielded mixed results. Tafalla (2007) reported that male partici-

pants playing the game *DOOM* (id Software, 1993) with the soundtrack scored almost twice as many points, compared to those playing without sound. The soundtrack to this game consists of chilling music that closely mirrors onscreen events, and the sounds of weapons, heavy breathing, and screams. Male participants also experienced greater arousal in the sound condition, as indicated by increased heart rate. Playing the game with the sound track led to more stress in female participants, as measured by systolic and diastolic blood pressure. Similarly, Hébert, Béland, Dionne-Fournelle, Crête, and Lupien (2005) examined the effects of the musical soundtrack (i.e., techno music that was built into the game) on stress levels while playing *Quake III* (id Software, 1999). Significantly higher cortisol levels, indicating higher stress, were found for participants playing the game with music than those playing in silence. Hébert et al. (2005) switched off all sound effects in both the music and silent conditions, and thus their study demonstrated that music alone can contribute significantly to stress levels while playing a video game.

Yamada, Fujisawa, and Komori (2001) asked participants to play a car racing game accompanied by the music that was built into the game, several other pieces of music selected by the experimenters, or in a silent condition. In contrast to Tafalla's (2007) finding that the presence of music dramatically boosted performance, Yamada et al. (2001) found that the presence of some music (including the original musical soundtrack of the game) had a negative effect on performance. In particular, "dark, agitated" music tended to lead to the weakest performance, and seemed to interfere most with gamers' ability to concentrate on the race. The best scores, as measured by lap time, were earned in the *silent* condition.

Another study by Wolfson and Case (2000) examined the effects of background color (red/blue) and loudness of the video game audio (loud/soft) in a simple experimenter-designed game. While loudness of the audio alone had little impact, participants gave significantly higher ratings in response to the question 'Do you think you played well?' after sessions combining a red background paired with loud audio. However, this was based only on the perception of having played more successfully. Analyses of the actual performance scores yielded only a main effect of color, with less errors being made when playing with red background (regardless of sound level).

The games used in Tafalla (2007) and Hébert et al.'s (2005) studies were First-Person Shooters, in which the player takes on the role of an avatar who must navigate elaborate environ-

ments in search of a several enemies who must be defeated by employing a number of different strategies, similar to Role-Playing and Adventure games. In comparison, Wolfson and Case's (2000) game involved hitting a ball with a paddle, and Yamada et al.'s (2001) driving game was based on the singular goal of completing laps as quickly as possible. Thus, complexity of task may be an important variable mediating the effects of sound and music on performance.

While several studies have examined the effects of alternating soundtracks or switching sound on and off, few have employed subtler manipulations of video game audio – for example, separating sound effects from music. Nacke, Grimshaw, and Lindley (2010) separated diegetic sound (that is, sounds originating from the fictional universe within the game environment, such as audio linked to characters and objects) from the non-diegetic musical soundtrack of the first-person shooter game *Half-Life 2* (Valve Corporation, 2004). The presence of diegetic sound led to higher ratings of game experience such as positive affect, competence, immersion, challenge, and lower ratings of negative affect. The presence of the musical soundtrack in addition to diegetic sound led to lower ratings for flow experience, and to the highest ratings for feelings of tension. In another study by Lipscomb and Zehnder (2005), participants playing the *Lord of the Rings: The Two Towers* (Stormfront Studios, 2002) with the musical soundtrack and sound effects that accompany the game rated the overall game experience as more colorful, more dangerous, less relaxed, and less simple than those who played it with the sound effects alone.

Similarly, few researchers have focused on the effects of music that is not built into the game. For instance, recent research by Cassidy and MacDonald (2009) addressed the effects of self-selected music tracks on performance in video games, in which participants were asked to bring their own CDs to listen to while playing a game. The researchers exposed each participant to one of five different levels of sound while playing a driving video game: silence, car-only sounds, self-selected music brought in by the participants, and experimenter-selected music, which were divided into two levels of arousal (high and low). Cassidy and MacDonald found that self-selected music significantly improved performance (e.g., fewer driving errors, faster race times), and players' gaming experience (e.g., enjoyment of the driving experience). They also noted that high-arousal experimenter-selected music had an adverse effect on players, and performances suffered as a result. In their study, the sound effects of the car were present in all music conditions, so these findings can be attributed to differences in the music alone.

As apparent from the studies we have discussed, different video game genres vary with respect to how sound is incorporated into the game, and therefore also the degree to which the player can control the audio. Zehnder and Lipscomb (2006) coded 159 games from different genres according to the options they offer players to control elements of sound, such as volume controls for sound effects and music, and whether the musical soundtrack can be selected from a playlist. They found that Racing/Driving and Simulation genres are more likely to allow players to control sound effects and music than Action/Adventure and Role-Playing Game (RPGs) genres. The lack of control over music and absence of popular music in RPGs and Action/Adventure games suggests that customized, built-in music for those games is more central to the gameplay – with greater use of interactive and adaptive audio, and sometimes also kinetic-gestural audio interaction – than in other genres. Findings from studies employing First-Person Shooters (e.g., Hébert et al., 2005; Nacke et al., 2010; Tafalla, 2007) also suggest that sound that is internal to the game may play a more important role in contributing to players' excitement and successful gaming experience in genres comparable to the RPG or Action/Adventure genres than Driving/Racing games.

The Present Study

The few scattered studies in this area point to the need for further research in order to better understand the role of sound on performance and the gaming experience. To this end, the present study examines the effects of built-in audio supplied by the game and superfluous background music on players' performance and the quality of their gaming experience while playing the adventure role-playing game, *The Legend of Zelda: Twilight Princess* (2006) on the Nintendo Wii console. Specifically, our conditions were: game play accompanied by sound from the television screen and speakers in the remote control (i.e., normal playing conditions), remote control sounds only, silence, and unrelated background music played on a boombox (not linked to the player's actions or the events unfolding on the screen).

Our study extends the present literature by employing an adventure role-playing game, a genre that has not received much attention in previous research addressing video game audio. More importantly, our study compares the effects of (1) built-in video game audio that is *contingent on* the player's actions and events on the screen (such as sounds of sword slashes, auditory warnings of approaching enemies, and music that signals that one is entering a new territory within the virtual environment), and (2) a musical soundtrack that is *unrelated* to the player's actions or to events unfolding in the game (therefore referred to as *Non-contingent* Music). While previous studies have compared sound conditions versus silence, it is not known whether the player is really integrating the moment-by-moment audio cues and feedback into their game play, or whether the mere absence of silence is sufficient to influence performance and overall quality of the game experience. By providing two conditions (silence, and non-contingent music) to compare to playing conditions with built-in audio provided by the game, we may gain greater insight into whether it is the contingent and interactive nature of video game audio that accounts for differences in performance or perceptions of the game, or whether an irrelevant musical backdrop is sufficient to affect performance and the subjective experience of a game. Finally, the innovation of the Wii console allowed to study the effects of video game sound in a context in which kinetic-gestural audio interaction plays a more prominent role than in games used in previous studies. Specifically, the Wii console's controller provides an added dimension of video game audio by emitting sounds linked to the movements of the player. This enabled us to examine if avatar-specific sounds emitted by the Wii remote alone (e.g., sword slashes in conjunction with the player's and avatar's movements) can affect performance or game experience.

Given the rich variety of audio cues supplied by this game (as shown previously in Table 1), and a few studies indicating that auditory cues may facilitate performance in more complex or elaborate video games (e.g., Nacke et al., 2010; Tafalla, 2007), we predicted that decreasing levels of built-in video game sound in *Twilight Princess* would lead to a corresponding decrease in performance scores and ratings for the quality of the gaming experience. The effects of the (non-contingent) unrelated background music are harder to predict. As the music is not contingent on player's actions or events within the game, its presence may have little or no effect on facilitating performance. Alternatively, music could affect performance by serving as a distraction (e.g., Yamada et al., 2001), or by optimizing performance (e.g., Cassidy & MacDonald, 2009).

METHOD

Participants

A total of 23 participants took part in the study. Twelve were Kalamazoo College undergraduates (mean age = 20.13 years, SD = 1.47), 10 were Brigham Young University undergraduates (mean

age = 23.73 years, SD = 1.57), and one was a high school senior (age = 18.0 years). Only 20 participants were included in the final sample as three participants from BYU were dropped because they failed to complete at least one cluster of tasks in a play session. All others completed at least one cluster during every play session. The dropped participants were replaced with two students from Kalamazoo College and one high school senior. As sex was not a variable of interest in the present study, and as previous studies have found distinct differences in frequency of playing among males and females when employing convenience samples (e.g., see Grimshaw, Lindley, & Nacke, 2008), we included only males in this study.

Participants were recruited through e-mails and campus postings and carefully screened for several criteria. Specifically: (1) Participants had to have some familiarity with role-playing games and with the Wii console in order to qualify for the study. Otherwise, they may have struggled with the gameplay and found it difficult to advance. (2) In order to most clearly see the effects of removing audio cues during play, we wanted to observe participants who were exploring a new virtual environment and solving puzzles they had never encountered before. Therefore, potential recruits were excluded if they had ever played or observed somebody else playing *Twilight Princess* prior to participating in this study.

Prequestionnaire: A pre-questionnaire revealed that more than half of the participants (n= 13) spent two to 10 hours playing video games on a weekly basis. The participants did not play RPGs often, and most (n = 14) reported playing RPGs for less than four hours a week. However, all 20 participants in the final sample were familiar with *The Legend of Zelda* series, and had played an average of 3.63 of the 14 available games at the time of the study. The participants' level of experience with the *Legend of Zelda* series ranged from three participants who had played zero games to one participant who had played 11 games. They also had limited experience with the Wii. The majority (*n* = 13) reported that they spent less than two hours weekly playing the Wii console. Given the variability of experience with the Wii and with this series, it was important to employ a method that accounts for individual differences in participants' levels of experience. Our repeated measures design enabled us to account for these differences, as discussed in our description of the procedure.

Stimuli and Apparatus

Console and game. The game selected was *The Legend of Zelda: Twilight Princess* (Nintendo, 2006) for the Wii console. Five 'episodes'[1] were used: 'Gerudo Desert,' 'Forest Temple,' 'Eldin Province Under Twilight,' 'Goron Mines,' and 'Sacred Grove/Temple of Time.' 'Gerudo Desert' was used as a practice session. All other sessions were played in the experimental conditions. The participants played as the character Link, the series' human protagonist, for all sessions. In 'Eldin Province under Twilight,' 'Sacred Grove/Temple of Time,' and 'Gerudo Desert,' players could also play as a wolf. These levels were selected for their linear structure, the ease with which they allowed us to examine players' performance and their graduated levels of difficulty. As shown previously in Table 1, each level also incorporates a rich variety of audio cues. Table 2 provides descriptions of the episodes and examples of objectives given to participants. All sessions were played on a Nintendo Wii Entertainment System connected to an INSIGNIA NS-LCD19 LCD Television.

Sound and music. The sound used in the Full Sound and Partial Sound conditions consisted of the audio that is built into the game, emitted by the screen and/or the Wii remote. The music for the non-contingent sound condition consisted of short digital compositions from the musical soundtrack of *Twilight Princess*, taken from excerpts not corresponding to the levels included in our study. (All sound and music materials are described in detail in the 'Experimental Sessions'

section and Appendix A). The compact disc was played on a SONY CFD-G55 CD-radio cassette recorder placed under the television set.

Measures

Performance. Scoring guides were constructed to measure participants' progress and ability to respond effectively to the demands of the game while they played. The measures consisted of (1) the number of tasks completed, (2) the speed of task completion, (3) number of hits on the player that incurred damage, and (4) the number of 'continues' players were forced to use (as explained below). Point scores were assigned for the successful completion of tasks (arranged, for convenience, into *clusters of tasks*). Participants also received points for how quickly they completed each task (referred to as *time points* in this study). The number of times players fell or were damaged by enemies, obstacles, traps, or environmental dangers resulted in points being subtracted from a set number of points allotted for *hits*. Finally, whenever a player lost all available life force in the game and was therefore forced to use a '*continue*', a point penalty was incurred.

Many games use the number of tasks completed, speed of level completion and amount of hits taken to define a player's success, and our measures reflected these prevalent gameplay features. The game's audio was also intertwined with these measures (e.g., a set of rising tones to accompany the collection of key items, a clicking timer to inform the player of how long they have to complete a task or loud warnings when too many hits have left a player near 'death'). Examining performance through these measures allowed us not only to quantify participants' success while completing a level, but also to assess the degree to which participants were able to complete the challenges of a virtual environment efficiently and unscathed across the different sound conditions.

Post-game questionnaire. A questionnaire was constructed to assess the overall quality of the player's gaming experience, and was administered after each session. The 30-item post-game questionnaire consisted of continuous rating scales for telepresence, focused attention, time distortion, and flow, adapted from measures used in previous studies (as shown in Appendix B). In addition, the researchers asked questions on enjoyment of the session and self-appraisal of performance, and created scales for control and effectance, and identification with avatar and emotion. Each scale consisted of a line of 140 mm, with labels such as 'Strongly Disagree' and 'Strongly Agree' on either side. During coding, two research assistants measured the distance from the leftmost end of the scale to the 'X' marked by the participants.

Procedure and Design

The procedure employed a repeated measures design, with each participant completing one orientation session and playing the game in four experimental conditions in four subsequent sessions. In a repeated measures design, each participant serves as his or her own control because the design allows for the effects of each experimental condition to be seen within a single participant. In this way, we can separate the effects of experimental condition from individual differences. In addition, because repeated measures designs result in more data points per participant, sample sizes can be relatively small and still provide sufficient statistical power. We controlled for potential carryover effects by employing a Latin squares design that counterbalanced the order of the experimental conditions across participants, as described in more detail in our Experimental Sessions section.

Each participant was run individually in a small laboratory equipped with a television, a small boombox, and a comfortable couch. As our laboratory is a relatively sound-proofed 'room within a room' located in a building that was usually vacant during the sessions, there was little to no ambient noise. Each session was approximately one hour

in length, thus sessions for the full sample took a total of over 100 hours to run.

Practice session. The first of the five sessions was a practice meeting. Participants played for 45 minutes with audio from the television and the Wii remote (i.e., in normal playing conditions). They were informed that involvement in all sessions would automatically enter them in a tournament, and that the winner would receive a new copy of the *Twilight Princess* game and 50 dollars cash. (Because our participants were required to complete a practice session and four experimental sessions, there was risk of participant fatigue and attrition. We developed the tournament methodology to help avoid fatigue, as an incentive to complete all sessions and to motivate participants to play competitively as they would in a real-world setting). Participants also completed a pre-questionnaire to assess their previous video game experience, and signed an agreement stating that they would not play *Twilight Princess* or consult strategy guides for this game until the study was completed. After the practice meeting, the participants returned to the lab for four experimental sessions on four consecutive days.

Experimental sessions. The four experimental conditions will be referred to as Full Sound, Partial-Sound, No Sound, and Non-contingent Music:

1. The Full Sound condition featured *Twilight Princess* with audio from both the television and the Wii remote (i.e., normal playing conditions). The full range of game audio includes sounds emitted by the *remote* such as sounds of weapons (e.g., when using the remote as a sword), sounds made when playing as the wolf character (jumping, attacking), and sounds of a character (Midna) giggling, serving as a cue to inform the player of access points to important areas. In addition, the *television screen* sounds double some of the remote sounds, and also adds a rich musical score that responds to the player's actions, some music linked to

certain items, and ambient sounds in the virtual environment. Thus the video game audio richly encompasses interactive, adaptive, and kinetic-gestural audio as described by Collins (2007) in our previous discussion. (A catalogue of built-in audio cues for the levels used in the study is provided in Table 1 in our introduction).

2. The Partial-Sound condition involved playing the video game with audio from the Wii remote only (emitting the sounds as described above).

3. The No Sound condition had no audio at all.

4. In the Non-contingent Music condition, participants played the video game accompanied by music playing in the background on a boom-box, *without any audio from the television screen or the Wii remote corresponding to their actions or events unfolding in the game.* The music consisted of short digital compositions (orchestral music, without lyrics) from the musical soundtrack of *Twilight Princess* (Minegishi, Ohta, & Kondo, 2006; also available at http://www.thehylia.com/soundtrack-tp.php). Six of the tracks – *not related to any of the levels used in the study* - were looped on a 60-minute compact disc in the order shown in Appendix A. Music that was metrically regular and repetitive in thematic material, with few abrupt changes in tempo, key, or dynamics, was selected so that it would not be distracting to players. No sound effects were included in the music.

The pairing of the sound conditions with the four game levels for each of the 20 participants was determined by a Latin Square design (Box, Hunter, & Hunter, 1978). Specifically, the order in which each participant experienced the four sound conditions was counterbalanced with game level across the 20 participants. It should be noted, however, that the order of the game levels (or 'episodes') for the experimental sessions stayed consistent due to the graduated scheme of the episodes.

Before every experimental session, participants were reminded of the tournament and encouraged to do their best. They were also told: "During these 4 sessions, you may sometimes be playing under special conditions. If you notice anything different today, don't stop - just keep playing." Researchers also collected participants' time-keeping devices so they would not be able to keep track of time while playing.

Participants played for 45 minutes per session. Researchers sat behind participants to observe game play without distracting them. If players lost all their 'life,' they were instructed to use a 'continue' and keep playing. Players were also given a hint if they spent longer than 22.5 minutes on a task. After participants completed each session each day, they filled out the post-game questionnaire. As they were leaving, researchers made seemingly casual remarks such as, "By the way - I think you're somewhere towards the top so far." This bogus feedback was used as an equalizer, with the intention that players' perceptions of how they were doing in relation to others would be somewhat similar and to motivate them to continue to do their best. After the final session, participants also ranked the four experimental sessions based on perceived duration of the play period, and were individually debriefed.

RESULTS

Previous Gaming Experience and Overall Rankings

Only one item in the pre-questionnaire addressing participants' previous video game experience was found to serve as a reliable predictor for overall ranking and overall score for the 20 participants included in the study. The number of games previously played in the *Legend of Zelda* series was the only reliable predictor for overall ranking, $r(20)$

= -.60, p <.01, and overall score (grand sum of performance scores for all four episodes), $r(20)$ =.59, p <.01. In other words, the more *Legend of Zelda* games a participant had played before, the closer to rank 1 (top score) and the higher the overall score. The number of hours spent playing other role-playing games, playing Nintendo Wii, and playing video games in general, were not significantly correlated with overall ranking or overall score.

Effects of Sound Manipulation

Performance measures. A one-way repeated measures analysis of variance was run for each performance measure, with sound condition as the within-subjects factor. Surprisingly, no significant effects were found for sound condition on total performance points, time points, cluster points, or hit points. (No effects for order of exposure to the sound conditions were found in this or any of the analyses conducted). The performance scores were run as raw scores and also converted into ordinal data, and neither analysis yielded significant results.

The only significant finding for sound condition was for the number of 'continues' used during play, $F(3, 57) = 3.34$, p <.026. As a continue allows a gamer to keep playing when one would otherwise have run out of power and would have had to quit the game, this is an important finding. As shown in Table 3 and as predicted, most continues were requested in the No Sound condition ($M = 2.6$, $SD = 2.21$, range = 0 to 7), followed by Partial-Sound ($M = 2.1$, $SD = 1.41$, range = 0 to 5), and then Full Sound condition ($M = 1.45$, $SD = 1.67$, range = 0 to 5). Surprisingly, however, participants used the least number of continues in the Non-contingent Music condition ($M = 1.0$, $SD = 1.52$, range = 0 to 6).

Recalculated performance data. Because the number of 'continues' varied with sound condition, we computed the *number of clusters* (i.e., groups of tasks) completed and the *amount of*

Table 3. Effects of sound condition on performance measures

Sound Condition	Total Score		Time Points		Cluster Points		Hit Points		Number of Continues Used	
	Mean	SD	Mean	SD	Mean	SD	Mean	SD	Mean	SD
Full Sound	227.43	90.93	90.13	45.15	116.5	44.49	26.1	9.68	1.45*	1.67
Partial-Sound	232.67	84.5	97.37	37.32	124	43.425	20.5	12.25	2.1*	1.41
No Sound	196.45	85.27	74.845	39.39	103.5	40.82	26.95	8.31	2.6*	2.21
Non-contingent Music	248	92.57	99.25	43.25	128.95	46.07	25.55	13.12	1*	1.52
Total Score	226.14	88.72	90.4	41.73	118.24	43.98	24.78	11.09	1.79	1.805

*p <.05

time played that the participants would have earned without continues. Doing this gives us a more accurate measure of participants' performance in each condition, without the help of extending play when they had already run out of 'life'. The *recalculated number of clusters* was computed by counting all clusters (full and partial) a participant finished until the first continue was used. The *recalculated playing time* was determined by the length of time participants played before using the first continue. Similar to the method used with the *number of clusters* completed, if multiple continues were used during a cluster, then the time taken to complete the cluster was divided by the number of continues used.

One-way repeated measures ANOVAs were run for the *number of clusters* completed and the *amount of time* played (using the recalculated measures, as described above). Sound condition was used as the within-subjects factor. Significant effects were found for both the *number of clusters* completed, $F(3, 57) = 3.17, p < .05$, and the *amount of time* played, $F(3, 57) = 3.7, p < .05$. Surprisingly, participants did best overall in the Non-contingent Music condition, as they completed an average of 2.6 clusters ($SD = .33$) and played an average of 33.3 minutes ($SD = 3.42$ minutes) before using a continue. For clusters completed, participants did next best in the Full Sound condition ($M = 2.05$, $SD = .32$), then in the Partial-Sound condition ($M = 1.64, SD = .24$), and finally in the No Sound condition ($M = 1.36, SD = .29$). Results were similar for time spent playing, as participants played second longest in the Full Sound condition ($M = 30.3$ minutes, $SD = 3.63$). However, participants did play for slightly longer in the No Sound condition ($M = 20.53$ minutes, $SD = 3.84$) than they did in the Partial-Sound condition ($M = 19.405$ minutes, $SD = 2.66$). These findings show that the presence of sound *did* in fact enhance performance with respect to the number of 'continues' needed, and the number of tasks players completed and the amount of time they were able to play before running out of 'life'.

Perception of duration of play. There was also a significant relationship between sound condition and participants' perception of the length of the play sessions. This pertains to the item given to participants at the conclusion of the final session: "Please rank your sessions according to how long they seemed to be (1 = shortest; 4 = longest)." Sound condition had a significant effect on perceived session duration rankings, $\chi^2(19) = 13.56, p = .004$, phi coefficient $= .61$. As expected, participants indicated that the Full Sound sessions seemed shortest to them (Mean Ranking = 1.79), while the No Sound session felt longest (Mean Ranking = 3.32), and the Partial-Sound condition (Mean Ranking = 2.42) and Non-contingent Music condition (Mean Ranking = 2.47) were ranked in between.

Post-game ratings. Finally, there were no significant effects of sound condition on any of the ratings in our post-game questionnaire, which included enjoyment of game, self-appraisal of performance, telepresence, focused attention, time distortion, flow, identification with avatar, and control/effectance. This was largely due to the variability across participants in their ratings of the same sound conditions. That is, participants seemed to differ a great deal from each another in how they experienced each of the sound conditions.

Episode Effects

Of secondary interest to this study was the question of whether performance and aspects of the gaming experience varied with the specific episodes (or levels) of the game. The four episodes used in the experimental sessions are described in Table 2 in our Method section. It should be noted that although sound conditions were carefully counterbalanced between participants, the order of episodes was kept constant (i.e., each participant always played in the order of episode 1 to 4). It would not have been sensible to randomize episodes due to the graduated structure of the levels.

Table 2. Descriptions of video game episodes used in the study

Episode	Description
Episode 0 (Training): Episode 1: Episode 2: Episode 3: Episode 4:	*Gerudo Desert* features the game's protagonist and playable character, Link, exploring a large desert, bandit camp, and abandoned prison. The only objectives given to players were to learn how to play the game. As players move through the level, they are attacked by sandworms, bandits and skeleton soldiers. Used as the practice level. *Forest Temple* features Link exploring the first dungeon of the game, which is a temple in the forest. The main objectives given to players were to save all the monkeys and defeat Ook the Bad Baboon. Eight monkeys are imprisoned and scattered throughout the temple and after rescuing monkeys, the monkeys begin to assist players in accessing new areas and finding secrets. *Eldin Province under Twilight* features Link, in wolf form, exploring a mountain village trapped in twilight. Twilight causes the village to appear dark and transforms local creatures into enemies. The main objectives for players were to remove the influence of twilight by locating invisible twilit insects and defeating them. Special instructions were given to participants on how to perform a long-range jump that could not be practiced in earlier sessions. *Goron Mines* features Link exploring a forge inside an active volcano. The main objectives for players were to locate key shards carried by Goron elders and defeat Dangoro the Goron, a large guard that protects one of the treasures in the level. There are multiple traps throughout the level, which can be deactivated temporarily. While deactivated, a non-diegetic timer sounds to inform the player of how long is left before the trap reactivates. *Sacred Grove/Temple of Time* features Link exploring a hidden forest and temple. The main objectives for players were to locate the skull kid and find the Temple of Time. In order to find the skull kid, the player must look for light emitted from the skull kid's lantern and the music coming from a flute the skull kid plays. The music the skull kid plays is an excerpt from the non-diegetic music playing during the level. Defeating the skull kid allows the player to find the temple.

Performance measures. To reveal any episode effects for performance on the game, a series of one-way, repeated measures analyses of variance were conducted. In each case, one of the performance scores was used as the dependent variable and the episode variable was the independent variable. All tests on performance scores (and subscores) yielded significant results: Total score, $F(3, 57) = 15.01$, $p < .001$, time points, $F(3, 57) = 20.50$, $p < .001$, cluster points, $F(3, 57) = 16.55$, $p < .001$, hit points, $F(3, 57) = 9.12$, $p < .001$, and number of continues, $F(3, 57) = 13.21$, $p < .001$. The means are shown in Table 4. Participants did best in Episode 4 across all performance scores. Participants' next best performance scores occurred during Episode 1 and then Episode 3, although these were reversed for some performance measures. As shown in Table 4, participants tended to score by far the lowest time points and lowest overall performance points and completed the fewest tasks in Episode 2. The higher number of 'hits' (i.e., damage to oneself) and 'continues' also reflect a weak performance for Episode 2.

Potential explanations for the low scores for this episode are addressed in our Discussion section.

Post-game ratings. Episode effects were also found for some measures in the post-game questionnaire assessing the overall quality of participants' gaming experience. Among the main variables of interest in the ratings were our measures of 'telepresence,' or the sense of being more present in the virtual environment than in one's real physical setting. A repeated measures multivariate analysis of variance was conducted, with session as the independent variable and the set of eight telepresence measures (shown in Appendix B) as the dependent variables. A significant multivariate effect was found for telepresence, F approx. $(3, 57) = 1.8$, $p = .018$. Follow-up univariate tests found a significant effect for Question 10, $F(3, 57) = 5.76$, $p = .002$. This item was "While playing, the world created by the game was more real or present for me compared to the 'real world'" (Strongly disagree-Strongly agree). Means for this question steadily rose with each subsequent episode, beginning with episode 1 ($M = 47.65$, $SD = 24.64$). Means continued to increase in

Table 4. Effects of Episodes on Performance Measures

Episode Number	Total Score***		Time Points**		Cluster Points**		Hit Points**		Number of Continues Used**	
	Mean	SD	Mean	SD	Mean	SD	Mean	SD	Mean	SD
Episode 1	248.69	92.34	102.13	42.88	126.25	45.65	24.15	6.34	1.15	1.35
Episode 2	155.66	56.04	52.66	21.95	80.95	25.63	32.2	6.54	3.05	2.16
Episode 3	241.93	82.46	98.525	41.16	127.75	43.54	25.55	8	2.45	1.47
Episode 4	257.27	84.65	108.27	34.31	138	36.97	17.2	15.66	.5	.76

**$p < .001$

episode 2 ($M = 57.65$, $SD = 26.54$) and episode 3 ($M = 67.45$, $SD = 37.74$). Participants' ratings were highest in their final episode of play, episode 4 ($M = 70.25$, $SD = 28.86$). This increase in means across the four sessions suggests that increased interaction with the game over time may heighten the experience of perceiving the virtual world as more real, regardless of factors such as sound.

Other variables of general interest to our study were the 'Control and Effectance' ratings, which referred to the player's perception of their ability to control their avatar and feel that they were a causal agent within the virtual environment. To see what effect episode had on experiencing 'Control and Effectance', a repeated measures multivariate analysis of variance was conducted on the five items in this measure. A Significant multivariate effect for Control and Effectance was found, F approx. $(3, 57) = 2.96$, $p < .001$. Follow-up univariate tests revealed a significant effect for Question 29, $F(3, 57) = 3.83$, $p = .014$. This item was, "While playing, I felt a strong sense of mission or clear goals in mind" (Strongly disagree-Strongly agree). For this question, participants felt that they had the strongest sense of mission in episode 2 ($M = 110$, $SD = 20.08$), followed by Episode 3 ($M = 100.05$, $SD = 17.97$), Episode 1 ($M = 93.1$, $SD = 30.94$), and finally Episode 4 ($M = 87.2$, $SD = 26.5$). This finding is surprising as participants tended to perform worst in Episode 2, but found it to be the episode for which they had the clearest goals. The converse was also found, as participants felt they did not have a strong sense of mission in Episode 4, even though they performed best in that episode. This suggests that having a strong sense of mission or clear set of goals during episodes may be independent of actual performance.

Other Findings

As we were also interested in performance and quality of gaming experience more generally, we conducted additional analyses that did not focus on effects of sound. Due to space constraints, we report only one of our additional findings here.

Enjoyment, self-appraisal, and performance scores. Pearson *r* correlations were conducted with three measures of central importance to video gaming research: enjoyment of the game, self-appraisal of performance, and actual performance (total performance score). Correlations revealed positive relationships between self-appraisal of performance and actual performance, $r(80) = .43$, $p < .001$, and self-appraisal of performance and enjoyment, $r(80) = .67$, $p < .001$. There was also a marginally significant positive relationship between enjoyment and actual performance, $r(80) = .22$, $p = .053$. The positive (though only moderate) relationships between self-appraisal and enjoyment suggest that many gamers are fairly accurate in self-assessments of their own performance (even when given positive bogus feedback), and these assessments are often related to how much they enjoy playing. However, the weaker relationship between enjoyment and actual performance suggests that enjoyment may not always be tied to how well one is playing, and that self-appraisal of performance has a stronger relationship with enjoyment of the game.

DISCUSSION

Our central question on the effects of video game audio on performance and game experience has real-world relevance. Gamers who share living quarters with others often play with the sound off or volume turned down, or with their own or others' music playing in the background. The possible effects of these playing conditions on performance are sure to be on their minds. Further, this question is of interest to game developers and sound designers. How important is video game audio to performance, enjoyment, and the overall experience of a role-playing game such as *Twilight Princess*? Overall, the findings of our study do not suggest any simple relationships

between video game audio and performance or quality of the game experience. As discussed in detail below, what emerged is a picture that is more complex and open to individual variation than we had anticipated.

Effects of Contingent and Non-Contingent Sound on Performance

Our initial analysis revealed only one significant finding for the effects of sound on performance, but it was of central importance. Specifically, participants' use of 'continues' (needed when a player runs out of 'life') varied with sound condition: Participants used the least 'continues' in the Non-contingent Music condition, followed by the Full Sound and Partial-Sound conditions, and used the highest number of 'continues' when playing the game with No Sound. In other words, as the presence of built-in audio decreased, participants were forced to use more 'continues' in order to keep playing, as they made more mistakes and performance faltered when sound cues were not available. At first, we failed to find differences in other performance measures between sound conditions because the 'continues' may have allowed participants to compensate for weak performances. However, when we recalculated the performance data to assess each participant's performance only until the first 'continue' was used, we found that participants completed more tasks and played significantly longer in the Non-contingent Music, followed by Full Sound condition, and finally by Partial-Sound and No Sound conditions (although these last two were reversed for length of play). For instance, participants played an average of 33.3 minutes and 30.3 minutes in the Non-contingent Music and Full Sound conditions, compared to only 19.4 and 20.5 minutes in the Partial-Sound and No Sound conditions, before running out of 'life' and having to use their first 'continue.' These subsequent analyses confirmed that sound *did* indeed facilitate performance, compared to playing in silence (see also Jørgensen, 2008a).

An unexpected and striking finding of this study was that the highest performance scores were not earned in the conditions with built-in audio, but when playing with background music that was *unrelated* to the player's actions or events in the game. Specifically, players earned the highest means for total performance score and most performance subscores, and needed the fewest 'continues' in the Non-contingent Music condition. The music track, played by a boombox underneath the television set, consisted of music from a CD of the original musical soundtrack of *Twilight Princess* (from levels not included in our study, and without any sound effects or other audio cues). As this music was not linked to the actions made with the controller or any events unfolding on screen - and thus provided no audio cues to aid in task completion or guide the player through the virtual environment - one might expect performance scores for playing with non-contingent music to be closer to those for the silent condition. However, these two conditions were the most dissimilar with respect to the performance means.

Though somewhat surprising, this finding is in line with some studies that show that music can enhance performance, most notably in spatiotemporal tasks (e.g., Nantais & Schellenberg, 1999; Rauscher, Shaw, & Ky, 1995). Some studies suggest that preference for the music may also play a role in whether music will enhance performance (e.g., Nantais & Schellenberg, 1999). Accordingly, a study by Cassidy and MacDonald (2008) found that players performed best and reported greatest enjoyment and positive mood change when playing a Wii Star Wars game with music they themselves had chosen, compared with experimenter-selected music or the musical soundtrack provided by the game (see also Cassidy & MacDonald, 2009). Background music may enhance performance through general mechanisms such as modulation of mood or arousal (e.g., Schellenberg, Nakata, Hunter, & Tamato, 2007; Thompson, Schellenberg, & Husain, 2001) and

may therefore have more sweeping effects across different proficiency levels than finer manipulations of video game sound.

Video Game Audio and Cognitive Load

Why did the 'full sound' condition fail to yield the best performance scores? While it provides many cues that facilitate play, video game audio also includes many sound effects and musical features that are not directly relevant to completing tasks – but are added to make the game more interesting or immersive. Information that adds enjoyment or appeal but is conceptually irrelevant has been referred to as 'seductive details' (Garner, Brown, Sanders, & Menke, 1992). As seductive details increase *cognitive load* and compete for limited cognitive resources in working memory while not adding information directly relevant to a task, they can detrimentally affect learning and performance especially in multimedia formats (e.g., see Sweller's (1999)*cognitive load theory*, and Mayer's (2009)*cognitive theory of multimedia learning*).

Another way the 'full sound' condition may have added extraneous cognitive load on the player is by splitting attention, as the participant must resolve audio coming from two spatial locations (remote control and screen), and integrate these cues with visual information on the screen to make them meaningful. Further, there may be a *redundancy effect* due to some overlap between the two sound sources (e.g., sounds made by the avatar's sword and bow-and-arrow are doubled on remote and screen; others are emitted by only one source), and some audio cues double information available in the visual display. Redundant information may add extraneous cognitive load on the working memory of the player (see Leahy, Chandler, & Sweller, 2003, for similar findings in the context of multimedia instruction). This was reflected in our initial performance data based on the entire play sessions (not just counting performance until the first 'continue'). Aside from number of 'continues' used, playing with sound emitted from one source (remote control only) yielded slightly higher overall means for total performance scores, time points, number of tasks completed and avoiding damaging hits than when playing with both screen and remote control sounds. During their first five sessions playing *Twilight Princess*, participants played surprisingly well with minimal sound cues – mainly linked to the actions of the avatar – provided by the remote control alone.

Why did the 'non-contingent' music in our study also not diminish performance by adding 'cognitive load' with the addition of 'seductive' background music? Moreno and Mayer (2000) found that participants learning information presented as animation and narration with background music performed more poorly than those learning by animation and narration alone. Although the music was irrelevant to the task, the learners could not ignore it as important information was also being presented in the auditory mode. Thus irrelevant information competed with task-relevant information for limited resources in auditory working memory. Likewise, Brünken, Plass, and Leutner (2004) found that performance in a dual-task procedure suffered when participants had to process images accompanied by both relevant narration and irrelevant background music, but not when processing only visual information with unrelated background music alone.

This scenario can be compared to the 'full sound' condition in the present study – which included both task-relevant and irrelevant auditory information (that is, useful audio cues, warnings, feedback, and meaningful musical motifs, as well as sound and music features that are added only to make the game more engaging and immersive) – versus the non-contingent background music that was entirely irrelevant to the game. The background music in both Brünken et al.'s (2004) study and our present study may have failed to 'seduce' players' attention away from the game as it could

easily have been 'tuned out' by participants as it conveyed no information relevant to the game play. Brünken and colleagues proposed that "the background music alone does not impose load on auditory working memory, perhaps because – as it contains no relevant information – it is not related to the process of knowledge construction. Therefore, the background music alone has *no cognitive load* implications" (p. 130). On the other hand, the built-in audio in the present study included both task-relevant and irrelevant information, adding a burden to players working at the limits of their cognitive capacities while figuring out a rather complex new game.

Highly arousing music – such as music played at a fast tempo – has also been shown to disrupt performance on driving games (Cassidy & MacDonald, 2009; North & Hargreaves, 1999). One of the authors of the present study (a music researcher) therefore selected tracks from the *Twilight Princess* musical soundtrack that were metrically regular and moderate in tempo, and did not include sharp changes in tempo or loudness, pauses, *staccato*, or other features that draw listeners' attention to music (e.g., see Tan & Kelly, 2004; Tan & Spackman, 2005). As it provided a pleasant and non-distracting stream of continuous sound, the background music in the present study may have been moderately arousing and thus more enhancing to performance than playing in silence (see Roth & Smith, 2008). At the same time, the lack of contingency to the game play meant players did not have to actively attend to the background music track, conserving cognitive resources for the task at hand.

As players get used to a game, cognitive load should be gradually reduced, freeing up attentional resources to allocate to relevant audio cues. Therefore, contingent sound may be increasingly helpful to players as they advance in the game, and we may expect to see performance while playing with full built-in audio to eventually exceed performance while playing with unrelated background music for most players.

Effects of Sound on Quality of Gaming Experience

Surprisingly, no significant effects were found in the present study for sound condition on ratings for enjoyment of game, self-appraisal of performance, telepresence, focused attention, time distortion, flow, identification with avatar, or control and effectance. The wide variances in ratings for the same sound conditions suggest that gamers are not a homogeneous group, but respond differently to the same playing conditions. However, several other studies have suggested that sound can facilitate presence and emotion (Västfjäll, 2003) and perceptions of the overall game experience (e.g., Grimshaw, Lindley, & Nacke, 2008; Nacke, Grimshaw, & Lindley, 2010; Zehnder & Lipscomb, 2006). For instance, Grimshaw et al. (2008) and Nacke et al. (2010) used a Game Experience Questionnaire (recently devised by Ijsselsteijn, Poels, & deKort, 2008, and unavailable at the time of our study). These studies yielded positive effects of presence of sound on aspects of gameplay experience (such as positive affect, competence, immersion, challenge (Nacke et al., 2010)).

It should be noted that in the present study, participants' post-session rankings of perceived duration of sessions showed that No Sound condition felt like it was the longest, whereas the Full Sound condition was perceived to be the shortest session. Thus, there is some indication that participants *may* have been more immersed or absorbed in the game when playing with full sound than when playing in other conditions.

A Comment on Individual Differences

The present study highlights the challenges of processing multisensory cues during the initial stages of playing an elaborate adventure role-playing game. Informally, we noticed some interesting individual differences when examining the

performance profiles of all 23 participants who completed the study.[2] Specifically, we noted that five of the seven top players earned their highest or second highest scores when playing in the Full Sound condition, while only four of the remaining 16 participants earned their highest or second-highest score in the Full Sound condition. These findings[3] suggest that the most successful gamers may pay more attention to audio cues or are more successful in incorporating them into their play than the average player, at least during the early stages in the game.

According to the congruence-associationist model (see Cohen, 2009) as applied to multimedia contexts, the eye tends to focus on visual elements that are temporally or semantically congruent with elements in sound or music. The majority of participants in our study, however, seemed to rely heavily on visual information when completing tasks and navigating the virtual environment during the initial stages of learning a new game. When audio cues were provided, we observed that many participants did not stop to investigate what they meant, or slowed down in their tracks but were unsuccessful at incorporating the audio 'clue' into their subsequent actions. Episode 2, in particular, posed a challenge to our participants as they had to find *invisible* enemies who could be located primarily through audio cues (e.g., the sound of enemies moving on a wall or flying). Similarly, few players could defeat an invisible ghost in Episode 4. As the cues were not also provided in the visual information on screen, responding effectively to auditory cues was not only important but essential to advancing through these levels. The fact that the absence or presence of built-in sound did not have a strong effect on performance in Episode 2 suggests again that most participants were not using auditory cues effectively to guide their game play.

As hinted in our data, one strategy that may distinguish top performers from the majority of players is the ability to integrate audio cues effectively into one's game play. The most proficient players may play a truly *audio-visual* game from the outset, and swiftly developing strategies that incorporate task-relevant information conveyed by *both sound and images* may be a key to becoming a more successful player.

Coda

As Collins (2007) has observed, "studies and theories of video games have, for the most part, disregarded the audio. While there has been a scattering of articles published sporadically in the last few years, video game audio remains largely unexplored" (p. 263). The present study contributes to the sparse literature on the role of sound in video games, and points to the challenges of processing multisensory cues in an elaborate adventure role-playing game. Among the practical findings that emerged is the discovery that when it comes to video game audio, 'more is not always better' - especially during the initial stages of learning a new game. Further, we discovered that gamers are not a homogeneous group but respond quite differently to the same playing conditions at various stages of a new game. Thus, allowing players to tailor the audio to fit their preferences and the demands of a particular game, as well as the flexibility to modulate these settings as they advance in a game, may lead to optimal performance conditions and the most positive gaming experience. An increasing number of games and platforms allow for the independent control of background music and sound effects (allowing players to set the balance), and for the incorporation of self-selected music tracks. It seems that the industry is recognizing the importance of game audio to players' enjoyment of the game experience, and is empowering players to customize sound conditions to fit their preferences. The ability to configure video game audio in increasingly flexible ways also provides future researchers with exciting opportunities to further explore how sound shapes and enriches the video game experience.

ACKNOWLEDGMENT

The authors thank Matthew Vazquez, McKay Stevens, and Robert Hansen for their assistance in running the procedure; Allison Jacobs, Katherine Keegan, Jessica Messerschmidt, and Emily Adelstein for help with data entry; and all 23 students who participated in the study. We are especially grateful to Scotty D. Craig, Robert Batsell Jnr., Kristie McAlpine, and anonymous reviewers for helpful comments on earlier drafts.

REFERENCES

Atari Inc. (1972). *Pong (Arcade software)*. Sunnyvale, CA: Atari Inc.

Barfield, W., & Weghorst, S. (1993). The sense of presence within virtual environment: A conceptual framework. In Salvendy, G., & Smith, M. (Eds.), *Human computer interaction: Applications and case studies* (pp. 699–704). Amsterdam: Elsevier.

Bizarre Creations. (2007). *Project Gotham Racing 4 (Xbox software)*. Redmond, WA: Microsoft Game Studios.

Blue Tongue Entertainment. (2008). *de Blob* (Wii software). Agoura Hills, CA: THQ.

Box, G. E. P., Hunter, W. G., & Hunter, S. J. (1978). *Statistics for experimenters*. New York: John Wiley & Sons.

Brünken, R., Plass, J. L., & Leutner, D. (2004). Assessment of cognitive load in multimedia learning with dual-task methodology: Auditory load and modality effects. *Instructional Science*, *32*, 115–132. doi:10.1023/B:TRUC.0000021812.96911.c5

Cassidy, G., & MacDonald, R. A. R. (2008, August). Music and videogame play: The effects of self-selected and experimenter-selected music on performance and experience. In L. Mitchell (Ed.), *Music and health: Empirical investigations and theoretical constructs. Proceedings for the 2008 International Conference of Music Perception and Cognition*, Hokkaido University, Japan. Australia: Causal Productions.

Cassidy, G. G., & MacDonald, R. A. R. (2009). The effects of music choice on task performance: A study of the impact of self-selected and experimenter-selected music on driving game performance and experience. *Musicae Scientiae, 13*, 357–386.

Chen, H., Wigand, R. T., & Nilan, M. (2000). Exploring web users' optimal flow experiences. *Information Technology & People, 13*, 263–281. doi:10.1108/09593840010359473

Cohen, A. J. (2009). Music as a source of emotion in film. In Juslin, P., & Sloboda, J. (Eds.), *Oxford handbook of music and emotion: Theory, research, applications* (pp. 879–908). Oxford, UK: Oxford University Press.

Collins, K. (2007). An introduction to the participatory and non-linear aspects of video games audio. In Hawkins, S., & Richardson, J. (Eds.), *Essays on sound and vision* (pp. 263–298). Helsinki, Finland: Helsinki University Press.

Csikszentmihalyi, M. (1975). *Beyond boredom and anxiety: The experience of play in work and games*. San Francisco, CA: Jossey-Bass.

Garner, R., Brown, R., Sanders, S., & Menke, D. (1992). "Seductive details" and learning from text. In Renninger, K. A., Hidi, S., & Krapp, A. (Eds.), *The role of interest in learning and development* (pp. 239–254). Hillsdale, NJ: Erlbaum.

Ghani, J. (1995). Flow in human computer interactions: Test of a model. In Carey, J. (Ed.), *Human factors in information systems: Emerging theoretical bases* (pp. 291–311). Norwood, NJ: Ablex.

Grimshaw, M., Lindley, C. A., & Nacke, L. (2008, October). *Sound and immersion in the first-person shooter: Mixed measurement of the player's sonic experience*. Paper presented at the meeting meething of Audio Mostly, Piteå, Sweden.

Hébert, S., Béland, R., Dionne-Fournelle, O., Crête, M., & Lupien, S. J. (2005). Physiological stress response to video-game playing: The contribution of built-in music. *Life Sciences, 76*, 2371–2380. doi:10.1016/j.lfs.2004.11.011

id Software. (1993). *DOOM* (Computer software). Mesquite, TX: id Software.

id Software. (1999). *Quake III Arena* (Computer software). Santa Monica, CA: Activision.

Ijsselsteijn, W., Poels, K., & deKort, Y. A. W. (2008). *The Game Experience Questionnaire: Development of a self-report measure to assess player experiences of digital games*. Eindhoven, The Netherlands: TU Eindhoven.

Jørgensen, K. (2008a). Left in the dark: Playing computer games with the sound turned off. In Collins, K. (Ed.), *From Pac Man to pop music: Interactive Audio in Games and New Music* (pp. 163–176). Aldershot, UK: Ashgate.

Jørgensen, K. (2008b). Audio and gameplay: An analysis of PvP battlegrounds in World of Warcraft. *Game Studies, 8*(2). Retrieved August 17, 2009, from http://gamestudies.org/0802/articles/jorgensen

Kim, T., & Biocca, F. (1997). Telepresence via television: Two dimensions of telepresence may have different connections to memory and persuasion. *Journal of Computer-Mediated Communication, 3*(2). Retrieved April 27, 2009, from http://jcmc.indiana.edu/vol3/issue2/kim.html

Leahy, W., Chandler, P., & Sweller, J. (2003). When auditory presentations should and should not be a component of multimedia instruction. *Applied Cognitive Psychology, 17*, 401–418. doi:10.1002/acp.877

Lipscomb, S. D., & Zehnder, S. M. (2005). Immersion in the virtual environment: The effect of a musical score on the video gaming experience. *Journal of Physiological Anthropology and Applied Human Science, 23,* 88–95.

Long, A. (2000). *The Legend of Zelda – retroview.* Retrieved April 1, 2009, from http://www.rpgamer.com/games/zelda/z1/reviews/z1strev1.html

Mayer, R. E. (2009). *Multimedia learning* (2nd ed.). New York: Cambridge University Press.

McDonald, G. (2008). *A history of video game music.* Retrieved August 1, 2008, from http://www.gamespot.com/features/6092391/p-6.html

Minegishi, T., Ohta, A., & Kondo, K. (2006). *The Legend of Zelda: Twilight Princess: Original soundtrack.* Kyoto, Japan: Nintendo.

Moreno, R., & Mayer, R. E. (2000). A coherence effect in multimedia learning: The case for minimizing irrelevant sounds in the design of multimedia instructional messages. *Journal of Educational Psychology, 92,* 117–320. doi:10.1037/0022-0663.92.1.117

Nacke, L. E., Grimshaw, M. N., & Lindley, C. A. (2010). More than a feeling: Measurement of sonic user experience and psychophysiology in a first-person shooter game. *Interacting with Computers, 22*(5)..doi:10.1016/j.intcom.2010.04.005

Nantais, K. M., & Schellenberg, E. G. (1999). The Mozart effect: An artifact of preference. *Psychological Science, 10,* 370–373. doi:10.1111/1467-9280.00170

Nicovich, S. G., Boller, G. W., & Cornwell, T. B. (2005). Experienced presence within computer-mediated communications: Initial explorations on the effects of gender with respect to empathy and immersion. *Journal of Computer-Mediated Communication, 10*(2). Retrieved August 9, 2009, from http://jcmc.indiana.edu/vol10/issue2/nicovich.html

Nintendo. (1998). *The Legend of Zelda: Ocarina of Time* (Nintendo 64 software). Redmond, WA: Nintendo.

Nintendo. (2006). *The Legend of Zelda: Twilight Princess* (Wii software). Redmond, WA: Nintendo.

North, A. C., & Hargreaves, D. J. (1999). Music and driving game performance. *Scandinavian Journal of Psychology, 40,* 285–292. doi:10.1111/1467-9450.404128

Rauscher, F. H., Shaw, G. L., & Ky, K. N. (1995). Listening to Mozart enhances spatial-temporal reasoning: Towards a neurophysiological basis. *Neuroscience Letters, 185,* 44–47. doi:10.1016/0304-3940(94)11221-4

Rollings, A., & Adams, E. (2003). *On game design.* Berkeley, CA: New Riders.

Roth, E. A., & Smith, K. H. (2008). The Mozart effect: Evidence for the arousal hypothesis. *Perceptual and Motor Skills, 107,* 396–402. doi:10.2466/PMS.107.6.396-402

Schellenberg, E. G., Nakata, T., Hunter, P. G., & Tamoto, S. (2007). Exposure to music and cognitive performance: Tests of children and adults. *Psychology of Music, 35,* 5–19. doi:10.1177/0305735607068885

Shin, N. (2006). Online learner's 'flow' experience: An experimental study. *British Journal of Educational Technology, 37,* 705–720. doi:10.1111/j.1467-8535.2006.00641.x

Skadberg, Y. X., & Kimmel, J. R. (2004). Visitors' flow experience while browsing a web site: Its measurement, contributing factors and consequences. *Computers in Human Behavior, 20,* 403–422. doi:10.1016/S0747-5632(03)00050-5

Slater, M., Usoh, M., & Steed, A. (1994). Depth of presence in virtual environment. *Presence (Cambridge, Mass.), 3,* 130–144.

Stockburger, A. (2003). The game environment from an auditive perspective. In Copier, M., & Raessens, J. (Eds.), *Level up: Digital games research conference*. Utrecht, The Netherlands: Utrecht University, Faculty of Arts.

Stormfront Studios. (2002). *The Lord of the Rings: the Two Towers (Playstation software)*. Redwood City, CA: Electronic Arts.

Sweller, J. (1999). *Instructional design in technical areas*. Camberwell, Australia: ACER Press.

Tafalla, R. J. (2007). Gender differences in cardio-vascular reactivity and game performance related to sensory modality in violent video game play. *Journal of Applied Social Psychology*, *37*, 2008–2023. doi:10.1111/j.1559-1816.2007.00248.x

Tan, S. L., & Kelly, M. E. (2004). Graphic representations of short musical compositions. *Psychology of Music*, *32*(2), 191–212. doi:10.1177/0305735604041494

Tan, S. L., & Spackman, M. P. (2005). Listeners' judgments of the musical unity of structurally altered and intact musical compositions. *Psychology of Music*, *33*(2), 133–153. doi:10.1177/0305735605050648

Thompson, W. F., Schellenberg, E. G., & Husain, G. (2001). Arousal, mood, and the Mozart effect. *Psychological Science*, *12*, 248–251. doi:10.1111/1467-9280.00345

Västfjäll, D. (2003). The subjective sense of presence, emotion recognition, and experienced emotions in auditory virtual environments. *Cyberpsychology & Behavior*, *6*, 181–188. doi:10.1089/109493103321640374

Vestal, A., O'Neill, C., & Shoemaker, B. (2008). *The history of Zelda*. Retrieved April 1, 2009, from http://www.gamespot.com/gamespot/features/video/hist_zelda/index.html

Wolfson, S., & Case, G. (2000). The effects of sound and colour on responses to a computer game. *Interacting with Computers*, *13*, 183–192. doi:10.1016/S0953-5438(00)00037-0

Yamada, M., Fujisawa, N., & Komori, S. (2001). The effect of music on the performance and impression in a racing game. *Journal of Music Perception and Cognition*, *7*, 65–76.

Zehnder, S. M., & Lipscomb, S. D. (2006). The role of music in video games. In Voderer, P., & Bryant, J. (Eds.), *Playing video games: Motives, responses and consequences* (pp. 241–258). Mahwah, NJ: Lawrence Erlbaum.

ENDNOTES

[1] The term 'episode' is used in this paper to refer to what is usually referred to as 'levels' of the *Twilight Princess* game. This is to avoid confusion with the levels as labeled in the game.

[2] This observation is based on all 23 participants, including the three lowest-scoring participants who were excluded from the rest of the analyses (see description of participants in Method section).

[3] It should be noted that our sample was too small to conduct statistical analyses on trends described in this paragraph. Thus we report patterns in the data that warrant further study.

APPENDIX A

Music Used in the Non-contingent Music Condition

A 60-minute compact disc was made of the following music taken from the compact disc: T. Minegishi, A. Ohta, & K. Kondo (2006): *The Legend of Zelda: Twilight Princess*. Original Soundtrack. Kyoto: Nintendo. The musical pieces were arranged in the following order: 1-1 2 3 2 4 5 6 2 3-3 2 1-1 2 3 2 4 5 6 2 3-3 2 1-1 2 3 2 4 5 6 2 3-3 2 (Numbers correspond to the tracks listed below.)

1. *Lake Hylia*. Track 90.
2. *Ordon Ranch*. Track 15.
3. *Ordon Village*. Track 9.
4. *Hyrule Castle Town*. Track 97.
5. *Tobias and Geremias*. Track 98.
6. *S.T.A.R. Game Room*. Track 102.

APPENDIX B

Post-game questionnaire.

Questionnaire Items		
Themes	**Items**	**References**
Telepresence: Focused attention: Time Distortion: Flow: Identification with avatar and emotion: Control and effectance:	When the game ended, I felt like I came back to the "real world" after a journey. The television came to me and created a new world for me, and that world suddenly disappeared when the game ended. While playing, I felt I was in the world the game created. While playing, I never forgot that I was in the middle of an experiment. While playing, my body was in the room, but my mind was inside the world created by the game. While playing, the world created by the game was more real or present for me compared to the "real world." The world created by the game seemed to me only "something I saw" rather than "somewhere I visited." While playing, my mind was in the room, not in the world created by the game. While playing the game, I was not distracted. When interrupted by the research assistant, I felt annoyed. While playing the game, I couldn't seem to concentrate. While playing the game, I was unaware of what was going on around me. I was unconscious of the passing of time while playing the game. It felt like time flew while I was playing the game. I was totally involved in what I was doing. I seemed to be cut off from the "real world" that was physically around me. I was really quite oblivious to my surroundings after I got going. I felt less aware of myself and my problems. My character's personality is a lot like my own. I felt many of the emotions that my character might have been feeling. While playing, I felt emotionally involved in the events happening in the virtual world around my character. It was easy to control the actions and movements of my character. After doing something or going somewhere, I often did not know where it was the right thing to do. Many events happened often without warning and caught me by surprise. While playing, I felt a strong sense of mission or clear goals in mind. While playing, I felt unsure about what to do or somewhat lost.	Kim & Biocca, 1997 (drawing from Barfield & Weghorst, 1993; Slater, Usoh, & Steed, 1994); Nicovich, et al. 2005 Shin, 2006 (drawing from Ghani, 1995) Shin, 2006; Skadberg & Kimmel, 2004 Chen, Wigand, & Nilan, 2000 (drawing from Csikszentmihalyi, 1975) The present authors The present authors

This work was previously published in International Journal of Gaming and Computer-Mediated Simulations, Volume 2, Issue 3, edited by Richard E. Ferdig, pp. 1-23, copyright 2010 by IGI Publishing (an imprint of IGI Global).

Chapter 11
Measuring Student Perceptions:
Designing an Evidenced Centered Activity Model for a Serious Educational Game Development Software

Leonard A. Annetta
North Carolina State University, USA

Shawn Y. Holmes
North Carolina State University, USA

Meng-Tzu Cheng
North Carolina State University, USA

Elizabeth Folta
North Carolina State University, USA

ABSTRACT

As educational games become more pervasive, the evolution of game design software is inevitable. This study looked at student perceptions of teacher created Serious Educational Games as part of a project striving to create a game development software where teachers and students create games as part of educational activities. The objective was to use evidence from student perceptions to inform further development of the software. A mixed method design ascertained data from 181 male and 178 females from 33 teacher created games. Results indicate that the software is relatively effective by the supporting documentation and training lacked in several areas. This information led to the creation of a commercial game development software set for release in 2010.

INTRODUCTION

Creating and infusing video games into school curricula has potential to motivate students to explore content once viewed as boring or undesirable. Current research suggests that because today's students have grown up in the digital age, they will spend as many if not more hours engaging in online games than in formal face-to-face instruction (Foreman, 2003; Neal, 2003; Prensky, 2001;

DOI: 10.4018/978-1-4666-0029-4.ch011

Rejeski, 2002). The fascination with *Pong*™ in the 1970's is today paralleled by the popularity of video games where players can compete against one another or together to reach a common goal.

As a result, some believe that video game technology will inevitably replace a significant amount of traditional instruction—lectures, tests, and note taking (Neal, 2003). The *2008 Project Tomorrow* survey, a national nonprofit organization committed to supporting and promoting the effective use of science, math, and technology resources in K-12 education, reported that online video gaming is one of the technologies that students use most frequently—and that educational gaming is one of the emerging technologies that students would most like to see implemented in their schools. However, only 10% of teachers reported adopted gaming as an instructional tool (eSchool News, 2008).

Serious Educational Games (author) are not only deeply engaging, but provide a natural forum for technology integration with dynamic visual representations of the natural world. Video gamesmanship represents conscious, deliberate mental and physical activity and promotes active learning by shifting players into the participant role (Bowman, 1982). Dickey (2000) and Duffy and Cunningham (1996) agree that a major goal of constructivist learning environments is to find activities that support *dialogical interchange and reflexivity*. When well-designed, gaming has the properties of the most effective instructional situations: experiential, inquiry-based, and providing continuous user feedback, while promoting self-efficacy, goal-setting, and team learning (Bransford, Brown, & Cocking, 1999). Virtual reality research suggests participation in a 3D environment supports the constructivist instructional paradigm and may bridge the gap between experiential learning and information representation (Bricken & Byrne, 1994; Dede, 1995).

When students create games with support by teachers in terms of content accuracy, time allowed, and recognition of the work involved

and this technology becomes part of the school culture—students become more engaged in the content as well as proficient producers in the digital world. They are thereby simultaneously introduced to modeling and design through immersion in the virtual space.

Purpose of the Study

This study was couched in an evidenced centered design proof of concept project based on activity theory where a software package was developed to allow for easy Serious Educational Game creation by teachers and students. The software development platform was developed as a mod of the popular Half-Life 2 game engine where games could be easily created for instructional purposes. Elite teachers (Kenan Fellows-to be explained more in-depth later) were participants in the study. After two years of professional development and testing of the software, students played the games created by these teachers. The goal of the study was to solicit student feedback to inform the next phase of the software design and the professional development model using an innovative technology. The research question thus became: What characteristics from student perceptions and attitudes after game play influence future game software design?

RATIONALE

Activity Theory

The oldest tradition of activity theory has its roots in the classical German philosophy of Kant and Hegel, which emphasized both developmental and historical ideas and the active and constructive roles of humans. Later on, the more contemporary philosophy of Marx and Engels elaborated the concept of activity further. Until the 1920s and 1930s, it was actually brought up by the Russian psychologists Vygotsky and Leont'ev, and Luria

(Kuutti, 1996). Today, activity theory has become a cross-disciplinary research approach that serves as a powerful sociocultural and sociohistorical lens through which we can analyze most forms of human activities (Engeström, 2000; Jonassen & Rohrer-Murphy, 1999).

Scientific knowledge especially the application of the information-processing branch of cognitive psychology has been used to explain human-computer interaction (HCI) for some time. When technology is designed to fit the needs of users in the real world and too much emphasis is placed on human action as the unit of analysis, the importance of context is often left out of consideration (Kaptelinin, 1996a; Kuutti, 1996). In other words, since human actions are always situated in a real world context, research results that place too much emphasis on isolating human actions from real-life situations are no longer sufficient to cover practical design. Users activities and the tasks they seek to perform within those activities are both important considerations when it comes to the technology designs and HCI (Constantine, 2006; Norman, 2005).

Recently, activity theory has evoked much attention among researchers and HCI designers in bridging the gap between research results and practical design. An activity refers to a basic unit of analysis including individual actions and a minimal meaningful context into which those individual actions are situated. Activity theory then provides a framework for understanding human practices with both individual and social levels interlinked at the same time (Kuutti, 1996). Kaptelinin (1996b) also contended that "one of the most important claims of activity theory is

that the nature of any artifact can be understood only within the context of human activity – by identifying the ways people use this artifact, the needs it serves, and the history of its development" (p. 46).

The original perspective of human activity is represented as Figure 1. The subject is the individual or group of actors engaged in the activity. The object is a solution of a problem or a purpose that is sought by the subject. In other words, the activity is performed by the subject and motivated by the object. Moreover, the object just can be achieved by the mediation of tools. Within a transformational process, then the outcome could be yielded.

Based on the original model, Engeström (1999) later developed a more systematic structure of human activity by adding three more elements to the bottom of the triangle (Figure 2). Community is the social context to which the subject belongs and in where all activities take places. Rules are any socio-cultural and procedural factors that constrain or allow activities to occur and to interact with other community members. Finally, the division of labor is the differentiated responsibilities that community members share while the subject is participating in the activity (Constantine, 2006; Yamagata-Lynch, 2007). This structure of human activity gives emphasis on the inseparable relationship between activities and the environmental context these activities situated.

Activity theory consists of several basic principles which are associated with various aspects of the whole activity and hence should be considered as an integrated system (Kaptelinin &

Figure 1. The original perspective of human activity (adapted from Engeström, 1987)

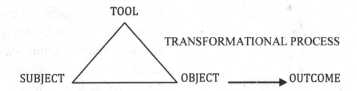

Figure 2. The structure of human activity (adapted from Engeström et al., 1999)

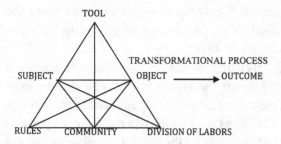

Nardi, 1997). Activity includes a set of goal-directed conscious actions that contribute to the fulfillment of the object, and actions are composed of chains of automatic operations, which provide an adjustment of actions to current situations (Figure 3). The relationship among activities, actions, and operations are dynamically changed (Constantine, 2006; Jonassen, 2000).

Kaptelinin and Nardi (1997) argued that "human beings live in a reality that is objective in a broad sense: the things that constitute this reality have not only the properties that are considered objective according to natural sciences but socially/culturally defined properties as well" (pp. 158-159). In other words, activity theory posits that socially/culturally defined properties do objectively exist in real life situations regardless of whether or not we can sense it. Therefore, the context in which humans live is full of meanings and gives activity a specific direction. This is the focus of our game design thrust. We want the activity to be informed by life experience while

Figure 3. A hierarchical structure of human activity (adapted from Engeström et al., 1999)

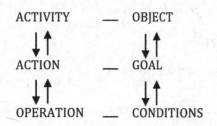

teaching the designer about vocational implications within the activity.

Activity has both internal and external properties that cannot be analyzed separately. Internalization transforms external activities back to internal, which provides a means for people to internally simulate the potential interactions with the reality and/or to predict the possible consequences without actually manipulating real objects. On the other hand, the transformation of internal into external activities is called externalization. When an internalized action needs to be repaired or when activities need to be externally performed in order to be coordinated between several people, externalization is often required (Kaptelinin & Nardi, 1997). In game design this process is operationalized when storyboards externalize into the digital environment.

Activities cannot be fully understood if the history of its development has not been analyzed (Kuutti, 1991). Kaptelinin and Nardi (1997) suggested that the development of an activity is a dynamic process; it is also a general research methodology. Hence, in order to get a clear picture of the context in which activities are situated, the formative experiment, which combines active participation with monitoring of the developmental changes, should be conducted instead of traditional laboratory experiments. Hence, usability and feasibility testing is a necessity and subsequent iterations of each game needs to be built for a success final product.

Similarly, the disparity between traditional academic research and research based on practical experience has evoked much criticism in the area of gaming and simulations (Kriz & Hense, 2006). According to Kriz and Hense (2006), traditional academic research has focused on developing and improving domain-specific knowledge by using simulations and games in experimental environments, while the practical experience has involved the transfer and dissemination of knowledge using specific simulation games with clearly defined, designated audiences in a defined context of use.

Especially for the issue regarding the use and design of gaming and simulations for educational purposes, many learning sciences researchers now argue that learning cannot be seen as merely outcomes of a learning activity which can be investigated in the laboratory settings any more. Learning refers to the learning activity itself, it is dynamic and continues to change. Hence, inspired by the claims of activity theory, the main aim of evaluative approaches is no more to merely test the learning outcomes of games and simulations. What needs to be assessed is not only whether a simulation works but also how and why it works in a given context (Kriz & Hense, 2006; Van Eck, 2007). Shelton and Wiley (2007) even predicted, "Perhaps we should adopt a view of pure contextuality, simply creating designs and games that work for specific situations within specific domains, and not concerning ourselves with the development of context-free recipes that anyone can use in any situation" (p. 1). Teachers created games in context by applying real world situations through a problem based approach that aligned with their respective curricula. That was the thrust of the activities of this study.

To this end, activity theory provides a conceptual framework for understanding human activity and the use of tools/artifacts. As it pertains to activity theory, design-based research gives a systematic methodology of experimenting with innovative designs in real-world practices to develop theories of learning and teaching that account for the multiple interactions of people acting in a complex social setting (Barab & Squire, 2004).

Evidence Centered Design

Evidence Centered Design (ECD) provides us with a conceptual framework for a coherent assessment design that supports a broad range of activity types. Based on evidentiary reasoning, ECD ensures that the assessment and its interpretation support the intention of the assessment (Mislevy, Almond, & Lukas, 2003). The framework is applicable to games that evoke behaviors that are evidence for key skills, knowledge and abilities. The design of the assessment must show standard interpretations of the evoked behavior and how it constitutes as evidence of what is being assessed. Emphasizing consideration of targeted inferences, and the evidence required for inferences, along with the specific relationships between design and delivery processes, the final design using ECD provides specifications for implementation and delivery.

The design of the assessment begins by understanding what is being measured. Analysis of the domain being measured to identify specific domain related claims about the students is the next step in the process. This guides the evidence to be modeled by the students on which the claims are built. The ECD framework links the relationship between the claims to be made, the proficiency of the students, the evidence showing these claims and the situations used to elicit the evidence about the claims for the development of the assessment capable of producing valid and relevant results (Williamson, Steinberg, Mislevy, & Behrens, 2003).

The Four-Process Delivery model informs ECD and provides a generic framework for test delivery:

1. Activity Selection – what the next task should be and when to stop the process. This is accomplished in our model by a cascading model of development from teacher to students.

2. Presentation Process – presenting the task and supporting documents for the task. When students play the final product we then get a sense as to how to build curriculum or future activities around the game.

3. Response Process- identifying observable outcomes for a particular task (scoring process). Assessment is key to any educational initiative. If learning is the ultimate goal then the game goal and in world assessment has to align.

4. Summary scoring process- accumulating the observable outcomes across several tasks. This is where our use of the AIM SOLO taxonomy is key. We can get a snapshot of student understanding regardless of the game.

These four steps, which we used in this study, provided the research team with a structure that ensures reliability in the assessment activities when the activities are replicated.

We further used a Cognitive Task Analysis (CTA). CTA is supported by ECD and is a process of investigating the knowledge and strategies used by examinees at targeted ability levels to solve specific tasks. CTA is used to obtain evidence related to the anticipated assessment claims, yields observable errors, misconceptions, and successes. Moreover, we took into account Shelton's (2007) argument that the following elements of effective instructional games emphasize the pedagogy and engagement factors within the scenario of what makes for *essential criteria* and added our modification (shown in bold):

- Addresses a learning issue
  - Complex – requiring a level of depth beyond what one sees in simple "walk-through instruction"
  - Intentional – directed instruction aimed at identified problems, but may be exploratory in nature
  - Subject matter that has historically been difficult to teach and/or difficult for students to learn
- Contains learning objectives or goals
  - Explicit or implicit, depending on how they fit within the flow of the scenario
  - Align with national and/or state content standards
- Includes participants with constraints (rules)
  - Not observers, requires a level of interaction
  - Includes an environment with constraints (rules)
  - Students/player becomes constructor or level or entire game where game rules are redeveloped
- Contrived for other-world experiences, and/or
- Mimics real-world processes, sequences, etc.
- Understanding careers in content specific scenarios
- Operates by a facilitating mechanism – includes required hardware, software, and non-computer based resources
- Requires activity
  - Interactive (contains feedback, adaptation, choice)
  - Autonomous (embedded information)
  - Interactivity is a function of assessment and vice versa
- Based on non-random outcomes
  - Sequences of events produce a predictable, or sometimes unpredictable outcome, ultimately tied to learning goals
  - Events within a scenario may have random qualities
- Repeatable (different choices may produce different outcomes)
- Scalable
  - Internal – the simulation may be expanded to include multiple players
  - External – the platform may be developed to include multiple scenarios based on similar instructional objectives
- Contains representations not possible / affordable to experience in the "real world"
- Cost-effective

We make the argument that both Activity Theory and ECD are critical frameworks for Serious

Educational Game design. What follows are the methodologies we employed and a description of how these two respective frameworks influenced the results.

METHODS

With a keen eye on activity theory and ECD, the following methodologies drove this study and the subsequent enhanced software and professional development design. A posttest only, mixed method design was employed to ascertain student perceptions of a cascading ECD of teacher created games as part of a funded research project. The goal of the study was to ascertain evidence from the design activities (i.e., student response to the innovation) that would inform the research team as to how the software and future teacher professional development would need to evolve.

The Serious Educational Game software was designed as a drag-and-drop environment using principles of visual and object oriented programming to allow game developers to create visually and technically enticing games without the need for the customary expertise of a game studio. The professional development of the teachers in this project emphasized the limitations of the software and that by allowing for one person to be the programmer, designer, artist, etc. the end products would not necessarily be at the same immersion level as a commercial game. Although never explicitly stated, the aforementioned activity theory and ECD frameworks were the back bone to the teacher professional development on SEG design.

Setting of the Study

This mixed-methods study was set in one urban high school and one rural middle school. The goal of the research project was to impact students in grades 5 through 9. These two schools were chosen for the study because they had teachers

who were part of the Kenan Fellows Program. The Kenan Fellows program advances knowledge in numerous fields of scientific and mathematical discovery and pedagogical content knowledge through a rigorous application and review process. Kenan Fellows go through two years of inquiry teaching professional development and leadership training. Only the best of the best become Kenan Fellows and thus we were fortunate to have two at the participating schools who through their leadership training impacted the remaining 31 teachers who created Serious Educational Games. These final 33 (of the 75 teachers in the project) were chosen because the research team thereby ensuring reliable measures rated their games similarly.

A Cascading ECD Model

Using the iterative processes of activity theory, a cascading ECD model was incorporated into this study. We first trained a small group of five Kenan Fellows who after one year helped us train another group of 15 Kenan Fellows. Finally, these 20 Kenan Fellows helped us train the final 55 teachers on SEG design and development. As previously mentioned, these 75 teachers all had their students play their games. We used the four-part ECD model (Williamson, Steinberg, Mislevy, & Behrens, 2003) in each level of teacher professional development. Teachers were trained to this with the end in mind when selecting an activity, presenting the final build to students, embedding assessment in world, and gathering student feedback. The results from this study were shared with teachers so they could work with students to further develop their SEGs.

Sample

The student participants in this study were composed of 181 male and 178 females from the participating schools. Forty-seven percent were Caucasian, 23% African-American, 2% Native American, 3%, and Asian, 25% reported as other.

Of the 359 students, 50% came from grade 8, 16% grade 6, 16% grade 7, 9% grade 9, and 8% grade 5. The middle school students were all enrolled in academic level science courses while the high school students were from Algebra one classes.

Data Collection and Instrumentation/ Research Design

Data was collected in two phases. The first phase was through a post game experience Structure of Observed Learning Outcomes taxonomy (SOLO) (Biggs and Collis, 1982). A SOLO taxonomy is a systematic way of classifying learner responses. The SOLO model is a hierarchy of five levels of conceptual understanding: Prestructural, Unistructural, Multistructural, Relational, and Extended Abstract. Each partial construction or level is a foundation for further learning upon which to build (Biggs, 2003). Prestructural responses have no organization and normally make no sense. Unistructural responses are simple with obvious connections, but lack the understanding of their significance. Multistructural responses continue to make more connections between parts, but still lack the major connection and its significance. Relational level responses show that the learner understands the significance of the information and finally, extended abstract responses show not only the connections and understanding of the concept, but learners also make connections beyond the subject area and are able to generalize the ideas. Simply put, the responses progress from having no understanding (Prestructural) to 'surface level' understanding (Unistructural and Multistructural) to finally 'deep level' understanding (Relational and Extended Abstract) (Minogue & Jones, 2009). SOLO taxonomy has been used as an evaluation tool in several aspects of education from the evaluation of student understanding (Minogue & Jones, 2009; Hodges & Harvey, 2003) to the development of curricula (Brabrand & Dahl, 2009).

For the purposes of this study, we adopted the AIM SOLO taxonomy developed by Minogue and Jones (2009) (see Appendix A). Since student participants played different teacher created games, we used this SOLO taxonomy because it was technology focused and provided the student perceptions and attitudes that would eventually drive future software design.

The second phase of data collection was qualitative in nature. Interviews were conducted sequentially and conversational. This allowed researchers to deeply probe into the points of view of the student participants (Marshall & Rossman, 1995). Four students were randomly selected and interviewed for approximately ten minutes each. These students were racially and ethnically diverse (1 Hispanic, 1 African American, 1 Asian and 1 Caucasian) and were either 13 or 14 years of age. These structured, open-ended interviews (Creswell & Plano Clark, 2007) occurred immediately following the school day in which student played the Algebra-based game designed and created by their teacher. An 11-item interview protocol was constructed (Appendix B) to guide the inquiries and serve as leading questions. Based on student participant response, the interviewer solicited probing questions and all responses were synthesized based on two researchers reviewing the interview transcripts.

Data Analysis

Frequency responses from 359 students playing games created by 33 teachers were calculated based on prompts from the AIM SOLO taxonomy. Coupled with the interviews, these frequencies begin to shed light on teacher game design effectiveness as perceived by the student game players.

Interview transcripts were analyzed through inductive analysis and creative synthesis to "discover important patterns, themes, and interrelationships" (Patton, 2002, pp. 40-41). Glaser (1965) indicated that data can only be accurate through combinations of observing, talking with participants, and reading written responses from participants in the pursuit of gaining the trust of participants. Johnson and Onwuegbuzie (2004) indicated that researchers look for induction, deduction, and abduction, bridging the qualitative and quantitative methodologies. Induction was used to identify patterns, while deduction and abduction were used to test ideas and express explanations in order to understand results respectively.

RESULTS

Treatment Analysis

Results from the AIM SOLO taxonomy (Table 1) suggests that teacher created games, and thus the software package, were relatively effective. This is based on the assumption that the majority of responses fall between *Somewhat Agree* and *Strongly Agree*.

The majority of the students (66%) perceived they could recall and use the information in the teacher created game in which they played. They

Table 1. Frequency responses to the AIM SOLO taxonomy

Questions	Strongly Disagree	Disagree	Somewhat Disagree	Somewhat Agree	Agree	Strongly Agree
I was able to recall and use information presented in the program following its use.	14%	10%	10%	26%	30%	10%
I am more interested in this topic after using the program.	13%	11%	13%	31%	22%	10%
I feel that the reading level of the program was appropriate.	6%	6%	8%	23%	36%	21%
I was able to navigate through the program without difficulty.	18%	15%	14%	20%	17%	16%
The screen directions are consistent and easy to follow.	13%	10%	17%	22%	24%	14%
I felt that I was able to control pace and sequence of the program.	12%	11%	13%	27%	26%	11%
I believe that the graphics and animation enhanced the material presented in the program.	7%	8%	14%	26%	29%	16%
I believe that I have learned a lot about science/math by participating in this activity.	20%	18%	15%	24%	18%	5%
I feel that the graphics and animation did NOT make the program any more interesting.	22%	27%	19%	14%	7%	11%
This program was different from the types of things we typically do in science class.	6%	7%	11%	20%	25%	31%
I do NOT feel any more interested in this topic after using the program.	17%	27%	21%	15%	9%	11%
I was NOT able to remember and use information presented in the program following its use.	14%	29%	19%	17%	11%	10%
I found the program confusing and difficult to navigate through.	20%	24%	14%	18%	10%	14%

were also more interested (63%) in the respective science or math topic, which was the backbone to the game they played. Because there was such a diverse group of students in the project (i.e., second language learners), reading level was a concern and was addressed through the design of the software and subsequent teacher professional development. To this end, 80 percent of the students felt the reading level was adequate. Only fifty-three percent thought the games were easily navigated. Student participants clearly agreed that this mode of instruction was different from normal class activity. Most intriguing, however, was the result from the question asking the perception of student learning in their respective game. 53 percent reported that they didn't think they learned content from playing the game while 47 percent did. This will be an important discussion topic.

The next question of the AIM SOLO taxonomy asked student to rate the activity overall on a scale from 1-10. Ten percent of the students rated it as a 10, 6.7% (9), 15% (8), 14.8% (7), 12.5% (6), 15% (5), 5.6% (4), 5% (3), 6.7% (2), and 8.6% (1).

The final question of the AIM SOLO taxonomy ask students if they perceived using teacher created games in the classroom as more interesting, about the same or less interesting to them (Table 2). Students reported being more interested in Serious Educational Games then listening to a teacher's presentation and making a model about the topic embedded in the game. They were indifferent when comparing their experience to watching a movie about the topic and were split on their interest as compared to studying a diagram about the topic.

Most notably was that students reported that their game play experience was less interesting to them than reading a book.

Results from the interviews suggested the students all liked their classes while three also reported enjoying Astronomy, Earth Science, Creative Writing equally as much as math. They all rated liking science or math between 7 and 10 when asked if they could rate the level of their science enjoyment after playing the teacher created game. All students agreed that their favorite part of class were projects and problem solving. A probing question was asked based on the response to this leading question.

Since three of you answered "projects" can you give me an idea of these projects? What are they?

We receive a project from an actual company like we did projects for NASA, big companies like that ask us for our help.

It is very rewarding. This is not like a regular math class where you come in and do 50 problems a day.

We made goggles, irrigation fields, programming. And for Algebra I we made a pool, how much it would be in real life, now we are designing our own city, we did Peruvian dating.

When asked whether or not they used computers, all four students said they use them almost everyday.

Students were then probed if they liked that and why. Their responses were:

Table 2. Final AIM SOLO question

	More interesting	About the same	Less interesting
A teacher's presentation on this topic	49%	31%	20%
Watching a movie about this topic	39%	37%	24%
Reading about this topic	39%	17%	44%
Making a model about this topic	42%	32%	26%
Studying a diagram about this topic	38%	23%	39%

It is better than writing down the problems on paper.

I would write it down on paper. Because it took me such a long time to figure out the square root sign.

I would rather use the computer because like last year we had to write about 10 pages of notes, and your hand gets really tired.

When asked how the computer is generally used in the class prior to playing the teacher created games, students responded that their computers were used for schoolwork but also for note taking, instant messaging and playing online games without teachers knowing. All four students emphatically reported playing computer and/or video games at home. They further reported that they play computer and/or video games each day but the response rate fluctuated. They agreed that their play spikes on the weekends but clearly chatting with friends is above gaming in their priority list. On average, however, students reported playing computer and/or video games between 15-25 hours per week. They all reported liking their teacher's games but all had recommendations as to how to make it better. This is another important aspect of discussion.

When probed about game characteristics they enjoyed, or not, students reported the following:

I liked how you had to climb on the side of the building, I liked how the signs helped you, but you could fall off and crash to the ground.

I like how the numbers helped you get back to where you were if you fell down. I liked the controls.

I didn't like that you had to use the mouse. It would have been better if we could use the keyboard mouse.

I had to keep switching hands using the mouse.

It didn't have weapons.

I didn't mind the mouse but I didn't like that you had to right click on the mouse. And if you left clicked it broke the game. And I would have like to have more people in the game.

I didn't like that you had to have something in the center of the screen to click on it.

Interestingly, when asked how their perceptions toward science and math class would change if they played video games in their class more often, students said:

I would like math class more (all said like it more).

It would be good because more people would pay attention to it, than the work on the board, they would be more involved in it and learn more.

Everybody already has video games on their flash drives they should just make it official.

Of particular interest was the response to the last leading question. This asked about math problems in the games. All students said the problems were easy but one response spoke to failure.

The problems were pretty easy and if you didn't want to do the math you could just go back to the beginning if you got the answer wrong. That actually made the game more fun when you had to keep starting over.

This final statement, which was resonated by others in this class, added a new twist to activity development. There needed to be a penalty for students who purposely got answers wrong so they could redo game activities that seemed fun to them.

DISCUSSION

Although student participants reported positively to most of the AIM SOLO and interview prompts, it was the testimony given regarding the perceived learning and feedback to game design that was most intriguing. Further, this feedback carried the most weight toward future software and professional development design.

One main focus to the teacher professional development regarding Serious Educational Game design and infusion into the classroom was the notion of learning becoming stealthy. That is a good game would not make students think they were learning but rather they were simply playing in class. The AIM SOLO results illustrated the majority (53%) of the 359 students didn't think they learned from the game that was created by their teacher. This was seen as a major positive finding since that was an overarching goal of the Activity Theory and ECD design project. It is important to reiterate that the AIM SOLO population was students in classrooms from 33 of the 75 teachers in the project. This group was chosen because project staff members rated these games as being equivalent based on an SEG scoring rubric designed for the purposes of this project.

What this tells us is that there are clear components of some of these games that met or exceeded the goals of being educational; yet stealthy. Moreover, this informed the research team that this was more of a training delivering issue then it was a software issue. To this end the software is only as good as the training and those using it for educational purposes. This finding is crucial in the further development of this software in that the research team needs to enhance its delivering and documentation so that end users better understand the pedagogical implications of Serious Educational Games. This is the evidence that further informs activity. Finally, this finding also implies that the scoring rubric may also need to be re-evaluated.

From the interviews we learned that student participants felt a need to be involved in the design process. Students wanted to inform the teacher as to how to improve the game. This confirmed that most teachers are not gamers and thus, missed the "fun" of Serious Educational Games. These results informed a second iteration of game design where students enhanced the teacher created games and became the constructors of their own knowledge.

It can be gleaned from the interview transcripts that students felt that if they played more games in school then they would like class more. Since most students already sneak games in class maybe teachers and school administrators should allow them to play SEGs created by teachers who were properly trained in video game design. Students also reached what is known as pleasurable frustration in most cases; where a challenge is exciting yet difficult. If a student got an answer wrong and had to go back to game start then they seemed to enjoy going through the original challenges again. This idea of repetitive education supports learning theory on several levels. Albeit unexpected, the response that students intentionally got problems wrong so they could redo game challenges were a bit disconcerting yet informative as this notion of Activity Theory and ECD evolves.

Other responses that aided in enhancing the game creation software dealt with interface issues. Students didn't like the mouse control; specifically using the right-click to move the camera. Also, they didn't like that objects weren't easily clickable suggesting bonding boxes need to be enlarged. They liked the signs the teacher put in the game to help them recall information if they were sent back to game start. Their favorite part of class was the problem solving and projects. This helped confirm that the documentation and training in its current form reached teachers to design game narratives that provided authentic examples and problems in which their respective students could relate (important aspects of both Activity Theory and ECD). Maybe the most telling response was that students rated their classes between a 7-10. From cursory feedback in other studies, most students would not rate their science or math classes that high. This also confirmed for us the enjoyment and class satisfaction Serious Educational Games bring to the teaching repertoire.

CONCLUSION

The evidence-centered design of this project ensured that the assessment and its interpretation supported the intention of the assessment (Mislevy, Almond, & Lukas, 2003). Through cognitive task analysis, this study obtained evidence related to the anticipated assessment claims, yielded observable errors, and successes. Grounded in activity theory and evidenced centered design, these results spring boarded the research team to new funding that focused on the student as designer (leaving the teacher as content expert and pedagogical facilitator), ECD, and a scalable commercial software package called *Adventure Lab*. Set to be released in the summer of 2010, *Adventure Lab* takes into account an activity theory design that fits the needs of users in the real world and places more emphasis on context then on human action as the unit of analysis (Kaptelinin, 1996a; Kuutti, 1996). Further *Adventure Lab* documentation and training models have user activities and the tasks they seek to perform within those activities at the forefront of the software design and HCI (Constantine, 2006; Norman, 2005).

REFERENCES

Annetta, L. A. (2008). Serious Educational Games []. Amsterdam, The Netherlands: Sense Publishers.]. *Theory into Practice*, 83.

Barab, S., & Squire, K. (2004). Design-based research: Putting a stake in the ground. *Journal of the Learning Sciences*, *13*(1), 1–14. doi:10.1207/s15327809jls1301_1

Biggs, J. B. (2003). *Teaching for quality learning at university*. Maidenhead, UK: Open University Press.

Biggs, J. B., & Collis, K. F. (1982). *Evaluating the quality of learning: The SOLO taxonomy*. New York: Academic Press.

Bowman, R. F. (1982). A Pac-Man theory of motivation: Tactical implications for classroom instruction. *Educational Technology*, *22*(9), 14–17.

Brabrand, C., & Dahl, B. (2009). Using the SOLO taxonomy to analyze competence progression of university science curricula. *Higher Education*, *58*, 531–549. doi:10.1007/s10734-009-9210-4

Bransford, J. D., Brown, A. L., & Cocking, R. R. (Eds.). (1999). *How people learn: Brain, mind, experience, and school*. Washington, DC: National Academy Press.

Bricken, M., & Byrne, C. M. (1994). Summer students in virtual reality: A pilot study on educational applications of virtual reality. In Wexelblat, A. (Ed.), *Virtual Reality: Applications and explorations* (pp. 199–218). Boston: Academic.

Constantine, L. L. (2006). *Activity Modeling: Toward a pragmatic integration of activity theory with usage-centered design*. Retrieved November 24, 2009, from http://www.foruse.com/articles/activitymodeling.pdf

Creswell, J., & Plano Clark, V. (2007). *Designing and conducting mixed methods research*. Thousand Oaks, CA: Sage Publications.

Dede, C. (1995). The evolution of contructivist learning environments: Immersion in distributed virtual worlds. *Educational Technology*, *35*(5), 46–52.

Dickey, M. D. (2000). *3D virtual worlds and learning: An analysis of the impact of design affordances and limitations of Active Worlds, blaxxum interactive, and OnLive! Traveler; and a study of the implementation of Active Worlds for formal and informal education.* Columbus, OH: The Ohio State University.

Duffy, T. M., & Cunningham, D. J. (1996). Constructivism: Implications for the design and delivery of instruction. In Jonassen, D. H. (Ed.), *Handbook of Research for Educational Communications and Technology.* New York: MacMillan.

Engeström, Y. (1987). *Learning by expanding: An activity-theoretical approach to developmental research.* Helsinki, Finland: Orienta-Konsultit Oy.

Engestrom, Y. (2000). Activity theory as a framework for analyzing and redesigning work. *Ergonomics, 43*(7), 960. doi:10.1080/001401300409143

Engeström, Y., Miettinen, R., & Punamäki, R.-L. (Eds.). (1999). *Perspectives on activity theory.* Cambridge, UK: Cambridge University Press.

Foreman, J. (2003, July-August). Next generation: Educational technology versus the lecture. *EDUCASE,* 12-22. Retrieved from http://web.reed.edu/cis/tac/meetings/Next%20Generation%20Ed%20Tech.pdf

Glaser, B. (1965). The constant comparative method of qualitative analysis. *Social Problems, 12*(4), 436–445. doi:10.1525/sp.1965.12.4.03a00070

Hodges, L. C., & Harvey, L. C. (2003). Evaluation of student learning in organic chemistry using the solo taxonomy. *Journal of Chemical Education, 80,* 785–787. doi:10.1021/ed080p785

Johnson, R., & Onwuegbuzie, A. (2004). Mixed methods research: A research paradigm whose time has come. *Educational Researcher, 33*(7), 14–26. doi:10.3102/0013189X033007014

Jonassen, D. H. (2000). Revisiting activity theory as a framework for designing student-centered learning environment. In Jonassen, D. H., & Land, S. M. (Eds.), *Theoretical foundations of learning environments* (pp. 89–121). Mahwah, NJ: Lawrence Erlbaum Associate.

Jonassen, D. H., & Rohrer-Murphy, L. (1999). Activity theory as a framework for designing constructivist learning environments. *Educational Technology Research and Development, 47*(1), 61–79. doi:10.1007/BF02299477

Kaptelinin, V. (1996a). Activity theory: Implication for human-computer interaction. In Nardi, B. A. (Ed.), *Context and consciousness: Activity theory and human-computer interaction* (pp. 103–116). Cambridge, MA: MIT Press.

Kaptelinin, V. (1996b). Computer-mediated activity: Functional organs in social and developmental contexts. In Nardi, B. A. (Ed.), *Context and consciousness: Activity theory and human-computer interaction* (pp. 45–68). Cambridge, MA: MIT Press.

Kaptelinin, V., & Nardi, B. A. (1997). Activity theory: Basic concepts and applications. In *Proceedings of CHI '97* (pp. 158-159).

Kriz, W. C., & Hense, J. U. (2006). Theory-oriented evaluation for the design of and research in gaming and simulation. *Simulation & Gaming, 37*(2), 268–283. doi:10.1177/1046878106287950

Kuutti, K. (1991). *The concept of activity as a basic unit of analysis for CSCW research.* Paper presented at the Second European Conference on Computer-Supported Cooperative Work.

Kuutti, K. (1996). Activity theory as a potential framework for human-computer interaction research. In Nardi, B. A. (Ed.), *Context and consciousness: Activity theory and human-computer interaction* (pp. 17–44). Cambridge, MA: MIT Press.

Marshall, C., & Rossman, G. (1995). *Designing qualitative research* (2nd ed.). Thousand Oaks, CA: Sage.

Minogue, J., & Jones, G. (2009). Measuring the impact of Haptic feedback using the SOLO taxonomy. *International Journal of Science Education, 31,* 1359–1378. doi:10.1080/09500690801992862

Mislevy, R., Almond, R., & Lukas, J. (2003). *Brief intro to Evidence-Centered Design* (CSE Tech. Rep. No. 632). The National Center for Research on Evaluation, Standards, Student Testing (CRESST).

Neal, L. (2003). *Predictions for 2003: e-learning's leading lights look ahead*. Retrieved February 22, 2004, from http://www.elearnmag.org/subpage/sub_page.cfm/article_pk=6541&page_number_nb=17title-COLUMN

Norman, D. (2005). Human-centered design considered harmful. *Interaction, 12*(4), 12–19. doi:10.1145/1070960.1070976

Patton, M. (2002). *Qualitative research and evaluation methods*. Thousand Oaks, CA: Sage Publications.

Prensky, M. (2001). *Digital Game-Based Learning*. New York: McGraw-Hill.

Rejeski, D. (2002). *Gaming our way to a better future*. Retrieved February 22, 2004, from http://www.avault.com/developer/getarticle.asp?name=drejeski1

Shelton, B. (2007). Designing educational games for activity-goal alignment. In Shelton, B., & Wiley, A. (Eds.), *Educational design and use of computer simulation games* (pp. 103–130). Sense Publishers.

Shelton, B. E., & Wiley, D. A. (2007). Introduction. In Shelton, B. E., & Wiley, D. A. (Eds.), *Modeling and simulations for learning and instruction: The design and use of simulation computer games in education* (pp. 1–2). The Netherlands: Sence Publishers.

Van Eck, R. (2007). Six ideas in search of a discipline. In Shelton, B. E., & Wiley, D. A. (Eds.), *Modeling and simulations for learning and instruction: The design and use of simulation computer games in education*. The Netherlands: Sence Publishers.

Williamson, D., Bauer, M., Steinberg, L., Mislevy, R., & Behrens, J. (2003, April). *Creating a complex measurement model using evidence centered design*. Paper presented at American Educational Research Association/NCME conference, Chicago.

Yamagata-Lynch, L. C. (2007). Confronting analytical dilemmas for understanding complex human interactions in design-based research from a cultural-historical activity theory (CHAT) gramework. *Journal of the Learning Sciences, 16*(4), 451–484.

APPENDIX A

Figure 4. AIM SOLO taxonomy

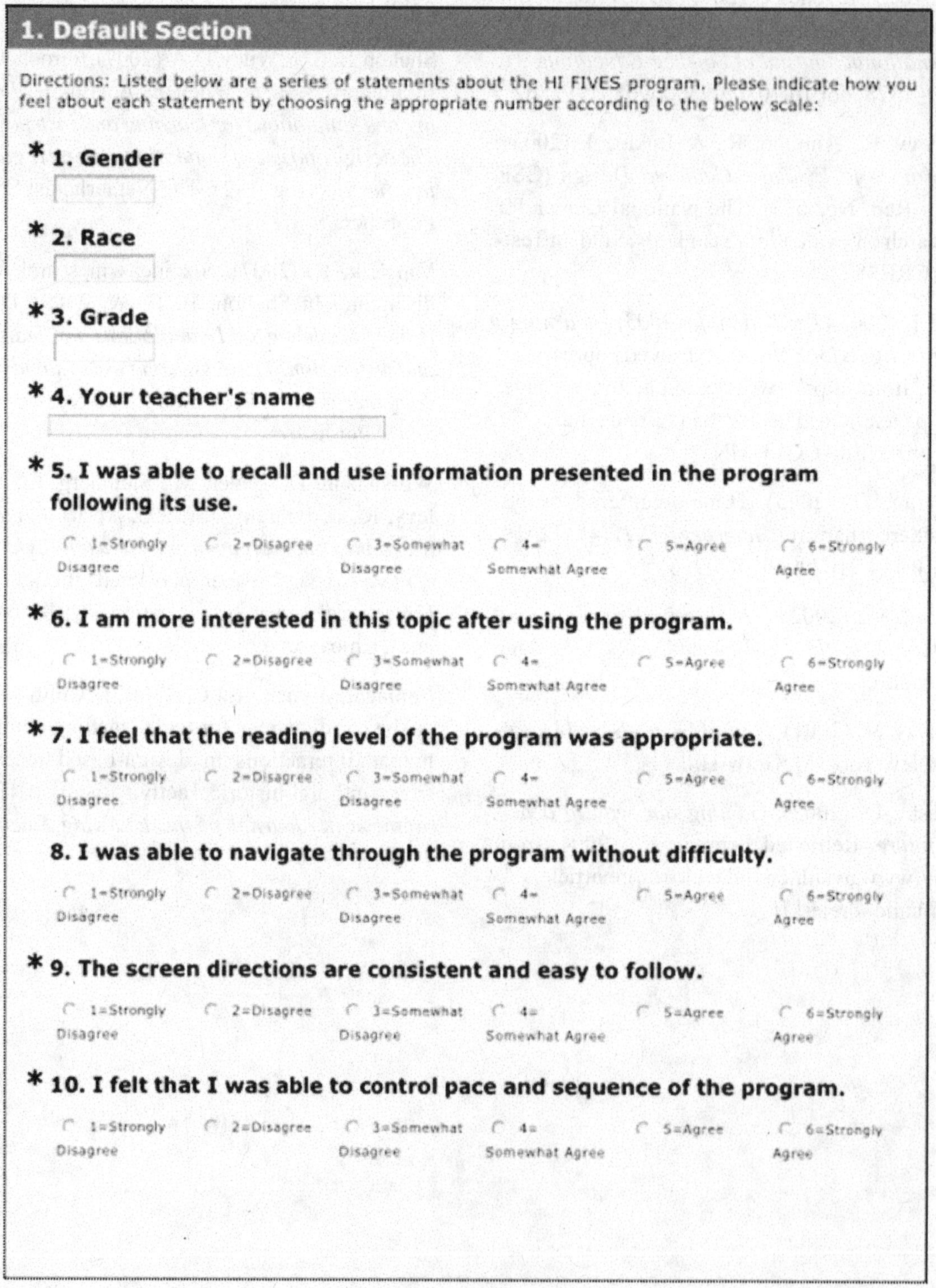

1. Default Section

Directions: Listed below are a series of statements about the HI FIVES program. Please indicate how you feel about each statement by choosing the appropriate number according to the below scale:

* 1. Gender

* 2. Race

* 3. Grade

* 4. Your teacher's name

* 5. I was able to recall and use information presented in the program following its use.

    ○ 1=Strongly Disagree   ○ 2=Disagree   ○ 3=Somewhat Disagree   ○ 4= Somewhat Agree   ○ 5=Agree   ○ 6=Strongly Agree

* 6. I am more interested in this topic after using the program.

    ○ 1=Strongly Disagree   ○ 2=Disagree   ○ 3=Somewhat Disagree   ○ 4= Somewhat Agree   ○ 5=Agree   ○ 6=Strongly Agree

* 7. I feel that the reading level of the program was appropriate.

    ○ 1=Strongly Disagree   ○ 2=Disagree   ○ 3=Somewhat Disagree   ○ 4= Somewhat Agree   ○ 5=Agree   ○ 6=Strongly Agree

8. I was able to navigate through the program without difficulty.

    ○ 1=Strongly Disagree   ○ 2=Disagree   ○ 3=Somewhat Disagree   ○ 4= Somewhat Agree   ○ 5=Agree   ○ 6=Strongly Agree

* 9. The screen directions are consistent and easy to follow.

    ○ 1=Strongly Disagree   ○ 2=Disagree   ○ 3=Somewhat Disagree   ○ 4= Somewhat Agree   ○ 5=Agree   ○ 6=Strongly Agree

* 10. I felt that I was able to control pace and sequence of the program.

    ○ 1=Strongly Disagree   ○ 2=Disagree   ○ 3=Somewhat Disagree   ○ 4= Somewhat Agree   ○ 5=Agree   ○ 6=Strongly Agree

Figure 5.

11. I believe that the graphics and animation enhanced the material presented in the program.

◯ 1=Strongly Disagree   ◯ 2=Disagree   ◯ 3=Somewhat Disagree   ◯ 4= Somewhat Agree   ◯ 5=Agree   ◯ 6=Strongly Agree

* 12. I believe that I have learned a lot about science by participating in this activity

◯ 1=Strongly Disagree   ◯ 2=Disagree   ◯ 3=Somewhat Disagree   ◯ 4= Somewhat Agree   ◯ 5=Agree   ◯ 6=Strongly Agree

* 13. I feel that the graphics and animation did NOT make the program any more interesting.

◯ 1=Strongly Disagree   ◯ 2=Disagree   ◯ 3=Somewhat Disagree   ◯ 4= Somewhat Agree   ◯ 5=Agree   ◯ 6=Strongly Agree

* 14. This program was different from the types of things we typically do in science class.

◯ 1=Strongly Disagree   ◯ 2=Disagree   ◯ 3=Somewhat Disagree   ◯ 4= Somewhat Agree   ◯ 5=Agree   ◯ 6=Strongly Agree

* 15. I do NOT feel any more interested in this topic after using the program.

◯ 1=Strongly Disagree   ◯ 2=Disagree   ◯ 3=Somewhat Disagree   ◯ 4= Somewhat Agree   ◯ 5=Agree   ◯ 6=Strongly Agree

* 16. I was NOT able to remember and use information presented in the program following its use.

◯ 1=Strongly Disagree   ◯ 2=Disagree   ◯ 3=Somewhat Disagree   ◯ 4= Somewhat Agree   ◯ 5=Agree   ◯ 6=Strongly Agree

* 17. I found the program confusing and difficult to navigate through.

◯ 1=Strongly Disagree   ◯ 2=Disagree   ◯ 3=Somewhat Disagree   ◯ 4= Somewhat Agree   ◯ 5=Agree   ◯ 6=Strongly Agree

* 18. On a scale of 1-10, with a 1 being not at all interesting and a 10 being extremely interesting, how would you rate this program? Choose the number of your choice below.

◯ 1   ◯ 2   ◯ 3   ◯ 4   ◯ 5   ◯ 6   ◯ 7   ◯ 8   ◯ 9   ◯ 10

Figure 6.

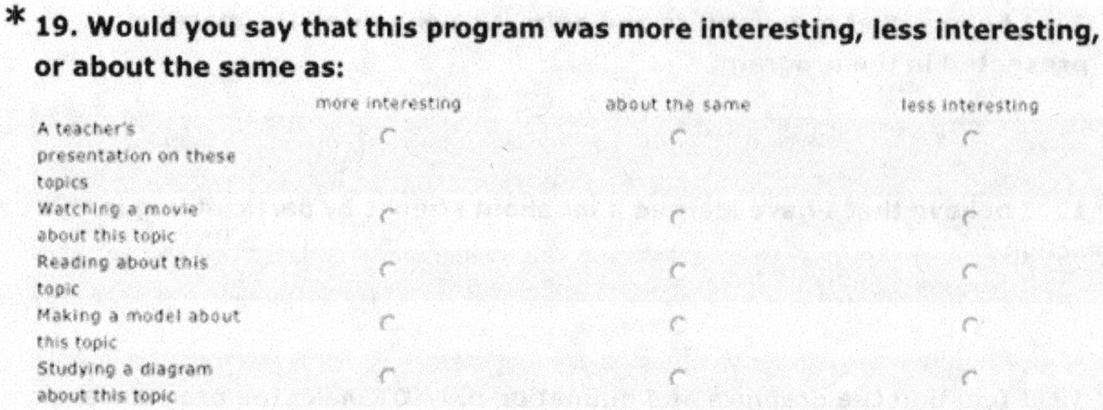

* 19. Would you say that this program was more interesting, less interesting, or about the same as:

	more interesting	about the same	less interesting
A teacher's presentation on these topics	○	○	○
Watching a movie about this topic	○	○	○
Reading about this topic	○	○	○
Making a model about this topic	○	○	○
Studying a diagram about this topic	○	○	○

APPENDIX B

1. What is your favorite class?
2. How much do you like science (or math) class? If you could rate your math class on a scale from 1-10 what would it be?
3. What is your favorite part of science (or math) class?
4. Do you use the computer a lot in class? Do you like it?
5. What do you use the computer for when you use it?
6. Do you play computer and/or video games at home?
7. How many hours per day would you say you play? Okay how about per week?
8. Did you like playing Mr./Mrs.... Game?
9. Why did you or did you not like it?
10. If you played video games in science (or math) class more often, how would that change your response to question 2?
11. Did the game make you do the math in the problems?

This work was previously published in International Journal of Gaming and Computer-Mediated Simulations, Volume 2, Issue 3, edited by Richard E. Ferdig, pp. 24-42, copyright 2010 by IGI Publishing (an imprint of IGI Global).

Chapter 12
Computer-Generated Three-Dimensional Training Environments:
The Simulation, User, and Problem-Based Learning (SUPL) Approach

Michael Garrett
Edith Cowan University, Australia

Mark McMahon
Edith Cowan University, Australia

ABSTRACT

Problem-based learning is an instructional strategy that emphasises the accumulation and development of knowledge via an active and experiential based approach to solving problems. This pedagogical framework can be instantiated using gaming technology to provide learners with the ability to control their learning experience within a dynamic, responsive, and visually rich three-dimensional virtual environment. In this regard, a conceptual framework referred to as the Simulation, User, and Problem-based Learning (SUPL) approach has been developed in order to inform the design of 3D simulation environments based on gaming technology within a problem-based learning pedagogy. The SUPL approach identifies a series of design factors relative to the user, the problem-solving task, and the 3D simulation environment that guide the learning process and facilitate the transfer of knowledge. This paper will present a simulation environment design according to this conceptual framework for a problem-solving task within the context of an underground mine emergency evacuation. The problem-solving task will be designed to satisfy learning objectives that relate to the development of knowledge and skills for emergency evacuation of the Dominion Mining's Challenger mining operation located in South Australia.

DOI: 10.4018/978-1-4666-0029-4.ch012

INTRODUCTION

Computer-generated three-dimensional (3D) simulation environments allow users to experience real, recreated, abstract, or imaginary environments that may be of impractical size, infeasible distance, prohibitive cost, or too significant a hazard to experience in person (Baylis, 2000). As such, 3D simulation environments provide safe and effective tools for education and training, enabling the development of knowledge and skills for use in real world environments. Most importantly, the virtual environment can authentically represent aspects of the real world to enhance learning transfer (Brown, Collins, & Duguid, 1989; Dobson et al., 2001).

The technical development of 3D environments has been heavily influenced by innovations within the gaming industry, where high consumer demand has driven rapid advancements in associated hardware and software technologies. This is particularly evident with regard to First Person Shooter (FPS) games, where the player is provided with a first person perspective of a three dimensional environment. FPS games are typically characterised as being on the cutting edge of gaming technology in terms of visual fidelity and performance, and have amongst the highest of expectations placed upon them by the gaming public. The abilities of 3D gaming technologies, in particular the game engines used to power FPS games, have not gone unnoticed, with proponents of computer assisted learning recognising the potential of these technologies to function as simulation environments. This has given rise to the serious games movement, which focuses on the application of gaming technologies and concepts for simulation and learning purposes. FPS game engines have been successfully used to this end in fields such as architecture, defence, mining, and occupational health and safety (Bonk & Dennen, 2005; Malhorta, 2002; Mantovani, Gamberini, Martinelli, & Varotto, 2001; Orr, Filigenzi, & Ruff, 2003).

In order to facilitate learning in a simulation environment, the environment must go beyond modelling the system to provide goals and guidance for the end user (de Jong et al., 1998; Withers, 2005). One such framework that is consistent with the experiential and user-focussed nature of 3D simulation environments is that of problem-based learning. The process of solving problems and the subsequent knowledge that is acquired during the learning process supports the generation of contextual knowledge for use in future applications (Hmelo-Silver, 2004). Problem-based learning promotes active, transferable learning whereby learners use the task to develop a strategic model that can go beyond the specific problem to solve future problems (Barrows & Tamblyn, 1980).

2. PROBLEM-BASED LEARNING WITHIN A 3D SIMULATION ENVIRONMENT

Problem-based learning is an approach to learning that is situated in problem-solving experience and consistent with experiential-based learning (Hmelo-Silver, 2004). Two fundamental postulates drive problem-based learning; that learning through problem solving is more effective in the creation of bodies of knowledge usable in the future, and that problem-solving skills are more important than memory skills (Barrows & Tamblyn, 1980). Problem-based learning uses problems as the stimulus and focus for student activity and differs from other instructional methods in that it begins with problems rather than with the exposition of disciplinary knowledge (Boud & Feletti, 1997). Problem-solving forms the primary process through which learning takes place. This is influenced by both factors internal to the problem solver, in terms of their existing knowledge, skills, and experience, and external in terms of the variable characteristics and representation of the problem (Jonassen, 2000; Lee, 2004; Newell & Simon, 1972; Smith, 1988; Zhang, 1991).

Problem-based learning is successful only if the scenarios that learners engage in are of high quality, whereby learners are led to a particular area of study in order to achieve specified learning objectives which have been defined in advance (Wood, 2003). These scenarios need to be provided in a format that allows the learner to challenge and develop their reasoning skills and stimulate their self-directed study (Barrows & Tamblyn, 1980). Problem-based learning scenarios should also facilitate the learner's ability to evaluate their skills and knowledge in working with the problem (Barrows & Tamblyn, 1980; Hmelo-Silver, 2004). The design variables to be considered in this regard thus relate to the format and presentation of the problem and the manner in which the learning process is directed and controlled (Arts,

Gijselaers, & Segers, 2002; Barrows, 1986). This takes place in conjunction with an understanding of the affordances of technology in presenting the problem as well as the extent to which the problem-solving task is structured to accommodate the background and needs of the user.

The framework presented in Figure 1 was derived from a review of the literature (see Sections 2.1 through 2.4) that explored the interplay between:

- The characteristics of the user
- The nature of the problem-solving task, and;
- The affordances and limitations of 3D simulation environments;

Figure 1. Simulation, User, and Problem-based Learning (SUPL) approach

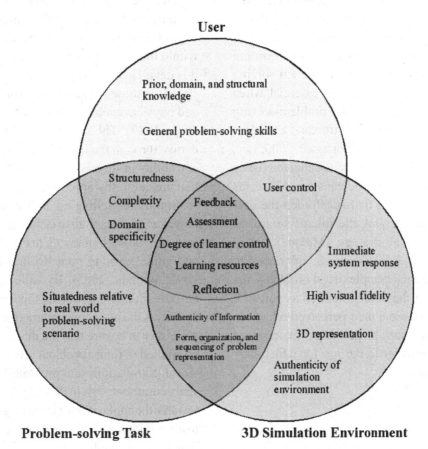

This framework, referred to as the Simulation, User, and Problem-based Learning (SUPL) approach, identifies a series of design factors which guide the learning process and facilitate the transfer of knowledge relative to user, problem-solving task, and 3D simulation environment components. Central to all three components are the aspects of problem-based learning which mediate the learning process.

2.1 Accommodating the Needs of Users

While rarely under the control of the designer, a range of user characteristics can impact greatly on the quality of learning and need to be taken into consideration. Such characteristics can be categorised according to cognitive and metacognitive factors; motivational and affective factors; developmental and social factors; and individual differences (American Psychological Association, 1997). To a certain extent, these characteristics are dependent on the context in which learning takes place. Learners' existing problem-solving skills and prior knowledge are essential when considering the nature of the problem-solving task in terms of the level of structure, complexity, and domain specificity (Jonassen, 2000; Lee, 2004; Smith, 1988). Similarly, the characteristics of the environment must be considered in terms of the level of control that is afforded the user as well as understanding the role of control as a key motivational strategy (Malone, 1980). Understanding user requirements with regard to the representational complexity of problems, the extent to which they are structured as part of a learning sequence and their perceived relevance necessary precursors to providing experiences that promote transfer to the job for which they are being trained.

2.2 Problems that Support Learning Transfer

A simulation represents a real world system to foster the transfer of knowledge and to develop conclusions that provide insight into the behaviour of the real world system being modelled (McHaney, 1991; Towne, 1995). The success of a simulation is often measured by the degree of knowledge transfer and is only of value if the skills addressed and improved upon in the simulation environment are required in the operational environment that is being modelled (A. L. Alexander, Brunye, Sidman, & Weil, 2005). Representing the system and it's underlying behaviour facilitates this objective, with the assumption being that a faithful representation will encourage knowledge transfer between the simulation environment and the real world system.

This assumption is consistent with Brown, Collins, and Duguid's (1989) theory of situated cognition which asserts that knowledge is situated within the activity, context and culture in which it is developed and used. Such activity promotes cognition through the deliberate use of the social and physical context of the environment (Brown et al., 1989). The communities of practice that evolve through the interplay between experience and ability in situated cognition ensure outcomes that are culturally appropriate.

Simply modelling an authentic environment however is not enough to ensure learning without an instructional framework to effectively support and guide learning (van Rosmalen, 1994; Tait, 1994; Withers, 2005). By utilising a problem-based learning framework in this regard, authentic activity is the basis for encouraging the reflection necessary to ensure that the developed skills can be applied to future problem scenarios in the real world. Simulations and problem-based learning share common goals in that they are both directed towards the application of knowledge and concepts to new situations. Thus, problems can be provided that replicate authentic tasks and enhance the potential for transfer inherent in problem-based learning.

2.3 Leveraging from the Affordances of 3D Environments

Computer-generated 3D environments based on FPS game engines are an appropriate means for simulating real world environments based on their ability to represent three dimensional spaces at a high visual quality while allowing the user fluid control of the virtual environment. Simulation environments of this nature utilise Euclidean geometry to describe the objects within them, and as such, can be used to construct scale representations of real world spaces, preserving dimensions, perspective, and relative distances to scale. Furthermore, the potential for high visual fidelity inherent in this type of environment can be used to depict a realistic virtual space where the behaviour of objects and their subsequent relationships with each other and the user can be represented appropriately, whilst also providing the user with a sense of presence and immersion (Gernmanchis, Cartwright, & Pettit, 2005; Sadowski & Stanney, 2002; Shiratuddin & Thabet, 2002).

Given these capabilities, 3D environments based on FPS gaming technology are well suited to the representation of real world tasks that may involve movement and orientation, complex object manipulation, or decision making in a three dimensional space (Munro et al., 2002). Furthermore, the scripting languages and other programmable constructs inherent in FPS game engines provide the ability to structure and facilitate instruction in accordance with a problem-based learning pedagogy, where assessment, feedback, learning resources, control of the learning process, and reflection can be provided for.

3. CONTEXT OF THE SIMULATION DESIGN

Dominion Mining has acknowledged the potential of a computer-generated simulation environment of the Challenger underground gold mine to be utilised as part of their emergency training procedures for underground vehicle fire scenarios.

The Challenger underground gold mine consists of a main shaft, referred to as the decline, which descends in a spiral configuration parallel to the main ore body with smaller sub-shafts protruding into the ore body in order to facilitate extraction. The decline descends in twenty metre vertical increments, with each level being labelled according to its depth below the entrance to the mine. Each level has a vent rise, for controlling air flow within the mine, and an escape rise, which is a ladder that allows personnel to climb the twenty metre vertical distance between levels of the mine rapidly in the event that access to, or usage of, the main decline is obstructed during an emergency. Figure 2 and Figure 3 demonstrate the structure of the Challenger mine and interior, respectively.

Dominion employees who enter the underground mine at Challenger are outfitted with standard equipment that includes a personal radio if not working with a mining vehicle, a cap lamp, which is a light that is attached to the helmet, and a self rescuer, which is a portable gas mask which provides oxygen for use when there is a lack of breathable air within the mining environment. The duration of the oxygen supply provided by a self rescuer is contingent on the level of physical activity of the person who is wearing it.

Dominion's existing emergency evacuation procedures direct personnel to locate one of several refuge chambers that are located throughout the mine in the event of a fire. These refuge chambers provide a safe haven for personnel while they await rescue and are self contained, with their own battery power supply and oxygen cylinders independent to the power and air that is provided from the surface. The method advocated by Dominion

Figure 2. Cross-sectional diagram of the Challenger mine

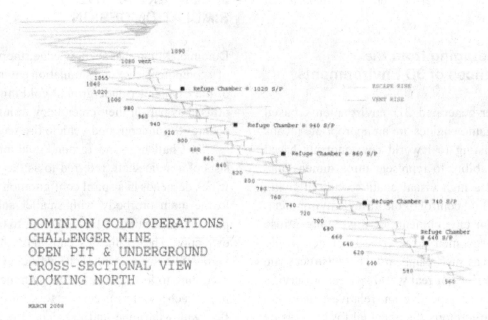

for reaching a refuge chamber in the event of an emergency evacuation underground is specified in detail during induction training for personnel at the Challenger mine. In the event that personnel become aware that an emergency evacuation has been declared they are instructed to:

Figure 3. Interior image from the Challenger mine taken on the decline on level 920

- Evacuate immediately to the nearest refuge chamber to the area in which they are working, walking down the decline if possible;
- Not attempt to walk past or extinguish the fire unless it is small and they are confident to do so;
- Not use escape rises during a fire under any circumstances except where there is a blockage to the main decline which needs to be cleared in order to reach a refuge chamber, and;
- Utilise a self rescuer if smoke is encountered along the way to the nearest refuge chamber.

4. DESIGN OF A CORRESPONDING SIMULATION ENVIRONMENT

Design documentation was developed using components of the Document-Oriented Design and Development for Experiential Learning (DODDEL) model (McMahon, 2009), which is a flexible document-orientated model for the design of serious games. With reference to the SUPL approach proposed in this paper, components of the DODDEL model were used to structure the design process, which consisted of:

- A situation analysis of the underground fire emergency evacuation scenario at the Challenger mine, encompassing the aims and outcomes of a corresponding simulation environment, the subsequent learning approach to be adopted, and an examination of the learner and the context in which learning would occur, and;
- The subsequent development of a detailed design proposal which identified the specific concepts, challenges and feedback and relevant game approach.

Key to the DODDEL model is the iterative nature of the elements within the above components and the fact that they articulate from broad design to detailed specifications in a manner that supports specific milestones with regard to documented output. The design is articulated below with reference to the role of the SUPPL approach in informing the design decisions required for each stage.

4.1 Situation analysis

A situation analysis is used as the basis for the exploration of design. Such analysis is used to identify the aims and learning outcomes of the product as well as the user attributes and contextual requirements that will affect the product design in a manner where each of the elements inform each other (McMahon, 2009).

4.1.1 Aims and Outcomes

A general set of aims and outcomes were derived which identified the attributes that needed to be instilled in the learner for emergency evacuations during underground fire scenarios in the Challenger mine. The SUPL approach was adopted to guide the development of these aims and outcomes, which are listed below, and required a focus on the situatedness of the learning outcomes relative to the real world task.

Organisational aims of the simulation environment

- Augment existing training;
- Provide personnel with a more realistic depiction of an emergency evacuation scenario, and;
- Improve decision making during an emergency evacuation of the Challenger mine.

Learning outcomes of the simulation environment

- Know the layout, structure, and organisation of the Challenger mining environment ;
- Understand the role and appropriate application of the self rescuer and cap lamp;
- Understand the function of and appropriate application of refuge chambers and escape rises, and;
- Perform an emergency evacuation procedure during an underground fire at Challenger.

The identification of learning outcomes allows consideration of the authentic elements that will need to be accommodated in the 3D simulation environment. These are explored in greater detail in Sections 4.2.1.1 and 4.2.2.1.

4.1.2 Learning Approach

The 3D simulation environment will be instantiated in accordance with the SUPL approach described in this paper. As such, learning activity will focus on problem-solving with the goal of developing transferable knowledge in accordance with the aims and outcomes identified in Table 1 and Table 2. The SUPL approach indicates that this process will require a contextually authentic representation of the Challenger mining environment as well as an appropriately situated problem-solving task in order to facilitate learning transfer. The nature of this problem-solving task will also need to be characterised such that it is consistent with the prior problem-solving knowledge and experience of learners.

4.1.3 Learner and Context

An understanding of the learner and the context in which learning occurs is crucial in enabling the design to cater to the needs of the target audience (McMahon, 2009). Achieving such an understanding entails an examination of the attributes of the learner as well as the constraints and affordances

Table 1. Questions and responses posed to the learner via the facilitator construct

Learner action	Question or response posed to learner	Impact
User heading in the wrong direction	Asks the learner if they are sure they are heading in the right direction	Learner re-assesses their current bearing
User continues to head in the wrong direction	Tells the learner that they are headed in the wrong direction and to turn around immediately	Learner turns around and knows that their objective is not in the direction that they were previously heading
User encounters smoke	Asks the learner what they should do when they first encounter smoke	Learner considers the appropriate course of action based on their induction training
User encounters smoke and is in danger of dying because they have not equipped their self-rescuer	Tells the learner to equip their self-rescuer immediately or they will succumb to the smoke	Learner equips their self rescuer
User getting too close to a vehicle fire	Tells the learner that they are getting too close to the fire	Learner re-assesses their current bearing
Use of escape rise	Asks the learner whether it was necessary to use the escape rise	Learner considers whether it was necessary to climb the escape rise in order to reach a refuge chamber
Remaining self-rescuer capacity	Tells the learner when their self-rescuer gets to 50%, 10%, and 0% oxygen capacity respectively	Learner attempts to reach a refuge chamber as soon as possible
Interruption of external oxygen and power supplies	Tells the learner that external supplies of oxygen and power have been interrupted	Learner knows that the refuge chamber lights will be red instead of green

Table 2. Learning objectives for the simulation environment

Learning objective	Relevant knowledge	Relevant skills
Recognition of an emergency evacuation scenario	An emergency evacuation may be signalled via radio communication or by the release of stench gas	
Awareness of the primary goal during an emergency evacuation scenario	The primary objective for any personnel working within the mine once an emergency evacuation has been declared is to retreat to the nearest refuge chamber as quickly and safely as possible	
Awareness of the locations of refuge chambers within the mine	Refuge chambers are located on levels 1020, 940, 860, 800, and 740 within the Challenger mine. The flashing lights mounted on refuge chambers indicate their presence when in close proximity	
Awareness of the locations of escape rises within the mine	Escape rises are located in the sub-shafts on every level of the Challenger mine with their direction indicated via reflective green signs	
Understanding the layout and structure of the mine	Each level of the mine is separated by distances of 20 metres vertically, or 140 metres on a 1:7 decline. Each level of the mine is labelled according to its vertical distance from the main portal starting at 1200 and descending in intervals of 20 metres	
Performance of the emergency evacuation procedure	Park up all vehicles, go to the nearest refuge chamber, and utilise self rescuers if required. Personnel should also not attempt to walk past or extinguish the fire unless it is small and they are confident to do so.	Identifying the ideal refuge chamber Navigating to a refuge chamber safely and efficiently Utilising a self rescuer effectively
Application of visual cues that can assist navigation	Depth markings, reflective signage, refuge chamber lights, and other assorted infrastructure	Navigating to a refuge chamber safely and efficiently
Application of escape rises	Escape rises provide access between levels of the mine and are intended to only be used when the decline is blocked in the event of a fire	Navigating to a refuge chamber safely and efficiently
Application of the self rescuer	Self contained personal oxygen supply for use in situations where the level of breathable air in the surrounding environment is not sufficient. Provides 100 minutes of oxygen at low physical exertion, 30 minutes at medium physical exertion, and 10 minutes at high physical exertion	Utilising a self rescuer effectively
Awareness of the function and capabilities of the cap lamp	Directional light attached to the miner's helmet which provides 30 hours of light at low beam setting, and 15 hours at high beam setting	
Awareness of the environmental conditions that can affect the ability to reach a refuge chamber	Fire, smoke, external power failure, external oxygen supply failure, insufficient oxygen in the mining environment, and lighting conditions in the mining environment	Navigating to a refuge chamber safely and efficiently

of the environment in which the product will be used (McMahon, 2009).

The SUPL approach categorises learner attributes within a problem-based learning context according to prior knowledge, domain knowledge, structural knowledge, and general problem-solving skills. Whilst the full extent of these attributes cannot be known with complete certainty and variance is likely to exist between learners due to differing degrees of experience at Challenger, the induction training that all Dominion personnel are required to undertake does establish a common foundation which can be used to inform problem selection in a manner that is consistent with the learners' level of understanding of the subject domain. Induction training establishes knowledge of:

- The layout, structure, and organisation of the Challenger mine, including the locations of escape rises and refuge chambers;
- The emergency procedures which mandate evacuation to the nearest refuge chamber in the event of a fire underground;
- The function and operational duration of the cap lamp and self rescuer, and;
- The actions that may be required during an emergency evacuation.

To ensure the preparedness of learners to engage in the environment, external factors that may impact on the capacity of the product to deliver outcomes within an organisational framework also need to be considered. In the context of the Challenger mine site, this includes the necessity of individual work on a single dedicated desktop computer allocated for this purpose. This computer will be brand new and built specifically for 3D graphics applications with hardware that allows the simulation environment to run without any performance issues.

The environment will necessarily be a standalone one, with guidance provided through the product itself with learners being excused from their normal duties to undertake the training. In this manner, a facilitator type construct will be directed to pose predefined questions to the learner, call for certain content to be displayed, or put the simulation into a certain state under specific circumstances which are triggered in response to input or changing system wide variables (Munro et al., 2002). Table 1 details the predefined questions posed to the learner by the facilitator construct.

4.2 Design Proposal

The design proposal is as an extension of the situation analysis which proposes a general approach to meet the needs of the product that have been previously elicited (McMahon, 2009). This proposal identifies the type of product and the approach that will be implemented, the specific concepts

that underpin the broad learning outcomes, and the nature of cause and effect interaction within the product (McMahon, 2009).

4.2.1 Game Approach

The game approach situates the product in a genre and identifies some basic criteria for its look and feel, setting up expectations about the activities that will be undertaken by the learner as well as the setting and context in which this will occur (McMahon, 2009). Given the learning approach described in Section 4.1.1, the game will consist of a three-dimensional simulation of the Challenger mining environment during an underground fire emergency in which the learner will undertake problem-solving activity from a first person perspective. The SUPL approach suggests that representing the context, setting, and activity of such a scenario in order to affect learning transfer is contingent on the ability of the 3D simulation environment to authentically depict the real world space whilst providing the user with sufficient control over their experience.

4.2.1.1 The 3D Simulation Environment

An authentic simulation demands that issues relating to physical and functional fidelity are addressed in order to facilitate transfer between the simulation environment and the real world system that is being modelled (Stone, 2008; Williams, 2003). To this end, the simulation environment will utilise the three-dimensional perspective and high visual fidelity provided by gaming technology to create a perceptible representation of the Challenger mining environment during an underground fire emergency. In order for this to be achieved, the following elements will need to be represented with high visual fidelity:

- The spatial characteristics of the mine shafts;

- The visual cues that aid navigation within the mining environment;
- Refuge chambers and escape rises;
- Lighting and shadows, and;
- Fire and smoke.

Accurate geometry of the shafts as well as high quality 3d models will be required to represent the refuge chambers, escape rises, and the mine itself with sufficient physical fidelity in order to preserve an adequate spatial and visual model of the mine. Visual cues will also need to be represented with high visual fidelity in order to assist way-finding and navigation within the virtual mine. The environmental conditions which impact problem resolution will also need to be represented with sufficient fidelity such that they are instantly recognisable and can be negotiated accordingly.

The key functional fidelity for this product is defined by the need for an authentic sense of movement through the virtual mine with regards to their speed and the inclination of the terrain. Furthermore, the relationship between the physical effort required to traverse the mining environment and the subsequent depletion of the self rescuer oxygen supply will also need to be represented. This fidelity will be enhanced through environmental factors that can impact resolution such as the spread of smoke within the mine.

Issues of functional fidelity identified by the SUPL approach also relate to the manner in which the learner interacts with the system and the immediacy with which it responds to their input. The learner will need to be provided with capabilities and methods for interaction within the virtual mine that model those which would be available to them during a real world emergency evacuation, including:

- The ability to walk and run throughout the simulation environment at speeds which approximate those in the real world environment;

- The ability to orient themselves with full 360 degrees of freedom;
- The ability to climb up and down escape rises;
- The ability to equip a self rescuer, and;
- The ability to change the beam settings on their cap lamp from low to high, and vice-versa.

These methods for interaction will need to be such that no perceptible delay will exist between the learner's input and the system response. In this manner, interaction will be sustained within the simulation environment whilst also fostering the learner's sense of presence and perceived ownership over the learning process.

4.2.2 Specific Concepts

Achieving the aims and outcomes of the product requires identifying all of the underpinning knowledge and skills (McMahon, 2009). Table 2 details the specific learning objectives of the simulation environment that have been derived from the aims and outcomes identified during the situation analysis.

Having established the specific concepts underpinning the broader aims and outcomes of the training simulation and the knowledge and experience of the learners who will be using it, it is now possible to determine an appropriate problem-solving task in accordance with the SUPL approach.

4.2.2.1 The Problem-Solving Task

Determining the characteristics of the problem-solving task and the nature of the challenge that lies therein is necessary towards the satisfaction of learning objectives as the composition of a problem not only shapes the problem-solver's perception of the problem-solving task, but also the problem-solving skills and abilities that may be required in order to solve it (Jonassen, 2000;

Lee, 2004; Taylor, 1975). The SUPL approach suggests that the characteristics of a problem that are significant in this regard are structuredness, complexity, domain specificity, situatedness relative to the real world problem-solving task being modelled, authenticity of information, and the manner in which the problem is represented.

The problem-solving task will consist of three domain specific problem-solving instances in which the learner will be tasked with evacuating from a virtual representation of the Challenger mining environment under emergency conditions. The learner will be provided with initial information that is intended to replicate that which would be provided by an emergency evacuation order, but each successive problem-solving instance will see less information provided in this manner as progress is made (see Table 3). Furthermore, the three problem-solving instances will also become successively more complex as changing environmental conditions will require increased deliberation from the learner in order to achieve resolution (see Table 4).

The problem-solving task will be closely situated relative to the emergency evacuation process within the real world Challenger mine. The vir-tual mining environment itself will embody the spatial characteristics, visual cues, and environmental conditions of the real world mine such that the spatial knowledge that is developed will be situated relative to the real world mine. Evidence of a human presence will also be exhibited within the virtual mining environment in order to increase the situated nature of the simulation, including the depiction of mining vehicles and the audible radio messages they emit during an emergency evacuation.

Information provided to the learner during the problem-solving task will be as authentic as possible with regard to the real world scenario, both in terms of its content and method of delivery. The initial information provided to the learner detailed in Table 4 will be presented using audio cues to represent the personal radio over which personnel would actually receive an emergency evacuation order. Where authenticity is difficult to implement, more abstract mechanisms will be used to communicate important information that is relevant to the problem-solving task to the user, such as the icons depicting the extent of their movement, the status of their cap lamp and self rescuer, and the inclination of the terrain.

Table 3. Structuredness of problem-solving instances within the simulation environment

Problem-solving instance	Initial information provided to the learner	Unknown or uncertain elements in the problem equation
1	• Emergency evacuation declaration • Potential environmental conditions • Location of vehicle fire • Location of smoke • Goals of the problem-solving task • User's initial starting location • Location of nearest refuge chambers	• Appropriate method for reaching a refuge chamber
2	• Emergency evacuation declaration • Potential environmental conditions • Location of vehicle fire • Location of smoke • Goals of the problem-solving task	• User's initial starting location • Location of nearest refuge chambers • Appropriate method for reaching a refuge chamber
3	• Emergency evacuation declaration • Potential environmental conditions • Goals of the problem-solving task	• Location of smoke and vehicle fire • User's initial starting location • Location of nearest refuge chambers • Appropriate method for reaching a refuge chamber

Table 4. Complexity of problem-solving instances within the simulation environment

Problem-solving instance	Learner's starting position	Smoke and fire	Possible outcomes
1	Level 760 decline	Not reachable by the learner	1) Learner successfully reaches a refuge chamber
2	Level 780 sub-shaft	Fire is blocking the learner's access to the decline on Level 780. Smoke is confined to an area close to the fire and is spreading slowly.	1) Learner successfully reaches a refuge chamber 2) Failure due to contact with fire 3) Failure due to being overcome by smoke
3	Level 820 sub-shaft	Fire is blocking the decline between Level 800 and Level 780. Smoke is prevalent throughout large sections of the mine and is spreading quickly.	1) Learner successfully reaches a refuge chamber 2) Failure due to contact with fire 3) Failure due to being overcome by smoke

A number of aspects of the problem-solving task were identified as requiring high fidelity representation within the simulation environment:

- Declaration of an emergency evacuation;
- Location of refuge chambers;
- Spatial characteristics of the virtual mining environment, including the depiction of visual cues that can aid navigation;
- Inclination of the terrain, the speed at which it can be traversed, and the respective levels of physical effort required to do so;
- Environmental conditions that can affect the ability to reach a refuge chamber;
- Function and capabilities of the self rescuer, cap lamp, and personal radio, and;
- Lighting conditions of the virtual mining environment;

Representing these aspects of the problem-solving scenario with sufficient fidelity will rely on the scripting and programming abilities of the selected gaming technology as well as its ability to represent three-dimensional environments with high visual fidelity.

4.2.3 Challenges and Feedback

A rigorous approach to designing challenge and feedback is necessary to ensure that activity is goal directed and leads to positive consequences for the learner (McMahon, 2009). The SUPL approach mandates that challenge and feedback be integrated within the problem-solving task such that there is a degree of uncertainty perceived by the learner which is alleviated via the provision of relevant corrective feedback towards the achievement of the learning objectives (Johnstone, 2001; Newell & Simon, 1972; Norman & Schmidt, 1992).

Each successive problem-solving instance will scaffold the learner through increasing complexity and a greater level of independent learning (see Table 2). Control of the learning process will be shared between the simulation environment and the learner, which is appropriate given that whilst the learners' prior knowledge and experience has been established with some assurance during the situation analysis, their understanding of the problem-based learning process is not known with any degree of certainty (Davis, 1973). Thus, the learner will be granted the freedom to interact freely within the three-dimensional environment using the abilities at their disposal (see Section 4.2.1.1), but the simulation environment will structure and facilitate the learning process as described in Section 4.2.2.1. The nature of learning resources will also vary to include explicit instructions as well as implicit cues, requiring the learner to assume greater responsibility for identifying and using resources as the simulation progresses.

The scripting capabilities inherent in gaming technology provide a means by which to create a facilitator like construct within the simulation environment that can respond to learner action in order to guide the problem-based learning process. In this manner, specific user actions can be set to trigger responses from the simulation environment in the form of questions or responses in order to guide the development of higher order thinking by encouraging learners to justify their thinking and externalise their self-reflection (Barrows & Tamblyn, 1980; Hmelo-Silver, 2004; Savery & Duffy, 2001), such as when the user encounters smoke or utilises an escape rise. Questions posed to the user by the simulation environment can be used to redirect the user in the event of inappropriate action, such as when they continue to move in the wrong direction, fail to equip their self rescuer when smoke is encountered, or are too close to a vehicle fire, thus meeting the requirement of effective facilitation in preventing the learner from going off track or stalling within a problem. (Hmelo-Silver, 2004).

The feedback provided by the task environment, which consists of the physical environment that can either directly or indirectly constrain or suggest different methods by which to solve a given problem (Dunbar, 1998), can be incorporated into the simulation environment itself. Feedback detailing movement speed, the current inclination of the terrain, and the subsequent level of physical effort being exerted is required to assist the learner in understanding the relationships between these concepts and how it effects their ability to evacuate safely from the virtual mine. Similarly, the task environment will also need to provide the user with feedback relating to the status of the self rescuer, cap lamp, and personal radio, as well as inform them when they are close enough to an escape rise to climb it.

Assessment measures can also be used to provide feedback that is tied directly to the challenge and give the learner the ability to monitor their performance (McMahon, 2009; Pederson & Williams, 2004; Rushton, 2005). Such measures should be designed to test the learner's ability to fulfil the predefined learning objectives as well as assist in the appropriate learning of pertinent knowledge within a problem-based learning environment such as that advocated by the SUPL approach (Davis, 1973; Norman, 1997). Given the learning objectives detailed in Table 1, a corresponding series of assessment measures that allow the learner to monitor their performance during the problem-solving task will be presented to the learner at the conclusion of each problem-solving instance, consisting of:

- The outcome of the problem-solving instance;
- Elapsed time;
- Total physical effort exerted;
- Total distance travelled;
- Remaining self rescuer capacity;
- Whether the ideal refuge chamber was selected;
- Whether the ideal path was taken to this refuge chamber;
- Whether escape rise usage was appropriate;
- Whether self rescuer usage was appropriate;

At completion of each stage, customised reflective question prompts based on user performance will be provided to have learners reflect on the strategies for learning, as well as what they learned and how it could be reapplied in future situations (Grunefeld & Silen, 2000; Hmelo-Silver, 2004; Savery & Duffy, 2001). Table 5, Table 6, and Table 7 detail the reflective question prompts to be presented to the learner at the conclusion of each problem-solving scenario accordingly:

Table 5. Reflective questions posed to the learner at the conclusion of the first problem-solving instance

Reflective Questions	Context
1. Which factors are important in choosing the ideal refuge chamber during an emergency evacuation? 2. Which route through the mine provides the safest and most efficient access to refuge chambers? 3. Why do you think that it is important to evacuate to a refuge chamber using minimal physical effort? 4. When is it appropriate to use escape rises during an emergency evacuation? 5. When is it appropriate to equip your self-rescuer during an emergency evacuation?	User successfully reaches a refuge chamber

Table 6. Reflective questions posed to the learner at the conclusion of the second problem-solving instance

Reflective Questions	Context
1. Which factors do you consider when choosing which refuge chamber to evacuate to during an emergency? 2. Which route provides the safest and most efficient access to this refuge chamber? 3. What impact does your level of physical effort have on the duration of oxygen supply provided by your self-rescuer? 4. What is the preferred method for clearing blockages to the main decline? 5. When should you equip your self-rescuer during an emergency evacuation?	User successfully reaches a refuge chamber
1. When should you equip your self-rescuer during an emergency evacuation? 2. What impact does your level of physical effort have on the duration of oxygen supply provided by your self-rescuer? 3. How can you best manage your self-rescuer in order to prolong the supply of oxygen? 4. Which route provides the safest and most efficient access to refuge chambers? 5. What degree of impact does climbing escape rises have on the duration of oxygen supplied by your self-rescuer?	User succumbs to smoke, resulting in failure
1. Under which circumstances should use of the main decline be avoided? 2. How can blockages on the main decline be cleared? 3. Which route provides the safest and most efficient access to refuge chambers? 4. What environmental cues indicate the presence of fire? 5. When should you equip your self-rescuer during an emergency evacuation?	User makes contact with fire, resulting in failure

Table 7. Reflective questions posed to the learner at the conclusion of the third problem-solving instance

Reflective Questions	Context
1. Which environmental cues can be used to determine your location within the mine? 2. How can knowledge of the slope of the terrain assist in navigating towards a refuge chamber during low visibility conditions? 3. Which environmental cues indicate the interruption of air and power supplied to the mine from the surface? 4. What is the preferred direction of travel along the decline during an emergency evacuation? 5. When is it appropriate to travel in the opposite direction?	User successfully reaches a refuge chamber
1. Which environmental cues can be used to determine your location within the mine? 2. How can knowledge of the slope of the terrain assist in navigating towards a refuge chamber during low visibility conditions? 3. At what point should you equip your self-rescuer during an emergency evacuation? 4. How does physical effort affect the duration of oxygen supply provided by your self-rescuer? 5. How can you best manage your level of physical effort in order to prolong the supply of oxygen?	User succumbs to smoke, resulting in failure
1. Which environmental cues can be used to determine your location within the mine? 2. How can knowledge of the slope of the terrain assist in navigating towards a refuge chamber during low visibility conditions? 3. Which route provides the safest and most efficient way to reach refuge chambers within the mine? 4. Under which circumstances should use of the main decline be avoided? 5. How can blockages on the main decline be cleared?	User makes contact with fire, resulting in failure

5. CONCLUSION

This paper has argued for the development of problem-based serious games using the SUPL approach. Specifically, a focus on an integrative process to design that focuses on the nature of the problem-solving task, user needs and attributes and the capabilities of 3D simulation technology is suggested as a means to guide the learning process and ensure effective transfer of training to the real world. A 3D simulation environment based on gaming technology will be utilised as a training platform to present an authentic and high fidelity representation of emergency evacuation scenario at the Challenger mine within a problem-based learning pedagogy. Research will be conducted around the implementation of the product to gauge its value in developing the knowledge and skills required to operate effectively during a real world underground fire emergency evacuation within the Challenger mining environment, as well as to ascertain the validity of the SUPL approach as a tool to guide the design of problem-based learning using 3D simulation technology.

At the time of writing, a working prototype has been completed according to the design detailed in this paper and has been deployed to the Challenger facility for evaluation.

REFERENCES

Alexander, A. L., Brunye, T., Sidman, J., & Weil, S. A. (2005). *From gaming to training: A review of studies on fidelity, immersion, presence, and buy-in and their effects on transfer in pc-based simulations and games. DARWARS Training Impact Group*. Retrieved June 9, 2008, from http://www.darwars.com/downloads/DARWAR%20 Paper%2012205.pdf

American Psychological Association. (1997). *Learner-Centered Psychological Principles*. Retrieved October 1, 2009, from http://www.apa.org/ed/lcp2/lcp14.html

Arts, J. A. R., Gijselaers, W. H., & Segers, M. S. R. (2002). Cognitive effects of an authentic computer-supported, problem-based learning environment. *Instructional Science, 30*, 465–495. doi:10.1023/A:1020532128625

Barrows, H. S. (1986). A taxonomy of problem-based learning methods. *Medical Education, 20*, 481–486. doi:10.1111/j.1365-2923.1986.tb01386.x

Barrows, H. S., & Tamblyn, R. M. (1980). *Problem-based learning: An approach to medical education*. New York: Springer.

Baylis, W. T. (2000). The use of virtual reality in training and education. *Logistics Spectrum, 34*(4), 25–28.

Bonk, C. J., & Dennen, V. P. (2005). Massive multiplayer online gaming: A research framework for military training and education. *Office of the Under Secretary of Defence for Personnel and Readiness*. Retrieved June 17, 2008, from http://blogoehlert.typepad.com/eclippings/files/GameReport_Bonk_final.pdf

Boud, D., & Feletti, G. (1997). Changing problem-based learning: Introduction to the. In Boud, D., & Feletti, G. (Eds.), *The challenge of problem-based learning* (2nd ed.). London: Kogan Page.

Brown, J. S., Collins, A., & Duguid, P. (1989). Situated cognition and the culture of learning. *Educational Researcher, 18*(1), 32–42.

Charlin, B., Mann, K., & Hansen, P. (1998). The many faces of problem-based learning: A framework for understanding and comparison. *Medical Teacher, 20*(4), 323–330. doi:10.1080/01421599880742

Davis, G. A. (1973). *Psychology of problem-solving: Theory and practice.* New York: Basic Books.

de Jong, T., van Joolingen, W. R., Swaak, J., Veermans, K., Limbach, R., & King, S. (1998). Self-directed learning in simulation-based discover environments. *Journal of Computer Assisted Learning, 14*(1), 235–246. doi:10.1046/j.1365-2729.1998.143060.x

Dobson, M. W., Pengelly, M., Sime, J. A., Al-baladejo, S. A., Garcia, E. V., & Gonzales, F. (2001). Situated learning with co-operative agent simulations in team training. *Computers in Human Behavior, 17*(1), 547–573. doi:10.1016/S0747-5632(01)00023-1

Dunbar, K. (1998). Problem Solving. In Bechtel, W., & Graham, G. (Eds.), *A companion to Cognitive Science.* London: Blackwell.

Germanchis, T., Cartwright, W., & Pettit, C. (2005). Using computer gaming technology to explore human wayfinding and navigation abilities within a built environment. In *Proceedings of the XXII International Cartographic Conference* (pp. 11-16). A Coruna, Spain: Globabl Congresos.

Grunefeld, H., & Silen, C. (2000, November). *Problem based learning compared to project organized learning.* Retrieved June 2, 2008, from http://www.utwente.nl/itbe/owk/publicaties/docenten/doc00-39.pdf

Hmelo-Silver, C. E. (2004). Problem-based learning: What and how do students learn? *Educational Psychology Review, 16*(3), 235–266. doi:10.1023/B:EDPR.0000034022.16470.f3

Johnstone, A. H. (2001). Can problem solving be taught? *University Chemistry Education, 5*(2), 69–73.

Jonassen, D. H. (2000). Toward a Design Theory of Problem Solving. *Educational Technology Research and Development, 48*(4), 63–86. doi:10.1007/BF02300500

Lee, Y. (2004). *Student perceptions of problems' structuredness, complexity, situatedness, and information richness and their effects on problem-solving performance.* Unpublished doctoral dissertation, Florida State University, FL.

Malhorta, P. (2002). *Issues involved in real-time rendering of virtual environments.* Unpublished master's thesis, Virginia Polytechnic Institute and State University, VA.

Malone, T. (1981). Towards a theory of intrinsically motivating instruction. *Cognitive Science, 4*, 333–369. doi:10.1207/s15516709cog0504_2

Mantovani, G., Gamberini, L., Martinelli, M., & Varotto, D. (2001). Exploring the suitability of virtual environments for safety training: Signals, norms and ambiguity in a simulated emergency escape. *Cognition Technology and Work, 3*(1), 33–41. doi:10.1007/PL00011519

McHaney, R. (1991). *Computer simulation: A practical perspective.* San Diego, CA: Academic Press.

McMahon, M. (2009). The DODDEL Model:Flexible Document-Oriented Model for the Design of Serious Games. In Connolly, T., Stansfield, M., & Boyle, L. (Eds.), *Games-Based Learning Advancements for Multi-Sensory Human Computer Interfaces: Techniques and Effective Practices* (pp. 98–118). Hershey, PA: IGI Global. doi:10.4018/978-1-60566-360-9.ch006

Munro, A., Breaux, R., Patrey, J., & Sheldon, B. (2002). Cognitive aspects of virtual environment design. In Stanney, K. M. (Ed.), *Handbook of virtual environments: Design, implementation, and applications* (pp. 415–434). Mahwah, NJ: Lawrence Erlbaum.

Newell, A., & Simon, H. A. (1972). *Human problem solving*. Englewood Cliffs, NJ: Prentice-Hall.

Norman, G. R. (1988). Problem-solving skills, solving problems and problem-based learning. *Medical Education, 22*, 279–286. doi:10.1111/j.1365-2923.1988.tb00754.x

Norman, G. R. (1997). Assessment in problem-based learning. In Boud, D., & Feletti, G. (Eds.), *The challenge of problem-based learning* (2nd ed., pp. 263–268). London: Kogan Page.

Norman, G. R., & Schmidt, H. G. (1992). The psychological basis of problem-based learning: A review of the evidence. *Academic Medicine, 67*(9), 557–565. doi:10.1097/00001888-199209000-00002

Orr, T. J., Filigenzi, M. T., & Ruff, T. M. (2003). *Desktop virtual reality miner training simulator. Centres for Disease Control and Prevention.* Retrieved June 17, 2008, from http://whitepapers.silicon.com/0,39024759,60018207p,00.htm

Pederson, S., & Williams, D. (2004). A comparison of assessment practices and their effects on learning and motivation in a student-centered learning environment. *Journal of Educational Multimedia and Hypermedia, 13*(1).

Rushton, A. (2005). Formative assessment: a key to deep learning? *Medical Teacher, 27*(6), 509–513. doi:10.1080/01421590500129159

Sadowski, W., & Stanney, K. (2002). Presence in virtual environments. In Stanney, K. M. (Ed.), *Handbook of virtual environments: Design, implementation, and applications* (pp. 791–806). Mahwah, NJ: Lawrence Erlbaum.

Savery, J. R. (2006). Overview of Problem-based learning: Definitions and Distinctions. *The Interdisciplinary Journal of Problem-based Learning, 1*(1), 9–20.

Savery, J. R., & Duffy, T. M. (2001). *Problem based learning: An instructional model and its constructivist framework (CRLT Tech. Rep.).* Bloomington, Indiana: Indiana University.

Shiratuddin, M. F., & Thabet, W. (2002). Virtual office walkthrough using a 3d game engine. *International Journal of Design Computing.* Retrieved June 18, 2008, from http://faculty.arch.usyd.edu.au/kcdc/ijdc/vol04/papers/shira/ijdc_final_journal.pdf

Smith, M. U. (1988). *Toward a unified theory of problem solving: A view from biology.* Paper presented at the Annual Meeting of the American Educational Research Association, New Orleans, LA.

Stone, R. J. (2008). *Human factors guidelines for interactive 3d and games-based training systems design.*

Tait, K. (1994). Discourse: The design and production of simulation-based learning environments. In de Jong, T., & Sarti, L. (Eds.), *Design and production of multimedia simulation-based learning material.* Dordrecht, The Netherlands: Kluwer Academic Publishers.

Taylor, R. N. (1975). Perception of problem constraints. *Management Science, 22*(1), 22–29. doi:10.1287/mnsc.22.1.22

Towne, M. D. (1995). *Learning and instruction in simulation environments.* Englewood Cliffs, NJ: Educational Technology Publications.

van Rosmalen, P. (1994). SAM, simulation and multimedia. In de Jong, T., & Sarti, L. (Eds.), *Design and production of multimedia simulation-based learning material.* Dordrecht, The Netherlands: Kluwer Academic Publishers.

Williams, V. (2003). Designing simulations for learning. *E-Journal of Instructional Science and Technology, 6*(1), 50–71.

Withers, D. (2005). *Authoring tools for educational simulations (Tech. Rep.)*. Burnaby, Canada: Simon Fraser University.

Wood, D. F. (2003). Problem based learning. *British Medical Journal*, *326*, 328–330. doi:10.1136/bmj.326.7384.328

Zhang, J. (1991). The interaction of internal and external representations in a problem solving task. In *Proceedings of the Thirteenth Annual Cognitive Science Society*. Hillsdale, NJ: Lawrence Erlbaum.

This work was previously published in International Journal of Gaming and Computer-Mediated Simulations, Volume 2, Issue 3, edited by Richard E. Ferdig, pp. 43-60, copyright 2010 by IGI Publishing (an imprint of IGI Global).

Chapter 13
Friendship, Closeness and Disclosure in Second Life

Don Heider
Loyola University Chicago, USA

Adrienne L. Massanari
Loyola University Chicago, USA

ABSTRACT

3-D virtual realms offer places for people to go interact, play games, and even do business. As these realms themselves become more sophisticated, the number of participants grows and the level and type of social interactions change. Meanwhile, scholars race to try to keep up. There is a growing, but still developing literature about interaction in virtual world. This paper explores communication and social intimacy in one such world, Second Life. In this paper, results of a four year ethnography in Second Life reveal findings that refute earlier research on computer-mediated communications, and support others while offering new findings to contribute to the growing body of knowledge.

SECOND LIFE AND STUDIES INTO OTHER VIRTUAL ENVIRONMENTS

"Most friendship is feigning, most loving mere folly." William Shakespeare, As You Like It

Second Life (SL) is a sophisticated offshoot of early text-based MUDs (multi-user dungeons) and MOOs (MUD, object oriented) that allows multiple players to connect and interact in online

environment. As of 2008, around 90,000 active subscribers use *Second Life* regularly (Woodcock, 2008). Unlike many of the more popular MMOGs (massively-multiplayer online games), like *World of Warcraft*, SL it is more of a virtual world [a "synchronous, persistent network of people, represented as avatars, facilitated by networked computers" (M. W. Bell, 2008)] than a videogame per-se, as there are no formal rules or goals for interactions within the environment, nor are there NPCs (non-player characters) with whom a player must interact to solve puzzles or

DOI: 10.4018/978-1-4666-0029-4.ch013

achieve goals within the environment. Instead, *Second Life* encourages user participation through content creation (Herman, Coombe, & Kaye, 2006), and the "goal" for most players is both the exploration of this vast environment and social interaction with others.

Early discussions of text-based virtual environments/online games often tried to counter the popular media's construction of these spaces as somehow "not real" or without real-world consequences (Dibbell, 1998; Turkle, 1995). And yet, work by many of these scholars tended to fall into same trap of claiming that "in virtual reality, you are whatever you say you are" (McRae, 1996, p. 245) – an argument that has since been problematized by others who note that "real world" issues of race, gender, and power still mark the interactions that happen online (Gonzalez, 2000; Kolko, 2000; Nakamura, 2000, 2002; Silver, 2000).

While *Second Life* is not traditionally considered a game, much of the work within the game studies field offers important insights into understanding the interactions that occur in virtual environments. The variety of topics covered recently within the field of game studies underscores Aarseth's (2006) suggestion that games deserve broad examination in-and-of themselves: in-game economics (Castronova, 2003, December 2001); the media's framing of virtual environments (Squire, 2002); how games can be read as cultural artifacts (Greenfield, 1994) and from a textual studies perspective (Jones, 2008); what we learn when playing (DiSalvo, Crowley, & Norwood, 2008; Gee, 2003; Simkins & Steinkuehler, 2008); how sexuality and race and gender are inscribed in popular games (Cassell & Jenkins, 1998; Consalvo, February 2003); the discourse around gaming addiction (Golub & Lingley, 2008); and fan-based modifications (mods) of games (Postigo, 2007). These studies seek to understand games and virtual environments as important cultural artifacts – ones that both reflect and challenge commonly held beliefs about what goes on during our face-to-face (FTF) interactions with others.

CMC AND INTERPERSONAL RELATIONSHIPS

Early scholarship on computer-mediated communication (CMC) argued that the lack of nonverbal cues would not foster relationships as deeply as face-to-face communication would (Thurlow, Lengel, & Tomic, 2004), despite anecdotal evidence that it was possible to create deep community ties and forge strong bonds with others online (Baym, 1998; Rheingold, 1993; Turkle, 1995). Models such as social presence theory (Short, Williams, & Christie, 1976) and media richness theory (Daft & Lengel, 1986) emphasized that the lack of paralinguistic cues in CMC would necessarily lead to much less effective and less efficient communication. Much of the early press coverage reinscribed this discourse, emphasizing the inherent superiority of offline communication and suggesting that online behavior little impact on individuals in the "real world" (Bell, 2001).

These theoretical models were later rejected as reductionist oversimplifications in favor of offering more nuanced perspectives regarding online interpersonal communication. These perspectives included the social information processing model, which suggests that both CMC and FTF interaction are equally driven by the same "relational motivators" (Walther, 1992). Some of these motivators, such as our desire to be liked by our conversational partners, mean that over time CMC can facilitate the development of deep emotional bonds between individuals. Walther (1996) terms this kind of communication "hyperpersonal," and suggests that it is likely to occur "when users experience commonality and are self-aware, physically separated, and communicating via a limited-cues channel that allows them to selectively self-present and edit; to construct and reciprocate representations of their partners and relations without the influence of environmental reality" (p. 33).

As Nancy Baym (2006) argues, the idea that CMC offers fewer social cues than FTF interactions is still important to current online interpersonal research, but the emphasis has shifted away from simple comparisons between the two mediums. Instead, research has focused on deepening our understanding of how individuals work around and/or integrate these potential limitations into their interpersonal communication online. For example, Walther's social information processing theory argues that individuals will adjust their interactions given the limitations of online communication – especially if it's predominately text-based (Walther, Loh, & Granka, 2005).

Many other recent studies in this area rely heavily on Erving Goffman's (1959) work on self-presentation as a performance involving what he terms frontstage and backstage behaviors. Goffman's suggestion that individuals constantly engage in impression management in their interactions with others has been particularly influential for researchers interested in the relationship between CMC and identity (Bechar-Israeli, 1995; boyd, 2007; Huffaker & Calvert, 2005; Liu, 2007). One of the key features of most online interactions is that they occur asynchronously, which allows individuals the luxury of time to focus on impression management and engage in potential self-censorship (Walther, 1996). In addition, the pseudo-anonymous nature of most online communities – where individuals use the same username/avatar to interact with the environment over time – allows for some reputational and other contextual clues about the person's prior interactions to shape future conversations with others (Donath, 1999). Thus, CMC provides important tools for self-expression and impression management that both mirror and challenge our understandings of how identity is performed in offline contexts.

SELF-DISCLOSURE IN CMC

Altman and Taylor's (1973) theory of social penetration suggests that individuals must engage in a process of self-disclosure if their relationships are to deepen beyond superficial interactions.

Typically, self-disclosure is reciprocal early on in relationships where we seek some affinity with the other – meaning we are likely to disclose personal information about ourselves when our conversational partner also discloses such information. Altman and Taylor argued that our personalities are analogous to the layers of an onion; the outer layers contain superficial demographic information (race/ethnicity, gender, appearance) and our superficial likes and dislikes, while the protected inner layers contain much more personal information about our values, goals, aspirations, and beliefs. Social penetration theory suggests that we will gradually reveal these deeper layers of the "onion"/personality over time – that is, assuming we wish to have more than a superficial relationship with the other person. CMC presents significant challenges to this theory. Online environments, with their lack of physical contextual cues, strip away most of the outer layers of the personality that we may use to establish affinity and liking with others. Instead, we establish must trust in our relationships and disclose information about ourselves without most physical cues being readily apparent.

In terms of FTF communication, researchers have long suggested that there are quantifiable differences in the type, amount, and quality of self-disclosure between same-gender conversational partners. However, recent meta-analysis of self-disclosure research (Dindia, 2002) suggests the difference in the ways in which men and women disclose information is actually minimal, and that the quality and type of self-disclosure between same- and different-gendered conversational partners varies little (Ferris & Roper, 2002). The content of the information exchanged may impact these findings, however. For example, a recent study of adolescents suggested that both the level of anonymity guaranteed within a particular online environment and the gender of the individual may impact a person's willingness to engage in self-disclosing behavior with others – with males being generally more likely to disclose information of a sexual nature online than females, especially if the interactions remain fully anonymous (Chiou, 2006).

Another important factor impacting our willingness to engage in online self-disclosure is if the relationship has the potential to traverse the online/offline boundary. As one of Henderson and Gilding (2004) observe in their investigation of how trust forms in computer-mediated interpersonal relationships, our levels of self-disclosure are higher online – especially if there's little chance of a FTF meeting. When describing one of their informant's perspectives on the issue, they write: "Leanne was…more likely to disclose online than in 'real life' because online friends '"supposedly" live far away' and 'your problems aren't going to really come back to you every time you physically see the person'" (Henderson & Gilding, 2004, p. 499). So, our desire to self-disclose is altered not only by whether or not it is occurring via CMC or through FTF communication, but the medium of our anticipated future interactions (Ramirez, Jr. & Zhang, 2007).

THE IMPACT OF AVATARS ON SOCIAL INTERACTION WITHIN VIRTUAL ENVIRONMENTS

Much of the work regarding interpersonal relationships online focuses on predominately text-based mediums, such as e-mail, instant messaging (IM), Internet Relay Chats (IRC), and message boards/ newsgroups. As Kollock and Smith (1999) note, online communication "strips away many of the cues and signs that are a part of face-to-face interaction. This poverty of signals is both a limitation of resource, making certain kinds of interaction more difficulty but also providing room to play with one's identity" (p. 9). Avatars – or "any visual representation of a user in an online community" (Hemp, 2006, p. 50) – can provide additional contextual clues regarding an individual's online identity that may be apparent in solely text-based

CMC. One would also assume that this additional physical information (representing the personality's outer layers) might encourage us to engage in a kind self-disclosure online that mirrors that which occurs FTF. However, the role that avatars play in these interactions is complex. Despite our assumption that more realistic avatars are likely to result in greater levels of self-disclosure between individuals, and increase the possibility that we can "trust" the our conversation partners more, research suggests otherwise. For example, an early experimental study into avatars showed that photographs within virtual workgroups did not actually increase the levels of affinity between communication partners in the long-term (Walther, Slovacek, & Tidwell, 2001) – suggesting it is actually the textual interaction between individuals, rather than basic physical cues – that potentially strengthens the bond between CMC partners. An more recent study supported the idea that individuals tend to disclose more information when interacting with less realistic-looking avatars (low similarities in form) than with photorealistic representations of the other individual (such as a live digital camera feed) (Bailenson, Yee, Merget, & Schroeder, 2006). Clearly, the mediating effect that avatars might have on individuals' willingness to self-disclose in an online environment like *Second Life* has yet to be fully understood.

Other work focuses on the ways in which avatar behavior connects to physical behavior outside the gaming/virtual environment. For example, recent research suggests that offering visual cues within virtual environments connecting players' behaviors to their avatars' movement (for example, having the avatar mime typing when an individual is chatting with another player) improves coordination between players (Moore, Gathman, Ducheneaut, & Nickell, 2007). Additionally, a study conducted in *Second Life* found that certain FTF nonverbal behaviors, such as the physical distance between individuals having a conversation, are often mirrored within the game world (Yee, Bailenson, Urbanek, Chang,

& Merget, 2007). Studies such as these suggest that perpetuating a simple "real world vs. game world" dichotomy is overly simplistic, as the on- and offline world comingle within and through player/avatar interactions.

Avatar behavior is critical to the notion of copresence, or our sense of being with other individuals inside the virtual environment (Bailenson et al., 2006). Zhao (2003) argues that to successfully become immersed in the virtual environment, and truly experience copresence, requires a suspension of disbelief on the part of players. Thus, avatars serve an important function within worlds like *Second Life* – both as expressions of individual identities, and as agents of copresence. To be a truly effective agent (and maximize a sense of copresence within the virtual environment), Bailenson, Yee, Merget, and Schroeder (2006) argue that the avatar needs to share either high levels of behavioral or form characteristics with the individual controlling it. So, while some level of fidelity between an individual's offline behavior and her avatar's actions is likely to increase our sense of copresence online, and possibly lead to more meaningful relationships with other players, there is a point at which too much realism actually detracts from an individual's willingness to disclose information more about themselves.

METHOD

This research is the result of four years spent immersed in Second Life, a 3-d virtual world owned and operated by Linden Lab. The primary researcher spent an average of 10-20 hours a week in the world totaling over 3,000 hours of observation time. The advantage of an ethnographic approach is being able to witness first hand social behavior and interaction. As Lindlof puts it: "The validity of participant observation derives from *being there* (his emphasis) (1995, p. 135)." As Tom Boellstorff has written about trying to understand places like Second Life: "Actual-world sociality

cannot explain virtual -world sociality (2008, p. 63)." Thus he argues, as do we, the only way to understand social interactions in a virtual world is to accept these worlds on their own terms. Thus one of the best ways to gain an understanding of them is to be immersed in them.

When the primary researcher first entered Second Life, there was a strong anti-research sentiment among residents. Apparently a number of researchers had entered the world initially and people were worn out from inquiries. This, added to a Linden Lab policy that stated all research proposals had to be pre-approved by the company, led the researcher to initially keep his research identity anonymous. Eventually Linden lifted the company's research approval requirements. As the primary researcher became more familiar with people in world, he revealed his identity as a college professor and researcher. All of the people quoted in this piece were aware they were being interviewed for research; still we chose to give their avatars pseudonyms for added protection

The researcher participated in many different sub-groups in the world in an effort to gain an understanding of a broad cross section of the different activities and participants involved in the Second Life. Over a dozen different avatars and accounts were used to collect data through participant observation. Different avatars were created primarily to be able to blend into Second Life's many diverse subgroups. There are groups such as elves (people who role play based upon an amalgam of literature about elves), doms/subs (the most popular of these groups were based on a series of novels by John Norman), and furries (where people live through avatars that resemble real and fictitious animals) to name but a few. However, the bulk of the research done for this piece was done in what we call the mainstream culture of Second Life, which is where the majority of the residents spend the bulk of their time, and these are areas not ruled by or associated with any specific set of sub-group rules or beliefs.

The primary researcher took classes, played games, worked in several in-world business, operated his own small business, joined a number of groups and frequented popular in-world destinations to gain a better understand of day-to-day life in this virtual world. The method used was that of ethnography, where the researcher as best as they can, takes on characteristics, habits, and nuances of the local culture in order to gain a better understanding of the world being studied (Adler & Adler, 1987).

Conversational interviews were conducted with hundreds of residents on a variety of topics over the four year research period. The researcher built a social network by finding a few residents who served as initial guides and helpers upon first entering the world, then contacts were added from there, more or less in what's often called snowballing (Berg, 2004, p. 171). On the topic discussed in this article, more in-depth interviews were done with 30 residents. The interviews were open ended, primarily because the researchers have found that unstructured interviews in participant observations often lead to more depth and breadth of responses (Fontana & Frey, 1994). Interview varied in length from 30 minutes to just over an hour.

Because of the length of time spent in Second Life, data was gathered on several different areas of inquiry surrounding questions about identity, communication and social relationships. This article represents findings in just one of those areas.

DISCUSSION

In his book "Social Relationships," David Argyle sets out four well-established variables of friendship: proximity, similarity, rewardingness, and self-disclosure (Argyle, 1998). Places like Second Life (SL) offer new variations on these established variables.

Take, for instance, *proximity*. People in SL come from all corners of the U.S. and a large array of other countries including the U.K., France, Hol-

land, Germany, Brazil, Mexico, Australia, China, Japan, South Korea, Turkey, and Israel, to name but a few. What computers have done is allow people from disparate locales to be in proximate locations with the aid of the technology. Second Life is certainly a prime example of this. Thus the idea of proximity has changed when it comes to friendship. One can certainly still be friends with the next-door neighbor. But virtual worlds such as Second Life now also allow one to become friends with someone is only virtually proximate.

Similarity, as seen now through the frame of a virtual setting, raises some interesting new questions as well. There of course are some built in similarities between people in a virtual world, because those participating in these places all are willing and interested to try spending time in a virtual environment. You can also tell a number of things based on decisions made by people in these environments. Where do they spend time? What appearance did they choose for their avatar? How do they behave in these virtual settings? All of these have rough parallels in real world settings. But all of these pertain to choices people make once they enter a virtual world such as SL. In real life, some things are not so easily effected by choice – especially physical appearance or where time is spent. These may be governed by a complex grid of things like genetic predisposition or economic mobility. So one could argue that the freedom of choice, the ease of options may help people more easily find people with similar outlooks than perhaps in everyday life. In SL, for instance, if you see an avatar with whickers, an elonged snout, claws and a tail, this may tell you something about the person's interest in furry culture, a genre in SL built around living as an animal. Second Life allows people, through avatars, to be more overt about interests and choices.

Rewardingness means roughly what rewards or positive results you get from the time you spend in a relationship. It can be something as simple as; when you call a friend, do they call you back? Second Life offers an atmosphere where you can choose to answer people or not. Though generally, even though almost all messages are typed, not spoken, people will most often respond, like they might in real life conversation. The ability too, to keep track of messages and answer is easier in SL than often in real life. And because of the ease of carrying things in a stored inventory in a virtual world, giving people something instantly is much easier than in real life. People often pass friends and acquaintances items, such as clothing, gadgets, or animations. These are just two examples of the kinds of rewards gained from building relationships in SL.

What we're most interested in is that fourth category of *self-disclosure*. In observations over these four years we noticed a significant difference in people's willingness to self-disclose than in normal everyday real life encounters, and thus, social relationships often have a different quality in Second Life than in a non-virtual world. The rest of this article will explore the idea of *self-disclosure* in Second Life.

MORE FRIENDS, CLOSER FRIENDS, FASTER

One is struck when entering SL at the amount and level of complexity of social relationships. It is largely a social world, with a tremendous amount of social interaction. For instance, many people have taken on partners (there is an option where to get "partnered" with another avatar wherein their name will appear within your profile, it's the Second Life form of getting married) and these partners rarely denote a relationship outside of the virtual world.

In other instances, people join families, groups of people unrelated outside of SL who then take on roles of father, mother, grandfather, aunt, cousin, etc. To remain a member in good standing in one of these family groups takes some work and attention. Often they are made up of fifteen or more people and just learning who all the people are

and what their role is (sister, father-in-law, etc.) takes some time. Then often people come and go, adding to the level of complexity. And just like a real family there are the rivalries, jealousies, dysfunctions, infighting, so to know at any given time who is and isn't getting along almost require a flow chart.

Others people in SL have formed groups around an interest (live music, art, a particular sexual practice, fans of a movie, etc.) and these groups may meet regularly and even purchase a plot of land where they can be together on a regular basis.

In the midst of these social relationships, we experienced firsthand, and also heard from many varied respondents, that people got closer to one another as a more rapid pace than in real life relationships, and people self disclosed much more.

Omg yes, within my first few months in world I couldn't believe what people were telling me about their lives. Especially when I was working at the club, people would come in and we would strike up a conversation in IM and before long I was hearing their life stories in incredible detail. (Xeke Howe interview *Avatars were assigned pseudonyms to protect the respondent's identity)

Howe also reported that people were disclosing to him many intimate details about their lives without him necessarily reciprocating. This would contradict Altman and Taylor's theory of social penetration, which posits that people disclose more as their conversational partner reveals more.

It felt like at times what it might like to be a bartender or hairdresser and hear people's stories all the time, or maybe even what it might be like to be a priest and hear confession. (Howe interview)

Hearing confession may be an apt analogy, given the anonymity of that religious practice in real life and the anonymity of virtual worlds such as SL. All of the thirty people we interviewed in world on this topic agreed that there was a phenomenon wherein people established more inmate friends at a rate faster than they had experienced in their lives outside of Second Life. This led us to want to identify this phenomenon, and to think about why it occurs in a virtual world

FACTICIUS CONTINGO

For purposes of discussion, we have decided to call this phenomenon of strong, close relationships which develop in virtual realms facticius contingo, Latin meaning to touch someone closely in an artificial realm.

We would argue that four different factors contribute to facticius contingo to provide the necessary means for such a phenomenon to take place. They are: *anonymity, time compression, lack of physical appearance, and word dependence.*

Anonymity

Second Life is an anonymous world. When you join, you make up whatever first name you choose and then pick a last name from a rotating list of choices. Each avatar, once created, has a profile – a set of pages anyone can see if you simply click on them. Each member chooses what, if anything, to write in these few, small pages. People often write something about their avatar. There is one page titled 1st life, meaning people's life outside of the virtual world. Very few people offer much information about their real lives on this page. There is a space for a real photo of yourself, but again, it is fairly unusual to see a real photo of the person behind the avatar.

This means when you meet someone and get to know them, there is a big difference between that meeting in real life and a virtual life. In real life if you meet someone at work or in your neighborhood, chances are good you will see that person again, often frequently. You may even have a continuing relationship with them. Thus, it's most often in everyday life, common *not* to

initially disclose too much information about yourself other than the superficial facts. Telling someone about a past indiscretion or embarrassing episode most likely won't happen because of the fear people have about how they might be perceived and received in the future. In SL, you have the choice whether you want to ever see that avatar again in the future.

Interviewer: do you get closer to people in sl, faster, than in rl?
Kayleen Kinski: yes
Interviewer: so why is that?
Kayleen Kinski: cause you cant see them!
Kayleen Kinski: lol
Interviewer: so how does that help?
Kayleen Kinski: cause you dont have to face them, look them in the eye, meet them again if you dont want to
Kayleen Kinski: all of the above
Kayleen Kinski: they're just ships in the night

One person described it as a similar situation as to when you sit someone on a plane and you strike up a conversation and talk for two hours, freely, often because you know you will never see the person again. The anonymity of SL plays a large part in people's willingness to self-disclose and that self-disclosure itself is a key link in why people may get closer in this setting. This also supports what other researchers have discovered, such as Henderson and Gilding (2004) who found that levels of self-disclosure increase if there is little chance of meeting face-to-face. This level of anonymity adds a dimension of comfort and sense of safety when it comes to self-disclosure in Second Life.

Time Compression

Anyone who has spent time in a 3-d virtual world knows that time can fly by. It's not difficult to enter one of these realms and lose all track of time. In Second Life, there is a sun and moon and days cycle through, but at a pace about three times faster than the real life lunar cycle. Although you can reset the day and night cycle, it's not common among residents to do so. This may have something to do with the effect described by Zhao (2003), of people in these environments suspending belief to become immersed in the world and be truly co present. Csikszentmihalvi (1975) has also described Flow Theory, wherein people have complete and energized focus in an activity such as a game. This may also help to explain the quick passing of time.

In this way, the acceleration of days and nights is reflected in relationships. In SL when you spend say an hour with someone, it feels as if you have been with them for considerably longer. People you've known for a week, you feel as if you have known them for months. A year in one of these places seems like several years. Why is this so? It may be to the fact that the primary activity for most people in these places in social interaction. That social interaction comes in the form of words. There are plenty of activities in SL, animations that replicate a broad range of activities from riding in a balloon, to racing down a ski slope, sky diving, or firing weapons. But all of it seems a bit empty done alone. So the primary activity in Second Life is communicating, even when there are other on-screen activities taking place.

Take for instance, the example of a dance club. In real life if one goes out dancing, even with friends, communication is somewhat difficult because of the loud volume of music. To be heard you often have to shout. In SL dance clubs the music can blare, but you can still "hear" people because almost conversation is typed and appears on screen. So a dance club becomes a highly social place where there a group conversation going on onscreen in "public" plus often people are conducting "private" conversations by typing message to other avatars in IM.

In work, in social settings, at home, those conversations are generally shorter and often interrupted by other activities. This may account

for why two hours talking to someone in SL may seem to residents like 8 hours in real life. Or why having a relationship with someone for a week may seem like a month. "The way time feels here, it just intensifies whatever connection you feel for someone, its hard to describe, but it happens a lot" (Amy Oletta interview).

There's another part to the time-compression factor contributing to people getting closer, faster in this virtual world. This also means that friendships and other relationships might end more rapidly. Like a meteor, they burst into existence, burn with intensity, and then are gone:

Researcher: do you get closer to people, faster here than in rl?
Kelly Grey: yes i think so
Kelly Grey: and then more intense
Kelly Grey: and then faster break-ups
Researcher: why is that do you think?
Kelly Grey: cause there is no real physical contact
Kelly Grey: it is just words
Kelly Grey: and when someone gets tired
Kelly Grey: they can easily disappear

Based on observations, it's not uncommon to see people partner and un-partner in a few weeks. Even with a high divorce rate in the real world, the rate with which partners split in SL appears to be much more frequent and much more rapid. The primary researcher had over a dozen acquaintances and friends in SL who were partnered and un-partnered multiple times over just the course of a year. This isn't always the case of course, and some people did stay together for longer stretches of time and even eventually meet face-to-face. But based on observations this was by far the exception.

Lack of Physical Appearance

Initially researchers believed that the lack of physical presence would impede computer mediated communication. They suspected that the lack of social cues, facial expressions, gestures, etc. would limit the depth and quality of interaction. What they hadn't counted on is that often the lack of those social cues, plus the lack of seeing the appearance of a person might not hinder but instead facilitate interaction. Often times the presence of an avatar rather than the presence of a real person gives people the opportunity to fill in the blanks with their own imagination.

Interviewer: do you think people get closer here faster than rl?
Zelda Moore: yes
Interviewer: why
Zelda Moore: because in rl you are judgmental of a person and their appearance
Zelda Moore: here its a clean slate
Interviewer: is that all there is to it?
Zelda Moore: well you i think emotions play more in sl
Interviewer: why
Zelda Moore: well
Zelda Moore: the fantasy of not really seeing or knowing the other person
Interviewer: what does that do
Zelda Moore: the mystery
Zelda Moore: of it all
Interviewer: your imagination
Zelda Moore: yes

Avatars, of course, have their own appearance. But few have any imperfections. Given that an avatar is the result of a series of choices, they do serve a symbolic role, as do the choices we make in normal life about our appearance. SL gives you much more opportunity for those choices. Bailensen, Yee, Merget, and Scrhoeder (2006) found that people tend to disclose more when interacting with less realistic avatars. Though people in SL may have created avatar that somehow resemble their real life appearance, few favor photo realism. So in this way, people not seeing a photo or cam representation of whom they are interacting with likely increases their comfort to

disclose more about themselves. An interesting area for further study would be to do a more in-depth comparison the impact of real life and avatar appearance on social interactions.

Just Words

Imagine a world where all you do is talk to people *all* the time. You've imagined what used to be a MOO or MUD and what now 3-d virtual worlds are. Given the amount of conversation, it's difficult to talk to someone for long and not begin telling things about yourself or self-disclosing. What we say and thin is tied closely to who we are. That includes details like how old we are, where we live, our gender, religious beliefs, social position, vocation, etc. It's almost impossible to sustain a conversation of any length without eventually telling people more and more about yourself.

People can and do keep some personal details out of conversation, but it's not the norm. As has been discussed in earlier research (Heider, 2009) the majority of people in Second Life build avatars that resemble themselves and their behavior also reflects who they are in real life. So given the amount of talk that makes up time in SL, it's no surprise then that there is considerable self-disclosure and often at a faster rate than we might experience in our daily lives.

But for some all the talking has another effect, even to bring out their conversational skills after they spend time in SL and go back to their normal existence:

Leyla Luhr: I've found that my RL people skills have improved from being here. you?
Interviewer: hmmmm
Interviewer: im a bit pushy in rl
Interviewer: maybe its helped my tolerance?
Leyla Luhr: SL has certainly made it easier for me to talk to people
Interviewer: interestihng
Interviewer: why do you think so?

Leyla Luhr: SL is like being parachuted into the middle of a very fun and close party. How would you feel?

Leyla Luhr: I felt incredibly insecure

Leyla Luhr: and then I reliased that all I needed to do was stop thinking about myself

Interviewer: nods

Leyla Luhr: and just talk from the heart to the people I met

So spending time in a world where talking is the primary activity both contributes to the speed people may get close, and it may have other effects as well, including for at least one person, a heightened ability to talk comfortably with strangers in a social setting.

CONCLUSION

Technology has, for some time, had an impact on human communication. The telegraph and telephone changed the way a person could get a message to another person over great distances, and communicating via telegraph or telephone had different qualities related to the medium. More recently email and instant messaging have brought another dimension to human contact as has the internet in general and as we have examined in this study, virtual online worlds specifically.

After spending four years observing and participating in human interactions in a virtual space, the authors sought to understand how human relationships might be different in a world such as Second Life. More research is needed in this and other areas related to virtual worlds. Research and theory in this area are still developing.

Early theory about how computers might affect communication predicted less effective and less meaningful interaction. But we found in some cases, just the opposite, where people in disparate locales formed close relationships in ways that might not occur through face-to-face interactions.

As virtual realms continue to develop and evolve, researchers begin to get a better understanding what it means to spend time in these places. In this piece we have begun to try to address some of the qualities of social relationship in one virtual world, Second Life. We suggest that *anonymity, time compression, lack of physical appearance, and word dependence* all contribute to a phenomenon wherein people at a rapid rate get close to other people, a phenomenon we are calling facticius contingo.

One thing is clear after spending four years in SL that is these places continue to be important to the people who choose to participate. They are more than places people go to be amused or entertained. People develop social interactions they find meaningful, compelling and gratifying. As one informant said:

Kayleen Kinski: but now i have two lives

Kayleen Kinski: most of the time sl is on but im doing stuff in rl anyway

Interviewer: is this place as important to you as rl?

Kayleen Kinski: hmm, not

Kayleen Kinski: no*

Kayleen Kinski: but it would be hard to give up

Kayleen Kinski: i'd have to go thru withdrawals for a bit

REFERENCES

Aarseth, E. (2006). How we became postdigital: From cyberstudies to game studies. In Silver, D., & Massanari, A. (Eds.), *Critical cyberculture studies* (pp. 37–46). New York: NYU Press.

Adler, P., & Adler, P. (1987). *Membership Roles in Field Research*. Thousand Oaks, CA: Sage Publications.

Altman, I., & Taylor, D. (1973). *Social penetration: The development of interpersonal relationships*. New York: Holt, Rinehart and Winston.

Argyle, M. (1998). *Social Relationships*. London: Blackwell Publishing.

Bailenson, J. N., Yee, N., Merget, D., & Schroeder, R. (2006). The effect of behavioral realism and form realism of real-time avatar faces on verbal disclosure, nonverbal disclosure, emotion recognition, and copresence in dyadic interaction. *Presence (Cambridge, Mass.)*, *15*(4), 359–372. doi:10.1162/pres.15.4.359

Baym, N. (1998). The emergence of on-line community. In Jones, S. G. (Ed.), *CyberSociety 2.0: Revisiting computer-mediated communication and community* (pp. 35–68). Thousand Oaks, CA: Sage.

Baym, N. (2006). Interpersonal life online. In L. A. Lievrouw & S. Livingstone (Eds.), *The handbook of new media* (Student ed., pp. 35-54). Thousand Oaks, CA: Sage.

Bechar-Israeli, H. (1995). From <Bonhead> to <cLoNehEAd>: Nicknames, play, and identity on Internet Relay Chat. *Journal of Computer-Mediated Communication*, *1*(2). Retrieved from http://jcmc.indiana.edu/vol1/issue2/bechar.html.

Bell, D. (2001). *An introduction to cybercultures*. London: Routledge.

Bell, M. W. (2008). Toward a definition of "virtual worlds" (Electronic Version). *Journal of Virtual Worlds Research*, *1*. Retrieved December 21, 2008, from http://journals.tdl.org/jvwr/article/view/283

Berg, B. (2004). *Qualitative Research Methods for the Social Sciences* (5th ed.). Boston: Pearson.

Boellstorff, T. (2008). *Coming of Age in Second Life; An Anthropologist Explores the Virtually Human*. Princeton: Princeton University Press.

Boyd, D. (2007). Why youth (heart) social network sites: The role of networked publics in teenage social life. In Buckingham, D. (Ed.), *MacArthur Foundation Series on Digital Learning – Youth, Identity, and Digital Media Volume*. Cambridge, MA: MIT Press.

Cassell, J., & Jenkins, H. (1998). *From Barbie to Mortal Kombat: Gender and computer games*. Cambridge, MA: The MIT Press.

Castronova, E. (2001, December). *Virtual Worlds: A First-Hand Account of Market and Society on the Cyberian Frontier* (No. 618).

Castronova, E. (2003). On virtual economies (Electronic Version). *Game Studies, 3*. Retrieved December 22, 2008, from http://www.gamestudies.org/0302/castronova/

Chiou, W.-B. (2006). Adolescents' sexual self-disclosure on the Internet: Deindividuation and impression management. *Adolescence*, *41*(163), 547–561.

Consalvo, M. (2003, February). *It's a queer world after all: Studying The Sims and sexuality*. New York: GLAAD Center for the Study of Media and Society.

Csikszentmihalyi, M. (1975). *Beyond Boredom and Anxiety: Experiencing Flow in Work and Play*. San Francisco, CA: Jossey-Bass.

Daft, R. L., & Lengel, R. H. (1986). Organizational information requirements, media richness and structural design. *Management Science*, *32*(5), 554–571. doi:10.1287/mnsc.32.5.554

Dibbell, J. (1998). *My tiny life: Crime and passion in a virtual world*. New York: Henry Holt and Company, Inc.

Dindia, K. (2002). Self-disclosure research: Knowledge through meta-analysis. In Allen, M. (Ed.), *Interpersonal Communication Research: Advances Through Meta-analysis* (pp. 169–185). Mahwah, NJ: Lawrence Erlbaum Associates.

DiSalvo, B. J., Crowley, K., & Norwood, R. (2008). Learning in context: Digital games and young black men. *Games and Culture*, *3*(2), 131–141. doi:10.1177/1555412008314130

Donath, J. S. (1999). Identity and deception in the virtual community. In Smith, M. A., & Kollock, P. (Eds.), *Communities in cyberspace* (pp. 29–59). London: Routledge.

Ferris, S. P., & Roper, S. (2002). Same and mixed-gender intimacy in a virtual environment. *Qualitative Research Reports in Communication*, 47-55.

Fontana, A., & Frey, J. (1994). Interviewing: The Art of Science. In Denzien, N., & Lincoln, Y. (Eds.), *Handbook of Qualitative Research* (pp. 361–376). Thousnad Oaks, CA: Sage Publications.

Gee, J. P. (2003). *What video games have to teach us about learning and literacy*. New York: Palgrave Macmillan.

Goffman, E. (1959). *The presentation of self in everyday life*. New York: Doubleday.

Golub, A., & Lingley, K. (2008). "Just like the Qing empire": Internet addiction, MMOGs, and moral crisis in contemporary China. *Games and Culture*, *3*(1), 59–75. doi:10.1177/1555412007309526

Gonzalez, J. (2000). The appended subject: Race and identity as digital assemblage. In Kolko, B. E., Nakamura, L., & Rodman, G. B. (Eds.), *Race in cyberspace* (pp. 27–50). New York: Routledge.

Greenfield, P. (1994). Video games as cultural artifacts. *Journal of Applied Developmental Psychology*, *15*, 3–12. doi:10.1016/0193-3973(94)90003-5

Heider, D. (2009). *Living Virtually; Researching Virtual Worlds*. New York: Peter Lang.

Hemp, P. (2006, June 1). Avatar-based marketing. *Harvard Business Review*, 48–57.

Henderson, S., & Gilding, M. (2004). 'I've never clicked this much with anyone in my life': Trust and hyperpersonal communication in online friendships. *New Media & Society*, *6*(4), 487–506. doi:10.1177/146144804044331

Herman, A., Coombe, R. J., & Kaye, L. (2006). Your Second Life? Goodwill and the performativity of intellectual property in online gaming. *Cultural Studies*, *20*(2/3), 184–210. doi:10.1080/09502380500495684

Huffaker, D. A., & Calvert, S. L. (2005). Gender, identity, and language use in teenage blogs. *Journal of Computer-Mediated Communication*, *10*(2). Retrieved from http://jcmc.indiana.edu/vol10/issue2/huffaker.html.

Jones, S. E. (2008). *The meaning of video games*. London: Routledge.

Kolko, B. E. (2000). Erasing @race. In Kolko, B. E., Nakamura, L., & Rodman, G. B. (Eds.), *Race in cyberspace* (pp. 213–232). New York: Routledge.

Kollack, P., & Smith, M. A. (1999). Communities in cyberspace. In Smith, M. A., & Kollock, P. (Eds.), *Communities in cyberspace* (pp. 3–25). London: Routledge.

Lindlof, T. (1995). *Qualitative Communication Research Methods* (3rd ed.). Thosand Oaks, CA: Sage Publications.

Liu, H. (2007). Social network profiles as taste performances. *Journal of Computer-Mediated Communication*, *13*(1). http://jcmc.indiana.edu/vol13/issue1/liu.html.

McRae, S. (1996). Coming apart at the seams: Sex, text, and the virtual body. In Cherney, L., & Weise, E. R. (Eds.), *Wired women: Gender and new realities in cyberspace*. Seattle: Seal Press.

Moore, R. J., Gathman, E. C. H., Ducheneaut, N., & Nickell, E. (2007, April 28-May 3). *Coordinating joint activity in avatar-mediated interaction*. Paper presented at the Human Factors in Computing Systems (CHI 2007), San Jose, CA.

Nakamura, L. (2000). "Where do you want to go today?": Cybernetic tourism, the Internet, and transnationality. In Kolko, B. E., Nakamura, L., & Rodman, G. B. (Eds.), *Race in Cyberspace* (pp. 15–26). New York: Routledge.

Nakamura, L. (2002). *Cybertypes: Race, ethnicity, and identity on the Internet*. New York: Routledge.

Postigo, H. (2007). Of mods and modders: Chasing down the value of fan-based digital games modifications. *Games and Culture, 2*(4), 300–313. doi:10.1177/1555412007307955

Ramirez, A. Jr, & Zhang, S. (2007). When Online Meets Offline: The Effect of Modality Switching on Relational Communication. *Communication Monographs, 74*(3), 287–310. doi:10.1080/03637750701543493

Rheingold, H. (1993). *The virtual community: Homesteading on the electronic frontier* (1st ed.). Reading, MA: Addison-Wesley.

Short, J., Williams, E., & Christie, B. (1976). *The social psychology of telecommunications*. London: Wiley.

Silver, D. (2000). Margins in the wires: Looking for race, gender, and sexuality in the Blacksburg Electronic Village. In Kolko, B. E., Nakamura, L., & Rodman, G. B. (Eds.), *Race in cyberspace* (pp. 133–150). New York: Routledge.

Simkins, D. W., & Steinkuehler, C. (2008). Critical ethical reasoning and role-play. *Games and Culture, 3*(3/4), 333–355. doi:10.1177/1555412008317313

Squire, K. (2002). Cultural framing of computer/video games [Electronic Version]. *Game Studies, 2*. Retrieved December 22, 2008, from http://www.gamestudies.org/0102/squire/

Thurlow, C., Lengel, L., & Tomic, A. (2004). *Computer mediated communication: Social interaction and the Internet*. London: Sage.

Turkle, S. (1995). *Life on the screen: Identity in the age of the Internet*. New York: Simon and Schuster.

Walther, J. B. (1992). Interpersonal effects in computer-mediated interaction: A relational perspective. *Communication Research, 19*(1), 52–90. doi:10.1177/009365092019001003

Walther, J. B. (1996). Computer-mediated communication: Impersonal, interpersonal, and hyperpersonal interaction. *Communication Research, 23*(3), 3–43. doi:10.1177/009365096023001001

Walther, J. B., Loh, T., & Granka, L. (2005). Let me count the ways: The interchange of verbal and nonverbal cues in computer-mediated and face-to-face affinity. *Journal of Language and Social Psychology, 24*(1), 36–65. doi:10.1177/0261927X04273036

Walther, J. B., Slovacek, C. L., & Tidwell, L. C. (2001). Is a picture worth a thousand words?: Photographic images in long-term and short-term computer-mediated communication. *Communication Research, 28*(1), 105–134. doi:10.1177/009365001028001004

Woodcock, B. (2008). *MMOG Active Subscriptions: 0-120,000*. Retrieved December 23, 2008, from http://www.mmogchart.com/Chart3.html

Yee, N., Bailenson, J. N., Urbanek, M., Chang, F., & Merget, D. (2007). The unbearable likeness of being digital: The persistence of nonverbal social norms in online virtual environments. *Journal of CyberPsychology and Behavior, 10*, 115–121. doi:10.1089/cpb.2006.9984

Zhao, S. (2003). Toward a taxonomy of copresence. *Presence (Cambridge, Mass.), 12*(5), 445–455. doi:10.1162/105474603322761261

This work was previously published in International Journal of Gaming and Computer-Mediated Simulations, Volume 2, Issue 3, edited by Richard E. Ferdig, pp. 61-74, copyright 2010 by IGI Publishing (an imprint of IGI Global).

Chapter 14
Computer Gaming Scenarios for Product Development Teams

Andrew J. Wodehouse
University of Strathclyde, UK

William J. Ion
University of Strathclyde, UK

ABSTRACT

In this paper, computer gaming approaches are introduced as a viable means to structure the interaction of a product development team during concept generation. During concept generation, teams gather large amounts of information before generating new ideas and concepts. Digital technologies mean that relevant information can be sourced faster than ever, but this does not necessarily migrate into the activity of concept creation. It is suggested that cues from computer games can help integrate information as well as individuals more effectively, resulting in better conceptual output. A range of game types are evaluated with a view to their possible utilization in support of concept design. Two scenarios for the implementation of gaming methods are proposed, and one refined scenario identified as having potential for further development.

INTRODUCTION

In product development, concept design is the process undertaken when trying to develop solutions for a given problem. This encompasses the formation of design requirements, the generation of ideas, and the selection of an embodied concept. Associated activities are often undertaken

by groups in a collaborative setting, and despite the fact this is typically a fuzzy process based around sketch work and discussion, a number of formal tools and techniques to support the process (Cross, 1994; French, 1985; Pahl & Beitz, 1995; Pugh, 1991; Ulrich & Eppinger, 1995).

The most popular approach to concept generation in industry today is brainstorming. Popularized by Osborn (1953) in the 1950s, brainstorming consists of a group of people working together in

DOI: 10.4018/978-1-4666-0029-4.ch014

a non-critical environment to generate a high number of ideas. Although there are many variations, there is generally a facilitator, fixed timescale and whiteboard or appropriate writing implements. Organizations such as IDEO (Kelley, 2006) have made this approach central to their corporate culture, and such is its popularity brainstorming is often used as shorthand for any meeting where groups try to develop some ideas. This can be to its detriment when groups undertake the activity informally and half-heartedly with disappointing results. Other criticisms include that it can be personality-driven, with the loudest participants dominating, that the quality of ideas can be suffer given the pressure for quantity, and the lack of opportunity to develop idea threads within a session can be frustrating.

Progressive Creative Methods

In order to address these shortcomings, a number of progressive methods (Shah, Kulkarni, & Vargas-Hernandez, 2000) have emerged that provide a degree of structure for teams while still allowing participants to develop their own ideas. An example of a progressive design method is the 6-3-5 Method (Rohrbach, 1969). Also known as Brainwriting was developed as an alternative to brainstorming. The name reflects the format, in that a team of 6 participants sketch 3 ideas every 5 minutes. After each five minute round, the concepts are passed round to the adjacent participant. The team is then able to draw on others' ideas for inspiration as they wish. If all participants complete the session properly, a 30 minute session should produce 108 ideas. The focus of the technique is therefore on quantity – the results of the session would then be used for further concept development and evaluation. A sample of part of a 6-3-5 session is shown in Figure 1.

Access to Information

While progressive methods go some way towards structuring concept design work while allowing

Figure 1. Sample of a 6-3-5 session

creative thinking, a major shortcoming is the lack of information use as ideas are being generated. Access to appropriate information, principles, exemplars and context have been shown to be important in creating well-substantiated concepts and acting as stimuli for discussion (Benami & Jin, 2002; Chuang & Chen, 2008). The digitization of such information has many advantages: it can be conveniently accessed, revised and edited easily, stored with minimal physical overheads, and communicated instantly across distance. As advances in computer hardware and software continue apace, and with the exponential growth of the Internet meaning previously arcane information is now readily available, the challenge is to find effective approaches to presenting and using digital information for concept design.

While more logical methods such as TRIZ (Altshuller, Altov, & Shulyak, 1994; Rantanen & Domb, 2002) make use of past solutions and prior knowledge when tackling design problems. They are also highly prescriptive in how a problem should be approached. This paper therefore aims to develop theoretical frameworks for improved use of information in progressive concept design approaches by utilizing characteristics of a field where highly engaging and effective information use are essential: computer games.

Utilising Computer Games

According to Manninen (2003), the interactive experience can be made more rich using forms which are "large, versatile, flexible and focused on the content"- precisely the area where the computer games industry has garnered vast expertise and in which innovative techniques could be implemented. Recent studies have shown that gaming simulation can enhance understanding of organizational culture, structure, and processes (Kriz, 2003), and that the playing of computer games can be helpful in establishing procedural habits (Gee, 2003). The computer gaming industry continues to go from strength to strength, with its global value expected to rise in value by 50 percent between 2006 and 2011 from $31.6 billion to $48.9 billion (PwC, 2006). This has led to significant resources being spent on the creation of interfaces which are rich, engaging and fun, and provides a strong indicator of how people can best interact with digital information and each other in the future (Friedman, 2006).

The shift towards using games constructively is reflected in the burgeoning area of game-based learning (Prensky, 2001), where the main applications are of a business or task orientated nature. Simulation games, in particular, are becoming increasingly common in business and teaching business (Faria & Wellington, 2004). McDaniel et al. (2006) suggest that the designing of games as well as their playing lend themselves to the learning of project management, providing contrast between theory and practice. Projects such as the Microsoft-MIT funded Games-to-Teach project (MIT and Microsoft Corporation, 2005) indicate that this will be applied to many other areas of learning as the field evolves.

Despite this movement to utilizing their obvious potential, until now there has been relatively little study into how some of the qualities of computer games could be applied to the context of design (Ip & Jacobs, 2004; Squire, 2002;

Wodehouse & Bradley, 2006). This paper therefore seeks to address two main questions:

- How can computer gaming techniques and strategies be used to enhance information use in concept design?
- What framework or methods can be used to combine and utilize the most desirable features of these games?

CHARACTERISTICS OF COMPUTER GAMES

The playing of games is an innate human trait, and is apparent in many aspects of society from the imaginary games played by children in the playground to sports spectacles played out in front thousands. The traditional forms of game played by small groups, such as chess, cards or board games, utilize information to greater or lesser extent. They all have rule sets and knowledge held by each participant which is then shared with the rest of the group in a structured way. These forms of game remain popular, but it is in the digital arena where radical innovation is pushing the boundaries of what can be achieved in complex worlds where large amounts of information are discovered, shared in the user experience. Further, the mode of interactivity engendered by digital communication is part of the modern mindset, with computer users demanding a higher and more sophisticated level of engagement in these environments than ever before (Gee, 2003). Prensky coined the term "digital natives" to highlight the first generation to grow up immersed in a digital world, highlighting the fact that they "think and process information fundamentally differently".

He points to the preference for speed of information, parallel processing and multi-tasking, graphics over text, random access as afforded by hypertext and links, networks, instant gratification and rewards, and games and gameplay as characteristics of this generation. As a result, they expect digital environments not to just emulate traditional forms (such as static web pages replicating newspapers, and the Solitaire computer game replicating the card game) but to provide a platform for them to engage and interact in profound ways with both information and other people. In recent years, the power of the Internet is becoming apparent as it is used by these digital natives in a way it was not previously. This can be illustrated in the shift from Web 1.0 to Web 2.0 (O'Reilly, 2005). Although Web 2.0 brands such as YouTube and Facebook have only recently penetrated the mainstream, many have their eye on the next phase of development, dubbed Web 3.0 or the "Semantic Web". In this vision, computers will become a kind of personal assistant, connecting aspects of our digital lives with innate intelligence, and trawling the Internet to respond to our information, social and entertainment needs. It is clear, then, that digital environments and computer gaming provide opportunities for better use of information use in design contexts. *Motivation, structure* and *interaction* are discussed below as aspects of computer games which can lead to better information use, and subsequently used to structure the evaluation of scenarios developed in Section 4.

Motivation

The motivation engendered by computer games is one of its primary attractions for use in the design context: if using information stored in a digital library can be made even remotely as attractive as playing a computer game, an increase in uptake could be expected. The concerns of parents whose children spend endless hours trying to master the latest games are indicative of the hold they can exert over players. Davis and Carini (2004) emphasize the strong link between fun and engagement in their work developing heuristics for designing fun in video games, and this is clearly a desirable element for any interaction proposed. Considering the interaction purely as

'fun', however, is not altogether appropriate for the business and productivity context – an overly-relaxed approach to a task is not sustainable in arenas where deadlines and targets continue to define the pace of work.

Csikszentmihalyi (1997) has developed the concept of 'flow' to describe how individuals are motivated by particular tasks. He describes the normal, relaxed condition of the mind as one of "informal disorder", and emphasizes the need for focus in order to "pursue mental operations to any depth". When this level of concentration is attained, we find that we can 'lose' ourselves in a task. Most people have experienced this, usually when undertaking an activity they enjoy. It is particularly common when engaging in something creative, such as drawing, when time can seem to disappear. Csikszentmihalyi identifies the quality of this experience when undertaking a task as a function of the relationship between its challenge and the skill required. The optimal experience, or flow, occurs when both variables are high (Figure 2).

Malone (1981) suggests that challenge depends on "goals with uncertain outcomes", describing fantasy and curiosity as elements of intrinsically motivating games. Sweetser and Wyeth (2005) highlight that challenge is often identified as the most important aspect of computer game design: it should have a suitable level of challenge "not discouragingly hard or boringly easy". They have developed a method of analyzing the enjoyment of computer games by relating them to Csikszentmihalyi's concept of flow called GameFlow – a model for evaluating player enjoyment in games. Chen (Chen, 2007) also applies Csikszentmihalyi's ideas to the field of computer games, suggesting that many games follow a prescriptive path too challenging for the novice or too easy for the expert, taking them out of their respective flow zones. She, like Malone, suggests that this can be overcome by incorporating choices for the player during the game. However, it is also stressed that these choices are embedded inside the core

Figure 2. Finding flow

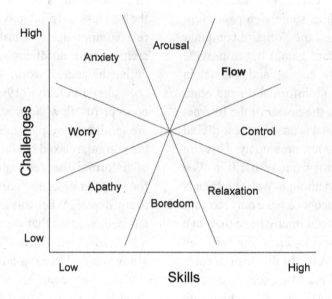

activities to ensure the flow is never interrupted - too many choices for the player or computer to deal with can lead to an interrupted or fragmented experience.

If the role of a gaming element is to assist participants in actually reaching the flow state when undertaking a task, it is desirable that it is integrated into the task itself rather than being an incongruous addition that moves players from one task to the next. For example, in The Monkey Wrench Conspiracy (Prensky, 2001), the player designs implements in a CAD program to help them complete an adventure in space. The incentive of using the tools for the gaming element is the motivation for completing the CAD tutorials in good time. It is necessary to ensure these elements are carefully balanced to ensure the user is not simply offered chunks of "fun" play as a carrot to endure tedious tasks. In this example, attention could be given to the process of actually designing the implements to make it more appealing.

Interaction

As Apperley (2006) notes, interactivity is a very broad term that cannot be applied to unite all computer games. There is very little structural and organizational commonality between different games, particularly in terms of the aesthetic look and feel. Additionally, completely different paradigms of gameplay, graphics, scoring and strategies may be required, even within genres. Manninen (2001) has attempted to identify and categorize the main forms of interaction involved in the playing of the gamut of computer games in an "Interaction Taxonomy" (Figure 3). As well as providing a loose framework to categorize the forms of interaction in multiplayer games, these individual categories draw attention to the different ways information can be communicated in the game environment.

Although factual information can be effectively communicated through speech and the written word, much emotional and contextual communication relies on the reading of more subtle signs and clues. Mehrabian's (1981) commonly quoted "7%-38%-55% Rule" suggests that in any face-to-face communication there are three

Figure 3. Taxonomy of interaction forms (Manninen, 2001)

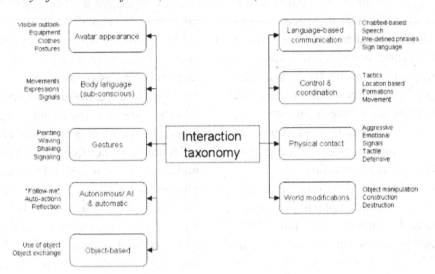

elements: words, tone of voice and body language, with the importance of each being 7%, 38% and 55% respectively. Although these findings were in the context of people talking about feelings and emotions, it highlights the fact that words spoken are only a component part of any interaction. Communicating in the virtual environment of computer games presents obstacles in conveying the nuances of tone of voice and especially body language given the current limitations in technology and for any platform to be successful, it must provide the adequate means for participants to communicate the information required to complete tasks. For different concept design approaches, different forms of communication have precedence. For example, brainstorming is often verbal in nature, whereas the 6-3-5 Method relies on sketchwork to share ideas. It is therefore necessary for any gaming intervention to be attuned to the information required to be shared by participants using a particular design approach.

In their studies of MMORPGs (Massive Multiplayer Online Role-Playing Games), Ducheneaut and Moore (2004) use the term "macroing" for players progressing through the online world on autopilot, completing the tasks necessary to advance in the game and not bothering to interact with the hundreds of other players present in the games's social areas. They suggest that the overwhelming number of people and information were important factors in this. On the other hand, they also observed players who engaged in rich interaction. They go on to highlight issues such as space in the virtual environment, the level of information presented, and appropriate rewards as ways to encourage strong social behavior in MMORPGs. It is necessary, then, to use the design activity and any gaming element as the focus of the group. From a CSCW perspective, Gutwin and Greenberg's (2002) examination of how small groups perform concept design work in medium-sized groupware environments focused on the importance of an "awareness of others", emphasizing how individuals move regularly between individual and shared activities.

The opportunities provided by the virtual gaming world for participants to use avatars and take on roles can potentially be a powerful way to address this need for "workspace awareness". Westecott (2003) emphasizes the importance of roles in gameplay and describes how in games, the player can be regarded as a "first-person actor" where they must take the role of a character and interact with environments and other players.

This provides the opportunity to build and support social structures in a game space that can be task-orientated. Similar analogies describing the design of the game experience as a stage for characters to interact (Laurel, 2004) have also been applied. Given the personal nature of creativity and idea generation, the management and use of such avatars can potentially be used to provide different levels of anonymity or shielding from criticism where necessary or desired.

While competition has been cited as a key element in the enjoyment of playing computer games (Vorderer, Hartmann, & Klimmt, 2003), the achievement orientation and perceived competence of individuals has been highlighted as a significant factor in how well players respond (Tauer & Harackiewicz, 1999). Given that the concept design task is fundamentally co-operative in nature, the idea of introducing competition is attractive in the sense that if all individuals are motivated, confident and engaged it could further stimulate and subsequently enhance their work. If this is not the case, however, there is the risk of alienating individuals within the task, and in the virtual setting it is easy for players to withdraw from engaging as suggested by the macroing phenomenon in MMORPGs.

Structure

Computer games provide a structured framework through which players must navigate, but unlike the strictly linear narrative of a film or book, each game is played in a different manner. Players are repeatedly presented with a wide range of concepts and scenarios which they must rapidly assimilate and select from in order to progress, and although games vary in their linearity and narrative scope, in all of them participation by the player is fundamental. Newman (2002) describes how in the virtual environment, the act of interfacing with the system is a part of a continuous feedback loop where the player must be seen as "both implied

by, and implicated in, the construction and composition of the experience".

The decisions, whether they be the split-second choices made in the midst of an action game or a tactical choice associated with a strategy game, made by the player make each experience unique. It has been suggested that controlling the allowable inputs and outputs of games could allow action and reflection to be configured for optimal decision making (Manninen, 2003). The decisions made by players can be inhibited by an imbalance in game variables such as time restrictions vs. information load, action components vs. strategy interludes, and narrative thread vs. flexibility. Structuring the game to balance these various elements and ensure players remain in the "flow" state is integral to the gaming experience. Similarly in engineering design, the overall process structure has periods of divergence and convergence during which information and ideas are generated and evaluated accordingly. If these are imbalanced it is likely to result in a compromised output. How this balance is achieved for different game genres is, then, particularly relevant to understanding how an optimized flow experience can be obtained for the concept design task.

For the team situation, the lack of facility for vivid communication can be problematic. It has been suggested that existing design teams using groupware to facilitate collaboration should build compensatory structures into the design process to allow teams to overcome these barriers (Mark & Wulf, 1999). These compensatory structures, however, should not interfere with the flow of a design session – if they can be absorbed into the structure of gameplay, the team potentially benefits from better engagement as well as more controlled information exchange.

Modern computer games often consist of vastly complex worlds that contain large amounts of information. With rules of gameplay often being very involved, it is interesting to note how game developers have addressed the issue of conveying these key information elements to players in an engaging way. Gee (2003) describes the experience of opening the instructions or manual for a new game and on first examination it can seem impenetrable. After spending a while playing the game, however, the attention of the player is captured, motivation increases and they are more likely to engage with what was previously difficult material. In addition, it can be used in a number of different ways, such as referring to it for details to enhance their play. As the industry evolves, however, thick instruction manuals are being eschewed in favor of integrated starter levels, introductory characters and cut-away sequences that prime the player and teach different aspects of the game as it is actually played. In the design context, the requirement to find and apply information that is related to the conceptual development of a recently formed or gestating idea is likely to be more productive than generic searches on a particular topic.

As the field of game studies develops, an argument that has recently emerged is between "ludolology" and "narratology" as approaches for the analysis of games (Frasca, 1999). Ludologists focus on game mechanics and the element of play as the essence of the game, whereas narratologists argue that games are closely linked to stories and emphasize their importance in giving games meaning. There has been continuing debate on the merits of this delineation (Frasca, 2003; Pearce, 2005) with a general consensus emerging that most games have a blend of these two elements, particularly in the realm of computer games where complex combinations of avatars, animation and immersion are used (Apperley, 2006). Regarding concept design, the element of narratology lends itself well to the contextualization of the design problem and in assisting with navigating through the various stages expected of the designer to reach a design solution. Integrating engaging ludological elements which will potentially enhance levels of information use by participants, however, presents a greater challenge. In essence, can designing truly be a game?

Summary of Characteristics of Computer Games

Computer games have been shown to have a number of potential benefits for team utilization of information during the concept design task. Three key characteristics of computer games are increased *motivation* of participants, controlled *interaction* during collaboration, and adding *structure* to the completion of tasks. To better understand how these characteristics are manifested in typical computer games, a selection were systematically evaluated.

REVIEW OF COMPUTER GAMES

Primary evaluation of a number of contemporary computer games took place to examine the relevant feature sets, game structures and interface designs in information-rich environments. Evaluations of games have used a range of approaches, including quantitative methods (Ip & Jacobs, 2004), surveys of large numbers of players (Vorderer et al., 2003), and analysis of characteristics based on aggregating magazine reviews (Pinelle, Wong, & Stach, 2008). However, it has been suggested that the value systems created by players in the playing of games are best understood through in-depth studies (Barr, Noble, & Biddle, 2006). Given the specific nature of the application of the gaming interactions, it was felt this was the most appropriate approach, and therefore primary evaluation of a number of games was undertaken. Four genres (*strategy, simulation, role playing* and *action*) were identified (Apperley, 2006), and exemplars from each played. Table 1 lists the games which were selected for closer examination, and also provides synopsis of each. Recognized as being games of excellence and/or popularity in their respective genres, they were selected as examples where the gameplay and information-rich environments have been tightly interwoven to provide an engaging user experience. The mechanisms used to do so have additionally been captured in Table 1.

Table 1. Games selected for evaluation of information use

Genre	Game	Description	Information use
Strategy	Age of Empires III	Conquer other civilizations, accumulate wealth by trading and diplomacy, build and defend empires.	Tactical and responsive decisions based on analysis of shared game board. Information not shared across players, but communication facilities can co-ordinate actions. Additional information generally presented in toolbars on periphery of main board.
Simulation	Sim City 4	Build houses, shops and amenities to create a city and then manage utilities and resources to help it develop. The city and its inhabitants will respond to every decision made.	Focus on micro- and macro-management of complex data sets. Continual monitoring of conditions and statistics required. Information continually provided through game AI 'advisors', ability to review historical data. Sophisticated toolbar, dialog box layouts.
Role-playing	Oblivion: The Elder Scrolls IV	Interact with a richly colored environment and a large cast of characters through structured dialogue. Based around a series of puzzles, and features drama, intrigue and humor.	Information pieced together from various aspects of the game world to solve puzzles and challenges. Verbal and physical interaction with range of AI characters. Inventories of maps, tips, conversations and so on assist with application of information to game context. A number of statistical screens (weapons, health etc.) must also be monitored.
Action	Super Mario Bros. 3	Navigate a fast-moving 2D cartoon environment by running and jumping over various obstacles. Completing each stage moves the player closer to achieving the mission to stop the evil Bowser.	Control of avatar is easy to learn and mesmeric in use. Sequence of levels memorized with practice and necessary for progress to higher levels. Little formal communication, although two-player mode allows for degree of co-operation. A number of statistics are displayed (lives, pointes earned etc.) though not central to game.

DEVELOPMENT OF NEW INTERACTIONS

To better understand how these mechanisms could be adapted, two different scenarios for concept design were developed. Using the 6-3-5 Method's principle of concept exchange as a basis, gaming aspects were introduced to examine how a progressive interaction could be improved and the quality of concepts enhanced through the integration of information searching tasks. It was decided to base these around the strategy and action genres to allow two contrasting scenarios to be developed – one based on decision making and the other skill. These are outlined in more detail below, with storyboards included for each.

Using Strategy

Scenario 1 (Figure 4) uses aspects of strategy and simulation games by using a shared, dynamic board to dictate the tasks undertaken by the players. These include information searching and information use tasks related to specific information items. The engagement engendered by the shared board, and the integration of information retrieval with idea generation, make this scenario distinct from the 6-3-5 Method, which relies simply on sharing ideas amongst the team.

In terms of *motivation* for playing, strategy games rely less on pressure and more on engagement: decisions are continually being made as an intricate situation builds, with the player becoming more and more involved. The "arousal" and "control" terms used by Csikszentmihalyi may therefore be more appropriate in this instance. Players attempt to cross the board from one side to the other by linking boxes (information items) to circles (concepts). Other players' squares can be destroyed using 'requirement bombs' – players must consider how best to prevent others crossing while they make progress themselves.

Control and co-ordination, world modification and language-based communication (as identified

Figure 4. Scenario 1

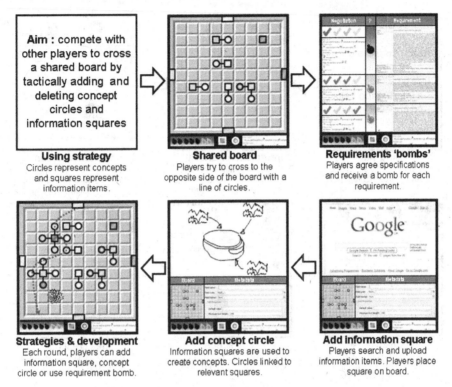

Using strategy
Circles represent concepts and squares represent information items.

Shared board
Players try to cross to the opposite side of the board with a line of circles.

Requirements 'bombs'
Players agree specifications and receive a bomb for each requirement.

Strategies & development
Each round, players can add information square, concept circle or use requirement bomb.

Add concept circle
Information squares are used to create concepts. Circles linked to relevant squares.

Add information square
Players search and upload information items. Players place square on board.

by Manninen) would be the primary forms of *interaction* between participants. Although in this instance the board has been rendered somewhat crudely with squares representing information and circles concepts, it could be simulated in a more complex way similar to games such as *Sim City*. This would allow more sophisticated communication of the nature of the concepts and information contained on the board. Additionally, communication with others is possible through the tools (e.g., chat or messaging) provided in the panel at the bottom of the screen.

A ludological approach is prevalent in the *structure* of the scenario: the board and the decisions related to the game are central to the organization of the participants and allocation of the tasks. Players enter different game modes depending on what task they are undertaking, but continually return to the game board as the situation evolves.

Using Action

Scenario 2 (Figure 5) also explicitly introduces information searching as part of the concept design activity, utilising two action-based sequences that relate to design activities. Players are firstly required to search for information items, which are represented as balls. They are motivated to collect as much information as possible as they have more balls to drop on other players in the following game sequence. They are then required to create ideas for the information balls they were struck by. The motivation to develop concepts is to allow them to drop these as boxes on other players for further development. The task and game sequence repeats, with the aim of providing a strong link between the different elements.

Action games are generally reliant on dexterity and skill in undertaking highly context-specific challenges for *motivation*, making the integration of productive content difficult. It can be

Figure 5. Scenario 2

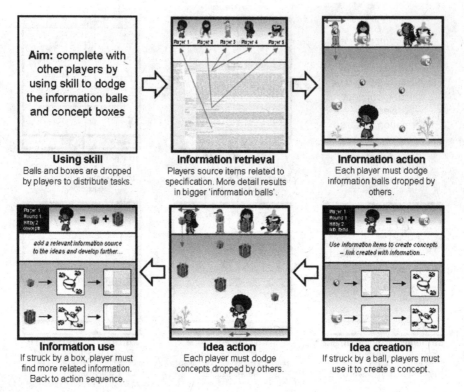

Using skill
Balls and boxes are dropped by players to distribute tasks.

Information retrieval
Players source items related to specification. More detail results in bigger 'information balls'.

Information action
Each player must dodge information balls dropped by others.

Information use
If struck by a box, player must find more related information. Back to action sequence.

Idea action
Each player must dodge concepts dropped by others.

Idea creation
If struck by a ball, players must use it to create a concept.

expected that participants will reach the 'flow' state when undertaking the action-based sequences. Achieving the same in the searching and designing tasks is more unpredictable – the use of time limits and quality control measures could be ways of introducing mild anxiety or arousal measures that assist motivation. It is the linkage of the action-based sequences to the productivity sequences that is, however, the greatest challenge for such games, and this scenario attempts to do so by ensuring the detail of information or ideas produced improve their chances in the action sequences through the sizes of balls or boxes.

The *interaction* of players occurs primarily in the intensity of the action-based sequences. The competitive nature of these can be viewed as beneficial in spurring on players to produce better material, but could be counterproductive if a spirit of overall harmony and co-operation is affected. Many of the more subtle modes of communication described by Manninen such as body language and gesture are not utilized in this scenario. While this could affect the ability of a team of strangers to bond, it does focus the attention of players on the content rather than personalities.

Regarding *structure*, action games tend to have a loose narratology, even if it is not the focus of the player. Short-term goals tend to dominate. It would not be feasible, however, to develop a new action game specific for each design problem to be solved. It is therefore appropriate to consider how engaging action-based sequences can be embedded into concept design in a way which is repeatable (i.e., not project-specific) but still meaningfully integrated.

DEVELOPMENT OF DESIGN INTERACTION

Given their conceptual nature, a detailed formal analysis was not appropriate for the scenarios.

Instead, the broad game characteristics explored at the beginning of this paper were utilized to help identify a general direction for development. The strategy-based Scenario 1 was found to be strong due to the controlled and on-going interactions of the game being suited to the design context. However, there were a number of aspects which required strengthening, particularly regarding motivation to engage with the game through characteristics such as risk and pressure: it remained somewhat limited in terms of the forced interaction and motivation between players, and it was felt the board did not sufficiently integrate information and ideas across the team. Although the action-based Scenario 2 was felt to be particularly promising in terms of user engagement, concerns persisted about the feasibility of these being meaningful parts of the player experience rather than appendages to the actual design tasks.

To address these limitations, it was felt that a more sophisticated way to ensure players were forced to use judgment when reviewing the concepts of other players, while maintaining a balance of competition and co-operation across the team, was deemed necessary. This led to an exploration of game theory, which has, over the last fifty years, emerged as a major interdisciplinary approach to studying the way people interact (Hamburger, 1979). Its origins are in the field of mathematics, but its ideas have been applied in a range of areas such as economics and other behavioral sciences. It is primarily concerned with the decisions made and strategies used by individuals as they pursue their own interests, leading to conflict or compe-

titions within groups or social structures. Some games, such as chess, are by their nature very competitive as the players' interests are in direct conflict. Such games are called zero sum games, because if we add up the wins and losses, with losses being negative (i.e., +1 for the winner, -1 for the loser, 0 for a draw) we find that the end result will always be zero. In a non-zero-sum game, however, players' interests are not always in direct conflict so there is the opportunity for mutual gain. Probably the most famous example of a game where this is the case is the Prisoner's Dilemma, developed by Flood and Dresher when working at RAND Corporation in the early 1950s.

The name Prisoner's Dilemma comes from the original scenario for the problem: it consists of two prisoners, who are held in separate cells, accused of being complicit in a particular crime. The aim for the captors is to convince one of the prisoners to implicate the other by giving evidence against them. If both prisoners choose to give evidence (defect) then the judge is in no doubt of their guilt and sentences them to three years in prison each. If neither prisoner gives evidence (co-operate) then the judge has less clear indication of guilt and sentences them to only one year each. If one prisoner, however, defects and the other does not the judge will allow the defector to go free while sentencing the other prisoner to five years. The reward structure for the game is summarized in Table 2.

In his seminal book on the subject *"The Evolution of Co-operation"*, Robert Axelrod (1990) outlines how this model can be used to help de-

Table 2. Reward structure for Prisoner's dilemma

		Player B	
		Co-operate	Defect
Player A	Co-operate	R=3, R=3 Reward for mutual cooperation	S=0, T=5 Sucker's payoff, and temptation to defect
	Defect	T=5, S=0 Temptation to defect and sucker's payoff	P=1, P=1 Punishment for mutual defection

NB: The payoffs to Player A are listed first

scribe human patterns of co-operation. He describes how he invited researchers worldwide to submit a computer program to play an iterated version of the Prisoner's Dilemma, and uses this as the basis of discussion on society and human collaboration in general, citing examples from trench warfare in World War I to biological systems. Given the fact that many of the elements in conceptual design are typically individual tasks within a group or organizational context, for example finding relevant information or creating a concept sketch, there seemed to be potential for harnessing the strategies associated with the Prisoner's Dilemma.

Although game theory has not yet been widely embraced by the design community, there are a few relevant instances. Matthews and Chesters have developed an 'Information Pump' (2006) using modified Prisoner's Dilemma interaction. This is a method for extracting feedback from product users that awards participants points for the information they supply. The interaction is fairly involved, consisting of 'encoders' who have knowledge of the product in question and 'dummies' who do not. The encoders make statements about the product and the other participants then make judgments on their validity and how others will react. Despite the complexity of the approach, the authors report positive feedback to their initial studies.

It has also been suggested how the Prisoner's Dilemma could motivate learning in the design studio (Shih, Hu, & Chen, 2006). In this instance, it was used to model the interaction between students assessed individually but working in the social studio space. The dilemma was whether a student would choose to share information they had sourced individually with their colleagues or not. Even though this was a theoretical proposition, the authors suggest that structuring and restructuring of learning groups will take place based on the effectiveness of cooperation between individuals. In both these examples, this tension between cooperation and competition of participants was

attractive, and ways to incorporate similar mechanisms in the context of concept design teams were subsequently explored.

Using Judgment

A revised scenario (Figure 6) incorporating elements of the Prisoner's Dilemma was subsequently constructed as a way to encourage participants to interact by evaluating each others' concepts. This approach differs from the traditional Prisoner's Dilemma in that it is no longer just about iterations of co-operation and defection, but also about players' judgment in evaluating the concepts. This shift in emphasis is reflected in a change in terminology: *interaction* (as opposed to *game*), and *participants* (as opposed to *players*) are considered more appropriate in reference to the activity of the team, and are additionally more suited to use in business contexts in which it is hoped the interaction will be used.

The interaction was brought further back into the realm of more traditional design methods by placing it on a shared grid similar to that used in the 6-3-5 Method (although players move diagonally across the board rather than completing rows). The interaction consists of rounds, and for each round all participants must have either produced a concept or found a relevant information item. When reviewing each others' concepts, the participants have to decide whether it should be developed or rejected. Information searching and concept development tasks are subsequently allocated, based on the premise that participants gravitate towards sketching and "ideator" activity over research and "collector" activity (Puccio, 1999). As the interaction progresses, a linked grid of information and ideas emerge that shows links, development and rationale over a session.

Figure 6. Revised scenario

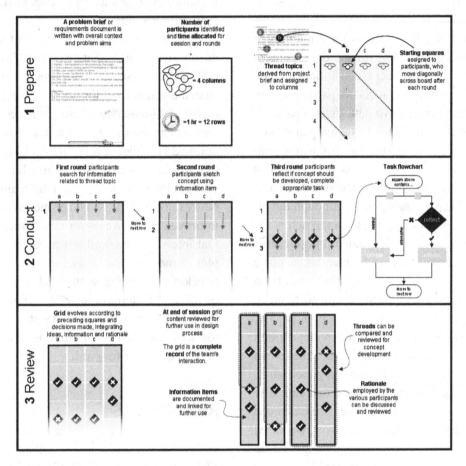

CONCLUSION

The stated aims of this paper were to explore *how computer gaming techniques could be used to enhance information use in product development teams*, and to *suggest frameworks for their application*. A review of relevant gaming literature as well as an examination of computer gaming genres (including the testing of four titles for illustration) has revealed a number of characteristics in motivation, interaction and structure that are applicable to the design team. Two scenarios were developed to the storyboard level to visualize the implementation of certain characteristics, and to deliver a number of tangible suggestions on how gaming interventions can be made in the design team context. Finally, utilizing additional ideas

from game theory to optimize team engagement, a refined proposal for the implementation of a structured approach to concept design has been outlined. This can be considered a development of existing progressive concept design methods – in particular the 6-3-5 Method. While the resulting interaction is not a game in the conventional sense, it is cognizant of the qualities they offer, and incorporates information search and concept evaluation activities in a way that other concept design methods would not normally encompass. Furthermore the output is a combination of information and conceptual work, linked and categorized according to the design context.

Utilization

This research has implications for a number of disciplines. Firstly, for product development teams involved in concept generation, a new approach is presented that allows participants to gather information and evaluate ideas in parallel. The structure is simple but has a number of key benefits – it ensures that information is relevant, at the point of need and utilized. In addition, it shares ideas and information across the team in a structured and engaging way. Although developed with designers in mind, the approach is applicable to any organization undertaking creative problem solving. Initial tests have taken place with range of industries and feedback has been generally positive, with the traceability offered by the shared grid proving particularly popular. The storyboard presented in Figure 6 provides enough information for a team to undertake their own concept generation session using a paper-based grid to share sketches and information items. The benefits of the approach, however, are enhanced when all information and sketchwork is shared digitally. Some initial prototyping using a set-up of Microsoft OneNote to provide real-time document sharing in conjunction with digital tablets to capture sketchwork has been carried out with reasonable success. The long-term aim for the research, however, is the programming and testing of a bespoke computer-based tool to facilitate the approach.

Additionally, the theoretical ideas presented suggest a number of relationships and cross-linkages between computer games and their application to teamworking. Some of these have been encapsulated in the two initial scenarios developed for the concept design context, but a broader range of game genres and different applications remain to be explored. It is hoped that researchers from a range of academic backgrounds can use this initial work as a basis to develop new insights into how games can be augmented with more established literature in areas such as management, psychology, and creativity.

Finally, as games developers continue to produce virtual worlds that are visual, information-rich, and engaging it is important that there is a shared awareness of the activities undertaken in traditional industries where games could potentially enhance current practices. This research has outlined a number of ways in which the principles of computer games could be adapted and integrated with typical design tasks to help teams produce better informed ideas. The proposed incremental improvement of an existing design method shows that interventions need not necessarily be complex or radical – they may simply involve games developers working with practitioners to draw on relevant features or techniques that they know to be effective. It is hoped that this work points towards how such collaborations could form and be applied going forward.

REFERENCES

Altshuller, G., Altov, H., & Shulyak, L. (1994). *TRIZ, the theory of inventive problem solving.* Worcester, MA: Technical Innovation Center Inc.

Apperley, T. H. (2006). Genre and game studies: Toward a critical approach to video game genres. *Simulation & Gaming, 37*(1), 6–23. doi:10.1177/1046878105282278

Axelrod, R. (1990). *The Evolution of Co-operation.* London: Penguin Books.

Barr, P., Noble, J., & Biddle, R. (2006). Video game values: Human-computer interaction and games. *Interacting with Computers, 19*, 180–195. doi:10.1016/j.intcom.2006.08.008

Benami, O., & Jin, Y. (2002). *Creative stimulation in conceptual design.* Paper presented at the ASME 2002 Design Engineering Technical Confereces and Computer and Information in Engineering Conference, Montreal, Canada.

Chen, J. (2007). Flow in Games (and Everything Else). *Communications of the ACM, 50*(4), 31–34. doi:10.1145/1232743.1232769

Chuang, Y., & Chen, L. L. (2008). How to rate 100 visual stimuli efficiently. *International Journal of Design, 2*(1), 31–43.

Cross, N. (1994). *Engineering Design Methods, Strategies for Product Design.* Chichester, UK: John Wiley & Sons.

Csikszentmihalyi, M. (1997). *Finding Flow: The Psychology of Engagement with Everyday Life.* New York: BasicBooks.

Davis, S. B., & Carini, C. (2004, September 6-10). *Constructing a Player-Centred Definition of Fun for Video Games Design.* Paper presented at the HCI 2004, Leeds, UK.

Ducheneaut, N., & Moore, R. J. (2004, November 6-10). *The social side of gaming: a study of interaction patterns in a massively multiplayer online game.* Paper presented at the CSCW, Chicago.

Faria, A. J., & Wellington, W. J. (2004). A survey of simulation game users, former-users, and never-users. *Simulation & Gaming, 35*(2), 178–207. doi:10.1177/1046878104263543

Frasca, G. (1999). Ludology Meets Narratology. Similitude and Differences between (Video) games and Narrative. *Parnasso, 3*, 365–371.

Frasca, G. (2003, November 4-6). *Ludologists Love Stories, Too: Notes from a Debate that Never Took Place.* Paper presented at the Level Up: Digital Games Research Conference, Utrecht, The Netherlands.

French, M. (1985). *Conceptual Design for Engineers.* London: The Design Council/ Springer Verlag.

Friedman, T. L. (2006). *The World Is Flat.* London: Penguin Books.

Gee, J. P. (2003). *What Video Games Have to Teach Us About Learning and Literacy.* New York: Palgrave Macmillan.

Gutwin, C., & Greenberg, S. (2002). A Descriptive Framework of Workspace Awareness for Real-Time Groupware. *Computer Supported Cooperative Work, 11*, 411–446. doi:10.1023/A:1021271517844

Hamburger, H. (1979). *Games as models of social phenomena.* San Francisco, CA: W. H. Freeman and Company.

Ip, B., & Jacobs, G. (2004). Quantifying Game Design. *Design Studies, 25*, 607–624. doi:10.1016/j.destud.2004.02.001

Kelley, T. (2006). *The Ten Faces of Innovation: Strategies for Heightening Creativity.* London: Profile Books.

Kriz, W. C. (2003). Creating effective learning environments and learning organizations through gaming simulation design. *Simulation & Gaming, 34*(4), 495–511. doi:10.1177/1046878103258201

Laurel, B. (Ed.). (2004). *Design Research: Methods and Perspectives.* Boston: MIT Press.

Malone, T. W. (1981). Toward a Theory of Intrinsically Motivating Instruction. *Cognitive Science, 4*, 333–369. doi:10.1207/s15516709cog0504_2

Mannien, T. (2003). Interaction Forms and Communicative Actions in Multiplayer Games. *The International Journal of Computer Game Research, 3*(1).

Manninen, T. (2001, September 10-14). *Rich Interaction in the Context of Networked Virtual Environments- Experiences Gained from the Multi-player Games Domain.* Paper presented at the HCI 2001/ IHM 2001, Lille, France.

Manninen, T. (2003). Interaction Forms and Communicative Actions in Multiplayer Games. *Game Studies, 3*(1).

Mark, G., & Wulf, V. (1999). Changing interpersonal communication through groupware use. *Behaviour & Information Technology, 18*(5), 385–395. doi:10.1080/014492999118968

Matthews, P. C., & Chesters, P. E. (2006). Implementing the Information Pump using accessible technology. *Journal of Engineering Design, 17*(6), 563–585. doi:10.1080/09544820600646629

McDaniel, R., Fiore, S. M., Greenwood-Erickson, A., Scielzo, S., & Cannon-Bowers, J. A. (2006). Video Games as Learning Tools for Project Management. *The Journal of the International Digital Media and Arts Association, 3*(1), 78–91.

Mehrabian, A. (1981). *Silent Messages: Implicit Communication of Emotions and Attitudes* (2nd ed.). Belmont, CA: Wadsworth, Inc. MIT and Microsoft Corporation (Producer). (2005, July 12). *Games-to-teach project*. Retrieved from http://cms.mit.edu/games/education/proto.html

Newman, J. (2002). The Myth of the Ergodic Videogame: Some thoughts on player-character relationships in videogames. *Game Studies, 2*(1).

O'Reilly, T. (2005). *What is Web 2.0*. Retrieved August 4, 2009, from http://oreilly.com/web2/archive/what-is-web-20.html

Osborn, A. (1953). *Applied Imagination: Principles and Procedures of Creative Problem Solving*. New York: Charles Scribner's Sons.

Pahl, G., & Beitz, W. (1995). *Engineering Design, A Systematic Approach*. Bath, UK: Springer.

Pearce, C. (2005, June 16-20). *Theory wars: an argument against arguments in the so-called ludology/narratology debate*. Paper presented at the Changing Views: Worlds in Play, Digital Games Research Association Conference, Vancouver, Canada.

Pinelle, D., Wong, N., & Stach, T. (2008). *Heuristic Evaluation for Games: Usability Principles for Video Game Design*. Paper presented at the CHI 2008, Florence, Italy.

Prensky, M. (2001). *Digital Game-Based Learning*. New York: McGraw-Hill.

Puccio, G. J. (1999). Creative Problem Solving Preferences: Their Identification and Implications. *Creativity and Innovation Management, 8*(3), 171–178. doi:10.1111/1467-8691.00134

Pugh, S. (1991). *Total Design*. Reading, UK: Addison-Wesley.

PwC. (2006). *Global Entertainment and Media Outlook: 2006–2010*. Retrieved from http://www.pwc.com

Rantanen, K., & Domb, E. (2002). *Simplified TRIZ: new problem-solving applications for engineers and manufacturing professionals*. Boca Raton, FL: St. Lucie Press. doi:10.1201/9781420000320

Rohrbach, B. (1969). Kreativ nach Regeln. *Absatzwirtschaft, 12*, 73–75.

Shah, J. J., Kulkarni, S. V., & Vargas-Hernandez, N. (2000). Evaluation of Idea Generation Methods for Conceptual Design: Effectiveness Metrics and Design of Experiments. *Journal of Mechanical Design, 122*(4), 377–385. doi:10.1115/1.1315592

Shih, S.-G., Hu, T.-P., & Chen, C.-N. (2006). A game theory-based approach to the analysis of cooperative learning in design studios. *Design Studies, 27*, 711–722. doi:10.1016/j.destud.2006.05.001

Squire, K. (2002). Cultural Framing of Computer/Video Games. *Game Studies, 2*(1).

Sweetser, P., & Wyeth, P. (2005). GameFlow: A Model for Evaluating Player Enjoyment in Games. *ACM Computers in Entertainment, 3*(3).

Tauer, J. M., & Harackiewicz, J. M. (1999). Winning Isn't Everything: Competition, Achievement Orientation, and Intrinsic Motivation. *Journal of Experimental Social Psychology*, *35*, 209–238. doi:10.1006/jesp.1999.1383

Ulrich, K. T., & Eppinger, S. D. (1995). *Product Design and Development* (3rd ed.). New York: McGraw-Hill.

Vorderer, P., Hartmann, T., & Klimmt, C. (2003, September 25-27). *Explaining the enjoyment of playing video games: the role of competition.* Paper presented at the International Conference on Entertainment Computing, Pittsburgh, Pennsylvania.

Westecott, E. (2003). Game Forms for New Outcomes. In Laurel, B. (Ed.), *Design Research: Methods and Perspectives* (pp. 129–134). Cambridge, MA: MIT Press.

Wodehouse, A. J., & Bradley, D. A. (2006). Gaming techniques and the product development process: commonalities & cross-applications. *Journal of Desert Research*, *5*(2), 155–171. doi:10.1504/JDR.2006.011360v

This work was previously published in International Journal of Gaming and Computer-Mediated Simulations, Volume 2, Issue 3, edited by Richard E. Ferdig, pp. 75-92, copyright 2010 by IGI Publishing (an imprint of IGI Global).

Chapter 15
Adaptive Interactive Narrative Model to Teach Ethics

Rania Hodhod
University of York, UK

Daniel Kudenko
University of York, UK

Paul Cairns
University of York, UK

ABSTRACT

Promoting ethical, responsible, and caring young people is a perennial aim of education. Efforts have been made to find ways of teaching other than traditional ones like games and role play. Narrative-based computer games are engaging learning platforms that allow collaboration of humans and computers in the creation of innovative experiences. In this paper, the authors examine the design of an adaptive, interactive narrative model that uses a student model to provide an individualized story-path and an individualized learning process. In this regard, the authors comprise strong learning objectives underpinned by effective story telling. The adaptive narrative model has been deployed in the educational game environment, AEINS, along with the use of the Socratic Method and pedagogical agents to support teaching in the ethics domain. Evaluation results indicate the usefulness of the design and provide evidence on the development of moral reasoning and the transfer of moral virtues to its users.

INTRODUCTION

Computer game worlds have become more complex over the years as computer technology has evolved. It is a very dynamic field that has moved on significantly since the simplicity of Pong with many improvements and expansions. Since the

1950s, computer and cognitive scientists have developed the idea that the computer can be used by a student to learn independently and that computer programs can teach a student. For example, McGrenere (1996) investigated whether games could be utilized to assist learning. Others have explored the appropriate game types and game elements to be used as educational tools (Amory et al., 1999). Some researchers consider educational

DOI: 10.4018/978-1-4666-0029-4.ch015

games only effective if the interaction is monitored and directed by teachers (Klawe, 1998) or if the games are integrated with other more traditional activities such as pencil-and-paper exercises. Other researchers believe that effectiveness is related to the features, preferences and behavior of a particular user (McGrenere, 1996).

In the last few decades, games became a strong supplement to teaching by virtue of their concrete experiences leading to learning. Studies on the use of games in education (Amory et al., 1999; Shaffer, 2005; Gee, 2005; Tan et al., 2005; Gómez-Martín et al., 2005; Fasili & Michalakopoulos, 2005; Egenfeldt-Neilson, 2005; Shaffer, 2006; Gee, 2006) have proven that games constitute a medium that motivates students to try to develop their knowledge while they put it into practice. Instead of being taught about topics, students are engaged with the topics and play them out. Within such environments, players can learn while being engaged in an entertainment activity (Maragos & Grigoriadou, 2005) and thereby create their own experiences and get feedback on their specific actions in a safe environment (Egenfeldt-Neilson, 2005).

Of course, not all users share the same preferences or styles when interacting with a game or when solving game-problems. This leads to the importance of adaptation in the sense that the behavior of each play-instance of a game depends on the actions of an individual player. Student modeling plays a central role in providing a personalized learning process for the individual student by considering his needs, strengths and weaknesses. The telling of stories within these environments has an important role in engaging the player, transferring tacit knowledge to the student and supporting adaptation through providing personalized implicit feedback that fosters self reflection and helps the students to discover any course of contradiction themselves.

Stories and interactive narrative have been used for a long time now to entertain children and teach them, for example, in classrooms for primary and secondary school curricula, both on their own and as a support for other subjects (Bolton, 1999; Bayon et al., 2003). In an article, Simpson (1998) emphasizes the importance of stories in our lives and their role in tightening human relationships: ``*Stories are connections to the past and yet carry us into the future; they speak of relationships, of human connections, and to what gives a quality to our lives.*'' This has been also emphasized through role playing and discussions that have been used effectively in helping students to transfer their knowledge and beliefs into actions, in addition to helping them to see how their decisions affect other people and things (McBrien & Brandt, 1997).

Interactive narrative allows teachers to introduce sensitive issues in a safe and stimulating way. It has proven to be successful in creating enriching experiences for its users, sparking problem-solving skills, individual and group decision-making skills, and encouraging pupils to develop strategies to deal with different issues in different disciplines. For these reasons, interactive narrative has mainly been used as a common tool to teach in ill-defined domains such as design, history, law and ethics. The Socratic Method is the most widely used pedagogy in telling these stories.

Ethics and citizenship is an important ill-defined domain that can not be easily taught through dictating concepts. It needs more than the traditional methods of teaching to allow the children to draw the required analogies and relate them to their real life experiences. According to Kohlberg, if children get engaged in enough independent thinking they will eventually begin to formulate conceptions of rights, values, and principles by which they evaluate existing social arrangements (Colby et al., 1983; Willard et al., 1996).

We argue that the development of virtues requires practicing the same way other skills such as reading or writing do. In addition, learning about ethical virtues is different from applying them. As Watson (2003) clarifies: ``*Getting high scores in an ethical course does not guarantee at all the actual behavior of that student.*'' This goes well with our opinion that children need to practice moral reasoning by involving them in different moral situations, though within a safe environment, which allows them to act according to their beliefs. Accordingly, presenting the effect of their actions on themselves and others may help them to eventually begin to formulate their own conceptions of rights, values and principles. Another important point Watson (2003) mentioned is the desire for good: "*The trick lies not solely with knowing what is right and good but also in building a love for the good and the worthwhile*" Watson points out that by giving the students the chance to see successful people do what is right and good, chances are better that students will be biased to follow suit themselves than they might otherwise. In other words, students can even advance to the kinds of thinking that characterize some of the great moral leaders and philosophers who have at times advocated civil disobedience in the name of universal ethical principles (Crain, 1985).

This paper focuses on the role of the student model to provide an adaptive, interactive narrative model within which students can express their characters through problem solving, decision making, and conflict resolution present in moral dilemmas. The proposed model has been applied to AEINS, a learning environment that allows the student to practice various moral virtues. The environment involves the students in interactive moral dilemmas that focus on virtues and moral exemplars. The students are involved in independent thinking processes that help them to identify what is good and bad. Moreover, the paper discusses how learning theories, such as Bloom's Taxonomy, Keller's ARCS model and Gagné's Principles assisted and guided the design and the implementation of AEINS. It also focuses on the role of the Socratic Method as a teaching pedagogy, and the role of pedagogical agents in supplying the educational process. AEINS promotes the acquisition of skills and knowledge in a pleasant interactive way, as shown from the evaluation results.

ADAPTIVE INTERACTIVE NARRATIVE

Interactive narrative is an engaging learning medium that allows collaboration of humans and computers in the creation of innovative experiences. Interactive narrative can be seen as an engaging hook where the player feels in control and can see his actions affecting how the story unfolds.

A model of dual narrative that combines dynamically generated and graph structured narratives has been designed. The dynamically generated narrative generates a story that is not a part of a learning objective but rather as a step of making contact. It serves the purposes of transitioning between objectives and increasing causal relatedness, thus improving cohesiveness (Niehaus & Reidl, 2009). Planning has been used to generate the dynamic narrative as it is more variable than the other types and able to generate different narratives for different users, and also different narratives for a single user on subsequent play turns. In other words, for every possible way the student can violate the story plan, an alternative story plan is generated.

Scripted narrative is another type of narrative generation that can be seen as a good representation for semi-directed stories that allow following the student's actions and make an assessment on them, in the form of a step by step follow up. It is characterized by the presence of unexpected ends that raise the student's curiosity during the interaction course. Although scripting narrative is a hard process that can be time consuming, it allows defining decision points that reflect the student's mental state at the time of the interaction. Ideally, each path in the scripted narrative is a story in which the protagonist is the student in the role of making moral decisions. This kind of narrative allows students to pursue different procedures for solving the problem, which arises from allowing different perspectives based on students' perceptions and interpretations of the nature of the problem (Shin & McGee, 2003).

Adaptation to individual users in computer-based learning environments has been successfully applied previously. Student modeling is the core of this process that mainly aims to guide the adaptive learning process based on the student's current skills. It aims at identifying the student's characteristics, needs, and situation in an automatic way, using student's behaviour and actions in order to automatically infer the relevant information (Graf et al., 2009) and provides tailored feedback. A reliable student model is necessary, but getting enough information about a student is quite challenging (Graf et al., 2008). For instance, it is a big challenge gathering the information that would allow the system to identify a student who was confused.

Overall, then, the suggested model manages to integrate both dynamically generated narrative and scripted narratives to form one continuous story. The dynamically generated narrative engages the student and ties scripted narratives together in one dramatic coherent story from the start to the end. The scripted narratives allow pursuing different story paths with unexpected ends and the use of the student model that assesses the student's actions and helps to provide a personalized learning process. The continuous story allows the presence of evolving agents that play an important role as pedagogical facilitators. The student's understanding gained through this process is situated in their experience and can best be evaluated in terms relevant to this experience (Thomas & Young, 2007). The model has been applied to the educational game, AEINS, to evaluate the validity of the model.

AEINS

The AEINS architecture has been designed in a way that allows the generation of interactive narrative at run time, forming the main story, and is flexible enough to allow the presentation of interactive teaching moments based on the current student model.

AEINS is an adaptive educational game that aims to foster character education. AEINS is a problem solving environment that helps 8-12 year old children to be engaged effectively in interactive moral dilemmas. AEINS main aim is to allow students to practice various moral virtues and exercise resolving moral conflicts. In other words, it aims to give the students the opportunity to move from the state of making moral judgments to the state of taking moral actions, from the knowing state to the doing state, which we consider an important step in moral education.

As seen in Figure 1, AEINS architecture consists of six modules; four modules to serve the educational targets and two modules for generating the story and storing information about the story world. AEINS starts by generating a story within which the student can act and affect how the story unfolds. Based on the student's actions the world model state changes, the new state is presented to the student through the presentation module. To initialize the student model, the student is asked to choose his friends from the agents inhabiting the world.

Based on the current student model together with the domain model, the pedagogical model decides which moral dilemma (teaching moment) to present next to the student. Each teaching moment is associated with educational and narrative prerequisites that need to be satisfied in order for the teaching moment to be presented. If the current state of the world allows the presentation of the teaching moment (TM), the student can start the interaction with the TM right away. If this is not the case, the story generator develops a plan that after execution will move the current world state to a state that allows the TM to be presented as part of the main story. Thereby, the TM would be logically and coherently interleaved. Manipulating the teaching moment's priority is done through production rules as follows:

Figure 1. AEINS Architecture

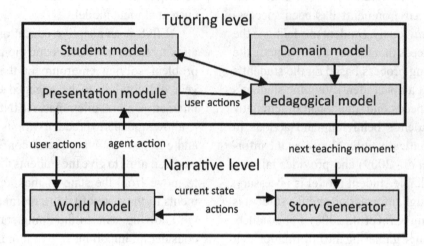

Trigger: teaching moment X_1 has not been presented
and teaching moment X_2 has not been presented
and value Y is not held by the user
and value X is held by the user
Action: set priority to teaching moment X_2

The capital letters in the rules represents variables and the representation denotes that if (a) a specific pattern of teaching moments has not been presented to the student yet and (b) user holds certain values and does not hold others, then the action part of the rule executes and the next teaching moment is prioritised.

The pedagogical model tracks and assesses the student's actions and updates the student model accordingly. Research suggests that students benefit from being encouraged to consider a collection of evidence and coordinate their theoretical ideas with supporting or contradictory evidence as they engage in argumentation (Koslowski, 1996; Bell & Linn, 2000; Shin & McGee, 2003). In addition, students must have opportunities to choose among different options and to reason which criteria lead to the option chosen (Kuhn, 1993). AEINS follows these approaches in designing the pedagogical model and uses Socratic Dialogue as it has been shown to be a highly effective approach to help children develop new ideas and gain new

insights (Elkind & Sweet, 1997). With ill-defined problems, development is a change in the way a person thinks and not is a case of acquiring more knowledge. Therefore, the pedagogical model has been developed in the form of production rules that give the system specific cognitive operations to reason about the student and the teaching process. The model specifies how a student ideally would use the system and how the system reacts to his actions. According to the student's actions, the model assesses the student's skills and adjusts the student model accordingly. In order to design the pedagogical model, the problem's structure and what exactly needed to be modeled has to be specified. An example of the pedagogical model assessment rules is as follows:

If action ("TM_1", "agree_to_lie")
and if action ("TM_1", "insist_to_lie")
and if action ("TM_1", "lie_for_friend_sake")
and if action ("TM_1", "agree_lying_is_bad)
Then skill ("do_not_lie", "acquired", 0.5)

The teaching moments are crucial components of AEINS that aim to provide concrete settings for the student to practice abstract concepts. They can be thought of as a variety of ethical problems that require tough decisions. The idea behind the current design is based on analyzing moral dilemmas and transforming them to story graph structures, and then specifying the decision points that should reflect the required skills. While designing the teaching moments, we took into account that they should emphasize good models and examples, after which the students could hopefully model their own behavior. Ideas from Kohlberg's dilemmas and other moral situations designed specifically for school students were used to author the teaching moments. Analyzing these situations and transforming them to graph structures is not a straight forward process. In fact, it can be considered the bottleneck of the system's development phases.

The Socratic Method as the Teaching Pedagogy

Students of all ages use questions in their learning of topics (http://question.eu/). Questions act as the means to make a transition from the observation and hypothesis stage. The Socratic Method is one way of using questions in order to develop moral thinking and provides opportunities for personal discovery through problem solving. In classroom environments, the Socratic Method is dramatic and entertaining. It triggers lively classroom discussion and can help students make choices based on what is right instead of what they can get away with. It allows an appropriate amount of choices during ill-structured and authentic investigations that lead to the development of inquiry skills (Avner et al., 1980).

The Socratic Method displays its strengths when the students make a bad choice. Through discussion, students should then be forced to face the contradictions present in any course of action that is not based on principles of justice or fairness (Troup, n.d.). This method requires a delicate balance between letting the students make decisions, and demonstrating the limits in their reasoning (Nucci, 2008). Finally, 'raising the stake', which is defined as introducing consequences, is a tactic followed if a student sticks with the unethical

choice. For example, if we would like students to investigate the effects of stealing, we could pose the problem of shoplifting and ask what they would do if they were the owners.

In Lynch et al. (2008), it has been shown that even in domains where it is impossible to make sharp distinctions between good and bad solutions due to the lack of ideal solutions or a domain theory, solution differences are meaningful. In our opinion, the students' different answers to a Socratic Dialogue are also meaningful and reflect their own beliefs and thoughts. The Socratic Method has been applied previously in the intelligent tutoring system, CIRCISM-TUTOR that teaches how the cardiovascular reflex system stabilizes blood pressure functions (Kim, 1989; Yang et al., 2000). It has been shown that applying the Socratic Method positively influences the learning process. The Socratic Method can be woven in interactive narrative contexts and this has proven to be successful in creating enriching experiences for its users.

AEINS uses misconception in favor of the learning process, where it had been shown that when students face evidence that they believe to be true is, in fact, false and a misconception, students often are interested in resolving the discrepancy (Bergin, 1999). AEINS also words the question from the perspective of the student to provide a meaningful context and facilitate the activation of prior knowledge. This technique has shown its usefulness in the learning process as shown in Anderson and Pichert (1978). For example, if we would like students to investigate stealing effects, we could pose the problem of shoplifting and what if they were the owners themselves.

AEINS uses the Socratic Method as its main teaching pedagogy. The Socratic Method has been easily weaved into the teaching moments' story lines. It provides a medium that encourages the student to think critically in order to solve the discrepancies encountered in the moral situations presented to them. Evaluation of AEINS shows positive and encouraging results from using this method. The Socratic Method forces the student to face the contradictions present in any course of action that is not based on principles of justice or fairness. The voice of Socrates comes from the moral agent participating in the current teaching moment. When the student performs a wrong choice, a text dialogue starts between the moral agent and the student that tries to emphasize the wrong beliefs and encourage the good actions. The moral agent presents opinions and asks questions in order to lead the student to discover for themselves any contradiction(s) present in any course of action that is not based on moral principles. The dialogues continue till the story ends with either a negative reward or a positive one based on the student model. The student model is updated after each student's action. However this information is only used by the pedagogical model after the teaching moment ends.

It has been also noticed that raising the stakes strategy in the Socratic Method forces the students to think differently, consider issues that were not considered before and see things from different perspectives. Actually this is interesting because this means that the medium was able to allow practicing the required skills rather than dictated them to the students.

Pedagogical Agents in AEINS

Agents are entities that can perform a task or a set of tasks. Pedagogical agents are those agents that can communicate and interact in learning environments. They can have a set of normative teaching goals and plans for achieving these goals (e.g., teaching strategies) (Giraffa & Viccari, 1998) and associated resources in the learning environment (Thalmann et al., 1997).

The purpose of educational agents is not to perform tasks for users or to simplify tasks, but rather to help users learn how to accomplish tasks (Sklar, 2003). Agents, with different roles, have been used in many intelligent tutoring systems to support education. For example agents can be used to observe the students actions and assess them, in addition to providing feedback, explanations and demonstrations to the student (Hospers et al., 2003; Abbas & Sawamura, 2009). Others have used emotional agents to support student system interactions and provide human-like tutoring (Nkambou, 2006; Neji et al., 2008).

Giraffa and Viccari (1998) have pointed out some interesting properties for agents that allow them to act as life-like characters, such as having mobility to go to different physical places, be flexible and accept other agents' interventions, have personalities, have social ability via some kind of agent communication language, act proactively and have some kind of reactivity. These life-like agents have significant motivational benefits and can also play an important pedagogical role by acting as virtual learning companions (Maragos & Grigoriadou, 2005) and increase problem solving effectiveness by providing students with customized advice (Lester et al., 1997). Agents that hold one or more of these properties enrich the learning environment by being believable active and reactive characters and engage the student in the educational process without interfering.

The game-like nature of AEINS allows the incorporation of non-playing characters and objects in the AEINS story world. The non-playing characters can be referred to as semi-autonomous agents where on one hand they are able to act and react according to their state and the current world state. On the other hand, the story generator can dictate, when required, what they should do in order to preserve the coherence and dramatic tension of the whole story. The presence of a continuous story with characters' personalities evolving during the story helps with the mental and emotional engagement of the student.

The AI of the non-playing characters is represented in the form of rules. These rules can be modified during the story as a result of certain actions. For example, a character who is a friend to the student can become an enemy as a result of a student action, or an unethical character can change to become a good character as a result of some interactions with the surrounding world.

The student and the agents are responsible for the story unfolding based on their actions. When it is time to present a teaching moment, the currently involved agents in the main story will take the corresponding roles (that fits their current personalities and relationship to the student). If there is a role that is still needed, but there is no agent to take that role, the story world with the assistance of the story generator will allow the inclusion of another agent smoothly through the narrative.

As mentioned previously, the predominant teaching pedagogy is the Socratic Method. The Socratic Voice is used by the moral agent to provide discussion, hints and feedback to the student. The text dialog produced encourages the student to think critically in order to solve the discrepancies encountered in the moral situation(s) they are facing. In addition, students have opportunities to choose among different options and to reason which criteria lead to the option chosen (Kuhn, 1993). When the teaching moment ends, the student along with the non-playing characters are free to act again influencing how the main story unfolds.

Learning Theories in AEINS

Incorporating learning theories in the design of educational learning environments has its positive effects. It helps and leads the way to implementing well-structured learning objects into the learning environment to meet its intended educational goals. This leads to the student acquiring the required new skills or knowledge. There are three theories that appear to be most closely aligned with the generally accepted game design principles: Bloom's Taxonomy (Bloom & Krathwohl, 1956), Keller's ARCS model (Keller, 1987) and Gagné's Principles of instruction (Gagné et al., 2005). Gagne's three principles for successful instruction are as follows:

Providing instruction on the set of component tasks that build toward a final task. This principle is tackled in designing the teaching moments, where coaching is afforded using the Socratic Method and by providing personalized feedback. Such a teaching strategy contributes to the building of skills required for mastering the task.

Ensuring that each component task is mastered. This principle was attempted in AEINS through the use of the pedagogical model that tracks the student's learning process and evaluates his moves. Accordingly, if the component is still not mastered, the model chooses another educational object that attempts to address the misconceptions the student has.

Sequencing the component tasks to ensure optimal transfer to the final task. This principle has been addressed by representing the domain model using hierarchal frames that allow partial ordering of the domain concepts and defining the relationships between them.

The second learning theory used was Bloom's taxonomy. Bloom was determined to develop a practical means for classifying curriculum goals and learning objectives. This has been divided into six levels; knowledge, comprehension, application, analysis, synthesis, and evaluation. We argue that AEINS is capable of attempting the higher levels of Bloom's taxonomy. Through being involved and interacting in moral situations (teaching moments), the student is able to see the moral values (concepts) involved in the situation context, and see in what pattern they are framing the situation. Accordingly, he is able to aggregate parts together, evaluate the situation and make judgments about the value of ideas. Based on the idea pictured, he started acting to solve the problem encountered. These skills are part of the higher levels; analysis, evaluation and synthesis.

The last learning theory inspiring this work is Keller's ARCS model, which relies on four foundational categories that are to be applied when designing instructional activities. ARCS is an acronym that represents these four classes:

Attention, Relevance, Confidence/Challenge, and Satisfaction/Success. The details of how each attribute has been attempted are as follows:

Attention is an aspect that relates to gaining and keeping the student's attention. AEINS presentation module addressed this aspect by capturing the student's attention through a graphical user interface. Curiosity arousal is achieved through involving the student in the story generation where he is able to affect how the story unfolds. Moreover, AEINS used teaching moments with a series of thought provoking questions, and having different endings based on the student's actions.

Relevance is an aspect that relates to the students' need to be able to understand implicitly how the activity relates to their current situation, and/or to them personally. This is the first step in most instructional design models that rely on an understanding of student attributes as a part of the analysis process. AEINS tackled this attribute by designing and implementing teaching moments that contextually discuss situations the student is familiar with or there is high probability for the student to face at some point. To present the student with the appropriate teaching moment, a motive matching procedure is done through initializing the student model based on the first interactions between the student and the system. Based on this, the educational material that suits the student skills level is presented. The teaching moment story is evolved based on the student's actions. This gives the student the chance to see that the upcoming activities are based on his own actions and decisions.

Confidence/Challenge is an attribute that aims to provide the right level of challenge to the student. If students believe they are, somehow, incapable of achieving the objectives because it will take too long, or, conversely, that the challenge is beneath them, their motivation will most assuredly decrease. AEINS has various teaching moments that tackle different student knowledge levels. Based on the student model, the appropriate teaching moment that targets the current level of

the student's knowledge and skills is presented. The student has control over his virtual character that is able to act and influence the story within every single teaching moment.

Satisfaction/Success is an attribute that calls for students to attain some type of satisfaction or reward from the learning experience. AEINS attempted this by providing positive and negative rewards as part of its teaching pedagogy. These rewards take the form of formative and summative feedback that is part of the teaching strategy within the teaching moments.

ANALYTICAL EVALUATION

The student model is the central component to provide adaptivity in the designed model. In the design of the scripted narratives (teaching moments), we assume that all student misconceptions are expressed in the interaction with the system (e.g., lying when the student believes that lying is okay). The student model has been evaluated using the following assumptions:

- The student modeling has a positive result if the process is able to determine correctly the participant's misconceptions or missing conceptions that underlie unethical action or choice, and provides the appropriate feedback.
- The student modeling has a negative result if the process fails or is unable to determine the participant's misconceptions and consequently does not provide the right feedback corresponding to the participant's actions.

The level of success of the student model component depends on how comprehensive the implemented rules are and the rules complexity for determining the participant's misconceptions. A well designed student model offers good help for a class instructor to use to categorize the participants in his/her class. It also gives the instructor a guide to the most suitable dilemma to prepare for the next class, for example, a dilemma that tackles misconceptions of most of the class participants. Moreover, personalized reports can be produced at the end of the student-game interaction that can help the tutor to easily identify the most common students' misconceptions.

It has been found that the presence of the student model allows a personalized learning process where the teaching moments were presented to the student according to his needs; some of the teaching moments are not be presented if the learner's skills do not require it. With the absence of the student model, the teaching moments will be presented in a certain order to all the students without any consideration to individual differences and needs. With this evidence, it can be said that the student modeling can positively affect the learning process.

EMPIRICAL EVALUATION

A full study has been completed to test AEINS for different criteria such as the technical infrastructure, its functioning, its ability to support or enable specific activities, and to generate predicted educational outcomes. The study was conducted on 20 children aged 8 to 12 year old to test the hypothesis of building an educational game that is able to develop new thoughts of the participants in promoting character education. The children were of different origins and had different cultural backgrounds, for example Egypt, UK, China, Malaysia and Fiji. In each assignment, the student has been left to explore and interact with the system at their own pace. The student is not merely learning about a process or concept undertaken by an ethics teacher, but he experiences that process for himself.

In designing this study, it was determined that the best way to approach it was to rely on a qualitative research method. This is due to the fact that qualitative research methods are ideal

for getting into users' thoughts, and that is what exactly needed to satisfy the aim and objectives listed above. In each assignment, the participant was left to explore and interact with the system at their own pace. The children were monitored during their interaction with AEINS to see if one of the following appears: engagement, losing interest, forget about the outside world, boredom. The participants were then interviewed. The interviews were semi structured based upon a pre-defined schedule to gain feedback from the participants about the way they perceived the game. All discussions were recorded in order to be analyzed in detail later.

According to what AEINS aims to achieve and the data provided, it has been found that it will not be interesting to tackle every single question on its own as sometimes some questions did not produce enough rich data. Instead the results are organized around the main themes reflected by the data. These themes are: AEINS Architecture and implementation, Social aspects in AEINS, and Learning deployed in AEINS and educational achievements.

For the purpose of this paper we are going to focus only on the evaluation results of the learning deployed in AEINS and educational achievements. This theme is very important as it tends to show that AEINS is an effective learning environment and is able to deliver effective learning, in other words develop the participant's reasoning process.

The use of Socratic Method as the teaching pedagogy shows success. In every teaching moment, since the voice of Socrates comes from one of the involved characters, usually one of the student's friends, it pushes the student to think harder to solve the discrepancy inherent in these situations. For example, from P11's log file, it has been found that the student traversed the following path in the shoplifting dilemma: agree to help his friend to take a chocolate bar without paying for it, then undertake a discussion with the good moral character that uses the Socratic Voice. The discussion ends by a change in the student behavior where he admitted he did a mistake and asked his friend to return the chocolate. Such attitude reflects the power of the Socratic Method in forcing the student to face the contradictions present in any course of action not based on good moral principles. In the interview with P11, he mentioned that he did make a mistake by helping Gina (the immoral character in the shoplifting dilemma) to take the chocolate. This goes well with the results obtained from the log file.

One participant liked the fact that she can interact with the teaching moments and was able to see the effect of her decisions on herself and others. This interviewee asked to restart the game when she was faced with the negative consequences as a result of one of her choices. This shows that although the feedback was implicitly provided in the story, it managed to deliver the message (you did something wrong). In the post interview, it seems that the interviewee had an explicit representation about taking stuff. This appears in her final comment: P13:"Taking other people stuff is stealing and we should not take something without asking first."

We claim that the interactive teaching moments were able to provide the appropriate hints about various moral actions and situate the students in different mental and emotional states. Moreover, this allows the student to attempt higher-order thinking skills from the adapted version of Bloom's taxonomy such as Analysis. For example, the participants were analyzing the situations where conflict exists, and tried to find a solution to the current dilemma. For example, P4: "It was difficult to make a decision as this can make my friend upset."

The participants also related the ideas to the real world and by applying their beliefs. For example, Participant 17 was choosing nearly all bad actions. Accordingly he was faced with negative consequences as feedback. He said during the interview P17:"I hope there was no law." This shows that, although he chose to carry out unethical actions, the feedback made him think of the law and the consequences of such actions in real life. Another interesting point raised while talking to participant 5 was that they were able to show high intellectual reasoning to provide support to their acts. For example, Participant 5 does not like to disagree with his friends because they become angry with him. "I do not want them to stop being my friend." When asked if they even do wrong things, he replied "Yes, because everyone does wrong stuff." However, Participant 5 does not seem to be worried about other things rather than losing a friend. We claim that this illustrates some ideas transfer as a result of interacting with AEINS. The following quote supports this claim: "I used to lie on my little sister to get out of trouble, now I think with lying I can be in a bigger trouble." When asked about what he is going to do now, he answered: "Tell the truth."

Transferring knowledge to the real world is the main aim of AEINS although this is very difficult to be assessed as it needs very long term evaluation. However, the interviews provided some insight about what AEINS has achieved in this area. It has been shown that some of the students are thinking about taking the experiences from the game to real experiments. For example, when one participant was asked about what she thinks she will take away from this experience, she answered P7:"I will think about the situations I have been involved in and what can happen if I really get involved into one." Another participant commented: P6:"I think this can help me solving school problems." These quotes show the possibility of learning transfer and the sparking of new thoughts and/or deeper ones. This also fits well with Gee (2004) in that when people are faced with a new situation in the world, aspects or elements of this situation remind them of aspects or elements of experiences they have had in the past. They use these elements of past experience to think about the new situation. Sometimes they can just apply past experience pretty much as is to the new situation, other times they have to adapt past experience to be able to apply it.

The evaluation also raised some interesting issues that need to be addressed in the case of multiplayer environment including the communication between the different players and the effect of their actions not only on the non-playing characters but also on each other. Other issues are the effect of using a natural language processing engine and the benefit that can be acquired from using such platform in the classroom environment.

CONCLUSION

Educational games area gained much attention in the last few decades for its powerful engaging property and the ability of these platforms to deliver learning in various domains. They offer an advantage over traditional schooling, where connection between perception and action that is a highly prototypical form of knowledge, can be represented in the following form of production rules: If this is the current situation, do these. Therefore, immersing the student in a (simulated) environment provides a much richer experience than a worksheet or other homework assignment could.

Different narrative techniques provide various advantages. This paper highlights the synergy of integrating both dynamic narrative and scripted narrative techniques and how a student model can be used to provide an adaptive, interactive narrative model. The model has been applied to the educational environment, AEINS, which interacts with every single participant on an individualized basis. AEINS offers a compelling virtual world and virtual identity, at some level, where deep learning may occur. Moreover, it managed to provide adaptation based on the student's explicit actions and the inferred intentions. AEINS has been built considering the learning theories of Gagne's Events of Instruction, Bloom's Taxonomy and Keller's ARCS Motivational Model. By considering the learning theories in the design and the implementation phases of AEINS, the learning tasks were implemented according to authentic learning frames.

In summary, the AEINS system tightly integrates gaming and learning whereby the boundaries between both are blurred. It can be noticed that the children were able to build a powerful bridge between their real identity and this virtual identity in the game. They did have emotional responses that transfer their real world responses to the game. This goes quite well with Gee's discussion about learning and identity and his illustration about the importance of the ability of children to build these bridges in order not to make the learning imperiled. The students were actively participating in the construction of their knowledge in a way that can be also applied to other ill-defined domains, for example, history and cultural competence.

Finally, AEINS evaluation shows promising results and provides support for the effectiveness of the use of evolving characters and the Socratic Method in supporting the educational process in ill-defined domains.

REFERENCES

Abbas, S., & Sawamura, H. (2009). Developing an argument learning environment using agent-based ITS (ALES). In *proceedings of The Second International Conference on Educational Data Mining (EDM09)*, Cordoba, Spain.

Amory, A., Naicker, K., Vincent, J., & Adams, C. (1999). The use of Computer Games as an educational tool: 1. Identification of appropriate game types and game elements. *British Journal of Educational Technology, 30*(4), 311–322. doi:10.1111/1467-8535.00121

Anderson, R. C., & Pichert, J. W. (1978). Recall of previously un-recallable information following a shift in perspective. *Journal of Verbal Learning and Verbal Behavior, 17*, 1–12. doi:10.1016/S0022-5371(78)90485-1

Avner, A., Moore, C., & Smith, S. (1980). Active external control: A basis for superiority of CBI. *Journal of Computer-Based Instruction, 6*(4), 115–118.

Bayon, V., Wilson, J. R., Stanton, D., & Boltman, A. (2003). Mixed reality storytelling environments. *Virtual Reality Journal, 7*(1).

Bell, P., & Linn, M. C. (2000). Scientific arguments as learning artifcats: Designing for learning from the web with KIE. *International Journal of Science Education, 22*(8), 797–817. doi:10.1080/095006900412284

Bergin, D. A. (1999). Influences on classroom interest. *Educational Psychologist Journal, 34*(2), 87–98. doi:10.1207/s15326985ep3402_2

Bloom, B. S., & Krathwohl, D. R. (1956). Taxonomy of educational objectives: The classification of educational goals, by a committee of college and university examiners. In *Handbook 1: Cognitive domain*. New York: Longmans.

Bolton, G. (1999). *Acting in classroom drama: A critical analysis*. London: Heinemann.

Colby, A., Kohlberg, L., Gibbs, J., & Lieberman, C. (1983). A longitudinal study of moral judgment. *Journal of Monographs of the Society for Research in Child Development, 48*.

Crain, W. (1985). *Theories of development. Kohlberg's stages of moral development* (pp. 118-136).

Egenfeldt-Neilson, S. (2005, February). *Beyond Edutainment: Exploring the educational potential of computer games*. Unpublished doctoral dissertation, University of Copenhagen, Copenhagen, Denmark.

Elkind, D. H., & Sweet, F. (1997). The Socratic Approach to Character Education. [html]. *Educational Leadership, 2*, Retrieved from http://www.goodcharacter.com/Article.

Fasli, M., & Michalakopoulos, M. (2005). Supporting active learning through game-like exercises. In *Proceedings of the Fifth IEEE International Conference on Advanced Learning Technologies (ICALT05)* (pp. 730-734).

Gagné, R. M., Wager, W. W., Golas, K. G., & Keller, J. M. (2005). *Principles of instructional design* (4th ed.). Toronto, ON: Thomson Wadsworth.

Gee, J. P. (2005). Learning by design: Good video games as learning machines. *ELearning Journal, 2*(1).

Gee, J. P. (2006). Are video games good for learning? In *Proceedings of the Curriculum Corporation 13th National Conference*. Retrieved from http://www.curriculum.edu.au/verve/_resources/Gee_Paper.pdf

Giraffa, L., & Viccari, R. (1998). The use of agents techniques on intelligent tutoring systems. *In Proceedings of the XVIII International Conference of the Chilean Computer Science Society*.

Gómez-Martín, M. A., Gómez-Martín, P. P., & González-Calero, P. A. (2004). Game-Driven Intelligent Tutoring Systems. In M. Rauterberg (Ed.), *Proceedings of the ICEC 2004* (LNCS 3166, pp. 108-113).

Graf, S., Yang, G., & Lin, T., & Kinshuk. (2008). The relationship between learning styles and cognitive traits - Getting additional information for improving student modeling. *Journal of Computers in Human Behavior, 24*, 122–137. doi:10.1016/j.chb.2007.01.004

Graf, S., Yang, G., Lin, T., & Kinshuk. (2009). Automatic, global and dynamic student modeling in a ubiquitous learning environment. *Knowledge Management & E-Learning: An International Journal, 1*(1).

Hospers, M., Kroezen, E., & Nijholt, A. op den Akker, R., & Heylen, D. (2003). Developing a generic agent-based intelligent tutoring system. In *Proceedings of the Third IEEE International Conference on Advanced Learning Technologies (ICALT'03)*.

Keller, J. M. (1987). Development and use of the ARCS model of instructional design. *Journal of Instructional Development, 10*(3), 2–10. doi:10.1007/BF02905780

Kim, N. (1989). *Circsim-tutor: an Intelligent Tutoring System for Circulatory Physiology.* Chicago: Illinois Institute of Technology.

Klawe, M. (1998). *When Does the Use of Computer Games and Other Interactive Multimedia Software Help Students Learn Mathematics?* Paper presented at the Department of Computer Science, the University of British Columbia, BC, Canada.

Koslowski, B. (1996). *Theory and Evidence: The Development of Scientific Reasoning.* Cambridge, MA: MIT Press.

Kuhn, D. (1993). Science as Argument: Implications for Teaching and Learning Scientific Thinking. *Scientific and Educational Journal, 77*(3), 319–337. doi:10.1002/sce.3730770306

Lester, J., Converse, S., Stone, B., Kahler, S., & Barlow, T. (1997). Animated pedagogical agents and problem-solving effectiveness: A large-scale empirical evaluation. In *Proceedings of the 8th World Conference on Artificial Intelligence in Education*, Kobe, Japan.

Lynch, C., Pinkwart, N., Ashley, K., & Aleven, V. (2008, June). What do argument diagrams tell us about students' aptitude or experience? A statistical analysis in an ill-defined domain. In *Proceedings of the workshop held during ITS-2008, the 9th international Conference on Intelligent Tutoring Systems*, Montreal, Canada.

Maragos, K., & Grigoriadou, M. (2005). Towards the design of intelligent educational gaming systems. In *Proceedings of the AIED workshop5, held at the 12th International Conference on Artificial Intelligence in education*, Amsterdam.

McBrien, J. L., & Brandt, R. S. (1997). *The Language of Learning: A Guide to Education Terms* (pp. 17–18). Alexandria, VA: Association for Supervision and Curriculum Development.

McGrenere, J. L. (1996, June). *Design: Educational Electronic Multi-Player Games: A Literature Review.* Paper presented at the Department of Computer Science, University of British Columbia, BC, Canada.

Neji, M., Ben ʾAmmar, M., Alimi, A. M., & Gouardères, G. (2008). Agent-Based framework for affective intelligent tutoring systems. In Woolf et al. (Eds.), *Proceedings of the ITS2008* (LNCS 5091, pp. 665-667).

Niehaus, J., & Riedl, M. (2009). Toward scenario adaptation for learning. In *Proceedings of the 14th International Conference on Artificial Intelligence in Education (AIED09)*.

Nkambou, R. (2006). Towards affective intelligent tutoring system, Workshop on Motivational and Affective Issues in ITS. In *Proceedings of the 8th International Conference on Intelligent Tutoring Systems (ITS 2006)* (pp. 5-12).

Nucci, L. (2008). *An Overview of Moral Development and Moral Education.* Retrieved from http://tigger.uic.edu/~lnucci/MoralEd/overview.html

Shaffer, D. W. (2005). *Multisubculturalism: Computers and the end of progressive education.* Retrieved from: http://coweb.wcer.wisc.edu/cv/papers/multisubculturalism-draft1.pdf

Shaffer, D. W. (2006). Epistemic frames for epistemic games. *Computers and Education Journal, 46*(3), 223-234. Retrieved from http://dx.doi.org/10.1016/j.compedu.2005.11.003

Shin, N., & McGee, S. (2003). *Designers Should Enhance learners' Ill-Structured Problem-Solving Skills*. Retrieved from http://vdc.cet.edu/entries/illps.htm

Simpson, D. E. (1998). Dilemmas in palliative care education. *Palliative Medicine Journal, 12*.

Sklar, E. (2003). Agents for education: when too much intelligence is a bad thing. In *Proceedings of the second international joint conference on Autonomous agents and Multiagent systems (AAMAS '03)*, Melbourne, Australia (pp. 1118-1119). New York: ACM.

Tan, J., Beers, C., Gupta, R., & Biswas, G. (2005). Computer Games as Intelligent Learning Environments: A River Ecosystem Adventure. In C. K. Looi, et al. (Eds.), Artificial Intelligence in Education. Amsterdam: IOS Press.

Thalmann, D., Noser, H., & Huang, Z. (1997). Autonomous Virtual Actors Based on Virtual Sensors. In Trappl, R., & Petta, P. (Eds.), *Creating Personalities for Synthetic Actors: towards autonomous personality agents*. Berlin: Springer Verlag. doi:10.1007/BFb0030568

Thomas, J. M., & Young, M. (2007). Becoming Scientists: Employing Adaptive Interactive Narrative to Guide Discovery Learning. In *Proceedings of the AIED-07 Workshop on Narrative Learning Environments*, Marina Del Rey, California, USA.

Troup, P. (n.d.). *Understanding Student Development Theories as Multicultural*. Retrieved from http://www1.umn.edu/ohr/prod/groups/ohr/@pub/@ohr/documents/asset/ohr_68497.pdf

Upper Saddle River, N. J. Prentice Hall International. Retrieved from http://faculty.plts.edu/gpence/html/kohlberg.htm

Willard, C. A., Woods, J., Van Eemeren, F. H., Walton, D. N., & Zarefsky, D. (1996). *Fundamentals of argumentation theory: A handbook of historical backgrounds and contemporary developments*. Mahwah, NJ: Lawrence Erlbaum Associates.

This work was previously published in International Journal of Gaming and Computer-Mediated Simulations, Volume 2, Issue 4, edited by Richard E. Ferdig, pp. 1-15, copyright 2010 by IGI Publishing (an imprint of IGI Global).

Chapter 16
Bio–Affective Computer Interface for Game Interaction

Jorge Arroyo-Palacios
University of Sheffield, UK

Daniela M. Romano
University of Sheffield, UK

ABSTRACT

Affective bio-feedback can be an important instrument to enhance the game experience. Several studies have provided evidence of the usefulness of physiological signals for affective gaming; however, due to the limited knowledge about the distinctive autonomic signatures for every emotion, the pattern matching models employed are limited in the number of emotions they are able to classify. This paper presents a bio-affective gaming interface (BAGI) that can be used to customize a game experience according to the player's emotional response. Its architecture offers important characteristics for gaming that are important because they make possible the reusability of previous findings and the inclusion of new models to the system. In order to prove the effectiveness of BAGI, two different types of neural networks have been trained to recognize emotions. They were incorporated into the system to customize, in real-time, the computer wallpaper according to the emotion experienced by the user. Best results were obtained with a probabilistic neural network with accuracy results of 84.46% on the training data and 78.38% on the validation for new independent data sets.

INTRODUCTION

Physiological signals offer a promising medium to interact in a natural and intuitive way with the game environment. In addition of being reliable, sensible and provide real time feedback, physiological signals offer an insight into hu-man's physical and mental state which can be used to enrich the game interaction. Common physiological measures already used in gaming or Human Computer Interaction (HCI) include: cardiovascular, electrodermal, muscular tension, ocular, skin temperature, brain activity and respiration measures. The game industry has already seen their potential and several research studies

DOI: 10.4018/978-1-4666-0029-4.ch016

have been conducted to investigate the best way to use them.

One of the earliest commercial examples of a bio-adaptive interface used in commercial games can be seen in "Tetris 64", released for the Nintendo 64 platform. In "Tetris 64" a sensor is placed at the player's ear to monitor the heart rate, the game speeds up or slows down depending on the player's cardiovascular activity. A more modern commercial example is "Relax & Race" by Vyro games. In "Relax & Race" the game takes the form of a race between two characters: stress and the player. The game senses the electrodermal activity (EDA) of the player and increases the speed of the character as the player relaxes.

There are also several research studies that explore physiological signals in gaming. Toups et al. (2006) for example use electrodermal and electromyographic (EMG) activity as an indication of increased attention, effort and stress in team game play. In their game, the computer opponents sense the physiological signals and pursue players with higher activation levels. One interesting feature of this study was that the physiological information was provided to the team coordinator thus he could modify the game strategy. Another study that also uses EDA and EMG activity was carried out by Predinger et al. (2006) where the emotional response of a character was adapted according to physiological responses of the player in a virtual card game.

Gilleade et al. (2005) proposed that the identification of emotions, through physiological signals, can provide means to the Artificial Intelligence (AI) of the game for automatically: i) assist (e.g., when the player is frustrated), challenge (e.g., when the player is bored), emote (to enhance the game experience of the player). In their studies they developed a game that monitors the cardiovascular activity to increase or decrease the number of threats in a game.

Educational games and tutoring systems have also employed the use of physiological signals to provide affective feedback to the system and adapt according to the student emotional state (Conati, 2002).

Research in brain activity has lead to the creation of brain-computer interfaces (BCI) which have been used as a game interface control for an immersive 3D gaming environment (Lalor et al., 2005) and for moving a ball on a table in Brainball (Hjelm & Browall, 2000). Ko et al. (2009) presented the emotion recognition capabilities for games of three currently available portable BCI devices: NIA, Emotive EPOC and Mind Set.

Respiration measures have also been used to interact with games. Arroyo and Romano (2009) developed a simple balloon game where the player blows up a virtual balloon with his chest expansion and contraction while breathing. Table 1 presents a summary of some games that recognize emotions by the use of physiological signals.

There are two important observations from the literature reviewed:

i) Most of the emotion recognition systems (ERS) follow an ad hoc strategy (i.e., they provide a solution designed for a specific problem or task, non generalizable, and which is not easily adaptable to other purposes).

ii) There are very few multi-category discrimination emotion recognition systems implemented in real-time. All the emotion recognition systems of the games presented in Table 1 are aimed to identify the presence or absence of a particular emotion, or to discriminate among small sets of opposite emotions.

Nowadays, games are being produced for a great variety of domains including: entertainment, training, medical therapies, education and socialization. Users are more demanding in their expectations, and current games involve more photographic realism, cinematic sequences and new interaction methods. Emotions recognition systems can contribute to enhance the emotional

Table 1. Use of physiological signals in games.

Game	Signal	Detect	Emotion	Action
Tetris 64	HR	Increase	Anxiety	Game slows down (normal mode) Game speeds up (reverse mode)
		Decrease	Relaxation	Game speeds up (normal mode) Game slows down (reverse mode)
Relax & Race	SR	Increase	Relaxation	Character slows down
		Decrease	Anxiety	Character speeds up
PhysiRogue (Toups et al., 2006)	EDA, EMG	Increase	Attention, effort, stress.	Opponents pursue players with highest activation levels
Card game (Prendinger et al., 2006)	EDA, EMG	Increase	High arousal, negative valence	If player makes progress agent shows: -joy (empathic mode) -fear (negative empathic mode)
Similar to Missile Command (Gilleade et al., 2005)	HR	Increase	Over stimulation	Reduce number of threats.
		Decrease	Lack of engagement	Increase number of threats
Prime Climb (Conati, 2002)	EMG, EDA, HR	Specific changes	Reproach, shame and joy	Depending on emotion, agent can intervene in game.
Brain ball (Hjelm & Browall, 2000)	Brain activity	Specific changes	Relaxation	Ball is moved
Blow up balloon (Arroyo-Palacios & Romano, 2009)	RSP	Increase and decrease	None	Virtual balloon is blown up
Relax to Win (Bersak et al., 2001)	SR	Increase	Relaxed	Character slows down
		Decrease	Anxious	Character speeds up

HR = Heart rate SR = Skin Resistance EMG = Electromyographic Activity RSP = Respiration EDA = Electrodermal Activity

experience; however, their current construction strategy is expensive, time-consuming, limited (in discrimination capabilities) and does not allow the reusability of tools and previous findings.

In this paper the architecture, implementation and validation of a flexible multi-category emotion recognition system is presented. Specifically, this paper contributes to the research efforts in affective gaming by presenting:

- Implementation of a real-time multi-category emotion recognition system.
- A flexible and scalable architecture that facilitates the integration of findings from other studies.
- Real-time classification results from two machine learning algorithms.

- A simple application that adapts the desktop wallpaper according to the emotional state of the user.

VARIABLE PARAMETERS IN EMOTION RECOGNITION SYSTEMS

Set of Emotions

Depending on the type of application or game, different sets of discrete emotions need to be considered. For instance, adventure/action games might need the identification of emotions such as: enjoyment, frustration, anxiety, boredom. As suggested in (Conati, 2002) shame might need to be considered in learning/training games. Social games such as Second Life could find useful to include in the recognition emotions such as: love, anger and sadness. For horror games such as Dead Space, FEAR and Resident Evil, fear and anxiety might need to be recognized.

Besides the use of discrete emotions, researchers have also proposed the use of dimensional models for representing emotions in games (Peter & Herbon, 2006). In this way a set of emotion for a game could be composed by the following 4 affective states: 1) positive valence – high arousal, 2) positive valence – low arousal, 3) negative valence – high arousal, and 4) negative valence – low arousal.

Measures and Features to Analyze

Common physiological measures already used in gaming or HCI include: cardiovascular, electrodermal, muscular tension, ocular, skin temperature, brain activity and respiration measures. Each of these measures can be more or less convenient depending on the type of game and emotions to be recognized. From these measures, several features can be calculated from various analysis domains including: statistics, frequency domain, geometric analysis, multiscale sample entropy and sub-band spectra. Reviewing some relevant studies in HCI it can be seen that they have privileged the use of different physiological measures over others, and have extracted different numbers of features to analyze. For instance, Kim and Andre (2008) extracted a total of 110 features from 4 sensors: EMG, ECG, SC and RSP; Picard et al. (2001) extracted 40 features from EMG, BVP, RSP and SC; Nasoz et al. (2004) used GSR, temperature and HR signals.

Times to Analyze

Another variable parameter among the emotion recognition systems in the literature concerns to the time window used to analyze the physiological signals. For instance, Picard et al. (2001) used a time window of 100 seconds from the end of each emotion segment to analyze all the signals in their first data set; Kim and Andre (2008) segmented their data in samples of 160 seconds by taking the middle part of each signal; Nasoz et al. (2004) used a time frame of 7 seconds when the emotion was most likely to be experienced.

Approaches for Physiological Pattern Classification

Pattern Matching

The emotion recognition systems in the games listed in Table 1 are implemented following a pattern matching approach. Following this strategy, the system detects the presence of the constituents of a rigidly specified pattern in the physiological data. The classification process can be based on existing models describing the relationship between psychology and physiology, like for example the model proposed by Cacioppo and Tassinary (1990) or use empirical findings from literature, for example, Stemmler (1989). The dilemma is to decide which model and physiological definitions, the system should be based on.

Table 2 illustrates some patterns of heart rate associated to emotions from different studies that a computer system could use to discriminate a set of three emotions composed by fear, joy and anger.

Table 2. Patterns associated to emotions from different studies.

Author	Signal	Fear	Sadness	Happiness
Christie (2002)	Heart rate	Increase	Decrease	Decrease
Ekman et al. (1983)	Heart rate	Increase (high)	Increase (high)	Increase (low)
Frederickson et al. (2000)	Heart rate	Increase	Decrease	No significant difference

A vast number of studies in psychology document the autonomic responses to emotions. However not all of them followed the same methodology. Unfortunately, the differences are present in critical elements of the study such as: model and set of emotions investigated, stimuli used to evoke the emotions, physiological measures, features extracted, and type of analysis on the data (already highlighted in Arroyo-Palacios & Romano, 2008). As a result some discrepancies remain among their findings, as it can be observed in Table 2 and, in more detail, in the compilation of physiological responses to specific emotions in (Cacioppo, Klein, Berntson, & Hatfield, 1993; Zajonc & McIntosh, 1992).

Despite the discrepancies among psychological studies, in the gaming literature pattern matching techniques have demonstrated to be practical especially for: i) determining the presence or absence of a particular emotion, or ii) discriminating small sets of opposite affective states. Additionally pattern matching offers important characteristics for a real time interaction such as simple implementation and very fast computation.

Pattern Recognition

Another approach that can be used to implement emotion recognition for gaming is pattern recognition. It implies the training of a system to recognize a set of affective states corresponding to a particular emotional model. The machine learning model receives as input labeled sets of physiological data and then it is trained to detect the patterns associated to each emotion. The model is then able to classify new sets of physiological data into specific emotions. As a result, a physiological definition for different affective states has been obtained through empirical data. The advantage of this approach is that it offers ecological validity on the emotions recognized (the settings during the pattern recognition process can be identical or similar to the classification settings) and provides good classification rates among several emotions,

as showed in several offline HCI studies (Haag, Goronzy, Schaich, & Williams, 2004; J. Kim & Andre, 2008; K. H. Kim, Bang, & Kim, 2004; T. Kim, Shin, & Shin, 2009; Nasoz et al., 2004; Picard et al., 2001).

Despite the advantages of this approach it has not been fully exploited by the game industry, perhaps due to concerns that might arise as consequence of:

- The time that a pattern recognition process takes (depending on the processing power, algorithms and quantity of data, it can take up to several hours or days.
- Difficulties to reuse the system for other purposes or to reuse the finding from other studies.
- Few studies show good results from user independent and real-time implementations (e.g., Leon, Clarke, Callaghan, & Sepulveda, 2007).
- Lack of guided principles for its application.
- Lack of physiological affective databases to train the systems.

In the research presented in this paper some of these concerns have been addressed.

IMPORTANCE OF FLEXIBILITY IN ERS

There is a wide range of applications where emotion recognition systems can be very useful however the development of such system for a particular situation is complex, multifaceted and very time-consuming. It requires taking into consideration theoretical, methodological, technical, and some other aspects.

The ad hoc strategy followed so far has proven good classification results; nevertheless, the reusability of systems and findings is very difficult and the comparison of results among experiments carried out in different labs is almost impossible.

The flexibility in an emotion recognition system would facilitate its use in different type of applications, allow the reusability of findings and facilitate the comparison of results. It would be also possible to use the classification strategy that best suit to our application. Moreover, the research community is continuously proposing new theories and providing new discoveries. A flexible architecture on the set of emotions, physiological signals, time windows and classification strategy would also allow scalability for the inclusion of advances in emotion research.

Table 3 presents some machine learning based emotion recognition studies where different parameters were considered for the classification of emotions.

BAGI: DESIGN AND IMPLEMENTATION

One of the most important characteristics of BAGI is its architecture which allows: flexibility, scalability, multi-category discrimination and real time affective feedback. The innovative aspect resides in the classification module which provides two important characteristics: i) flexibility to receive different configurations in the parameters mentioned in section 2 and ii) ability to incorporate different models obtained through a machine learning process for a real time multi-category discrimination. Figure 1 presents the architecture of BAGI.

The following subsections briefly present the modules involved in BAGI, with a more detailed description of the classification module.

Acquisition of Physiological Data

The equipment selected for the acquisition of the physiological data was Procomp Infiniti by Thought Technology. It offers important characteristics such as: user-friendly sensors, real time feedback, and connectivity with other applications. The Procomp Infiniti is an eight channel, multi-modal device for real time computerized biofeedback and data acquisition. It has 8 sensor inputs with two channels sampled at 2048 samples/second (s/s) and six channels sampled at 256 s/s.

Table 3. Different parameters in offline emotion recognition studies

Study	Emotions	Time window	Measures	Analysis technique
(J. Kim & Andre, 2008)	High arousal, low arousal, positive valence, negative valence	160 seconds	EMG, ECG, EDA, RSP (110 features)	LDA, Binary tree model
(Picard et al., 2001)	No emotion, anger, hate, grief, platonic love, romantic love, joy, reverence.	100 seconds	EMG, BVP, RSP, EDA (40 features)	SFFS, FP, SFFS-FP
(Nasoz et al., 2004)	Sadness, anger, fear, surprise, frustration, amusement	7 seconds	EDA, ST, HR	KNN, DFA, MBP
(T. Kim et al., 2009)	Fear, neutral, joy	50 seconds	ECG	K-means based expectation maximization
(Haag et al., 2004)	Valence and arousal	2 seconds	ECG, BVP, EDA, EMG, RSP, ST	NN trained with resilient propagation
(K. H. Kim et al., 2004)	Sad, stress, anger, surprise	50 seconds	ST, EDA, ECG, BVP	SVM

EMG = Electromyographic Activity HR = Heart Rate SFFS= Sequential Floating Forward Selection ECG = Electrocardiographic Activity ST = Skin Temperature NN = Neural Network EDA = Electrodermal Activity LDA = Linear Discriminant Analysis SVM = Support Vector Machine RSP = Respiration MBP = Marquardt Backpropagation FP = Fisher Projection BVP = Blood Volume Pulse Activity KNN = K-Nearest Neighbour DFA = Discriminant Function Analysis

Figure 1. Architecture of BAGI

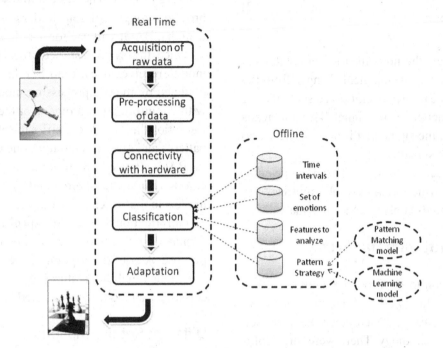

Pre-Processing

The pre-processing module focused in two main tasks: i) the application of noise reduction algorithms to clean the signals, and ii) the construction of vectors with the values of the different physiological measures.

Although there are several techniques that could be applied to clean the signals and facilitate the analysis, simple and fast algorithms that could contribute to the effectiveness of the system without compromising its real-time capabilities had to be considered. For this reason, the noise in the signals was reduced using a moving average filter. A moving average filter smoothes the data by replacing the data points of a signal by averaging the value of a selected number of d adjacent points, Equation (1) illustrates a 3-point smooth:

$$Sj = \frac{Yj-1+Yj+Yj+1}{d} \tag{1}$$

where S_j is the jth point in the smoothed signal, Y_j the jth point in the original signal, and d is a positive integer called smooth width or averaging factor. The higher the number of d, the less variability will be observable in the resulting signal.

This filter was computed directly on the signals by using the smoothing algorithm function provided by Biograph Infiniti software.

The construction of vectors was carried out to facilitate the analysis and classification process. The first step was the extraction of 5 statistical features from the signals: mean, standard deviation, coefficient of variation, maximum and minimum.

The next step involved the normalization of the signals, a common practice in the emotion physiology literature, as a consequence of the physiological differences among individuals. The relation of change (ρ) was obtained by comparing the extracted features of each signal during the stimuli ($f_{stimuli}$) with the extracted features of each signal during baseline ($f_{baseline}$).

$$\rho = \frac{fstimuli}{fbaseline} \qquad (2)$$

In this way, the normalization facilitates the identification of physiological changes from the baseline to one particular emotional state: If $\rho > 1$ it means an increase in the signal, if $\rho < 1$ it means a decrease in the signal and if $\rho = 1$ it means no change in the signal.

Finally, each vector is composed of one emotional label and the normalized values corresponding to the signals considered for the analysis.

Connectivity with Hardware

The connection to the Procomp equipment was actually done through the Biograph Infiniti with the aid of a Software Development Kit provided by Thought Technology. There were three components involved in the implementation of the connectivity with Biograph Infiniti: C++ classes, XML file and Connection Instrument.

Classification

First, at the initial setup, the classification module receives the intervals of time, set of emotions, features to analyze and the pattern strategy for classification. For the pattern strategy this module can receive models from two types of sources: i) existing rigid pattern matching models from literature and ii) models obtained through a machine

learning process. The system allows the user to browse through different folders and select the data that BAGI will use for the classification.

Once the system started, the classification module receives in real-time the relation of change obtained by the pre-processing module. Finally with the information provided at the initial configuration the module classifies the physiological patterns and gives as an output one emotion.

BAGI allows the incorporation of new sets of emotions, intervals of times and pattern matching models to the system. The only constraint is that this information must be in a specific but simple format. A simple text editor can be used for this purpose. A brief description of the implementation of the flexibility features of the system in the classification module is provided below.

Different Set of Emotions

In BAGI the user specifies the set of emotions to classify; this set can vary in the number and labels of affective states. In order to do this, a simple text file with the emotions can be created, and saved into the system. Figure 2 presents two sets of affective states that can be used for classification.

Flexible Time Window

Following the same strategy, BAGI enables the user to specify the time window for the analysis. The user can create a file in simple text editor

Figure 2. Two sets of emotions for the BAGI system

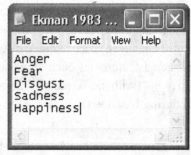
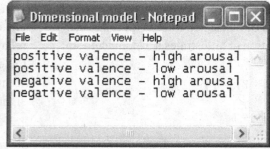

with the time intervals, indicating the starting and ending time (in milliseconds) for each section to analyze. The system reads the file and let a timer know about the intervals, the first two values in the file represent the start and ending time for the baseline and the following pairs of values represent the start and ending time of the sections to analyze.

The calculated values of the first interval are stored as the baseline for a user and at the end of the following intervals the system processes the physiological signals and gives as an output an emotion. Figure 3 presents an example of a file containing the time intervals of a session.

Pattern Matching Models

Different pattern matching models can be used with BAGI. They just need to follow a specific format as for example the one illustrated in Table 4.

The values presented in Table 4 correspond to normalized values obtained by comparing a feature of a signal during the stimuli with the same feature during the baseline, as explained previously in Equation (2).

The two values in each channel (CH1 and CH2) in Figure 4 represent the ranges in the physiological signals that will characterize a particular emotion. For instance, the pattern of fear is specified in this model as 20% to 100% increase in the HR signal, and a 20% to 500% increase in the SC signal.

Figure 3. Time intervals for the analysis of signals

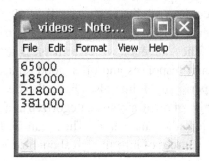

Table 4. Example of pattern matching model

ID	CH1		CH2	
Anger	1.2	2	0.9	2
Fear	1.2	2	1.2	5
Disgust	0.5	1	1.2	2
Sadness	0.5	1	0.9	1.1
Joy	0.9	1.1	1	1.3

The pattern matching files can be easily created in a program like for example Microsoft Excel and saved with a .csv extension.

Multi-Category Discrimination in Real-Time

The key to achieve effective and real-time emotion recognition is the ability of the system to incorporate information obtained from an offline process. In this way, it is possible to use machine learning models for multi-category discrimination and use them for real-time classification.

Different types of neural networks were trained, wrapped into .dll and .h files and integrated in the system. In this way, BAGI calls trained neural networks and performs real-time classification. Following this procedure new pattern recognition models can also be included in the system.

Game Adaptation

The adaptation module receives as an input the emotion provided by the classification module and matches the emotion with a predefined action in the game. After that it establishes a connection and, if required, instructs the game to perform any adjustment.

Figure 4. Target emotions in valence and arousal dimensions

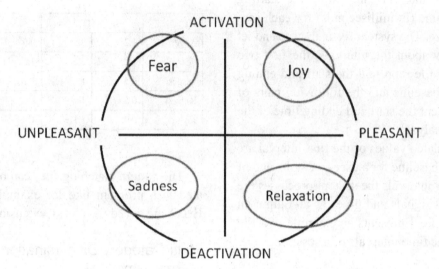

EXPERIMENTAL VALIDATION OF BAGI

The validation of BAGI consisted in three stages. First the multi-category discrimination in real-time was tested. For this purposes an experiment was carried out to collect physiological and emotional data, to train our machine learning model and classify physiological signals in real-time.

In order to test the process of game adaptation, a computer application that customizes the computer desktop wallpaper according to the emotion of the user was developed.

Finally, in order to validate the flexibility of BAGI a series of black box tests were carried out to evaluate different: set of emotions, times to analyze the signals, physiological measures and pattern strategies.

The three stages of the validation are described in the following subsections.

Real-Time Multi-Category Discrimination

As a first step on the validation of the multi-category discrimination in real-time of BAGI, a series of experiments to gather physiological

and emotional data were conducted. After that, machine learning models were trained and implemented to achieve real-time emotion classification.

The target emotions to be recognized by the system in this experiment included: relaxation, joy, sadness and fear. They were selected because each of the emotions are localized in one different quadrant in the circumplex model of emotions (Russell, 1980). Figure 4 illustrates the target emotions in the valence and arousal dimensions.

The physiological measures considered for this study included cardiovascular, electrodermal and respiration measures. From these measures a total of 17 signals were extracted using the Biograph Infiniti software.

To create a database of physiological responses to emotional stimuli, highly evocative video clips from movies were used.

Video clips have been widely used as stimuli in Psychology studies (e.g., Averill, 1969; Gross & Levenson, 1995) and in HCI (e.g., Nasoz et al., 2004). They have shown effectiveness to elicit emotional responses and offer good control for the experiment. Films also, have the desirable properties of being already categorized and being dynamic rather than static. There can be found several sources of information about movies and plenty websites where thousands of users vote and rate films and video clips from different genres (e.g., The Internet Movie Database, Yahoo movies, Youtube).

In order to select the most evocative video clips for the participants, the following procedure was undertaken. First, three types of sources that could provide titles of highly evocative video clips for our four target emotions were considered: i) previous studies; ii) websites with massive rates of video clips; and iii) recommendations from our research group and one media expert. Some criteria used for the selection include: self explanatory clips, highly evocative, short dialogues, length of clips. At the end, a corpus of 30 clips that fulfilled these conditions was gathered. Finally a pilot study was carried out with a group of 17 participants to select the best 12 video clips (3 clips for each target emotion).

Experiment Setup

At the beginning of the session the participant was briefed about the purpose of the experiment and signed a consent form. The electrodermal and cardiovascular sensors were placed in the fingers and the respiration sensor around the chest of the participant. During the experiment the participant was sat down in front of a desk with a questionnaire. Two minutes of baseline were recorded from the participant while he was watching a relaxing video, then 12 more video clips were projected in a 10ft by 8ft screen with the lights off. It was decided to use this big screen, instead of a common PC monitor, in order to get greater emotional responses. Studies recompiled in (Lombard & Ditton, 1997) support that more emotional responses are obtained when larger screens are used to present the stimuli.

The videos had an average of 3 minutes length each. After each video presentation the participants had 30 seconds to report his emotional experience in the questionnaire. The session lasted for an hour in total and there was just one participant per session. The session was video recorded to corroborate the emotions reported with the facial expressions of the participants. A total of 61 participants volunteered for this experiment.

Feature Selection

There were different motivations to carry out a feature selection process in our study. One of the most important was due to a restriction from the Biograph Infiniti software when connecting with third-party applications in real-time. In other words, the software that comes with the Procomp equipment, can create up to 8 connections through which only 8 signals can be passed from the Biograph Inifiniti to the emotion recognition system. Having extracted a total of 17 signals for analysis, it was necessary to select 8 signals that discriminate better the target emotions. Additionally, the feature selection process can improve the performance of the leaning model and recognition system by:

- Enhancing the generalization capabilities.
- Speeding up the learning and classification process.
- Improving the model interpretability.

The feature selection process was carried out offline, using a stepwise algorithm to select the best 8 features. Table 5 presents the 8 most important variables obtained from our analysis.

Training Results

With the selected variables, machine learning models were designed to automatically recognize the physiological patterns from the emotions experienced by participants. A supervised learning approach was followed to deduce a function from our training data and predict a class label. Two types of models were trained to recognize the patterns of the target emotions: i) Neural Network (NN) trained with a backpropagation algorithm and ii) Probabilistic Neural Network (PNN).

Table 5. Variables obtained from feature selection analysis.

No.	Variable	Importance
1	Raw signal from BVP sensor	100.00
2	Amplitude from BVP	97.900
3	Respiration Period	81.486
4	Heart Rate	67.175
5	Raw signal from respiration sensor	34.112
6	Skin Resistance	23.702
7	Low Frequency % power	18.646
8	Ratio LF/HF	18.281

From the 61 participants some interruptions in the recording of the physiological data were observed in 2 participants. Although the information could be recovered and reconstructed, it was decided to discard it from the analysis to reduce any external bias.

A total of 708 training vectors were constructed from the 59 participants and 12 video clips considered for the analysis. The video clips were grouped in 4 categories, according to the target emotions, and there were 177 vectors for each category. Each vector contained the emotion reported by the participant and the normalized values for the 8 physiological signals presented in Table 5.

From the training process we achieved a total classification accuracy of 62.42% with the backpropagation NN and 84.46% with PNN. Table 6 and Table 7 present the confusion matrices of the NN and the PNN.

In order to assess the generalization capabilities of our predictive models on new independent data sets, a leave one out cross validation technique was used. From the evaluation of the trained models a total classification accuracy of 54.94% on the NN trained with backpropagation and a 78.38% on the PNN was obtained. The confusion

Table 6. Confusion matrix for the backpropagation NN

Actual category	Predicted category			
	Relaxation	Joy	Sadness	Fear
Relaxation	100 (56.49%)	28	35	14
Joy	15	137 (77.4%)	17	8
Sadness	28	18	93 (52.54%)	38
Fear	13	13	39	112 (63.27%)

Table 7. Confusion matrix for the PNN

Actual category	Predicted category			
	Relaxation	Joy	Sadness	Fear
Relaxation	151 (85.31%)	15	8	3
Joy	14	156 (88.13%)	3	4
Sadness	14	6	139 (78.53%)	18
Fear	5	3	17	152 (85.87%)

Table 8. Confusion matrix for the validation of the backpropagation NN

Actual category	Predicted category			
	Relaxation	Joy	Sadness	Fear
Relaxation	102 (57.62%)	26	33	16
Joy	27	123 (69.49%)	16	11
Sadness	36	21	65 (36.72%)	55
Fear	17	15	46	99 (55.93%)

Table 9. Confusion matrix for the validation of the PNN

Actual category	Predicted category			
	Relaxation	Joy	Sadness	Fear
Relaxation	143 (80.79%)	18	13	3
Joy	22	145 (81.92%)	5	5
Sadness	18	8	127 (71.75%)	24
Fear	8	8	21	140 (79.09%)

matrices of the validation of these two models are presented in Table 8 and Table 9.

Real-Time Bio-Affective Feedback

For testing the real-time recognition and adaptation capabilities a very simple application that adapts the desktop wallpaper according to the emotion recognized by the system was built. The replay capabilities of Procomp with the video recordings from the sessions were used to simulate the real-time acquisition of physiological signals from 59 participants of our experiment. Then, the BAGI was connected to the application that customizes the desktop wallpaper. Two types of models for real time classification were tested: one pattern matching model based on the findings from Ekman et al. (1983) and one machine learning model trained with the PNN. Both models were able to successfully classify physiological signals in

real-time and adapt the computer wall paper to the emotion recognized. Table 10 presents a description of the wallpapers assigned to each emotion and an example of BAGI performing real-time adaptation is presented in Figure 5.

Table 10. Customization of the wallpaper

Figure 5 a) shows the default computer wallpaper when the participant is starting the experiment; Figure 5 b) illustrates how BAGI customize the computer wallpaper as soon as it recognizes joy.

Flexible Architecture

The flexibility of BAGI has been tested using the black box testing method. The detailed tests carried out on BAGI are presented in Table 11.

The results obtained from the black box tests demonstrated the flexibility of BAGI to work with

Figure 5. a) Participant at beginning of experiment; b) BAGI customizing wallpaper according to emotion

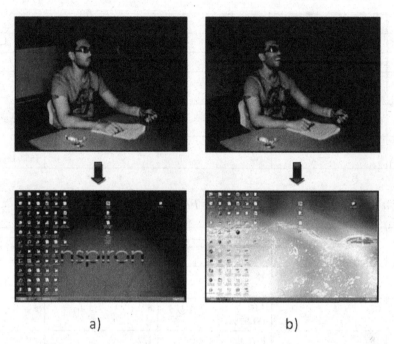

a)   b)

Emotion recognized	Wallpaper colour
Relaxation	White
Joy	Blue
Sadness	Gray
Fear	Yellow

Table 11. Flexibility black box tests on BAGI

Test	Details
Set of emotions	System tested with 3 different sets of emotions with different number of emotions and labels.
Time intervals	System tested using 3 different time intervals for the analysis of the signals: 10, 120 and 180 seconds.
Physiological measures	System tested using 3, 5 and 8 different physiological measures.
Pattern matching models	System tested with 3 different pattern matching models.
Machine learning models	System tested with 1 NN trained with back-propagation algorithm and 1 PNN.

different affective sets, time intervals, measures and psycho-physiological models.

CONCLUSION AND FUTURE WORK

At the present time, when the game industry is looking for more immersive interactive techniques and ways to improve the artificial intelligence, affective recognition systems can play an important part as an instrument to enhance the game experience.

Physiological signals have been already used to recognize emotions in games; nevertheless the pattern matching approach commonly followed is not practical for the recognition among several emotions.

The feasibility of the use of physiological signals with machine learning techniques has already been proved by several offline HCI studies. However the implementation of such systems in a real-time application is not a straightforward task.

In this study a user independent real-time emotion recognition system that could be used for gaming was presented. The architecture of BAGI facilitates the reusability of previous findings and the integration of new models.

An experiment to gather emotional and physiological data was carried out with 61 participants. The results from the questionnaires showed that the video clips used as a stimuli effectively evoked the four target emotions in the most of the participants.

From the three sensors used to record the physiological signals a total of 17 signals were extracted. And due to the real-time connectivity limitations of the equipment with third-party computer applications the best 8 signals that discriminate our data were selected.

Two machine learning models were trained to recognize the physiological patterns of 4 emotions, having the best results with a PNN with classification accuracy of 84.46% on the training data and 78.38% when it was cross-validated. The two machine learning models were implemented on the system for a real time classification. Finally, a simple application that customizes the desktop wallpaper to the emotional state of the user was developed. The results from our study provide evidence of the feasibility of the use of BAGI as an interface for gaming.

Although the training models can be claimed to apply just to classify emotions experienced while watching video clips, the methodology used in this study can be used to train models for different types of stimuli. And the architecture of BAGI allows the inclusion of these new trained models to perform a real-time classification.

An interesting future study would be the utilization of a model trained with stimuli to classify emotional responses evoked by other type of stimuli (e.g., use a model trained with video clips to classify emotions evoked by pictures). There are already some differences in the physiological patterns, for the same emotions using different stimuli, in the psychology literature; however there is no empirical evidence in the literature of

machine learning models attempting to classify emotions evoked by different types of stimuli.

Our future work will involve the training of a machine learning model in a game context and its inclusion to BAGI. Hopefully, with the affective feedback provided by BAGI it will be possible to reinforce the AI of the game and enhance the emotional experience.

ACKNOWLEDGMENT

J.A.P. would like to thank CONACYT and SEP for their financial support.

REFERENCES

Arroyo-Palacios, J., & Romano, D. (2008). *Towards a Standardization in the Use of Physiological Signals for Affective Recognition Systems.* Paper presented at the Measuring Behavior 2008, Maastricht, The Netherlands.

Arroyo-Palacios, J., & Romano, D. (2009). *Exploring the Use of a Respiratory-Computer Interface for Game Interaction.* Paper presented at the IEEE Consumer electronics Society Games innovation Conference, London.

Averill, J. R. (1969). Autonomic response patterns during sadness and mirth. *Psychophysiology*, *5*, 399–414. doi:10.1111/j.1469-8986.1969.tb02840.x

Bersak, D., McDarby, G., Augenblick, N., McDarby, P., Daragh, M., Brian, M., et al. (2001). *Intelligent Biofeedback using an Immersive Competitive Environment.* Paper presented at the Designing Ubiquitous Computing Games Workshop, Atlanta, GA.

Cacioppo, J. T., Klein, D. J., Berntson, G. G., & Hatfield, E. (1993). The Psychophysiology of Emotion. In M. Lewis & J. M. Haviland (Eds.), *Handbook of Emotions* (pp. 119-142).

Cacioppo, J. T., & Tassinary, L. G. (1990). Inferring Psychological Significance from Physiological Signals. *The American Psychologist, 45*, 16–28. doi:10.1037/0003-066X.45.1.16

Christie, I. C. (2002). *Multivariate Discrimination of Emotion-Specific Autonomic Nervous System Activity.* Blacksburg, VA: Virginia Polytechnic Institute and State University.

Conati, C. (2002). Probabilistic Assessment of User's Emotion in Educational Games. *Applied Artificial Intelligence, 16*, 555–575. doi:10.1080/08839510290030390

Ekman, P., Levenson, R. W., & Friesen, W. V. (1983). Autonomic nervous system activity distinguishes among emotions. *Science, 221*, 1208–1210. doi:10.1126/science.6612338

Fredrickson, B. L., Mancuso, R. A., Branigan, C., & Tugade, M. M. (2000). The Undoing Effect of Positive Emotions. *Motivation and Emotion, 24*(4), 237–258. doi:10.1023/A:1010796329158

Gilleade, K. M., Dix, A., & Allanson, J. (2005). *Affective Videogames and modes of Affective Gaming: Assist Me, Challenge Me, Emote Me.* Paper presented at the Digital Games Research Association (DiGRA).

Gross, J. J., & Levenson, R. W. (1995). Emotion elicitation using films. *Cognition and Emotion, 9*(1), 87–108. doi:10.1080/02699939508408966

Haag, A., Goronzy, S., Schaich, P., & Williams, J. (2004). Emotion Recognition Using Bio-sensors: First Steps towards an Automatic System. In *Affective Dialog Systems (LNCS 3068).* Berlin: Springer. doi:10.1007/978-3-540-24842-2_4

Hjelm, S. I., & Browall, C. (2000). *Brainball - using brain activity for cool competition.* Paper presented at the 1st Nordic Conference on Human-Computer Interaction.

Kim, J., & Andre, E. (2008). Emotion Recognition Based on Physiological Changes in Music Listening. *IEEE Transactions on Pattern Analysis and Machine Intelligence, 30*(12), 2067–2083. doi:10.1109/TPAMI.2008.26

Kim, K. H., Bang, S. W., & Kim, S. R. (2004). Emotion recognition system using short-term monitoring of physiological signals. *Medical & Biological Engineering & Computing, 42*, 419–427. doi:10.1007/BF02344719

Kim, T., Shin, D., & Shin, D. (2009). *Towards an Emotion Recognition System based on Biometrics.* Paper presented at the International Joint Conference on computational Sciences and Optimization.

Ko, M., Bae, K., Oh, G., & Ryu, T. (2009). *A Study on New Gameplay Based on Brain-Computer Interface.* Paper presented at the Digital Games Research Association (DiGRA).

Lalor, E. C., Kelly, S. P., Finucane, C., Burke, R., Smith, R., & Reilly, R. B. (2005). Steady-State VEP-Based Brain-Computer Interface Control in an Immersive 3D Gaming Environment. *EURASIP Journal on Applied Signal Processing, 19*, 3156–3164. doi:10.1155/ASP.2005.3156

Leon, E., Clarke, G., Callaghan, V., & Sepulveda, F. (2007). A user-independent real-time emotion recognition system for software agents in domestic environments. *Engineering Applications of Artificial Intelligence, 20*(3), 337–345. doi:10.1016/j.engappai.2006.06.001

Lombard, M., & Ditton, T. (1997). At the Heart of It All: The Concept of Presence. *Journal of Computer-Mediated Communication, 3*(2).

Nasoz, F., Alvarez, K., Lisetti, C. L., & Finkelstein, N. (2004). Emotion recognition from physiological signals using wireless sensors for presence technologies. *International Journal of Cognition. Technology and Work, 6*(1), 4–14. doi:10.1007/s10111-003-0143-x

Peter, C., & Herbon, A. (2006). Emotion representation and physiology assignments in digital systems. *Interacting with Computers*, *18*, 139–170. doi:10.1016/j.intcom.2005.10.006

Picard, R. W., Vyzas, E., & Healey, J. (2001). Toward Machine Emotional Intelligence: Analysis of Affective Physiological State. *IEEE Transactions on Pattern Analysis and Machine Intelligence*, *23*(10), 1175–1191. doi:10.1109/34.954607

Prendinger, H., Becker, C., & Ishizuka, M. (2006). A study in Users' Physiological Response to an Empathic Interface Agent. *International Journal of Humanoid Robotics*, *3*(3), 371–391. doi:10.1142/S0219843606000801

Russell, J. A. (1980). A circumplex model of affect. *Journal of Personality and Social Psychology*, *39*, 1161–1178. doi:10.1037/h0077714

Stemmler, D. (1989). The autonomic differentiation of emotions revisited: Convergent and discriminant validation. *Psychophysiology*, 617–632. doi:10.1111/j.1469-8986.1989.tb03163.x

Toups, Z. O., Graeber, R., Kerne, A., Tassinary, L., Berry, S., Overby, K., et al. (2006). *A Design for Using Physiological Signals to Affect Team Game Play*. Paper presented at the Augmented Cognition International.

Zajonc, R. B., & McIntosh, D. N. (1992). Some Promising Questions and Some Questionable Promises. *Psychological Science*, *3*(1), 70–74. doi:10.1111/j.1467-9280.1992.tb00261.x

Chapter 17
Evaluating User Experience of Actual and Imagined Movement in BCI Gaming

Bram van de Laar
University of Twente, The Netherlands

Boris Reuderink
University of Twente, The Netherlands

Danny Plass-Oude Bos
University of Twente, The Netherlands

Dirk Heylen
University of Twente, The Netherlands

ABSTRACT

Most research on Brain-Computer Interfaces (BCI) focuses on developing ways of expression for disabled people who are not able to communicate through other means. Recently it has been shown that BCI can also be used in games to give users a richer experience and new ways to interact with a computer or game console. This paper describes research conducted to find out what the differences are between using actual and imagined movement as modalities in a BCI game. Results show that there are significant differences in user experience and that actual movement is a more robust way of communicating through a BCI.

INTRODUCTION

In the field of BCI, brain activity is recorded and automatically interpreted to be applied in various applications. Measuring brain activity is already well known in medicine using the electroencepha-logram (EEG). EEG is a proven method, which has a number of advantages over other methods: it is non-invasive, has a high temporal resolution, does not require a laboratory setting, is relatively cheap, and it is even possible to create wireless EEG head-sets.

BCI systems need to make decisions based on very short segments of EEG data to make it

DOI: 10.4018/978-1-4666-0029-4.ch017

useful for different applications such as wheelchairs, robots, and personal computers. In the case of software applications, BCI can be used as an additional modality of control, for evaluation of the user or the application, or to build adaptive user interfaces (Nijholt et al., 2008a).

Games are usually the first applications to adopt new paradigms, driven by the gamers' continuing search for novelty and challenges (Nijholt et al., 2008b). Apart from them being a suitable platform to bring this new interaction modality to the general population, games also provide a safe and motivational environment for patients during training or rehabilitation (Graimann et al., 2007; Leeb et al., 2007b). Research has shown that using BCI instead of the conventional mouse and keyboard can add to the user experience by making a game more challenging, richer, and more immersive (Oude Bos & Reuderink, 2008). This was done by comparing keyboard control with BCI control for a simple game called BrainBasher, and evaluating the user experience with the Game Experience Questionnaire (IJsselsteijn et al., 2007). Both this game and this questionnaire were also used for the research described here, comparing actual and imagined movement.

Before BCI can be adopted by the general population there are still a number of issues that need to be addressed: artifacts in the recorded brain data (signals that do not stem from the brain), inter and intra-subject variability, inter and intra-session variability, long training periods, low transfer rates (of commands), and the phenomenon that some people are unable to use a BCI at all (Sannelli et al., 2008). Apart from that, more attention from the Human Computer Interaction community is required on how this new input modality influences the user experience, and how the interaction can be improved (Lecuyer et al., 2008).

While most research into using movement for BCI has focused on imagined movement, some clinical research shows that actual movement in fact elicitates a more pronounced and therefore better discernable signal in the motor cortex (McFarland et al., 2000).

Actual movement can also be used with other interfaces than a BCI. Interfaces such as a motion tracking system, for example, which are probably more reliable at this moment. One big potential advantage of a BCI however is that the measured brain signals are always preceding actual muscle activity at the limbs, and can be measured before the muscles activate. This advantage is amplified by the onset of a potential in preparation of a movement, the so called Bereitschaftspotential, or Readiness Potential (Kornhuber & Deecke, 1965; Shibasaki et al., 2006). A very useful aspect of the RP is the lateralized readiness potential (LRP), where the preparation of left-sided movement is reflected in a potential occurring at the right motor cortex, and vice-versa. Krauledat et al. (2004) show that this lateralized readiness potential can be used to classify actual movement even before the movement itself is carried out. This could give a gamer an advantage over other interfaces especially in fast paced, highly reactive games.

But using BCI can also provide other benefits. While measuring brain activity for detection of movement, whether actual or imagined, other information can be derived from the brain as well, such as the user's mental and emotional state. This could be used to make smarter applications which are more aware of the user.

RELATED WORK

A few BCI games based on imagined or actual movement do already exist. A first-person shooter game in which the user could move using the keyboard, and turn by imagined movement was designed. Players learned to control the BCI by experimenting; no instructions were given beforehand. Other examples include the virtual environments of Leeb et al. (2005) the board game of Kayagil et al. (2007) and the game BrainBasher

(Oude Bos & Reuderink, 2008) that we used in this study.

Both actual and imagined movement can be used for BCIs. Obviously, actual movement is a more natural and intuitive way for users to communicate and express themselves. All these games involve movement tasks, and are based on a neurological process known as Event-Related Desynchronization (ERD) (Pfurtscheller, 2001). ERD is detectable as a decrease in power in the β-frequency band on corresponding motor cortices. Before use the BCI has to be adapted to person-specific examples of the ERD using machine learning techniques.

Actual movement is characterized by a more pronounced and reliable signal in the motor cortex (McFarland et al., 2000). This more pronounced signal is a very welcome advantage in the world of BCI where every extra percent of accuracy is appreciated.

When looking at the success of the Nintendo Wii, it becomes clear that actual movement is well enjoyed by gamers. Moreover, imagined movement in adulthood is not as trivial as actual movement is. Although for example professional sportsmen and musicians use imaginary movement for training an actual motor skill it still is not as trivial to do as actual movement jeannerod1994. Though one can think of various applications in which imagined movement is used, these are almost always associated with skills which require a lot of training. Actual movement might therefore be a more natural and easier way of interacting with a BCI.

METHODS

The main question in this study is whether there are differences between imagined and actual movement in a BCI gaming environment. Some of the differences that will be looked into are the gaming experience for the user and the detectability of the signal from the EEG. We also looked at the generalizability of these BCI modalities for different user groups based on demographical characteristics.

Experiment Setup

To answer these questions an experiment has been carried out in which users communicate with the BCI game BrainBasher (Oude Bos & Reuderink, 2008) using both kinds of movement. First, users fill in a form regarding demographics including handedness as well as characteristics that could influence their ability to focus on the task (like alcohol and caffeine consumption habits). This data is used to check for group differences during analysis. Our experiment consists of two parts: actual movement and imagined movement. The order of performing actual and imagined movement is randomly assigned for each subject. Each part consists of two sessions. For the experiment design see Figure 1.

For the system to be able to recognize the user's actions, a training session is required to create a user-specific classifier. This is followed by a game session, after which the subject fills in a user experience questionnaire. This questionnaire has been designed based on the Game Experience Questionnaire (GEQ) developed at the Game Experience Lab in Eindhoven ijsselsteijn2007. With this information the user experience for actual and imagined movement can be compared. Between all sessions are breaks in which the user can relax for a minute or two.

The experiment is set up as a randomized cross-over experiment to eliminate sequence and learning effects induced by the succession of both tasks (Byron et al., 1980). The subjects are randomly assigned to either group A or group B, taking care that both groups in the end have an equal number of subjects. Both groups perform the same tasks ('receive the same treatment') but in a different order. In Figure 1 this crossover design can be clearly seen halfway the diagram. After all experiments are done we compare the results of

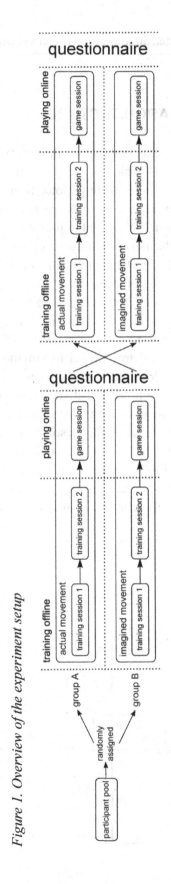

Figure 1. Overview of the experiment setup

the actual movement sessions versus the results of the imagined movement game sessions. The new questionnaire has also been evaluated so it can be used for assessments of other BCI games and other BCI paradigms.

The setup is situated in a normal office environment, in contrast to a shielded room. This setting was chosen deliberately as it is a more representative setting for home use. Besides this, the EEG system used has active electrodes which pick up a lot less noise than passive electrodes would. During the experiments themselves, only the researcher and the subject will be in the room. This way, distractions will be kept to a minimum, while still being able to provide help when needed.

BRAIN BASHER

The BCI game used for this research is Brain-Basher (Oude Bos & Reuderink 2008). The goal of this game is to perform specific brain actions as quickly as possible. For each correct and detected action you score a point. Game control is achieved by two mental tasks: left hand movement versus right hand movement. For the actual movement task both hands are laid on the desk in front of the user. When the appropriate stimulus appears they have to perform a simple tapping movement with their whole hand. When performing the imagined movement task users are instructed to imagine the same movement, without actually using any of their hand muscles.

Before the user can play however, they will have to undergo a training session in which stimuli (in the form of symbols denoting the user actions, see Figure 2) and breaks are alternated. During the stimulus the subject performs the indicated action: movement of the left or right hand. The user is instructed to stay relaxed and not to move, excluding the break periods, to prevent artifacts in the EEG. This is of course with the exception of the hand movement in the case of the actual movement sessions. In our system, the training

Figure 2. The symbols for left and right hand movement

consists of two short sessions, taking ten minutes in total. The EEG data from both training sessions are concatenated and used for training the classifier of the BCI system.

During the game session the user is instructed to take care that they carry out precisely the same movement (be it actual or imagined) as in the preceding training session. The difference is that they have to react as fast as they can to each new symbol popping up by performing the action right away. Bashing a symbol is accomplished when the classifier recognizes the action, according to a confidence level of at least 60%. Every bash results in one point added to their total score. The goal of the game is to bash as many symbols in the allocated three minutes, to achieve a maximum score (Figure 3).

BRAIN ARCHITECTURE

As already explained earlier, the system is trained on the ERD which is generated by planning, imagining and executing motor functions. This signal comes from the motor cortex in which the movement for every limb is prepared. The motor cortex is the most backward positioned part of the frontal lobe, stretching in a narrow band from the ears to the top of the scalp.

We used a 32 electrode setup to measure the ERDs. These electrodes are fitted into the small plastic holes of an EEG cap. The small holes are filled with electrolytic gel to provide a proper electrical (low inductance) connection to the scalp on which the potentials can be measured. The cap has to be set up by someone else than the user, because all the plastic holes have to be filled with gel by hand. Although the part of the brain the ERDs can be measured is quite small, we used the full set of 32 electrodes to use spatial filtering and to eliminate sources of noise outside

Figure 3. A game session

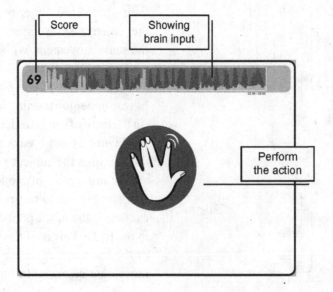

Figure 5. Photograph of an EEG cap in use

the head. Setting up the system will take somewhere between 10 and 15 minutes. In Figure 5 the system with the cap, the electrodes and the game BrainBasher can be seen in action.

The BrainBasher BCI

A schematic view of the total system is shown in Figure 4. The user interacts with the system by executing brain actions, and also by keyboard to traverse the menu. Brain activity is acquired with a BioSemi EEG setup using 32 electrodes, sampled at 256Hz. For training the system, examples of the ERD for both the left hand and right hand are used to train a classifier to be used during the online game session. The EEG data is processed as shown in Figure 6. First the raw data is re-referenced to the common average reference (CAR) by subtracting the mean of all channels to remove far away sources of noise (Ludwig et al., 2008). After re-referencing a bandpass-filter isolates the frequency range (8-30Hz) in which the ERD occurs. Then we train spatial filters (spatial filters operate in the space domain, as opposed to filtering in the frequency domain) to suppress irrelevant signals with the common spa-

tial patterns (CSP) algorithm (Koles et al., 1991) to isolate activity on the motor cortices. Now that we have filtered the signal both in the time domain and in the spatial domain, we calculate the energy of the signal by taking its variance. A Linear Discriminant Analysis (LDA) is applied to make a final prediction based on these band power features. After training the BCI generates a new prediction every quarter of a second, based on the real-time EEG data. These predictions are used to play the game.

BCI Performance Evaluation

After the training session, we evaluate the accuracy of the classifier by a cross-validation procedure. It is to be expected that a classifier has to have a certain minimum performance for pleasurable experience. Another frequently used performance measure for BCIs is the information transfer rates (ITR), representing communicated information measured in bits per minute. The ITR more directly expresses the utility of a BCI for a user that intends to use the BCI to communicate, and is preferable to other measures because it combines both the quality and the speed of the

Figure 4. BrainBasher system view

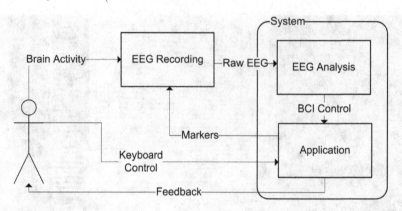

Figure 6. BrainBasher BCI pipeline

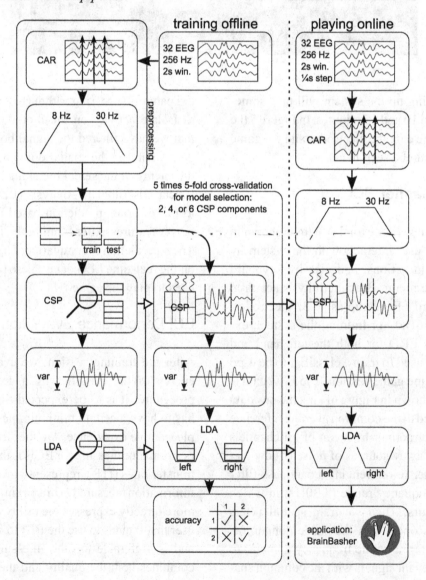

BCI into a single performance measure. Current BCI are reported to obtain ITRs of up to 10-25 bits per minute (Wolpaw et al., 2002).

The ITR is estimated by calculating how much information the predictions of the BCI give on the intentions of the users (the ground truth), know as the mutual information I:

$$I(X;Y) = \sum_{y \in Y} \sum_{x \in X} p(x,y) \log_2 \frac{p(x,y)}{p_1(x)p_2(y)} \qquad (1)$$

where X and Y are the (discrete) predictions and the ground truth respectively, $p(x, y)$ is the joint probability distribution function of X and Y, and $p_1(x)$ and $p_2(y)$ are the marginal probability distribution functions of X and Y respectively. Mutual information measures the decrease in uncertainty in a signal Y (the desired action) given signal X (a derivation of the EEG).

The duration of a trial is needed to calculate the ITR in bits per minute from the mutual information as follows:

$$ITR = 60 \times \frac{I(X;Y)}{\Delta t} \qquad (2)$$

where Δt is the time in seconds between one trial and the next, assuming their class labels are independent of each other.

Questionnaire Design

To evaluate the user experience a questionnaire based on the GEQ (IJsselsteijn et al., 2007) is developed. Although the GEQ consists of a lot of useful questions for evaluating various games, its main purpose is evaluating complex and immersive 3D virtual games. Therefore the questionnaire has been adapted to evaluate the user experience especially in BCI games. Questions that are not applicable, (e.g., the questions about the storyline, the complexity and the flow of the

game) were left out. On the other hand we added questions, specifically on the amount of control the user experiences. The amount of control is a trivial aspect when using mouse and keyboard. These are reliable ways of communicating with the computer compared to a BCI system which is not so reliable. Also items about user concentration and alertness were added. This is an important aspect because users will have to concentrate to use a BCI game and possibly get tired more quickly than normal.

The questionnaire consists of statements to which users can respond on a 5 point Likert-scale ranging from `completely disagree' to `completely agree'. Some examples of items in the questionnaire might be: ``I liked playing the game.", ``I felt the computer recognized my actions." or ``I'm exhausted."

To analyse the results of the questionnaire, we will use Cronbach's Alpha cronbach1951. Alpha is a measure of internal consistency. It is (to a certain extent) a measure of how reliably a scale constructed out of the selected items will measure one concept. This does not necessarily mean that you are measuring the concept you intended to measure, therefore further (qualitative) validation is needed. Alpha is only an estimator of reliability: it measures to what extent the different items are correlating and are consistent, taking subject and environment variance into account. In this research the Standardized Alpha will be used because we want to sum standard scores to construct scales from Likert scale items. A commonly accepted threshold for Alpha of 0.7 is the goal for every scale (Cortina, 1993).

Results

First we describe the demographics of the test subject pool, then we analyse the questionnaire used for evaluation. Using the results from the questionnaire we can look at the differences in user experience between actual and imagined movement.

Participants

Twenty healthy persons participated as test subjects in this study. The average age across the group was 26.8 (standard deviation: 12.3, minimum: 13 and maximum: 58). Of the twenty participants 10 (50%) were male and 10 (50%) were female. Test subjects were randomly assigned to either group A or group B. Group A would do imagined movement as their first task and actual movement second, group B would do exactly the opposite. Each group had ten (50%) participants. 19 (95%) participants were Dutch, 1 (5%) participant German. Apart from standard demographics we also asked participants their handedness, because this characteristic might be of influence: 5 (25%) participants were dominantly left-handed 15 (75%) were right-handed. 14 (70%) received an education higher than average. Computer usage and game experience varied a lot among participants: 8 (40%) participants used a PC for more than six hours a day, 5 (25%) used a computer on a less than daily basis. The same variance goes for game experience: 2 (10%) played games two hours a day, 8 (40%) on a weekly basis, 6 (30%) on a monthly basis and 4 (20%) never played a video game.

Questionnaire Construction

All participants filled in the questionnaire after both tasks without missing any questions. The responses on the same items for both movement tasks were stored in the same respective variables for scale analyses and in separate variables to analyse the differences in user experience between both tasks. Scale reliability analysis was carried out in order to evaluate if the newly developed questionnaire would be useful as a reliable tool to assess user experience in BCI games. The total user experience questionnaire consisted of 42 items over 8 scales. Each item consists of responses to a statement on the user's experience on a 5 point Likert-scale.

Some items were recorded to avoid an expected negative correlation. Correcting the scales for items that did not contribute to the scales consistency, e.g. deleting items with a low or negative Inter-Item Correlation, Standardised Alpha's ranged from 0.620 to 0.865 and all scales consisted of at least three items.

To evaluate the usefulness and dimensionality of the resulting scales, a factor analysis was done on all scales separately. Factor analysis is a multivariate analysis technique which can be used to analyse data with "large sets of correlated variables [..]" and as such can be usefull "as a means of examining and describing the internal structure of the covariance and correlation matrices involved". The method used in the factor analysis called Principal Components Analysis (PCA) yields one or more linear combinations of variables in which the maximum explained variance in the data is attained. If one is looking for unidimensionality, then the first extracted component, id est, the one which explains the most variance, should explain by far the most variance in the data.

Looking at our data the first principal components extracted by the factor analyses of every scale explained more than 56% of the variance in the data, except for the Negative Experiences scale. Scree plots catell1977 also indicated strong unidimensionality across all scales except for the Negative Experiences scale, which turned out to be a two dimensional scale. Scree plots can be used for an heuristical evaluation of the number of relevant components in a factor analysis. These plots are constructed by plotting the value of each successive eigenvalue against the rank order. The point at which a strong 'knee' occurs can be used as the cutoff for the number of dimensions. This gave a confirmation for the earlier findings. An obvious knee shape could be seen in all plots except for the Negative Experiences scale.

The corrected questionnaire consisted of 32 items divided over 8 scales. An overview of all corrected scales with their respective Alpha's and variance explained by the first dimension in factor

Table 1. Constructed Scales including alpha and variance explained by 1th principal component

Construction of Scales			
	No. of items	Alpha	Var. explained
Alertness	3	0.783	70.4%
Challenge	5	0.777	56.4%
Control	3	0.783	69.9%
Goals	3	0.754	67.7%
Fatigue	3	0.759	67.6%
Immersion	3	0.620	57.0%
Negative Experiences	5	0.638	41.9%
Positive Experiences	7	0.865	55.8%

Table 2. Paired t-Tests Scales, comparing imagined and actual movement

Differences of Imagined vs. Actual Movement				
	Diff of avg	StDev	t	Sig (2-tail)
Alertness	-.65	1.20	-2.42	03
Challenge	.40	.83	2.17	04
Control	-.30	1.34	-1.00	33
Goals	-.18	.50	-1.63	12
Fatigue	.40	1.11	1.62	12
Immersion	-.15	.60	-1.12	28
Negative Experiences	.00	.59	00	1.00
Positive Experiences	-.24	.89	-1.22	24

analysis can be found in Table 1. The variance explained by the first factor measures to what extent a scale is measuring only one underlying attribute or construct.

Differences in User Experience

The final corrected scales were used to compare the user experience for users performing both kinds of movements. A direct comparison by means of paired t-tests was done. The results of these test can be seen in Table 2. The first column is the difference of the means of both scales, the second column is the total standard deviation, the third the t-score and the last column is the two-tailed significance of the difference. The data show that the differences in the user experience for the Alertness as well as the Challenge scales are significant. Actual movement scored significantly higher on the Alertness scale (t(19)=-2.42, p=0.03) which could be attributed to mental tiring process of performing imagined movement. The same trend is also shown in the Fatigue scale, while there is no significant difference between actual and imagined movement (p=0.12). One possible explanation for this can be found in the correlation between the Fatigue and Alertness

scale. These show a strong negative correlation in actual movement (r=-0.707, p<0.001). Challenge also significantly differs between both kinds of movement (t(19)=2.17, p=0.04). User experience data therefore indicates that performing imagined movement is more of a challenge than actual movement is.

Performance

Using the error rate calculated by the classifier from the EEG data we can compare the performance achieved on different subjects. For each subject two error rates are available, one for actual and one for imagined movement. The average rate for actual movement is 38.67%, while the average error rate for imagined movement is 42.28%. A Wilcoxon signed-rank test showed that actual movement error rates are significantly lower ($W_+(20)$) = 48, p = 0.0328). Looking at performance across different groups there are no significant differences between men and women in actual (t(19)=0.584, p=0.570) or imagined (t(19)=0.205, p=0.840) movement. Comparing left handed with right handed test subjects also didn't show any significant differences in actual or imagined movement (t(19)=-0.876, p=0.403 and t(19)=0.99, p=0.923 respectively).

The Information Transfer Rate or ITR is another performance measure we calculated for every subject. This makes our results more comparable with other BCI's as well it is more informative than purely an accuracy rate. Note that the ITRs are calculated just for the training data and that therefor the maximum achievable ITR is 15 bits per minute. In the actual game session the bitrate can be higher, for the best subjects probably over 30 bits per minute. It is however difficult to give accurate numbers for this prediction because our BCI is self paced without a definite time window.

The calculated ITRs can be seen in Table 3 (due to an unfortunate loss of data we were not able to calculate the ITR for all subjects).

These findings support the accuracy measure in that actual movement provides a more usable signal on average.

CONCLUSION AND DISCUSSION

Results from this study showed that differences in user experience and in performance between

Table 3. ITR for actual and imagined movement for all subjects (in bits/minute), missing data is marked with x

ITR for all subjects					
Subject	AM	IM	Subject	AM	IM
A1	3.8	4.2	B1	2.0	4.1
A2	8.7	2.3	B2	2.6	2.1
A3	2.4	2.0	B3	3.8	2.1
A4	4.5	3.8	B4	4.8	10.5
A5	6.5	3.8	B5	6.0	2.3
A6	4.1	1.8	B6	2.6	4.2
A7	2.3	2.3	B7	2.7	5.3
A8	3.3	3.9	B8	2.3	2.3
A9	x	2.4	B9	5.1	1.7
A10	x	x	B10	5.7	2.6

actual and imagined movement in BCI gaming do exist. Actual movement produces a more reliable signal while the user stays more alert. On the other hand, imagined movement is more challenging.

To be able to assess the differences in user experience between actual and imagined movement, we developed a questionnaire for evaluating BCI games. While this questionnaire was found to be a numerically grounded tool to be used in this setting, further research for validation is needed.

User experience data from this questionnaire showed two significant differences. Users found more challenge in performing imagined movement. This might be due to a higher error rate, which makes sense; looking at the average error rate, it is harder to perform imagined movement. If we assume imagined movement is a skill that can be learned this might be an advantage for using imagined movement. Gamers are always looking for challenges and limitations that they can overcome by practice (Nijholt et al., 2008b).

On the other hand, for a few test subjects, the BCI system could not correctly recognize any movement. This corresponds to an error rate of 50%, in which case simple random `guessing' would be as good as classification. Participants who achieved a high error rate also were not able to score any game points (other than maybe by chance). This is an issue that frustrates the user and is something that has to be resolved for wider acceptance of BCI gaming. This problem of not being able to be understood by a BCI is referred to as BCI illiteracy (Sannelli et al., 2008).

One could argue that perhaps the feedback of the movement classification in the top bar in the game screen could be a distraction. This could affect the performance in a negative way. On the other hand, the feedback bar can actually improve performance, as the users can see how close they are to the wanted classification. This improves their awareness of how to best perform the mental task, and also functions are a motivator when they are close to the target.

Alertness is the other scale in which a difference was found. This alertness has to do with the state of mind of the user after they played the game. The fact that they felt less alert after performing imagined movement is explainable. Imaginary movement requires more concentration and is a less natural action to perform. Doing something you do everyday does not tire you as much as doing something completely new. This was also reflected in the Fatigue scale, which scored slightly higher for imagined movement.

The generalizability over various demographic groups was good and there were no significant differences in performance. While there have been some anecdotal findings that women would be better in communicating through a BCI, results show no significant differences between men and women. Data also did not show any differences between left and right handed people. While the gathered data does not provide a clear view on how age is related to performance in the game, one might hypothesize that imagined movement is a skill of young children who mimic movements of others. A child sees someone performing a certain movement that can be of advantage to the child, for example grabbing something, they then try to perform it themselves. This probably is a skill that fades over time when a person gets older. While at a higher age humans are still able to mimic movements, it takes more time to learn them. This is possibly a ground for older people not performing well at imagined movement in general. Altough it was made clear to every subject what kind of movement they had to imagine and how they could do it, some people still reported that they struggled with the concept of imagining a movement.

Future work could include research into the different ways of imagining movement. As McFarland et al. (2000) already explain: when given the instruction to imagine a movement, most people will try to sense the movement. Other kinds of imagination (e.g., visualizing the movement) might activate different cortical areas. Some users might even prefer to visualize a movement if they find it more natural or less tiring. Evaluating the performance and user experience of these different tasks are a valuable addition.

The developed questionnaire seems to be a instrument that can aid us in evaluating differences in user experience between different modalities for BCI, but it might also be of interest for evaluation of BCI games other than BrainBasher. Then further research on the validity and generalizability of the questionnaire is needed.

Although the game works in an online manner and the classification algorithm is fast enough to be computed real-time, there always is an inherent delay in feedback. This is due to the fact that the classification algorithm needs a measurement of EEG data of a few seconds. Currently this measurement is two seconds. The consequence is that users get feedback of what they did with a a delay of up to two seconds. This delay sometimes leads to confusion and a lower positive affect towards the system. Due to differences in brain signals and quality of recordings, it is possible that some users were able to produce a recognizable brain action faster (with less delay) than other users regardless of the fixed two seconds window. For example, if the CSP filters are able to separate the relevant signals better for one subject than an other, less noise is present in the two seconds window, and the classifier can be relatively certain about the class of the performed brain action even if the signal is only present in the last fragment of the classification window. In the presence of more noise, a larger part of the classification window needs to contain the signal for a positive detection, resulting in higher response times. The current problem that response times can be higher than with ordinary kinds of interfaces also call for inovative game design. If the game is designed for usage with a BCI, the user should still be able to get immersed into the game, instead of being distracted by the slower response of the system. On the other hand, a BCI can provide new kinds of games, using the users mental state (e.g., relaxation level, emotions) as a part of the game itself and in such a way create an even more immersive world than is possible using a mere keyboard and mouse (Tan & Nijholt, 2010).

Future research might include shortening the response time of the underlying system of the game and finding out what this does for acceptance of and positive affection towards the BCI. Other BCI for movement, such as the LRP could also be explored to reduce the response delay. Preliminary research by Reuderink et al. (2010) indicates that the LRP of actual movements is already recognizable before a button press can be detected. Furthermore, the LRP can still be recognized reliably at rates of two strokes per second. This last property would make BCIs usable in fast paced games, which is something that traditional BCIs do not allow for.

Because of the similarities in brain activity between actual and imagined movement and the somewhat lacking of intuitivity for imagined movement one might suggest using actual movement as a training for using imagined movement. The user of the BCI can get accustomed to using movements for communications and at the same time trying to imagine the movement. With the acquired data from the actual movement, the imagined movement could be classified.

ACKNOWLEDGMENT

The authors gratefully acknowledge the support of the BrainGain Smart Mix Programme of the Dutch Ministry of Economic Affairs and the Dutch Ministry of Education, Culture, and Science. We would also like to thank all the people who were willing to submit precious time to being a test subject for our experiments.

REFERENCES

Brown, B. W. Jr. (1980). The crossover experiment for clinical trials. *Biometrics*, *36*(1), 69–79. doi:10.2307/2530496

Catell, R. B., & Vogelmann, S. (1977). A comprehensive trial of the scree and Kg criteria for determining the number of factors. *Multivariate Behavioral Research*, *12*(3), 289–325. doi:10.1207/s15327906mbr1203_2

Cortina, J. (1993). What is coefficient Alpha? an examination of theory and applications. *The Journal of Applied Psychology*, *78*(1), 98–104. doi:10.1037/0021-9010.78.1.98

Cronbach, L. (1951). Coefficient alpha and the internal structure of tests. *Psychometrika*, *16*(3), 297–334. doi:10.1007/BF02310555

Graimann, B., Allison, B., & Gräser, A. (2007). New applications for non-invasive brain-computer interfaces and the need for engaging training environments. In *Proceedings of the BRAINPLAY 07 BCI and Games Workshop at ACE*.

IJsselsteijn, W., de Kort, Y., Poels, K., Jurgelionis, A., & Bellotti, F. (2007). Characterising and Measuring User Experiences in Digital Games. In *Proceedings of the International Conference on Advances in Computer Entertainment Technology*.

Jeannerod, M. (1994). The representing brain neural correlates of motor intention and imagery. *The Behavioral and Brain Sciences*, *17*, 187–245. doi:10.1017/S0140525X00034026

Kayagil, T. A., Bai, O., Lin, P., Furlani, S., Vorbach, S., & Hallett, M. (2007). Binary EEG control for two-dimensional cursor movement: An online approach. In *Proceedings of the IEEE/ICME International Conference on Complex Medical Engineering* (pp. 1542-1545).

Koles, Z. J. (1991). The quantitative extraction and topographic mapping of the abnormal components in the clinical EEG. *Electroencephalography and Clinical Neurophysiology*, *79*(6), 440–447. doi:10.1016/0013-4694(91)90163-X

Kornhuber, H., & Deecke, L. (1965). Hirnpotential¨anderungen bei Willk¨urbewegungen und passiven Bewegungen des Menschen: Bereitschaftspotential und reafferente Potentiale. *Pfl¨ugers Archiv European Journal of Physiology*, *284*(1), 1–17. doi:10.1007/BF00412364

Krauledat, M., Dornhege, G., Blankertz, B., Losch, F., Curio, G., & M¨uller, K.-R. (2004). Improving speed and accuracy of braincomputer interfaces using readiness potential features. In *Proceedings of the 26th Annual International Conference of the IEEE EMBS* (Vol. 26, pp. 4511-4515).

Lawley, D. N., & Maxwell, A. E. (1962). Factor Analysis as a Statistical Method. *Journal of the Royal Statistical Society. Series D*, *12*(3), 209–229.

Lecuyer, A., Lotte, F., Reilly, R., Leeb, R., Hirose, M., & Slater, M. (2008). Brain-computer interfaces, virtual reality, and videogames. *Computer*, *41*(10), 66–72. doi:10.1109/MC.2008.410

Leeb, R., Keinrath, C., Friedman, D., Guger, C., Neuper, C., Garau, M., et al. (2005). Walking from thoughts: Not the muscles are crucial but the brain waves! In *Proceedings of the 8th Annual International Workshop on Presence* (pp. 25-32).

Leeb, R., Lee, F., Keinrath, C., Scherer, R., Bischof, H., & Pfurtscheller, G. (2007). Brain-Computer Communication: Motivation, Aim, and Impact of Exploring a Virtual Apartment. *IEEE Transactions on Neural Systems and Rehabilitation Engineering*, *15*(4), 473–482. doi:10.1109/TNSRE.2007.906956

Ludwig, K. A., Miriani, R. M., Langhals, N. B., Joseph, M. D., Anderson, D. J., & Kipke, D. R. (2009). Using a Common Average Reference to Improve Cortical Neuron Recordings From Microelectrode Arrays. *Journal of Neurophysiology*, *101*(3), 1679–1689. doi:10.1152/jn.90989.2008

McFarland, D., Miner, L., Vaughan, T., & Wolpaw, J. (2000). Mu and Beta Rhythm Topographies During Motor Imagery and Actual Movements. *Brain Topography*, *12*(3), 177–186. doi:10.1023/A:1023437823106

Nijholt, A., Tan, D., Allison, B., Milan, J., & Graimann, B. (2008a). Brain-computer interfaces for HCI and games. In *Proceedings of the CHI '08 extended abstracts on Human factors in computing systems* (pp. 3925-3928). New York: ACM.

Nijholt, A., Tan, D., Pfurtscheller, G., Brunner, C., Millán, J., & Allison, B. (2008b). Brain-Computer Interfacing for Intelligent Systems. *IEEE Intelligent Systems*, *23*(3), 72–79. doi:10.1109/MIS.2008.41

Oude Bos, D., & Reuderink, B. (2008). Brainbasher: a BCI game. In P. Markopoulos, J. Hoonhout, I. Soute, & J. Read (Eds.), *Proceedings of the International Conference on Fun and Games 2008*, Eindhoven, The Netherlands (pp. 36-39).

Pfurtscheller, G. (2001). Functional brain imaging based on ERD/ERS. *Vision Research*, *41*(10-11), 1257–1260. doi:10.1016/S0042-6989(00)00235-2

Pineda, J. A., Silverman, D. S., Vankov, A., & Hestenes, J. (2003). Learning to control brain rhythms: making a brain-computer interface possible. *IEEE Transactions on Neural Systems and Rehabilitation Engineering*, *11*(2), 181–184. doi:10.1109/TNSRE.2003.814445

Reuderink, B., Poel, M., & Nijholt, A. (2010). *The impact of loss of control on the performance of a movement BCI.*

Sannelli, C., Braun, M., Tangermann, M., & Müller, K.-R. (2008). Estimating noise and dimensionality in BCI data sets: Towards BCI illiteracy comprehension. In *Proceedings of the 4th International Brain-Computer Interface Workshop and Training Course 2008*.

Shibasaki, H., & Hallett, M. (2006). What is the bereitschaftspotential? *Clinical Neurophysiology*, *117*, 2341–2356. doi:10.1016/j.clinph.2006.04.025

Tan, D., & Nijholt, N. (2010). *Brain-Computer Interfaces. Applying our Minds to Human-Computer Interaction*. New York: Springer Verlag.

Wolpaw, J. R., Birbaumer, N., McFarland, D. J., Pfurtscheller, G., & Vaughan, T. M. (2002). Braincomputer interfaces for communication and control. *Clinical Neurophysiology*, *113*, 767–791. doi:10.1016/S1388-2457(02)00057-3

This work was previously published in International Journal of Gaming and Computer-Mediated Simulations, Volume 2, Issue 4, edited by Richard E. Ferdig, pp. 33-47, copyright 2010 by IGI Publishing (an imprint of IGI Global).

Chapter 18
Towards Games for Knowledge Acquisition and Modeling

Stijn Hoppenbrouwers
Radboud University Nijmegen, The Netherlands

Bart Schotten
Radboud University Nijmegen, The Netherlands

Peter Lucas
Radboud University Nijmegen, The Netherlands

ABSTRACT

Many model-based methods in AI require formal representation of knowledge as input. For the acquisition of highly structured, domain-specific knowledge, machine learning techniques still fall short, and knowledge elicitation and modelling is then the standard. However, obtaining formal models from informants who have few or no formal skills is a non-trivial aspect of knowledge acquisition, which can be viewed as an instance of the well-known "knowledge acquisition bottleneck". Based on the authors' work in conceptual modelling and method engineering, this paper casts methods for knowledge modelling in the framework of games. The resulting games-for-modelling approach is illustrated by a first prototype of such a game. The authors' long-term goal is to lower the threshold for formal knowledge acquisition and modelling.

INTRODUCTION

In this paper we propose and illustrate an approach to knowledge acquisition and formalisation that does not primarily address the formal structures to be delivered, but rather the *process* of conceptualization and modelling, yielding formal models. We discuss the general idea of games-for-modelling,

and also present an initial prototype as an example and basic proof of concept.

Formal knowledge models of some sort are essential in AI and related fields, not just as part of the theoretical foundations of the fields, but also for application: computation based on knowledge structures inherently demands some artefacts, which may vary from "lightweight formalisations" (e.g., diagrams or strictly structured text) to expressions with formal semantics. Focus in

DOI: 10.4018/978-1-4666-0029-4.ch018

most cases (in research as well as practice) is on the syntax and semantics of the formal artefacts, and on associated reasoning methods to apply the artefacts to problems. Obtaining such formal models is nowadays tackled in AI by using some knowledge acquisition (KA) and modelling method, such as CommonKADS, which suggests a step-wise approach, starting with informal, conceptual representations and methods and refining these until a formal model is obtained (Schreiber et al., 1999). Although such methods were initially proposed as solutions to the *Knowledge-Acquisition Bottleneck* (KAB), experience shows that this KAB is as real as it was more than two decades ago when it was first mentioned (Hayes-Roth, Waterman, & Lenat, 1983). The enormous increase in the volume of knowledge discovery from data and machine learning research during the last decade, which was largely motivated by the appeal of *automatic* knowledge acquisition from data (Berthold & Hand, 1999), is evidence that the KAB is still prominent today.

Within our current focus, the most urgent KAB aspects are the following:

- It is hard to make knowledge explicit, and even harder to formalise it;
- The domain experts required for this job are usually not available for lengthy involvement in KA activities, nor do they possess the required modelling and formalisation skills;
- The expert knowledge engineers/modellers that could be hired to do the modelling job are few and expensive. Breaking the KAB by structurally employing expert modellers will only work in the most urgent of cases, covered by unusually large allocation of resources.

Many of the promises of AI concern a global user community of organisations and citizens that will never have access to expensive knowledge engineering experts. This will simply prevent many of the promises with respect to the wide availability of knowledge-based AI solutions from being fulfilled and, furthermore, it casts doubts on the future of enterprises like the semantic web.

The practical problem of the KAB presents us with challenges that are important and interesting enough to warrant focused academic efforts for understanding and alleviating the problem. As acknowledged by Wagner (Wagner, 2006), in fields like software engineering, information system engineering, and enterprise engineering, we are also confronted with KAB-like problems on a large scale, and consequently solutions are actively sought there, too.

In our research we work towards development of alternatives for existing knowledge acquisition and modelling methods. One idea we are exploring is to look at formal knowledge modelling activities as *games* (or, more modestly put, 'game-like procedures'), forcing ourselves to look at contextualised, operational modelling in which human factors are inevitably included. Because the way in which we employ games for formal knowledge modelling involves human-computer interactions (HCI), these games-for-modelling systems can best be tested using HCI-like evaluation methods, including existing methods specifically aimed at game evaluation. This combination, games-for-modelling and exploitation of HCI methods for evaluation, is, to the best of our knowledge, new to AI.

After providing an overview of related work, we will argue in favour of this approach, explain how methods can be viewed and designed as games, and provide an example of such a game, in the form of a first prototype. The paper is rounded off with conclusions of what has been achieved so far, and we offer a sketch of envisioned future work.

RELATED WORK

We need to be clear about two distinct categories in Knowledge Acquisition (KA): *automated* and *manual*. The first category uses knowledge discovery from data and machine learning techniques to derive models (Berthold & Hand, 1999), the second depends on the construction of models by hand (aided by tools), by individuals or teams. Although there are certainly many situations where knowledge discovery from data and machine learning can be very useful, the fact must be faced that learning technology will not resolve the KAB for cases in which highly domain specific knowledge (ultimately kept in individuals' minds) has to be made explicit and formalised.

Early work on Knowledge Acquisition by Newell and Simon mainly focused on elicitation of verbal data collected from domain experts in the act of solving problems, called *think-aloud protocols* (Newell & Simon, 1972). Useful knowledge was subsequently extracted from the protocols, using a technique called *protocol analysis*. Although the intention of protocol analysis was to obtain representations that could be manipulated by a computer, little attention was given to the actual semantics of the representations. The innovation by Newell and Simon was mainly to introduce techniques to computer science that were originally developed in the area of psychology in an attempt to close the gap between computers and humans.

As mentioned above, in knowledge engineering, perhaps the foremost comprehensive method is CommonKADS (Schreiber et al., 1999), though many more exist. The essential idea is to work from informal, yet conceptually rich, models towards more formal models (using for example predicate logic), using a selection from a given set of *problem solving methods*. Problem solving methods can be best seen as generic methods that are aimed at solving particular tasks, such as diagnosis. A problem solving method can be instantiated for a particular domain, and the result then is a system that is able is to solve the task for a particular problem in the domain. Despite the huge number of people years that were invested in CommonKADS projects, only a limited collection of problem-solving methods is now offered by the CommonKADS methodology. The researchers who were originally involved in the development of CommonKADS are no longer active in this area, and the methodology has never become the industry standard of knowledge acquisition and modelling. Today, knowledge modelling in AI is often called 'ontology building'; partly because of greater emphasis on the modelling of descriptive knowledge, using so-called description logics, than on problem solving (Cristani & Cruel, 2005).

Roughly similar approaches are widely used in system development, e.g., RUP (Kruchten, 2000), typically in combination with the UML (Booch, Rumbaugh, & Jacobson, 1998). They all make use of roughly defined, iterative phases in the modelling process, from exploration and informal sketching to formalization and implementation; also, they all, to a stronger or lesser degree, suggest or prescribe specific artefacts (descriptions, models) for particular phases and purposes, often involving strong structuring and/or specific modelling languages.

Useful as all this is (though the number and diversity of specific modelling languages is rampant), such deliverable-oriented textbook methods only provide limited help for non-expert modellers in the actual execution of their modelling tasks; they still require considerable study and above all practice to be mastered. The availability of tools provides some help, but currently such tools are usually highly technical model editors that require in-depth technical knowledge and advanced abstraction skills, and do not actively assist in the act of conceptualisation and formalization of the models. In other words, they support *model-centric modelling* instead of *modeller-centric modelling*.

An additional problem with domain specific, manual KA is posed by the social context of domain specific knowledge modelling, which in many cases calls for intensive negotiation and validation of models by heterogeneous teams of stakeholders. In line with this, there is increasing interest in approaches for *collaborative modelling* (Knock & Rittgen, 2009; Rittgen, 2009). Related issues are on the agenda in context of the Web 2.0 effort, and also in ontology engineering (Diaz, Baldo, & Canals, 2006).

In (Wagner, 2006; Hoppenbrouwers, Proper, & van der Weide, 2005; Veldhuijzen van Zanten, Hoppenbrouwers, & Proper, 2004), a conversation-based approach to knowledge modelling is suggested; in this vein, actual systems for modelling support have been created and studied, e.g., Wiki-based approaches (Wagner, 2006) and a negotiation-based approach (Rittgen, 2009), the latter of which is most closely related to our own work, and in fact is an exception in that it does focus on the (conversational) process of modelling, or rather on supporting it. Yet it still positions model editing (UML) as a central activity, assuming basic, diagram-oriented modelling skills to be available in the participants.

In view of the considerable challenge posed by the KAB, and focusing on manual KA, we find a dissatisfying lack of interest in issues that prevent real-life, operational modelling from becoming successful. In addition to focusing on representational issues (still the mainstream topic in literature on modelling), we believe that the situated act of modelling itself warrants study (starting from initial, sketchy conceptualization and moving on to actual formalization), including any relevant human factors involved. We may, for example, look at things like usability/playability, learnability, even enjoyability, but also, of course, at effectiveness and efficiency.

WHY GAMES?

Let us briefly explain what we mean by the *game metaphor*. People often refer to activities, tasks, or challenges (even complex, elaborate ones) as games, e.g., "the game of politics", "the game we play in this firm", "that sort of practice is not our game". At times, this referential metaphor is extended into actual identification or introduction of game aspects: competition, scores, declaration of winners/losers, rules, and so on. It seems justified, even fruitful, to use the game metaphor as well as actual game design as instruments in the study and development of tools for modelling support: games for modelling. This is in line with the newly established and flourishing field of 'Serious Gaming', prominently including management games (Elgood, 1993). We will now elaborate on our proposal to apply the game metaphor to thinking about modeller-oriented support systems for knowledge modelling.

In (Hoppenbrouwers, van Bommel, & Järvinen, 2008), a number of arguments are developed in favour of approaching the creation of operational methods/tools/procedures for modelling as game design. We briefly list the main arguments below:

Make formal modelling available to non-modellers As discussed, if the use of AI based on domain-specific models is to really take off, large scale and low-threshold formal modelling *will* be required. An obvious but non-trivial way to proceed is to create software applications that make creation of required models as painless and efficient as possible: bring lightweight formal modelling to the masses through the virtual world emerging on the internet, and by shaping such applications as games or game-like procedures.

Improve motivation of modellers In the wake of (Von Ahn, 2006), who managed to harness the creative energies of great numbers of on-line game players to perform "human computing", we believe it would be very helpful from both a methodological and a productivity point of view to make modelling more attractive (challenging, enjoyable), and thereby boost modelling in order to answer the needs and help bring AI to its full utilitarian potential. We believe games are a highly promising way of doing so.

Improve quality of models More in line with common objectives in the field of knowledge modelling, a gaming setup may help improve the quality of the products of modelling, both *textual* (the models as such) and *contextual* (knowledge, understanding, agreement etc. across communities involved with models and modelling). Useful strategies for modelling can be built into the game design (e.g., shaped as sub-games, tasks, challenges) or be left to the participants (the players' strategies), as best fits the situation. Work in the open source community at least suggests that collaborative activities may result in high quality outcome.

Tooling: virtual environments for collaborative modelling The relation between digital tools/environments for modelling and digital games is obvious. Video games are highly advanced interactive systems. Completely virtual work environments may not be accepted on a large scale yet, but completely virtual multi-player games most certainly are. It is conceivable that the knowledge modelling tools and environments of the future shall feature serious game characteristics.

Apart from the above arguments that focus on the support of actual, operational modelling, there is one that concerns research and development methodology with respect to games for modelling:

Research and development approach: improving performance by improving game design The game metaphor as well as the actual application of game design theoretical concepts will help *focus on the relevant research questions* concerning model oriented interaction systems and duly constrained modelling. Games can be tried and tested on various audiences, providing ample and well-structured data on interactions and results, and thus offer an empirical hold on modelling processes that otherwise would be much harder to obtain in large volumes. This will enable modelling-oriented research using evaluative approaches from AI and HCI.

GAMES EMBODYING METHODS

For the link between methods (viewed by us as interactive systems for modelling support) and games-for-modelling, we turn to Game Design Theory. Järvinen (Hoppenbrouwers, van Bommel,

& Järvinen, 2008) provides clear concepts for analyzing and designing games that help greatly in performing game design (and therefore also aid method and tool engineering in a gaming context). Below we list generic game elements according to Järvinen, and add the equivalent thereof for the construction of methods.

1. **Components**: objects that the player is able to manipulate and possess in the course of the game. In methods this corresponds to any objects manipulated in the modelling process, typically brief fragments of natural language text (even individual terms) and elements of diagrams, including instantiations of modelling concepts. These are in fact the items now manipulated by means of editors; however, we believe that the explicit incorporation of more fine-grained *intermediary deliverables* in the process (related to taking smaller steps in conceptualization and formalization) will add to the number of different game components.

2. **Rules**: constraints that cover each individual possibility and constraint that a game has to offer for its players, including *set goals* and *procedures*. Such constraints restrict the liberty of action of the modeller; one could say the rules constitute the method.

3. **Environment**: the stage for game play. For example: a board, a field, or a virtual environment in a digital game. In operational methods, this can range from a meeting room to a whiteboard to a digital editor; in a completely digital (virtual) setting, interactive and possibly collaborative tools will be involved. Editor-like environments may be used, but beyond these, series of assignments may also be executed in less technical settings resembling virtual game boards or even 3D worlds.

4. **Game mechanics**: describe possible means with which the player can interact with game elements as she is trying to influence game

285

states in order to complete a series of goals. For example: throwing in basketball, hitting in tennis; in more verbal games (and more relevant to our sort of gaming), proposing, asking, rejecting, and so on. The link with interaction mechanisms in operational modelling is obvious, but do note that game mechanics are not at all part of traditional (textbook) methods. In a conversation-oriented approach, the mechanisms associated with "verbal games" apply quite directly.

5.   **Theme**: game theme is the subject matter that is used in contextualizing the rule set and its game elements to other meanings than those which the game system as an information system requires. For example: real-estate market in Monopoly, or a fictional context, or a historical event. For methods, setting themes is quite unusual so far (except for the actual, real modelling context as such). An inspiring yet rather radical idea for a theme would be, for example, *performing magic*, since this metaphorically corresponds nicely to applied knowledge modelling: "in order to get something (some service, information, prediction, and so on) you have to describe something precisely, conforming to procedures that the magic practice demands (ritual) and using the appropriate magical language."

6.   **Information**: what the system and players need to know; the game state communicated. For example, a scoreboard, or a screen display, and/or component attributes such as value or number. In operational models, this can be the state of the model and procedural knowledge, but also feedback to the modellers (players) on the model (model checking, AI-based analyses) and the modelling process (status, progress, results, efficiency, etc.).

7.   **Interface**: the tools to access game elements via game mechanics when direct (i.e., physical) access to game objects is impossible.

For example, game pads, dance mats, mouse, steering wheels, etc. Though in operational modelling, rather standard games/systems interfacing is obvious, more innovative forms of interfacing may be worthwhile considering (e.g., 3D physical interfacing ('data gloves') or 'surface computing').

8.   **Player(s)**: the human factor in the game; their behaviour, mood, abilities and skills, relationship with games, game tastes. In modelling, this of course applies to modellers or other participants, and their competencies, interests, expertise, and preferences. Interestingly, player characteristics may be linked to specific roles, expertise, concerns, and preferences of participants (stakeholders) in the modelling process.

9.   **Context**: the physical location of the game, the time, players' personal histories, and other informal, external aspects to the game system that possibly affect the experience of playing the game. In modelling, this refers to the situational aspects of a particular modelling task and session.

At least the following elements are minimally required to design a game (constituting a working *definition*):

a)   **components** complemented with **constraints** governing their behaviour,

b)   an **information structure** to store the game states and component attributes and relations,

c)   at least one **game mechanic** to give players something to do, and

d)   a **goal** that the mechanics are designed to help completing, combined with **end or victory conditions**.

Goal setting is a key aspect of rule setting in games. In line with this, designing interactive games for modelling can be fruitfully driven by *goals of modelling*. This concerns both *utility goals* (i.e., what the model/modelling is useful for) and *modelling goals* (i.e., sub-goals pertaining to details of the modelling process as such).

The typical *utility* goals are system analysis and understanding, system simulation, and system development (including automated generation), but they also include organisational and individual learning and consensus building; ultimately, they relate to typical strategic business goals involving investment and some sort of gain (commercial or otherwise). This aspect is too often ignored when academics get involved in actual application of KA.

For an overview of key *modelling* goals we refer to (van Bommel, Hoppenbrouwers, Proper, & Roelofs, 2008). The chief goals are:

- **Creation goals**: which items (documents, objects, conceptualizations) are to be delivered when playing the game (van Bommel, Hoppenbrouwers, Proper, & Roelofs, 2008);
- **Grammar goals**: which language rules (syntax, vocabulary, possibly also semantics) does the player need to comply to;
- **Validation goals**: what sort of agreements, about which items, and between whom, is required in the game.

A number of sub-goals can be distinguished underneath the main goals, like argumentation goals, sense making goals, proof goals, abstraction goals, and so on.

Goals, sub-goals, and combinations of goals can be set for concrete modelling sessions or activities, involving one or more participants. *End goals* may be worked towards via *intermediary goals*. Strategies and techniques can be selected and deployed to achieve specific goals for concrete situations (van Bommel, Hoppenbrouwers, Proper, & Roelofs, 2008), in line with goals set but also with resources available and capacities and attitudes of participants. Once clear goals are set, and made more concrete by means of the definition of (a hierarchy of) combined assignments, challenges, etc., we can move towards actual game design. Importantly, the assignments given to the players need not overtly reflect the utility goals or even the modelling goals that the game designers have in mind. Any assignment that appropriately focuses, guides, and stimulates the player(s) will do. In fact, creative invention of (combinations of) appropriate assignments is key to successful game design.

This brings us to an issue that is possibly the one farthest removed from classical thinking about modelling: motivation. In the gaming world (both academic and industrial), much purposeful thought has gone into ways of making games captivating (Salen & Zimmerman, 2003). Indeed, game designers have now become so good at this that severe game addiction is sometimes the result. If we allow ourselves to run with the devil for at least a few yards, we might learn something about how to make dull or hard tasks more pleasantly challenging, more easily learnable and doable, and generally more effective. Perhaps modelling does not always have to be *great fun*, but we may at least succeed in making it *less boring* or *more positively challenging* for an audience not intrinsically motivated by the challenges of creating good formal models. The game design approach to the support of modelling thus creates opportunities for *designing motivation*.

GUIDING CONCEPTUALIZATION

Contrary to what is often assumed, knowledge modelling is not only a matter of translating informal into formal language (Hoppenbrouwers, 2008). Clearly, some creation of (details of) knowledge will often also be involved. Furthermore, formalization requires rational, 'clean' construction of representations according to utilitarian rather than linguistic/associative principles. It entails rationally governed construction (engineering) of conceptual structures conforming to conceptual patterns dictated by some chosen formalism. Such rational construction needs to take place before actual, final formal representations are produced, and possibly even independently of a specific formal syntax and semantics. Skilled formalists can perform such analysis and construction implicitly, and thus can produce formal representations (though perhaps sketchy ones) as an immediate product. Laymen need a much gentler, stepwise form of guiding and structuring.

If procedures for achieving this can be successfully created, lightweight formalization can be achieved without confronting a player with any form of mathematics, or even semi-formal diagrams. Models are then not elicited directly, but indirectly. After a guided conversation in which specific knowledge descriptions are elicited stepwise, conform rational principles governed by well-defined goals for modelling, it should be possible to automatically derive formal representations based on structured fragments of conceptualisations (small natural language or simple visualizations), and the strictly governed

relations between them. Abstraction then is a matter of filtering out the relevant concepts at type and instance level.

From a method perspective this will force us to look at "pre-formal", *intermediary* products that may include information that does not belong in the end product, but which is used to *derive* the end product (formal model) by means of reasonably basic reasoning.

For example, as illustrated in the middle column of Figure 1, a Business Process Model in the standard notation BPMN (Business Process Modelling Notation (Object management Group, 2006)) typically shows an ordering of activities, e.g., activities D and E must be completed before activity F can be started. However, the reason why this is the case is that D and E respectively produce entities n and o that are needed in F (resulting in what is technically called an "AND-join"). This is illustrated by the text in the leftmost and rightmost columns of Figure 1, in which these

Figure 1. Dependency information underlying a basic process model

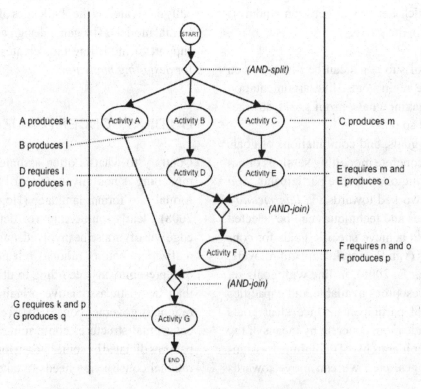

entities and dependencies are made explicit. However, such dependencies and entities are not made explicit in regular BPMN diagrams, even if they are crucial for creating a useful, 'good' one. As a consequence, the entities and dependencies involved are usually left implicit and exist only in the head of the modeller. Even if the objects in the process are made explicit, perhaps in another model, they are not explicitly used as a basis for deriving (or *accounting for*) AND-joins.

This idea inspired our prototype of a game-for-modelling (discussed below). Exploration of possibilities has only just begun.

A GAME PROTOTYPE

The game discussed in this section is the result of the MSc dissertation project of Bart Schotten (Information Science, Radboud University Nijmegen). We emphasize it is a very first, and therefore rather limited, attempt at developing a 'modeling wizard'. We do not claim the prototype to be directly useful for even the simplest of real-world (process) modelling tasks. We do, however, believe it has already taught us much about how to approach interactive systems for guided modeling. We will first provide an illustrated overview of a simple but typical course of gameplay using the prototype. Following our discussion in "Games Embodying Methods", we give a brief decomposed overview of the game design along the lines of Game Design Theory. The static pictures look very much like those one might expect from a regular graphical editor; the difference lies in the act of modelling as such; for this, a real demo or, even better, actual experience in playing the game would be required. Also note that the example presented is meant to explain the main game mechanics reflecting the rationale pattern presented in the previous section. It is a toy example that was also used in the tests for the initial, exploratory game round, but most assignments used for testing the game were more complex.

The external (utilitarian) purpose of the game is to get the player to describe a basic task accurately, in terms of its *steps* (which is the term the game uses for 'activities'). The game looks somewhat like a normal modelling tool, but provides more guidance for stepwise thinking and (most importantly) does not require abstract thinking about AND splits and joins: it merely inquires about what is needed for a step (i.e., *ingredients*), what items come out of it (i.e., *products*), and (optionally) what change is inflicted on some item in the course of the step (a *link*). The game-like properties of the procedure (please be aware of the fact that it is, after all, a methodical procedure dressed up as a game) are the following:

1) The game can only be finished if the player fulfils a minimal set of demands, because only then the required information can be derived;
2) The player gets immediate feedback on what she is doing, using graphics and sound; also, a score is calculated and made visible;
3) How long the player plays is reflected in the score, while the time is visibly ticking away, thus introducing mild time pressure;
4) The player is (hopefully) motivated or entertained by the setup and gameplay, besides being guided.

The player has the option of being shown extra (currently rather minimal) guiding and explanatory remarks, meant to help novice players understand the game and not miss some finer points. In the example pictures, we have excluded these (i.e., switched them off), except in the first illustration (Figure 2). In addition to the optional guidelines, hints are also shown on the bottom of the screen when the player moves his mouse over any object (standard). This is not visible in the figures.

At the beginning of the game the interface provides the player with only one button, allowing the player to create a new step (the order in which the steps are created is of no significance).

Figure 2. Creating a step

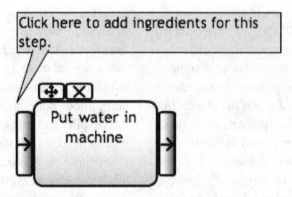

When a new step is created it appears as a rectangle that the player can drag around; the next thing to do is to give the step a name (Figure 2). A guideline for this is to describe the step in no more than four words.

Not visible in the illustration is the brief appearance of a green, animated number "10" drifting away from the activity symbol, indicating that 10 points have been scored by this action. There is also an accompanying sound.

Next, the player has to add "items needed" (*ingredients*) and "items created" (*products*) to the step. Each ingredient that is added to a step also shows up in a list in the top left of the screen (Figure 3). If required, items from this list can be dragged to any new step (re-use). This minimizes repetitive typing, provides a clear overview of

items introduced so far, and encourages consistent use of terminology.

Next, clicking on a small bubble to the right of an ingredient and then clicking on a bubble next to a product of the same step connects the ingredient with the product; again there is a (rather funny and appropriate) sound effect. This creates a "link" (Figure 4). A link creates a conceptual space in which to fit extra information about what happens to an ingredient during the step. This is the most crucial aspect of eliciting the dependencies that feed the derivation of AND-splits and joins.

As a conceptual aid, the player may describe the change by filling in the pattern "this ingredient is being..." The common grammatical trick is that the player provides a verb that can also be

Figure 3. Adding needed and created items

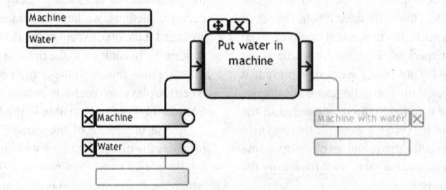

Figure 4. Adding a state change attribute

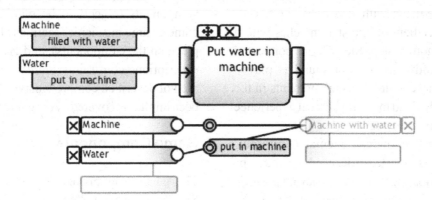

used as an adjective, and therefore as an attribute of the item (describing a relevant state of it): a *precondition* (though this term is not used in communication with the player). This is useful because if the item is also used in another step, the game will recognize that the item has certain attributes, and provides the player with the simple option to select one or more existing attributes as relevant to the step (illustrated as part of Figure 5, "filter::put in machine").

Another option for describing a link (and its underlying precondition) is to combine two ingredients in a pattern known from data modelling: ingredient A [with ingredient B] and ingredient B [in ingredient A]. An extra (advanced) option the player has here is to graphically connect the links, which automatically renders this precondition description pattern (not illustrated).

When the player has described multiple steps this way, the game derives the connections between the steps. Each step has a set of ingredients with

Figure 5. A connection is found

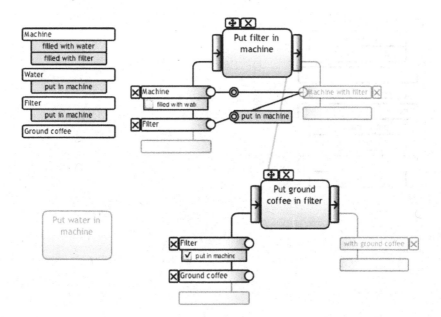

possible preconditions and a set of products as well as ingredients with added preconditions. When an ingredient of one step matches with a product of another step, the two are connected (Figure 5), and a triumphant sound is played (taDAA!). These main 'scoring' moments in the game attestedly lead to a mild but real experience of satisfaction in the player.

Optionally, the game can automatically visualize the derived suggested order of connected steps by moving ('floating') them to a relevant position when they are not manipulated by the player. However, note that this does not amount to the visualization of flow as in an actual flow chart. A flow chart is derived from the above diagram later (outside the game as such).

The player can only finish the game when all the steps she created are connected to at least one other step, but can carry on until the model is complete; this is up to the player to decide (Figure 6). This is the chief *minimal end condition* of the game (it declares when the game is allowed to end, not when the game has to end; this is a common feature of many known end conditions).

We will now briefly describe the main game components (objects to be manipulated in the game), game mechanics (actions allowed to take place on the components), and game rules (goal descriptions, constraints, score system). The rules are not described comprehensively, as they have been implicitly covered by the gameplay overview.

Game Components

The game components are: Task Name field, Step Symbol with Step Description, Ingredient boxes and Precondition Ticks, Product Boxes, Link Circles and Boxes, and Item/precondition List Boxes.

Game Mechanics

First, there are game mechanics for filling in various textual fields: Step Name, Step Description, Ingredients, Products, Link Descriptions. There are also non-textual mechanics: Creating Steps, adding and deleting Ingredients/Products, dragging Item List Boxes to Ingredient or Product

Figure 6. Finished

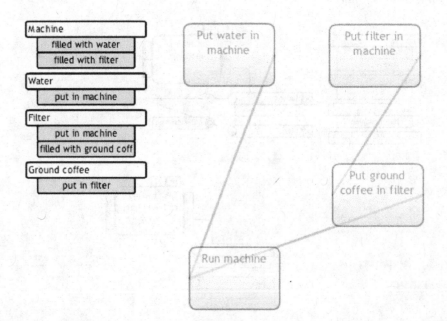

Boxes, ticking Preconditions, and linking Ingredients with Products.

Layout functions are left out here since they are auxiliary to actual gameplay. They belong to the game interface, which we further disregard here (but see the illustrations for a visual impression).

Game Rules: Goals, Assignments; End Condition

The (internal) goal of the game is to score points by creating a stepwise description of some task, within possibilities and rules as embedded in and constrained by the interface. The core conceptual goal is to identify and link dependencies between products and ingredients of steps. Mandatory result: two interconnected steps (minimal end condition), implying at least one product matching one ingredient, so the game cannot be ended without some ingredients and products being entered. Importantly, the absolute end condition is that the player herself "calls it quits" when the model is finished (complete). The game as such does therefore not provide means to decide when the game is finished, only when it is not. Note that this is not unheard of in the Gaming world: many modern role playing video games can in principle be played *ad infinitum*.

Game Rules: Score System

The scores are calculated as follows:

- 100 points for each step.
- 100 points for each connection between two steps.
- 10 points for each ingredient, product or link.

Deleting a step leads to a reduction of the score with 100 points. The final score is the sum of the score so far, minus half a point for every second played. However, the amount of points deducted based on the elapsed time can never be more than half of the amount of points scored.

After the Game: Deriving a BMPN Diagram

Besides the game as such, we also implemented a simple algorithm (Figure 7) for deriving a BPMN-like structure from the information gathered. Instead of generating an actual diagram (Figure 8), we decided that for this prototype an XML-based format, XPDL (Workflow Management Coalition, 2008) would suffice. A number of existing process modelling tools can generate diagrams based on an XPDL file.

GAME DEVELOPMENT AND EVALUATION

The development process was performed within the design science paradigm (Hevner, Ram, March, & Park, 2004), in a standard development cycle involving design, implementation, testing and improving the design. Testing was not always done extensively in the initial development stages, but as the game evolved from little more than a list of rules to a digital, more graphical game, more systematic evaluation took place.

We initially tried to stay away from automating the game, focusing instead on a pen and paper approach ("board game"). This gave us the chance to think through the basic setup and rules, without getting lost in details of implementation. However, the down sides of board gaming also became apparent soon. Playing and therefore testing the game proved to be a tedious experience for both the facilitator and the player, mostly because of active relations and dependencies between items, which had to be updated manually.

The first digital version of the game soon appeared, based on a standard spreadsheet implementation, which at least took the task of calculating the score out of the hands of the facilitator, and

Figure 7. Algorithm to find dependencies between step

```
#Start by finding the sets of input and output items
  for each step:

  for each ingredient
      for each precondition
      if precondition is selected
        add "precondition_ingredient" to input set
      if no preconditions are selected
        add "ingredient" to input set

  for each product
    if product is relevant
        add "product" to output set
    for each link
      if link is not empty
        add "link_ingredient" to output set

  # Whether a product is "relevant" (not overwritten by
  # a link and not present as an ingredient) is known
  # beforehand. A link always has a reference to its
  # corresponding ingredient and product.

  # Next, find the connections between the steps

  for each step x, y
    if x not equal to y
    and  input x that equals output y
      step x depends on step y
```

Figure 8. Generated BPMN Diagram (implemented only as XPDL)

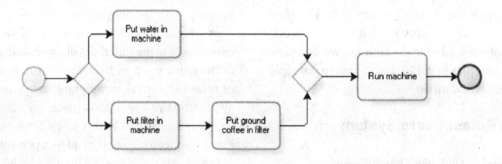

also made the entering of information by the player much easier. This allowed us to perform the first (successful) tests with 'outsiders' (i.e., players other than ourselves), proving that the game system was viable in principle, and that players could at least get through the game.

It became increasingly clear to us at this point that the expectations for and experience of playing an actual computer game rely not just on its rules, but also on flowing interaction, animation and sound. The choice was made to rebuild the game from scratch in Actionscript 3.0 (Adobe Labs, 2009), which, after a few iterations, led to the current prototype, which indeed started to 'feel more like a game'.

The game was elaborately tested on ten players: five with little to no prior process modelling experience, and five players with significant such experience. Each test player played the game three times. The first two times, simple, standard tasks were described: first, "making coffee" and second, "repairing a flat bicycle tyre". These are tasks everyone in the test population was familiar with, the second generally being a little more complicated than the first. The third game was played with a task of the player's own choice.

The players were given as little introduction as possible, forcing them to rely on the explanation provided by the game system. Admittedly, some subtle hints were sometimes given during the game if a player was really stuck. The players were asked to 'think aloud' as much as possible and to voice their possible frustrations or confusion. The attending game developer wrote down observations and interesting comments.

Afterwards the players were given a questionnaire, consisting of 25 statements (with five possible responses, ranging from "strongly disagree" to "strongly agree") and three open questions. The purpose of the questionnaire was to get an idea of the players' general experience. The statements hardly go into aspects unique to this particular game. Examples are: "I was satisfied with the result when I was done" and "I felt the score was a fair representation of how well I was doing". The statements are based on known properties of successful games, described in game design literature (Järvinen, 2008; Salen & Zimmerman, 2003; Desurvire, Caplan, & Toth, 2004) and on general usability heuristics (Nielsen, 2009).

We aimed for our observations and player comments, as well as the results of the questionnaire, to inform us about the differences between players with and without process modelling experience, with respect to success in and perception of the game. We also looked for differences in player perception when playing the game for the second or third time. In general, we were obviously also interested in whether or not the game was properly designed, and in particular in needs or wishes for further improvement. Note that our game was a very first attempt of creating a game-for-modelling, so finding out what does *not* work was expected to be a prominent part of our effort.

LESSONS LEARNED

Our observations suggest that there is indeed a noticeable difference between players with and without modelling experience. Despite our intentions to make the game playable for players with little or no expertise in modelling, most of those players found it hard to get started. It took them a while to understand what was meant by "task", "step", "ingredient" and "product". It was somewhat of a surprise to us that people by nature do not seem to make a sharp distinction even between actions and objects: sometimes they confuse the name of a step with its products, or describe substeps instead of ingredients.

Generally the game has a fairly hard time forcing people towards the 'correct' way of thinking, if they are not inclined that way already. For example, while the game is supposed to be played by listing steps, some people naturally start describing a task by listing ingredients. They even search for workarounds to do this, such as creating a 'superstep' encompassing the whole task, or describing a first step 'fetch all ingredients'.

Most experienced players fare better, quickly grasping the concept of the game, although sometimes after some initial confusion. In contrast with the less experienced players, they list ingredients only in their head, and then quickly switch to describing steps. Not surprisingly, experienced players are also more conscious of issues pertaining to abstraction.

When it comes to learning to play the game, the one thing we can clearly observe is the moment that players really 'get the hang of it'. Experienced players generally start working quickly and efficiently near the end of the first game or at the beginning of the second, while less experienced players are still struggling during the second game, and only pick up pace during the third. On the up side, given that playing the game does not take all that much time and effort, this could still be considered reasonably rapid learning.

A further interesting observation is that advanced functions of the game are generally not used. Players simply look for the easiest way to succeed in the game. Only one player used preconditions in his description. The results of the questionnaire suggest that experienced modellers were less satisfied with their results than inexperienced modellers. All players felt there was a trick to easily getting a high score, but still mostly thought that the score was a fair representation of how well they did. This suggests that the "trick" (whatever it was) was not actually used. This suggests that achieving a high the score system was not perceived as the main goal of playing the game, which is just as well (see "what went not so well" below).

There was very little variation in how easy players thought it was to get started (most answers were neutral), but surprisingly the experienced players were on average less satisfied with the amount of context-sensitive help.

The first open question of the questionnaire ("What was, according to you, the most important goal in the game?") turned out particularly interesting because it made visible the players' perception of the conflict between game-internal and game-external goals. The question was stated somewhat vaguely on purpose, and results in a variety of answers, such as: "scoring points" (pure game-internal), "finding out what the links between steps are" (basic game-external), and "judging how well people can model" (extreme external: concerning reflection on the modelling process).

What Went Well

It is encouraging that players generally do not take very long to learn how to play the game, and how to produce a reasonable task description. It seems that the main strength of the game is that it provides players with tangible feedback based on what they are doing, giving them at least a general sense of direction in the modelling process. This is an improvement over having to explain goals of modelling in abstract terms to people with little process modelling experience.

Aside from a few specific problems, the players seem to be satisfied with the current interface. By keeping things simple it manages to provide a good overview of the whole task description within one screen, and the feedback it provides by using graphics and sound seems to work well.

What Went Not So Well

We cannot honestly say that the current score system properly represents the various quality aspects of modelling. Players recognized that they did not really have to provide sensible input to get a good score. There is certainly much room for improvement here: the score system should directly encourage players to 'do the right thing'. Also, completeness is not covered by the scoring system, leaving it to intrinsic motivation of the player.

Two ways of improving this seem possible. First, we might introduce objective quality measurements using calculations or quality rules checking to determine a score. For some aspects, such as syntactic quality conditions (superfluous preconditions etc.), AI techniques may be deployed. Second, some form of third party validation of results might be introduced (a jury of sorts), reflecting common practice in modelling. A similar approach has been tested in collaborative modelling (Rittgen, 2009). This is in line with our plans to work towards multi-player games for modelling as suggested in (Hoppenbrouwers, 2008).

It is somewhat disappointing that even though the scope of the game was already limited, most players did not use the advanced functionality, in particular the preconditions. Players could be encouraged to do this by providing them with examples of the use of more complicated features, but we avoided such exemplification so far. Instead we used a wizard-like system to get players started, which is easy to understand, but is limited when things get more complicated. A tutorial-like series of assignments is being considered for the future.

A more specific problem we encountered concerns the use of links between ingredients and products within a step. If preconditions are not used, the purpose of these links is unclear to players and they consistently tend to forget about them. In fact, there are no clear rules concerning when links are required, so the confusion is entirely understandable. This is something that still requires attention. We have been considering ways of avoiding explicit linking altogether.

CONCLUSION AND FUTURE WORK

We discussed a Gaming approach to methods for knowledge elicitation and formalisation, in view of attempts to break, or at least widen, the Knowledge Acquisition Bottleneck. We discussed our perspective on the KAB, presented arguments for introducing the Game Metaphor, discussed the link between game design and operational method design.

We also demonstrated and discussed a very first prototype of a 'game for modelling' focusing on eliciting dependencies between products/ingredients of steps as the basis for an elementary process flow with AND-joins. This is in fact a very first implementation of the idea of a "modelling wizard". We described the game as such, and the process of developing and evaluating it.

We finished with the outcome of our evaluation, observations, and lessons learned. In particular we concluded that though the game worked reasonably well, it is not "intuitively playable" at this point. Arguably, this means we failed to achieve our main goal. However, this being a first attempt, we are by no means discouraged, and believe we have demonstrated what a game-for-modelling might look like and –in some respects– what it should perhaps not look like. In the mean time, we consider our first proof of concept a modest success: the game exists, is playable, renders sufficiently usable

results, and is considered moderately satisfying by the players. It now serves as a platform from which further explorations can depart.

Whether modelling can ever be remotely as much fun as a dedicated entertainment game remains to be seen, but we can certainly learn a lot in this respect from how games are designed. A good game is more than just a goal to work towards. It lets you know what interactions are at your disposal, it lets you explore what effect your actions have on the game world, and it gives you a sense of how well you are doing. Similarly, a good modelling process requires more than just a language and a model to work towards.

Future research will, of course, include further development of the game, and of similar games. We consider various directions for doing so. Improvement of this actual prototype is a possibility, but we are also interested in developing more text-oriented versions. In addition, we consider expansion of the concepts to be elicited by the game, possibly by combining a number of sub-games (covering different modelling rationales).

A PhD project has recently started at our department which aims at the creation of a larger, much more developed game, better rooted in theory and practice involving game design theory and game psychology, cognition (in particular pertaining to abstraction and conceptualization), but also AI (reasoning about information gathered, after the game but also during the game).

Evaluation of games played is a key aspect of the development cycle, and requires extra attention in any effort that claims to engage in "design science". Another ongoing PhD project (Ssebuggwwo, Hoppenbrouwers, & Proper, 2009) focuses on advanced evaluation of interactive modelling sessions (including both collaborative and solo modelling), and methodological results will be used to improve evaluation of games played.

REFERENCES

Adobe Labs. (2009). *Actionscript 3.0 Specification*.

Berthold, M., & Hand, D. J. (1999). *Intelligent Data Analysis, an Introduction*. Berlin: Springer Verlag.

Booch, G., Rumbaugh, J., & Jacobson, I. (1998). *The Unified Modelling Language User Guide*. Reading, MA: Addison-Wesley.

Cristani, M., & Cruel, R. (2005). A Survey on Ontology Creation Methodologies. *International Journal on Semantic Web and Information Systems, 1*(2), 49–69.

Desurvire, H., Caplan, M., & Toth, J. (2004). Using heuristics to evaluate the playability of games. In *Proceedings of CHI'04, on Human factors in computing systems*, Vienna, Austria (pp. 1509-1512). New York: ACM.

Diaz, A., Baldo, G., & Canals, G. (2006). Co-Protégé: Collaborative Ontology Building with Divergences. In *Proceedings of the 17th International Conference on Database and Expert Systems Applications* (pp. 156-160). Washington, DC: IEEE Computer Society.

Elgood, C. (1993). *Handbook of Management Games*. Aldershot, UK: Gower Publishing.

Hayes-Roth, F., Waterman, D., & Lenat, D. (1983). *Building Expert Systems*. Reading, MA: Adison-Wesley.

Hevner, A., Ram, S., March, S., & Park, J. (2004). Design Science in Information Systems Research. *Management Information Systems Quarterly, 28*(1), 75–105.

Hoppenbrouwers, S. (2008). Community-based ICT Development as a Multi-Player Game. In *Proceedings of International Conference "What is an Organization? Materiality, Agency and Discourse"*. Montreal, Canada: University of Montreal.

Hoppenbrouwers, S., Proper, H., & van der Weide, T. (2005). Formal Modelling as a Grounded Conversation. In G. Goldkuhl, M. Lind, & S. Haraldson (Eds.), *Proceedings of the 10th International Working Conference on the Language Action Perspective on Communication Modelling (LAP'05)* (pp. 139-155). Linköping: Linköpings Universitet and Hogskolan I Boras.

Hoppenbrouwers, S., van Bommel, P., & Järvinen, A. (2008). Method Engineering as Game Design: an Emerging HCI Perspective on Methods and CASE Tools. In *Proceedings of EMMSAD'08, Exploring Modelling Methods for System Analysis and Design, held in conjunction with CAiSE'08*, Montpellier, France.

Järvinen, A. (2008). *Games without Frontiers, Theories and Methods for Game Studies and Design*. Unpbulished doctoral dissertation, University of Tampere, Finland.

Knock, N., & Rittgen, P. (Eds.). (2009). *International Journal of e-Collaboration, Special Issue on Collaborative Business Information System Development, 5*(4), 37-52.

Kruchten, P. (2000). *The Rational Unified Process: An Introduction*. New York: Addison-Wesley.

Newell, A., & Simon, H. (1972). *Human Problem Solving*. Englewood Cliffs, NJ: Prentice-Hall.

Nielsen, J. (n.d.). *How to Conduct a heuristic Evaluation*. Retrieved 2009, from http://staff.unak.is/not/nicolaw/courses/hci/HCILab7papers.pdf

Object management Group (OMG). (2006). *BPMN 1.0, OMG Final Adopted Specification*.

Rittgen, P. (2009). Collaborative Modelling – A Design Science Approach. In *Proceedings of the 42nd Hawaii International Conference on System Sciences (HICSS-42)* (p. 10). Washington, DC: IEEE Computer Society.

Salen, K., & Zimmerman, E. (2003). *Rules of Play, Game Design Fundamentals*. Cambridge, MA: MIT Press.

Schreiber, A. T., Akkermans, J. A., Anjewierden, A., De Hoog, R., Shadbolt, N., Van de Velde, W., & Wielinga, B. (1999). *Knowledge Engineering and Management: The CommonKADS Methodology*. Cambridge, MA: MIT Press.

Ssebuggwawo, D., Hoppenbrouwers, S. J. B. A., & Proper, H. (2009). Evaluating Modeling Sessions Using the Analytic Hierarchy Process. In *Proceedings of the 2nd IFIP WG8.1 Working Conference on The Practice of Enterprise Modeling, PoEM 2009* (pp. 69-83). Berlin: Springer.

van Bommel, P., Hoppenbrouwers, S., Proper, H., & Roelofs, J. (2008). Concepts and Strategies for Quality of Modelling. In Halpin, T., Krogstie, J., & Proper, H. (Eds.), *Innovations in Information Systems Modelling, Methods and Best Practices* (pp. 167–189). Hershy, PA: IGI Global.

Veldhuijzen van Zanten, G., Hoppenbrouwers, S., & Proper, H. (2004). System Development as a Rational Communicative Process. *Journal of Systemics, Cybernetics and Informatics, 4*(2).

Von Ahn, L. (2006). Games with a Purpose. *Computer, 39*(6), 92–94. doi:10.1109/MC.2006.196

Wagner, C. (2006). Breaking the Knowledge Acquisition Bottleneck Through Conversational Knowledge Management. *Information Resources Management Journal, 19*(1), 70–83.

Workflow Management Coalition. (2008). *XPDL 2.1 Complete Specification*.

This work was previously published in International Journal of Gaming and Computer-Mediated Simulations, Volume 2, Issue 4, edited by Richard E. Ferdig, pp. 48-66, copyright 2010 by IGI Publishing (an imprint of IGI Global).

Chapter 19
Automated Event Recognition for Football Commentary Generation

Maliang Zheng
University of York, UK

Daniel Kudenko
University of York, UK

ABSTRACT

The enjoyment of many games can be enhanced by in-game commentaries. In this paper, the authors focus on the automatic generation of commentaries for football games, using Championship Manager as a case study. The basis of this approach is a real-time mapping of game states to commentary concepts, such as "dangerous situation for team A". While in some cases it is feasible to provide such a mapping by hand-coding, in some cases it is not straight-forward because the meaning of the concepts cannot be easily formalized. In these cases, the authors propose to use inductive learning techniques that learn such a mapping from annotated game traces.

INTRODUCTION

Watching game action on the screen can be made more exciting by providing additional commentary with the pictures. This is the case for many game genres. For example, in-game battle reports that comment on the current situation in real-time strategy games and highlight especially heroic actions by individual troops clearly can enrich the game experience and make it more immersive.

Even though passionate commentary is a desirable game feature, generating automated commentary is a significant technical challenge. In the football domain, ROCCO (Voelz et al., 1998) and MIKE (Tanaka-Ishii et al., 1998a) are two attempts to generate live commentary from game simulator data. Although ROCCO and MIKE are different in terms of system structure,

DOI: 10.4018/978-1-4666-0029-4.ch019

both solutions classify the events by matching them against hand-crafted propositional models (patterns) (Andrè, 1994). Therefore, the accuracy of classification solely relies on the correctness and completeness of the predefined conditions, and may be degraded dramatically when handling more complex occurrences, according to Gosling (1995). For instance, the existing solutions occasionally misclassify a player's kick action as a shot at goal when he merely intends to pass the ball to the teammate who is nearer to the goal. Furthermore, most models of events are so complicated that they consist of many rules, for example, ROCCO uses 8 rules to define the ball-transfer event (Voelz et al., 1998). Thus, the generation of reliable models by hand is rather inefficient and may even be infeasible for a large number of more complex events.

In this paper, we present our work on automatically generating commentary rules using inductive learning techniques. Specifically, we focus on in-game real-time commentary for simulated football games within Championship Manager, a highly popular title developed by Beautiful Games Studios (Eidos). In this game, the player steps into the role of a football team manager, purchasing and selling players, as well as overseeing their training progress. The football matches themselves are simulated based on player statistics. The player only watches the simulation and cannot interfere.

To generate the commentary, we first collected commentary concepts, such as "dangerous attack" from football news reports and other sources. We then attempted to manually implement direct mappings from game state to the set of commentary concepts (i.e., an *event recognition* mechanism). While for some concepts we were able to do so, for other concepts it turned out to be infeasible. Instead, we used an inductive learner to map hand-annotated game states selected from trace data, to generate the mapping function (classifier).

In this paper, we discuss our approach and present the empirical results on a few case studies, which show the successful application of machine learning to commentary concept generation. While our research has been focused on football and Championship Manager, the methods can be easily transferred to other games, as long as game trace data is readily available.

The paper is structured as follows. We first present the Championship Manager game, and the structure of the game traces. We then discuss our general approach, followed by examples of hand-coded commentary mappings and inductively learned mappings. We finish the paper with a summary and an outlook to future work.

CHAMPIONSHIP MANAGER

This section briefly summarizes our experimental domain, the Championship Manager game (CM[1]) 2008, presenting both the trace data specification and the game log simulation aspects.

Within CM, football matches are simulated. Similar to a real football match, there are four officials operating on the field and two teams competing to get the ball into the opposing goal. Each team comprises a maximum of eleven players; but the substitution is unlimited during the play.

The data extracted from each simulated football match is saved in a text file (Figure 1) that specifies the respective *spatial information* and *action description* of moving objects (i.e., *players, officials,* and *ball)*. The pitch coordinate has its origin at the centre mark, the x axis runs across the pitch from top to bottom, the y axis points up to the sky, and the z axis runs from left goal to right goal. Therefore, for every *sample period* (stated in the file's header part), the moving object's *position* is indicated in a three-dimensional space[2] as a decimal fraction with a sign. In addition, the player's *facing angle* is recorded and measured in degrees, which starts from the z axis and clockwise increases in the xz plane.

The samples capturing the above spatial information are recorded regularly at discrete time points from the start of the match until its end. In

Figure 1. The trace data and Euclidian space of the Championship Manager game

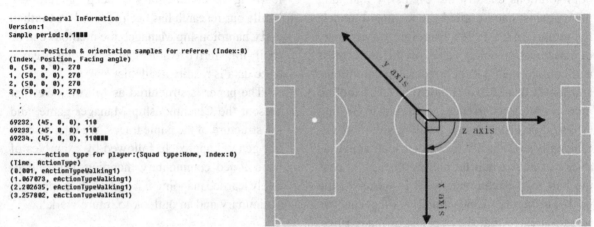

```
---------General Information
Version:1
Sample period:0.1███

---------Position & orientation samples for referee (Index:0)
(Index, Position, Facing angle)
0, (50, 0, 0), 270
1, (50, 0, 0), 270
2, (50, 0, 0), 270
3, (50, 0, 0), 270
    :
    :
69232, (45, 0, 0), 110
69233, (45, 0, 0), 110
69234, (45, 0, 0), 110███

---------Action type for player:(Squad type:Home, Index:0)
(Time, ActionType)
(0.001, eActionTypeWalking1)
(1.067073, eActionTypeWalking1)
(2.202635, eActionTypeWalking1)
(3.257802, eActionTypeWalking1)
```

contrast, action descriptions, which involve the event *time* and related *action type,* are recorded only at the occurrences of pre-defined events.

CM implements a number of common events (corner ball) and defines more than 200 types of actions in its game log, including elementary actions of officials and players elementary actions, (e.g., signalling a corner) as well as actions referring to the ball (e.g., kick, drop, dribble kick, head, and pick up).

The existing commentary system of CM appears to be decent in describing play-by-play events (e.g., "Wayne Rooney moves the ball left to Cristiano Ronaldo"), which make up the bulk of the generated commentary. However, commentaries on individual players' actions (e.g., "good save") are missing, and evaluations of play situations are oversimplified (e.g., a pass is classified as "superb" simply if the ball is received by another teammate without an opponent touching it).

MACHINE LEARNING

Machine learning (ML) is used in commentary generation to automatically generate models that map states to commentaries rather than having a designer hand-code the rules, which may turn out to be infeasible in many cases. Considering the fact that no single learning algorithms is universally powerful, our study was conducted on three representative algorithms, namely C4.5 (Quinlan, 1993), Naive Bayes (Denis et al., 2006), and K-Nearest Neighbor (Dasarathy, 1991). The following discussion will mainly focus on the first two algorithms which achieve better performance in our case study.

The C4.5 algorithm constructs a decision tree in top-down direction starting by placing an attribute at the root node. The node is then expended with branches, each of which associates with a subset of training examples for every possible value of the attribute. For continuous-valued attributes, the algorithm automatically converts them into threshold-based Boolean attributes. In other words, the nodes of such attributes allow only binary split. The same process is repeated recursively in every branch until all reach the leaf nodes, which include examples with identical classification. For both the attribute at the node and the value of the threshold, the selection prefers the one that produces the greatest information gain, which measures the reduction in the impurity in a collection of examples caused by the partition according to a given attribute or threshold. In the end, the algorithm creates an approximation of the target function in form of a decision tree; the new instance has to be sorted down to one of leaf nodes and thereby classified as the unique class shared by all examples.

In contrast to explicitly searching through the space of possible hypotheses, the Naive Bayes algorithm (NB) provides a statistical approach and, in addition, estimates explicit probabilities for hypotheses. Given a new instance described by the attribute values $\langle a_1, a_2 \ldots a_n \rangle$, among a finite set V the classifier is to find the most probable target value, v_{MAP}.

$$v_{MAP} = \arg\max_{v_j \in V} P(v_j \mid a_1, a_2 \ldots a_n)$$
$$= \arg\max_{v_j \in V} \frac{P(a_1, a_2 \ldots a_n \mid v_j) P(v_j)}{P(a_1, a_2 \ldots a_n)}$$

Besides the denominator term can be eliminated as a constant, provided the assumption that all attributes are conditionally independent the above equation can be further simplified as

$$v_{NB} = \arg\max_{v_j \in V} P(v_j) \prod_i P(a_i \mid v_j),$$

where $P(v_j)$ and $P(a_i|v_j)$ are estimated by counting the frequency of various attribute-value pairs occur with each class type within the training examples. For numeric attributes, the process assumes that their values are fitting with the normal distribution. Therefore,

$$P(a_i \mid v_j) = \frac{1}{\sqrt{2\pi}\sigma} e^{-\left[(a_i - \mu)^2 / 2\sigma^2\right]}$$

where $P(a_i|v_j)$ equals to the probability density function for a normal distribution with mean μ and standard deviation σ. Finally, the classifier assigns the target value v_{NB} to this new instance.

In short, these two algorithms share a common feature in classification efficiency, which is crucial for the game application. On the other hand, they are mutually complementary: the learning classifier of the C4.5 has merit in generating understandable rules but vulnerable to irrelevant attributes, while the NB is known for its robustness in practical application yet at risk of being overly restricted by presuming that all attributes are independent.

GENERAL APPROACH

The process of event recognition starts from the collection of commentary concepts, followed by the construction of the mapping between game states and target concepts. In order to enrich the communicable information and to minimize the potential ambiguity, the concepts were selected from multiple sources, such as live text commentary offered by Sky Sports, BBC live in EURO 2008, the Laws of the Game published by FIFA, and many others.

According to the recognition difficulty of football concepts, they are classified into two groups: one group contains the events/concepts that are recognizable easily by hand-coded rules, and the other one includes the concepts that require more sophisticated approaches (in our case, inductive learning methods). To make a proper partition, every candidate event must be firstly redefined as a set of attributes which can expressively summarize the characteristics of the concepts (details are presented in the case study section). While some events can be precisely determined by certain attribute-value pair(s) (see the following section), the rest are conjectured using models built through the learning process.

Instead of exercising human-crafted rules, the inductive learning methods use models learned from labelled training examples to recognize commentary concepts. For every target concept, the trainer firstly identifies its occurrence while watching the simulation, and then all related attributes paired with values, which are calculated in this specific setting, are saved as a training instance. In our experiment fifty matches were simulated, and the sampling process was performed repeatedly.

Next, the process is to compile the input dataset of the learning schemes with training instances. It is crucial to finding a subset of attributes that is predictive and succinct, since the inclusion of irrelevant or redundant attributes may impair the learning process in terms of efficiency and accuracy. In other words, including all attributes into dataset does not necessarily result in the best learning performance. We addressed this problem by enumerating the possible attribute combinations. While some combinations appear to be semantically disintegrated, the merit of others which can hardly be assessed by observation is to be measured through their performance in learning.

Before fed into the Weka (Hall et al., 2009) workbench for constructing the learning classifiers, the data used in training have to be deliberately devised if necessary. For instance, although both learning algorithms are extended to accept and operate on numeric values of attributes, discretizing such data by hand to certain extent can contribute the learning process.

The learning is run on datasets which involve various attribute combinations. Among all candidate classifiers, the evaluation is carried out as to their accuracy over future examples and the probable error in this accuracy estimate. Two measures - 10-fold cross-validation (Michie et al., 1994; Mitchell, 1997) and standard error computation (Gosling, 1995) - were therefore applied. To do the cross-validation, the dataset was equally split into 10 non-overlapping partitions, where each partition includes roughly the same distribution of categories as the full dataset does. Then, each of the ten parts was left out for testing and the learning scheme trained on the remaining nine partitions. As a result, the learning procedure was executed 10 times on different training sets $(s_1, s_2,..., s_{10})$, and the estimated error rate of the classifier over unseen instances (E_S) is the average of such 10 error estimates $(e_{s1}, e_{s2}, ..., e_{s10})$ according to the holdout sets. On the other hand, the standard error represents the amount of deviation of E_S from the error rate of the classifier over the entire unknown distribution D of examples (E_D), and is estimated by

$$SE = s / \sqrt{n},$$

Where n is the sample size and s is the sample standard deviation defined as follow:

$$s = \sqrt{\frac{1}{n-1} \sum_{i=1}^{n} (e_{si} - E_S)^2}.$$

In the comparison of two classifiers, the standard error interval (i.e., $E_S \pm SE$) measures the statistical significance of difference between two E_S s: one classifier with smaller value of E_S is not more accurate than the other if their intervals overlap.

Until the accuracy of the classifiers stops growing, some further tuning can be performed on the dataset. Such techniques involve reconstituting the dataset with duplicated instances, reordering the instances in the dataset, and so forth. Though there is no guarantee that such refinements could increase the accuracy of the classifiers, minor improvement can be observed occasionally in our experiment. Finally, the most accurate classifier is therefore adopted for every target concept.

Figure 2 shows a screenshot of our commentary system. Once a game log file has been loaded, the simulation components in the top right of the screen are accordingly initialized: red and blue points on the pitch stand for the competing, the four yellow points denote the officials, and another point symbolizes the football. As long as the match proceeds, the recognized events (i.e., the commentary) will instantly pop up at the left part of the screen. The match status data (i.e., substitutions) and system control options are also available at the bottom of the screen.

Figure 2. Screen shot of the football commentary system

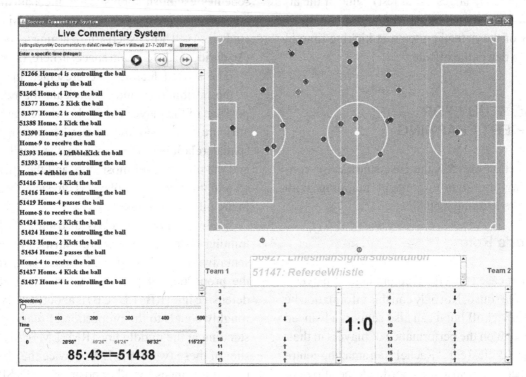

HAND-CODED COMMENTARY CONCEPTS

This section uses two examples to illustrate how the mapping between trace data and target concepts is implemented by hand-coding. One of the elementary concepts in football commentary is the *ball controller*. The relevant attributes to decide whether a player A controls the ball are:

• A is acting on the ball
• The last ball action was issued by A & A is still in the ball's zone (the circular region centred at the ball's location with a given radius)

Because the classification merely depends on the values of these two attributes, the state-to-concept mapping can be hand-coded. The first attribute is determined by the ball controller at a specific moment, and the information can be retrieved from the ball action section of trace data. However, the second attribute's value re-

quires further data processing: a queue is used to store the playing history of the ball controller, and the distance between player A and the ball is calculated.

Another commentary concept, "player A is the offside offender", can be defined as:

• A line referee has raised the flag for an offside offence
• Player A's teammate has kicked the ball
• When the ball was kicked, player A is standing at offside position

Similar to the former case, this commentary concept can be announced when all three attributes are evaluated as true. The value for the first attribute can be directly inferred from the referee action section of the trace data. The second attribute is decided by the squad type of the most recent ball actor. For the third attribute, the process firstly sorts the players' record by their z coordinate value team by team. Then, it only has to compare the largest (smallest) value of the attacking team with the first two largest (smallest) values of the defending team at kicking time in order to detect the offside.

CASE STUDY FOR CONCEPT LEARNING

This section presents the case studies[3] for constructing the state-to-concept mapping with inductive learning methods.

Player's Role

The first case concerns recognizing the player's role in the squad. Not only can this information be given at kickoff but it can also support advanced judgement on the performance of players in their assigned duties (e.g., "Rachel is an amazing centre defender"). Because the coordinate positions of each role could vary as the team's tactic changes, finding the proper cut-off points is important but clumsy by hand. For instance, a centre midfielder may be stationed in front of the back defenders for defensive reason, while his position may move up near to the forwarder to assist attacking. As mentioned in the earlier section, the learning

schemes establish sophisticated mechanisms to automate the analysis of numeric data. This case study is to test how exactly the learning technique can divide up the domain space, in here, the roles.

The related features are presented in Table 1: the attribute #1 and #2 indicate the relative position of the player within the whole team, the attribute #3 and #4 are the another measures of spatial relationships relative to the goalkeeper and the player at leftmost side, and the attribute #5 and #6 specify the player's physical location in the pitch coordinate.

Table 2 shows the class distribution of the training instances, which are statistically representative of problem space, in here, player roles: the proportion of players who standing at the defensive line (RB+LB+CB) is about 36%, which roughly equals to the proportion of players who standing at the middle line (RM+LM+CM). The sum of these two terms is also twice the proportion of instances for other positions (CF+SP).

In football squad, the left side or right side roles are as to the direction of opponent's goal. For example, the position of the left back in a left-side team falls in the negative part of the x-axis, while its counterpart in a right-side team has positive value in the x-axis. Thus, without unifying the values of location attributes in the dataset,

Table 1. Attributes of the Player A's role

No.	Attributes	Values
1	Distance between the A's position and the mean line of the squad (z-axis)	$\langle numeric \rangle$: $z_A - \dfrac{1}{n}\displaystyle\sum_{i=0}^{n} z_i$
2	Distance between the A's position and the mean line of the squad (x-axis)	$\langle numeric \rangle$: $x_A - \dfrac{1}{n}\displaystyle\sum_{i=0}^{n} x_i$
3	Distance between the A's position and the farthest position z_1 in the team (z-axis)	$\langle numeric \rangle$: $z_1 - z_A$
4	Distance between the A's position and the farthest position x_j in the team (x-axis)	$\langle numeric \rangle$: $x_j - x_A$
5	A's position (x-axis)	$\langle numeric \rangle$: from trace
6	A's position (z-axis)	

Table 2. Classes distribution in sample dataset

Roles/ Item	Goal-Keeper (GP)	Right-Back (RB)	Left-Back (LB)	Centre-Back (CB)	CentreMid-dleField (CM)	LeftMiddle-Field (LM)	RightMiddle-Field (RM)	CentreFor-ward (CF)	Sweeper (SP)
Propor-tion in Sample	9%	9%	9%	18%	18.18%	9%	9%	12.12%	6%

Table 3. Estimated error rate of the learning models

Error (%)	1,2,3,4	1,2,5,6	1,2,3,4,5,6
C4.5	25 (±1.15)	10.17 (±0.71)	11.36 (±0.34)
NB	29.54 (±1.33)	20.33 (±1.29)	20.45 (±0.90)

The classification error rates of the models built from different datasets with the C4.5 and the NB are illustrated in Table 3. In this case, the statistics reveal that the model induced from the dataset involves attribute #1, #2, #5, and #6 tends to be much more accurate in prediction, and the up bound of estimated error rate is significantly reduced to 10.88%. Therefore, this model is eventually adopted.

The decision tree structure of the model is presented in Figure 3. The threshold values at each branching nodes are computed from training data and used as the decision conditions for sorting the new instances down. The auto-analysis scheme efficiently splits the range of attribute values into several sections, and keeps the branches short from the root to the leaves, in which the classification result is specified.

the learning space is doubled. Even worse, the sparse training data cause that the information gains of branching at location attributes are underestimated, and that inferior attributes may instead be examined at top nodes. We resolved such inconsistency by mapping all positions of right-side-squad players into its opposing side.

Figure 3. The C4.5 decision tree for classifying player's role

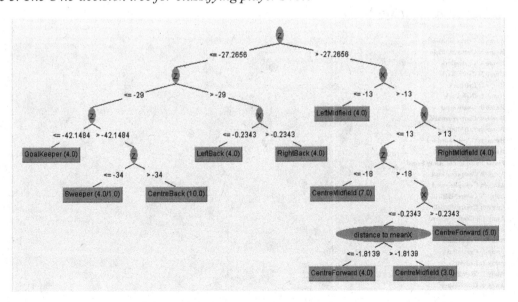

The Figure 4 is a screenshot about the classification of players' role at kickoff. In this case, besides that the formations of two teams are different, the position of the centre midfielder in the left-side team is much forward than in the right-side team. The result shows that the model correctly identifies the players' role.

Ball Receiver

The ball is frequently passed in each football match. Human observers are able to identify the possible path of the pass and recognize its intending receivers as soon as the ball is kicked out. Besides that this assumption directly derives the commentary (e.g., "player X runs to the ball"), such understanding is also conducive to identify the player's kicking intention for either passing the ball or a direct shot at the goal. On the other hand, finding a path for the ball pass based on common practice can also generate a subjective commentary as most commentators do, especially when the ball is intercepted in an unexpected path (e.g., "the ball should be passed to player Y").

The prediction of the ball receiver is mostly based on the analysis of situation on the pitch with good domain understanding. An intuitive

solution is to maintain a decision structure, the target values of which include all off-the-ball teammates. However, in football game, the situation on the pitch is highly dynamic; the events, such as, substitution, send off, and injury account for the variation in the players. As an alternative to predicting the teammate to whom this ball will be passed, the problem is converted into classifying whether any of other players could be the receiver (potentially more than one predicted receiver).

As shown in Table 4, eight of attributes are mostly intimate to the final classification: the attribute #3 indicates the direction of ball kicking, the attribute #4 implies specific power/direction of ball passing; the attribute #5 signals the intention of ball receiving, the attribute #6 measures the spatial relationship between the ball controller and teammates, the attribute #7 assesses the likelihood of being intercepted, and the attribute #8 evaluates the opportunity of ball passing.

In order to promote the learning process, rather than using numeric coordinate positions, the values of the player's location attributes (#1,#2) are discretized and assigned as one of nine nominal subareas (Figure 5). Basically, the ball is passed due to various intentions, which include breaking loose, clearance, set the pace, etc. One

Figure 4. Player's role classification

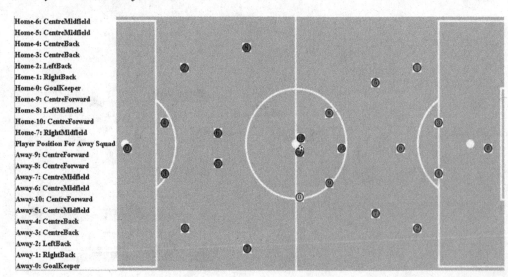

Table 4. Attributes of the ball-pass path (from player A to player B)

No.	Attributes	Values
1	Sender A's location	⟨DL,DM,DR,ML,MM, MR,FL,FM,FR⟩
2	Receiver B's location	
3	Sender A's facing direction	⟨numeric⟩: from trace
4	Sender A's action	⟨numeric⟩: from trace
5	Receiver B's action	
6	Angle between sender A and receiver B	⟨numeric⟩:arctan $(|y_A\text{-}y_B|/|x_A\text{-}x_B|)$
7	The risk of nterception	⟨numeric⟩: the number of opponents inside the rectangular region that A and B are standing at the opposite corners
8	The distance between receiver B and his closest defender D	⟨numeric⟩: $\sqrt{(x_B - x_D)^2 + (y_B - y_D)^2}$

concern about the data is that the positions of players (senders and receivers) are usually scattered over the pitch coordinate even though the pass is driven by the same purpose. For example, the attacker controlling the ball in FR is very likely to make a cross pass toward his teammate waiting in the penalty area, FM.

Without doing such discretizing there may exist a couple of instances with the identical classification result, whereas their values of the attributes (#1,#2) are considerably different. For that matter, the location attributes are very likely to be ignored by the conventional learning methods as the irrelevant attributes.

The attributes are combined as long as they are semantic coherent. For example, the combination (#1,#2,#3,#6) tries to capture the absolute spatial relations between the ball sender and the ball receiver through attribute #1 and #2, while attribute #3 together with attribute #6 implies the interaction if exists between players before the ball passing. The Table 5 presents the most accurate models that can be derived from the datasets which involve various attribute combinations.

In this experiment, we tried to refine the training data, such as, resample the data with replacement. Nevertheless, the attempts could hardly raise the accuracy of the models substantially. So,

Figure 5. Discretizing location data

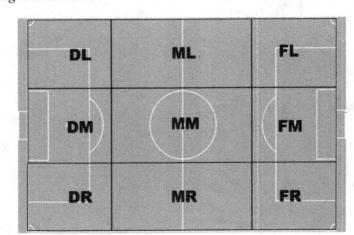

Table 5. Estimated error rate of the learning models

	C4.5 Error (%)	NB Error (%)
1,2,3,4,5,6,7,8	21.88 (±1.18)	23.43 (±0.66)
1,2,3,6,7,8	21.88 (±1.18)	20.31 (±0.91)
1,2,3,4	31.25 (±0.35)	29.68 (±0.94)
1,2,3,6	31.25 (±0.35)	26.56 (±0.38)
3,4,5,6,7,8	20.31 (±2.20)	26.56 (±1.61)
5,6,7,8	18.75 (±0.71)	26.56 (±0.94)

the model induced from the dataset which involves attribute #5, #6, #7, and #8 is adopted.

Granted that the estimated error rate of this model is higher than others, the result is still reasonable. On many occasions, the choice of the receiver for the ball passing can be very flexible, even human observers are incapable to make a precise prediction. However, for such specific situations as only a teammate is standing in the open space ahead of penalty area, the receiver can certainly be determined. In Figure 6, the model correctly predicts that the ball is passed to the centre forward (red-10) in the counter attack. On the contrary, the Figure 7 shows a negative example

as the ball is indeed passed to the red-5, although the red-10 is at good position for shooting.

Offside Trap

The concept - *Offside trap* - is often mentioned in the real commentary; it is also the precondition for judging whether the attacker successfully beats the trap. In order to correctly recognize the trap, the system must acquaint the normal occasions on which the defending team has the intention to exercise this tactic, for instance, the attacker is about to make a long pass from backfield or midfield to the goal side. It is a highly challenging work for the hand-coded approach to define such implicit scene by rules, but an interesting experiment for the learning techniques.

The relevant attributes are listed in Table 6 attribute #1 explores the possible relationship between the level of the defensive line and the offside trap (e.g., when the team's defensive line is high, the defenders could play the trap to against the counter attacks and generally cutting down on conceding goals), attribute #2 indicates the progress of the attack (e.g., if the ball is already in the goal side, the back's forward motion may be less probably for playing the trap but blocking the attack), attribute

Figure 6. Ball receiver (true classification)

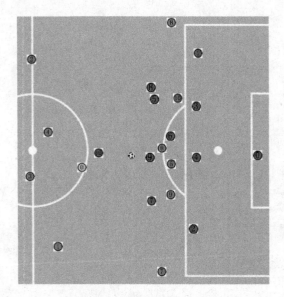

Figure 7. Ball receiver (false classification)

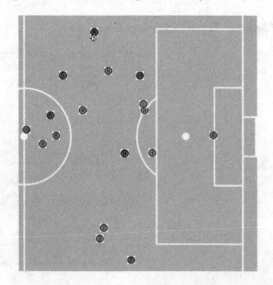

Table 6. Attribute Set for Offside Trap

No.	Attributes	Values
1	Mean of defender's positions in z-axis $\{z_1, z_2 \ldots z_n\}$	$\langle\text{numeric}\rangle: \dfrac{1}{n}\displaystyle\sum_{i=0}^{n} z_i$
2	Distance of the ball from mean defensive line	$\langle\text{numeric}\rangle: z_{ball} - \dfrac{1}{n}\displaystyle\sum_{i=0}^{n} z_i$
3	Distance between forward player A and opposing player B standing second closest to the goal	$\langle\text{numeric}\rangle: z_B - z_A$
4	Mean of defender's facing directions $\{a_1, a_2 \ldots a_n\}$	$\langle\text{numeric}\rangle: \dfrac{1}{n}\displaystyle\sum_{i=0}^{n} a_i$

#3 evaluates the technical condition to perform the tactic (e.g., if the distance is too far or forward has already stood at the offside position, it does not make sense to for backs to launch the trap), and attribute #4 captures the mutual interaction between the defenders.

The candidate datasets made up by various attribute combinations are fed into the learning schemes. The test results in Table 7 show that the NB generally outperforms the C4.5 in recognizing the trap when learning from the same dataset. One explanation for this fact is that the small size of attribute set restricts the effectiveness of the C4.5 in sorting the instance into the correct leaf. On the other hand, those attributes (#2,#3,#4) fit well

Table 7. Estimated error rate of the learning models

	C4.5 Error (%)	NB Error (%)
1,2,3,4	12.28 (±1.69)	10.52 (±0.96)
2,3,4	22.81 (±1.48)	8.77 (±1.16)
1,3,4	12.28 (±1.69)	10.52 (±0.96)
3,4	24.56 (±1.31)	8.77 (±1.16)
1,2	45.61 (±1.35)	36.84 (±1.10)
1,2,4	21.05 (±1.93)	17.54 (±1.32)
1,2,3	17.54 (±0.62)	17.54 (±0.38)
2,3	36.84 (±2.02)	19.29 (±0.70)

with the probability based approach as fitting with the assumption of independence. In the end, the model induced by the NB from either the attribute set (#2,#3,#4) or the set (#3,#4) qualifies for predicting the offside trap.

Figure 8, Figure 9, Figure 10, and Figure 11 demonstrate the course that the defending team (in blue) is playing a successful offside trap. The red-7 intercepts the ball originally controlled by the blue-18 at 4225 seconds since the game started. At 4227 seconds, our classifier correctly detects the trap along with that the backs (in blue) are running forward. In Figure 10, such trend becomes conspicuous while the red-7 is dribbling the ball: the 3 of 4 blue defenders previously standing behind the red-9 overtake him and the distance between the middle line and the defensive line of the defending team is shortened. The prediction is eventually justified by the scene that the red-9 stands at the offside position when his teammate, the red-7, passes the ball.

Summary

Our experiment covers three categories of commentary concepts – scene narrative, player's intentions, and tactic detection. The examples presented in case studies demonstrate that the learning models are acute for the evident occur-

Figure 8. Offside trap (at time point 4225sec.)

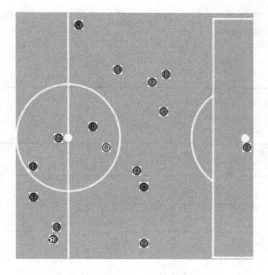

Figure 9. Offside trap (at time point 4227sec.)

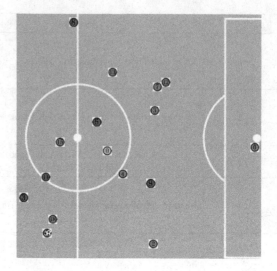

Figure 10. Offside trap (at time point 4229sec.)

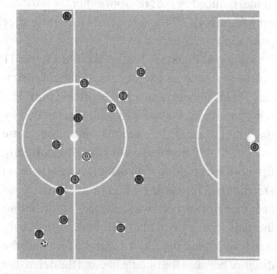

Figure 11. Offside trap (at time point 4232sec.)

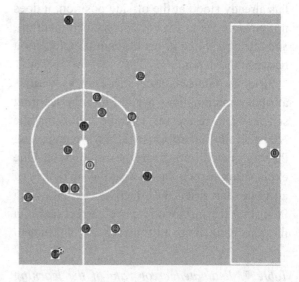

rences, the classifications of which make up the bulk of commentary. Even though the classifications may be incorrect in some cases without knowing factors outside the pure match trace (e.g., a player's personal data), those plausible statements can occasionally be uttered like the view of the commentator and thereby help enliven the commentary.

We believe that the learning based approach is reliable for recognizing commentary concepts in the CM. Compared with hand-coding methods; our approach releases the developer from designing rules in poor readability. The mappings instead are developed in a palpable manner that the developer needs to pick up the training instances and to compose the dataset. When proceeding to data analysis phase, the process executes automatically; the classic inductive learning methods at best ensures that the outcome fits the target concept over the training data. In a word, the simplified process promotes the applicability of the new approach.

In sum, not only does this learning based approach demonstrate promising application in the CM context, but also it can be generalized in larger scope. Since the CM is a simulated game, of which trace data are scaled down from real soccer games, the general approach remains instrumental though the data used for training need to be reprocessed (e.g., scale up in proportion). Of course, the fundamental condition for migrating this approach to other applications in the domain of soccer is that they can provide input data in similar quality.

RELATED WORK

Simulated football games provide a good test bed for Artificial Intelligence; many research projects use this as their evaluation domain (Kitano et al., 1997). Commentary generation is one of the challenges being tackled. It mainly includes game analysis, presentation planning and verbalization. Image analysis (Herzog & Wazinski, 1994; Yow, 1995) for recognizing events from video streams was developed before the availability of the simulated soccer domain, which circumvents the difficulty to process the image in real-time. Most existing attempts to the game analysis are conducted in the domain of RoboCup[4]. Similar to CM, the input data generated by RoboCup is in low-level quantitative form; however, rather than establishing direct relationships between raw data and all commentary concepts, most practices start by extracting fundamental concepts from raw data (Stolarski, 2006), and organizes concepts in a hierarchical way. In other words, the event recognition process can be developed incrementally, and usually commences with modelling the basic actions. Techniques for recognizing the play-by-play events involve state machines, propositional rules, and quantitative analysis (Andrè et al., 1994; Sedaghat et al., 2005; Tovinkere & Qian, 2001). Aside from event description, other commentary concepts require advanced methods with analyti-

cal functions. To perform an evaluation on the actions of players, some mathematical methods such as statistics, Ball-play Chains, and Voronoi Diagrams (Tanaka-Ishii, 1998a) are applied. In addition, through defining necessary preconditions and their intended effects, certain intentions of players are recognizable by incrementally instantiated plan hypotheses (Retz-Schmidt, 1991). As an alternative to these manually crafted models, we propose our approach to automatically generate such mappings.

The generation of the actual commentary text is a topic beyond the scope of this paper. To maximize the reported information and to amuse users with vivid commentary, a planning unit must be implemented to select the most valuable events. Factors, such as, succinctness, saliency, and topicality (Andrè et al., 1988) are taken into account. Thus, when crucial events (e.g., "goal kick") happen, interruption and abbreviation can be simulated with the mechanism of template-matching (Tanaka-Ishii et al., 1998b); when events are absent, some background commentaries are spiced. Finally, the commentary can be presented to users in natural language, e.g., using speech synthesizer. In addition, the Byrne system (Binsted & Luke, 1998) incorporates facial simulation for communication.

CONCLUSION AND OUTLOOK

In this paper, we have described an approach to in-game commentary generation, which is based on the mapping of states to commentary concepts. We showed that while some concepts can be produced by hand-coded mappings, other concepts require a more sophisticated approach. Specifically, we propose the application of inductive learning, and the results of our case studies show the feasibility of this approach for the integration of high-level scene analysis and intelligent classification.

In order to deploy our approach to a real game, more concept categories need to be tackled, and integrated into the commentary generation system. Also, the sophistication of the text generation can be improved (so far commentary text is based on a small set of simple templates).

In future work, we intend to add some specialized attributes, such as personal skills and playing condition, in the learning classifier. We also plan to extend the approach to other game genres, such as real-time strategy.

ACKNOWLEDGMENT

We thank Beautiful Games Studios for providing the trace data used in our study, and specifically Alex Whittaker for his assistance.

REFERENCES

Andrè, E., Herzog, G., & Rist, T. (1988). On the Simultaneous Interpretation of Real World Image Sequences and their Natural Language Description: The System SOCCER. In *Proceedings of the 8th ECAI*, Munich, Germany (pp. 449-454).

Andrè, E., Herzog, G., & Rist, T. (1994). Multimedia Presentation of Interpreted Visual Data. In P. Mc Kevitt (Ed.), *Proceedings of AAAI-94 Workshop on Integration of Natural Language and Vision Processing*, Seattle, WA (pp. 74-82).

Binsted, K., & Luke, S. (1998). Character Design for Soccer Commentary. In *Proceedings of the second International Workshop on RoboCup*, Paris (pp. 23-35).

Dasarathy, B. V. (Ed.). (1991). *Nearest Neighbor (NN) Norms: NN Pattern Classification Techniques*. Washington, DC: IEEE Computer Society Press.

Denis, F., Magnan, C. N., & Ralaivola, L. (2006). Efficient learning of Naive Bayes classifiers under class-conditional classification noise. In *Proceedings of the 23rd international conference on Machine learning* (pp. 265-272).

Gosling, J. (1995). *Introductory Statistics*. Glebe, Australia: Pascal Press.

Hall, M., Frank, E., Holmes, G., Pfahringer, B., Reutemann, P., & Witten, I. H. (2009). The WEKA Data Mining Software: An Update. *SIGKDD Explorations*, *11*(1). doi:10.1145/1656274.1656278

Herzog, G., & Wazinski, P. (1994). Visual TRAnslator: Linking perceptions and natural language descriptions. In. *Proceedings of the Artificial Intelligence Review*, *8*, 175–187. doi:10.1007/BF00849073

Kitano, H., Asada, M., Kuniyoshi, Y., Noda, I., Osawa, E., & Matsubara, H. (1997). RoboCup: A challenge problem for AI. *AI Magazine*, *18*(1), 73–85.

Michie, D., Spiegelhalter, D. J., & Taylor, C. C. (Eds.). (1994). *Machine Learning, Neural and Statistical*. New York: Ellis Horwood.

Mitchell, T. (1997). *Machine Learning*. New York: McGraw-Hill.

Quanlan, J. (1993). *C4.5: programs for machine learning*. San Francisco, CA: Morgan Kaufmann.

Retz-Schmidt, R. (1991). Recognizing Intentions, Interactions, and Causes of Plan Failures. *User Modeling and User-Adapted Interaction*, *1*, 173–202. doi:10.1007/BF00154477

Sedaghat, M. N., Gholami, N., Iravanian, S., & Kangavari, M. R. (2005). Design and Implementation of Live Commentary System in Soccer Simulation Environment. In *RoboCup 2004: Robot Soccer World Cup VIII* (pp. 602–610). Berlin: Springer.

Stolarski, D. (2006). Conceptual Representation for a Soccer Commentary Generator. In *RoboCup 2005: Robot Soccer World Cup IX* (pp. 496–503). Berlin: Springer. doi:10.1007/11780519_46

Tanaka-Ishii, K., Hasida, K., & Noda, I. (1998b). Reactive Content Selection in the Generation of Real-Time Soccer Commentary. In *Proceedings of. COLING-ACL'98*, Montreal, Canada (pp. 1282-1288).

Tanaka-Ishii, K., Noda, I., Frank, I., Nakashima, H., Hasida, K., & Matsubara, H. (1998a). Mike: An Automatic Commentary System for Soccer. In *Proceedings of ICMAS-98, Int. Conf. On Multi-agent Systems*, Paris (pp. 285-292).

Tovinkere, V., & Qian, R. J. (2001). Detecting semantic events in Soccer Games: towards a complete solution. In. *Proceedings of International Conference on Multimedia and Expo ICME, 2001*, 1040–1043.

Voelz, D., Andrè, E., Herzog, G., & Rist, T. (1998). Rocco: A RoboCup Soccer Commentator System. In Asada, M., & Kitano, H. (Eds.), *RoboCup-98: Robot Soccer World Cup II*. Berlin: Springer.

Witten, I., & Frank, E. (2005). *Data Mining: practical machine learning tools and techniques* (2nd ed.). San Francisco, CA: Morgan Kaufmann.

Yow, D., Yeo, B.-L., Yeung, M., & Liu, B. (1995). Analysis and Presentation of Soccer Highlights from Digital Video. In *Proceedings of 2nd Asian Conf. on Computer Vision (ACCV'95)*.

ENDNOTES

[1] CM2008 is a football-management simulation published by Eidos Interactive Limited. http://www.championshipmanager.co.uk/

[2] CM2008 only provides a two-dimensional simulation, so the value for the y-axis always equals 0.

[3] The case study only uses CM2008's output data for sample generation, and the events to be recognized are not part of the simulator

[4] RoboCup™ is an international project that uses soccer as a central topic of research. More information is available at: http://www.robocup.org/

This work was previously published in International Journal of Gaming and Computer-Mediated Simulations, Volume 2, Issue 4, edited by Richard E. Ferdig, pp. 67-84, copyright 2010 by IGI Publishing (an imprint of IGI Global).

Compilation of References

Aarseth, E. (2006). How we became postdigital: From cyberstudies to game studies. In Silver, D., & Massanari, A. (Eds.), *Critical cyberculture studies* (pp. 37–46). New York: NYU Press.

Abbas, S., & Sawamura, H. (2009). Developing an argument learning environment using agent-based ITS (ALES). In *proceedings of The Second International Conference on Educational Data Mining (EDM09)*, Cordoba, Spain.

Adler, P., & Adler, P. (1987). *Membership Roles in Field Research*. Thousand Oaks, CA: Sage Publications.

Adobe Labs. (2009). *Actionscript 3.0 Specification*.

Alexander, A. L., Brunye, T., Sidman, J., & Weil, S. A. (2005). *From gaming to training: A review of studies on fidelity, immersion, presence, and buy-in and their effects on transfer in pc-based simulations and games. DARWARS Training Impact Group*. Retrieved June 9, 2008, from http://www.darwars.com/downloads/DARWAR%20 Paper%2012205.pdf

Altman, I., & Taylor, D. (1973). *Social penetration: The development of interpersonal relationships*. New York: Holt, Rinehart and Winston.

Altshuller, G., Altov, H., & Shulyak, L. (1994). *TRIZ, the theory of inventive problem solving*. Worcester, MA: Technical Innovation Center Inc.

American Psychological Association. (1997). *Learner-Centered Psychological Principles*. Retrieved October 1, 2009, from http://www.apa.org/ed/lcp2/lcp14.html

Amory, A. N. K. V. J., & Adams, C. (1999). The use of computer games as an educational tool: identification of appropriate game types and game elements. *British Journal of Educational Technology*, *30*(4), 311–321. doi:10.1111/1467-8535.00121

Anderson, R. C., & Pichert, J. W. (1978). Recall of previously un-recallable information following a shift in perspective. *Journal of Verbal Learning and Verbal Behavior*, *17*, 1–12. doi:10.1016/S0022-5371(78)90485-1

Andrè, E., Herzog, G., & Rist, T. (1988). On the Simultaneous Interpretation of Real World Image Sequences and their Natural Language Description: TheSystem SOCCER. In *Proceedings of the 8th ECAI*, Munich, Germany (pp. 449-454).

Andrè, E., Herzog, G., & Rist, T. (1994). Multimedia Presentation of Interpreted Visual Data. In P. Mc Kevitt (Ed.), *Proceedings of AAAI-94 Workshop on Integration of Natural Language and Vision Processing*, Seattle, WA (pp. 74-82).

Annetta, L. A. (2008). Serious Educational Games []. Amsterdam, The Netherlands: Sense Publishers.]. *Theory into Practice*, 83.

Apperley, T. H. (2006). Genre and game studies: Toward a critical approach to video game genres. *Simulation & Gaming*, *37*(1), 6–23. doi:10.1177/1046878105282278

Argyle, M. (1998). *Social Relationships*. London: Blackwell Publishing.

Aristotle. (1992). Poetics (S. H. Butcher, Trans.). In H. Adams (Ed.), *Critical theory since Plato* (pp. 49-66). Fort Worth, TX: Harcourt Brace Jovanovich College Publishers.

Arroyo-Palacios, J., & Romano, D. (2008). *Towards a Standardization in the Use of Physiological Signals for Affective Recognition Systems*. Paper presented at the Measuring Behavior 2008, Maastricht, The Netherlands.

Arroyo-Palacios, J., & Romano, D. (2009). *Exploring the Use of a Respiratory-Computer Interface for Game Interaction.* Paper presented at the IEEE Consumer electronics Society Games innovation Conference, London.

Arts, J. A. R., Gijselaers, W. H., & Segers, M. S. R. (2002). Cognitive effects of an authentic computer-supported, problem-based learning environment. *Instructional Science, 30*, 465–495. doi:10.1023/A:1020532128625

Atari Inc. (1972). *Pong (Arcade software).* Sunnyvale, CA: Atari Inc.

Averill, J. R. (1969). Autonomic response patterns during sadness and mirth. *Psychophysiology, 5*, 399–414. doi:10.1111/j.1469-8986.1969.tb02840.x

Avner, A., Moore, C., & Smith, S. (1980). Active external control: A basis for superiority of CBI. *Journal of Computer-Based Instruction, 6*(4), 115–118.

Axelrod, R. (1990). *The Evolution of Co-operation.* London: Penguin Books.

Bailenson, J. N., Yee, N., Merget, D., & Schroeder, R. (2006). The effect of behavioral realism and form realism of real-time avatar faces on verbal disclosure, nonverbal disclosure, emotion recognition, and copresence in dyadic interaction. *Presence (Cambridge, Mass.), 15*(4), 359–372. doi:10.1162/pres.15.4.359

Barab, S. A. (2009, June). *Transformational Play: Why Educators Should Care About Games.* Paper presented at Games, Learning and Society, Madison, WI.

Barab, S. A., Dodge, T., Ingram-Goble, A., Volk, C., & Peppler, K. (2009). *Pedagogical dramas and transformational play: Narratively-rich games for learning.* Manuscript submitted for publication.

Barab, S., & Jackson, C. (2006). From Plato's Republic to Quest Atlantis: The role of the philosopher-king. *Technology, Humanities, Education, Narrative [THEN] Journal, 2.*

Barab, S., Dodge, T., Tuzun, H., Job-Sluder, K., Jackson, C., Arici, A., et al. (2007). The Quest Atlantis Project: A socially-responsive play space for learning. In B. E. Shelton & D. A. Wiley (Eds.), *The educational design and use of simulation computer games* (pp. 159-186). Rotterdam, The Netherlands: Sense Publishers.

Barab, S. A., Arici, A., & Jackson, C. (2005). Eat your vegetables and do your homework: A design-based investigation of enjoyment and meaning in learning. *Educational Technology, 65*(1), 15–21.

Barab, S. A., Cherkes-Julkowski, M., Swenson, R., Garrett, S., Shaw, R. E., & Young, M. (1999). Principles of self-organization: Ecologizing the learner-facilitator system. *Journal of the Learning Sciences, 8*(3-4), 349–390. doi:10.1207/s15327809jls0803&4_2

Barab, S., Sadler, T., Heiselt, C., Hickey, D., & Zuiker, S. (2007). Relating Narrative, Inquiry, and Inscriptions: A Framework for Socio-Scientific Inquiry. *Journal of Science Education and Technology, 16*(1), 59–82. doi:10.1007/s10956-006-9033-3

Barab, S., & Squire, K. (2004). Design-based research: Putting a stake in the ground. *Journal of the Learning Sciences, 13*(1), 1–14. doi:10.1207/s15327809jls1301_1

Barab, S., Thomas, M., Dodge, T., Carteaux, R., & Tuzun, H. (2005). Making learning fun: Quest Atlantis, a game without guns. *Educational Technology Research and Development, 53*(1), 86–108. doi:10.1007/BF02504859

Barab, S., Thomas, M., Dodge, T., Squire, K., & Newell, M. (2004). Critical design ethnography: Designing for change. *Anthropology & Education Quarterly, 35*(2), 254–268. doi:10.1525/aeq.2004.35.2.254

Barab, S., Zuiker, S., Warren, S., Hickey, D., Ingram-Goble, A., & Kwon, E.-J. (2007). Situationally embodied curriculum: Relating formalisms and contexts. *Science Education, 91*(5), 750–782. doi:10.1002/sce.20217

Barfield, W., & Weghorst, S. (1993). The sense of presence within virtual environment: A conceptual framework. In Salvendy, G., & Smith, M. (Eds.), *Human computer interaction: Applications and case studies* (pp. 699–704). Amsterdam: Elsevier.

Barrows, H. S. (1986). A taxonomy of problem-based learning methods. *Medical Education, 20*, 481–486. doi:10.1111/j.1365-2923.1986.tb01386.x

Barrows, H. S., & Tamblyn, R. M. (1980). *Problem-based learning: An approach to medical education.* New York: Springer.

Barr, P., Noble, J., & Biddle, R. (2006). Video game values: Human-computer interaction and games. *Interacting with Computers*, *19*, 180–195. doi:10.1016/j.intcom.2006.08.008

Barsalou, L. W. (2008). Grounded Cognition. *Annual Review of Psychology*, *59*, 617–645. doi:10.1146/annurev.psych.59.103006.093639

Baylis, W. T. (2000). The use of virtual reality in training and education. *Logistics Spectrum*, *34*(4), 25–28.

Baym, N. (2006). Interpersonal life online. In L. A. Lievrouw & S. Livingstone (Eds.), *The handbook of new media* (Student ed., pp. 35-54). Thousand Oaks, CA: Sage.

Baym, N. (1998). The emergence of on-line community. In Jones, S. G. (Ed.), *CyberSociety 2.0: Revisiting computer-mediated communication and community* (pp. 35–68). Thousand Oaks, CA: Sage.

Bayon, V., Wilson, J. R., Stanton, D., & Boltman, A. (2003). Mixed reality storytelling environments. *Virtual Reality Journal, 7*(1).

Bazin, A. (1971a). *What is cinema? Vol I.* (H. Gray, Trans.). Berkeley, CA: University Of California Press. (Original Works Published 1940-1955).

Bazin, A. (1971b). *What is cinema? Vol II.* (H. Gray, Trans.). Berkeley, CA: University Of California Press. (Original Works Published 1940-1955).

Bechar-Israeli, H. (1995). From <Bonhead> to <cLoNe-hEAd>: Nicknames, play, and identity on Internet Relay Chat. *Journal of Computer-Mediated Communication*, *1*(2). Retrieved from http://jcmc.indiana.edu/vol1/issue2/bechar.html.

Bell, M. W. (2008). Toward a definition of "virtual worlds" (Electronic Version). *Journal of Virtual Worlds Research*, *1*. Retrieved December 21, 2008, from http://journals.tdl.org/jvwr/article/view/283

Bell, D. (2001). *An introduction to cybercultures*. London: Routledge.

Bell, P., & Linn, M. C. (2000). Scientific arguments as learning artifcats: Designing for learning from the web with KIE. *International Journal of Science Education*, *22*(8), 797–817. doi:10.1080/095006900412284

Benami, O., & Jin, Y. (2002). *Creative stimulation in conceptual design.* Paper presented at the ASME 2002 Design Engineering Technical Confereces and Computer and Information in Engineering Conference, Montreal, Canada.

Benelli, C., & Yongue, B. (1995). Supporting young children's motor skills. *Childhood Education, 71*(4), 217–220.

Berg, B. (2004). *Qualitative Research Methods for the Social Sciences* (5th ed.). Boston: Pearson.

Bergin, D. A. (1999). Influences on classroom interest. *Educational Psychologist Journal, 34*(2), 87–98. doi:10.1207/s15326985ep3402_2

Berrenberg, J. L., & Prosser, A. (1991). The create-a-game exam: a method to facilitate student interest and learning. *Teaching of Psychology, 18*(3), 167–167. doi:10.1207/s15328023top1803_9

Bersak, D., McDarby, G., Augenblick, N., McDarby, P., Daragh, M., Brian, M., et al. (2001). *Intelligent Biofeedback using an Immersive Competitive Environment.* Paper presented at the Designing Ubiquitous Computing Games Workshop, Atlanta, GA.

Berthold, M., & Hand, D. J. (1999). *Intelligent Data Analysis, an Introduction*. Berlin: Springer Verlag.

Biggs, J. B. (2003). *Teaching for quality learning at university*. Maidenhead, UK: Open University Press.

Biggs, J. B., & Collis, K. F. (1982). *Evaluating the quality of learning: The SOLO taxonomy*. New York: Academic Press.

Binsted, K., & Luke, S. (1998). Character Design for Soccer Commentary. In *Proceedings of the second International Workshop on RoboCup*, Paris (pp. 23-35).

Birchfield, D., Ciufo, T., Minyard, G., Qian, G., Savenye, W., Sundaram, H., et al. (2006). *SMALLab: A Mediated Platform for Education.* Paper presented at ACM SIGGRAPH, Boston.

Bizarre Creations. (2007). *Project Gotham Racing 4 (Xbox software)*. Redmond, WA: Microsoft Game Studios.

Bjork, S., & Holopainen, J. (2004). *Patterns in game design (game development series)*. Boston: Charles River Media.

Bloom, B. S., & Krathwohl, D. R. (1956). Taxonomy of educational objectives: The classification of educational goals, by a committee of college and university examiners. In *Handbook 1: Cognitive domain*. New York: Longmans.

Blue Tongue Entertainment. (2008). *de Blob* (Wii software). Agoura Hills, CA: THQ.

Boellstorff, T. (2008). *Coming of Age in Second Life; An Anthropologist Explores the Virtually Human*. Princeton: Princeton University Press.

Bolton, G. (1999). *Acting in classroom drama: A critical analysis*. London: Heinemann.

Bonanno, P., & Kommers, P. A. M. (2008). Exploring the influence of gender and gaming competence on attitudes towards using instructional games. *British Journal of Educational Technology, 39*(1), 97–109.

Bonk, C. J., & Dennen, V. P. (2005). Massive multiplayer online gaming: A research framework for military training and education. *Office of the Under Secretary of Defence for Personnel and Readiness*. Retrieved June 17, 2008, from http://blogoehlert.typepad.com/eclippings/files/GameReport_Bonk_final.pdf

Booch, G., Rumbaugh, J., & Jacobson, I. (1998). *The Unified Modelling Language User Guide*. Reading, MA: Addison-Wesley.

Bordwell, D. (1985). *Narration in the fiction film*. Madison, WI: University Of Wisconsin Press.

Bordwell, D., Staiger, J., & Thompson, K. (1985). *The classical Hollywood cinema*. New York: Columbia University Press. doi:10.4324/9780203358818

Bottino, R. M., Ferlino, L., Ott, M., & Tavella, M. (2007). Developing strategic and reasoning abilities with computer games at primary school level. *Computers & Education, 49*, 1272–1286. doi:10.1016/j.compedu.2006.02.003

Boud, D., & Feletti, G. (1997). Changing problem-based learning: Introduction to the. In Boud, D., & Feletti, G. (Eds.), *The challenge of problem-based learning* (2nd ed.). London: Kogan Page.

Bowman, D., Kruijff, E., Laviola, J., & Poupyrev, I. (2000, July 23-28). An introduction to 3d user interface design. Paper presented at SIGGRAPH 2000, New Orleans, Louisiana.

Bowman, R. F. (1982). A Pac-Man theory of motivation: Tactical implications for classroom instruction. *Educational Technology, 22*(9), 14–17.

Box, G. E. P., Hunter, W. G., & Hunter, S. J. (1978). *Statistics for experimenters*. New York: John Wiley & Sons.

Boyd, D. (2008). Why youth "heart" social network sites: The role of networked publics in teenage social life. In D. Buckingham (Ed.), *Youth, identity, and digital media* (pp. 119-142). Cambridge, MA: MIT Press.

Brabrand, C., & Dahl, B. (2009). Using the SOLO taxonomy to analyze competence progression of university science curricula. *Higher Education, 58*, 531–549. doi:10.1007/s10734-009-9210-4

Bransford, J. D., Brown, A. L., & Cocking, R. R. (Eds.). (2000). *How people learn: Brain, mind, experience, and school*. Washington, DC: National Academy Press.

Bransford, J. D., Brown, A. L., & Cocking, R. R. (Eds.). (1999). *How people learn: Brain, mind, experience, and school*. Washington, DC: National Academy Press.

Bricken, M., & Byrne, C. M. (1994). Summer students in virtual reality: A pilot study on educational applications of virtual reality. In Wexelblat, A. (Ed.), *Virtual Reality: Applications and explorations* (pp. 199–218). Boston: Academic.

Brown, A. L. (1996). Design experiments: Theoretical and methodological challenges in creating complex interventions in classroom settings. *Journal of the Learning Sciences, 2*(2), 141–178. doi:10.1207/s15327809jls0202_2

Brown, B. W. Jr. (1980). The crossover experiment for clinical trials. *Biometrics, 36*(1), 69–79. doi:10.2307/2530496

Brown, J. S., Collins, A., & Duguid, P. (1989). Situated cognition and the culture of learning. *Educational Researcher, 18*(1), 32–42.

Brozik, D., & Zapalska, A. (2000). The restaurant game. *Simulation & Gaming, 31*(3), 407–416. doi:10.1177/104687810003100305

Bruckman, A. (2006). Analysis of log file data to understand behavior and learning in an online community. In J. Weiss, J. Nolan, J. Hunsinger, & P. Trifonas (Eds.), *The International handbook of virtual learning environments* (pp. 1449-1465). New York: Springer.

Bruckman, A. (2000). Situated support for learning: Storm's weekend with Rachael. *Journal of the Learning Sciences*, *9*(3), 329–372. doi:10.1207/S15327809JLS0903_4

Bruner, J. (2002). *Making stories: Law, literature, life.* New York: Farrar, Straus and Giroux.

Brünken, R., Plass, J. L., & Leutner, D. (2004). Assessment of cognitive load in multimedia learning with dual-task methodology: Auditory load and modality effects. *Instructional Science*, *32*, 115–132. doi:10.1023/B:TRUC.0000021812.96911.c5

Bryant, J. A., Akerman, A., & Drell, J. (in press). Diminutive subjects, design strategy, and driving sales: Preschoolers and the Nintendo DS. *Game Studies*.

Buckingham, D., & Willett, R. (2006). *Digital generations: Children, young people, and new media*. Mahwah, NJ: Lawrence Erlbaum Associates.

Buckingham, D., & Burn, A. (2007). Game literacy in theory and practice. *Journal of Educational Multimedia and Hypermedia*, *16*(3), 323–349.

Bukatko, D., & Daehler, M. W. (2001). *Child Development: A thematic approach* (4th ed.). Boston: Houghton Mifflin.

Cacioppo, J. T., Klein, D. J., Berntson, G. G., & Hatfield, E. (1993). The Psychophysiology of Emotion. In M. Lewis & J. M. Haviland (Eds.), *Handbook of Emotions* (pp. 119-142).

Cacioppo, J. T., & Tassinary, L. G. (1990). Inferring Psychological Significance from Physiological Signals. *The American Psychologist*, *45*, 16–28. doi:10.1037/0003-066X.45.1.16

Carlson, K., & Guynup, S. (2002). Avatar as content delivery platform. *Future Generation Computer Systems*, *17*, 65–71.

Carroll, N. (1985). The power of movies. *Daedalus*, *114*, 79–103.

Cassell, J., & Jenkins, H. (1998). *From Barbie to Mortal Kombat: Gender and computer games*. Cambridge, MA: The MIT Press.

Cassidy, G., & MacDonald, R. A. R. (2008, August). Music and videogame play: The effects of self-selected and experimenter-selected music on performance and experience. In L. Mitchell (Ed.), *Music and health: Empirical investigations and theoretical constructs. Proceedings for the 2008 International Conference of Music Perception and Cognition*, Hokkaido University, Japan. Australia: Causal Productions.

Cassidy, G. G., & MacDonald, R. A. R. (2009). The effects of music choice on task performance: A study of the impact of self-selected and experimenter-selected music on driving game performance and experience. *Musicae Scientiae*, *13*, 357–386.

Castronova, E. (2001, December). *Virtual Worlds: A First-Hand Account of Market and Society on the Cyberian Frontier* (No. 618).

Castronova, E. (2003). On virtual economies (Electronic Version). *Game Studies*, *3*. Retrieved December 22, 2008, from http://www.gamestudies.org/0302/castronova/

Castronova, E. (2005). *Synthetic worlds: The business and pleasure of gaming*. Chicago: University of Chicago Press.

Catell, R. B., & Vogelmann, S. (1977). A comprehensive trial of the scree and Kg criteria for determining the number of factors. *Multivariate Behavioral Research*, *12*(3), 289–325. doi:10.1207/s15327906mbr1203_2

Charlin, B., Mann, K., & Hansen, P. (1998). The many faces of problem-based learning: A framework for understanding and comparison. *Medical Teacher*, *20*(4), 323–330. doi:10.1080/01421599880742

Chen, D., & Stroup, W. (1993). General Systems Theory: Toward a Conceptual Framework for Science and Technology Education for All. *Journal of Science Education and Technology*, *2*(3), 447–459. doi:10.1007/BF00694427

Chen, H., Wigand, R. T., & Nilan, M. (2000). Exploring web users' optimal flow experiences. *Information Technology & People*, *13*, 263–281. doi:10.1108/09593840010359473

Chen, J. (2007). Flow in Games (and Everything Else). *Communications of the ACM*, *50*(4), 31–34. doi:10.1145/1232743.1232769

Childress, M. D., & Braswell, R. (2006). Using massively multiplayer online role-playing games for online learning. *Distance Education, 27*(2), 187–196. doi:10.1080/01587910600789522

Chiou, W.-B. (2006). Adolescents' sexual self-disclosure on the Internet: Deindividuation and impression management. *Adolescence, 41*(163), 547–561.

Christie, I. C. (2002). *Multivariate Discrimination of Emotion-Specific Autonomic Nervous System Activity.* Blacksburg, VA: Virginia Polytechnic Institute and State University.

Chuang, Y., & Chen, L. L. (2008). How to rate 100 visual stimuli efficiently. *International Journal of Design, 2*(1), 31–43.

Clark, K. A., & Sheridan, K. (2009, April). *Game Design Communities: Exploring a Model for Underserved Students.* Paper presented at the Annual Conference of the American Education Research Association, San Diego, CA.

Clarke, J., & Dede, C. (2007). MUVEs as a powerful means to study situated learning. In C. Chinn, G. Erkins, and S. Puntambekar (Eds.), *Proceedings of CSCL 2007: Of mice, minds and society*, New Brunswick, NJ (pp. 144-147).

Clark, R. E. (1983). Reconsidering research on learning from media. *Review of Educational Research, 53*, 445–459.

Clark, R. E. (1994). Media will never influence learning. *Educational Technology Research and Development, 42*(2), 21–29. doi:10.1007/BF02299088

Cohen, A. J. (2009). Music as a source of emotion in film. In Juslin, P., & Sloboda, J. (Eds.), *Oxford handbook of music and emotion: Theory, research, applications* (pp. 879–908). Oxford, UK: Oxford University Press.

Cohen, J. (1988). *Statistical power and analysis for the behavioral sciences* (2nd ed.). Hillsdale, NJ: Lawrence Erlbaum Associates.

Colby, A., Kohlberg, L., Gibbs, J., & Lieberman, C. (1983). A longitudinal study of moral judgment. *Journal of Monographs of the Society for Research in Child Development, 48.*

Collins, K. (2007). An introduction to the participatory and non-linear aspects of video games audio. In Hawkins, S., & Richardson, J. (Eds.), *Essays on sound and vision* (pp. 263–298). Helsinki, Finland: Helsinki University Press.

Comolli, J. (1996). Machines of the visible. In Druckrey, T. (Ed.), *Electronic culture: technology and visual representation* (pp. 109–117). New York: Aperture Books.

Conati, C. (2002). Probabilistic Assessment of User's Emotion in Educational Games. *Applied Artificial Intelligence, 16*, 555–575. doi:10.1080/08839510290030390

Connolly, T. M., Stansfield, M., & Hainey, T. (2007). An application of games-based learning within software engineering. *British Journal of Educational Technology, 38*(3), 416–428. doi:10.1111/j.1467-8535.2007.00706.x

Consalvo, M. (2003, February). *It's a queer world after all: Studying The Sims and sexuality.* New York: GLAAD Center for the Study of Media and Society.

Constantine, L. L. (2006). *Activity Modeling: Toward a pragmatic integration of activity theory with usage-centered design.* Retrieved November 24, 2009, from http://www.foruse.com/articles/activitymodeling.pdf

Cornett, S. (2004, April 24-29). The usability of massively multiplayer online roleplaying games: Designing for new users. In *Proceedings of the SIGCHI conference on Human factors in computing systems (SIGCHI 2004)*, Vienna, Austria (Vol. 6, pp. 703-710). New York: ACM Publishing.

Cortina, J. (1993). What is coefficient Alpha? an examination of theory and applications. *The Journal of Applied Psychology, 78*(1), 98–104. doi:10.1037/0021-9010.78.1.98

Crain, W. (1985). *Theories of development. Kohlberg's stages of moral development* (pp. 118-136).

Creswell, J., & Plano Clark, V. (2007). *Designing and conducting mixed methods research.* Thousand Oaks, CA: Sage Publications.

Cristani, M., & Cruel, R. (2005). A Survey on Ontology Creation Methodologies. *International Journal on Semantic Web and Information Systems, 1*(2), 49–69.

Cronbach, L. J. (1951). Coefficient alpha and the internal structure of tests. *Psychometrika, 16*(3), 297–334. doi:10.1007/BF02310555

Cross, N. (1994). *Engineering Design Methods, Strategies for Product Design*. Chichester, UK: John Wiley & Sons.

Csikszentmihalyi, M. (1975). *Beyond Boredom and Anxiety: Experiencing Flow in Work and Play*. San Francisco, CA: Jossey-Bass.

Csikszentmihalyi, M. (1985). Emergent motivation and the evolution of the self. In Kleiber, D. A., & Maehr, M. (Eds.), *Advances in motivation and achievement (Vol. 4*, pp. 93–119). Greenwich, CT: JAI Press.

Csikszentmihalyi, M. (1997). *Finding Flow: The Psychology of Engagement with Everyday Life*. New York: BasicBooks.

Csikszentmihalyi, M. (2001). *Flow: The psychology of optimal experience*. New York: Harpers & Row.

Csikszentmihalyi, M., & Hermanson, K. (1999). Intrinsic motivation in museums: why does one want to learn? In Hooper-Greenhill, E. (Ed.), *The educational role of the museum* (2nd ed., pp. 146–160). New York: Routledge.

Daft, R. L., & Lengel, R. H. (1986). Organizational information requirements, media richness and structural design. *Management Science*, *32*(5), 554–571. doi:10.1287/mnsc.32.5.554

Dasarathy, B. V. (Ed.). (1991). *Nearest Neighbor (NN) Norms: NN Pattern Classification Techniques*. Washington, DC: IEEE Computer Society Press.

Davis, S. B., & Carini, C. (2004, September 6-10). *Constructing a Player-Centred Definition of Fun for Video Games Design*. Paper presented at the HCI 2004, Leeds, UK.

Davis, G. A. (1973). *Psychology of problem-solving: Theory and practice*. New York: Basic Books.

De Crespigny, R. (2003). The Three Kingdoms and western Jin: A history of China in the third century AD. *Faculty of Asian Studies, 1*, 1-36. Retrieved July 18, 2008, from http://www.anu.edu.au/asianstudies/decrespigny/3KWJin.html

De Jong, T., & van Joolingen, W. R. (1998). Scientific discovery learning with computer simulations of conceptual domains. *Review of Educational Research, 68*(2), 179–201.

de Jong, T., van Joolingen, W. R., Swaak, J., Veermans, K., Limbach, R., & King, S. (1998). Self-directed learning in simulation-based discover environments. *Journal of Computer Assisted Learning, 14*(1), 235–246. doi:10.1046/j.1365-2729.1998.143060.x

Dede, C., & Ketelhut, D. J. (2003). *Designing for motivation and usability in a museum-based multi-user virtual environment*. Paper presented at the American Educational Research Association Conference, Chicago.

Dede, C., Ketelhut, D. J., & Ruess, K. (2002). *Motivation, usability and learning outcomes in a prototype museum-based multi-user virtual environment*. Paper presented at the 5th International Conference of the Learning Sciences, Seattle, WA.

Dede, C. (1995). The evolution of contructivist learning environments: Immersion in distributed virtual worlds. *Educational Technology*, *35*(5), 46–52.

Dede, C. (2005). Why design-based research is both important and difficult. *Educational Technology*, *45*(1), 5–8.

DeKoven, B. D. (1978). *The well-played game: A player's philosophy*. New York: Anchor Books.

Denis, F., Magnan, C. N., & Ralaivola, L. (2006). Efficient learning of Naive Bayes classifiers under class-conditional classification noise. In *Proceedings of the 23rd international conference on Machine learning* (pp. 265-272).

Desurvire, H., Caplan, M., & Toth, J. (2004). Using heuristics to evaluate the playability of games. In *Proceedings of CHI'04, on Human factors in computing systems*, Vienna, Austria (pp. 1509-1512). New York: ACM.

Dewey, J., & Bentley, A. F. (1949). *Knowing and the known*. Boston: Beacon.

Diaz, A., Baldo, G., & Canals, G. (2006). Co-Protégé: Collaborative Ontology Building with Divergences. In *Proceedings of the 17th International Conference on Database and Expert Systems Applications* (pp. 156-160). Washington, DC: IEEE Computer Society.

Dibbell, J. (1998). *My tiny life: Crime and passion in a virtual world*. New York: Henry Holt and Company.

Dickey, M. D. (2000). *3D virtual worlds and learning: An analysis of the impact of design affordances and limitations of Active Worlds, blaxxum interactive, and OnLive! Traveler; and a study of the implementation of Active Worlds for formal and informal education.* Columbus, OH: The Ohio State University.

Dindia, K. (2002). Self-disclosure research: Knowledge through meta-analysis. In Allen, M. (Ed.), *Interpersonal Communication Research: Advances Through Meta-analysis* (pp. 169–185). Mahwah, NJ: Lawrence Erlbaum Associates.

DiSalvo, B. J., Crowley, K., & Norwood, R. (2008). Learning in context: Digital games and young black men. *Games and Culture, 3*(2), 131–141. doi:10.1177/1555412008314130

Dobson, M. W., Pengelly, M., Sime, J. A., Albaladejo, S. A., Garcia, E. V., & Gonzales, F. (2001). Situated learning with co-operative agent simulations in team training. *Computers in Human Behavior, 17*(1), 547–573. doi:10.1016/S0747-5632(01)00023-1

Donath, J. S. (1999). Identity and deception in the virtual community. In Smith, M. A., & Kollock, P. (Eds.), *Communities in cyberspace* (pp. 29–59). London: Routledge.

Dourish, P. (2001). *Where the action is: The foundations of embodied interaction.* Cambridge, MA: MIT Press.

Ducheneaut, N., & Moore, R. J. (2004, November 6-10). *The social side of gaming: a study of interaction patterns in a massively multiplayer online game.* Paper presented at the CSCW, Chicago.

Ducheneaut, N., Yee, N., Nickell, E., & Moore, R. (2006). Building an MMO with Mass Appeal: A Look at Gameplay in World of Warcraft. *Games and Culture, 1*(4), 281–317. doi:10.1177/1555412006292613

Duffy, T. M., & Cunningham, D. J. (1996). Constructivism: Implications for the design and delivery of instruction. In Jonassen, D. H. (Ed.), *Handbook of Research for Educational Communications and Technology.* New York: MacMillan.

Dunbar, K. (1998). Problem Solving. In Bechtel, W., & Graham, G. (Eds.), *A companion to Cognitive Science.* London: Blackwell.

Duncan, S. (2009, June). *"Here's My Shootorial!": The Scaffolding of Game Design on Kongregate.* Paper presented at Games, Learning and Society, Madison, WI.

Edwards, A. L. (1957). *Techniques of attitude scale construction.* New York: Appleton-Century Crofts.

Egenfeldt-Neilson, S. (2005, February). *Beyond Edutainment: Exploring the educational potential of computer games.* Unpublished doctoral dissertation, University of Copenhagen, Copenhagen, Denmark.

Egenfeldt-Nielsen, S. (2007). Third generation educational use of computer games. *Journal of Educational Multimedia and Hypermedia, 16*(3), 263–281.

Ekman, P., Levenson, R. W., & Friesen, W. V. (1983). Autonomic nervous system activity distinguishes among emotions. *Science, 221*, 1208–1210. doi:10.1126/science.6612338

Elgood, C. (1993). *Handbook of Management Games.* Aldershot, UK: Gower Publishing.

Elkind, D. H., & Sweet, F. (1997). The Socratic Approach to Character Education. [html]. *Educational Leadership, 2*, Retrieved from http://www.goodcharacter.com/Article.

Elrad, T., Filman, R. E., & Bader, A. (2001). Aspect-oriented programming: Introduction. *Communications of the ACM, 44*(10), 29–32. doi:10.1145/383845.383853

Engeström, Y. (1987). *Learning by expanding: An activity-theoretical approach to developmental research.* Helsinki, Finland: Orienta-Konsultit Oy.

Engestrom, Y. (2000). Activity theory as a framework for analyzing and redesigning work. *Ergonomics, 43*(7), 960. doi:10.1080/001401300409143

Engeström, Y., Miettinen, R., & Punamäki, R.-L. (Eds.). (1999). *Perspectives on activity theory.* Cambridge, UK: Cambridge University Press.

Erlandson, B., & Nelson, B. (2008). *The Effect of Collaboration Modality on Cognitive Load in a Situated Inquiry Environment.* Paper presented at the American Educational Communication and Technology Conference, Orlando, FL.

Faria, A. J., & Wellington, W. J. (2004). A survey of simulation game users, former-users, and never-users. *Simulation & Gaming, 35*(2), 178–207. doi:10.1177/1046878104263543

Fasli, M., & Michalakopoulos, M. (2005). Supporting active learning through game-like exercises. In *Proceedings of the Fifth IEEE International Conference on Advanced Learning Technologies (ICALT05)* (pp. 730-734).

Fauconnier, G., & Turner, M. (2002). *The Way We Think: Conceptual Blending and the Mind's Hidden Complexities*. New York: Basic Books.

Feldon, D. F., & Kafai, Y. B. (2008). Mixed methods for mixed reality: Understanding users' avatar activities in virtual worlds. *Educational Technology Research and Development, 56*, 575–593. doi:10.1007/s11423-007-9081-2

Ferris, S. P., & Roper, S. (2002). Same and mixed-gender intimacy in a virtual environment. *Qualitative Research Reports in Communication*, 47-55.

Fields, D. A., & Kafai, Y. B. (2008). Knowing and throwing mudballs, hearts, pies, and flowers: A connective ethnography of gaming practices. In V. Jonker, A. Lazonder, & C. Hoadley (Eds.), *Proceedings of the Eighth International Conference of the Learning Sciences*, Utrecht, The Netherlands.

Fields, D. A., & Kafai, Y. B. (in press). Navigating life as an avatar: The shifting identities-in-practice of a girl player in a tween virtual world. In C. C. Ching & B. Foley (Eds.), *Constructing identity in a digital world*. Cambridge, UK: Cambridge University Press.

Fields, D. A., & Kafai, Y. B. (in press). Understanding Player Participation and Practices in Virtual Worlds: A Proposal for Qualitative Analyses of Log File Data. In D. Thomas (Ed.), *Research methods in virtual worlds*. Cambridge, MA: MIT Press.

Fields, D. A., & Kafai, Y. B. (2009). A connective ethnography of peer knowledge sharing and diffusion in a tween virtual world. *International Journal of Computer-Supported Collaborative Learning, 4*(1), 47–68. doi:10.1007/s11412-008-9057-1

Flanagan, M., & Nissenbaum, H. (2007). A Game Design Methodology to Incorporate Social Activist Themes. In *Proceedings of CHI 2007* (pp. 181-190). New York: ACM Press.

Fletcher, J. D., & Tobias, S. (2005). The Multimedia Principle. In R. E. Mayer (Ed.), *The Cambridge Handbook of Multimedia Learning* (pp. 117-133). New York: Cambridge University Press.

Fontana, A., & Frey, J. (1994). Interviewing: The Art of Science. In Denzien, N., & Lincoln, Y. (Eds.), *Handbook of Qualitative Research* (pp. 361–376). Thousnad Oaks, CA: Sage Publications.

Foreman, J. (2003, July-August). Next generation: Educational technology versus the lecture. *EDUCASE*, 12-22. Retrieved from http://web.reed.edu/cis/tac/meetings/Next%20Generation%20Ed%20Tech.pdf

Frasca, G. (2003, November 4-6). *Ludologists Love Stories, Too: Notes from a Debate that Never Took Place*. Paper presented at the Level Up: Digital Games Research Conference, Utrecht, The Netherlands.

Frasca, G. (1999). Ludology Meets Narratology. Similitude and Differences between (Video) games and Narrative. *Parnasso, 3*, 365–371.

Fredrickson, B. L., Mancuso, R. A., Branigan, C., & Tugade, M. M. (2000). The Undoing Effect of Positive Emotions. *Motivation and Emotion, 24*(4), 237–258. doi:10.1023/A:1010796329158

French, M. (1985). *Conceptual Design for Engineers*. London: The Design Council/ Springer Verlag.

Friedman, T. L. (2006). *The World Is Flat*. London: Penguin Books.

Gagné, R. M., Wager, W. W., Golas, K. G., & Keller, J. M. (2005). *Principles of instructional design* (4th ed.). Toronto, ON: Thomson Wadsworth.

Gallahue, D. L., & Ozmun, J. C. (1995). *Understanding motor development: Infants, children, adolescents, adults* (3rd ed.). Madison, WI: Brown and Benchmark Publishers.

Games, A. (2008). *Assessing Game-Based Literacies: The Role of Task Constraints on Strategic Meaning Making Within Gamestar Mechanic*. Paper presented at Games, Learning and Society, Madison, WI.

Garner, R., Brown, R., Sanders, S., & Menke, D. (1992). "Seductive details" and learning from text. In Renninger, K. A., Hidi, S., & Krapp, A. (Eds.), *The role of interest in learning and development* (pp. 239–254). Hillsdale, NJ: Erlbaum.

Garris, R., Ahlers, R., & Driskell, J. E. (2002). Games, motivation, and learning: A research and practice model. *Simulation & Gaming, 33*(4), 441–467. doi:10.1177/1046878102238607

Gee, J. P. (2003). *What video games have to teach us about learning and literacy.* New York: Palgrave MacMillan.

Gee, J. P. (2005). Learning by design: Good video games as learning machines. *ELearning Journal, 2*(1).

Gee, J. P. (2006). Are video games good for learning? In *Proceedings of the Curriculum Corporation 13th National Conference.* Retrieved from http://www.curriculum.edu. au/verve/_resources/Gee_Paper.pdf

Gee, J. P. (2006). *Games and Learning: Issues, Perils, and Potentials. A Report to the Spencer Foundation.* Retrieved August 2, 2008, from http://iop.onearmedman. com/content/Gee_Spencer_report_2006.pdf

Gee, J. P. (2007). *Good Video Games and Good Learning: Collected Essays on Video Games, Learning and Literacy.* New York: Peter Lang Publishing.

Gelernter, D. (1993). *Mirror worlds: Or the day software puts the universe in a Shoebox... how it will happen and what it will mean.* Oxford, UK: Oxford University Press.

Gentner, D., & Nielson, J. (1996). The anti-mac interface. *Communications of the ACM, 39*(6), 70–82. doi:10.1145/232014.232032

Germanchis, T., Cartwright, W., & Pettit, C. (2005). Using computer gaming technology to explore human wayfinding and navigation abilities within a built environment. In *Proceedings of the XXII International Cartographic Conference* (pp. 11-16). A Coruna, Spain: Globabl Congresos.

Ghani, J. (1995). Flow in human computer interactions: Test of a model. In Carey, J. (Ed.), *Human factors in information systems: Emerging theoretical bases* (pp. 291–311). Norwood, NJ: Ablex.

Gilleade, K. M., Dix, A., & Allanson, J. (2005). *Affective Videogames and modes of Affective Gaming: Assist Me, Challenge Me, Emote Me.* Paper presented at the Digital Games Research Association (DiGRA).

Giraffa, L., & Viccari, R. (1998). The use of agents techniques on intelligent tutoring systems. *In Proceedings of the XVIII International Conference of the Chilean Computer Science Society.*

Glaser, B. (1965). The constant comparative method of qualitative analysis. *Social Problems, 12*(4), 436–445. doi:10.1525/sp.1965.12.4.03a00070

Glaser, B. G. (1998). *Doing grounded theory: Issues and discussions.* Mill Valley, CA: Sociology Press.

Glenberg, A. M., Gutierrez, T., Levin, J., Japuntich, S., & Kaschak, M. P. (2004). Activity and Imagined Activity Can Enhance Young Children's Reading Comprehension. *Journal of Educational Psychology, 96*(3), 424–436. doi:10.1037/0022-0663.96.3.424

Goffman, E. (1959). *The presentation of self in everyday life.* New York: Doubleday.

Golub, A., & Lingley, K. (2008). "Just like the Qing empire": Internet addiction, MMOGs, and moral crisis in contemporary China. *Games and Culture, 3*(1), 59–75. doi:10.1177/1555412007309526

Gómez-Martín, M. A., Gómez-Martín, P. P., & González-Calero, P. A. (2004). Game-Driven Intelligent Tutoring Systems. In M. Rauterberg (Ed.), *Proceedings of the ICEC 2004* (LNCS 3166, pp. 108-113).

Gonzalez, J. (2000). The appended subject: Race and identity as digital assemblage. In Kolko, B. E., Nakamura, L., & Rodman, G. B. (Eds.), *Race in cyberspace* (pp. 27–50). New York: Routledge.

Gosling, J. (1995). *Introductory Statistics.* Glebe, Australia: Pascal Press.

Graf, S., Yang, G., Lin, T., & Kinshuk. (2009). Automatic, global and dynamic student modeling in a ubiquitous learning environment. *Knowledge Management & E-Learning: An International Journal, 1*(1).

Graf, S., Yang, G., & Lin, T., & Kinshuk. (2008). The relationship between learning styles and cognitive traits - Getting additional information for improving student modeling. *Journal of Computers in Human Behavior, 24,* 122–137. doi:10.1016/j.chb.2007.01.004

Graimann, B., Allison, B., & Gr¨aser, A. (2007). New applications for non-invasive brain-computer interfaces and the need for engaging training environments. In *Proceedings of the BRAINPLAY 07 BCI and Games Workshop at ACE.*

Greenfield, P. (1994). Video games as cultural artifacts. *Journal of Applied Developmental Psychology, 15,* 3–12. doi:10.1016/0193-3973(94)90003-5

Gresalfi, M., Barab, S. A., Siyahhan, S., & Christensen, T. (2009). Virtual worlds, conceptual understanding, and me: Designing for consequential engagement. *Horizon, 17*(1), 21–34. doi:10.1108/10748120910936126

Grimshaw, M., Lindley, C. A., & Nacke, L. (2008, October). *Sound and immersion in the first-person shooter: Mixed measurement of the player's sonic experience.* Paper presented at the meeting meething of Audio Mostly, Piteå, Sweden.

Gross, J. J., & Levenson, R. W. (1995). Emotion elicitation using films. *Cognition and Emotion, 9*(1), 87–108. doi:10.1080/02699939508408966

Grove, J., & Williams, H. (1998). Explorations in virtual history. In Monteith, M. (Ed.), *IT for learning enhancement.* Lisse, The Netherlands: Swets & Zeitlinger.

Grunefeld, H., & Silen, C. (2000, November). *Problem based learning compared to project organized learning.* Retrieved June 2, 2008, from http://www.utwente.nl/itbe/owk/publicaties/docenten/doc00-39.pdf

Gutwin, C., & Greenberg, S. (2002). A Descriptive Framework of Workspace Awareness for Real-Time Groupware. *Computer Supported Cooperative Work, 11,* 411–446. doi:10.1023/A:1021271517844

Haag, A., Goronzy, S., Schaich, P., & Williams, J. (2004). Emotion Recognition Using Bio-sensors: First Steps towards an Automatic System. In *Affective Dialog Systems (LNCS 3068).* Berlin: Springer. doi:10.1007/978-3-540-24842-2_4

Hake, R. R. (1998). Interactive-engagement vs Traditional Methods: A Six-Thousand-Student Survey of Mechanics Test Data for Introductory Physics Courses. *American Journal of Physics, 66,* 64–74. doi:10.1119/1.18809

Hall, M., Frank, E., Holmes, G., Pfahringer, B., Reutemann, P., & Witten, I. H. (2009). The WEKA Data Mining Software: An Update. *SIGKDD Explorations, 11*(1). doi:10.1145/1656274.1656278

Hamburger, H. (1979). *Games as models of social phenomena.* San Francisco, CA: W. H. Freeman and Company.

Harel Caperton, I. (2005). "Hard fun:" The essence of good games AND good education. *Telemedium Journal of Media Literacy.*

Harel Caperton, I. (2009). The New Literacy is Game Literacy. In *Proceedings of TEDGlobal,* Oxford, UK. Retrieved from http://www.worldwideworkshop.org/pdfs/Idit_Ted_Lecture.pdf

Harel Caperton, I., & Sullivan, S. (2009, June). *Students' Development of Contemporary Core Competencies through Making Educational Web Games.* Paper presented at Games, Learning and Society, Madison, WI.

Harel Caperton, I., Kraus, L., Sullivan, S., & Reynolds, R. (2008). *Globaloria: Social Media Networks for Learning Through Game Production With a Social Purpose.* Paper presented at Games, Learning and Society, Madison, WI.

Harel Caperton, I., Oliver, A., & Sullivan, S. (2009). *Globaloria in West Virginia: Empowering students with 21st-century digital literacy though a game-making learning network.* New York: World Wide Workshop Foundation. Retrieved from http://WorldWideWorkshop.org/reports

Harel, I. (1988). *Software design for learning: Children's learning fractions and Logo programming through instructional software design.* Unpublished doctoral dissertation, MIT Media Laboratory.

Harel, I. (1989, September). Learning About Learning. *Newsweek.*

Harel, I. (1991). *Children Designers: Interdisciplinary constructions for learning and knowing mathematics in a computer-rich school.* Norwood, NJ: Ablex.

Harel, I. (1996). Learning Skills for the New Millennium: The three X's. In *21st-Century Learning*, MaMaMedia.com.

Harel, I. (1997). Clickerati kids, who are they? *21ˢᵗ Century Learning*. Retrieved from http://www.mamamedia.com

Harel, I. (1999). And a Child Shall Lead Them: Young kids show the benefits of a new affinity with technology. *CONTEXT: Man & Machine.*

Harel, I. (2002). Learning new-media literacy: A new necessity for the Clickerati Generation. *Telemedium Journal of Media Literacy.*

Harel, I., & Papert, S. (1991). (Eds.). *Constructionism.* Norwood, NJ: Ablex.

Harel, I., Oliver, A., & Sullivan, S. (2008). *Implementing Globaloria in West Virginia: Results from Pilot Year-1.* New York: World Wide Workshop Foundation. Retrieved from http://www.worldwideworkshop.org/reports

Harel, I., & Papert, S. (1990). Software design as a learning environment. *Interactive Learning Environments*, *1*(1), 1–32. doi:10.1080/1049482900010102

Hart, S. G., & Staveland, L. E. (1988). Development of a multi-dimensional workload rating scale: Results of empirical and theoretical research. In P. A. Hancock & N. Meshkati (Eds.), *Human mental workload,* (pp.139-183). Amsterdam, The Netherlands: Elsevier.

Hayes, E., Johnson, B. Z., Lammers, J. C., & Lee, Y. (2009, April). *Taking the SIMS Seriously: Play, Identity, and Girls' IT Learning.* Paper presented at the Annual Conference of the American Education Research Association, San Diego, CA.

Hayes, E. (2008). Game content creation and IT proficiency: An exploratory study. *Computers & Education*, *51*(1), 97–108. doi:10.1016/j.compedu.2007.04.002

Hayes-Roth, F., Waterman, D., & Lenat, D. (1983). *Building Expert Systems.* Reading, MA: Adison-Wesley.

Hébert, S., Béland, R., Dionne-Fournelle, O., Crête, M., & Lupien, S. J. (2005). Physiological stress response to video-game playing: The contribution of built-in music. *Life Sciences*, *76*, 2371–2380. doi:10.1016/j.lfs.2004.11.011

Heider, D. (2009). *Living Virtually; Researching Virtual Worlds.* New York: Peter Lang.

Heim, M. (2001). The avatar and the power grid. *Mots Pluriels,* *19*(2001).

Heim, M. (1998). *Virtual realism.* Oxford, UK: Oxford University Press.

Hemp, P. (2006, June 1). Avatar-based marketing. *Harvard Business Review,*48–57.

Henderson, L., Klemes, J., & Eshet, Y. (2000). Just playing a game? Educational simulation software and cognitive outcomes. *Journal of Educational Computing Research*, *22*(1), 105–129. doi:10.2190/EPJT-AHYQ-1LAJ-U8WK

Henderson, S., & Gilding, M. (2004). 'I've never clicked this much with anyone in my life': Trust and hyperpersonal communication in online friendships. *New Media & Society*, *6*(4), 487–506. doi:10.1177/146144804044331

Herman, A., Coombe, R. J., & Kaye, L. (2006). Your Second Life? Goodwill and the performativity of intellectual property in online gaming. *Cultural Studies*, *20*(2/3), 184–210. doi:10.1080/09502380500495684

Herzog, G., & Wazinski, P. (1994). Visual TRAnslator: Linking perceptions and natural language descriptions. In. *Proceedings of the Artificial Intelligence Review*, *8*, 175–187. doi:10.1007/BF00849073

Hestenes, D. (1996). *Modeling Methodology for Physics Teachers.* Paper presented at the International Conference on Undergraduate Physics, College Park, MD.

Hestenes, D. (2006). *Notes for a Modeling Theory of Science Cognition and Instruction.* Paper presented at the GIREP Conrerence, Modeling and Physics and Physics Education.

Hestenes, D. (1992). Modeling Games in the Newtonian World. *American Journal of Physics*, *60*, 732–748. doi:10.1119/1.17080

Hevner, A., Ram, S., March, S., & Park, J. (2004). Design Science in Information Systems Research. *Management Information Systems Quarterly*, *28*(1), 75–105.

Hjelm, S. I., & Browall, C. (2000). *Brainball - using brain activity for cool competition.* Paper presented at the 1st Nordic Conference on Human-Computer Interaction.

Hmelo-Silver, C. E. (2004). Problem-based learning: What and how do students learn? *Educational Psychology Review*, *16*(3), 235–266. doi:10.1023/B:EDPR.0000034022.16470.f3

Hodges, L. C., & Harvey, L. C. (2003). Evaluation of student learning in organic chemistry using the solo taxonomy. *Journal of Chemical Education*, *80*, 785–787. doi:10.1021/ed080p785

Hoppenbrouwers, S. (2008). Community-based ICT Development as a Multi-Player Game. In *Proceedings of International Conference "What is an Organization? Materiality, Agency and Discourse"*. Montreal, Canada: University of Montreal.

Hoppenbrouwers, S., Proper, H., & van der Weide, T. (2005). Formal Modelling as a Grounded Conversation. In G. Goldkuhl, M. Lind, & S. Haraldson (Eds.), *Proceedings of the 10th International Working Conference on the Language Action Perspective on Communication Modelling (LAP '05)* (pp. 139-155). Linköping: Linköpings Universitet and Hogskolan I Boras.

Hoppenbrouwers, S., van Bommel, P., & Järvinen, A. (2008). Method Engineering as Game Design: an Emerging HCI Perspective on Methods and CASE Tools. In *Proceedings of EMMSAD '08, Exploring Modelling Methods for System Analysis and Design, held in conjunction with CAiSE '08*, Montpellier, France.

Hospers, M., Kroezen, E., & Nijholt, A. op den Akker, R., & Heylen, D. (2003). Developing a generic agent-based intelligent tutoring system. In *Proceedings of the Third IEEE International Conference on Advanced Learning Technologies (ICALT '03)*.

Hsu, H.-Y., & Wang, S.-K. (in press). Using gaming literacies to cultivate new literacies. *Simulation & Gaming*.

Huffaker, D. A., & Calvert, S. L. (2005). Gender, identity, and language use in teenage blogs. *Journal of Computer-Mediated Communication*, *10*(2). Retrieved from http://jcmc.indiana.edu/vol10/issue2/huffaker.html.

Hutchins, E. (1995). *Cognition in the Wild* (Vol. 1). Cambridge, MA: MIT Press.

Hutchison, D. (2007). Video games and the pedagogy of place. *Social Studies*, *98*(1), 35–40. doi:10.3200/TSSS.98.1.35-40

id Software. (1993). *DOOM* (Computer software). Mesquite, TX: id Software.

id Software. (1999). *Quake III Arena* (Computer software). Santa Monica, CA: Activision.

IJsselsteijn, W., de Kort, Y., Poels, K., Jurgelionis, A., & Bellotti, F. (2007). Characterising and Measuring User Experiences in Digital Games. In *Proceedings of the International Conference on Advances in Computer Entertainment Technology*.

Ijsselsteijn, W., Poels, K., & deKort, Y. A. W. (2008). *The Game Experience Questionnaire: Development of a self-report measure to assess player experiences of digital games*. Eindhoven, The Netherlands: TU Eindhoven.

Inal, Y., & Cagiltay, K. (2007). Flow experiences of children in an interactive social game environment. *British Journal of Educational Technology*, *38*(3), 455–464. doi:10.1111/j.1467-8535.2007.00709.x

Institute of Play. (2007). *What are gaming literacies*? Retrieved November 15, 2008, from http://www.instituteofplay.com/node/71

Ip, B., & Jacobs, G. (2004). Quantifying Game Design. *Design Studies*, *25*, 607–624. doi:10.1016/j.destud.2004.02.001

Järvinen, A. (2003, November). Making and breaking games: a typology of rules. In C. Marinka & R. Joost (Eds.), Level up conference proceedings (pp. 68–79). Utrecht, The Netherlands: University of Utrecht.

Järvinen, A. (2008). *Games without Frontiers, Theories and Methods for Game Studies and Design*. Unpbulished doctoral dissertation, University of Tampere, Finland.

Jeannerod, M. (1994). The representing brain neural correlates of motor intention and imagery. *The Behavioral and Brain Sciences*, *17*, 187–245. doi:10.1017/S0140525X00034026

Jenkins, H. (2006). *Convergence culture: Where old and new media collide*. New York: New York University Press.

Johnson, R., & Onwuegbuzie, A. (2004). Mixed methods research: A research paradigm whose time has come. *Educational Researcher*, *33*(7), 14–26. doi:10.3102/0013189X033007014

Johnstone, A. H. (2001). Can problem solving be taught? *University Chemistry Education, 5*(2), 69–73.

Jonassen, D. H. (2000). Revisiting activity theory as a framework for designing student-centered learning environment. In Jonassen, D. H., & Land, S. M. (Eds.), *Theoretical foundations of learning environments* (pp. 89–121). Mahwah, NJ: Lawrence Erlbaum Associate.

Jonassen, D. H. (2000). Toward a Design Theory of Problem Solving. *Educational Technology Research and Development, 48*(4), 63–86. doi:10.1007/BF02300500

Jonassen, D. H., & Rohrer-Murphy, L. (1999). Activity theory as a framework for designing constructivist learning environments. *Educational Technology Research and Development, 47*(1), 61–79. doi:10.1007/BF02299477

Jones, S. E. (2008). *The meaning of video games.* London: Routledge.

Jørgensen, K. (2008b). Audio and gameplay: An analysis of PvP battlegrounds in World of Warcraft. *Game Studies, 8*(2). Retrieved August 17, 2009, from http://gamestudies.org/0802/articles/jorgensen

Jørgensen, K. (2008a). Left in the dark: Playing computer games with the sound turned off. In Collins, K. (Ed.), *From Pac Man to pop music: Interactive Audio in Games and New Music* (pp. 163–176). Aldershot, UK: Ashgate.

Jorgenson, A. (2004, October 23-27). Marrying HCI/usability and computer games: A preliminary look. In *Proceedings of the third Nordic conference on Human-computer interaction (NordiCHI 2004),* Tampere, Finland (Vol. 82, pp. 393-396). New York: ACM Publishing.

Juul, J. (2005). *Half real.* Boston: MIT Press.

Kafai, Y. B. (1995). *Minds in Play: Computer game design as a context for children's learning.* Hillsdale, NJ: Lawrence Erlbaum Associates.

Kafai, Y. B. (2008). Gender play in a tween gaming club. In Y. B. Kafai, C. Heeter, J. Denner, & J. Sun (Eds.), *Beyond Barbie & Mortal Kombat: New perspectives on gender and gaming* (pp. 111-124). Cambridge, MA: MIT Press.

Kafai, Y. B., & Giang, M. (2007). Virtual playgrounds: Children's multi-user virtual environments for playing and learning with science. In T. Willoughby & E. Wood (Eds.), *Children's Learning in a Digital World* (pp. 196-217). Oxford, UK: Blackwell Publishing.

Kafai, Y. B., & Resnick, M. (Eds.). (1996). *Constructionism in Practice: Designing, thinking, and learning in a digital world.* Mahwah, NJ: Lawrence Erlbaum Associates.

Kafai, Y. B., Feldon, D., Fields, D. A., Giang, M., & Quintero, M. (2007). Life in the times of Whypox: A virtual epidemic as a community event. In C. Steinfield, B. Pentland, M. Ackerman, & N. Contractor (Eds.), *Proceedings of the Eighth Conference of Computer Supported Collaborative Learning,* New Brunswick, NJ (pp. 196-205).

Kafai, Y. B. (2006). Playing and making games for learning: Instructionist and constructionist perspectives for game studies. *Games and Culture, 1*(1), 36–40. doi:10.1177/1555412005281767

Kaptelinin, V., & Nardi, B. A. (1997). Activity theory: Basic concepts and applications. In *Proceedings of CHI '97* (pp. 158-159).

Kaptelinin, V. (1996a). Activity theory: Implication for human-computer interaction. In Nardi, B. A. (Ed.), *Context and consciousness: Activity theory and human-computer interaction* (pp. 103–116). Cambridge, MA: MIT Press.

Kaptelinin, V. (1996b). Computer-mediated activity: Functional organs in social and developmental contexts. In Nardi, B. A. (Ed.), *Context and consciousness: Activity theory and human-computer interaction* (pp. 45–68). Cambridge, MA: MIT Press.

Kayagil, T. A., Bai, O., Lin, P., Furlani, S., Vorbach, S., & Hallett, M. (2007). Binary EEG control for two-dimensional cursor movement: An online approach. In *Proceedings of the IEEE/ICME International Conference on Complex Medical Engineering* (pp. 1542-1545).

Ke, F. (2008). A case study of computer gaming for math: Engaged learning from gameplay? *Computers & Education, 51*(4), 1609–1620. doi:10.1016/j.compedu.2008.03.003

Keller, J. M. (1987). Development and use of the ARCS model of instructional design. *Journal of Instructional Development, 10*(3), 2–10. doi:10.1007/BF02905780

Kelley, T. (2006). *The Ten Faces of Innovation: Strategies for Heightening Creativity*. London: Profile Books.

Ketelhut, D. J., Dede, C., Clarke, J., & Nelson, B. (2007). Studying Situated Learning in a Multi-User Virtual Environment. In E. Baker, J. Dickieson, W. Wulfeck & H. O'Neil (Eds.), *Assessment of Problem Solving Using Simulations* (pp. 37-58). New York: Lawrence Erlbaum Associates.

Ketelhut, D. J. (2007). The impact of student self-efficacy on scientific inquiry skills: An exploratory investigation in River City, a multi-user virtual environment. *Journal of Science Education and Technology, 16*(1), 99–111. doi:10.1007/s10956-006-9038-y

Kiczales, G., Lamping, J., Mendhekar, A., Maeda, C., Lopes, C., Loingtier, J.-M., et al. (1997). Aspect-oriented programming. In *Proceedings of Ecoop '97 object-oriented programming* (pp. 220-242).

Kim, T., & Biocca, F. (1997). Telepresence via television: Two dimensions of telepresence may have different connections to memory and persuasion. *Journal of Computer-Mediated Communication, 3*(2). Retrieved April 27, 2009, from http://jcmc.indiana.edu/vol3/issue2/kim.html

Kim, T., Shin, D., & Shin, D. (2009). *Towards an Emotion Recognition System based on Biometrics*. Paper presented at the International Joint Conference on computational Sciences and Optimization.

Kim, J., & Andre, E. (2008). Emotion Recognition Based on Physiological Changes in Music Listening. *IEEE Transactions on Pattern Analysis and Machine Intelligence, 30*(12), 2067–2083. doi:10.1109/TPAMI.2008.26

Kim, K. H., Bang, S. W., & Kim, S. R. (2004). Emotion recognition system using short-term monitoring of physiological signals. *Medical & Biological Engineering & Computing, 42*, 419–427. doi:10.1007/BF02344719

Kim, N. (1989). *Circsim-tutor: an Intelligent Tutoring System for Circulatory Physiology*. Chicago: Illinois Institute of Technology.

Kitano, H., Asada, M., Kuniyoshi, Y., Noda, I., Osawa, E., & Matsubara, H. (1997). RoboCup: A challenge problem for AI. *AI Magazine, 18*(1), 73–85.

Klawe, M. (1998). *When Does the Use of Computer Games and Other Interactive Multimedia Software Help Students Learn Mathematics?* Paper presented at the Department of Computer Science, the University of British Columbia, BC, Canada.

Klopfer, E. (2008). *Augmented learning: Research and design of mobile educational games*. Cambridge, MA: MIT Press.

Knestis, K. (2008). *Understanding Globaloria as the subject of research: An agenda for future study*. Charleston, WV: Edvantia, Inc.

Knock, N., & Rittgen, P. (Eds.). (2009). *International Journal of e-Collaboration, Special Issue on Collaborative Business Information System Development, 5*(4), 37-52.

Ko, M., Bae, K., Oh, G., & Ryu, T. (2009). *A Study on New Gameplay Based on Brain-Computer Interface*. Paper presented at the Digital Games Research Association (DiGRA).

Koles, Z. J. (1991). The quantitative extraction and topographic mapping of the abnormal components in the clinical EEG. *Electroencephalography and Clinical Neurophysiology, 79*(6), 440–447. doi:10.1016/0013-4694(91)90163-X

Kolko, B. E. (2000). Erasing @race. In Kolko, B. E., Nakamura, L., & Rodman, G. B. (Eds.), *Race in cyberspace* (pp. 213–232). New York: Routledge.

Kollack, P., & Smith, M. A. (1999). Communities in cyberspace. In Smith, M. A., & Kollock, P. (Eds.), *Communities in cyberspace* (pp. 3–25). London: Routledge.

Kornhuber, H., & Deecke, L. (1965). Hirnpotential¨anderungen bei Willk¨urbewegungen und passiven Bewegungen des Menschen: Bereitschaftspotential und reafferente Potentiale. *Pfl¨ugers Archiv European Journal of Physiology, 284*(1), 1–17. doi:10.1007/BF00412364

Koslowski, B. (1996). *Theory and Evidence: The Development of Scientific Reasoning*. Cambridge, MA: MIT Press.

Kozma, R. B. (1994). The Influence of Media on Learning: The Debate Continues. *School Library Media Research, 22*(4). Retrieved July 29, 2008, from http://www.ala.org/ala/aasl/aaslpubsandjournals/slmrb/editorschoiceb/infopower/ALA_print_layout_1_202756_202756.cfm

Kozma, R. B. (1991). Learning with media. *Review of Educational Research, 61*, 179–211.

Krauledat, M., Dornhege, G., Blankertz, B., Losch, F., Curio, G., & M¨uller, K.-R. (2004). Improving speed and accuracy of braincomputer interfaces using readiness potential features. In *Proceedings of the 26th Annual International Conference of the IEEE EMBS* (Vol. 26, pp. 4511-4515).

Kriz, W. C. (2003). Creating effective learning environments and learning organizations through gaming simulation design. *Simulation & Gaming, 34*(4), 495–511. doi:10.1177/1046878103258201

Kriz, W. C., & Hense, J. U. (2006). Theory-oriented evaluation for the design of and research in gaming and simulation. *Simulation & Gaming, 37*(2), 268–283. doi:10.1177/1046878106287950

Kruchten, P. (2000). *The Rational Unified Process: An Introduction*. New York: Addison-Wesley.

Kuhn, D. (1993). Science as Argument: Implications for Teaching and Learning Scientific Thinking. *Scientific and Educational Journal, 77*(3), 319–337. doi:10.1002/sce.3730770306

Kuutti, K. (1991). *The concept of activity as a basic unit of analysis for CSCW research*. Paper presented at the Second European Conference on Computer-Supported Cooperative Work.

Kuutti, K. (1996). Activity theory as a potential framework for human-computer interaction research. In Nardi, B. A. (Ed.), *Context and consciousness: Activity theory and human-computer interaction* (pp. 17–44). Cambridge, MA: MIT Press.

Lainema, T., & Makkonen, P. (2003). Applying constructivist approach to educational business games: Case REALGAME. *Simulation & Gaming, 34*(1), 131–149. doi:10.1177/1046878102250601

Lalor, E. C., Kelly, S. P., Finucane, C., Burke, R., Smith, R., & Reilly, R. B. (2005). Steady-State VEP-Based Brain-Computer Interface Control in an Immersive 3D Gaming Environment. *EURASIP Journal on Applied Signal Processing, 19*, 3156–3164. doi:10.1155/ASP.2005.3156

Laurel, B. (1994). Placeholder: Landscape and narrative in virtual environments. *ACM Computer Graphics Quarterly, 28*(2), 118–126. doi:10.1145/178951.178967

Laurel, B. (Ed.). (2004). *Design Research: Methods and Perspectives*. Boston: MIT Press.

Lawley, D. N., & Maxwell, A. E. (1962). Factor Analysis as a Statistical Method. *Journal of the Royal Statistical Society. Series D, 12*(3), 209–229.

Leahy, W., Chandler, P., & Sweller, J. (2003). When auditory presentations should and should not be a component of multimedia instruction. *Applied Cognitive Psychology, 17*, 401–418. doi:10.1002/acp.877

Leander, K. M., & Lovvorn, J. F. (2006). Literacy networks: Following the circulation of texts, bodies, and objects in the schooling and online gaming of one youth. *Cognition and Instruction, 24*(3), 291–340. doi:10.1207/s1532690xci2403_1

Lecuyer, A., Lotte, F., Reilly, R., Leeb, R., Hirose, M., & Slater, M. (2008). Brain-computer interfaces, virtual reality, and videogames. *Computer, 41*(10), 66–72. doi:10.1109/MC.2008.410

Lee, K. M., Park, N., & Jin, S.-A. (2006). Narrative and interactivity in computer games. In P. Vorderer & J. Bryant (Eds.), *Playing video games: Motives, responses, and consequences* (pp. 259-274). Mahwah, NJ: Lawrence Erlbaum Associates.

Lee, Y. (2004). *Student perceptions of problems' structuredness, complexity, situatedness, and information richness and their effects on problem-solving performance*. Unpublished doctoral dissertation, Florida State University, FL.

Leeb, R., Keinrath, C., Friedman, D., Guger, C., Neuper, C., Garau, M., et al. (2005). Walking from thoughts: Not the muscles are crucial but the brain waves! In *Proceedings of the 8th Annual International Workshop on Presence* (pp. 25-32).

Leeb, R., Lee, F., Keinrath, C., Scherer, R., Bischof, H., & Pfurtscheller, G. (2007). Brain-Computer Communication: Motivation, Aim, and Impact of Exploring a Virtual Apartment. *IEEE Transactions on Neural Systems and Rehabilitation Engineering, 15*(4), 473–482. doi:10.1109/TNSRE.2007.906956

Lenhart, A., Kahne, J., Middaugh, E., Macgill, A. R., Evans, C., & Vitak, J. (2008). *Teens, Video Games and Civics: Teens' gaming experiences are diverse and include significant social interaction and civic engagement.* Washington, DC: Pew Internet and American Life Project. Nicholson, B., Alley, R., Green, J., & Lawson, D. (2009). *An Analysis of the Effects of a Technology Program on Students' Academic Performance: Are These Vygotsky's Children?* Huntington, WV: Marshall University.

Leon, E., Clarke, G., Callaghan, V., & Sepulveda, F. (2007). A user-independent real-time emotion recognition system for software agents in domestic environments. *Engineering Applications of Artificial Intelligence, 20*(3), 337–345. doi:10.1016/j.engappai.2006.06.001

Lester, J., Converse, S., Stone, B., Kahler, S., & Barlow, T. (1997). Animated pedagogical agents and problem-solving effectiveness: A large-scale empirical evaluation. In *Proceedings of the 8th World Conference on Artificial Intelligence in Education*, Kobe, Japan.

Leu, D. J. Jr, Kinzer, C. K., Coiro, J., & Cammack, D. (2004). Toward a theory of new literacies emerging from the Internet and other information and communication technologies. In Ruddell, R. B., & Unrau, N. (Eds.), *Theoretical models and processes of reading* (5th ed., pp. 1568–1611). Newark, DE: International Reading Association.

Lindlof, T. (1995). *Qualitative Communication Research Methods* (3rd ed.). Thosand Oaks, CA: Sage Publications.

Lipscomb, S. D., & Zehnder, S. M. (2005). Immersion in the virtual environment: The effect of a musical score on the video gaming experience. *Journal of Physiological Anthropology and Applied Human Science, 23*, 88–95.

Liu, H. (2007). Social network profiles as taste performances. *Journal of Computer-Mediated Communication, 13*(1). http://jcmc.indiana.edu/vol13/issue1/liu.html

Loenen, E. van, Bergman, T., Buil, V., Gelder, K., van, Groten, M., Hollemans, G., et al. (2007). Entertaible: A solution for social gaming experiences. In *Proceedings of Tangible play workshop, IUI conference*.

Lombard, M., & Ditton, T. (1997). At the Heart of It All: The Concept of Presence. *Journal of Computer-Mediated Communication, 3*(2).

Long, A. (2000). *The Legend of Zelda – retroview.* Retrieved April 1, 2009, from http://www.rpgamer.com/games/zelda/z1/reviews/z1strev1.html

Lopes, C. V., Dourish, P., Lorenz, D. H., & Lieberherr, K. (2003). Beyond aop: toward naturalistic programming. In *Proceedings of the Companion of the 18th annual ACM SIGPLAN conference on object-oriented programming, systems, languages, and applications (Oopsla'03)* (pp. 198-207). New York: ACM.

Ludlow, P., & Wallace, M. (2007). *The Second Life Herald: The Virtual Tabloid that Witnessed the Dawn of the Metaverse.* Cambridge, MA: MIT Press.

Ludwig, K. A., Miriani, R. M., Langhals, N. B., Joseph, M. D., Anderson, D. J., & Kipke, D. R. (2009). Using a Common Average Reference to Improve Cortical Neuron Recordings From Microelectrode Arrays. *Journal of Neurophysiology, 101*(3), 1679–1689. doi:10.1152/jn.90989.2008

Lutgens, F., Tarbuck, E., & Tasa, D. (2004). *Foundations of Earth Science* (4th ed.). Upper Saddle River, NJ: Prentice Hall.

Lynch, C., Pinkwart, N., Ashley, K., & Aleven, V. (2008, June). What do argument diagrams tell us about students' aptitude or experience? A statistical analysis in an ill-defined domain. In *Proceedings of the workshop held during ITS-2008, the 9th international Conference on Intelligent Tutoring Systems*, Montreal, Canada.

Malhorta, P. (2002). *Issues involved in real-time rendering of virtual environments.* Unpublished master's thesis, Virginia Polytechnic Institute and State University, VA.

Malone, M. R., & Lepper, M. R. (1987). Making learning fun. In R. E. Snow & M. J. Farr (Series Eds.) and R. E. Snow & J. F. Marshall (Vol. Eds.), *Aptitude, learning, and instruction: Vol.4 Conative and affective process analyses* (pp. 223-253). Hillsdale, NJ: Lawrence Erlbaum Associates.

Malone, T. W. (1981). Toward a theory of intrinsically motivating instruction. *Cognitive Science, 5*(4), 333–369. doi:10.1207/s15516709cog0504_2

Mandryk, R. L., & Maranan, D. S. (2002). False prophets: exploring hybrid board/video games. In *Proceedings of Chi '02 extended abstracts on human factors in computing systems* (pp. 640–641). New York: ACM.

Manninen, T. (2001, September 10-14). *Rich Interaction in the Context of Networked Virtual Environments- Experiences Gained from the Multi-player Games Domain.* Paper presented at the HCI 2001/ IHM 2001, Lille, France.

Manninen, T. (2003). Interaction Forms and Communicative Actions in Multiplayer Games. *Game Studies, 3*(1).

Manovich, L. (2001). *The language of new media.* Boston: MIT Press.

Mantovani, G., Gamberini, L., Martinelli, M., & Varotto, D. (2001). Exploring the suitability of virtual environments for safety training: Signals, norms and ambiguity in a simulated emergency escape. *Cognition Technology and Work, 3*(1), 33–41. doi:10.1007/PL00011519

Maragos, K., & Grigoriadou, M. (2005). Towards the design of intelligent educational gaming systems. In *Proceedings of the AIED workshop5, held at the 12ᵗʰ International Conference on Artificial Intelligence in education,* Amsterdam.

Mark, G., & Wulf, V. (1999). Changing interpersonal communication through groupware use. *Behaviour & Information Technology, 18*(5), 385–395. doi:10.1080/014492999118968

Marshall, C., & Rossman, G. (1995). *Designing qualitative research* (2nd ed.). Thousand Oaks, CA: Sage.

Matthews, P. C., & Chesters, P. E. (2006). Implementing the Information Pump using accessible technology. *Journal of Engineering Design, 17*(6), 563–585. doi:10.1080/09544820600646629

Mayer, R. E. (2005). Cognitive Theory of Multimedia Learning. In R. E. Mayer (Ed.), *The Cambridge Handbook of Multimedia Learning* (pp. 31-48). New York: Cambridge University Press.

Mayer, R. E., & Clark, R. C. (2007). Using Rich Media Wisely. In R. A. Reiser & J. V. Dempsey (Eds.) *Trends and Issues in Instructional Design and Technology* (pp. 311-322). Upper Saddle River, NJ: Pearson Education Inc.

Mayer, R. E. (1997). Multimedia learning: Are we asking the right questions? *Educational Psychologist, 32*(1), 1–19. doi:10.1207/s15326985ep3201_1

Mayer, R. E. (2009). *Multimedia learning* (2nd ed.). New York: Cambridge University Press.

Mayer, R. E., & Moreno, R. (2003). Nine Ways to Reduce Cognitive Load in Multimedia Learning. *Educational Psychologist, 38*(1), 43–52. doi:10.1207/S15326985EP3801_6

Mazalek, A., Reynolds, M., & Davenport, G. (2007, October). The tviews table in the home. In *Proceedings of the Second Annual IEEE International Workshop on Horizontal Interactive Human- Computer Systems (TABLETOP '07)* (pp. 52-59).

Mazzarella, S. R. (2005). *Girl wide web: Girls, the internet, and the negotiation of identity.* New York: Peter Lang.

McBrien, J. L., & Brandt, R. S. (1997). *The Language of Learning: A Guide to Education Terms* (pp. 17–18). Alexandria, VA: Association for Supervision and Curriculum Development.

McDaniel, R., Fiore, S. M., Greenwood-Erickson, A., Scielzo, S., & Cannon-Bowers, J. A. (2006). Video Games as Learning Tools for Project Management. *The Journal of the International Digital Media and Arts Association, 3*(1), 78–91.

McDonald, G. (2008). *A history of video game music.* Retrieved August 1, 2008, from http://www.gamespot.com/features/6092391/p-6.html

McFarland, D., Miner, L., Vaughan, T., & Wolpaw, J. (2000). Mu and Beta Rhythm Topographies During Motor Imagery and Actual Movements. *Brain Topography, 12*(3), 177–186. doi:10.1023/A:1023437823106

McGrenere, J. L. (1996, June). *Design: Educational Electronic Multi-Player Games: A Literature Review.* Paper presented at the Department of Computer Science, University of British Columbia, BC, Canada.

McHaney, R. (1991). *Computer simulation: A practical perspective.* San Diego, CA: Academic Press.

McMahon, M. (2009). The DODDEL Model:Flexible Document-Oriented Model for the Design of Serious Games. In Connolly, T., Stansfield, M., & Boyle, L. (Eds.), *Games-Based Learning Advancements for Multi-Sensory Human Computer Interfaces: Techniques and Effective Practices* (pp. 98–118). Hershey, PA: IGI Global. doi:10.4018/978-1-60566-360-9.ch006

McRae, S. (1996). Coming apart at the seams: Sex, text, and the virtual body. In Cherney, L., & Weise, E. R. (Eds.), *Wired women: Gender and new realities in cyberspace.* Seattle: Seal Press.

Mehrabian, A. (1981). *Silent Messages: Implicit Communication of Emotions and Attitudes* (2nd ed.). Belmont, CA: Wadsworth, Inc. MIT and Microsoft Corporation (Producer). (2005, July 12). *Games-to-teach project.* Retrieved from http://cms.mit.edu/games/education/proto.html

Michie, D., Spiegelhalter, D. J., & Taylor, C. C. (Eds.). (1994). *Machine Learning, Neural and Statistical.* New York: Ellis Horwood.

Miller, S. (2001). Aspect-oriented programming takes aim at software complexity. *IEEE Computer, 34*(4), 18–21.

Minegishi, T., Ohta, A., & Kondo, K. (2006). *The Legend of Zelda: Twilight Princess: Original soundtrack.* Kyoto, Japan: Nintendo.

Minogue, J., & Jones, G. (2009). Measuring the impact of Haptic feedback using the SOLO taxonomy. *International Journal of Science Education, 31,* 1359–1378. doi:10.1080/09500690801992862

Mislevy, R., Almond, R., & Lukas, J. (2003). *Brief intro to Evidence-Centered Design* (CSE Tech. Rep. No. 632). The National Center for Research on Evaluation, Standards, Student Testing (CRESST).

Mitchell, A., & Savill-Smith, C. (2004). *The use of computer and videogames for learning: A review of the literature.* London: Learning and Skills Development Agency. Retrieved July 31, 2008, from http://www.lsda.org.uk/files/PDF/1529.pdf

Mitchell, T. (1997). *Machine Learning.* New York: McGraw-Hill.

Moore, R. J., Gathman, E. C. H., Ducheneaut, N., & Nickell, E. (2007, April 28-May 3). *Coordinating joint activity in avatar-mediated interaction.* Paper presented at the Human Factors in Computing Systems (CHI 2007), San Jose, CA.

Moreno, R., & Mayer, R. E. (2000). A coherence effect in multimedia learning: The case for minimizing irrelevant sounds in the design of multimedia instructional messages. *Journal of Educational Psychology, 92,* 117–320. doi:10.1037/0022-0663.92.1.117

Mousavi, S., Low, R., & Sweller, J. (1995). Reducing cognitive load by mixing auditory and visual presentation modes. *Journal of Educational Psychology, 87,* 319–334. doi:10.1037/0022-0663.87.2.319

Munro, A., Breaux, R., Patrey, J., & Sheldon, B. (2002). Cognitive aspects of virtual environment design. In Stanney, K. M. (Ed.), *Handbook of virtual environments: Design, implementation, and applications* (pp. 415–434). Mahwah, NJ: Lawrence Erlbaum.

Murray, J. (1997). *Hamlet on the holodeck: The future of narrative in cyberspace.* Boston: MIT Press.

Nacke, L. E., Grimshaw, M. N., & Lindley, C. A. (2010). More than a feeling: Measurement of sonic user experience and psychophysiology in a first-person shooter game. *Interacting with Computers, 22*(5)..doi:10.1016/j.intcom.2010.04.005

Nakamura, L. (2000). "Where do you want to go today?": Cybernetic tourism, the Internet, and transnationality. In Kolko, B. E., Nakamura, L., & Rodman, G. B. (Eds.), *Race in Cyberspace* (pp. 15–26). New York: Routledge.

Nakamura, L. (2002). *Cybertypes: Race, ethnicity, and identity on the Internet.* New York: Routledge.

Nantais, K. M., & Schellenberg, E. G. (1999). The Mozart effect: An artifact of preference. *Psychological Science, 10,* 370–373. doi:10.1111/1467-9280.00170

Nardi, B., Ly, S., & Harris, J. (2007). Learning conversations in World of Warcraft. In *Proceedings of the 2007 Hawaii International Conference on Systems Science* (pp. 79). Washington, DC: IEEE Computer Society.

Nasoz, F., Alvarez, K., Lisetti, C. L., & Finkelstein, N. (2004). Emotion recognition from physiological signals using wireless sensors for presence technologies. *International Journal of Cognition. Technology and Work, 6*(1), 4–14. doi:10.1007/s10111-003-0143-x

National Council for the Social Studies. (1994). *The curriculum standards for Social Studies*. Retrieved July 18, 2008, from http://www.socialstudies.org/standards/

Neal, L. (2003). *Predictions for 2003: e-learning's leading lights look ahead*. Retrieved February 22, 2004, from http://www.elearnmag.org/subpage/sub_page.cfm/article_pk=6541&page_number_nb=17title-COLUMN

Needlman, A. R. D. (1996). Growth and development. In R. E. Behrman, R. M. Kliegman, & M. Arvin (Eds.), *Nelson textbook of pediatrics* (15th ed., pp. 30-72). Philadelphia: Saunders.

Neji, M., Ben Ammar, M., Alimi, A. M., & Gouardères, G. (2008). Agent-Based framework for affective intelligent tutoring systems. In Woolf et al. (Eds.), *Proceedings of the ITS2008* (LNCS 5091, pp. 665-667).

Nelson, B., Ketelhut, D. J., Clarke, J., Dieterle, E., Dede, C., & Erlandson, B. (2007). Robust design strategies for scaling educational innovations: The River City MUVE case study. In B. E. Shelton & D. A. Wiley (Eds.), *The Educational Design and Use of Computer Simulation*.

Nelson, B. (2007). Exploring the use of individualized, reflective guidance in an educational multi-user virtual environment. *Journal of Science Education and Technology, 16*(1), 83–97. doi:10.1007/s10956-006-9039-x

Nelson, B., & Erlandson, B. (2008). Managing Cognitive Load in Educational Multi User Virtual Environments: Reflection on Design Practice. *Educational Technology Research and Development, 56*, 619–641. doi:10.1007/s11423-007-9082-1

Nelson, B., & Ketelhut, D. J. (2007). Designing for Real-World Inquiry in Virtual Environments. *Educational Psychology Review, 19*(3), 265–283. doi:10.1007/s10648-007-9048-1

Nelson, B., Ketelhut, D. J., Clarke, J., Bowman, C., & Dede, C. (2005). Design-based research strategies for developing a scientific inquiry curriculum in a multi-user virtual enviroment. *Educational Technology, 45*(1), 21–27.

Newell, A., & Simon, H. (1972). *Human Problem Solving*. Englewood Cliffs, NJ: Prentice-Hall.

Newman, J. (2002). The Myth of the Ergodic Videogame: Some thoughts on player-character relationships in videogames. *Game Studies, 2*(1).

Nickelodeon. (2009). *iPhone & iPod Touch Consumer Research*. New York: Internal Data.

Nicovich, S. G., Boller, G. W., & Cornwell, T. B. (2005). Experienced presence within computer-mediated communications: Initial explorations on the effects of gender with respect to empathy and immersion. *Journal of Computer-Mediated Communication, 10*(2). Retrieved August 9, 2009, from http://jcmc.indiana.edu/vol10/issue2/nicovich.html

Niehaus, J., & Riedl, M. (2009). Toward scenario adaptation for learning. In *Proceedings of the 14th International Conference on Artificial Intelligence in Education (AIED09)*.

Nielsen, J. (n.d.). *How to Conduct a heuristic Evaluation*. Retrieved 2009, from http://staff.unak.is/not/nicolaw/courses/hci/HCILab7papers.pdf

Nijholt, A., Tan, D., Allison, B., Milan, J., & Graimann, B. (2008a). Brain-computer interfaces for HCI and games. In *Proceedings of the CHI '08 extended abstracts on Human factors in computing systems* (pp. 3925-3928). New York: ACM.

Nijholt, A., Tan, D., Pfurtscheller, G., Brunner, C., Millán, J., & Allison, B. (2008b). Brain-Computer Interfacing for Intelligent Systems. *IEEE Intelligent Systems, 23*(3), 72–79. doi:10.1109/MIS.2008.41

Nintendo. (1998). *The Legend of Zelda: Ocarina of Time* (Nintendo 64 software). Redmond, WA: Nintendo.

Nintendo. (2006). *The Legend of Zelda: Twilight Princess* (Wii software). Redmond, WA: Nintendo.

Nitsche, M. (2009). *Video game spaces: Image, play, and structure in 3d worlds*. Boston: MIT Press.

Nkambou, R. (2006). Towards affective intelligent tutoring system, Workshop on Motivational and Affective Issues in ITS. In *Proceedings of the 8th International Conference on Intelligent Tutoring Systems (ITS 2006)* (pp. 5-12).

Norman, D. (2005). Human-centered design considered harmful. *Interaction, 12*(4), 12–19. doi:10.1145/1070960.1070976

Norman, G. R. (1988). Problem-solving skills, solving problems and problem-based learning. *Medical Education, 22*, 279–286. doi:10.1111/j.1365-2923.1988.tb00754.x

Norman, G. R. (1997). Assessment in problem-based learning. In Boud, D., & Feletti, G. (Eds.), *The challenge of problem-based learning* (2nd ed., pp. 263–268). London: Kogan Page.

Norman, G. R., & Schmidt, H. G. (1992). The psychological basis of problem-based learning: A review of the evidence. *Academic Medicine, 67*(9), 557–565. doi:10.1097/00001888-199209000-00002

North, A. C., & Hargreaves, D. J. (1999). Music and driving game performance. *Scandinavian Journal of Psychology, 40*, 285–292. doi:10.1111/1467-9450.404128

NPD. (2008). *Kids & Consumer Electronics (Rep.).* NY: Port Washington.

NPD. (2009). *Kids & Gaming (Rep.).* NY: Port Washington.

Nucci, L. (2008). *An Overview of Moral Development and Moral Education.* Retrieved from http://tigger.uic.edu/~lnucci/MoralEd/overview.html

Nunnaly, J. (1978). *Psychometric theory.* New York: McGraw-Hill.

O'Neil, H. F., Wainess, R., & Baker, E. L. (2005). Classification of learning outcomes: Evidence from the computer games literature. *Curriculum Journal, 16*(4), 455–474. doi:10.1080/09585170500384529

Object management Group (OMG). (2006). *BPMN 1.0, OMG Final Adopted Specification.*

O'Reilly, T. (2005). *What is Web 2.0.* Retrieved August 4, 2009, from http://oreilly.com/web2/archive/what-is-web-20.html

Orr, T. J., Filigenzi, M. T., & Ruff, T. M. (2003). *Desktop virtual reality miner training simulator. Centres for Disease Control and Prevention.* Retrieved June 17, 2008, from http://whitepapers.silicon.com/0,39024759,60018207p,00.htm

Osborn, A. (1953). *Applied Imagination: Principles and Procedures of Creative Problem Solving.* New York: Charles Scribner's Sons.

Oude Bos, D., & Reuderink, B. (2008). Brainbasher: a BCI game. In P. Markopoulos, J. Hoonhout, I. Soute, & J. Read (Eds.), *Proceedings of the International Conference on Fun and Games 2008,* Eindhoven, The Netherlands (pp. 36-39).

Pagulayan, R. J., Keeker, K., Wixon, D., Romero, R., & Fuller, T. (2003). User-centered design in games. In Jacko, J., & Sears, A. (Eds.), *Handbook for human-computer interaction in interactive systems* (pp. 883–906). Hillsdale, NJ: Erlbaum.

Pahl, G., & Beitz, W. (1995). *Engineering Design, A Systematic Approach.* Bath, UK: Springer.

Paivio, A. (1986). *Mental Representations.* New York: Oxford University Press.

Paivio, A. (1991). Dual Coding Theory: Retrospect and Current Status. *Canadian Journal of Psychology, 45*, 255–287. doi:10.1037/h0084295

Papastergiou, M. (2009). Exploring the potential of computer and video games for health and physical education: A literature review. *Computers & Education, 53*, 603–622. doi:10.1016/j.compedu.2009.04.001

Papert, S. (1980). *Mindstorms: Children, computers and powerful ideas.* New York: Basic Books.

Papert, S. (1993). *The children's machine: Rethinking schools in the age of the computer.* New York: Basic Books.

Parchman, S. W., Ellis, J. A., Christinaz, D., & Vogel, M. (2000). An evaluation of three computer-based instructional strategies in basic electricity and electronics training. *Military Psychology, 12*(1), 73–87. doi:10.1207/S15327876MP1201_4

Patton, M. (2002). *Qualitative research and evaluation methods.* Thousand Oaks, CA: Sage Publications.

Pausch, R. (1994, April). What HCI designers can learn from video game designers. In *Proceedings of the Conference on Human Factors in Computing Systems (SIGCHI 1994)*. Boston, MA (pp.177-178). New York: ACM Publishers.

Pearce, C. (2005, June 16-20). *Theory wars: an argument against arguments in the so-called ludology/narratology debate.* Paper presented at the Changing Views: Worlds in Play, Digital Games Research Association Conference, Vancouver, Canada.

Pederson, S., & Williams, D. (2004). A comparison of assessment practices and their effects on learning and motivation in a student-centered learning environment. *Journal of Educational Multimedia and Hypermedia*, *13*(1).

Peter, C., & Herbon, A. (2006). Emotion representation and physiology assignments in digital systems. *Interacting with Computers*, *18*, 139–170. doi:10.1016/j.intcom.2005.10.006

Pfurtscheller, G. (2001). Functional brain imaging based on ERD/ERS. *Vision Research*, *41*(10-11), 1257–1260. doi:10.1016/S0042-6989(00)00235-2

Picard, R. W., Vyzas, E., & Healey, J. (2001). Toward Machine Emotional Intelligence: Analysis of Affective Physiological State. *IEEE Transactions on Pattern Analysis and Machine Intelligence*, *23*(10), 1175–1191. doi:10.1109/34.954607

Pineda, J. A., Silverman, D. S., Vankov, A., & Hestenes, J. (2003). Learning to control brain rhythms: making a brain-computer interface possible. *IEEE Transactions on Neural Systems and Rehabilitation Engineering*, *11*(2), 181–184. doi:10.1109/TNSRE.2003.814445

Pinelle, D., Wong, N., & Stach, T. (2008). *Heuristic Evaluation for Games: Usability Principles for Video Game Design.* Paper presented at the CHI 2008, Florence, Italy.

Pinkard, N. (2009). *Preparing Urban Youth to be Multiliterate*. Chicago: University of Chicago, Center for Urban School Improvement. Retrieved from http://iremix.org/3-research/pages/33-research-overview

Postigo, H. (2007). Of mods and modders: Chasing down the value of fan-based digital games modifications. *Games and Culture*, *2*(4), 300–313. doi:10.1177/1555412007307955

Poupyrev, I. (2000, July 23-28). 3D manipulation techniques. In the *Course Notes of the 27th International Conference on Computer Graphics and Interactive Technologies (SIGGRAPH 2000)*, New Orleans, LA.

Prendinger, H., Becker, C., & Ishizuka, M. (2006). A study in Users' Physiological Response to an Empathic Interface Agent. *International Journal of Humanoid Robotics*, *3*(3), 371–391. doi:10.1142/S0219843606000801

Prensky, M. (2001). *Digital Game-Based Learning*. New York: McGraw-Hill.

Professional Technology Temple. *Wikipedia*. Retrieved July 18, 2008, from http://en.wikipedia.org/wiki/Professional_Technology_Temple

Puccio, G. J. (1999). Creative Problem Solving Preferences: Their Identification and Implications. *Creativity and Innovation Management*, *8*(3), 171–178. doi:10.1111/1467-8691.00134

Pugh, S. (1991). *Total Design*. Reading, UK: Addison-Wesley.

PwC. (2006). *Global Entertainment and Media Outlook: 2006–2010*. Retrieved from http://www.pwc.com

Quanlan, J. (1993). *C4.5: programs for machine learning*. San Francisco, CA: Morgan Kaufmann.

Ramirez, A. Jr, & Zhang, S. (2007). When Online Meets Offline: The Effect of Modality Switching on Relational Communication. *Communication Monographs*, *74*(3), 287–310. doi:10.1080/03637750701543493

Rantanen, K., & Domb, E. (2002). *Simplified TRIZ: new problem-solving applications for engineers and manufacturing professionals*. Boca Raton, FL: St. Lucie Press. doi:10.1201/9781420000320

Rashid, A., & Moreira, A. (2006). Domain models are not aspect free. In *Proceedings of Model Driven Engineering Languages and Systems* (pp. 155-169).

Rauscher, F. H., Shaw, G. L., & Ky, K. N. (1995). Listening to Mozart enhances spatial-temporal reasoning: Towards a neurophysiological basis. *Neuroscience Letters, 185,* 44–47. doi:10.1016/0304-3940(94)11221-4

Reese, C., Duvigneau, M., Köhler, M., Moldt, D., & Rölke, H. (2003, February). Agent based settler game. In *Proceedings of agentcities agent technology competition (ATC03),* Barcelona, Spain. Agentcities.NET.

Reese, D. D. (2007). First steps and beyond: Series games as preparation for future learning. *Journal of Educational Multimedia and Hypermedia, 16*(3), 283–300.

Rejeski, D. (2002). *Gaming our way to a better future.* Retrieved February 22, 2004, from http://www.avault.com/developer/getarticle.asp?name=drejeski1

Retz-Schmidt, R. (1991). Recognizing Intentions, Interactions, and Causes of Plan Failures. *User Modeling and User-Adapted Interaction, 1,* 173–202. doi:10.1007/BF00154477

Reuderink, B., Poel, M., & Nijholt, A. (2010). *The impact of loss of control on the performance of a movement BCI.*

Revelle, G. L., & Medoff, L. (2002). Interface design and research process for studying the usability of interactive home-entertainment systems by young children. *Early Education and Development, 13*(4), 423–434. doi:10.1207/s15566935eed1304_6

Reynolds, R., & Harel Caperton, I. (2009a, June). *Development of Students' Six Contemporary Learning Abilities in Globaloria.* Paper presented at the Annual Conférence of the American Educational Research Association, San Diego, CA.

Reynolds, R., & Harel Caperton, I. (2009b, June). *Development of High School and Community College Students' Contemporary Learning Abilities in Globaloria.* Paper presented at the Annual Conference of the American Educational Research Association, San Diego, CA.

Rheingold, H. (1993). *The virtual community: Homesteading on the electronic frontier* (1st ed.). Reading, MA: Addison-Wesley.

Rideout, V. J., Vanderwater, E. A., & Wartella, E. A. (2003). *Zero to Six: Electronic Media in the Lives of Infants, Toddlers and Preschoolers.* Menlo Park, CA: Henry J. Kaiser Family Foundation.

Rideout, V., & Hamel, E. (2006). *The media family: Electronic media in the lives of infants, toddlers, preschoolers and their parents.* Menlo Park, CA: Henry J. Kaiser Family Foundation.

Rittgen, P. (2009). Collaborative Modelling – A Design Science Approach. In *Proceedings of the 42nd Hawaii International Conference on System Sciences (HICSS-42)* (p. 10). Washington, DC: IEEE Computer Society.

Robertson, J., & Good, J. (2005). Children's narrative development through computer game authoring. *TechTrend, 49*(5), 43–59. doi:10.1007/BF02763689

Robertson, J., & Howells, C. (2008). Computer game design: Opportunities for successful learning. *Computers & Education, 50,* 559–578. doi:10.1016/j.compedu.2007.09.020

Roesengren, K. S., Savelsbergh, G. J. P., & van der Kamp, J. (2003). Development and learning: A TASC-based perspective on the acquisition of perceptual-motor behaviors. *Infant Behavior and Development, 26,* 473–494. doi:10.1016/j.infbeh.2003.08.001

Rohrbach, B. (1969). Kreativ nach Regeln. *Absatzwirtschaft, 12,* 73–75.

Rollings, A., & Adams, E. (2003). *On game design.* Berkeley, CA: New Riders.

Rosenblatt, L. M. (1995). *Literature as exploration* (5th ed.). New York: Modern Language Association of America.

Roth, E. A., & Smith, K. H. (2008). The Mozart effect: Evidence for the arousal hypothesis. *Perceptual and Motor Skills, 107,* 396–402. doi:10.2466/PMS.107.6.396-402

Rouse, R. (2001). *Game design–theory and practice.* Sudbury, MA: Jones and Bartlett.

Rushton, A. (2005). Formative assessment: a key to deep learning? *Medical Teacher, 27*(6), 509–513. doi:10.1080/01421590500129159

Russell, J. A. (1980). A circumplex model of affect. *Journal of Personality and Social Psychology, 39,* 1161–1178. doi:10.1037/h0077714

Ryan, M.-L. (2001). *Narrative as virtual reality: Immersion and interactivity in literature and electronic media.* Baltimore: Johns Hopkins University Press.

Sadowski, W., & Stanney, K. (2002). Presence in virtual environments. In Stanney, K. M. (Ed.), *Handbook of virtual environments: Design, implementation, and applications* (pp. 791–806). Mahwah, NJ: Lawrence Erlbaum.

Salen, K. (Ed.). (2007). *The Ecology of Games: Connecting Youth, Games, and Learning.* Chicago: John D. and Catherine T. MacArthur Foundation.

Salen, K., & Zimmerman, E. (2004). *Rules of play.* Cambridge, MA: MIT Press.

Salen, K., & Zimmerman, E. (2006). *The game design reader: A rules of play anthology.* Cambridge, MA: MIT Press.

Salen, K. (2007). Gaming literacies: A game design study in action. *Journal of Educational Multimedia and Hypermedia, 16*(3), 301–322.

Salen, K., & Zimmerman, E. (2003). *Rules of Play, Game Design Fundamentals.* Cambridge, MA: MIT Press.

Salen, K., & Zimmerman, E. (2005). *The game design reader: A rules of play anthology.* Cambridge, MA: MIT Press.

Sanchanta, M. (2007, September 7). Nintendo's Wii takes console lead. *The Financial Times.* Retrieved October 29, 2001, from http://www.ft.com/home/us

Sanchez-Crespo, D. (2003). *Core techniques and algorithms in game programming.* New Riders Games.

Sannelli, C., Braun, M., Tangermann, M., & Müller, K.-R. (2008). Estimating noise and dimensionality in BCI data sets: Towards BCI illiteracy comprehension. In *Proceedings of the 4th International Brain-Computer Interface Workshop and Training Course 2008.*

Savery, J. R. (2006). Overview of Problem-based learning: Definitions and Distinctions. *The Interdisciplinary Journal of Problem-based Learning, 1*(1), 9–20.

Savery, J. R., & Duffy, T. M. (2001). *Problem based learning: An instructional model and its constructivist framework (CRLT Tech. Rep.).* Bloomington, Indiana: Indiana University.

Schellenberg, E. G., Nakata, T., Hunter, P. G., & Tamoto, S. (2007). Exposure to music and cognitive performance: Tests of children and adults. *Psychology of Music, 35,* 5–19. doi:10.1177/0305735607068885

Schreiber, A. T., Akkermans, J. A., Anjewierden, A., De Hoog, R., Shadbolt, N., Van de Velde, W., & Wielinga, B. (1999). *Knowledge Engineering and Management: The CommonKADS Methodology.* Cambridge, MA: MIT Press.

Sedaghat, M. N., Gholami, N., Iravanian, S., & Kangavari, M. R. (2005). Design and Implementation of Live Commentary System in Soccer Simulation Environment. In *RoboCup 2004: Robot Soccer World Cup VIII* (pp. 602–610). Berlin: Springer.

Seely Brown, J., & Adler, R. P. (2008). Minds on Fire: Open Education, the Long Tail, and Learning 2.0. *Educause Review.*

Shaffer, D. W. (2005). *Multisubculturalism: Computers and the end of progressive education.* Retrieved from: http://coweb.wcer.wisc.edu/cv/papers/multisubculturalism-draft1.pdf

Shaffer, D. W. (2006). Epistemic frames for epistemic games. *Computers and Education Journal, 46*(3), 223-234. Retrieved from http://dx.doi.org/10.1016/j.compedu.2005.11.003

Shaffer, D. W. (2006). *How computer games help children learn.* New York: Palgrave Macmillan.

Shah, J. J., Kulkarni, S. V., & Vargas-Hernandez, N. (2000). Evaluation of Idea Generation Methods for Conceptual Design: Effectiveness Metrics and Design of Experiments. *Journal of Mechanical Design, 122*(4), 377–385. doi:10.1115/1.1315592

Sheldon, L. (2004). *Character development and storytelling for games.* Boston: Thomson Course Technology.

Shelton, B. (2007). Designing educational games for activity-goal alignment. In Shelton, B., & Wiley, A. (Eds.), *Educational design and use of computer simulation games* (pp. 103–130). Sense Publishers.

Shelton, B. E., & Wiley, D. A. (2007). Introduction. In Shelton, B. E., & Wiley, D. A. (Eds.), *Modeling and simulations for learning and instruction: The design and use of simulation computer games in education* (pp. 1–2). The Netherlands: Sence Publishers.

Shibasaki, H., & Hallett, M. (2006). What is the bereitschaftspotential? *Clinical Neurophysiology, 117*, 2341–2356. doi:10.1016/j.clinph.2006.04.025

Shih, S.-G., Hu, T.-P., & Chen, C.-N. (2006). A game theory-based approach to the analysis of cooperative learning in design studios. *Design Studies, 27*, 711–722. doi:10.1016/j.destud.2006.05.001

Shin, N., & McGee, S. (2003). *Designers Should Enhance learners' Ill-Structured Problem-Solving Skills*. Retrieved from http://vdc.cet.edu/entries/illps.htm

Shin, N. (2006). Online learner's 'flow' experience: An experimental study. *British Journal of Educational Technology, 37*, 705–720. doi:10.1111/j.1467-8535.2006.00641.x

Shirai, A., Geslin, E., & Richir, S. (2007). *WiiMedia: Motion Analysis Methods and Applications Using a Consumer Video Game Controller.* Paper presented at the Sandbox: ACM Siggraph Symposium on Video Games, San Diego, CA.

Shiratuddin, M. F., & Thabet, W. (2002). Virtual office walkthrough using a 3d game engine. *International Journal of Design Computing.* Retrieved June 18, 2008, from http://faculty.arch.usyd.edu.au/kcdc/ijdc/vol04/papers/shira/ijdc_final_journal.pdf

Shneiderman, B. (2003). Why not make interfaces better than 3D reality? *IEEE Computer Graphics and Applications, 23*(6), 12–15. doi:10.1109/MCG.2003.1242376

Shneiderman, B., & Plaisant, C. (2004). *Designing the user interface: Strategies for effective human-computer interaction.* Reading, MA: Addison Wesley.

Short, J., Williams, E., & Christie, B. (1976). *The social psychology of telecommunications.* London: Wiley.

Siegler, R. (1991). *Children's Thinking* (2nd ed.). Englewood Cliffs, NJ: Prentice Hall.

Silk, K. J., Sherry, J., Winn, B., Keesecker, N., Horodynski, M. A., & Sayir, A. (2008). Increasing nutrition literacy: Testing the effectiveness of print, web site, and game modalities. *Journal of Nutrition Education and Behavior, 40*(1), 3–10. doi:10.1016/j.jneb.2007.08.012

Silver, D. (2000). Margins in the wires: Looking for race, gender, and sexuality in the Blacksburg Electronic Village. In Kolko, B. E., Nakamura, L., & Rodman, G. B. (Eds.), *Race in cyberspace* (pp. 133–150). New York: Routledge.

Simkins, D. W., & Steinkuehler, C. (2008). Critical ethical reasoning and role-play. *Games and Culture, 3*(3/4), 333–355. doi:10.1177/1555412008317313

Simpson, D. E. (1998). Dilemmas in palliative care education. *Palliative Medicine Journal, 12.*

Skadberg, Y. X., & Kimmel, J. R. (2004). Visitors' flow experience while browsing a web site: Its measurement, contributing factors and consequences. *Computers in Human Behavior, 20*, 403–422. doi:10.1016/S0747-5632(03)00050-5

Skalski, P., Lange, R. L., Tamborini, R., & Shelton, A. K. (2007). *Mapping the road to fun: Natural video game controllers, presence and game enjoyment.* Paper presented at the International Communication Association Conference, San Francisco, CA.

Sklar, E. (2003). Agents for education: when too much intelligence is a bad thing. In *Proceedings of the second international joint conference on Autonomous agents and Multiagent systems (AAMAS '03)*, Melbourne, Australia (pp. 1118-1119). New York: ACM.

SlashGear.com. (2009, January 16). *Nintendo Wii sales set new industry record.* Retrieved from http://www.slashgear.com/nintendo-wii-sales-set-new-industry-records-1630867/

Slater, M., Usoh, M., & Steed, A. (1994). Depth of presence in virtual environment. *Presence (Cambridge, Mass.), 3*, 130–144.

Slator, B. M., Hill, C., & Del Val, D. (2004). Teaching Computer Science with Virtual Worlds. *IEEE Transactions on Education, 47*(2), 269–275. doi:10.1109/TE.2004.825513

Smith, M. U. (1988). *Toward a unified theory of problem solving: A view from biology*. Paper presented at the Annual Meeting of the American Educational Research Association, New Orleans, LA.

Squire, K. (2002). Cultural framing of computer/video games [Electronic Version]. *Game Studies, 2*. Retrieved December 22, 2008, from http://www.gamestudies.org/0102/squire/

Squire, K. (2002). Rethinking the role of games in education. *Game Studies, 2*(1).

Squire, K. (2005). Changing the game: What happens when video games enter the classroom. *Innovate: Journal of Online Education, 1*(6). Retrieved July 28, 2008, from http://www.academiccolab.org/resources/documents/Changing%20The%20Game-final_2.pdf

Squire, K. (2009a). Designing Educational Systems for a Participatory Media Age. Presented at the *Annual Conference of the American Education Research Association*. San Diego, CA.

Squire, K. (2009b). What Happens When a Game Is a Curriculum? Lessons Learned From a Game-Based Curriculum. Presented at the *Annual Conference of the American Education Research Association*, San Diego, CA.

Squire, K. (2005). Educating the fighter. *Horizon, 13*(2), 75–88. doi:10.1108/10748120510608106

Squire, K. (2006). From content to context: Videogames as designed experience. *Educational Researcher, 35*(8), 19–29. doi:10.3102/0013189X035008019

Squire, K. D., & Jan, M. (2007). Mad City Mystery: Developing scientific argumentation skills with a place-based augmented reality game on handheld computers. *Journal of Science Education and Technology, 16*(1), 5–29. doi:10.1007/s10956-006-9037-z

Ssebuggwawo, D., Hoppenbrouwers, S. J. B. A., & Proper, H. (2009). Evaluating Modeling Sessions Using the Analytic Hierarchy Process. In *Proceedings of the 2nd IFIP WG8.1 Working Conference on The Practice of Enterprise Modeling, PoEM 2009* (pp. 69-83). Berlin: Springer.

Steimann, F. (2000). On the representation of roles in object- oriented and conceptual modelling. *Data & Knowledge Engineering, 35*(1), 83–106. doi:10.1016/S0169-023X(00)00023-9

Steimann, F. (2005). Domain models are aspect free. In Briand, L. C., & Williams, C. (Eds.), *Models* (pp. 171–185). New York: Springer.

Steinkeuhler, C. (2009a, April). *Digital Literacies for the Disengaged: Creating After-School Online Game-Based Learning Environments for Boys*. Presented at the Annual Conference of the American Education Research Association, San Diego, CA.

Steinkeuhler, C. (2009b, April). *A Topology of Literacy Practices in Virtual Worlds*. Presented at the Annual Conference of the American Education Research Association, San Diego, CA.

Steinkuehler, C. (2007). Massively multiplayer online gaming as a constellation of literacy practices. *E-learning, 4*(3), 297–318. doi:10.2304/elea.2007.4.3.297

Steinkuehler, C. A., & Duncan, S. (2009). Scientific habits of mind in virtual worlds. *Journal of Science Education and Technology, 17*(6), 530–543. doi:10.1007/s10956-008-9120-8

Stemmler, D. (1989). The autonomic differentiation of emotions revisited: Convergent and discriminant validation. *Psychophysiology*, 617–632. doi:10.1111/j.1469-8986.1989.tb03163.x

Stevens, R., Satwicz, T., & McCarthy, L. (2008). In-Game, In-Room, In-World: Reconnecting video game play to the rest of kids' lives. In K. Salen (Ed.), *The ecology of games: Connecting youth, games, and learning* (pp. 41-66). Cambridge, MA: MIT Press.

Stockburger, A. (2003). The game environment from an auditive perspective. In Copier, M., & Raessens, J. (Eds.), *Level up: Digital games research conference*. Utrecht, The Netherlands: Utrecht University, Faculty of Arts.

Stolarski, D. (2006). Conceptual Representation for a Soccer Commentary Generator. In *RoboCup 2005: Robot Soccer World Cup IX* (pp. 496–503). Berlin: Springer. doi:10.1007/11780519_46

Stone, R. J. (2008). *Human factors guidelines for interactive 3d and games-based training systems design*.

Stormfront Studios. (2002). *The Lord of the Rings: the Two Towers (Playstation software)*. Redwood City, CA: Electronic Arts.

Subrahmanyam, K., Greenfield, P. M., & Tynes, B. (2004). Constructing sexuality and identity in an internet teen chatroom. *Journal of Applied Developmental Psychology, 25*, 651–666. doi:10.1016/j.appdev.2004.09.007

Sutcliffe, A., Ryan, M., Doubleday, A., & Springet, M. (2000). Model mismatch analysis: Towards a deeper explanation of users' usability problems. *Behaviour & Information Technology, 19*(1), 43–55. doi:10.1080/014492900118786

Suzuki, L. K., & Calzo, J. P. (2004). The search for peer advice in cyberspace: An examination of online teen bulletin boards about health and sexuality. *Journal of Applied Developmental Psychology, 25*, 685–698. doi:10.1016/j.appdev.2004.09.002

Sweetser, P., & Wyeth, P. (2005). GameFlow: A Model for Evaluating Player Enjoyment in Games. *ACM Computers in Entertainment, 3*(3).

Sweller, J. (1999). *Instructional design in technical areas*. Camberwell, Australia: ACER Press.

Tafalla, R. J. (2007). Gender differences in cardiovascular reactivity and game performance related to sensory modality in violent video game play. *Journal of Applied Social Psychology, 37*, 2008–2023. doi:10.1111/j.1559-1816.2007.00248.x

Tait, K. (1994). DISCOURSE: The design and production of simulation-based learning environments. In de Jong, T., & Sarti, L. (Eds.), *Design and production of multimedia simulation-based learning material*, Dordrecht, The Netherlands: Kluwer Academic Publishers.

Taiwan Ministry of Education. (2008). *The curriculum standards for senior high school history study*. Retrieved July 18, 2008, from http://203.68.236.92/95course/content/98-01.pdf

Tamborini, R., & Skalski, P. (2006). The role of presence in the experience of electronic games. In P. Vorderer & J. Bryant (Eds.), *Playing video games: Motives, responses, and consequences* (pp. 225-240). Mahwah, NJ: Lawrence Erlbaum Associates.

Tan, D., Robertson, G., & Czerwinski, M. (2001). Exploring 3D navigation: Combining speed-coupled flying with orbiting. *SIGCHI'01, 3*(1), 418-425.

Tan, J., Beers, C., Gupta, R., & Biswas, G. (2005). Computer Games as Intelligent Learning Environments: A River Ecosystem Adventure. In C. K. Looi, et al. (Eds.), Artificial Intelligence in Education. Amsterdam: IOS Press.

Tanaka-Ishii, K., Hasida, K., & Noda, I. (1998b). Reactive Content Selection in the Generation of Real-Time Soccer Commentary. In *Proceedings of. COLING-ACL'98*, Montreal, Canada (pp. 1282-1288).

Tanaka-Ishii, K., Noda, I., Frank, I., Nakashima, H., Hasida, K., & Matsubara, H. (1998a). Mike: An Automatic Commentary System for Soccer. In *Proceedings of ICMAS-98, Int. Conf. On Multi-agent Systems*, Paris (pp. 285-292).

Tan, D., & Nijholt, N. (2010). *Brain-Computer Interfaces. Applying our Minds to Human-Computer Interaction*. New York: Springer Verlag.

Tan, S. L., & Kelly, M. E. (2004). Graphic representations of short musical compositions. *Psychology of Music, 32*(2), 191–212. doi:10.1177/0305735604041494

Tan, S. L., & Spackman, M. P. (2005). Listeners' judgments of the musical unity of structurally altered and intact musical compositions. *Psychology of Music, 33*(2), 133–153. doi:10.1177/0305735605050648

Tauer, J. M., & Harackiewicz, J. M. (1999). Winning Isn't Everything: Competition, Achievement Orientation, and Intrinsic Motivation. *Journal of Experimental Social Psychology, 35*, 209–238. doi:10.1006/jesp.1999.1383

Taylor, T. L. (2006). *Play between worlds: Exploring online game culture*. Cambridge, MA: MIT Press.

Taylor, R. N. (1975). Perception of problem constraints. *Management Science, 22*(1), 22–29. doi:10.1287/mnsc.22.1.22

Thai, A. M., Lowenstein, D., Ching, D., & Rejeski, D. (2009). *Game Changer: Investing in Digital Play to Advance Children's Learning and Health*. New York: Joan Ganz Cooney Center at Sesame Workshop.

Thalmann, D., Noser, H., & Huang, Z. (1997). Autonomous Virtual Actors Based on Virtual Sensors. In Trappl, R., & Petta, P. (Eds.), *Creating Personalities for Synthetic Actors: towards autonomous personality agents*. Berlin: Springer Verlag. doi:10.1007/BFb0030568

Thelen, E. (1995). Motor development: A new synthesis. *The American Psychologist, 50*(2), 79–95. doi:10.1037/0003-066X.50.2.79

Thomas, J. M., & Young, M. (2007). Becoming Scientists: Employing Adaptive Interactive Narrative to Guide Discovery Learning. In *Proceedings of the AIED-07 Workshop on Narrative Learning Environments*, Marina Del Rey, California, USA.

Thompson, W. F., Schellenberg, E. G., & Husain, G. (2001). Arousal, mood, and the Mozart effect. *Psychological Science, 12*, 248–251. doi:10.1111/1467-9280.00345

Thorne, B. (1993). *Gender play: Girls and boys in school*. New Brunswick, NJ: Rutgers University Press.

Thurlow, C., Lengel, L., & Tomic, A. (2004). *Computer mediated communication: Social interaction and the Internet*. London: Sage.

Toups, Z. O., Graeber, R., Kerne, A., Tassinary, L., Berry, S., Overby, K., et al. (2006). *A Design for Using Physiological Signals to Affect Team Game Play*. Paper presented at the Augmented Cognition International.

Tovinkere, V., & Qian, R. J. (2001). Detecting semantic events in Soccer Games: towards a complete solution. In. *Proceedings of International Conference on Multimedia and Expo ICME, 2001*, 1040–1043.

Towne, M. D. (1995). *Learning and instruction in simulation environments*. Englewood Cliffs, NJ: Educational Technology Publications.

Troup, P. (n.d.). *Understanding Student Development Theories as Multicultural*. Retrieved from http://www1.umn.edu/ohr/prod/groups/ohr/@pub/@ohr/documents/asset/ohr_68497.pdf

Turkle, S. (1995). *Life on the screen: Identity in the age of the Internet*. New York: Simon and Schuster.

Ulrich, K. T., & Eppinger, S. D. (1995). *Product Design and Development* (3rd ed.). New York: McGraw-Hill.

Upper Saddle River, N. J. Prentice Hall International. Retrieved from http://faculty.plts.edu/gpence/html/kohlberg.htm

van Bommel, P., Hoppenbrouwers, S., Proper, H., & Roelofs, J. (2008). Concepts and Strategies for Quality of Modelling. In Halpin, T., Krogstie, J., & Proper, H. (Eds.), *Innovations in Information Systems Modelling, Methods and Best Practices* (pp. 167–189). Hershy, PA: IGI Global.

Van Eck, R. (2007). Six ideas in search of a discipline. In Shelton, B. E., & Wiley, D. A. (Eds.), *Modeling and simulations for learning and instruction: The design and use of simulation computer games in education*. The Netherlands: Sence Publishers.

van Rosmalen, P. (1994). SAM, simulation and multimedia. In de Jong, T., & Sarti, L. (Eds.), *Design and production of multimedia simulation-based learning material*. Dordrecht, The Netherlands: Kluwer Academic Publishers.

Västfjäll, D. (2003). The subjective sense of presence, emotion recognition, and experienced emotions in auditory virtual environments. *Cyberpsychology & Behavior, 6*, 181–188. doi:10.1089/109493103321640374

Veldhuijzen van Zanten, G., Hoppenbrouwers, S., & Proper, H. (2004). System Development as a Rational Communicative Process. *Journal of Systemics, Cybernetics and Informatics, 4*(2).

Vestal, A., O'Neill, C., & Shoemaker, B. (2008). *The history of Zelda*. Retrieved April 1, 2009, from http://www.gamespot.com/gamespot/features/video/hist_zelda/index.html

Voelz, D., Andrè, E., Herzog, G., & Rist, T. (1998). Rocco: A RoboCup Soccer Commentator System. In Asada, M., & Kitano, H. (Eds.), *RoboCup-98: Robot Soccer World Cup II*. Berlin: Springer.

Vogel, J. J., Vogel, D. S., Cannon-Browers, J., Bowers, C. A., Muse, K., & Wright, M. (2006). Computer gaming and interactive simulations for learning: A meta-analysis. *Journal of Educational Computing Research, 34*(3), 229–243. doi:10.2190/FLHV-K4WA-WPVQ-H0YM

Von Ahn, L. (2006). Games with a Purpose. *Computer, 39*(6), 92–94. doi:10.1109/MC.2006.196

Vorderer, P., Hartmann, T., & Klimmt, C. (2003, September 25-27). *Explaining the enjoyment of playing video games: the role of competition.* Paper presented at the International Conference on Entertainment Computing, Pittsburgh, Pennsylvania.

Vorhaus, M. (2008). From gathering around TV to gathering around Wii. *Advertising Age, 79*(27), 18.

Wagner, C. (2006). Breaking the Knowledge Acquisition Bottleneck Through Conversational Knowledge Management. *Information Resources Management Journal, 19*(1), 70–83.

Walther, J. B. (1992). Interpersonal effects in computer-mediated interaction: A relational perspective. *Communication Research, 19*(1), 52–90. doi:10.1177/009365092019001003

Walther, J. B. (1996). Computer-mediated communication: Impersonal, interpersonal, and hyperpersonal interaction. *Communication Research, 23*(3), 3–43. doi:10.1177/009365096023001001

Walther, J. B., Loh, T., & Granka, L. (2005). Let me count the ways: The interchange of verbal and nonverbal cues in computer-mediated and face-to-face affinity. *Journal of Language and Social Psychology, 24*(1), 36–65. doi:10.1177/0261927X04273036

Walther, J. B., Slovacek, C. L., & Tidwell, L. C. (2001). Is a picture worth a thousand words?: Photographic images in long-term and short-term computer-mediated communication. *Communication Research, 28*(1), 105–134. doi:10.1177/009365001028001004

Wang, J. H. T. (2004). A study on gross motor skills of preschool children. *Journal of Research in Childhood Education, 19*(1), 32–43.

Wartella, E., & Robb, M. (2007). Young children, new media. *Journal of children and media, 1*(1), 35-44.

Washbush, J., & Gosen, J. (2001). An exploration of game-derived learning in total enterprise simulations. *Simulation & Gaming, 32*(3), 281–296. doi:10.1177/104687810103200301

Westecott, E. (2003). Game Forms for New Outcomes. In Laurel, B. (Ed.), *Design Research: Methods and Perspectives* (pp. 129–134). Cambridge, MA: MIT Press.

Whitehouse, P., Reynolds, R., & Harel Caperton, I. (2008). *The Development of a Research Framework to Examine Teacher Professional Development and Educator Experiences in Globaloria, Pilot Year 1.* West Virginia University and World Wide Workshop. Retrieved from http://www.WorldWideWorkshop.org/Reports

Wiebe, J., & Martin, N. J. (1994). The impact of computer-based adventure game achievement and attitudes in geography. *Journal of Computing in Childhood Education, 5*(1), 61–71.

Wildeman, H. H., Owston, R. D., Brown, C., Kushniruk, A., Ho, F., & Pitts, K. C. (2007). Unpacking the potential of educational gaming: A new tool for gaming research. *Simulation & Gaming, 38*(1), 10–30. doi:10.1177/1046878106297650

Wilensky, U. (2003). Statistical mechanics for secondary school: The GasLab modeling toolkit. *International Journal of Computers for Mathematical Learning, 8*(1), 1–41. doi:10.1023/A:1025651502936

Willard, C. A., Woods, J., Van Eemeren, F. H., Walton, D. N., & Zarefsky, D. (1996). *Fundamentals of argumentation theory: A handbook of historical backgrounds and contemporary developments.* Mahwah, NJ: Lawrence Erlbaum Associates.

Williams, D. (2006). Groups and Goblins: The social and civic impact of an online game. *Journal of Broadcasting & Electronic Media, 50*(4), 651–670. doi:10.1207/s15506878jobem5004_5

Williams, D., Consalvo, M., Caplan, S., & Yee, N. (in press). Looking for gender (LFG): Gender roles and behaviors among online gamers. *The Journal of Communication.*

Williams, D., Yee, N., & Caplan, S. (2008). Who Plays, How Much, and Why? A Behavioral Player Census of Virtual World. *Journal of Computer-Mediated Communication, 13*, 993–1018. doi:10.1111/j.1083-6101.2008.00428.x

Williamson, D., Bauer, M., Steinberg, L., Mislevy, R., & Behrens, J. (2003, April). *Creating a complex measurement model using evidence centered design.* Paper presented at American Educational Research Association/NCME conference, Chicago.

Williams, V. (2003). Designing simulations for learning. *E-Journal of Instructional Science and Technology*, *6*(1), 50–71.

Withers, D. (2005). *Authoring tools for educational simulations (Tech. Rep.)*. Burnaby, Canada: Simon Fraser University.

Witten, I., & Frank, E. (2005). *Data Mining: practical machine learning tools and techniques* (2nd ed.). San Francisco, CA: Morgan Kaufmann.

Wodehouse, A. J., & Bradley, D. A. (2006). Gaming techniques and the product development process: commonalities & cross-applications. *Journal of Desert Research*, *5*(2), 155–171. doi:10.1504/JDR.2006.011360

Wolfson, S., & Case, G. (2000). The effects of sound and colour on responses to a computer game. *Interacting with Computers*, *13*, 183–192. doi:10.1016/S0953-5438(00)00037-0

Wolpaw, J. R., Birbaumer, N., McFarland, D. J., Pfurtscheller, G., & Vaughan, T. M. (2002). Braincomputer interfaces for communication and control. *Clinical Neurophysiology*, *113*, 767–791. doi:10.1016/S1388-2457(02)00057-3

Woodcock, B. (2008). *MMOG Active Subscriptions: 0-120,000*. Retrieved December 23, 2008, from http://www.mmogchart.com/Chart3.html

Wood, D. F. (2003). Problem based learning. *British Medical Journal*, *326*, 328–330. doi:10.1136/bmj.326.7384.328

Workflow Management Coalition. (2008). *XPDL 2.1 Complete Specification*.

XKaileeX. (2003). Anti-virtual dating. *The Whyville Times*. Retrieved November 2, 2008, from Whyville.net.

Yamada, M., Fujisawa, N., & Komori, S. (2001). The effect of music on the performance and impression in a racing game. *Journal of Music Perception and Cognition*, *7*, 65–76.

Yamagata-Lynch, L. C. (2007). Confronting analytical dilemmas for understanding complex human interactions in design-based research from a cultural-historical activity theory (CHAT) gramework. *Journal of the Learning Sciences*, *16*(4), 451–484.

Yee, N., Bailenson, J. N., Urbanek, M., Chang, F., & Merget, D. (2007). The unbearable likeness of being digital: The persistance of nonverbal social norms in online virtual environments. *Journal of CyberPsychology and Behavior*, *10*, 115–121. doi:10.1089/cpb.2006.9984

Yow, D., Yeo, B.-L., Yeung, M., & Liu, B. (1995). Analysis and Presentation of Soccer Highlights from Digital Video. In *Proceedings of 2nd Asian Conf. on Computer Vision (ACCV'95)*.

Zacharia, Z. C. (2007). Comparing and combining real and virtual experimentation: an effort to enhance students' conceptual understanding of electric circuits. *Journal of Computer Assisted Learning*, *23*, 120–132. doi:10.1111/j.1365-2729.2006.00215.x

Zajonc, R. B., & McIntosh, D. N. (1992). Some Promising Questions and Some Questionable Promises. *Psychological Science*, *3*(1), 70–74. doi:10.1111/j.1467-9280.1992.tb00261.x

Zehnder, S. M., & Lipscomb, S. D. (2006). The role of music in video games. In Voderer, P., & Bryant, J. (Eds.), *Playing video games: Motives, responses and consequences* (pp. 241–258). Mahwah, NJ: Lawrence Erlbaum.

Zhang, J. (1991). The interaction of internal and external representations in a problem solving task. In *Proceedings of the Thirteenth Annual Cognitive Science Society*. Hillsdale, NJ: Lawrence Erlbaum.

Zhao, S. (2003). Toward a taxonomy of copresence. *Presence (Cambridge, Mass.)*, *12*(5), 445–455. doi:10.1162/105474603322761261

About the Contributors

Richard E. Ferdig is the RCET Research Professor and Professor of Instructional Technology at Kent State University. He works within the Research Center for Educational Technology and also the School of Lifespan Development & Educational Sciences. He earned his PhD in educational psychology from Michigan State University. At Kent State University, his research, teaching, and service focus on combining cutting-edge technologies with current pedagogic theory to create innovative learning environments. His research interests include online education, gaming, and what he labels a deeper psychology of technology. In addition to publishing and presenting nationally and internationally, Ferdig has also been funded to study the impact of emerging technologies.

Sara de Freitas is director of Research at the Serious Games Institute (SGI) – an international hub of excellence in the area of games, virtual worlds and interactive digital media for serious purposes, including education, health and business applications. Situated on the Technology Park at the University of Coventry, Sara leads an interdisciplinary and cross-university applied research group. Based as part of the largest commercial arm of any UK university, the SGI applied research group - with expertise in AI and games, visualization, mixed reality, augmented reality and location aware technologies – works closely with international industrial and academic research and development partners. Sara is currently working on the Technology Strategy Board-part-funded Serious Games – Engaging Training Solutions project developing three serious games demonstrators, and Chairs the UK Lab Group.

* * *

Adam Ingram-Goble is a doctoral student in the learning sciences program at Indiana University. Stemming from his master's work in computer science, Ingram-Goble is interested in the intersection of gaming, learning, and programming for contextualizing education. He has worked on the Quest Atlantis project since 2005, developing curricula and game elements, but has recently shifted his focus to placing the design tools of QA in the hands of its players.

Adrienne Massanari (amassanari@luc.edu) is an Assistant Professor of New and Digital Media in the School of Communication at Loyola University, where she serves as the Program Director for the Center for Digital Ethics and Policy. Her research interests include the social and cultural impacts of new media, information architecture and user-centered design, youth culture, and gaming.

Albert Ritzhaupt is an Assistant Professor of Instructional Technology at UNCW and taught the course Games, Simulations and Virtual Worlds offered in the Watson School of Education.

Amos Brocco obtained his Msc. in Computer Science (major) / Mathematics (minor) from the University of Fribourg (Switzerland) in 2005. Since the end of 2005 he is working as Ph.D. student with the Pervasive and Artificial Intelligence research group at the University of Fribourg. His thesis is focused on bio-inspired techniques for grid and peer-to-peer systems. His research interests are in the area of distributed swarm intelligence, adaptive network algorithms and bio-inspired techniques. His activities also include teaching assistance for undergraduate and post-graduate courses.

Andrew Wodehouse is a Lecturer in Design at the Department of Design Manufacture and Engineering Management at University of Strathclyde since September 2003. He graduated as an MEng in Product Design Engineering at the University of Glasgow/ Glasgow School of Art and Ing from the Hanzehogeschool Groningen, the Netherlands, before working as a product design engineer for a number of design consultancies, including Cambridge Consultants Ltd. Research projects include the Digital Libraries for Distributed Innovative Design Education and Teamwork (DIDET), and Knowledge and Information Management Through Life (KIM). His PhD focuses on digital information support for concept design.

Anna Akerman is an Assistant Professor of Communications at Adelphi University and a Visiting Scholar at New York University's Department of Psychology, where she received her Ph.D. in social and developmental psychology. As a Research Consultant with Nickelodeon/MTV Networks Kids & Family Group, she investigates the influence and role of mass media in children's lives. She has also worked with Sesame Workshop, Noggin, MediaKidz, and Scholastic.

Apostolos Malatras received the Diploma in Computer Science from the University of Piraeus, Greece, the MSc degree in Information Systems from the Athens University of Economics and Business, Greece, and the PhD degree in networking from the University of Surrey, UK. He is a Post-doctoral Fellow with the Pervasive and Artificial Intelligence research group, University of Fribourg, Switzerland. Prior to this position, he was a Senior Research Engineer with Thales Research and Technology, Berkshire, UK. He is the author and co-author of more than 25 research papers. His research interests focus on context awareness, network management, mobile ad hoc networks, service oriented architectures, wireless sensor networks, and communications middleware.

Bart Schotten works as an analyst / functional designer for Info Support, a Dutch IT company. In 2009 he earned his master's degree in Information Science at Radboud University Nijmegen, specializing in information architecture, with a particular interest in modeling. For his master's thesis he developed and tested the first working prototype of a game for the elicitation of basic process models.

Béat Hirsbrunner is full professor at the Department of Computer Science, and leader of the Pervasive and Artificial Intelligence (PAI) research group at the University of Fribourg (UNIFR). He has conducted research works on the topics of Context-aware Ubiquitous Computing, Human-Computer Interaction, and Multimodal Dialogue Management. He is currently responsible for teaching several courses of the Computer Science curriculum and in particular Distributed Systems and Ubiquitous Computing. He is author and co-author of more than 120 scientific publications.

Boris Reuderink, MSc, obtained his master degree in 2007, after spending time on different machine learning problems, including OCR of handwritten text on envelopes and the detection of laughter in audio-visual data. Brains and intelligence have always been his guiding interests. These interests can be combined his PhD position at the University of Twente, for which he focuses on making BCI function in real-world settings for healthy users. After expanding her computer science education with some subjects about neurophysiology, Danny Plass-Oude Bos did her internship at the University of Nijmegen in 2007, implementing physiological artifact detection in an online EEG-based BCI system. In 2008 she obtained her master title in Computer Science (Human-Computer Interaction specifically) on BrainBasher, looking into the user experience of using BCI for games. At the moment she is working as a PhD student at the University of Twente, still attempting to merge BCI with HCI by researching how BCI can be made a more intuitive means of interaction.

Bram van de Laar, MSc, obtained his Bachelor degree in Computer Science (2006) and Master degree in Human Media Interaction (2009). With a broad interest in technology, such as: 3D, games, video, networking, music, sounds, haptics, physical exertion and brain-computer interfacing in particular, Bram tries to create a synergy by exploiting different modalities. User experience and 'added value' play an important role in this philosophy. As a PhD student at the University of Twente Bram gets the opportunity to explore the possibilities in these areas.

Brian C. Nelson is an assistant professor of educational technology in the Graduate School of Education at Arizona State University. Dr. Nelson's research focuses on the theory, design, and implementation of computer-based learning environments, focusing on immersive games. An instructional designer and learning theorist, he has published and presented extensively on the viability of educational virtual environments for situated inquiry learning and assessment. Dr. Nelson was the project designer on the River City project through two NSF-funded studies, and is a co-principal investigator on the NSF-funded SAVE Science study with Drs. Ketelhut and Schifter. He is also co-PI on the MacArthur Foundation "21st Century Assessment" project, investigating new models for assessment in digital media-based learning environments, and co-PI on the NSF study "Scaffolding Understanding through Redesigning Games for Education (SURGE), investigating the use of an online game to teach physics. Dr. Nelson earned his Ed.D. at Harvard University.

Brock R. Dubbels has worked since 1999 as a professional in education and instructional design. His specialties include reading comprehension and instruction and assessment. His current focus is on the role of embodied cognition connected with digital literacies, game design, and play. From these perspectives he designs face-to-face, virtual, and hybrid learning environments, exploring new technologies for assessment, delivering content, creating engagement with learners, and investigating ways people approach learning. He is currently a research associate at the Center for Cognitive Science at the University of Minnesota. He is also the founder and principal learning architect at www.vgalt.com.

Camela Babson is a graduate student at the University of North Carolina Wilmington (UNCW), enrolled in a graduate course titled Games, Simulations and Virtual Worlds offered in the Watson School of Education.

Catherine Schifter is an associate professor in and chair of the Department of Curriculum, Instruction and Technology in Education in Temple University's College of Education. She has over 25 years of experience in teaching higher education science or computers for future teachers and, after 10 years of researching implementation of computers into classrooms, she has a clear understanding of how technology can support learning at all levels. She has served as principal investigator on five contracts with the School District of Philadelphia to assess implementation of technology-related federal grants into elementary- and middle-school classrooms to support literacy and mathematics education. Her recent scholarship has focused on distance learning and teachers' use of technology, the latter topic the subject of her current book, *Infusing Technology into the Classroom: Continuous Practice Improvement (2008)*. Professor Schifter received her PhD from the University of Pennsylvania.

Daniel Kudenko is a lecturer in Computer Science at the University of York, UK. His research areas are AI for interactive entertainment, machine learning (specifically reinforcement learning), user modeling, and multi-agent systems. In many of these areas he has collaborated with industrial partners in the entertainment and military sector, and has been involved in projects for Eidos, QinetiQ, as well as the Ministry of Defence. Dr. Kudenko has been heading a research group in York on AI for games and interactive entertainment, which works on topics ranging from interactive drama for entertainment and education to football commentary generation. Dr. Kudenko received a Ph.D. in machine learning in 1998 at Rutgers University, NJ. He has participated in several research projects at the University of York, Rutgers University, AT&T Laboratories, and the German Research Center for AI (DFKI) on various topics in artificial intelligence. Dr. Kudenko's work has been published in more than 70 peer-reviewed papers. He has served on multiple program committees and has been chairing a number of workshops, as well as co-edited three Springer LNCS volumes.

Daniela Romano, PhD, is a lecture in Computer Science at University of Sheffield and theme leader Virtual Reality within the Kroto Research Institute for Multidisciplinary Engineering Research, where she manages a team of researchers and the virtual laboratory lab. Virtual Reality research, is concerned with both the technology, which allows users to interact with a computer-simulated environment, the software for the seamless interface and the simulation most often 3D. As such my competences include 3D Graphics, Human-Computer Interaction (HCI), Cognitive Science, Software Engineering, Artificial Intelligence (AI) and Education. In particular she specialise in VR solutions for educational purposes, otherwise known as "Serious Games" and the simulation of complex environments using Agent Based Modelling. She has published over 60 articles in various areas related to the creation of believable virtual environments and serious games.

David Birchfield is an assistant professor in Arizona State University's School of Arts, Media and Engineering where he leads the K-12 Embodied and Mediated Learning Group. In this role he directs research and outreach activities for a team of interdisciplinary collaborators that span eight academic departments and includes a national network of school and community partners. His research is focused on interactivity and experiential media design as applied to creative and educational spaces. This work includ Fulvio Frapolli obtained his degree in Mathematics from the Swiss Federal Institute of Technology in Zurich (Switzerland) in 2004. Since 2005 he is working as Ph.D. student within the Pervasive and Artificial Intelligence research group at the University of Fribourg (Switzerland). His thesis is focused in providing an holistic board game development framework, which allows users to design and modify computer enhanced board games by means of a set of graphical tools that are supported by a well-defined conceptual model and a visual programming environment. His research interests are in the area of Human-Computer Interaction, Mixed-reality, Game Modeling, Games rules flexibility, Tabletop gaming, Tangible User Interaction. His activities also include teaching assistance for undergraduate and post-graduate courses.

DavidGibson is research assistant professor of computer science at the College of Engineering and Mathematical Sciences at the University of Vermont and co-principal investigator on the National Science Foundation funded *Global Challenge Award ITEST Project*. He is also the creator and project director of *simSchool* (www.simschool.org), a classroom flight simulator for training teachers funded currently by the Fund for the Improvement of Postsecondary Education. His recent books *Games and Simulations in Online Learning* (2006) and *Digital Simulations for Improving Education* (2008), address the potential for games and simulation-based learning. Gibson has help lead technology-based research and development projects since the early 1980's which have resulted in the development and deployment of electronic portfolios, online data gathering, analysis and representation software, and innovative e-learning platforms.

Deborah Fields is a doctoral candidate at UCLA in the division of Psychological Studies in Education. With extensive experience working in areas of informal education, Fields engages in research about learning *across* spaces, peer-to-peer learning & teaching, and play. These interests have guided her studies in virtual worlds, science, and math in both formal and informal contexts. Fields' recent work has been published in the *International Journal of Computer Supported Collaborative Learning*, the *International Journal of Science Education*, and *On Horizon*. She has a forthcoming book chapter coming out in *Constructing Identity in a Digital World* published by Cambridge University Press.

Diane Jass Ketelhut is an assistant professor of science education at Temple University's College of Education. Her research interests center on scientific inquiry, specifically looking at the effects of inquiry on science self-efficacy; using emerging technologies to deliver scientific inquiry curricula on student learning and engagement; professional development in scientific inquiry on helping teachers integrate scientific inquiry into their curricula; and different methods of assessing science and scientific inquiry. Her current federally-funded projects include "SAVE Science," an innovative game-based system for evaluating learning in science for middle school years, "Science in the City," a standards-based scientific inquiry after-school curriculum project for elementary and middle-school students, and e=mc^2, an alternative mid-career math and science middle school teacher education program. In her teaching, she provides students with scientific inquiry experiences, both technological and hands-on, meant to engage them and challenge them to confront their own preconceptions. She holds certification in secondary school science and was a science curriculum specialist and teacher (science and math) for grades 5-12 for 12 years. Diane received an Sc.B. in Bio-Medical Sciences from Brown University, an MEd in curriculum and instruction from the University of Virginia and her EdD in learning and teaching from Harvard University.

Don Heider (dheider@luc.edu) is the founding Dean & a Professor at Loyola University Chicago's School of Communication. Heider recently released edited volume *Living Virtually* explores politics, social behavior, journalism, and ethics in virtual worlds. Heider is a multiple Emmy-award winning producer and reporter who spent ten years in news before beginning a career in teaching.

Elizabeth Folta is a graduate student in Science Education at NC State University with a minor in Fisheries and Wildlife Science. Her research interests include educational gaming and technology in environmental education. Elizabeth plans finish her dissertation in early August 2010 and start her career as an Assistant Professor in Informal Biology Education at SUNY – College of Environmental Science and Forestry. She has worked in informal education for a number of years including a wildlife education center, National Parks, and National Wildlife Refuges.

Fulvio Frapolli obtained his degree in Mathematics from the Swiss Federal Institute of Technology in Zurich (Switzerland) in 2004. Since 2005 he is working as Ph.D. student within the Pervasive and Artificial Intelligence research group at the University of Fribourg (Switzerland). His thesis is focused in providing an holistic board game development framework, which allows users to design and modify computer enhanced board games by means of a set of graphical tools that are supported by a well-defined conceptual model and a visual programming environment. His research interests are in the area of Human-Computer Interaction, Mixed-reality, Game Modeling, Games rules flexibility, Tabletop gaming, Tangible User Interaction.His activities also include teaching assistance for undergraduate and post-graduate courses.

Idit Harel Caperton is a Founder and President of World Wide Workshop Foundation in NYC. A learning scientist, an educational technology innovator, and a social entrepreneur, Idit won numerous awards for her work, including the AERA 1992 Outstanding Book Award for *Children Designers*, the Computerworld-Smithsonian Award (1999), the Internet industry coveted Global Information Infrastructure Award (1999), and the 21st-Century Achievement Award on the MaMaMedia Peace Project from the Computerworld Honors Program (2002). Idit serves on the Advisory Boards of PBSKids, CUNY, ATLAS at CU Boulder, TIG, MEET, and Saybot LLC, as well as on Overseeing Visiting Committees at Harvard and MIT. She is known for her visionary work at the MIT Media Lab in the 80s and for founding MaMaMedia.com in the 90s, a pioneering kids Internet brand using technology for creative learning, innovation, and globalization through constructionist learning.

J. Alison Bryant is Chief Strategy Officer at Smarty Pants, a youth and family research and strategy firm. Prior to joining Smarty Pants, Dr. Bryant was Senior Research Director of Digital Research and Brand & Consumer Insights for the Nickelodeon/MTV Networks Kids & Family Group. She led Nick's efforts to understand the digital lives of kids and families, conducting research on a variety of digital platforms (online, console and handheld gaming, interactive television, mobile). Her Ph.D. is from the Annenberg School of Communication at the University of Southern California and before joining Nickelodeon she was an assistant professor of Telecommunications at Indiana University. She has published and presented extensively on media, kids and families, including two edited books: The Children's Television Community and Television and the American Family (2nd Ed). She is also associate editor for the Journal of Children & Media.

Jordana Drell is the Director of Preschool Games in the Nickelodeon Kids and Family Games Group. Jordana is responsible for Nick Jr. games across all platforms including, NicKJr.com, NickJrArcade. com, NickjrBoost.com, mobile, console and handheld. She produced the first game for preschoolers on the Wii, Diego Safari Rescue. Before joining Nickelodeon, Jordana was a Producer in the Interactive Group at Sesame Workshop where she produced numerous Flash games for Sesamestreet.com.

Jorge Arroyo-Palacios graduated from the Instituto Tecnológico de Ciudad Victoria (Mexico) with an honours BEng degree in Computer Systems in 2003. He awarded a scholarship from the Mexican Council of Science and Technology (CONACYT) to pursuit a postgraduate degree, and in 2004 he joined the University of Sheffield. He received the MSc degree in Advanced Computer Science in 2005 with his thesis work on the creation and population of virtual urban environments. Currently he is completing his PhD in the field of affective computing and holds a research assistant position at the Computer Science Department of the University of Sheffield. His research interests include: bio-affective interfaces, video games, virtual reality and artificial intelligence.

Katharine Daniels is a graduate student at the University of North Carolina Wilmington (UNCW), enrolled in a graduate course titled Games, Simulations and Virtual Worlds offered in the Watson School of Education.

Kristin Searle is a dual-degree doctoral student in the teaching, learning, and curriculum program at the Graduate School of Education and the Department of Anthropology at the University of Pennsylvania. She has studied and worked in a number of formal and informal learning contexts, including the American Indian Teacher Training Program and the Upward Bound Bridge/Jumpstart program, both at the University of Utah. More recently, she has begun to explore the educational applications of virtual worlds, looking specifically at Whyville.net. Throughout her work, Kristin is interested in how identities are produced and negotiated in educational contexts and beyond.

Leonard A. Annetta is an associate professor of Science Education at North Carolina State University, Dr. Annetta's research has focused on distance learning and the effect of instructional technology on science learning of teachers and students in rural and underserved populations. His research vigorously began to parlay the results of his dissertation into a pursuit of how synchronous interaction over the Web could propel distance learning in formal and informal settings. Understanding the popularity of online, multiuser video game play, Dr. Annetta began to use his past programming knowledge to build a virtual environment that became the platform for his current research agenda. Dr. Annetta has been awarded over $5 million in grants to support his work on distance learning and the use of Serious Educational Games as a vehicle for learning STEM content and STEM career awareness.

Maliang Zheng is a graduate student at the University of York in the Computer Science department. His research interests lie in the areas of machine learning and information extraction. Zheng joint the GIEDY (Game, Interactive, Entertainment and Drama at York) group and worked with Dr. Daniel Kudenko on mining the football match data to generate game commentary. He is currently a researcher of a leading software company, studying how to improve the customer satisfaction with the commercial products by including the data mining technology in analyzing the user behavior.

Mark McMahon is a Senior Lecturer and Program Director of Creative Industries and Contemporary Arts at Edith Cowan University where he also co-ordinates the Game Design & Culture and Digital Media courses. He has previously worked as a multimedia developer and instructional designer. His current research is in Serious Games, particularly the underlying psychology of learning and immersion as well as instructional design models to support Serious Game development.

Melissa Gresalfi is an assistant professor in learning sciences and cognitive science at Indiana University, and is the associate director of the Center for Research on Learning and Technology. Her work considers cognition and social context by examining student learning as a function of participation in activity settings. Following a situative perspective on learning, her work investigates how opportunities to learn are constructed in mathematics classrooms, and how, when, and why different students take up those opportunities. Her research has been funded by the MacArthur Foundation, the National Science Foundation, and the Spencer Foundation.

Meng-Tzu Cheng is an assistant professor in the Department of Biology at the National Changhua University in Taiwan. Her research interests have focused on creating and using video games and simulations as a teaching and learning tool that helps middle school students to learn the concepts of biology in a more fun and interesting way.

Michael Garrett is a Phd student currently studying at Edith Cowan University in Australia. His Phd studies focus on the application of three-dimensional gaming technologies within a problem-based learning framework for the purpose of providing training for real world scenarios. Michael has also conducted previous research in conjunction with the Royal Australian Navy to assess the viability of gaming technology for spatial awareness training with Collins class submarines.

Paul Cairns is a Senior Lecturer in Human Computer Interaction at the University of York. He is a Programme leader for the MSc in Human-Centred Interactive Technologies. His interests are in Human Computer Interaction generally but, with a background in mathematics, he is interested in statistical methods for understanding user behaviour and mathematical knowledge management. He has more recently developed an interest in understanding the positive experience of using interactive systems, in particular, understanding what it means to be immersed in videogames. Dr. Cairns is also very interested in research methods and with Anna Cox wrote: Cairns, P. and Cox, A.L. (2008) Research Methods for Human-Computer Interaction Cambridge University Press.

Peter J.F. Lucas is an associate professor with the Institute for Computing and Information Sciences at Radboud University Nijmegen, the Netherlands. He has been involved in research in Artificial Intelligence, in particular knowledge-based systems, since the beginning of the 1980s. He has contributed to this area by theoretical as well as applied research, the latter for the major part focusing on the field of medicine. His research interests include topics such as applied logic and theorem proving, knowledge representation, decision-support systems, model-based diagnosis, and Bayesian networks. He has extensively published in AI journals and conferences (more than 100 journal and conference publications), written and edited several books, organised a number of workshops in the field, and edited 6 thematic issues of journals on topics mentioned above.

Rania Hodhod is a Ph.D. student and a member of the Artificial Intelligence Research Group in the Computer Science Department at the University of York, with Departmental Overseas Research Studentship (DORS). Her aim is to create an adaptive educational interactive narrative drama by integrating intelligent tutoring systems main components to the interactive narrative environments. Rania got her Masters degree in computer and information sciences from Ain Shams University, Egypt. She also obtained a diploma on Tutoring in on-line learning environment from the E-Learning lab, Aalborg University, Denmark. Her research interests include e-learning, intelligent tutoring systems, educational games and user modeling. Within these areas, Rania has several publications in international conferences that have gained general interest. Rania was also responsible of developing and designing an online course in computer science during her participation in the European funded project, The Mediterranean Virtual University.

Robin Brooks is a graduate student at the University of North Carolina Wilmington (UNCW), enrolled in a graduate course titled Games, Simulations and Virtual Worlds offered in the Watson School of Education.

Sasha Barab is a professor in learning sciences, instructional systems technology and cognitive science at Indiana University. He holds the Barbara Jacobs Chair of Education and Technology, and is the Director of the Center for Research on Learning and Technology. He has received multiple grants from the National Science Foundation and the MacArthur Foundation. His research has resulted in dozens of peer-reviewed articles, chapters in edited books, and he is editor of the book *Designing for Virtual Communities in the Service of Learning*. He has also given plenary talks worldwide, and testified before Congress on the potential of advanced technologies to impact learning. His current work involves the design of rich learning environments, frequently with the aid of technology, that are created to assist children in developing their sense of purpose as individuals, as members of their communities, and as knowledgeable citizens of the world. This work is being used by tens of thousands of children worldwide.

Shawn Y. Holmes is a former high school biology teacher and an Assistant Professor in science education at North Carolina State University in the Department of Mathematics, Science, and Technology Education. Her area of research is in science teacher education, specifically helping science educators gain cultural competency through recognizing and implementing ethical actions. She uses computer simulations to influence perspective-taking skills of educators in various scenarios involving students in school environments.

Shiang-Kwei Wang (Ph.D. University of Georgia) is an Associate Professor of the Master of Science in Instructional Technology Program in the School of Education at the New York Institute of Technology. Her professional interests have been in the areas of technology integration in K-12 learning settings, the motivational impact of information and communication technologies (ICTs) on learning attitude and performance, as well as the design and development of interactive learning tools. She can be reached at skwang@nyit.edu. Her web site address is http://iris.nyit.edu/~skwang.

Stephen Guynup has been considered one of the most creative and controversial designers of online virtual worlds for the past 15 years. His past efforts include numerous conference presentations, including SIGGRAPH 1998, 1999, 2000, 2003, 2004, 2009 and will Chair the Web3D Art Gallery at SIGGRAPH 2010. He currently teaches Game Design for the Art Institute of Pittsburgh - Online Division.

Stijn J.B.A. Hoppenbrouwers is an assistant professor at the Institute for Computing and Information Sciences at Radboud University Nijmegen. In his research he focuses on the process of modeling in system development and knowledge engineering. Stijn has been involved in applied systems modeling research since the mid nineties, and took part in a number of academic and industrial projects, including the ArchiMate project. He has published well over 50 reviewed articles and chapters in conferences proceedings, books and journals, and has organized and chaired some international workshops and conferences. He is also an active member of the IFIP 8.1 workgroup. His primary topics of interest include information systems, information modeling, rule-based modeling, enterprise architecture modeling, method engineering, conceptualization, elicitation, and collaborative modeling.

Tyler Dodge is a doctoral candidate in the Department of Instructional Systems Technology at Indiana University. His current work reflects his enduring commitment to educating children and young adults. It involves the research and development of traditional and modern narrative media to empower youth and advance design knowledge. He has co-authored several articles and book chapters, presented at conferences and workshops, and taught at the high school and college levels. His dissertation research concerns the effects of media design on observational learning from characters.

William Ion is a Professor in the Department of Design, Manufacture and Engineering Management at the University of Strathclyde. He graduated from the University of Glasgow with an Honors degree in Mechanical Engineering. Prior to appointment at the University of Strathclyde in 1985 he spent periods with Barr and Stroud Ltd and Yarrow Shipbuilders Ltd. He has been an investigator on research projects in the areas of design tools and techniques and computer supported working in design, design education and rapid prototyping, and is Operations Director of the newly created Advanced Forming Research Centre (AFRC).

Yasmin B. Kafai is Professor of Learning Sciences at the Graduate School of Education at the University of Pennsylvania and co-executive editor of the *Journal of the Learning Sciences*. Her research focuses on the design and study of new learning and gaming technologies in schools, community programs and virtual worlds. Recent collaborations with MIT researchers have resulted in the development of Scratch, a media-rich programming environment for designers of all ages, to create and share games, art, and stories. Current projects examine creativity and IT in the design of computational textiles with urban youth. Kafai earned a doctorate from Harvard University while working at the MIT Media Lab.

Index